WESTERN MARXISM: AN INTRODUCTION

Classical and Contemporary Sources

BEN AGGER

University of Waterloo

GOODYEAR PUBLISHING CO., INC.
Santa Monica, California

Library of Congress Cataloging in Publication Data

AGGER, BEN.
 Western Marxism, an introduction.

 Bibliography: p. 345
 Includes index.
 1. Communism—History. 2. Socialism—History.
I. Title.
HX36.A538   335.4′09   78-21654
ISBN 0-87620-953-3
ISBN 0-87620-925-2 pbk.

Current Printing (last number):
10 9 8 7 6 5 4 3 2 1

ISBN: 0-87620-953-3 (case)
Y-9533-4 (case)
ISBN: 0-87620-925-2 (paper)
Y-9252-0 (paper)

Printed in the United States of America

For Guga,
whose interruptions
reminded me that
humanism is about people

Acknowledgements

I have many people to thank for helping me along the way towards this book. Foremost among these are my teachers. John O'Neill, Gad Horowitz, Miroslav Disman, Christian Bay and Robert E. Agger all helped me to think and write with clarity and with commitment to social change. They each in his own way showed me the possibility of a humane socialism, comprised of men and women who refuse to dominate others in the name of distant future liberation. They have taught me that socialism is a process as much as a product. And they showed me that critical thinkers, in the midst of bourgeois societies, can most effectively contribute to the creation of that kind of socialism by refusing to succumb either to value-free scholarship or to the Leninist ideology of state-socialism.

Gad Horowitz (of the University of Toronto) and Mark Kann (of the University of Southern California) read this book in various stages of the draft and both offered indispensable advice and encouragement. Horowitz urged me to rethink the nature of my Marxism and convinced me that the critique of ideology and class struggle are not disjunctive alternatives. Kann showed me, in his own work and through his appraisal of mine, that a North American Marxism, optimally attuned to liberal-democratic political culture, can be created.

I would like to thank the editorial and production staff at Goodyear who have made this book smooth sailing. It has been a pleasure to work with Jim Boyd, my editor at Goodyear, who has exhibited the patience and encouragement necessary to keep me at work on this rather lengthy project; and with Hal Humphrey in production, who has brought art to the book.

I would like to thank the many people who worked on manuscript preparation and who have suffered my hand-writing and sloppy typing en route to the final product. Diane Brouillette, Peggy Hibbard, Ursula Ortmann, Jean Spowart and Bev Taylor are to be commended for a job well done.

I would like to acknowledge with gratitude assistance I have received from the University Research Grant program at the University of Waterloo (funded by the Canada Council) and from the Department of Sociology of the University of Waterloo (whose chairman, Kenneth Westhues, has been more than generous in providing me with materials, typing and xeroxing facilities and, most important, an hospitable working environment).

Finally, I would like to thank my mother, Molly Blake, for teaching me to listen; Don Roebuck, for his friendship and discerning intelligence; Ray Morrow for his ceaselessly honest approach to my work and life; Dan Kubat and Ed Vaz for affording a quality of friendship that far surpasses mere collegiality; and Susan McDaniel, for showing me that dialectics is a way of seeing which lets the textures show through.

Ben Agger
Waterloo, Ontario, Canada

Contents

Acknowledgements **v**

Introduction: A North American Marxism **1**

1

Alienation, Contradiction, and Crisis in Marx's Dialectical Method

HISTORICAL OVERVIEW **5**

MARX'S VISION OF SOCIALIST EMANCIPATION **16**
   With excerpts from *Economic and Philosophical Manuscripts* by
   Karl Marx

MARX'S DIALECTICAL METHOD **27**
   With excerpts from *German Ideology* by Karl Marx and
   Friedrich Engels, including "Theses on Feuerbach"

MARX'S THEORY OF REVOLUTIONARY
COMMUNISM **35**
   With excerpts from *The Communist Manifesto* by Karl Marx
   and Friedrich Engels

MARX'S THEORY OF THE INTERNAL CONTRADICTIONS OF
CAPITALISM **43**
   With excerpts from *Capital,* Vol. I, by Karl Marx

MARX'S CRISIS THEORY **65**
   With excerpts from *Capital,* Vol. III, by Karl Marx

GUIDE TO FURTHER READING **73**

QUESTIONS FOR FURTHER DISCUSSION **74**

2
Twentieth-Century Reformers and Radicals: Scientific Marxism in the Second International

HISTORICAL OVERVIEW   75

Bernstein: EVOLUTIONARY SOCIALISM   87
With excerpts from *Evolutionary Socialism* by Eduard Bernstein

Kautsky: MARXISM AS ETHICS AND SCIENCE   91
With excerpts from *Ethics and the Materialist Conception of History* by Karl Kautsky

Kautsky: DEMOCRACY VERSUS DICTATORSHIP   94
With excerpts from *The Dictatorship of the Proletariat* by Karl Kautsky

Gramsci: THE PHILOSOPHY OF PRAXIS   99
With excerpts from *Prison Notebooks* by Antonio Gramsci

Luxemburg: THE MAJORITARIAN DICTATORSHIP OF THE PROLETARIAT   104
With excerpts from *The Junius Pamphlet* by Rosa Luxemburg and *Rosa Luxemburg Speaks*

Leninism: DIALECTICAL MATERIALISM AS A VANGUARD SCIENCE   111
With an excerpt from *What is to Be Done?* by V. I. Lenin

GUIDE TO FURTHER READING   114

QUESTIONS FOR FURTHER DISCUSSION   115

3
Hegelian Marxism I: The Role of Class Consciousness

HISTORICAL OVERVIEW   116

Lukács: ON CLASS CONSCIOUSNESS   126
With an excerpt from *History and Class Consciousness* by Georg Lukács

Korsch: PHILOSOPHY AND MARXISM   134
With an excerpt from *Marxism and Philosophy* by Karl Korsch

Horkheimer: TRADITIONAL AND CRITICAL THEORY   138
With an excerpt from *Critical Theory* by Max Horkheimer

The Frankfurt Institute for Social Research: IDEOLOGY AND THE ECLIPSE OF SUBJECTIVITY   139
With an excerpt from *Aspects of Sociology* by the Frankfurt Institute for Social Research

GUIDE TO FURTHER READING   143

QUESTIONS FOR FURTHER DISCUSSION   144

Hegelian Marxism II: The Theory of Domination

HISTORICAL OVERVIEW   145

Adorno: NEGATIVE DIALECTICS   156
    With excerpts from *Negative Dialectics* by Theodor Adorno

Horkheimer: ECLIPSE OF REASON   163
    With excerpts from *Eclipse of Reason* by Max Horkheimer

Horkheimer and Adorno: MARXISM AS POSITIVIST
MYTHOLOGY   170
    With excerpts from *Dialectic of Enlightenment* by Max
    Horkheimer and Theodor W. Adorno

Marcuse: ONE-DIMENSIONAL SOCIETY   175

Jacoby: SOCIAL AMNESIA   178
    With excerpts from *Social Amnesia* by Russell Jacoby

GUIDE TO FURTHER READING   187

QUESTIONS FOR FURTHER DISCUSSION   188

Eastern European Revisionism: Marxian Humanism

HISTORICAL OVERVIEW   189

Korać: ON SOCIALIST HUMANISM   203
    With an excerpt from "In Search of Human Society" by
    Veljko Korać, from *Socialist Humanism,* edited by Erich
    Fromm

Schaff: MARXIAN HUMANISM AND THE PROBLEM OF
HAPPINESS   209
    With excerpts from *Marxism and the Human Individual* by
    Adam Schaff

Marković: PARTICIPATORY DEMOCRACY AND
BUREAUCRACY   219
    With an excerpt from *From Affluence to Praxis* by Mihailo
    Marković

Stojanović: SELF-CRITIQUE OF SOCIALIST SOCIETY   225
    With an excerpt from *Between Ideals and Reality* by Svetozar
    Stojanović

GUIDE TO FURTHER READING   227

QUESTIONS FOR FURTHER DISCUSSION   228

Individualized Marxism: Class-Radicalism in the 1960s

HISTORICAL OVERVIEW **229**

Marcuse: FREUDIAN MARXISM **237**

Marcuse: THE NEW SENSIBILITY **244**

Sartre and Merleau-Ponty: EXISTENTIALIST MARXISM **248**
  With excerpts from *Search for a Method* by Jean-Paul Sartre, and *Sense and Non-Sense* by Maurice Merleau-Ponty

PHENOMENOLOGICAL MARXISM **257**
  With excerpts from "Phenomenological Marxism" by Paul Piccone

THE DIALECTICAL SENSIBILITY **260**
  With an excerpt from "Dialectical Sensibility I: Critical Theory, Scientism, and Empiricism" by Ben Agger

GUIDE TO FURTHER READING **266**

QUESTIONS FOR FURTHER DISCUSSION **267**

Returning to Crisis-Theory: The Many Faces of Modern Marxism

HISTORICAL OVERVIEW **268**

Miliband: STATE INTERVENTION **279**
  With an excerpt from *The State in Capitalist Society* by Ralph Miliband

Habermas: LEGITIMATION PROBLEMS IN LATE CAPITALISM **284**
  With excerpts from *Legitimation Crisis* by Jürgen Habermas

Braverman: AGAINST THE THEORY OF THE "NEW WORKING CLASS" **294**
  With excerpts from *Labor and Monopoly Capital* by Harry Braverman

Leiss: TECHNOLOGY, ECOLOGY, AND HUMAN NEEDS **307**
  With an excerpt from *The Limits to Satisfaction* by William Leiss

TOWARDS AN ECOLOGICAL MARXISM **316**

GUIDE TO FURTHER READING **339**

QUESTIONS FOR FURTHER DISCUSSION **340**

Glossary of Terms 341
Bibliography 345
Index 349

Introduction: A North American Marxism

It is early 1978. An author, a young sociology professor working near Toronto, is completing a book for North American undergraduate and graduate students. A publisher near Los Angeles is planning to publish the book, believing that a significant market exists for a work of this kind. The book is about Marxism.

The book's argument is that Marxism is not a fossil, to be displayed under glass in eastern and central European museums of natural history. It argues instead that Marxism potentially relates to the lives of students in North American universities as well as to American workers; that a non-authoritarian Marxism can be as North American as liberal democracy. It contends Marxism is a living theoretical system relevant wherever workers in offices and factories do not control the process and product of their work, but are merely wage-laborers.

Why do we write about Marxism in 1978, believing that it might be relevant to North Americans? Our answer, developed systematically in the course of this book, is that Marxism exists—must exist—because alienation exists. Alienation refers to the way in which human beings under capitalism do not control their work but instead are dominated by their work and by the requirements of the profit-system.

Marx analyzed capitalism in terms of the alienation it produced and in terms of the contradictions imbedded in the capitalist production process. He theorized that the maturation of these contradictions would cause the rate of profit to fall and require capitalists to fire many workers. These developments, emerging in deep-seated economic crises, would nudge the working class towards socialist revolution. It is our contention, summarized in Chapter 7, that alienation still exists (because capitalism exists, albeit in internationalist forms and based on monopoly, small capitalists having been systematically swallowed up by large) and that the "internal contradictions" of capitalism, as Marx termed them in *Capital,* remain. By internal contradictions Marx referred to the way in which he

1

felt that capitalism, logically, was destined to dig its own grave—on the basis of its domestic and international expansion and on the basis of its relentless accumulation of profit.

But Marxism, according to the understanding developed in this book, is not determinism: It requires the "free will" of workers who engage in socialist class-radicalism to seize upon deep economic crises and transform capitalism into socialism. Marx, according to our reading of his work in Chapter 1, did not say that socialism was inevitable; rather he argued that socialism was merely a possibility, the realization of which depended upon class consciousness and class-struggle. Many Marxists of the Second International, as we note in Chapter 2, below, ignored the necessity of class conscious class-radicalism, instead believing (in an act of faith) that socialism was a predetermined necessity, as inevitable as the sun rising in the east.

Why socialism has not dawned in the way that many early twentieth century Marxists hoped is the subject of this book. Our concern with dashed socialist expectations does not emerge from an attitude of cynicism about the possibility of benign human relationships; rather we want to investigate Marxian failures because we believe that the world needs creative, democratic Marxism today more than ever, in face of the deep economic, political, and ecological crises.

Thus we write *Western Marxism* not as a work of pure history but as a way of keeping history alive in the present. It is our contention that Marx's dialectical method can be applied to the framework of 1980s North America and utilized as an effective theoretical and political weapon of democratic socialist class-radicalism. In a personal sense, this attempt to recapture the past by fulfilling never-forgotten socialist aspirations was formed in the 1960s, when many young North Americans became dissatisfied with the complacency of the 1950s, with racial and sexist discrimination, and with the Indo-China war. It is our belief, amplified in Chapter 6, that the "individualist Marxism" of the 1960s, as we term it, was a profoundly energizing force for recapturing and reenlivening the Marxian dialectical method. Moreover, we contend, notably in Chapter 7, that the youthful Americanization of significant Marxist themes during the 1960s provides a unique opportunity to create a North American Marxism that blends American populism, non-authoritarian at its roots, with more traditional European socialist concerns. It is towards this synthesis of Marxism and American populism that we move in the course of this book.

While many who survey the 1960s from the perspective of hindsight state dogmatically that hippiedom and the New Left were momentary flights of middle-class student fancy, we contend that the work of theorists like Herbert Marcuse first augured this blending of democratic radicalism and European socialism. On the basis of Marcuse's work we develop the argument below that a democratically-minded, non-authoritarian socialist class-radicalism can be forged in the American context. This class-radicalism will be rooted in a new socialist-populist ideology that bends European socialist themes (such as class struggle) into the non-authoritarian American context, thus appealing to American workers who would otherwise view Marxism as another form of bureaucratic centralization, and equate socialism, wrongly, with the Soviet system.

In Chapter 7 we attempt to forge a Marxist—populist synthesis that borrows the radical democracy and anti-authoritarianism of the student and minority movements of the 1960s, theoretically vindicated in Marcuse's brilliant 1969 work

An Essay on Liberation, and combines them with a systematic theory of capitalist crisis-tendencies. We analyze a number of crisis-theories in Chapter 7, arguing that new opportunities are being created for socialist class-radicalism as the western "class compromise" further erodes, as the capitalist state falters in its attempt to mediate between business and labor, and as new ecological imperatives force the cooling down of the capitalist production process itself. Our position, amplified in Chapter 7, is that Marcusean Marxism did not go far enough towards systematically reconnecting American populism, with its anti-authoritarian majoritarianism, to European socialism and Marxism. For this reason, the 1960s did not see the creation, in North America or western Europe, of a concerted class-radicalism that could fundamentally challenge the faltering capitalist system.

This book draws on the radical exuberance of the 1960s, a spirit that still imbues this author with real optimism about socialist possibility. Yet this is not to forget that the capitalist class- and power-systems, no longer domestic but global in their reach, are exceedingly heavy weights on this socialist possibility. Optimism in the personal sense is not a theoretical category; socialist optimism, however, can and must be derived from the careful analysis of crisis-tendencies in advanced capitalism, on the basis of which new, cogent types of class-radicalism, motivated by a North American Marxist-populist ideology, can be built. We are theoretically optimistic that the deep crises of the late 1970s can be turned in a socialist direction — given correct theory, which grasps capitalist crisis in all its forms, and given a new ideology with which to stimulate and energize concerted class-radicalism.

North American Marxism, based on a coupling of the populist critique of what we call centralist bigness and the traditional socialist program, is not a form of individual "consciousness"; nor is it a personal "lifestyle," isolated from larger social forces. We do not offer the American student yet another intellectual fad the consumption of which will produce liberation or euphoria. Indeed one of the lessons of the 1960s was that radical exuberance can quickly turn into pathetic, cloying narcissism when it loses its sensitivity to the suffering and hopes of human beings. To become a North American Marxist, in the way that we eventually recommend, does not mean that one has achieved liberation and can ignore the very real suffering of those who are perhaps more directly exploited by capital.

While this book is about theory, we stress that theory without practice, without sensitivity to alienation and to the needs and rights of others, is a form of narcissism. In Chapter 4, we discuss the pitfalls of a purely intellectual Marxism, directed only towards the salvation of the theorist. A North American Marxism, if successful, will relate not to "liberation" in the abstract but to the day-to-day struggles of human beings and the themes that make life meaningful for them. Marxism, for Marx, was not a purely intellectual project, subject to narcissistic inner-direction, but a way of relating emancipatory theory and the vision of socialist possibility to the daily struggles of oppressed human beings.

It was noted, at the beginning, that a market for Marxism evidently exists on this continent, especially in the universities. It is the author's contention that the existence of this market says more about the 1970s and 1980s than does the apparent rush back towards the fraternity-and-football college cultures of the 1950s. Young people are not inured to economic, political, ecological, and human crisis, as media-makers would have us believe. They are cynical about a system that irrationally creates huge universities, fills them with students and then, just as suddenly, removes federal and state aid to higher education charging that most B.A. degrees are job-unrelated. They are still searching for ways to make sense of and transform an ugly, crazy world, creating a new one to which they can legitimately commit their futures. This book is addressed to them, in the hope that they can learn from the successes and failures of the socialist past and ultimately translate socialism and Marxism into the non-authoritarian framework of the North American experience.

1

Alienation, Contradiction, and Crisis in Marx's Dialectical Method

HISTORICAL OVERVIEW

Karl Marx outlined his theories of capitalism during the period of its earliest development. We term this period "early market capitalism," characterized by the relative immaturity of industrial production and technology, and by open markets for commodities in which supply and demand were allowed to find their own balance without the intervention and regulation of the nation-state. During this period of early market capitalism the "internal contradictions" between capital and labor were sharp, threatening the breakdown of the entire system. Marx initially believed that the temporary insurrection of the communists in Paris in 1871 signalled the dawning of a new revolutionary age. This optimism turned out to be somewhat exaggerated, as the Paris Commune collapsed shortly after its inception. Although Marx did not live to see a successful communist revolution, while living in London he was active in various political organizations, foremost of these being the First International, formed in 1864 and which collapsed as Marx and the anarchist Bakunin could not come to terms. Earlier, during the 1840s and 1850s, he and Engels were active in the underground Communist League.

Marx gradually abandoned the revolutionary model of the dictatorship of the proletariat and its violent seizure of power. His 1848 Communist Manifesto drew inspiration from the Blanquist and Jacobin traditions, stressing the radical rupture with the past that the communist revolution would represent. Yet later works such as Capital abandoned the Blanquist-Jacobin inspiration, drawn mainly from the French political experience of the 1789 revolution and its aftermath. Marx came to stress that revolutionary transformation must slowly build upon the full development of industrial production and upon the liberal-democratic social structure which accompanied industrialization in France, Britain, and the United States.

5

GENERAL INTRODUCTION

To understand western Marxism we must understand Marx's own dialectical method. Developments within western Marxism can be comprehended only in light of modifications and transformations of Marx's original theory of capitalism. It is convenient to divide Marx's theory into three elements:

1. A theory of alienation and a vision of human emancipation
2. A theory of the laws of capitalist social structure and their "internal contradictions"
3. A model of crisis that extends the logic of internal contradictions in empirical directions.

By internal contradictions Marx meant deep-seated structural elements of capitalism that predisposed the system to eventually produce severe and crippling crises. Thus he analyzed internal contradictions from the point of view of their implied, self-propelling logic. Marx suggested that capitalism was on a precarious footing in the way it organized its mode of production; he argued that the capitalist production process would create the conditions of economic crisis that would force a revolutionary working class to rebel against the system and to create socialism. The basic contradiction, according to Marx, was the contradiction between capital and labor. Marx's "general law of capital accumulation" explains the way in which the capitalist derives "surplus-value" from wage-labor, thus deepening the alienation of labor.

Marx did not suggest that the contradictions of capitalism would inevitably lead to socialism unless these contradictions emerged in empirical forms of economic and social crisis, to be acted upon by the revolutionary working class. Among the crisis-forms Marx noted were the tendency of the rate of profit to fall; the tendency towards the concentration and centralization of capital; the tendency of capitalism to create an "industrial reserve army" of periodically unemployed workers; and the tendency towards a severe disproportion between what Marx called "socialized labor processes" (growing division of labor, societal complexity, large-scale production, etc.) and the private accumulation of capital by a few large capitalists.

The first two features of Marx's dialectical method, his theory and critique of alienation and his theory of the "internal contradictions" of capitalism, were the most systematically developed aspects of his outlook. The crisis-theory was only briefly outlined in *Capital* and, earlier, in the *Communist Manifesto*. The first two features can be considered the backbone of Marx's dialectical method. He argued that an adequate understanding of capitalism depends upon (a) an analysis of the modalities and dimensions of human alienation, and (b) an analysis of the self-contradictory aspects of the capitalist system, the so-called "internal contradictions".

Most western Marxists today retain Marx's theory of alienation and his theory of internal contradictions. They see modern capitalism in terms of alienation and class struggle. Yet many Marxists do not accept Marx's specific crisis-theory, developed in the context of late nineteenth century Europe, for they do not believe that internal contradictions today manifest themselves in the same crisis-forms as sketched by Marx. In Chapter 7, we assess recent developments in crisis-theory that go significantly beyond Marx in this respect.

The unique feature of Marx's dialectical method was the notion that human beings create a social order that takes on an existence of its own and tends to break down (because of the maturation of its internal contradictions). Marx argued that capitalism could be comprehended in terms of its structural contradictions ("immanent laws", as he termed them); these "laws", once understood, could be transformed by overthrowing the capitalist order. Marx contended that these "immanent laws" of capitalism are not eternally given, in the way that the physical laws of motion are given, but are theoretically reconstructed reflections of an imperfect, self-contradictory social order.

While Marx's social science offered insights into the probable points of breakdown of capitalism, his early philosophical critique of alienation provided an understanding of the fundamental inequity of capitalism, in which work became estranged from the worker and owned and controlled by others. His later scientific theory, developed in the three volumes of *Capital,* outlined the "immanent laws" of the capitalist production process, showing how capitalism is a contradictory, self-undermining social order. His model of crisis, only sketched in broadest outline and not systematically developed, showed how alienated workers would ultimately revolt against the capitalist system and produce a non-alienated socialist order, building upon the crisis-forms generated by the maturation and manifestation of the internal contradictions.

It is crucial to note that Marx did not believe that the maturation of internal contradictions would inevitably lead to the final capitalist breakdown and the dawning of socialism. Contradictions *tend* (and only tend) to produce crises that must be understood and acted upon by the revolutionary working class. By themselves, the internal contradictions are logical and analytical categories that describe the imperfect, crisis-bound functioning of the capitalist system; they do not guarantee the arrival of socialism. In fact, as we will often note in this book, there have been only tenuous relationships between the levels of contradiction and crisis in the twentieth century, with capitalism often capable of postponing its eventual collapse by managing the crisis-tendencies that periodically emerge from the maturation of contradictions.

Marx's early writings, excerpted below, laid the groundwork for a general theory of alienation. Every human being, according to Marx, externalizes himself in nature, realizing his humanity by projecting outward his values, purposes, and aspirations. Freedom for Marx is the realization of human beings in their externalizing activity; alienation is the negation of freedom, the inability of the person to engage in self-realizing activity. Marx analyzed specific conditions under which human beings are not free to externalize their natures and purposes upon the world, developing his critique of capitalism on the basis of these few basic insights into the nature of labor.

Marx applied his general theory of alienation to the particular context of capitalism in which the means of production are privately owned. He felt that an entire class had been alienated under the capitalist mode of production, owing to their subservience to a wage-labor system controlled by capitalists. In a society predicated on the private ownership and control of the means of production, Marx contended, there could be no justice for the worker who owes his livelihood to the capitalist. Furthermore, Marx perceived structural contradictions that rendered capitalism crisis-bound and ultimately inoperative. In *Capital* Marx argued that with the advance of the capitalist production process, profit would inevitably shrink, forcing the capitalist to fire workers and thus create the seeds of working-class revolt.

Alienation under capitalism is both a subjective and objective condition: Marx pinned his belief in the possibility of revolution precisely on the worker's inability to tolerate too much alienation in the forms, then, of unemployment, destitution, and even starvation. In this sense, alienation can be consciously reversed by struggling workers who comprehend the possibility of their own liberation. Marx felt that the tendency of profit to shrink with the advance of the capitalist production process would eventually create the conditions of capitalism's destruction. Marx and Engels wrote the *Communist Manifesto* to urge workers to recognize the injustice of their condition and the possibility of transforming it and to act on that recognition to create a new socialist order.

Marx in this sense was both a social scientist and a partisan of political action; unlike many theorists before and after him, Marx did not sharply separate these two activities. He unified the scientific and political aspects of his critique of capitalism to provide a theory that could instruct workers about ways of overcoming alienation. He held that there is a dialectical relationship between economic structures (and their contradictions) and the human experience of alienation that, he contended, is the source of revolutionary class struggle. Marx rose above the pure description of capitalism as he abandoned the social scientist's conventional impartiality with respect to political and ethical values; he did not believe that his primary duty was as an impartial social scientist, albeit one who provides a relentless critique of the inequities of capitalism. He felt rather that his responsibility was to herald and to expedite socialist transformation, not as an individual with personal beliefs and values but as a revolutionary social scientist whose theory and research could inform workers about the possibility of class emancipation.

While most social scientists attempt to produce laws of social action, Marx believed that capitalism was not an eternal form of society but a distorted, destructive form that could be abolished. In this sense Marx tried to unmask social scientific "laws" as historically limited, partial replicas of a particular stage of social development capable of being radically transformed. Marx submitted that social science should not seek invariant laws of social action and social structure but rather the preconditions of human emancipation from the distorted "laws" of capitalism.

Marx believed that these "laws" sought by bourgeois social scientists were not causal statements that applied to every social order, like the law of gravity. He argued that they were ideological masks that deceived human beings about the temporary, historical character of capitalism. By inferring from the capitalist condition certain eternal, causal aspects of the human condition, Marx felt that bourgeois social scientists created a form of ideology and of what he termed "false consciousness," confusing capitalist "laws" with all social laws, past and future, thus giving workers no hope of changing the capitalist condition. He wanted both to disabuse workers of this false consciousness of capitalist "laws," which he contended were historically peculiar and not eternal, and to overthrow the "laws" by creating socialist freedom. Marx saw the laws sought by bourgeois social scientists as laws of *domination,* which bound workers to an alienated social condition.

Marx related alienation to the social and economic structures that cause that alienation. His was not merely a causal theory, however, for he also provided an account of the internal contradictions and probable crisis-tendencies of capitalism; he analyzed the structural conditions of human emancipation created by capitalism itself in its efforts to contain the internal contradictions that Marx argued were deep-seated (and ineradicable). Marx did not preach to the working class in a moralistic fashion but rather he explained possible scenarios and strategies of class struggle revealed by the maturation of the contradictions and resulting crisis-tendencies of capitalism.

In his own intellectual activity, Marx was both scrupulously honest about his political commitments and rigorously empirical in his scientific research. His three volumes of *Capital* stand today as models of systematic and careful scholarship. He did not believe that it was sufficient merely to deliver speeches to trade-union conventions rallying workers around the emotional cause of socialism. The emotions of revolutionary class struggle had to be harnessed theoretically and politically, he felt, through systematic theorizing about socialist possibilities and empirical research into crisis-tendencies.

Marx felt implicitly that there had to be a division of labor in revolutionary struggle, with some, like himself, producing the theory that could explain and orient class struggle; Marx and Engels felt that the working class required leadership and organization. A burning question in modern Marxism is the extent of the theorist's own personal commitment to radical change. Many worry that Marxist intellectuals are basically elitist and, in Lenin's phrase, members of a revolutionary vanguard, imposing their own prejudices on a pliant working class. Marx's own view was that the radical intellectual could contribute effectively to the socialist movement by providing theoretical and empirical analyses of internal contradictions, using these analyses to explain the worker's alienation and to articulate the possibility of overcoming it in structural and historical terms.

Marx's dialectical method links structural processes and personal processes: He felt that there would be no revolution unless alienated human beings acted to overcome social relations of subservience and domination; yet there would be no revolution unless human beings located their alienation in a theoretical framework that showed them how to work towards socialist change by recognizing and acting upon capitalist internal contradictions. Later Marxists have termed this the "dialectic of theory and praxis," the foundation stone of Marxist methodology.

Marx's method could be complete only when it joined a theory of alienation, a theory of internal contradictions and a model of crisis that linked the recognition of structural breakdown with active class struggle. Without a model of crisis and breakdown, there would be no basis for the formation of class consciousness and class struggle. Marx's method is not deterministic precisely because he does not equate the existence of capitalist internal contradictions with the development and socialist resolution of crisis-tendencies. The breakdown of the system is not inevitable, in spite of the existence of fundamental contradictions. Revolutionary struggle must actively hasten along the maturation of internal contradictions and their emergence in crisis-forms; without this class-conscious revolutionary activity, it would be impossible to move much beyond temporary interruptions in capitalist functioning towards the establishment of qualitatively new socialist relationships.

This book surveys western Marxism from the perspective of Marx's dialectical methodology. Each species of recent Marxian theory can be assessed in terms of its degree of determinism. We will discover that a fundamental division has emerged between those versions of Marxism that are deterministic and those versions that remain dialectical, stressing the necessity of voluntary class action to shepherd along the maturation of internal contradictions. Marxian determinists argue that internal contradictions, and resulting crisis-tendencies (e.g., depressions, high unemployment, falling profits and wages), are so severe that the capitalist system will collapse "automatically," without the active intervention of a class-conscious proletariat.

Our basic model of Marxism's intellectual history holds that we can understand twentieth century theoretical developments in terms of the shifting relationship between Marxian theory and class struggle. In those historical periods when internal contradictions are sharp and produce severe crises, Marxian theories tend to adopt a more scientific, deterministic character; when contradictions appear blunted, and when crisis is not triggered as a consequence, a non-deterministic Marxism emerges. As we will note in our subsequent chapters, many Marxists of one kind or the other have tended to exaggerate either the deterministic or voluntaristic dimension, reducing Marxism either to a fatalistic determinism or to philosophical pessimism. In our concluding chapter, we will attempt to develop a contemporary Marxism which joins revolutionary determinism and voluntarism in a single theory without sacrificing one or the other.

The first type of Marxism, arising in periods of acute crisis, is deterministic in character, suggesting that the revolution is inevitable; the second type of Marxism argues that human beings must attempt to liberate themselves even if there are no structural tendencies towards a broad social and economic crisis. Marx's own dialectical method joined a structural crisis-theory, revolving around his general law of capitalist accumulation coupled with an appreciation of the internal stress-points in the process of capitalist accumulation, and a vision of personal and collective emancipation. Without linking an appreciation of the stress-points of capitalism with a program of constructive class struggle, Marx felt that there would be little prospect of socialist transformation. The revolution, Marx implied, will not occur automatically; neither will the revolution be purely a result of human will, for in the absence of structural crisis-tendencies it is impossible to transform capitalism into socialism.

Our model of the historical vicissitudes of Marxian theory captures the shifting relationship between deterministic and voluntaristic dimensions of Marxism. To the extent to which the capitalist order is beset by crises and mass unrest the deterministic outlook will usually prevail; to the extent to which capitalism is relatively crisis-free, generating prosperity for most and keeping inflation and unemployment in check, the voluntaristic perspective will be adopted.

Deterministic Marxism emerged most clearly during the Second International (1899–1914), as we discuss in Chapter 2. After the First World War, however, Marxism gradually lost its direct relationship to the possibility of revolutionary transformation and became a more abstract and generalized critique of capitalist alienation; this process was accelerated during the period immediately following World War II when western Marxism underwent further revisions (see Chapters 3 and 4, especially). In recent years, as we note in our concluding Chapter 7, advanced capitalism has experienced severe dislocations resulting from the inability of government intervention in the economy to keep both unemployment and inflation at tolerable levels, and resulting from new ecological pressures on the capitalist production process, generating a renewed interest in crisis-theories.

The theory of the crisis, in Marxian formulations, lends itself to differing interpretations, producing both determinism and voluntarism: (a) the first interpretation suggests that because crisis is inevitable (or at least unavoidable) in a capitalist system, human beings need not actively intervene in hastening along the revolutionary process; (b) the second interpretation suggests that crisis is not inevitable and that human beings must engage in producing revolutionary transformations. Marx gave license, at different places and in different contexts within his own work, to both viewpoints. We suggest here that Marx's dialectical method requires a mixture of objective crisis-tendencies (whether these include falling rate of profit and periodic unemployment, or other tendencies appropriate to later types of industrial capitalism) and voluntaristic class struggle that moves crisis-bound social orders in a socialist direction. Certain Marxists in the 1960s adopted the second approach, suggesting that radical change will be purely a result of organized insurrection and consciousness-raising. In later chapters we will examine this issue at greater length, assessing contemporary forms of the relationship between personal liberation, structural crisis and socialist transformation.

Marx theorized that capitalist economic structures tend to self-destruct; this tendency, he felt, could be comprehended and then further advanced by members of the politically organized and class-conscious proletariat. However there could be no successful insurrection, as he learned from the fatal experience of the Paris Communards in 1871, without the pre-existence of structural crisis-tendencies. Marx did not believe that a tightly organized group of dedicated revolutionaries could successfully turn the system on its head without at the same time exploiting structural tendencies of that system to collapse. As we will argue below, notably in Chapter 7, personal liberation, when divorced from larger socialist movements and the analysis of structural crisis-tendencies, becomes purely an intellectual escape mechanism for the disaffected. It is virtually impossible to broaden personal rebellion into collective transformation without comprehending structural tendencies of crisis within which personal liberation might take place. Bluntly put: Good intentions are not enough to effect socialist change. Good intentions, while necessary, must be harnessed to a careful analysis of structural weaknesses and thus the possibilities of socialist transformation.

The history of western Marxism is a history of the alternating relationship between crisis-triggered revolutionary determinism and, in periods of political harmony and class compromise, pessimism about socialist change. Marx was neither a determinist nor an idealist; his dialectical method relates voluntaristic class-struggle to structural crisis-tendencies. It is a peculiarity of western Marxism that many Marxists have exaggerated either the deterministic or voluntaristic orientations, failing to combine them as Marx had done originally.

Efforts to revise and update Marxism have often failed because they have either rewritten Marxism as economic determinism (as in the Second International; see Chapter 2) or as a personal form of philosophical radicalism, impotent politically (as did members of the Frankfurt School; see Chapter 4). This is especially paradoxical in that, as we have argued, determinism often arose as a response to broad social and economic crisis. The paradox is that determinism, which adopts a passive political strategy, believing that the revolution is inevitable (purely a product of internal contradictions), responds fatalistically to deep crisis that, one might expect, would elicit exactly the opposite response from Marxists. Why does crisis often elicit determinism and not voluntarism? Our response, further developed in Chapter 2 when we examine the determinism of Kautsky and the Austro-Marxists, is that intense capitalist crisis has triggered determinism and not voluntarism because western Marxists did not appreciate the non-deterministic character of Marx's dialectical method, failing to appreciate the difference between internal contradictions and crisis-tendencies. Instead of recognizing deep capitalist crisis as a signal that class struggle must immediately take wing, Marxists like Kautsky saw impending deep crisis as positive proof that Marx was "correct" in (allegedly) predicting the "inevitable" collapse of capitalism. On this basis, Kautsky could passively adopt a deterministic perspective on capitalist crisis, failing to stimulate socialist class-radicalism.

Marx's method, while rooted in certain assumptions about the contradictions of capitalism, remained primarily an empirical methodology, oriented not to logical but to economic and political analysis. While capitalism is logically self-contradictory (i.e., structurally prone to breakdown), Marx did not *predict* the date of this collapse. He refrained from prediction in this regard not because his revolutionary meteorology was rudimentary but because his dialectical method was not deterministic. As a methodology of revolutionary transformation, Marxism required both theory and action; without theory, the class struggle would be aimless and utopian; without class-radicalism, Marxian theory would have no means of translating itself into reality, into socialism.

Western Marxists have often misinterpreted Marx as a determinist who ignored the voluntaristic basis of class struggle because they have failed to understand Marx's dialectical method, composed of a theory of alienation, a theory of contradictions, and a theory of crisis and appropriate class struggle. This misinterpretation is justified by Marx himself in numerous places in his writings where he characterized his method as "scientific socialism" and as a "natural science of history," creating the erroneous impression that his method, like the natural sciences, was deterministic. Our reconstruction of Marx's method in this chapter is based not on precise textual examination but on a reading of Marx's methodological intention, which remains insufficiently developed. When we read Marx as a dialectical theorist and not as a strict determinist or voluntarist we are reconstructing the general thrust of his theory in such a way as to see his method in terms of the three aforementioned components and not in terms of his periodic utterances about the determinism of his method.

It is our position, developed in Chapter 7, that Marxism can be relevant today only if the crisis-theory of Marx is substantially revised. We retain from Marx his critique of alienation and his understanding of capitalist internal contradictions (the foremost being the contradiction, in general terms, between capital and labor); we depart from original Marxism in arguing that forms of crisis and appropriate class-radicalism have changed with the further development of advanced monopoly capitalism. It is thus our intention not to provide a careful reading of Marx that establishes a single correct version of Marxist theory, valid for all time, but to establish a dialectical method that allows us to reconstruct that theory in historically and culturally relevant terms. It is our contention that there is no single or unique Marxism but a variety of theoretical possibilities, stemming from the open-minded reapplication of the dialectical method.

Marx did not systematize his method because he was preoccupied with the careful analysis of capitalist internal contradictions; he wanted to show that capitalism logically could not avoid breakdown. But this was a far cry from establishing the probable date of that breakdown in deterministic fashion. When

Marx said, as he often did, that the collapse of capitalism was "necessary" he meant necessary in a logical sense (and necessary for human freedom) but not in a scientific sense. The necessity of the revolution for Marx was not equivalent to the necessity of the law of gravity; it was merely a logical necessity, which Marx carefully developed in the three volumes of his *Capital.* Indeed, as we will note in our brief commentaries on the readings, Marx's optimism about the imminence of the socialist revolution appeared to fade between 1848, the date of publication of the *Communist Manifesto,* and about 1867, when he published the first volume of *Capital.* In his 1848 work, he and Engels spoke about the dawn of socialism as an imminent reality, not to be avoided. By the mid-1860s, Marx saw that capitalism had utilized a variety of mechanisms for postponing its crisis and collapse; thus, in *Capital,* Marx said nearly nothing about empirical models of probable crisis and the class struggle that would guide crisis in a socialist direction.

As we will demonstrate in our readings, Marx in *Capital* developed two contradictory arguments. On the one hand, he argued that capitalism was wracked by internal contradictions, the maturation of which would lead to a final system-wrenching crisis. This was an argument on the level of logical analysis. On the other hand, Marx showed that there are internal coping-mechanisms in capitalism that allow the system to counterattack such crisis-tendencies as falling rate of profit, stagnation, the creation of an overly disaffected industrial reserve army, and the like. In this sense, Marx showed empirically how capitalism could counteract the logic of a self-contradictory production and accumulation process.

Throughout Marx's final works runs this tension between the logical requirements of structural breakdown and the empirical tendencies of the system to avoid crisis. This distinction refers back to our earlier distinction between the levels of Marx's dialectical method: We noted that Marx distinguished between structural contradictions and empirical manifestations of crisis and breakdown. In dealing with internal contradictions, Marx presented a highly simplified breakdown of the elements of the capitalist system; it is possible to reduce his model in this respect to the contradiction between capital and labor (or, as Marx often phrased this, the contradiction between private appropriation and socialized production). Internal contradictions for Marx referred to deep-seated aspects of capitalism that logically predispose the system to collapse. Marx was saying that *if* the logic of contradiction is allowed to develop freely, in its natural fashion, *then* the breakdown would eventually occur. In this sense, his theory of contradictions was an ideal-type construction, possessing a logical elegance but often lacking close fit to the empirical world.

Many Marxists today read works such as *Capital* both as a logical analysis of internal contradictions (which it most certainly is) and as an empirical description of European capitalism in the 1860s and 1870s. While Marx obviously examined the empirical workings of capitalism, he did not attempt to describe European capitalism, and to chart its empirical tendencies towards collapse, in a rigorous and precise way. He attempted rather to provide a systematic logical analysis of deep structural contradictions. In this sense *Capital* is not a work about the precise empirical details of Germany or Britain in 1867 but a highly schematic analysis of capitalism as a moving structure of often-contradictory forces.

Those Marxists who read *Capital* as directly applicable to the real world, and not as a highly abstract schematization of reality, tend to adopt a deterministic outlook. They confuse the logical necessity of collapse and breakdown with an empirical necessity (confusing, as we noted above, the "laws" of capitalism with the law of gravity). This confusion results in the belief that Marx's *Capital* is a predictive statement, showing not that capitalism could collapse but that it *will* collapse, necessarily.

Other Marxists, as we will discuss in our Chapters 4 and 6, reject the logical analysis of contradictions altogether. Not only do they not read *Capital* as a precise empirical analysis of 1860s capitalism, they also do not accept Marx's logical schematization of internal contradictions (e.g., capital/labor). These Marxists abandon both the second and third levels of Marx's dialectical method, retaining only the theory and critique of alienation presented in the 1844 manuscripts (and excerpted below). For these Marxists, capitalism not only is not crisis-bound but it is also devoid of the deep structural contradictions Marx most systematically presented in *Capital.* Thus, for these Marxists, the reality of alienation becomes pervasive and inescapable as the relationship between theory and action is severed.

The position we develop in the course of this book is a middle position, between the Marxian determinism that treats socialism as a logical necessity and the Marxian scepticism that believes that contradictions have been permanently eliminated, allowing capitalism to glide along forever. The position advanced here is that modern Marxists must retain Marx's theories of alienation and contradiction while revising his crisis-theorizing. It is our contention that capitalism is not devoid of deep structural contradictions; but, while the contradictions remain, they take empirical forms not envisaged by Marx. In Chapter 7, we bring together different contemporary crisis-theories to round out this picture.

This middle position reads *Capital* as a valuable book, an interesting outline of possible forms of breakdown. However, it does not read *Capital* as a forecast of inevitable breakdown but rather as an account of the possibilities of preventing breakdown and expanding the capitalist production and accumulation process. Yet this middle position does not argue, on this basis, that the possibility of breakdown has disappeared entirely, that the system will last forever, gliding along endlessly. The middle position maintains that breakdown is possible but not inevitable; internal contradictions remain, along with the potential for the transformation of capitalism into socialism, but crisis is not an inevitable consequence of contradictions.

To remain Marxists, modern theorists, according to our argument, must adopt the middle position, retaining the theory of capitalist internal contradictions but not assuming either that crisis is an inevitable outcome of these contradictions or that crisis will take the same forms today (e.g., falling rate of profit) as in Marx's time. Our discussion, below, of the vicissitudes of western Marxism reveals that Marxism has moved from strict determinism (Kautsky) to, at the other extreme, utter abandonment of the Marxian theory of internal contradictions (the Frankfurt School). In our concluding Chapter, we will develop the so-called middle position, assessing current research into new models of crisis.

In our discussion of Marx's dialectical method that follows, the reader should look for two, apparently contradictory elements: (a) on the one hand, Marx argued that capitalism, as he saw it, would fall because the deep-seated internal contradictions would blossom forth in particular crisis-forms that the system, according to Volumes I and III of *Capital,* could not contain. Thus we read Marx on one level as proposing an empirical analysis of historically specific crisis-tendencies, relevant to late nineteenth century capitalism; (b) on the other hand, Marx can be read as generating a profound logical analysis of capitalist internal contradictions applicable to future forms of capitalism. In this sense his detailed analyses in *Capital* are not empirical but logical, showing that deep-seated internal contradictions can be temporarily (but probably not permanently) contained by the internal coping mechanisms of the capitalist system.

The second aspect of our reading of Marx will sustain our argument, later, that there is a serious difference between internal contradictions and the precise empirical forms in which contradictions emerge as system-wrenching crises. By conflating contradictions, on the logical level of analysis, with empirical crisis-forms scientific Marxists of the Second International mistakenly assumed that the system would break down deterministically, without active class struggle required to bend empirical crisis-tendencies into socialist transformation.

Those theorists of the Second International who thought capitalist crisis and socialist revolution to be "necessary" in early twentieth century Europe failed to distinguish between the logical and empirical levels of Marxian theory. The scientific Marxists like Kautsky read *Capital* as an empirical prediction and not as a logical-conceptual analysis of internal contradictions, from which crises would *not* inevitably spring. This is why Kautsky and other scientific Marxists did not map out an active role for the class-conscious proletariat, as did Lukács in response to the failure of the Second International's scientific Marxism; Kautsky believed, on the basis of Marx's allegedly empirical analysis in *Capital,* that internal contradictions were immediately being transformed into breakdown and socialist reconstruction, thus requiring no voluntaristic class-radicalism to shepherd along crisis-tendencies.

Similarly, the Frankfurt School, in the late 1940s and 1950s, surveying the post-war reconstruction of global capitalism, believed that capitalism had "solved" its structural contradictions, on the basis of which they dismissed the possibility of system-wrenching crises and socialist transformation via organized class-radicalism. The Frankfurt theorists (see Chapter 4, in particular) accepted Marx's critique of alienation but not his theory of internal contradictions or his crisis-theory and his sketch of voluntaristic class-radicalism to be initiated on the basis of the recognition of crisis.

In Chapter 6 we will examine recent attempts by theorists such as Herbert Marcuse to develop new types of class-radicalism that are optimally democratic in their organizational structures. The "individualist Marxists," as we term them, believe that internal contradictions still exist but that class-radicalism must take new directions from what Marx had in mind in the late nineteenth century. The reinterpretation of Marxism dealt with in Chapter 6, focused on the work of Marcuse, is important because it signals the first attempt to surpass the pessimism of the Frankfurt School. Marcuse reintroduced the theory of internal contradictions while attempting to revise crisis-models and appropriate types of class-radicalism.

The individualist Marxists, in the 1960s, paved the way for more systematic revisions of Marxian crisis-theory in the 1970s, dealt with in Chapter 7. Marcuse, Sartre, and Merleau-Ponty showed that it was possible to retain a theory of deep-seated structural contradictions while revising Marx's crisis-theory and strategies of class-radicalism. Our conclusion will attempt to bring together and systematize recent developments both in crisis-theory and in the articulation of strategies of contemporary class-radicalism.

Marx's dialectical method, introduced in this opening chapter, allows for a catholicity of theoretical approaches. Marxism has survived the Russian Revolution and the pessimism of the Frankfurt School without having abandoned Marx's method. His method, in this book, will provide a framework for analyzing the history and the future of western Marxism.

MARX'S VISION OF SOCIALIST EMANCIPATION

In the following passages, Marx argues that the worker's alienation results from the process whereby the "product of his labor" becomes an "alien object" to him. Alienation is not a property of *all* externalizing activity, for alienated labor "exists independently, *outside*" the worker, while externalizing labor need not take on an estranged existence. Marx here outlines his seminal theory of alienation, upon which he draws throughout his analysis of capitalism.

Marx argues that the worker becomes a "slave" of his work and its product; the more the worker produces, the less he has. He suggests that alienation is not merely a result of the alienation of the worker's product, its ownership and control by a capitalist. He outlines four features of alienated labor. The first feature exists, Marx argues, in the worker's "relationship with the product of his labor."

The second feature is the *external* character of work, the fact that work is imposed and not freely chosen. Marx suggests that the worker feels "at home only during his leisure-time," when his time is his own. In later chapters, notably Chapter 3 on Hegelian Marxism and Chapter 4 on the Frankfurt School's critique of instrumental rationality and domination, we will examine the further penetration of alienation into the realms of culture and leisure under advanced capitalism.

Marx criticizes the *forced* character of the work-activity under capitalism. The compulsion to work is imposed indirectly on the worker through the wage-labor system, in which he receives a barely adequate living-wage in return for the capitalist's right to dispose of the product of his labor-power. Human beings do not fulfill themselves creatively in work but treat work only as a means to an end, performed in return for a living-wage.

The third feature of alienated labor is the alienation of human species-life. The purpose of human species-activity, Marx asserts, is "free, conscious activity," not conceived as a means to an end (wage-labor) nor perceived as external to the worker, imposed by the false necessity of capitalism. Marx argues that men are distinguished from animals by the purposive character of human productive activity: "animals produce only themselves while man reproduces the whole of nature." Marx considers non-human nature to be the "inorganic body" of man, the canvas upon which men reproduce themselves "in accordance with the laws of beauty."

Species-life under a system of alienated labor is turned into a means of individual existence. In Chapter 5 on Marxian humanism, we will examine the ways in which certain dissident eastern European social philosophers have made this insight into human species-life the core of their "philosophy of praxis," opposing the rigid dominance and alienating character of Soviet state-socialism.

The fourth characteristic of alienation is the divorce of man from man, the destruction of human community under a system of capitalist wage-labor. Men relate to each other not as free and co-equal producers—and as participants in a self-regenerating communitarian species-life—but as units of labor, defined not by their total humanity but by their status and function in the production process. In Chapter 6 on individualized Marxism, we will examine the tendency to view modern alienation primarily as a function of the over-bureaucratization and oversocialization of the human being, resulting in his definition merely as an occupant of a narrow social-economic role. This critique broadens out into a critique of the loss of community that is a prevalent symptom of contemporary advanced capitalist alienation.

These four features of alienated labor reveal that Marx was equally as concerned with the process and activity of work, and its relation to human consciousness and personality, as with the relationship between the worker as a possessor of labor-power and his product. Many latter-day Marxists *reduce* Marx's theory of alienation to the exploitation of labor by capital, implying that the emancipation of labor will be purely a result of the repossession by the working class of the means and product of production. The excerpt below will demonstrate that Marx regarded the process and activity of production—the relation of man to himself, to his species-being and to other men—as being fully as important for speculating about human emancipation as the relation of the worker to his product.

Marx's solution to the problem of alienation was communism. He termed communism the "*definitive* resolution of the antagonism between man and nature, and between man and man"; alienation was the "riddle of history" to be solved by communism. Marx felt that communism would achieve the unity of man's species-life and his particular individuality. In addition, Marx felt that communism could unify the very personality of the human being, defragmenting human activities which, under capitalism, are subordinated to the interests of capital.

Marx asserts that private property makes men "stupid and partial," fracturing the inherent unity of man's creative interaction with the world. Each particular function (e.g., eating, drinking, working) is degraded into a means to an end, the mere preservation of the physical body, losing its potential to express an aspect of human personality. The physical senses, Marx argues, are separated from the intellectual senses, as manual and mental labor are divorced through the advance and deepening of the division of labor. The senses—potentially media for creative expression and experience—are reduced to the sense of "having," of mere possession.

Implicit in Marx's critique of the division between manual and mental labor is a notion of the alienating effects of the division of labor. For Marx this critique of the division of labor seemed to have two interrelated features: (a) on the one hand, Marx opposed and criticized the reduction of wage-laboring human beings to single, narrow economic roles (i.e., to the particular function they perform in the factory and office); (b) on the other hand, Marx opposed the internal fragmentation of labor in the plant, such that workers do not participate in the production and control of the whole product. The archetype of alienation in this sense is the assembly-line. Unfortunately, Marx's two-fold critique of the (capitalist) division of labor remained mere fragments inviting future development. In Chapter 7, we will present readings from Harry Braverman's *Labor and Monopoly Capital* that further develop a Marxist theory and critique of the division of labor (both in society at large and in the workplace and production process themselves).

Communism was equated by Marx with the overcoming of private property. By private property, Marx did not refer to all products but only to the industrial means of production, owned by capitalists. Communism, Marx felt, would emancipate the human senses, fundamentally altering man's relationship with nature, externalizing essential human purposes and designs. The senses are the bond between the free consciousness of men and this creative externalization.

Marx was deeply concerned that nature should not become a mere utility for men but that it should attain an aesthetic and even spiritual status. "Humanized nature" would gain emancipation along with human labor. Humanized nature would reflect and foster "humanized senses," allowing human beings to recapture their creative, self-creating relationship with nature.

In the section of the *Economic and Philosophical Manuscripts* excerpted below, Marx advances one of his most profound and original ideas. He suggests that human creativity has a double character: (a) on the one hand, it is productive, useful activity, externalizing objects (e.g., tools, factories, houses, works of art) that assume their own separate existence; (b) on the other hand, the things we make *remake* us, altering and deepening our perception of ourselves and the world. Marx implied that creativity and self-creativity could be unified under communism.

Marx indicates that productive work (i.e., activity which is useful to society, in general terms) need not be seen as antithetical to personally fulfilling, enjoyable creativity. At the core of Marx's vision of freedom lies the assumption that socially useful work can be organized democratically, without harsh authoritarian coordination or an overly refined division of labor (such that the worker *becomes* his function); and that this work need not be intrinsically unpleasant, or, as Marx phrased it, "external" to the worker — something to be escaped. This is a revolutionary sentiment for it contradicts the nearly universal assumption of most bourgeois social philosophers that human freedom can only reside *outside* of productive activity. Socialists before Marx, such as Robert Owen, also believed that work could be rendered creative; yet Marx was the first to make this assumption the core of his political and economic philosophy.

Furthermore, Marx did not feel that there had to be eternal "contradictions" between the needs of human and non-human nature. The dichotomy between "subject" and "object" — the philosophical equivalent of the dichotomy between human and non-human nature — was perceived by Marx to be false, *not* an essential component of the social world. He argued that class-stratified societies produce these dichotomies because they have alienated men from their productive and creative possibilities. Under communism, Marx argued, productivity and creativity need not be contradictory. Yet, he continued, dualisms such as these would not be overcome merely through philosophical introspection but rather through "practical means, . . . through the *practical* energy of man" (i.e., through revolutionary activity).

We shall begin from a *contemporary* economic fact. The worker becomes poorer the more wealth he produces and the more his production increases in power and extent. The worker becomes an ever cheaper commodity the more goods he creates. The *devaluation* of the human world increases in direct relation with the *increase in value* of the world of things. Labour does not only create goods; it also produces itself and the worker as a *commodity*, and indeed in the same proportion as it produces goods.

This fact simply implies that the object produced by labour, its product, now stands opposed to it as an *alien being,* as a *power independent* of the producer. The product of labour is labour which has been embodied in an object and turned into a physical thing; this product is an *objectification* of labour. The performance of work is at the same time its objectification. The performance of work appears in the sphere of political economy as a *vitiation* of the worker, objectification as a *loss* and as *servitude to the object,* and appropriation as *alienation.*

So much does the performance of work appear as vitiation that the worker is vitiated to the point of starvation. So much does objectification appear as loss of the object that the worker is deprived of the most essential things not only of life but also of work. Labour itself becomes an object which he can acquire only by the greatest effort and with unpredictable interruptions. So much does the appropriation of the object appear as alienation that the more objects the worker produces the fewer he can possess and the more he falls under the domination of his product, of capital.

All these consequences follow from the fact that the worker is related to the *product of his labour* as to an *alien* object. For it is clear on this presupposition that the more the worker expends himself in work the more powerful becomes the world of objects which he creates in face of himself, the poorer he becomes in his inner life, and the less he belongs to himself. It is just the same as in religion. The more of himself man attributes to God the less he has left in himself. The worker puts his life into the object, and his life then belongs no longer to himself but to the object. The greater his activity, therefore, the less he possesses. What is embodied in the product of his labour is no longer his own. The greater this product is, therefore, the more he is diminished. The *alienation* of the worker in his product means not only that his labour becomes an object, assumes an *external* existence, but that it exists independently, *outside himself,* and alien to him, and that it stands opposed to him as an autonomous power. The life which he has given to the object sets itself against him as an alien and hostile force.

Let us now examine more closely the phenomenon of *objectification;* the worker's production and the *alienation* and *loss* of the object it produces, which is involved in it. The worker can create nothing without *nature,* without the *sensuous external world.* The latter is the material in which his labour is realized, in which it is active, out of which and through which it produces things.

But just as nature affords the *means of existence* of labour, in the sense that labour cannot *live* without objects upon which it can be exercised, so also it provides the *means of existence* in a narrower sense; namely the means of physical existence for the *worker* himself. Thus, the more the worker *appropriates* the external world of sensuous nature by his labour the more he deprives himself of *means of existence,* in two respects: first, that the sensuous external world becomes progressively less an object belonging to his labour or a means of existence of his labour, and second, that it becomes progressively less a means of existence in the direct sense, a means for the physical subsistence of the worker.

In both respects, therefore, the worker becomes a slave of the object; first, in that he receives an *object of work,* i.e., receives *work,* and second, in that he receives *means of subsistence.* Thus the object enables him to exist, first as a *worker* and second, as a *physical subject.* The culmination of this enslavement is that he can only maintain himself as a *physical subject* so far as he is a *worker,* and that it is only as a *physical subject* that he is a worker.

(The alienation of the worker in his object is expressed as follows in the laws of political economy: the more the worker produces the less he has to consume; the more value he creates the more worthless he becomes; the more refined his product the more crude and misshapen the worker; the more civilized the product the more barbarous the worker; the more powerful the work the more feeble the worker; the more the work manifests intelligence the more the worker declines in intelligence and becomes a slave of nature.)

Political economy conceals the alienation in the nature of labour in so far as it does not examine the direct relationship between the worker (work) and production. Labour certainly produces marvels for the rich but it produces privation for the worker. It produces palaces, but hovels for the worker. It produces beauty, but deformity for the worker. It replaces labour by machinery, but it casts some of the workers back into a barbarous kind of work and turns the others into machines. It produces intelligence, but also stupidity and cretinism for the workers.

The direct relationship of labour to its products is the relationship of the worker to the objects of his production. The relationship of property owners to the objects of production and to production itself is merely a *consequence* of this first relationship and confirms it. We shall consider this second aspect later.

Thus, when we ask what is the important relationship of labour, we are concerned with the relationship of the *worker* to production.

So far we have considered the alienation of the worker only from one aspect; namely, *his relationship with the products of his labour*. However, alienation appears not merely in the result but also in the *process* of *production*, within *productive activity* itself. How could the worker stand in an alien relationship to the product of his activity if he did not alienate himself in the act of production itself? The product is indeed only the *résumé* of activity, of production. Consequently, if the product of labour is alienation, production itself must be active alienation—the alienation of activity and the activity of alienation. The alienation of the object of labour merely summarizes the alienation in the work activity itself.

What constitutes the alienation of labour? First, that the work is *external* to the worker, that it is not part of his nature; and that, consequently, he does not fulfil himself in his work but denies himself, has a feeling of misery rather than well-being, does not develop freely his mental and physical energies but is physically exhausted and mentally debased. The worker, therefore, feels himself at home only during his leisure time, whereas at work he feels homeless. His work is not voluntary but imposed, *forced labour*. It is not the satisfaction of a need, but only a *means* for satisfying other needs. Its alien character is clearly shown by the fact that as soon as there is no physical or other compulsion it is avoided like the plague. External labour, labour in which man alienates himself, is a labour of self-sacrifice, of mortification. Finally, the external character of work for the worker is shown by the fact that it is not his own work but work for someone else, that in work he does not belong to himself but to another person.

Just as in religion the spontaneous activity of human fantasy, of the human brain and heart, reacts independently as an alien activity of gods or devils upon the individual, so the activity of the worker is not his own spontaneous activity. It is another's activity and a loss of his own spontaneity.

We arrive at the result that man (the worker) feels himself to be freely active only in his animal functions—eating, drinking, and procreating, or at most also in his dwelling and in personal adornment—while in his human functions he is reduced to an animal. The animal becomes human and the human becomes animal.

Eating, drinking, and procreating are of course also genuine human functions. But abstractly considered, apart from the environment of human activities, and turned into final and sole ends, they are animal functions.

We have now considered the act of alienation of practical human activity, labour, from two aspects: (a) the relationship of the worker to the *product of labour* as an alien object which dominates him. This relationship is at the same time the relationship to the sensuous external world, to natural objects, as an alien and hostile world; (b) the relationship of labour to the *act of production* within *labour*. This is the relationship of the worker to his own activity as something alien and not belonging to him, activity as suffering (passivity), strength as powerlessness, creation as emasculation, the *personal* physical and mental energy of the worker, his personal life (for what is life but activity?), as an activity which is directed against himself, independent of him and not belonging to him. This is *self-alienation* as against the above-mentioned alienation of the *thing*.

We have now to infer a third characteristic of *alienated labour* from the two we have considered.

Man is a species-being not only in the sense that he makes the community (his own as well as those of other things) his object both practically and theoretically, but also (and this is simply another expression for the same thing) in the sense that he treats himself as the present, living species, as a *universal* and consequently free being.

Species-life, for man as for animals, has its physical basis in the fact that man (like animals) lives from inorganic nature, and since man is more universal than an animal so the range of inorganic nature from which he lives is more universal. Plants, animals, minerals, air, light, etc., constitute, from the theoretical aspect, a part of human consciousness as objects of natural science and art; they are man's spiritual inorganic nature, his intellectual means of life, which he must first prepare for enjoyment and perpetuation. So also, from the practical aspect, they form a part of human life and activity. In practice man lives only from these natural products, whether in the form of food, heating, clothing, housing, etc. The universality of man appears in practice in the universality which makes the whole of nature into his inorganic body: (a) as a direct means of life; and equally (b) as the material object and instrument of his life activity. Nature is the inorganic body of man; that is to say nature, excluding the human body itself. To say that man *lives* from nature means that nature is his *body* with which he must remain in a continuous interchange in order not to die. The statement that the physical and mental life of man, and nature, are interdependent means simply that nature is interdependent with itself, for man is a part of nature.

Since alienated labour: (a) alienates nature from man; and (b) alienates man from himself, from his own active function, his life activity; so it alienates him from the species. It makes *species-life* into a means of individual life. In the first place it alienates species-life and individual life, and second, it turns the latter, as an abstraction, into the purpose of the former, also in its abstract and alienated form.

For labour, *life activity*, *productive life*, now appear to man only as *means* for the satisfaction of a need, the need to maintain his physical existence. Productive life is, however, species-life. It is life creating life. In the type of life activity resides the whole character of a species, its species-character; and free, conscious activity is the species-character of human beings. Life itself appears only as a *means of life*.

The animal is one with its life activity. It does not distinguish the activity from itself. It is *its activity*. But man makes his life activity itself an object of his will and consciousness. He has a conscious life activity. It is not a determination with which he is completely identified. Conscious life activity distinguishes man from the life activity of animals. Only for this reason is he a species-being. Or rather, he is only a self-conscious being, i.e., his own life is an object for him, because he is a species-being. Only for this reason is his activity free activity. Alienated labour reverses the relationship, in that man because he is a self-conscious being makes his life activity, his *being*, only a means for his *existence*.

The practical construction of an *objective world*, the *manipulation* of inorganic nature, is the confirmation of man as a conscious species-being, i.e., a being who treats the species as his own being or himself as a species-being. Of course, animals also produce. They construct nests, dwellings, as in the case of bees, beavers, and ants. But they only produce what is strictly necessary for themselves or their young. They produce only in a single direction, while man produces universally. They produce only under the compulsion of direct physical needs, while man produces when he is free from physical need and only truly produces in freedom from such need. Animals produce only themselves, while man reproduces the whole of nature. The products of animal production belong directly to their physical bodies, while man is free in face of his product. Animals construct only in accordance with the standards and needs of the species to which they belong, while man knows how to produce in accordance with the standards of every species and knows how to apply the appropriate standard to the object. Thus man constructs also in accordance with the laws of beauty.

It is just in his work upon the objective world that man really proves himself as a *species-being*. This production is his active species-life. By means of it nature appears as *his* work and his reality. The object of labour is, therefore, the *objectification of man's species-life;* for he no longer reproduces himself merely intellectually, as in consciousness, but actively and in a real sense, and he sees his own reflection in a world which he has constructed. While, therefore, alienated labour takes away the object of production from man, it also takes away his *species-life,* his real objectivity as a species-being, and changes his advantage over animals into a disadvantage in so far as his inorganic body, nature, is taken from him.

Just as alienated labour transforms free and self-directed activity into a means, so it transforms the species-life of man into a means of physical existence.

Consciousness, which man has from his species, is transformed through alienation so that species-life becomes only a means for him. Thus alienated labour turns the *species-life of man,* and also nature as his mental species-property, into an *alien* being and into a *means* for his *individual existence*. It alienates from man his own body, external nature, his mental life and his *human* life. A direct consequence of the alienation of man from the product of his labour, from his life activity and from his species-life, is that *man* is *alienated* from other *men*. When man confronts himself he also confronts *other* men.

What is true of man's relationship to his work, to the product of his work and to himself, is also true of his relationship to other men, to their labour and to the objects of their labour.

In general, the statement that man is alienated from his species-life means that each man is alienated from others, and that each of the others is likewise alienated from human life.

Human alienation, and above all the relation of man to himself, is first realized and expressed in the relationship between each man and other men. Thus in the relationship of alienated labour every man regards other men according to the standards and relationships in which he finds himself placed as a worker.*

3. [*Communism* is the *positive* abolition of *private property*, of *human self-alienation*, and thus the real *appropriation* of *human* nature through and for man.] It is, therefore, the return of man himself as a *social*, i.e., really human, being, a complete and conscious return which assimilates all the wealth of previous development. [Communism as a fully developed naturalism is humanism and as a fully developed humanism is naturalism. It is the *definitive* resolution of the antagonism between man and nature, and between man and man. It is the true solution of the conflict between existence and essence, between objectification and self-affirmation, between freedom and necessity, between individual and species. It is the solution of the riddle of history and knows itself to be this solution.]

Thus the whole historical development, both the *real* genesis of communism (the birth of its empirical existence) and its thinking consciousness, is its comprehended and conscious process of becoming; whereas the other, still undeveloped, communism seeks in certain historical forms opposed to private property a *historical* justification founded upon what already exists, and to this end tears out of their context isolated elements of this development (Cabet and Villegardelle are pre-eminent among those who ride this hobby-horse) and asserts them as proofs of its historical pedigree. In doing so, it makes clear that by far the greater part of this development contradicts its own assertions, and that if it has ever existed its past existence refutes its pretension to *essential being*.

It is easy to understand the necessity which leads the whole revolutionary movement to find its empirical, as well as its theoretical, basis in the development of *private property*, and more precisely of the economic system.

This material, directly *perceptible* private property, is the material and sensuous expression of *alienated human* life. Its movement—production and consumption—is the *sensuous* manifestation of the movement of all previous production, i.e., the realization or reality of man. Religion, the family, the state, law, morality, science, art, etc., are only *particular* forms of production and come under its general law. The positive supersession of *private property*, as the appropriation of *human* life, is, therefore, the positive supersession of all alienation, and the return of man from religion, the family, the state, etc., to his *human*, i.e., social life. Religious alienation as such occurs only in the sphere of *consciousness*, in the inner life of man, but economic alienation is that of *real life* and its supersession, therefore it affects both aspects. Of course, the develop-

---

*From *Karl Marx: Early Writings* translated and edited by T.B. Bottomore. Copyright © 1963 by T.V. Bottomore. Used with permission of McGraw-Hill Book Company. Pp. 121–29.

ment in different nations has a different beginning according to whether the actual and *established* life of the people is more in the realm of mind or more in the external world, is a real or ideal life. Communism begins where atheism begins (Owen), but atheism is at the outset still far from being *communism;* indeed it is still for the most part an abstraction.

Thus the philanthropy of atheism is at first only an abstract *philosophical* philanthropy, whereas that of communism is at once *real* and oriented towards *action.*

We have seen how, on the assumption that private property has been positively superseded, man produces man, himself and then other men; how the object which is the direct activity of his personality is at the same time his existence for other men and their existence for him. Similarly, the material of labour and man himself as a subject are the starting-point as well as the result of this movement (and because there must be this starting-point private property is a historical necessity). Therefore, the *social* character is the universal character of the whole movement; *as* society itself produces *man* as *man*, so it is *produced* by him. Activity and mind are social in their content as well as in their *origin;* they are *social* activity and social mind. The *human* significance of nature only exists for *social* man, because only in this case is nature a *bond* with other *men*, the basis of his existence for others and of their existence for him. Only then is nature the *basis* of his own *human* experience and a vital element of human reality. The *natural* existence of man has here become his *human* existence and nature itself has become human for him. Thus *society* is the accomplished union of man with nature, the veritable resurrection of nature, the realized naturalism of man and the realized humanism of nature.

Social activity and social mind by no means exist *only* in the form of activity or mind which is directly communal. Nevertheless, communal activity and mind, i.e., activity and mind which express and confirm themselves directly in a *real association* with other men, occur everywhere where this direct expression of sociability arises from the content of the activity or corresponds to the nature of mind.

Even when I carry out *scientific* work, etc., an activity which I can seldom conduct in direct association with other men, I perform a *social,* because *human,* act. It is not only the material of my activity—such as the language itself which the thinker uses—which is given to me as a social product. My *own existence* is a social activity. For this reason, what I myself produce I produce for society, and with the consciousness of acting as a social being.

My universal consciousness is only the *theoretical* form of that whose *living* form is the real community, the social entity, although at the present day this universal consciousness is an abstraction from real life and is opposed to it as an enemy. That is why the *activity* of my universal consciousness as such is my *theoretical* existence as a social being.

It is above all necessary to avoid postulating "society" once again as an abstraction confronting the individual. The individual *is* the *social being.* The manifestation of his life—even when it does not appear directly in the form of a communal manifestation, accomplished in association with other men—is, therefore, a manifestation and affirmation of *social life.* Individual human life and species-life are not different things, even though the mode of existence of individual life is necessarily either a more *specific* or a more *general* mode of species-life, or that of species-life a *specific* or more *general* mode of individual life.

In his *species-consciousness* man confirms his real *social life,* and reproduces his real existence in thought; while conversely, species-life confirms itself in species-consciousness and exists for itself in its universality as a thinking being. Though man is a unique individual—and it is just his particularity which makes him an individual, a really *individual* communal being—he is equally the *whole,* the ideal whole, the subjective existence of society as thought and experienced. He exists in reality as the representation and the real mind of social existence, and as the sum of human manifestations of life.

Thought and being are indeed *distinct* but they also form a unity. *Death* seems to be a harsh victory of the species over the individual and to contradict their unity; but the particular individual is only a *determinate species-being* and as such he is mortal.

4. Just as *private property* is only the sensuous expression of the fact that man is at the same time an *objective* fact for himself and becomes an alien and non-human object for himself; just as his manifestation of life is also his alienation of life and his self-realization a loss of reality, the emergence of an *alien* reality; so the positive supersession of private property, i.e., the *sensuous* appropriation of the human essence and of human life, of objective man and of human *creations,* by and for man, should not be taken only in the sense of *immediate,* exclusive *enjoyment,* or only in the sense of *possession* or *having.* Man appropriates his manifold being in an all-inclusive way, and thus as a whole man. All his *human* relations to the world—seeing, hearing, smelling, tasting, touching, thinking, observing, feeling, desiring, acting, loving—in short, all the organs of his individuality, like the organs which are directly communal in form, are in their objective action (their *action in relation to the object*) the appropriation of this object, the appropriation of human reality. The way in which they react to the object is the confirmation of *human reality.* It is human effectiveness and human *suffering,* for suffering humanly considered is an enjoyment of the self for man.

Private property has made us so stupid and partial that an object is only *ours* when we have it, when it exists for us as capital or when it is directly eaten, drunk, worn, inhabited, etc., in short, *utilized* in some way. But private property itself only conceives these various forms of possession as *means of life,* and the life for which they serve as means is the *life* of *private property*—labour and creation of capital.

Thus *all* the physical and intellectual senses have been replaced by the simple alienation of *all* these senses; the sense of *having.* The human being had to be reduced to this absolute poverty in order to be able to give birth to all his inner wealth. (On the category of *having* see Hess in *Einundzwanzig Bogen.*)

The supersession of private property is, therefore, the complete *emancipation* of all the human qualities and senses. It is such an emancipation because these qualities and senses have become *human,* from the subjective as well as the objective point of view. The eye has become a *human* eye when its *object* has become a *human,* social object, created by man and destined for him. The senses have, therefore, become directly theoreticians in practice. They relate themselves to the thing for the sake of the thing, but the thing itself is an *objective human* relation to itself and to man, and vice versa. Need and enjoyment have thus lost their *egoistic* character and nature has lost its mere *utility* by the fact that its utilization has become *human* utilization.

Similarly, the senses and minds of other men have become my *own* appropriation. Thus besides these direct organs, *social* organs are constituted, in the form of society; for example, activity in direct association with others has become an organ for the manifestation of life and a mode of appropriation of *human* life.

It is evident that the human eye appreciates things in a different way from the crude, non-human eye, the human *ear* differently from the crude ear. As we have seen, it is only when the object becomes a *human* object, or objective *humanity*, that man does not become lost in it. This is only possible when man himself becomes a *social* object; when he himself becomes a social being and society becomes a being for him in this object.

On the one hand, it is only when objective reality everywhere becomes for man in society the reality of human faculties, human reality, and thus the reality of his own faculties, that all *objects* become for him the *objectification of himself*. The objects then confirm and realize his individuality, they are *his own* objects, i.e., man himself becomes the object. *The manner in which these objects* becomes his own depends upon the *nature of the object* and the nature of the corresponding faculty; for it is precisely the *determinate character* of this relation which constitutes the specific *real* mode of affirmation. The object is not the same for the *eye* as for the *ear*, for the ear as for the eye. The *distinctive character* of each faculty is precisely its *characteristic* essence and thus also the characteristic mode of its objectification, of its *objectively real*, living *being*. It is therefore not only in thought, but through *all* the senses that man is affirmed in the objective world.

Let us next consider the subjective aspect. Man's musical sense is only awakened by music. The most beautiful music has no meaning for the non-musical ear, is not an object for it, because my object can only be the confirmation of one of my own faculties. It can only be so for me in so far as my faculty exists for itself as a subjective capacity, because the meaning of an object for me extends only as far as the sense extends (only makes sense for an appropriate sense). For this reason, the *senses* of social man are *different* from those of non-social man. It is only through the objectively deployed wealth of the human being that the wealth of subjective *human* sensibility (a musical ear, an eye which is sensitive to the beauty of form, in short, senses which are capable of human satisfaction and which confirm themselves as human faculties) is cultivated or created. For it is not only the five senses, but also the so-called spiritual senses, the practical senses (desiring, loving, etc.), in brief, human sensibility and the human character of the senses, which can only come into being through the existence of *its* object, through humanized nature. The cultivation of the five senses is the work of all previous history. Sense which is subservient to crude needs has only a restricted meaning. For a starving man the human form of food does not exist, but only its abstract character as food. It could just as well exist in the most crude form, and it is impossible to say in what way this feeding-activity would differ from that of animals. The needy man, burdened with cares, has no appreciation of the most beautiful spectacle. The dealer in minerals sees only their commercial value, not their beauty or their particular characteristics; he has no mineralogical sense. Thus, the objectification of the human essence, both theoretically and practically, is necessary in order to *humanize* man's senses, and also to create the *human senses* corresponding to all the wealth of human and natural being.

Just as society at its beginnings finds, through the development of *private property* with its wealth and poverty (both intellectual and material), the materials necessary for this *cultural development,* so the fully constituted society produces man in all the plenitude of his being, the wealthy man endowed with all the senses, as an enduring reality. It is only in a social context that subjectivism and objectivism, spiritualism and materialism, activity and passivity, cease to be antinomies and thus cease to exist as such antinomies. The resolution of the *theoretical* contradictions is possible *only* through practical means, only through the *practical* energy of man. Their resolution is not by any means, therefore, only a problem of knowledge, but is a *real* problem of life which philosophy was unable to solve precisely because it saw there a purely theoretical problem.*

MARX'S DIALECTICAL METHOD

Two central components of Marx's dialectical materialism, as we noted in our general introduction to this chapter, are his vision of human emancipation under a communist order and his theoretical and empirical conception of historical change. Marx's dialectical method relates human consciousness to social-structural dynamics, generating a model of the *totality* of social processes. In opposition to pure materialism, which reduces history entirely to structural dynamics, Marx's materialism starts from concrete material conditions but does not at the same time ignore human consciousness, will, and motivation required to change those conditions. Social change for Marx is a product of the complex combination of structural dynamics and human purposes, irreducible either to wholly structural or wholly volitional factors.

A classical problem in the history of social science is the determination of the causality of social and political change. At opposite extremes are deterministic and idealistic explanations for change. Determinists view historical dynamics as possessing a logic of their own, while idealists see history in terms of the actions of individual human beings, whether of certain "great men" such as famous kings or passionate revolutionaries such as Lenin and Mao.

Marx took a middle position, arguing that social change is a product both of structural and motivational dynamics. In concrete terms, Marx believed that a socialist revolution would only occur (a) when the economic system was crisis-bound, threatening the collapse of the system of capitalist profit *and* (b) when human beings acted upon those conditions, grasping the opportunity to reorder society through collective action. He believed that a "dialectic"—or reciprocal interaction and feedback—existed between structural and volitional aspects of social change.

Marx's dialectical materialism refuted many of the idealist themes of German philosophy, especially that species inspired by G. W. F. Hegel. Marx attempted to combat German idealism by showing that material conditions of change had initial priority over volitional factors such as the consciousness of the speculative philosopher. Marx struggled against those in mid-nineteenth century Germany who believed that the world could be changed—or at least "transcended"—in the private mind of the thinking person. It appeared to Marx that German idealism *perpetuated* alienation by failing to convince the person of his responsibility for his own emancipation. In spite of the pretentions of idealist philosophers, material bondage to the profit-system remained.

---

*From *Karl Marx: Early Writings* translated and edited by T.B. Bottomore. Copyright © 1963 by T.V. Bottomore. Used with permission of McGraw-Hill Book Company. Pp. 155–62.

This critique of Hegel's idealist philosophy was the point of departure for Marx's theory and critique of ideology. The dialectical method, referred to above, was designed to debunk and demystify ideologies that kept the human being in harness to alienation. Ideology for Marx referred to any system of ideas that explains human alienation in terms of pregiven natural necessity ("fate" or "destiny," for example), or that ignores the very reality of alienation (e.g., the ideology of free enterprise in early capitalist societies argued that everyone, worker and capitalist alike, benefitted from capitalism). German idealists did not ignore alienation but rather suggested that alienation was an inevitable product of every social order that could be overcome only through the development of philosophical self-consciousness. Hegel's major works, the *Phenomenology of Mind* and *Science of Logic*, develop the categories for this transcendence of alienation. Marx opposed Hegel at the level of Hegel's basic assumptions about human existence.

Earlier, in our discussion of Marx's vision of human emancipation, we outlined Marx's concept of alienation. Hegel believed that every act of human self-externalization (e.g., work) alienated the product of that externalizing activity from the human being, inevitably decreasing human freedom (that is, control of the act and product of externalization). Hegel did not feel, however, that alienation was a permanent condition for he argued that rational philosophical self-consciousness (consciousness of the development of the human mind or spirit) could retrieve and overcome the act of self-alienation.

Marx also employed the concept of self-alienation *(Selbstentäusserung)* to characterize the act of externalization. However Marx argued that capitalist externalization had been narrowed into *labor* to be exchanged on the open market. Workers receive a living-wage from capitalists in return for the right to dispose of the worker's labor power. In this sense, Marx believed that alienation was comprised of the four features outlined earlier. He did not believe that alienation was a by-product of every act of human self-externalization (except in the trivial sense that all human activity externalizes products and works which then take on a separate existence from the human being). Idealists hold that alienation is a function of the separate reality of all material objects; dialectical materialists hold that alienation is a product of *domination*.

Hegelian idealism operated as a type of ideology that discouraged political activism by conceptualizing alienation as a perpetual aspect of the human condition. Marx opposed idealism on the grounds that it functioned ideologically, replacing political consciousness and action with an inner-directed philosophical self-consciousness. Bluntly put—to borrow Marx's formulation (excerpted below) from his *Theses on Feuerbach*—philosophy only interprets the world whereas revolutionary action changes the world.

Precisely here, at the crossroads of philosophy and praxis, Marxism takes two different (and, some contend, opposite) paths. Deterministic Marxists believe that philosophy is unnecessary for the cause of revolution, but other Marxists argue that praxis cannot successfully exist *without* philosophy. This takes us directly to the core of Marx's dialectical method. Marx created a theory and critique of ideology because he felt that ideological mystification was a crucial component of alienation. Indeed, the exploitation of the worker's labor-power could not take place without a degree of ideological deception. Marx and Engels' *German Ideology* (excerpted directly below) stands as their definitive statement of the dialectical method, outlining the relationship between ideology and alienation and, at the same time, possible forms of revolutionary change.

Marx and Engels took Hegelian idealism as seriously as they did because they felt that ideological mystification (in the form, specifically, of the philosophy of idealist transcendence developed most systematically by Hegel) was a crucial component of capitalist alienation. Before the working class could seize the revolutionary opportunity created by the maturation of the contradictions in capitalist economies, they must grasp the untruth of ideologies that either ignore the reality of exploitation or mystify it into an essential, inevitable aspect of the human condition. Marx fought Hegel on the grounds of Hegel's argument that human self-externalization always involves alienation: Marx offered instead a historical theory of the genesis of alienation, attempting to pierce the ideology of German idealism.

For Marx, every system of alienation produces an ideology, a system of self-justifying and self-serving explanations of its own rationality. Later western sociologists such as Karl Mannheim (in his seminal *Ideology and Utopia,* a book which directly contested the Marxian theory of ideology) argue that every social order produces a system of ideas and explanations with which to socialize its members. These are arguments at cross-purposes for Marx would not have disputed Mannheim's argument about the eternal necessity of shared social belief-systems (termed by the French sociologist Émile Durkheim the "collective consciousness" of societies). Marx did not equate social belief-systems in general with ideology in particular. Only class-stratified societies produce ideology, according to Marx, in order to protect, legitimate and rationalize their unequal balance between rulers and ruled.

Against the mystifications of ideology, Marx constructed a dialectical materialist theory of history which would have the potential to *enlighten* alienated workers about a mystified social reality. This enlightenment—and this fostering of class-consciousness, in particular—would put men in touch with their potential for creating a truly emancipated, democratically ordered society. Marx felt that ideology in early capitalism tended to degrade the potential of an active humanity to take control of social and economic institutions. Ideology, to summarize Marx's basic theory of alienation and its effects on human consciousness, denuded human beings of a certain intellectual and practical *competence* with respect to their ability to control their own lives.

In the excerpts offered below, from the *German Ideology,* Marx and Engels outline the aims of their dialectical method. *This method demystifies ideology by showing human beings the possibility of their own liberation.* "Men are the producers of their conceptions, ideas, etc.—real active men. . ." Marx and Engels lay the foundation for a materialist conception of history: "Its premises are men, not in any fantastic isolation or abstract definition, but in their actual, empirically perceptible process of development under definite conditions."

The production of ideas, of conceptions, of consciousness, is at first directly interwoven with the material activity and the material intercourse of men, the language of real life. Conceiving, thinking, the mental intercourse of men, appear at this stage as the direct efflux of their material behaviour. The same applies to mental production as expressed in the language of the politics, laws, morality, religion, metaphysics of a people. Men are the producers of their conceptions, ideas, etc.—real, active men, as they are conditioned by a definite development of their productive forces and of the intercourse corresponding to these, up to its furthest forms. Consciousness can never be anything else than conscious existence, and the existence of men is their actual life-process. If in all ideology men and their circumstances appear upside down as in a *camera obscura*, this phenomenon arises just as much from their historical life-process as the inversion of objects on the retina does from their physical life-process.

In direct contrast to German philosophy which descends from heaven to earth, here we ascend from earth to heaven. That is to say, we do not set out from what men say, imagine, conceive, nor from men as narrated, thought of, imagined, conceived, in order to arrive at men in the flesh. We set out from real, active men, and on the basis of their real life-process we demonstrate the development of the ideological reflexes and echoes of this life-process. The phantoms formed in the human brain are also, necessarily, sublimates of their material life-process, which is empirically verifiable and bound to material premises. Morality, religion, metaphysics, all the rest of ideology and their corresponding forms of consciousness, thus no longer retain the semblance of independence. They have no history, no development; but men, developing their material production and their material intercourse, alter, along with this their real existence, their thinking and the products of their thinking. Life is not determined by consciousness, but consciousness by life. In the first method of approach the starting-point is consciousness taken as the living individual; in the second it is the real living individuals themselves, as they are in actual life, and consciousness is considered solely as *their* consciousness.

This method of approach is not devoid of premises. It starts out from the real premises and does not abandon them for a moment. Its premises are men, not in any fantastic isolation or abstract definition, but in their actual, empirically perceptible process of development under definite conditions. As soon as this active life-process is described, history ceases to be a collection of dead facts as it is with the empiricists (themselves still abstract), or an imagined activity of imagined subjects, as with the idealists.

Where speculation ends—in real life—there real, positive science begins: the representation of the practical activity, of the practical process of development of men. Empty talk about consciousness ceases, and real knowledge has to take its place. When reality is depicted, philosophy as an independent branch of activity loses its medium of existence. At the best its place can only be taken by a summing-up of the most general results, abstractions which arise from the observation of the historical development of men. Viewed apart from real history, these abstractions have in themselves no value whatsoever. They can only serve to facilitate the arrangement of historical material, to indicate the sequence of its separate strata. But they by no means afford a recipe or schema, as does philosophy, for neatly trimming the epochs of history. On the contrary, our difficulties begin only when we set about the observation and the arrangement—the real depiction—of our historical material, whether of a past epoch or of the present. The removal of these difficulties is governed by premises which it is quite impossible to state here, but which only the study of the actual life-process and the activity of the individuals of each epoch will make evident. *

The dialectical method begins with "real men" and not abstract consciousness. Reality takes precedence over ideas, although ideas often help to form and

---

*From Karl Marx and Friedrich Engels, *The German Ideology* (New York: International Publishers, 1949), pp. 13-16.

to change reality. History must be understood as "a sum of productive forces, a historically created relation of individuals to nature and to one another, which is handed down to each generation from its predecessor..." Marx and Engels sketch the dialectic between material conditions and the human volition required to make and remake those conditions: "...circumstances make men just as much as men make circumstances."

This phrase is the essence of the dialectical method. It gives social structure and human volition an equal due, combining materialism and idealism into a synthetic two-dimensional system.

Our conception of history depends on our ability to expound the real process of production, starting out from the simple material production of life, and to comprehend the form of intercourse connected with this and created by this (i.e., civil society in its various stages), as the basis of all history; further, to show it in its action as State; and so, from this starting-point, to explain the whole mass of different theoretical products and forms of consciousness, religion, philosophy, ethics etc., etc., and trace their origins and growth, by which means, of course, the whole thing can be shown in its totality (and therefore, too, the reciprocal action of these various sides on one another). It has not, like the idealistic view of history, in every period to look for a category, but remains constantly on the real ground of history; it does not explain practice from the idea but explains the formation of ideas from material practice; and accordingly it comes to the conclusion that all forms and products of consciousness cannot be dissolved by mental criticism, by resolution into "self-consciousness" or transformation into "apparitions," "spectres," "fancies," etc., but only by the practical overthrow of the actual social relations which gave rise to this idealistic humbug; that not criticism but revolution is the driving force of history, also of religion, of philosophy and all other types of theory. It shows that history does not end by being resolved into "self-consciousness" as "spirit of the spirit," but that in it at each stage there is found a material result: a sum of productive forces, a historically created relation of individuals to nature and to one another, which is handed down to each generation from its predecessor; a mass of productive forces, different forms of capital, and conditions, which, indeed, is modified by the new generation on the one hand, but also on the other prescribes for it its conditions of life and gives it a definite development, a special character. It shows that circumstances make men just as much as men make circumstances.

This sum of productive forces, forms of capital, and social forms of intercourse, which every individual and generation finds in existence as something given, is the real basis of what the philosophers have conceived as "substance" and "essence of man." and what they have deified and attacked: a real basis which is not in the least disturbed, in its effect and influence on the development of men, by the fact that these philosophers revolt against it as "self-consciousness" and "the unique." These conditions of life, which different generations find in existence, decide also whether or not the periodically recurring revolutionary convulsion will be strong enough to overthrow the basis of all existing forms. And if these material elements of a complete revolution are not present (namely, on the one hand the existence of productive forces, on the other the formation of a revolutionary mass, which revolts not only against separate conditions of society up till then, but against the very "production of life" till then, the "total activity" on which it was based), then, as

far as practical development is concerned, it is absolutely immaterial whether
the "idea" of this revolution has been expressed a hundred times already; as the
history of communism proves.*

The dialectical method debunks ideology by attempting to substitute true
consciousness for false consciousness. "The ideas of the ruling class are in every
epoch the ruling ideas." Ideology serves the ruling class, and yet ideology can be
overcome through the rational analysis of revolutionary possibilities.

The ideas of the ruling class are in every epoch the ruling ideas: i.e., the class,
which is the ruling material force of society, is at the same time its ruling
intellectual force. The class which has the means of material production at its
disposal, has control at the same time over the means of mental production, so
that thereby, generally speaking, the ideas of those who lack the means of
mental production are subject to it. The ruling ideas are nothing more than the
ideal expression of the dominant material relationships, the dominant material
relationships grasped as ideas; hence of the relationships which make the one
class the ruling one, therefore the ideas of its dominance. The individuals
composing the ruling class possess among other things consciousness, and
therefore think. In so far, therefore, as they rule as a class and determine the
extent and compass of an epoch, it is self-evident that they do this in their whole
range, hence among other things rule also as thinkers, as producers of ideas,
and regulate the production and distribution of the ideas of their age: thus
their ideas are the ruling ideas of the epoch. For instance, in an age and in a
country where royal power, aristocracy and bourgeoisie are contending for
mastery and where, therefore, mastery is shared, the doctrine of the separation
of powers proves to be the dominant idea and is expressed as an "eternal law."
The division of labour, which we saw above as one of the chief forces of history
up till now, manifests itself also in the ruling class as the division of mental and
material labour, so that inside this class one part appears as the thinkers of the
class (its active, conceptive ideologists, who make the perfecting of the illusion
of the class about itself their chief source of livelihood), while the others'
attitude to these ideas and illusions is more passive and receptive, because they
are in reality the active members of this class and have less time to make up
illusions and ideas about themselves. Within this class this cleavage can even
develop into a certain opposition and hostility between the two parts, which,
however, in the case of a practical collision, in which the class itself is endangered, automatically comes to nothing, in which case there also vanishes the
semblance that the ruling ideas were not the ideas of the ruling class and had a
power distinct from the power of this class. The existence of revolutionary
ideas in a particular period presupposes the existence of a revolutionary class;
about the premises for the latter sufficient has already been said above.†

Marx and Engels in the excerpt above assert that there must be a revolutionary class before there are revolutionary ideas to energize the class towards

---

*From Karl Marx and Friedrich Engels, *The German Ideology* (New York: International Publishers, 1969), pp. 28–30.

†From Karl Marx and Friedrich Engels, *The German Ideology* (New York: International Publishers, 1969), pp. 39–40.

insurgent action. Marx here broke definitively with idealism that would have reversed this relationship. For Marx, the revolutionary class was to be created by structures of alienation that oppress the working class and benefit the capitalist class. Those most directly alienated from human possibilities can gain consciousness of the prospect of radical change only by recognizing and comprehending their own alienation. Well-intentioned reformers must not act merely on behalf of the alienated in the hope of effecting change externally: Change must spring from within the hearts and minds of those most directly enslaved by a class-stratified social order.

Finally, Marx in *Theses on Feuerbach* outlined the synthetic culmination of dialectical method, informed by his vision of human emancipation. Marx developed a concept of revolutionary praxis, completing his theoretical model. This model was comprised of three interrelated parts:

1. The vision of human emancipation under communism, sketched most clearly and forcefully in the *Economic and Philosophical Manuscripts* of 1844

2. The dialectical method of analyzing social reality, joining structural and volitional elements in one dynamic totality

3. A concept of revolutionary practice that involves the simultaneity of the transformation of social structure and human self-emancipation

In Thesis II Marx argues that "man must prove the truth," indicating that the dialectical method is interested not merely in understanding the functioning of capitalism but also in transforming it. This is a profound refutation of the traditionally value-free stance of the social scientist who argues that his primary mission *as* a scientist is to understand reality. Marx indicates in Thesis II that understanding must broaden out into the "proof" of this understanding, gauged in terms of revolutionary practice.

In Thesis III Marx criticizes pure materialism for forgetting "that circumstances are changed by men and that the educator himself must be educated." The dialectical method, as we recall, involves feedback between structural conditions (which prepare the seeds of revolution by oppressing one class to benefit another) and the subjective recognition of the possibility of revolutionary practice. Without grasping the possibility and necessity of radical change, there will be no "automatic" revolution. Furthermore, Marx cautions against an elitist type of social change movement, reminding that theoreticians must not only teach the working class but that they may also learn from the working class: Out of class struggle will spring the tools for improving that struggle.

Also contained in Thesis III is the ultimate formulation of the dialectical method. Marx defines revolutionary practice as the "coincidence of changing . . . circumstances and [self-changing] human activity." Later, in our Chapter 6 on individualized Marxism, we will encounter a similar definition, revised in more contemporary terms. While many traditional Marxists have concentrated on structural aspects of change, fewer have tried to understand what social transformation would *mean* for individual human beings. This linkage of the structural and subjective dimensions of revolutionary practice defines the non-deterministic character of Marx's dialectical method.

THESES ON FEUERBACH

I

The chief defect of all materialism up to now (including Feuerbach's) is that the object, reality, what we apprehend through our senses, is understood only in the form of the *object* or *contemplation;* but not as *sensuous human activity,* as *practice;* not subjectively. Hence in opposition to materialism the *active* side was developed abstractly by idealism—which of course does not know real sensuous activity as such. Feuerbach wants sensuous objects really distinguished from the objects of thought, but he does not understand human activity itself as *objective* activity. Hence, in *The Essence of Christianity,* he sees only the theoretical attitude as the true human attitude, while practice is understood and established only in its "dirty Jew" appearance. He therefore does not comprehend the significance of "revolutionary," of "practical-critical" activity.

II

The question whether objective truth is an attribute of human thought is not a theoretical but a *practical* question. Man must prove the truth, i.e., the reality and power, the "this-sidedness" of his thinking in practice. The dispute over the reality or non-reality of thinking that is isolated from practice is a purely *scholastic* question.

III

The materialistic doctrine concerning the changing of circumstances and education forgets that circumstances are changed by men and that the educator himself must be educated. This doctrine has therefore to divide society into two parts, one of which is superior to society.

The coincidence of the changing of circumstances and of human activity or self-changing can only be comprehended and rationally understood as *revolutionary practice.*

IV

Feuerbach starts out from the fact of religious self-estrangement, of the duplication of the world into a religious and a secular one. His work consists in resolving the religious world into its secular basis. But that the secular basis raises itself above itself and establishes for itself an independent realm in the clouds can be explained only through the cleavage and self-contradictions within this secular basis. The latter must therefore in itself be both understood in its contradiction and revolutionized in practice. Therefore after, e.g., the earthly family is discovered to be the secret of the heavenly family, one must proceed to destroy the former both in theory and in practice.

V

Feuerbach, not satisfied with *abstract thought,* wants contemplation, but he does not understand our sensuous nature as *practical,* human-sensuous activity.

VI

Feuerbach resolves the essence of religion into the essence of *man.* But the essence of man is no abstraction inherent in each separate individual. In its reality it is the *ensemble* (aggregate) of social relations.

Feuerbach, who does not enter more deeply into the criticism of this real

essence, is therefore forced:
1. To abstract from the process of history and to establish the religious temperament as something independent, and to postulate an abstract—*isolated*—human individual.
2. The essence of man can therefore be understood only as "genus," the inward, dumb generality which *naturally* unites the many individuals.

VII
Feuerbach therefore does not see that the "religious temperament" itself is a social product and that the abstract individual whom he analyses belongs to a particular form of society.

VIII
All social life is essentially *practical*. All the mysteries which urge theory into mysticism find their rational solution in human practice and in the comprehension of this practice.

IX
The highest point to which contemplative materialism can attain, i.e., that materialism which does not comprehend our sensuous nature as practical activity, is the contemplation of separate individuals and of civil society.

X
The standpoint of the old type of materialism is civil society, the standpoint of the new materialism is human society or social humanity.

XI
The philosophers have only *interpreted* the world differently, the point is, to *change* it.*

MARX'S THEORY OF REVOLUTIONARY COMMUNISM

In *The Communist Manifesto,* drafted in 1848, Marx and Engels outline the general assumptions of their theory of historical materialism. They develop the key concepts to be employed later in Marx's more detailed economic and political analysis of capitalism.

"Society . . . is more and more splitting up into two great hostile camps," bourgeoisie and proletariat. The manufacturing system took the place of the feudal guild system, ultimately creating a world market for capitalist goods. "Each step in the development of the bourgeoisie was accompanied by a corresponding political advance of that class." In the period of industrial capitalism, the state becomes merely "a committee for managing the . . . affairs of the . . . bourgeoisie."

The bourgeois order feverishly revolutionizes the technological foundations of production and expands into underdeveloped markets. The bourgeois system "creates a world after its own image."

---

*From Karl Marx and Friedrich Engels, *The German Ideology* (New York: International Publishers, 1969), pp. 197–99.

> Just as the bourgeois system burst forth from the feudal system, so Marx and Engels assert that the bourgeois order is sowing the seeds of its own destruction. This concept lies at the core of Marx's dialectical method, the notion that the capitalist order tends to produce periodic crises that eventually result in the breakdown of the social system. Marx and Engels liken capitalism to a "sorcerer who is no longer able to control the powers of the nether world whom he has called up by his spells."
>
> Workers under capitalism themselves become commodities. Work loses "all charm" for the worker, as he becomes "an appendage to the machine." Marx and Engels argue that the exploitation of the worker *increases.*

Our epoch, the epoch of the bourgeoisie, possesses, however, this distinctive feature: it has simplified the class antagonisms. Society as a whole is more and more splitting up into two great hostile camps, into two great classes directly facing each other: bourgeoisie and proletariat.

From the serfs of the Middle Ages sprang the chartered burghers of the earliest towns. From these burgesses the first elements of the bourgeoisie were developed.

The discovery of America, the rounding of the Cape, opened up fresh ground for the rising bourgeoisie. The East Indian and Chinese markets, the colonization of America, trade with the colonies, the increase in the means of exchange and in commodities generally, gave to commerce, to navigation, to industry an impulse never before known, and thereby, to the revolutionary element in the tottering feudal society, a rapid development.

The feudal system of industry, under which industrial production was monopolized by closed guilds, now no longer sufficed for the growing wants of the new markets. The manufacturing system took its place. The guild masters were pushed on one side by the manufacturing middle class; division of labor between the different corporate guilds vanished in the face of division of labor in each single workshop.

Meantime the markets kept ever growing, the demand ever rising. Even manufacture no longer sufficed. Thereupon steam and machinery revolutionized industrial production. The place of manufacture was taken by the giant, modern industry, the place of the industrial middle class by industrial millionaires, the leaders of whole industrial armies, the modern bourgeois.

Modern industry has established the world market, for which the discovery of America paved the way. This market has given an immense development to commerce, to navigation, to communication by land. This development has, in its turn, reacted on the extension of industry; and in proportion as industry, commerce, navigation, railways extended, in the same proportion the bourgeosie developed, increased its capital, and pushed into the background every class handed down from the Middle Ages.

We see, therefore, how the modern bourgeoisie is itself the product of a long course of development, of a series of revolutions in the modes of production and of exchange.

Each step in the development of the bourgeoisie was accompanied by a corresponding political advance of that class. An oppressed class under the sway of the feudal nobility, an armed and self-governing association in the medieval commune; here independent urban republic (as in Italy and Germany), there taxable "third estate" of the monarchy (as in France), afterwards, in the period of manufacture proper, serving either the semi-feudal or the absolute monarchy as a counterpoise against the nobility, and, in fact, cornerstone of the great monarchies in general, the bourgeoisie has at last, since the establishment of modern industry and of the world market, conquered for itself, in the modern representative state, exclusive political sway. The executive of the modern state is but a committee for managing the common affairs of the whole bourgeoisie.

The bourgeoisie, historically, has played a most revolutionary part.

The bourgeoisie, wherever it has got the upper hand, has put an end to all feudal, patriarchal, idyllic relations. It has pitilessly torn asunder the motley feudal ties that bound man to his "natural superiors," and has left remaining no other nexus between man and man than naked self-interest, than callous "cash payment." It has drowned the most heavenly ecstasies of religious fervor, of chivalrous enthusiasm, of Philistine sentimentalism in the icy water of egotistical calculation. It has resolved personal worth into exchange value and, in place of the numberless indefeasible chartered freedoms, has set up that single, unconscionable freedom—free trade. In one word, for exploitation, veiled by religious and political illusions, it has substituted naked, shameless, direct, brutal exploitation.

The bourgeoisie has stripped of its halo every occupation hitherto honored and looked up to with reverent awe. It has converted the physician, the lawyer, the priest, the poet, the man of science into its paid wage laborers.

The bourgeoisie has torn away from the family its sentimental veil, and has reduced the family relation to a mere money relation.

The bourgeoisie has disclosed how it came to pass that the brutal display of vigor in the Middle Ages, which reactionists so much admire, found its fitting complement in the most slothful indolence. It has been the first to show what man's activity can bring about. It has accomplished wonders far surpassing Egyptian pyramids, Roman aqueducts, and Gothic cathedrals; it has conducted expeditions that put in the shade all former exoduses of nations and crusades.

The bourgeoisie cannot exist without constantly revolutionizing the instruments of production, and thereby the relations of production, and with them the whole relations of society. Conservation of the old modes of production in unaltered form was, on the contrary, the first condition of existence for all earlier industrial classes. Constant revolutionizing of production, uninterrupted disturbance of all social conditions, everlasting uncertainty and agitation distinguish the bourgeois epoch from all earlier ones. All fixed, fast-frozen relations, with their train of ancient and venerable prejudices and opinions, are swept away, all new-formed ones become antiquated before they can ossify. All that is solid melts into air, all that is holy is profaned, and man is at last compelled to face with sober senses his real conditions of life and his relations with his kind.

The need of a constantly expanding market for its products chases the bourgeoisie over the whole surface of the globe. It must nestle everywhere, settle everywhere, establish connections everywhere.

The bourgeoisie has through its exploitation of the world market given a cosmopolitan character to production and consumption in every country. To the great chagrin of reactionists, it has drawn from under the feet of industry the national ground on which it stood. All old-established national industries have been destroyed or are daily being destroyed. They are dislodged by new industries, whose introduction becomes a life and death question for all civilized nations, by industries that no longer work up indigenous raw material, but raw material drawn from the remotest zones; industries whose products are consumed not only at home, but in every quarter of the globe. In place of the old wants, satisfied by the productions of the country, we find new wants, requiring for their satisfaction the products of distant lands and climes. In place of the old local and national seclusion and self-sufficiency we have intercourse in every direction, universal interdependence of nations. And as in material, so also in intellectual production. The intellectual creations of individual nations become common property. National one-sidedness and narrow-mindedness become more and more impossible, and from the numerous national and local literatures there arises a world literature.

The bourgeoisie, by the rapid improvement of all instruments of production, by the immensely facilitated means of communication, draws all, even the most barbarian, nations into civilization. The cheap prices of its commodities are the heavy artillery with which it batters down all Chinese walls, with which it forces the barbarians' intensely obstinate hatred of foreigners to capitulate. It compels all nations, on pain of extinction, to adopt the bourgeois mode of production; it compels them to introduce what it calls civilization into their midst, i.e., to become bourgeois themselves. In one word, it creates a world after its own image.

The bourgeoisie has subjected the country to the rule of the towns. It has created enormous cities, has greatly increased the urban population as compared with the rural, and has thus rescued a considerable part of the population from the idiocy of rural life. Just as it has made the country dependent on the towns, so it has made barbarian and semi-barbarian countries dependent on the civilized ones, nations of peasants on nations of bourgeois, the East on the West.

The bourgeoisie keeps more and more doing away with the scattered state of the population, of the means of production, and of property. It has agglomerated population, centralized means of production, and has concentrated property in a few hands. The necessary consequence of this was political centralization. Independent, or but loosely connected provinces, with separate interests, laws, governments and systems of taxation, became lumped together into one nation, with one government, one code of laws, one national class interest, one frontier, and one customs tariff.

The bourgeoisie, during its rule of scarce one hundred years, has created more massive and more colossal productive forces than have all preceding generations together. Subjection of nature's forces to man, machinery, application of chemistry to industry and agriculture, steam navigation, railways, electric telegraphs, clearing of whole continents for cultivation, canalization of rivers, whole populations conjured out of the ground—what earlier century had even a presentiment that such productive forces slumbered in the lap of social labor?

We see then: the means of production and of exchange, on whose foundation the bourgeoisie built itself up, were generated in feudal society. At a certain stage in the development of these means of production and of exchange, the conditions under which feudal society produced and exchanged, the feudal organization of agriculture and manufacturing industry, in one word, the feudal relations of property, became no longer compatible with the already developed productive forces; they became so many fetters. They had to be burst asunder; they were burst asunder.

Into their place stepped free competition, accompanied by a social and political constitution adapted to it, and by the economic and political sway of the bourgeois class.

A similar movement is going on before our own eyes. Modern bourgeois society with its relations of production, of exchange, and of property, a society that has conjured up such gigantic means of production and of exchange, is like the sorcerer who is no longer able to control the powers of the nether world whom he has called up by his spells. For many a decade past, the history of industry and commerce is but the history of the revolt of modern productive forces against modern conditions of production, against the property relations that are the conditions for the existence of the bourgeoisie and of its rule. It is enough to mention the commercial crises that by their periodic return put on its trial, each time more threateningly, the existence of the entire bourgeois society. In these crises a great part not only of the existing products but also of the previously created productive forces are periodically destroyed. In these crises there breaks out an epidemic that in all earlier epochs would have seemed an absurdity—the epidemic of overproduction. Society suddenly finds itself put back into a state of momentary barbarism; it appears as if a famine, a universal war of devastation had cut off the supply of every means of subsistence; industry and commerce seem to be destroyed; and why? Because there is too much civilization, too much means of subsistence, too much industry, too much commerce. The productive forces at the disposal of society no longer tend to further the development of the conditions of bourgeois property; on the contrary, they have become too powerful for these conditions, by which they are fettered, and as soon as they overcome these fetters they bring disorder into the whole of bourgeois society, endanger the existence of bourgeois property. The conditions of bourgeois society are too narrow to comprise the wealth created by them. And how does the bourgeoisie get over these crises? On the one hand, by enforced destruction of a mass of productive forces; on the other, by the conquest of new markets, and by the more thorough exploitation of the old ones. That is to say, by paving the way for more extensive and more destructive crises, and by diminishing the means whereby crises are prevented.

The weapons with which the bourgeoisie felled feudalism to the ground are now turned against the bourgeoisie itself.

But not only has the bourgeoisie forged the weapons that bring death to itself; it has also called into existence the men who are to wield those weapons—the modern working class—the proletarians.

In proportion as the bourgeoisie, i.e., capital, is developed, in the same proportion is the proletariat, the modern working class, developed—a class of laborers, who live only as long as they find work, and who find work only so long as their labor increases capital. These laborers, who must sell themselves piecemeal, are a commodity, like every other article of commerce, and are consequently exposed to all the vicissitudes of competition, to all the fluctuations of the market.

Owing to the extensive use of machinery and to division of labor, the work of the proletarians has lost all individual character and, consequently, all charm for the workman. He becomes an appendage of the machine, and it is only the simplest, most monotonous, and most easily acquired knack that is required of him. Hence the cost of production of a workman is restricted, almost entirely, to the means of subsistence that he requires for his maintenance and for the propagation of his race. But the price of a commodity, and therefore also of labor, is equal to its cost of production. In proportion, therefore, as the repulsiveness of the work increases, the wage decreases. Nay, more, in proportion as the use of machinery and division of labor increases, in the same proportion the burden of toil also increases, whether by prolongation of the working hours, by increase of the work exacted in a given time, or by increased speed of the machinery, etc.*

> Marx below clears up a fundamental misunderstanding surrounding his vision of communism. Instead of opposing the private appropriation and ownership of all things, Marx argues that he "merely" opposes the "miserable character" of capitalist wage-labor. Capitalists accumulate labor for its own sake, and for the sake of profit, whereas communists would utilize this accumulated labor as a "means to widen, to enrich, to promote the existence of the laborer."

The average price of wage labor is the minimum wage, i.e., that quantum of the means of subsistence which is absolutely requisite to keep the laborer in bare existence as a laborer. What, therefore, the wage laborer appropriates by means of his labor merely suffices to prolong and reproduce a bare existence. We by no means intend to abolish this personal appropriation of the products of labor, an appropriation that is made for the maintenance and reproduction of human life, and that leaves no surplus wherewith to command the labor of others. All that we want to do away with is the miserable character of this appropriation, under which the laborer lives merely to increase capital, and is allowed to live only in so far as the interest of the ruling class requires it.

In bourgeois society living labor is but a means to increase accumulated labor. In communist society accumulated labor is but a means to widen, to enrich, to promote the existence of the laborer.

In bourgeois society, therefore, the past dominates the present; in communist society the present dominates the past. In bourgeois society capital is independent and has individuality, while the living person is dependent and has no individuality.†

> Finally, Marx and Engels argue that the advent of communism would not signal the utter disintegration of a civilized social order; men will not sink into apathetic, narcissistic laziness. Communism would change the structure of the family, education, nationalism; it would not eliminate them. Marx and Engels attack the bourgeois ideology that transforms the existing institutions of capitalist society "into eternal laws of nature." They argue convincingly that an aspect of capitalist ideology involves the freezing of our historical imaginations such that we cannot *imagine* a different, better world. We are locked into habits of thought that tend to see the future entirely in terms of the present; capitalism,

---

*From Lewis Feuer, editor, *Basic Writings on Politics and Philosophy* (Garden City, N.Y.: Anchor Books, 1959), pp. 8–14.

†From Lewis Feuer, editor, *Basic Writings on Politics and Philosophy* (Garden City, N.Y.: Anchor Books, 1959), p. 22.

under the weight of these habits, appears to exhaust all human and social possibilities. Thus we inevitably equate capitalism with every conceivable social order, unable to speculate imaginatively about qualitatively different forms of family association, work, and culture. This theme will reappear in the context of our discussion, in Chapter 4, of the Frankfurt School's revision of Marxism in light of the new ideological social control mechanisms utilized in advanced capitalism.

It has been objected that upon the abolition of private property all work will cease and universal laziness will overtake us.

According to this, bourgeois society ought long ago have gone to the dogs through sheer idleness, for those of its members who work acquire nothing and those who acquire anything do not work. The whole of this objection is but another expression of the tautology that there can no longer be any wage labor when there is no longer any capital.

All objections urged against the communistic mode of producing and appropriating material products have, in the same way, been urged against the communistic modes of producing and appropriating intellectual products. Just as, to the bourgeois, the disappearance of class property is the disappearance of production itself, so the disappearance of class culture is to him identical with the disappearance of all culture.

That culture, the loss of which he laments, is, for the enormous majority, a mere training to act as a machine.

But don't wrangle with us so long as you apply, to our intended abolition of bourgeois property, the standard of your bourgeois notions of freedom, culture, law, etc. Your very ideas are but the outgrowth of the conditions of your bourgeois production and bourgeois property, just as your jurisprudence is but the will of your class made into a law for all, a will whose essential character and direction are determined by the economic conditions of existence of your class.

The selfish misconception that induces you to transform into eternal laws of nature and of reason, the social forms springing from your present mode of production and form of property, historical relations that rise and disappear in the progress of production, this misconception you share with every ruling class that has preceded you. What you see clearly in the case of ancient property, what you admit in the case of feudal property, you are of course forbidden to admit in the case of your own bourgeois form of property.

Abolition of the family! Even the most radical flare up at this infamous proposal of the Communists.

On what foundation is the present family, the bourgeois family, based? On capital, on private gain. In its completely developed form this family exists only among the bourgeoisie. But this state of things finds its complement in the practical absence of the family among the proletarians, and in public prostitution.

The bourgeois family will vanish as a matter of course when its complement vanishes, and both will vanish with the vanishing of capital.

Do you charge us with wanting to stop the exploitation of children by their parents? To this crime we plead guilty.

But, you will say, we destroy the most hallowed of relations when we replace home education by social.

And your education! Is not that also social, and determined by the social conditions under which you educate, by the intervention, direct or indirect, of society, by means of schools, etc.? The communists have not invented the intervention of society in education; they do but seek to alter the character of that intervention, and to rescue education from the influence of the ruling class.

The bourgeois claptrap about the family and education, about the hallowed co-relation of parent and child, becomes all the more disgusting, the more, by the action of modern industry, all family ties among the proletarians are torn asunder and their children transformed into simple articles of commerce and instruments of labor.

"But you communists would introduce community of women," screams the whole bourgeoisie in chorus.

The bourgeois sees in his wife a mere instrument of production. He hears that the instruments of production are to be exploited in common and, naturally, can come to no other conclusion than that the lot of being common to all will likewise fall to the women.

He has not even a suspicion that the real point aimed at is to do away with the status of women as mere instruments of production.

For the rest, nothing is more ridiculous than the virtuous indignation of our bourgeois at the community of women which, they pretend, is to be openly and officially established by the communists. The communists have no need to introduce community of women; it has existed almost from time immemorial.

Our bourgeois, not content with having the wives and daughters of their proletarians at their disposal, not to speak of common prostitutes, take the greatest pleasure in seducing each other's wives.

Bourgeois marriage is in reality a system of wives in common and thus, at the most, what the communists might possibly be reproached with is that they desire to introduce, in substitution for a hypocritically concealed, an openly legalized community of women. For the rest, it is self-evident that the abolition of the present system of production must bring with it the abolition of the community of women springing from that system, i.e., of prostitution, both public and private.

The communists are further reproached with desiring to abolish countries and nationality.

The workingmen have no country. We cannot take from them what they have not got. Since the proletariat must first of all acquire political supremacy, must rise to be the leading class of the nation, must constitute itself *the* nation, it is, so far, itself national, though not in the bourgeois sense of the word.

National differences and antagonisms between peoples are daily more and more vanishing, owing to the development of the bourgeoisie, to freedom of commerce, to the world market, to uniformity in the mode of production and in the conditions of life corresponding thereto.

The supremacy of the proletariat will cause them to vanish still faster. United action, of the leading civilized countries at least, is one of the first conditions for the emancipation of the proletariat.

In proportion as the exploitation of one individual by another is put to an end, the exploitation of one nation by another will also be put to an end. In proportion as the antagonism between classes within the nation vanishes, the hostility of one nation to another will come to an end.*

---

*From Lewis Feuer, editor, *Basic Writings on Politics and Philosophy* (Garden City, N.Y.: Anchor Books, 1959), pp. 23–26.

MARX'S THEORY OF THE INTERNAL CONTRADICTIONS OF CAPITALISM

Marx's theory of the internal contradictions of capitalism takes its most developed form in his 1867 work, *Capital*, notably in Volume I of that work. While his earlier works were primarily philosophical and historical, Marx's *Capital* is given over to a careful and detailed accounting of Marx's economic theory. This economic theory is nearly devoid of ethical and ideological polemics, being primarily a sustained argument about the inherently crisis-prone nature of the capitalist system. Marx in later works such as *Capital* does not relinquish his earlier speculative discussions of the character of human alienation and the meaning of emancipation; rather he mutes the philosophical dimension and amplifies the precise empirical and conceptual analysis of capitalism in order to develop a model of capitalist crisis and socialist transformation.

While volumes have been written about the relationship between Marx's "early" (philosophical) and "later" (economic) works, we prefer to read Marx as a "single" theorist, with differing emphases in his development as a student of capitalism. The later works build upon the earlier works; *Capital* develops Marx's understanding of the internal contradictions of capitalism, where earlier works concentrated on a more general theoretical appreciation of the nature of capitalist alienation. It will be recalled from our general introduction to this chapter that Marx's dialectical method consisted of a theory and critique of alienation, a theory of capitalist internal contradictions and a model of empirical crisis-tendencies and modes of transformation into socialism. *Capital* represents the second stage of the dialectical method, which concludes with a glimpse of Marx's empirical political sociology and his modelling of probable crisis-tendencies and modes of breakdown. It is our personal contention, amplified in our concluding chapter, that the first two components of Marxism are still valid—the theory of alienation and of internal contradictions—but that empirical theories of crisis and transformation have not yet been adequately developed to replace Marx's archaic notions (themselves inadequately developed). It could be said that our position is two-thirds Marxist! However it is our contention that a "real" Marxist is anyone who accepts Marx's fundamental understandings of alienation and internal contradictions, endemic to capitalist class society; the crisis-modelling must always be adjusted to particular stages in the historical development of capitalism (and cannot be written for all time).

An afterword to the second German edition of *Capital*, written in 1873, briefly summarizes Marx's dialectical method, stressing its differences from Hegel's idealism. Marx's method has three features:

1. It assumes the inevitable collapse of the existing social order.
2. It sees every social form as being in fluid movement, recognizing the historical roots of modern social reality.
3. Finally, it "lets nothing impose upon it," being revolutionary in spirit and oriented to the merging of theory and praxis.

My dialectic method is not only different from the Hegelian, but is its direct opposite. To Hegel, the life-process of the human brain, i.e., the process of thinking, which, under the name of "the Idea," he even transforms into an independent subject, is the demiurgos of the real world, and the real world is only the external, phenomenal form of "the Idea." With me, on the contrary, the ideal is nothing else than the material world reflected by the human mind, and translated into forms of thought.

The mystifying side of Hegelian dialectic I criticised nearly thirty years ago, at a time when it was still the fashion. But just as I was working at the first volume of "Das Kapital," it was the good pleasure of the peevish, arrogant, mediocre 'Επιγονοι who now talk large in cultured Germany, to treat Hegel in same way as the brave Moses Mendelssohn in Lessing's time treated Spinoza, i.e., as a "dead dog." I therefore openly avowed myself the pupil of that mighty thinker, and even here and there, in the chapter on the theory of value, coquetted with the modes of expression peculiar to him. The mystification whch dialectic suffers in Hegel's hands by no means prevents him from being the first to present its general form of working in a comprehensive and conscious manner. With him it is standing on its head. It must be turned right side up again if you would discover the rational kernel within the mystical shell.

In its mystified form, dialectic became the fashion in Germany, because it seemed to transfigure and to glorify the existing state of things. In its rational form it is a scandal and abomination to bourgeoisdom and its doctrinaire professors, because it includes in its comprehension and affirmative recognition of the existing state of things, at the same time also, the recognition of the negation of that state, of its inevitable breaking up; because it regards every historically developed social form as in fluid movement, and therefore takes into account its transient nature not less than its momentary existence; because it lets nothing impose upon it, and is in its essence critical and revolutionary.

The contradictions inherent in the movement of capitalist society impress themselves upon the practical bourgeois most strikingly in the changes of the periodic cycle, through which modern industry runs, and whose crowning point is the universal crisis. That crisis is once again approaching, although as yet but in its preliminary stage; and by the universality of its theatre and the intensity of its action it will drum dialectics even into the heads of the mushroom-upstarts of the new, holy Prusso-German empire.*

Marx's precise analysis of the workings of capitalism takes its departure from a few central concepts and assumptions. The most important of these is his notion of "labor-power," which the free worker sells to the capitalist on the open market in return for a living wage. "By labor-power ... is to be understood the aggregate of those mental and physical capabilities existing in a human being, which he exercises whenever he produces a use-value of any description." By "use-value" Marx meant anything that was produced for the sake of its sale or exchange.

Three conditions must exist for the worker to sell his labor-power to the capitalist.

1. The worker must own his labor; he must be legally free to sell it to the capitalist. In the feudal period, workers were not legally free to do so.

---

*From Karl Marx, *Capital,* Vol. I (Moscow: Progress Publishers, n.d.), p. 29.

2. The worker must sell his labor as a commodity that is then disposed of as the capitalist desires. The worker has no rights whatsoever to determine the disposition of his labor-power or of the commodities his labor-power produces.
3. The worker must be provided with the means of existence, usually in the form of a living wage. This cost is contained in the cost of the commodity his labor-power produces.

Marx dispels the myth that the market-bound relationship of worker to capitalist is a natural fact of history. "This relationship of worker to capitalist has no natural basis; . . . it is clearly the result of a past historical development . . ." Products do not appear as commodities until the social division of labor has been sufficiently advanced so that use-value is separated clearly from exchange-value. Furthermore, money must exist as a means of circulation. But both of these conditions can exist and have existed without the existence of capitalism. Capitalism is unique in that it presupposes the meeting in the marketplace of an owner of the means of production and a free worker willing to sell his labor-power in return for a wage.

The change of value that occurs in the case of money intended to be converted into capital cannot take place in the money itself, since in its function of means of purchase and of payment, it does no more than realise the price of the commodity it buys or pays for; and, as hard cash, it is value petrified, never varying. Just as little can it originate in the second act of circulation, the re-sale of the commodity, which does no more than transform the article from its bodily form back again into its money-form. The change must, therefore, take place in the commodity bought by the first act, M—C, but not in its value, for equivalents are exchanged, and the commodity is paid for at its full value. We are, therefore, forced to the conclusion that the change originates in the use-value, as such, of the commodity, i.e., in its consumption. In order to be able to extract value from the consumption of a commodity, our friend, Moneybags, must be so lucky as to find, within the sphere of circulation, in the market, a commodity, whose use-value possesses the peculiar property of being a source of value, whose actual consumption, therefore, is itself an embodiment of labour, and, consequently, a creation of value. The possessor of money does find on the market such a special commodity in capacity for labour or labour-power.

By labour-power or capacity for labour is to be understood the aggregate of those mental and physical capabilities existing in a human being, which he exercises whenever he produces a use-value of any description.

But in order that our owner of money may be able to find labour-power offered for sale as its commodity, various conditions must first be fulfilled. The exchange of commodities of itself implies no other relations of dependence than those which result from its own nature. On this assumption, labour-power can appear upon the market as a commodity, only if, and so far as, its possessor, the individual whose labour-power it is, offers it for sale, or sells it, as a commodity. In order that he may be able to do this, he must have it at his disposal, must be the untrammelled owner of his capacity for labour, i.e., of his person. He and the owner of money meet in the market, and deal with each other as on the basis of equal rights, with this difference alone, that one is buyer, the other seller; both, therefore, equal in the eyes of the law. The continuance of this relation demands that the owner of the labour-power should sell it only for a definite period, for if he were to sell it rump and stump, once for all, he would be selling himself, converting himself from a free man into a slave, from an owner of a commodity into a commodity. He must constantly look upon his labour-power as his own property, his own commodity, and this he can only do by placing it at the disposal of the buyer temporarily, for a definite period of time. By this means alone can he avoid renouncing his rights of ownership over it.

The second essential condition to the owner of money finding labour-power in the market as a commodity is this—that the labourer instead of being in the position to sell commodities in which his labour is incorporated, must be obliged to offer for sale as a commodity that very labour-power, which exists only in his living self.

In order that a man may be able to sell commodities other than labour-power, he must of course have the means of production, as raw material, implements, etc. No boots can be made without leather. He requires also the means of subsistence. Nobody—not even "a musician of the future"—can live upon future products, or upon use-values in an unfinished state; and ever since the first moment of his appearance on the world's stage, man always has been, and must still be a consumer, both before and while he is producing. In a socity where all products assume the form of commodities, these commodities must be sold after they have been produced, it is only after their sale that they can serve in satisfying the requirements of their producer. The time necessary for their sale is superadded to that necessary for their production.

For the conversion of his money into capital, therefore, the owner of money must meet in the market with the free labourer, free in the double sense, that as a free man he can dispose of his labour-power as his own commodity, and that on the other hand he has no other commodity for sale, is short of everything necessary for the realisation of his labour-power.

The question why this free labourer confronts him in the market, has no interest for the owner of money, who regards the labour-market as a branch of the general market for commodities. And for the present it interests us just as little. We cling to the fact theoretically, as he does practically. One thing, however, is clear—Nature does not produce on the one side owners of money or commodities, and on the other men possessing nothing but their own labour-power. This relation has no natural basis, neither is its social basis one that is common to all historical periods. It is clearly the result of a past historical development, the product of many economic revolutions, of the extinction of a whole series of older forms of social production.

So, too, the economic categories, already discussed by us, bear the stamp of history. Definite historical conditions are necessary that a product may become a commodity. It must not be produced as the immediate means of subsistence of the producer himself. Had we gone further, and inquired under what circumstances all, or even the majority of products take the form of commodities, we should have found that this can only happen with production of a very specific kind, capitalist production. Such an inquiry, however, would have been foreign to the analysis of commodities. Production and circulation of commodities can take place, although the great mass of the objects produced are intended for the immediate requirements of their producers, are not turned into commodities, and consequently social production is not yet by a long way dominated in its length and breadth by exchange-value. The appearance of products as commodities pre-supposes such a development of the social division of labour, that the separation of use-value from exchange-value, a separation which first begins with barter, must already have been completed. But such a degree of development is common to many forms of society, which in other respects present the most varying historical features. On the other hand, if we consider money, its existence implies a definite stage in the exchange of commodities. The particular functions of money which it performs, either as the mere equivalent of commodities, or as means of circulation, or means of payment, as hoard or as universal money, point, according to the extent and relative preponderance of the one function or the other, to very different stages in the process of social production. Yet we know by experience that a circulation of commodities relatively primitive, suffices for the production of all these forms. Otherwise with capital. The historical conditions of its existence are by no means given with the mere circulation of money and commodities. It can spring into life, only when the owner of the means of production and subsistence meets in the market with the free labourer selling his labour-power. And this one historical condition comprises a world's history. Capital, therefore, announces from its first appearance a new epoch in the process of social production.*

Marx describes the very process of labor as that of "acting on the external world and changing it ... [which also changes] man's own nature." Men develop their "slumbering powers" by interacting with nature. In a famous passage Marx describes the essential difference between animals and men; animals such as bees are masterful architects, yet this architecture is devoid of the "imagination" the human being brings to his tasks. Men plan their work while animals merely carry it out instinctively, in accordance with their built-in genetic codes. Further, Marx argues that the less a human being finds his work to be creative and fulfilling—"and the less, therefore, he enjoys it as something which gives play to his bodily and mental powers"—the more he must concentrate on his work, implicitly succumbing to it, and losing his mastery over it.

The capitalist buys labour-power in order to use it; and labour-power in use is labour itself. The purchaser of labour-power consumes it by setting the seller of it to work. By working, the latter becomes actually, what before he only was potentially, labour-power in action, a labourer. In order that his labour may re-appear in a commodity, he must, before all things, expend it on something useful, on something capable of satisfying a want of some sort. Hence, what the capitalist sets the labourer to produce, is a particular use-value, a specified article. The fact that the production of use-values, or goods, is carried on under the control of a capitalist and on his behalf, does not alter the general character of that production. We shall, therefore, in the first place, have to consider the labour-process independently of the

---

*From Karl Marx, *Capital*, Vol. (Moscow: Progress Publishers, n.d.), pp. 164–67.

particular form it assumes under given social conditions.

Labour is, in the first place, a process in which both man and Nature participate, and in which man of his own accord starts, regulates, and controls the material re-actions between himself and Nature. He opposes himself to Nature as one of her own forces, setting in motion arms and legs, head and hands, the natural forces of his body, in order to appropriate Nature's productions in a form adapted to his own wants. By thus acting on the external world and changing it, he at the same time changes his own nature. He develops his slumbering powers and compels them to act in obedience to his sway. We are not now dealing with those primitive instinctive forms of labour that remind us of the mere animal. An immeasurable interval of time separates the stage of things in which a man brings his labour-power to market for sale as a commodity, from that state in which human labour was still in its first instinctive stage. We pre-suppose labour in a form that stamps it as exclusively human. A spider conducts operations that resemble those of a weaver, and a bee puts to shame many an architect in the construction of her cells. But what distinguishes the worst architect from the best of bees is this, that the architect raises his structure in imagination before he erects it in reality. At the end of every labour-process, we get a result that already existed in the imagination of the labourer at its commencement. He not only effects a change of form in the material on which he works, but he also realises a purpose of his own that gives the law to his modus operandi, and to which he must subordinate his will. And this subordination is no mere momentary act. Besides the exertion of the bodily organs, the process demands that, during the whole operation, the workman's will be steadily in consonance with his purpose. This means close attention. The less he is attracted by the nature of the work, and the mode in which it is carried on, and the less, therefore, he enjoys it as something which gives play to his bodily and mental powers, the more close his attention is forced to be.*

> The inner dynamic of capitalist production is not labor pure and simple, the production of use-values. Capitalists employ labor in order to produce "surplus-value," which is the source of profit. This is value that is "greater than the sum of the values of the commodities used in its production." Without this concept, Marx's system would lose its dynamic and explanatory utility.

The product appropriated by the capitalist is a use-value, as yarn, for example, or boots. But, although boots are, in one sense, the basis of all social progress, and our capitalist is a decided "progressist," yet he does not manufacture boots for their own sake. Use-value is, by no means, the thing "qu'on aime pour lui-même" in the production of commodities. Use-values are only produced by capitalists, because, and in so far as, they are the material substratum, the depositories of exchange-value. Our capitalist has two objects in view: in the first place, he wants to produce a use-value that has a value in exchange, that is to say, an article destined to be sold, a commodity; and secondly, he desires to produce a commodity whose value shall be greater than the sum of the values of the commodities used in its production, that is, of the means of production and

---

*From Karl Marx, *Capital*, Vol. I (Moscow: Progress Publishers, n.d.), pp. 173–74.

the labour-power, that he purchased with his good money in the open market. His aim is to produce not only a use-value, but a commodity also; not only use-value, but value; not only value, but at the same time surplus-value.*

" . . .the value of labor-power, and the value which that labor-power creates in the labor process, are two entirely different magnitudes." This is the central analytic assumption of Marx's theory of capitalism. It explains *why* the capitalist is willing to employ labor-power in return for a living-wage: It is because the capitalist stands to make surplus-value from the labor-power he employs.

Let us now examine production as a creation of value.

We know that the value of each commodity is determined by the quantity of labour expended on and materialised in it, by the working-time necessary, under given social conditions, for its production. This rule also holds good in the case of the product that accrued to our capitalist, as the result of the labour-process carried on for him. Assuming this product to be 10 lbs. of yarn, our first step is to calculate the quantity of labour realised in it.

For spinning the yarn, raw material is required; suppose in this case 10 lbs. of cotton. We have no need at present to investigate the value of this cotton, for our capitalist has, we will assume, bought it at its full value, say of ten shillings. In this price the labour required for the production of the cotton is already expressed in terms of the average labour of society. We will further assume that the wear and tear of the spindle, which, for our present purpose, may represent all other instruments of labour employed, amounts to the value of 2s. If, then, twenty-four hours' labour, or two working-days are required to produce the quantity of gold represented by twelve shillings, we have here, to begin with, two days' labour already incorporated in the yarn.

We must not let ourselves be misled by the circumstances that the cotton has taken a new shape while the substance of the spindle has to a certain extent been used up. By the general law of value, if the value of 40 lbs. of yarn = the value of 40 lbs. of cotton + the value of a whole spindle, i.e., if the same working-time is required to produce the commodities on either side of this equation, then 10 lbs. of yarn are an equivalent for 10 lbs. of cotton, together with one-fourth of a spindle. In the case we are considering the same working-time is materialised in the 10 lbs. of yarn on the one hand, and in the 10 lbs. of cotton and the fraction of a spindle on the other. Therefore, whether value appears in cotton, in a spindle, or in yarn, makes no difference in the amount of that value. The spindle and cotton, instead of resting quietly side by side, join together in the process, their forms are altered, and they are turned into yarn; but their value is no more affected by this fact than it would be if they had been simply exchanged for their equivalent in yarn.

The labour required for the production of the cotton, the raw material of the yarn, is part of the labour necessary to produce the yarn, and is therefore contained in the yarn. The same applies to the labour embodied in the spindle, without whose wear and tear the cotton could not be spun.

Hence, in determining the value of the yarn, or the labour-time required for its production, all the special processes carried on at various times and in different places, which were necessary, first to produce the cotton and the

*From Karl Marx, *Capital*, Vol. I (Moscow: Progress Publishers, n.d.), p. 181.

wasted portion of the spindle, and then with the cotton and spindle to spin the yarn, may together be looked on as different and successive phases of one and the same process. The whole of the labour in the yarn is past labour; and it is a matter of no importance that the operations necessary for the production of its constituent elements were carried on at times which, referred to the present, are more remote than the final operation of spinning. If a definite quantity of labour, say thirty days, is requisite to build a house, the total amount of labour incorporated in it is not altered by the fact that the work of the last day is done twenty-nine days later than that of the first. Therefore the labour contained in the raw material and the instruments of labour can be treated just as if it were labour expended in an earlier stage of the spinning process, before the labour of actual spinning commenced.

The values of the means of production, i.e., the cotton and the spindle, which values are expressed in the price of twelve shillings, are therefore constituent parts of the value of the yarn, or, in other words, of the value of the product.

Two conditions must nevertheless be fulfilled. First, the cotton and spindle must concur in the production of a use-value; they must in the present case become yarn. Value is independent of the particular use-value by which it is borne, but it must be embodied in a use-value of some kind. Secondly, the time occupied in the labour of production must not exceed the time really necessary under the given social conditions of the case. Therefore, if no more than 1 lb. of cotton be requisite to spin 1 lb. of yarn, care must be taken that no more than this weight of cotton is consumed in the production of 1 lb. of yarn; and similarly with regard to the spindle. Though the capitalist have a hobby, and use a gold instead of a steel spindle, yet the only labour that counts for anything in the value of the yarn is that which would be required to produce a steel spindle, because no more is necessary under the given social conditions.

We now know what portion of the value of the yarn is owing to the cotton and the spindle. It amounts to twelve shillings or the value of two days' work. The next point for our consideration is, what portion of the value of the yarn is added to the cotton by the labour of the spinner.

We have now to consider this labour under a very different aspect from that which it had during the labour-process; there, we viewed it solely as that particular kind of human activity which changes cotton into yarn; there, the more the labour was suited to the work, the better the yarn, other circumstances remaining the same. The labour of the spinner was then viewed as specifically different from other kinds of productive labour, different on the one hand in its special aim, viz., spinning, different, on the other hand, in the special character of its operations, in the special nature of its means of production and in the special use-value of its product. For the operation of spinning, cotton and spindles are a necessity, but for making rifled cannon they would be of no use whatever. Here, on the contrary, where we consider the labour of the spinner only so far as it is value-creating, i.e., a source of value, his labour differs in no respect from the labour of the man who bores cannon, or (what here more nearly concerns us), from the labour of the cotton-planter and spindle-maker incorporated in the means of production. It is solely by reason of this identity, that cotton planting, spindle making and spinning, are capable of forming the component parts, differing only quantitatively from each other, of one whole, namely, the value of the yarn. Here, we have nothing more to do with the quality, the nature and the specific character of the labour, but merely with its quantity. And this simply requires to be calculated. We proceed upon the assumption that spinning is simple, unskilled labour, the average labour of a given state of society. Hereafter we shall see that the contrary assumption would make no difference.

While the labourer is at work, his labour constantly undergoes a transformation: from being motion, it becomes an object without motion; from being the labourer working, it becomes the thing produced. At the end of one hour's spinning, that act is represented by a definite quantity of yarn; in other words, a definite quantity of labour, namely that of one hour, has become embodied in the cotton. We say labour, i.e., the expenditure of his vital force by the spinner, and not spinning labour, because the special work of spinning counts here, only so far as it is the expenditure of labour-power in general, and not in so far as it is the specific work of the spinner.

In the process we are now considering it is of extreme importance, that no more time be consumed in the work of transforming the cotton into yarn than is necessary under the given social conditions. If under normal, i.e., average social conditions of production, *a* pounds of cotton ought to be made into *b* pounds of yarn by one hour's labour, then a day's labour does not count as 12 hours' labour unless 12 *a* pounds of cotton have been made into 12 *b* pounds of yarn; for in the creation of value, the time that is socially necessary alone counts.

Not only the labour, but also the raw material and the product now appear in quite a new light, very different from that in which we viewed them in the labour-process pure and simple. The raw material serves now merely as an absorbent of a definite quantity of labour. By this absorption it is in fact changed into yarn, because it is spun, because labour-power in the form of spinning is added to it; but the product, the yarn, is now nothing more than a measure of the labour absorbed by the cotton, If in one hour 1⅔ lbs. of cotton can be spun into 1⅔ lbs. of yarn, then 10 lbs. of yarn indicate the absorption of 6 hours' labour. Definite quantities of product, these quantities being determined by experience, now represent nothing but definite quantities of labour, definite masses of crystallised labour-time. They are nothing more than the materialisation of so many hours or so many days of social labour.

We are here no more concerned about the facts, that the labour is the specific work of spinning, that its subject is cotton and its product yarn, than we are about the fact that the subject itself is already a product and therefore raw material. If the spinner, instead of spinning, were working in a coal mine, the subject of his labour, the coal, would be supplied by Nature; nevertheless a definite quantity of extracted coal, a hundredweight for example, would represent a definite quantity of absorbed labour.

We assumed, on the occasion of its sale, that the value of a day's labour-power is three shillings, and that six hours' labour is incorporated in that sum; and consequently that this amount of labour is requisite to produce the necessaries of life daily required on an average by the labourer. If now our spinner by working for one hour, can convert 1⅔ lbs. of cotton into 1⅔ lbs. of yarn, it follows that in six hours he will convert 10 lbs. of cotton into 10 lbs. of yarn. Hence, during the spinning process, the cotton absorbs six hours' labour. The same quantity of labour is also embodied in a piece of gold of the value of three shillings. Consequently by the mere labour of spinning, a value of three shillings is added to the cotton.

Let us now consider the total value of the product, the 10 lbs. of yarn. Two and a half days' labour has been embodied in it, of which two days were contained in the cotton and in the substance of the spindle worn away, and half a day was absorbed during the process of spinning. This two and a half days' labour is also represented by a piece of gold of the value of fifteen shillings. Hence, fifteen shillings is an adequate price for the 10 lbs. of yarn, or the price of one pound is eighteen pence.

Our capitalist stares in astonishment. The value of the product is exactly equal to the value of the capital advanced. The value so advanced has not expanded, no surplus-value has been created, and consequently money has not been converted into capital. The price of the yarn is fifteen shillings, and fifteen shillings were spent in the open market upon the constituent elements of the product, or, what amounts to the same thing, upon the factors of the labour-process: Ten shillings were paid for the cotton, two shillings for the substance of the spindle worn away, and three shillings for the labour-power. The swollen value of the yarn is of no avail, for it is merely the sum of the values formerly existing in the cotton, the spindle, and the labour-power. Out of such a simple addition of existing values, no surplus-value can possibly arise. These separate values are now all concentrated in one thing; but so they were also in the sum of fifteen shillings, before it was split up into three parts, by the purchase of the commodities.

There is in reality nothing very strange in this result. The value of one pound of yarn being eighteenpence, if our capitalist buys 10 lbs. of yarn in the market, he must pay fifteen shillings for them. It is clear that, whether a man buys his house ready built, or gets it built for him, in neither case will the mode of acquisition increase the amount of money laid out on the house.

Our capitalist, who is at home in his vulgar economy, exclaims: "Oh! but I advanced my money for the express purpose of making more money." The way to Hell is paved with good intentions, and he might just as easily have intended to make money, without producing at all. He threatens all sorts of things. He won't be caught napping again. In future he will buy the commodities in the market, instead of manufacturing them himself. But if all his brother capitalists were to do the same, where would he find his commodities in the market? And his money he cannot eat. He tries persuasion. "Consider my abstinence; I might have played ducks and drakes with the 15 shillings; but instead of that I consumed it productively, and made yarn with it." Very well, and by way of reward he is now in possession of good yarn instead of a bad conscience; and as for playing the part of a miser, it would never do for him to relapse into such bad ways as that; we have seen before to what results such asceticism leads. Besides, where nothing is, the king has lost his rights; whatever may be the merit of his abstinence, there is nothing wherewith specially to remunerate it, because the value of the product is merely the sum of the values of the commodities that were thrown into the process of production. Let him therefore console himself with the reflection that virtue is its own reward. But no, he becomes importunate. He says: "The yarn is of no use to me; I produced it for sale." In that case let him sell it, or, still better, let him for the future produce only things for satisfying his personal wants, a remedy that his physician MacCulloch has already prescribed as infallible against an epidemic of overproduction. He now gets obstinate. "Can the labourer," he asks, "merely with his arms and legs, produce commodities out of nothing? Did I not supply him with the materials, by means of which, and in which alone, his labour could be embodied? And as the greater part of society consists of such ne'er-do-wells, have I not rendered society incalculable service by my instruments of production, my cotton and my spindle, and not only society, but the labourer also, whom in addition I have provided with the necessaries of life? And am I to be allowed nothing in return for all this service?" Well, but has not the labourer rendered him the equivalent service of changing his cotton and spindle into yarn? Moreover, there is here no question of service. A service is nothing more than the useful effect of a use-value, be it of a commodity, or be it of labour. But here we are dealing with exchange-value. The capitalist paid to the labourer a value of 3 shillings, and the labourer gave him back an exact equivalent in the value of 3 shillings, added by him to the cotton: He gave him value for value. Our friend, up to this time so purse-proud, suddenly assumes the modest demeanour of his own workman, and exclaims; "Have I myself not worked? Have I not performed the labour of superintendence and of overlooking the spinner? And does not this labour, too, create value?" His overlooker and his manager try to hide their smiles. Meanwhile, after a hearty laugh, he re-assumes his usual mien. Though he chanted to us the whole creed of the economists, in reality, he says, he would not give a brass farthing for it. He leaves this and all such like subterfuges and juggling tricks to the professors of Political Economy, who are paid for it. He himself is a practical man: and though he does not always consider what he says outside his business, yet in his business he knows what he is about.

Let us examine the matter more closely. The value of a day's labour-power amounts to 3 shillings, because of our assumption half a day's labour is embodied in that quantity of labour-power, i.e., because the means of subsistence that are daily required for the production of labour-power, cost half a day's labor. But the past labour that is embodied in the labour-power, and the living labour that it can call into action; the daily cost of maintaining it, and its daily expenditure in work, are two totally different things. The former determines the exchange-value of the labour-power, the latter is its use-value. The fact that half a day's labour is necessary to keep the labourer alive during 24 hours, does not in any way prevent him from working a whole day. Therefore, the value of labour-power, and the value which that labour-power creates in the labour-process, are two entirely different magnitudes; and this difference of the two values was what the capitalist had in view, when he was purchasing the labour-power. The useful qualities that labour-power possesses, and by virtue of which it makes yarn or boots, were to him nothing more than a conditio sine qua non; for in order to create value, labour must be expended in a useful manner. What really influenced him was the specific use-value which this commodity possesses of being *a source not only of value, but of more value than it has itself.* This is the special service that the capitalist expects from labour-power, and in this transaction he acts in accordance with the "eternal laws" of the exchange of commodities. The seller of labour-power, like the seller of any other commodity, realises its exchange-value, and parts with its use-value. He cannot take the one without giving the other. The use-value of labour-power, or in other words, labour, belongs just as little to its seller, as the use-value of oil after it has been sold belongs to the dealer who has sold it. The owner of the money has paid the value of a day's labour-power; his, therefore, is the use of it for a day; a day's labour belongs to him. The circumstance, that on the one hand the daily sustenance of labour-power costs only half a day's labour, while on the other hand the very same labour-power can work during a whole day, that consequently the value which its use during one day creates, is double what he pays for that use, this circumstance is, without doubt, a piece of good luck for the buyer, but by no means an injury to the seller.

Our capitalist foresaw this state of things, and that was the cause of his laughter. The labourer therefore finds, in the workshop, the means of production necessary for working, not only during six, but during twelve hours. Just as during the six hours' process our 10 lbs. of cotton absorbed six hours' labour, and became 10 lbs. of yarn, so now, 20 lbs. of cotton will absorb 12 hours' labour and be changed into 20 lbs. of yarn. Let us now examine the product of this prolonged process. There is now materialised in this 20 lbs. of yarn the labour of five days, of which four days are due to the cotton and the lost steel of the spindle, the remaining day having been absorbed by the cotton during the spinning process. Expressed in gold, the labour of five days is thirty shillings. This is therefore the price of the 20 lbs. of yarn, giving, as before, eighteenpence as the price of a pound. But the sum of the values of the commodities that entered into the process amounts to 27 shillings. The value of the yarn is 30 shillings. Therefore the value of the product is 1/9 greater than the value advanced for its production; 27 shillings have been transformed into 30 shillings; a surplus-value of 3 shillings has been created. The trick has at last succeeded; money has been converted into capital.

Every condition of the problem is satisfied, while the laws that regulate the exchange of commodities, have been in no way violated. Equivalent has been exchanged for equivalent. For the capitalist as buyer paid for each commodity, for the cotton, the spindle and the labour-power, its full value. He then did what is done by every purchaser of commodities; he consumed their use-value. The consumption of the labour-power, which was also the process of producing commodities, resulted in 20 lbs. of yarn, having a value of 30 shillings. The capitalist, formerly a buyer, now returns to market as a seller, of commodities. He sells his yarn at eighteenpence a pound, which is its exact value. Yet for all that he withdraws 3 shillings more from circulation than he originally threw into it. This metamorphosis, this conversion of money into capital, takes place both within the the sphere of circulation and also outside it; within the circulation, because conditioned by the purchase of the labour-power in the market; outside the circulation, because what is done within it is only a stepping-stone to the production of surplus-value, a process which is entirely confined to the sphere of production. Thus "tout est pour le mieux dans le meilleur des mondes possibles."

By turning his money into commodities that serve as the material elements of a new product, and as factors in the labour-process, by incorporating living labour with their dead substance, the capitalist at the same time converts value, i.e., past, materialised, and dead labour into capital, into value big with value, a live monster that is fruitful and multiplies.*

This long section details the process of the production of surplus-value or profit. In short, the worker in the example works for a full day without receiving full pay for the day's work. While the value of a day's work is 6 shillings in the

---

*From Karl Marx, *Capital*, Vol. I (Moscow: Progress Publishers, n.d.), pp. 181–89.

example, the worker is paid for only half of that day, a total of 3 shillings. The remaining 6 hours of his working day go towards transferring his labor-power into surplus-value; the capitalist expends 27 shillings to produce 20 lbs. of yarn but he is paid 30 shillings for it on the open market. The capitalist thus profits to the extent of the 3 shillings that represent the unpaid labor of the worker.

This is not to say, however, that Marx merely advocated returning the "extra" portion of surplus-value to the worker by replacing it in his pay-packet. Marx made it clear that the exploitation of labor was peculiarly "just"— representing *capitalist* justice, by which the worker receives a wage in return for the uses of his labor-power. Marx did not equate the exploitation of labor with theft (as did Proudhon) but rather indicated that it was the peculiar characteristic of labor-power that it could be converted into value greater than itself (i.e., greater than the wage the capitalist paid for its use). Thus capitalism was a paradoxically "just " system in that the worker's labor was not simply stolen but received a monetary compensation. Marx did not believe that property is theft; rather he believed that capitalist private property is *domination.* Capitalism alienates labor not because it "steals" surplus-value (for the worker, according to the capitalist justice of the free market, receives a "full" wage for his labor-power) but because it dominates, coordinates, and fragments that labor. This is crucial to Marx because it allows him to distinguish his theory of emancipation from that of Proudhon and other utopian socialists, who merely advocated the abolition of private property. Marx advocated the abolition of capitalist class society and the private ownership of the means of production (and not *all* property, personal and productive). Marx is saying here that capitalism is not a system created by malevolent human beings and that it can be changed by getting rid of those human beings in favor of more "generous" ones. Capitalism can only be abolished by emancipating labor from a wage-labor system which dominates it.

By mixing living labor with materialized dead labor (e.g., tools, commodities), "the capitalist . . . converts value . . . capital, into value big with value, a live monster that is fruitful and multiplies."

In determining the degree of exploitation of labor by capital, Marx developed the following formula:

$$\frac{s}{v} \text{ (or the rate of surplus-value)} = \frac{\text{surplus labor}}{\text{necessary labor}}.$$

Necessary labor is that labor required to produce the value of labor-power; surplus labor is labor not necessary, which creates value only for the capitalist. The ratio of surplus to necessary labor is a measure of the degree of capitalist exploitation of labor. It will be noted that by "exploitation" Marx was referring to narrowly economic concepts, involving the rate of production of surplus-value for the capitalist. Exploitation was only one component of the broader notion of alienation, the features of which were developed above.

We have seen that the labourer, during one portion of the labour-process, produces only the value of his labour-power, that is, the value of his means of subsistence. Now since his work forms part of a system, based on the social division of labour, he does not directly produce the actual necessaries which he himself consumes; he produces instead a particular commodity, yarn for example, whose value is equal to the value of those necessaries or of the money with which they can be bought. The portion of his day's labour devoted to this purpose, will be greater or less, in proportion to the value of the necessaries that he daily requires on an average, or, what amounts to the same thing, in proporation to the labour-time required on an average to produce them. If the value of those necessaries represent on an average the expenditure of six hours' labour, the workman must on an average work for six hours to produce that value. If instead of working for the capitalist, he worked independently on his own account, he would, other things being equal, still be obliged to labour for the same number of hours, in order to produce the value of his labour-power, and thereby to gain the means of subsistence necessary for his conservation or continued reproduction. But as we have seen, during that portion of his day's labour in which he produces the value of his labour-power, say three shillings, he produces only an equivalent for the value of his labour-power already advanced by the capitalist; the new value created only replaces the variable capital advanced. It is owing to this fact, that the production of the new value of three shillings takes the semblance of a mere reproduction. That portion of the working-day, then, during which this reproduction takes place, I call *"necessary"* labour-time, and the labour expended during that time I call *"necessary"* labour. Necessary, as regards the labourer, because independent of the particular social form of his labour; necessary, as regards capital, and the world of capitalists, because on the continued existence of the labourer depends their existence also.

During the second period of the labour-process, that in which his labour is no longer necessary labour, the workman, it is true, labours, expends labour-power; but his labour, being no longer necessary labour, he creates no value for himself. He creates surplus-value which, for the capitalist, has all the charms of a creation out of nothing. This portion of the working-day, I name surplus labour-time, and to the labour expended during that time, I give the name of surplus-labour. It is every bit as important, for a correct understanding of surplus-value, to conceive it as a mere congelation of surplus labour-time, as nothing but materialised surplus-labour, as it is, for a proper comprehension of value, to conceive it as a mere congelation of so many hours of labour, as nothing but materialised labour. The essential difference between the various economic forms of society between, for instance, a society based on slave-labour, and one based on wage-labour, lies only in the mode in which this surplus-labour is in each case extracted from the actual producer, the labourer.

Since, on the one hand, the value of the variable capital and of the labour-power purchased by the capital are equal, and the value of this labour-power determines the necessary portion of the working day; and since, on the other hand, the surplus-value is determined by the surplus portion of the working-day, it follows that surplus-value bears the same ratio to variable capital, that surplus-labour does to necessary labour, or in other words, the rate of surplus-value $\frac{s}{v} = \frac{\text{surplus labour}}{\text{necessary labour}}$. Both ratios, $\frac{s}{v}$ and $\frac{\text{surplus-labour}}{\text{necessary labour}}$, express the same thing in different ways; in the one case by reference to mate-rialised, incorporated labour, in the other by reference to living fluent labour.

The rate of surplus-value is therefore an exact expression for the degree of exploitation of labour-power by capital, or of the labourer by the capitalist.*

---

*From Karl Marx, *Capital*, Vol. I (Moscow: Progress Publishers, n.d.), pp. 208–209.

The worker thus is bound to the capitalist by the bond of wages, exchanged for disposable labor-power. This does not mean that the individual is "free" outside of labor-time. Marx asserts that the individual consumption of the worker (food, shelter, etc.) is itself a factor in the reproduction of capital and profit. The laborer produces himself through his consumption. Marx terms "productive consumption" that portion of individual consumption "which is requisite for the perpetuation of the class" and which serves to reproduce the worker's labor-power. "Unproductive consumption" is consumption for the sake of pleasure, beyond the bare minimum necessary for survival. "From a social point of view, therefore, the working class, even when not directly engaged in the labor process, is just as much an appendage of capital as the ordinary instruments of labor." This analysis shows that the worker is not "free" to withdraw his labor-power from the marketplace, for he must work in order to survive. Marx argues that the appearance of the worker's legal independence under capitalism is kept in place through the "fictio juris" of the contract: in substance, he argues, the worker is no freer than under the feudal system.

The capital given in exchange for labour-power is converted into necessaries, by the consumption of which the muscles, nerves, bones, and brains of existing labourers are reproduced, and new labourers are begotten. Within the limits of what is strictly necessary, the individual consumption of the working-class is, therefore, the reconversion of the means of subsistence given by capital in exchange for labour-power, into fresh labour-power at the disposal of capital for exploitation. It is the production and reproduction of that means of production so indispensable to the capitalist: the labourer himself. The individual consumption of the labourer, whether it proceed within the workshop or outside it, whether it be part of the process of production or not, forms therefore a factor of the production and reproduction of capital; just as cleaning machinery does, whether it be done while the machinery is working or while it is standing. The fact that the labourer consumes his means of subsistence for his own purposes and not to please the capitalist has no bearing on the matter. The consumption of food by a beast of burden is none the less a necessary factor in the process of production, because the beast enjoys what it eats. The maintenance and reproduction of the working-class is, and must ever be, a necessary condition to the reproduction of capital. But the capitalist may safely leave its fulfilment to the labourer's instincts of self-preservation and of propagation. All the capitalist cares for, is to reduce the labourer's individual consumption as far as possible to what is strictly necessary, and he is far away from imitating those brutal South Americans, who force their labourers to take the more substantial, rather than the less substantial, kind of food.

Hence both the capitalist and his ideological representative, the political economist, consider that part alone of the labourer's individual consumption to be productive, which is requisite for the perpetuation of the class, and which therefore must take place in order that the capitalist may have labour-power to consume; what the labourer consumes for his own pleasure beyond that part, is unproductive consumption. If the accumulation of capital were to cause a rise of wages and an increase in the labourer's consumption, unaccompanied by increase in the consumption of labour-power by capital, the additional capital would be consumed unproductively. In reality, the individual consumption of the labourer is unproductive as regards himself, for it reproduces nothing but the needy individual; it is productive to the capitalist and to the State, since it is the production of the power that creates their wealth.

From a social point of view, therefore, the working-class, even when not directly engaged in the labour-process, is just as much an appendage of capital as the ordinary instruments of labour. Even its individual consumption is, within certain limits, a mere factor in the process of production. That process, however, takes good care to prevent these self-conscious instruments from leaving it in the lurch, for it removes their product, as fast as it is made, from their pole to the opposite pole of capital. Individual consumption provides, on the one hand, the means for their maintenance and reproduction; on the other hand, it secures by the annihilation of the necessaries of life, the continued re-appearance of the workman in the labour-market. The Roman slave was held by fetters; the wage-labourer is bound to his owner by invisible threads. The appearance of independence is kept up by means of a constant change of employers, and by the *fictio juris* of a contract.*

> Marx develops the "general law of capitalist accumulation" as the backbone of his economic system. This general law suggests that there is a reciprocal relationship and feedback between capitalist accumulation and labor-power, with accumulation always the independent variable, and labor-power always the dependent variable.
>
> As the quantity of unpaid labor rises and is accumulated by the capitalist class, there must be an addition of paid labor in order to effect its conversion into additional capital. As this happens, wages rise. The rate of exploitation correspondingly falls; but, Marx asserts, it does not fall so low that capital is no longer "nourished". A reaction occurs, where a smaller part of revenue is capitalized and accumulation lags. Wages thus reverse their direction and the rate of exploitation again rises. Capitalism is a mode of production in which the worker exists in order to facilitate the self-expansion of capital and profit.

Either the price of labour keeps on rising, because its rise does not interfere with the progress of accumulation. In this there is nothing wonderful, for, says Adam Smith, "after these (profits) are diminished, stock may not only continue to increase, but to increase much faster than before. . . . A great stock, though with small profits, generally increases faster than a small stock with great profits." In this case it is evident that a diminution in the unpaid labour in no way interferes with the extension of the domain of capital.—Or, on the other hand, accumulation slackens in consequence of the rise in the price of labour, because the stimulus of gain is blunted. The rate of accumulation lessens; but with its lessening, the primary cause of that lessening vanishes. i.e., the dispro-portion between capital and exploitable labour-power. The mechanism of the process of capitalist production removes the very obstacles that it temporarily creates. The price of labour falls again to a level corresponding with the needs of the self-expansion of capital, whether the level be below, the same as, or above the one which was normal before the rise of wages took place. We see thus: In the first case, it is not the diminished rate either of the absolute, or of the proportional, increase in labour-power, or labouring population, which causes capital to be in excess, but conversely the excess of capital that makes exploitable labour-power insufficient. In the second case, it is not the increased

---

*From Karl Marx, *Capital*, Vol. I (Moscow: Progress Publishers, n.d.), pp. 537–38.

rate either of the absolute, or of the proportional, increase in labour-power, or labouring population, that makes capital insufficient; but, conversely, the relative diminution of capital that causes the exploitable labour-power, or rather its price, to be in excess. It is these absolute movements of the accumulation of capital which are reflected as relative movements of the mass of exploitable labour-power, and therefore seem produced by the latter's own independent movement. To put it mathematically: The rate of accumulation is the independent, not the dependent, variable; the rate of wages, the dependent, not the independent, variable. Thus, when the industrial cycle is in the phase of crisis, a general fall in the price of commodities is expressed as a rise in the value of money, and, in the phase of prosperity, a general rise in the price of commodities, as a fall in the value of money. The so-called currency school concludes from this that with high prices, too much, with low prices too little money is in circulation. Their ignorance and complete misunderstanding of facts are worthily paralleled by the economists, who interpret the above phenomena of accumulation by saying that there are now too few, now too many wage-labourers.

The law of capitalist production, that is at the bottom of the pretended "natural law of population," reduces itself simply to this: The correlation between accumulation of capital and rate of wages is nothing else than the correlation between the unpaid labour transformed into capital, and the additional paid labour necessary for the setting in motion of this additional capital. It is therefore in no way a relation between two magnitudes, independent one of the other: on the one hand, the magnitude of the capital; on the other, the number of the labouring population; it is rather, at bottom, only the relation between the unpaid and the paid labour of the same labouring population. If the quantity of unpaid labour supplied by the working-class, and accumulated by the capitalist class, increases so rapidly that its conversion into capital requires an extraordinary addition of paid labour, then wages rise, and, all other circumstances remaining equal, the unpaid labour diminishes in proportion. But as soon as this diminution touches the point at which the surplus-labour that nourishes capital is no longer supplied in normal quantity, a reaction sets in; a smaller part of revenue is capitalised, accumulation lags, and the movement of rise in wages receives a check. The rise of wages therefore is confined within limits that not only leave intact the foundations of the capitalistic system, but also secure its reproduction on a progressive scale. The law of capitalistic accumulation, metamorphosed by economists into pretended law of Nature, in reality merely states that the very nature of accumulation excludes every diminution in the degree of exploitation of labour, and every rise in the price of labour, which could seriously imperil the continual reproduction, on an ever-enlarging scale, of the capitalistic relation. It cannot be otherwise in a mode of production in which the labourer exists to satisfy the needs of self-expansion of existing values, instead of, on the contrary, material wealth existing to satisfy the needs of development on the part of the labourer. As, in religion, man is governed by the products of his own brain, so in capitalistic production, he is governed by the products of his own hand.*

Furthermore, Marx alleges that there exists a "law of the progressive increase in constant capital" (i.e., machines, plant) in proportion to variable

---

*From Karl Marx, *Capital*, Vol. I (Moscow: Progress Publishers, n.d.), pp. 580–82.

capital (i.e., the wages of labor). This means that from time to time the demand for human labor-power shrinks and workers must be laid off. Marx argues that capitalism requires an "industrial reserve army" in order to have ready sources of labor-power available when it needs them.

The accumulation of capital, though originally appearing as its quantitative extension only, is effected, as we have seen, under a progressive qualitative change in its composition, under a constant increase of its constant, at the expense of its variable constituent.

The specifically capitalist mode of production, the development of the productive power of labour corresponding to it, and the change thence resulting in the organic composition of capital, do not merely keep pace with the advance of accumulation, or with the growth of social wealth. They develop at a much quicker rate, because mere accumulation, the absolute increase of the total social capital, is accompanied by the centralisation of the individual capitals of which that total is made up; and because the change in the technological composition of the additional capital goes hand in hand with a similar change in the technological composition of the original capital. With the advance of accumulation, therefore, the proportion of constant to variable capital changes. If it was originally say 1:1, it now becomes successively 2:1, 3:1, 4:1, 5:1, 7:1, etc., so that, as the capital increases, instead of ½ of its total value, only 1/3, 1/4, 1/5, 1/6, 1/8, etc., is transformed into labour-power, and, on the other hand, 2/3, 3/4, 4/5, 5/6, 7/8, into means of production. Since the demand for labour is determined not by the amount of capital as a whole, but by its variable constituent alone, that demand falls progressively with the increase of the total capital, instead of, as previously assumed, rising in proportion to it. It falls relatively to the magnitude of the total capital, and at an accelerated rate, as this magnitude increases. With the growth of the total capital, its variable constituent or the labour incorporated in it, also does increase, but in a constantly diminishing proportion. The intermediate pauses are shortened, in which accumulation works as simple extension of production, on a given technical basis. It is not merely that an accelerated accumulation of total capital, accelerated in a constantly growing progression, is needed to absorb an additional number of labourers, or even, on account of the constant metamorphosis of old capital, to keep employed those already functioning. In its turn, this increasing accumulation and centralisation becomes a source of new changes in the composition of capital, of a more accelerated diminution of its variable, as compared with its constant constituent. This accelerated relative diminution of the variable constituent, that goes along with the accelerated increase of the total capital, and moves more rapidly than this increase, takes the inverse form, at the other pole, of an apparently absolute increase of the labouring population, an increase always moving more rapidly than that of the variable capital or the means of employment. But in fact, it is capitalistic accumulation itself that constantly produces, and produces in the direct ratio of its own energy and extent, a relatively redundant population of labourers, i.e., a population of greater extent than suffices for the average needs of the self-expansion of capital, and therefore a surplus-population.

Considering the social capital in its totality, the movement of its accumulation now causes periodical changes, affecting it more or less as a whole, now distributes its various phases simultaneously over the different spheres of production. In some spheres a change in the composition of capital occurs without increase of its absolute magnitude, as a consequence of simple centralisation; in others the absolute growth of capital is connected with absolute diminution of its variable constituent, or of the labour-power absorbed by it; in others again, capital continues growing for a time on its given technical basis, and attracts additional labour-power in proportion to its increase, while at other times it undergoes organic change, and lessens its variable constituent; in all spheres, the increase of the variable part of capital, and therefore of the number of labourers employed by it, is always connected with violent fluctuations and transitory production of surplus-population, whether this takes the more striking form of the repulsion of labourers already employed, or the less evident but not less real form of the more difficult absorption of the additional labouring population through the usual channels. With the magnitude of social capital already functioning, and the degree of its increase, with the extension of the scale of production, and the mass of the labourers set in motion, with the development of the productiveness of their labour, with the greater breadth and fulness of all sources of wealth, there is also an extension of the scale on which greater attraction of labourers by capital is accompanied by their greater repulsion; the rapidity of the change in the organic composition of capital, and in its technical form increases, and an increasing number of spheres of production becomes involved in this change, now simultaneously, now alternately. The labouring population therefore produces, along with the accumulation of capital produced by it, the means by which it itself is made relatively superfluous, is turned into a relative surplus-population; and it does this to an always increasing extent. This is a law of population peculiar to the capitalist mode of production:*

" . . .the laboring population always increases more rapidly than the conditions under which capital can employ this increase for its own self-expansion." The industrial reserve army exists as a check against rising wage demands on the part of employed workers. There is established an "accumulation of misery, corresponding with accumulation of capital." As the rich get richer, so the poor become more exploited: Workers are either laid off, and set adrift as members of the industrial reserve army, or they are forced to work longer hours at higher rates of productivity.

The greater the social wealth, the functioning capital, the extent and energy of its growth, and, therefore, also the absolute mass of the proletariat and the productiveness of its labour, the greater is the industrial reserve army. The same causes which develop the expansive power of capital, develop also the labour-power at its disposal. The relative mass of the industrial reserve army increases therefore with the potential energy of wealth. But the greater this reserve army in proportion to the active labour-army, the greater is the mass of a consolidated surplus-population, whose misery is in inverse ratio to its torment of labour. The more extensive, finally, the lazarus-layers of the working-class, and the industrial reserve army, the greater is official pauperism. *This is the absolute general law of capitalist accumulation.* Like all other laws it is modified

---

*From Karl Marx, *Capital*, Vol. I (Moscow: Progress Publishers, n.d.), pp. 589–92.

in its working by many circumstances, the analysis of which does not concern us here.

The folly is now patent of the economic wisdom that preaches to the labourers the accommodation of their number to the requirements of capital. The mechanism of capitalist production and accumulation constantly effects this adjustment. The first word of this adaptation is the creation of a relative surplus-population, or industrial reserve army. Its last word is the misery of constantly extending strata of the active army of labour, and the dead weight of pauperism.

The law by which a constantly increasing quantity of means of production, thanks to the advance in the productiveness of social labour, may be set in movement by a progressively diminishing expenditure of human power, this law, in a capitalist society—where the labourer does not employ the means of production, but the means of production employ the labourer—undergoes a complete inversion and is expressed thus: The higher the productiveness of labour, the greater is the pressure of the labourers on the means of employment, the more precarious, therefore, becomes their condition of existence, viz., the sale of their own labour-power for the increasing of another's wealth, or for the self-expansion of capital. The fact that the means of production, and the productiveness of labour, increase more rapidly than the productive population, expresses itself, therefore, capitalistically in the inverse form that the labouring population always increases more rapidly than the conditions under which capital can employ this increase for its own self-expansion.

We saw in Part IV., when analysing the production of relative surplus-value: within the capitalist system all methods for raising the social productiveness of labour are brought about at the cost of the individual labourer; all means for the development of production transform themselves into means of domination over, and exploitation of, the producers; they mutilate the labourer into a fragment of a man, degrade him to the level of an appendage of a machine, destroy every remnant of charm in his work and turn it into a hated toil; they estrange from him the intellectual potentialities of the labour-process in the same proportion as science is incorporated in it as an independent power; they distort the conditions under which he works, subject him during the labour-process to a despotism the more hateful for its meanness; they transform his life-time into working-time, and drag his wife and child beneath the wheels of the Juggernaut of capital. But all methods for the production of surplus-value are at the same time methods of accumulation; and every extension of accumulation becomes again a means for the development of those methods. It follows therefore that in proportion as capital accumulates, the lot of the labourer, be his payment high or low, must grow worse. The law, finally, that always equilibrates the relative surplus-population, or industrial reserve army, to the extent and energy of accumulation, this law rivets the labourer to capital more firmly than the wedges of Vulcan did Prometheus to the rock. It establishes an accumulation of misery, corresponding with accumulation of capital. Accumulation of wealth at one pole is, therefore, at the same time accumulation of misery, agony of toil, slavery, ignorance, brutality, mental degradation, at the opposite pole, i.e., on the side of the class that produces its own product in the form of capital.*

---

*From Karl Marx, *Capital*, Vol. I (Moscow: Progress Publishers, n.d.), pp. 603–604.

Marx ends Volume I of *Capital* with thoughts about the inevitability of capitalism's collapse. He argues that the centralization of capital is unavoidable, according to the general law of capitalist accumulation (surveyed above); along with this, the socialization of labor, as he calls it, will proceed apace. By socialization of labor Marx means the increasingly cooperative form of the working process, the technical application of science in production, the methodical cultivation of the soil, the transformation of tools and factories into instruments of labor usable only in common (growing division of labor and interdependence of labor), and the entanglement of workers in an international world market. Marx calls these the "immanent laws of capitalistic production."

As capital is increasingly concentrated in fewer and fewer hands, as the industrial reserve army grows, and as employed labor is increasingly subjugated and socialized to the requirements of capitalist accumulation, the working class moves toward insurrection. This class is "disciplined, united, organized by the very mechanism of the process of capitalist production itself." Finally, "the expropriators are expropriated."

What does the primitive accumulation of capital, i.e., its historical genesis, resolve itself into? In so far as it is not immediate transformation of slaves and serfs into wage-labourers, and therefore a mere change of form, it only means the expropriation of the immediate producers, i.e., the dissolution of private property based on the labour of its owner. Private property, as the antithesis to social, collective property, exists only where the means of labour and the external conditions of labour belong to private individuals. But according as these private individuals are labourers or not labourers, private property has a different character. The numberless shades, that it at first sight presents, correspond to the intermediate stages lying between these two extremes. The private property of the labourer in his means of production is the foundation of petty industry, whether agricultural, manufacturing, or both; petty industry, again, is an essential condition for the development of social production and of the free individuality of the labourer himself. Of course, this petty mode of production exists also under slavery, serfdom, and other states of dependence. But it flourishes, it lets loose its whole energy, it attains its adequate classical form, only where the labourer is the private owner of his own means of labour set in action by himself: the peasant of the land which he cultivates, the artisan of the tool which he handles as a virtuoso. This mode of production presupposes parcelling of the soil, and scattering of the other means of production. As it excludes the concentration of these means of production, so also it excludes co-operation, division of labour within each separate process of production, the control over, and the productive application of the forces of Nature by society, and the free development of the social productive powers. It is compatible only with a system of production, and a society, moving within narrow and more or less primitive bounds. To perpetuate it would be, as Pecqueur rightly says, "to decree universal mediocrity." At a certain stage of development it brings forth the material agencies for its own dissolution. From that moment new forces and new passions spring up in the bosom of society; but the old social organisation fetters them and keeps them down. It must be annihilated; it is annihilated. Its annihilation, the transformation of the individualised and scattered means of production into socially concentrated ones, of the pigmy property of the many into the huge property of the few, the expropriation of the great mass of the people from the soil, from the means of subsistence, and from the means of labour, this fearful and painful expropriation of the mass of the people forms the prelude to the history of capital. It comprises a series of forcible methods, of which we have passed in review only those that have been epoch-making as methods of the primitive accumulation of capital. The expropriation of the immediate producers was accomplished with merciless Vandalism, and under the stimulus of passions the most infamous, the most sordid, the pettiest, the most meanly odious. Self-earned private property, that is based, so to say, on the fusing together of the isolated, independent labouring-individual with the conditions of his labour, is supplanted by capitalistic private property, which rests on exploitation of the nominally free labour of others, i.e., on wage-labour.

As soon as this process of transformation has sufficiently decomposed the old society from top to bottom, as soon as the labourers are turned into proletarians, their means of labour into capital, as soon as the capitalist mode of production stands on its own feet, then the further socialisation of labour and further transformation of the land and other means of production into socially exploited and, therefore, common means of production, as well as the further expropriation of private proprietors, takes a new form. That which is now to be expropriated is no longer the labourer working for himself, but the capitalist exploiting many labourers. This expropriation is accomplished by the action of the immanent laws of capitalistic production itself, by the centralisation of capital. One capitalist always kills many. Hand in hand with this centralisation, or this expropriation of many capitalists by few, develops, on an ever-extending scale, the co-operative form of the labour-process, the conscious technical application of science, the methodical cultivation of the soil, the transformation of the instruments of labour into instruments of labour only usable in common, the economising of all means of production by their use as the means of production of combined socialised labour, the entanglement of all peoples in the net of the world-market, and with this, the international character of the capitalistic régime. Along with the constantly diminishing number of the magnates of capital, who usurp and monopolise all advantages of this process of transformation, grows the mass of misery, oppression, slavery, degradation, exploitation; but with this too grows the revolt of the working-class, a class always increasing in numbers, and disciplined, united, organised by the very mechanism of the process of capitalist production itself. The monopoly of capital becomes a fetter upon the mode of production, which has sprung up and flourished along with, and under it. Centralisation of the means of production and socialisation of labour at last reach a point where they become incompatible with their capitalist integument. Thus integument is burst asunder. The knell of capitalist private property sounds. The expropriators are expropriated.

The capitalist mode of appropriation, the result of the capitalist mode of production, produces capitalist private property. This is the first negation of individual private property, as founded on the labour of the proprietor. But capitalist production begets, with the inexorability of a law of Nature, its own negation. It is the negation of negation. This does not re-establish private property for the producer, but gives him individual property based on the acquisitions of the capitalist era: i.e., on co-operation and the possession in common of the land and of the means of production.

The transformation of scattered private property, arising from individual labour, into capitalist private property is, naturally, a process incomparably more protracted, violent, and difficult, than the transformation of capitalistic private property, already practically resting on socialised production, into socialised property. In the former case, we had the expropriation of the mass of the people by a few usurpers; in the latter, we have the expropriation of a few usurpers by the mass of the people.*

Marx concludes by showing that capitalism is a self-contradictory mode of production. The accumulation of capital, he has argued, inexorably creates a great mass of unemployed workers as the organic composition of capital changes, replacing variable capital (wages) with constant capital (plant and tools). The outcome of Marx's dialectical method is the conclusion that capitalism *cannot* survive, burdened as it apparently is with serious and ineradicable contradictions.

MARX'S CRISIS THEORY

These serious internal contradictions—resulting from the general law of capitalist accumulation and the tendency towards the concentration and centralization of capital and the corresponding swelling of the ranks of the industrial reserve-army and falling wages—were meant to emerge in a final cataclysm that capitalism could not avoid. Marx here opens Pandora's Box, suggesting to some of his followers that the breakdown of capitalism was inevitable and to others that capitalism must be actively negated by a class-conscious proletariat.

While we find Marx's theory of the internal contradictions of capitalism, contained mainly in Volume I of *Capital,* to be brilliant and incisive in its grasp of basic principles of the alienation and exploitation of labor, unfortunately the status of Marx's crisis theory is less clear. We will argue that the enduring contribution of Marxism is the vision of freedom and theory of internal contradictions and not the model of economic crisis Marx briefly presented in Volume III of *Capital,* especially in Chapter XXV of that work. Marx's description and diagnosis of alienation under early forms of capitalism makes *Capital* a profoundly path-breaking work. However Marx's model of the crisis of capitalism, and the subsequent transition to socialism, is inadequately developed and remains of limited interest for contemporary Marxists.

Again, this refers back to our analysis of Marx's dialectical method as the synthesis of a theory and critique of alienation, a theory of capitalism's internal contradictions, and an empirical model of crisis-tendencies and modes of transition to socialism. Our contention here is that the first two parts of the dialectical method are enduring (and will endure as long as capitalist alienation exists) but that the third part, crisis-modelling, continuously changes, requiring contemporary revisions of Marx's (sketchy) crisis-theory. Thus we must clearly separate the theory of internal contradictions from crisis-theory; the theory of internal contradictions might be seen as a *deeper* level of capitalist functioning than the model of crises. While internal contradictions remain—primarily the contradiction between capital and labor, as Marx generally expressed it—crisis-

---

*From Karl Marx, *Capital*, Vol. I (Moscow: Progress Publishers, n.d.), pp. 713–15.

forms change with the times. The project of twentieth century Marxism is to revise our understanding of these crisis-tendencies without abandoning other aspects of Marxist dialectical method (alienation and internal contradictions).

Marx's theory of crises remains generally irrelevant for the analysis of late capitalist society because Marx was so ambiguous and even self-contradictory in his original speculation about the transition to socialism. The theory of the breakdown, as it has been called, takes a variety of different forms in the writings of Marx and Engels. The diligent reader can find formulations in Marx about the necessity and inevitability of violent revolution as well as formulations about the possibility of gradual, nonviolent, even democratic-parliamentary transformations. These latter reflections appear more frequently during the later part of Marx's career, while the endorsement of violent revolution finds its most systematic exposition in Marx and Engels' 1848 *Communist Manifesto.*

This shift within Marx's own work should not be taken as evidence that he grew "soft" and conciliatory in his old age. It should instead be read as evidence of Marx's growing open-mindedness with respect to his analysis of crisis-forms. Instead of imposing one eternal model of crisis and transition upon historical dynamics, as Marx appeared to do earlier in his career when he suggested that the revolution would necessarily be a violent rupture with the past guided by a revolutionary dictatorship of the majority, Marx came to recognize the possibility of varied modes of breakdown and transformation. This is extremely important for contemporary Marxists inasmuch as it liberates us from subservience to a single authoritative version of radical change.

Volume I of *Capital* contains evidence that Marx did *not* believe that crisis was inevitable (or "automatic") in a capitalist system. There Marx argued that there was a continuous cycle between wages and capital accumulation; when wages rose in response to capital accumulation, profit would shrink, capital accumulation would slow and wages would gradually fall. As wages fell, profit could be increased—recall Marx's notion that profit could only be created by the extraction of surplus-value from labor. Thus Marx indicated that there was no inevitable tendency for profit to shrink to such a degree that the entire system of capital accumulation would be endangered. At the same time, Marx believed that there were built-in *tendencies* for profit to shrink and for the proletariat to become impoverished. Since Marx's death, there have been a variety of theories to account for the dynamics and causes of this projected collapse, termed variously the underconsumption theory (according to which capitalism cannot generate enough consumption to meet ever-rising commodity production), the disproportionality theory (according to which there is a contradiction between the increasingly socialized character of labor—the interdependence of productive functions and a growing division of labor—and the private character of capital accumulation, resulting in a type of economic anarchy), and the overproduction theory (the logical counterpart of the underconsumption theory).

Marx endorsed all three theories in different places in his writings. However he *also* appeared to endorse the concept of the noninevitability of capitalist breakdown. As Marx aged, he appeared to shy away from statements in *The Communist Manifesto* about the inevitability of crisis. Volume I of *Capital* provides no clearly articulated statement about why the system *must* collapse, given the logic and dynamic of capitalist accumulation.

Marx believed that collapse was not "necessary" in the sense that the earth rotates around the sun and will continue to do so for millions of years. He felt that collapse was necessary for human emancipation, an event without which aliena-tion would continue. Some contend that this non-necessitarian interpretation of Marxism robs Marxism of its powerful predictive power. However there is little textual evidence in Marx that allows us to pin down his so-called crisis theory in a definite and specific way. Marx is *more* convincing when he describes the ability of capitalism to reproduce itself endlessly through the cycle between wages and accumulation than when he argues that crisis and collapse are inevitable.

At this point we must raise perhaps the most fundamental issue in the history of Marxism. This issue has been characterized as the idea of Marxian determinism, or the idea of the scientific character of Marxism. In our general introduction to this chapter we suggested that Marxism has undergone numer-ous shifts from objective scientific to philosophical modes of analysis, each contingent on shifting structural and historical circumstances. We argued that Marxism tends to be scientific and deterministic when crisis-tendencies are sharp; similarly, Marxism becomes abstract and philosophical when capitalism appears self-sustaining and relatively crisis-free. We can now provide a more concrete discussion of this issue.

Marx at numerous times argued that Marxism charts the "natural laws" of capitalism; indeed, he characterized the central theme of Marxism as the "gen-eral law of capitalist accumulation". Marx did *not* mean that capitalism was a scientific specimen possessing eternal characteristics that could be inductively probed by observers who could then formulate testable hypotheses about the behavior of that specimen in quest of certain natural laws of its behavior. By natural laws Marx meant merely the typical patterns of development manifested by the capitalist system. The difference between pure materialism and dialectical materialism is that the latter is historical and thus seeks not eternal laws of behavior and nature but rather structural dynamics exhibited by historical phenomena. Marx was interested in depicting the behavior of capitalism because he wanted to create *new* "laws" of society. The so-called natural laws of capitalism, Marx felt, oppressed the human being and robbed him of substantive autonomy; Marx wished to *break* the dominance of capitalism's "natural laws" over human beings.

Thus when Marx talked about a Marxian science he did not mean that this science would have the same type of predictive capability as the natural or physical sciences. It would not map the laws of motion of capitalism in that sense. Instead, it would provide a diagnosis of capitalism in order to show human beings how the system might be purposefully changed. Marx believed that industrial society under capitalism was "sick" and could be cured. However the resolution of the illness would not come purely from the working out of the disease—according to pregiven natural laws—but rather from the activity of human beings acting with theoretical and political self-consciousness (as gravediggers, to follow through with our metaphor).

The laws Marx describes in Volumes I and III of *Capital* are not immutable: They can be *changed.* The central thesis in Volume I is the "general law of the accumulation of capital," describing the way in which the accumulation of capital relentlessly keeps wages low. The central thesis of Marx's theory of crisis is contained in Volume III of *Capital,* where he outlines the "law of the tendency of the rate of profit to fall." The second law in a sense *contradicts* the first law; it describes the *breakdown* of the general law of the accumulation of capital.

Volume III begins with Marx's differentiation of surplus-value from profit.

The rate of surplus-value is expressed by the ratio of surplus-value to variable capital (wages) : $\frac{s}{v}$. The rate of profit Marx suggests, is expressed by the ratio of surplus-value to total capital, or $\frac{s}{C}$. In other words, Marx asserts that the rate of profit is almost always smaller than the rate of surplus-value (the rate of the ex-ploitation of labor) because the former is a ratio of surplus-value to total capital, while the latter is the ratio of surplus-value to only a portion of capital, that rep-resented by variable capital, or wages.

Here, as at the close of the preceding chapter, and generally in this entire first part, we presume the amount of profit falling to a given capital to be equal to the total amount of surplus-value produced by means of this capital during a certain period of circulation. We thus leave aside for the present the fact that, on the one hand, this surplus-value may be broken up into various sub-forms, such as interest on capital, ground-rent, taxes, etc., and that, on the other, it is not, as a rule, identical with profit as appropriated by virtue of a general rate of profit, which will be discussed in the second part.

So far as the quantity of profit is assumed to be equal to that of surplus-value, its magnitude, and that of the rate of profit, is determined by ratios of simple figures given or ascertainable in every individual case. The analysis, therefore, first is carried on purely in the mathematical field.

We retain the designations used in Books I and II. Total capital C consists of constant capital c and variable capital v, and produces a surplus-value s. The ratio of this surplus-value to the advanced variable capital, or $\frac{s}{v}$, is called the rate of surplus-value and designated s'. Therefore $\frac{s}{v}$ =s', and consequently s=s'v. If this surplus-value is related to the total capital instead of the variable capital, it is called profit, p, and the ratio of the surplus-value s to the total capital C, or $\frac{s}{C}$, is called the rate of profit, p'. Accordingly,

$$p' = \frac{s}{C} = \frac{s}{c + v}.$$

Now, substituting for s its equivalent s'v, we find

$$p' = \frac{v}{C} = s' \frac{v}{c + v}.$$

which equation may also be expressed by the proportion

$$p':s' = v:C;$$

the rate of profit is related to the rate of surplus-value as the variable capital is to the total capital.

It follows from this proportion that the rate of profit, p', is always smaller than s', the rate of surplus-value, because v, the variable capital, is always smaller than C, the sum of v +c, or the variable plus the constant capital; the only, practically impossible case excepted, in which v=C, that is, no constant capital at all, no means of production, but only wages are advanced by the capitalist.*

The key to Marx's crisis-theory is his assumption that the capitalist mode of production implies a rising ratio of constant to variable capital, i.e., of machines, plant, and raw materials to wages. The so-called "organic composition of capital"

*From Karl Marx, *Capital*, Vol. III (Moscow: Foreign Languages Publishing House, 1962), pp. 49–50.

rises as capitalism advances; in turn, Marx argues that as this happens the rate of profit will tend to fall, even though the rate of surplus-value may stay the same or even rise temporarily. This argument rests on his theory about the rising organic composition of capital under the capitalist mode of production.

Assuming a given wage and working-day, a variable capital, for instance of 100, represents a certain number of employed labourers. It is the index of this number. Suppose £100 are the wages of 100 labourers for, say, one week. If these labourers perform equal amounts of necessary and surplus labour, if they work daily as many hours for themselves, i.e., for the reproduction of their wage, as they do for the capitalist, i.e., for the production of surplus-value, then the value of their total product=£200, and the surplus-value they produce would amount to £100. The rate of surplus-value, $\frac{s}{v}$, would =100%. But, as we have seen, this rate of surplus-value would nonetheless express itself in very different rates of profit, depending on the different volumes of constant capital c and consequently of the total capital C, because the rate of profit=$\frac{s}{C}$. The rate of surplus-value is 100%:

If c = 50, and v = 100, then p′ $= \frac{100}{150} = 66\frac{2}{3}\%$;

" c = 100, and v = 100, then p′ $= \frac{100}{200} = 50\%$;

" c = 200, and v = 100, then p′ $= \frac{100}{300} = 33\frac{1}{3}\%$;

" c = 300, and v = 100, then p′ $= \frac{100}{400} = 25\%$;

" c = 400, and v = 100, then p′ $= \frac{100}{500} = 20\%$.

This is how the same rate of surplus-value would express itself under the same degree of labour exploitation in a falling rate of profit, because the material growth of the constant capital implies also a growth—albeit not in the same proportion—in its value, and consequently in that of the total capital.

If it is further assumed that this gradual change in the composition of capital is not confined only to individual spheres of production, but that it occurs more or less in all, or at least in the key spheres of production, so that it involves changes in the average organic composition of the total capital of a certain society, then the gradual growth of constant capital in relation to variable capital must necessarily lead to *a gradual fall of the general rate of profit*, so long as the rate of surplus-value, or the intensity of exploitation of labour by capital, remain the same. Now we have seen that it is a law of capitalist production that its development is attended by a relative decrease of variable in relation to constant capital, and consequently to the total capital set in motion. This is just another way of saying that owing to the distinctive methods of production developing in the capitalist system the same number of labourers, i.e., the same quantity of labour-power set in motion by a variable capital of a given value, operate, work up and productively consume in the same time span an ever-increasing quantity of means of labour, machinery and fixed capital of all sorts, raw and auxiliary materials—and consequently a constant capital of an ever-increasing value. This continual relative decrease of the variable capital vis-a-vis the constant, and consequently the total capital, is identical with the pro-gressively higher organic composition of the social capital in its average. It is likewise just another expression for the progressive development of the social productivity of labour, which is demonstrated precisely by the fact that the same number of labourers, in the same time, i.e., with less labour, convert an ever-increasing quantity of raw and auxiliary materials into products, thanks to the growing application of machinery and fixed capital in general. To this growing quantity of value of the constant capital—although indicating the growth of the real mass of use-values of which the constant capital materially consists only approximately—corresponds a progressive cheapening of products. Every individual product, considered by itself, contains a smaller quantity of labour than it did on a lower level of production, where the capital invested in wages occupies a far greater place compared to the capital invested in means of production. The hypothetical series drawn up at the beginning of this chapter expresses, therefore, the actual tendency of capitalist production. This mode of production produces a progressive relative decrease of the variable capital as compared to the constant capital, and consequently a continuously rising organic composition of the total capital. The immediate result of this is that the rate of surplus-value, at the same, or even a rising, degree of labour exploitation, is represented by a continually falling general rate of profit. (We shall see later why this fall does not manifest itself in an absolute form, but rather as a tendency toward a progressive fall.) The progressive tendency of the general rate of profit to fall is, therefore, just *an expression peculiar to the capitalist mode of production* of the progressive development of the social productivity of labour. This does not mean to say that the rate of profit may not fall temporarily for other reasons. But proceeding from the nature of the capitalist mode of production, it is thereby proved a logical necessity that in its development the general average rate of surplus-value must express itself in a falling general rate of profit. Since the mass of the employed living labour is continually on the decline as compared to the mass of materialized labour set in motion by it, i.e., to the productively consumed means of production, it follows that the portion of living labour, unpaid and congealed in surplus-value, must also be continually on the decrease compared to the amount of value represented by the invested total capital. Since the ratio of the mass of surplus-value to the value of the invested total capital forms the rate of profit, this rate must constantly fall.*

> This "tendential law" is related to earlier aspects of Marx's theory of capitalism, contained mainly in Volume I of *Capital*. There he argued that there is a tendency for capital to be centralized and concentrated. Marx suggests that capitalist productivity implies a falling rate of profit *and* accelerated accumulation at the same time. Accumulation, he argues, hastens the falling rate of profit inasmuch as it breeds the concentration of labor and thus a higher organic composition of capital. In turn, the falling rate of profit forestalls the development of new, independent capitals and causes the centralization of capital by large capitalists. The system stagnates as profit rates fall and as capital is further centralized and concentrated. "It breeds over-production, speculation, crises, and surplus-capital alongside surplus-population."

We have seen in the first part of this book that the rate of profit expresses the rate of surplus-value always lower than it actually is. We have just seen that even a rising rate of surplus-value has a tendency to express itself in a falling rate of

---

*From Karl Marx, *Capital*, Vol. III (Moscow: Foreign Languages Publishing House, 1962), pp. 204–209.

profit. The rate of profit would equal the rate of surplus-value only if c = 0, i.e., if the total capital were paid out in wages. A falling rate of profit does not express a falling rate of surplus-value, unless the proportion of the value of the constant capital to the quantity of labour-power which sets it in motion remains unchanged or the amount of labour-power increases in relation to the value of the constant capital.

On the plea of analysing the rate of profit, Ricardo actually analyses the rate of surplus-value alone, and this only on the assumption that the working-day is intensively and extensively a constant magnitude.

A fall in the rate of profit and accelerated accumulation are different expressions of the same process only in so far as both reflect the development of productiveness. Accumulation, in turn, hastens the fall of the rate of profit, inasmuch as it implies concentration of labour on a large scale, and thus a higher composition of capital. On the other hand, a fall in the rate of profit again hastens the concentration of capital and its centralization through expropriation of minor capitalists, the few direct producers who still have anything left to be expropriated. This accelerates accumulation with regard to mass, although the rate of accumulation falls with the rate of profit.

On the other hand, the rate of self-expansion of the total capital, or the rate of profit, being the goad of capitalist production (just as self-expansion of capital is its only purpose), its fall checks the formation of new independent capitals and thus appears as a threat to the development of the capitalist production process. It breeds over-production, speculation, crises, and surplus-capital alongside surplus-population. Those economists, therefore, who, like Ricardo, regard the capitalist mode of production as absolute, feel at this point that it creates a barrier itself, and for this reason attribute the barrier to Nature (in the theory of rent), not to production. But the main thing about their horror of the falling rate of profit is the feeling that capitalist production meets in the development of its productive forces a barrier which has nothing to do with the production of wealth as such; and this peculiar barrier testifies to the limitations and to the merely historical, transitory character of the capitalist mode of production; testifies that for the production of wealth, it is not an absolute mode, moreover, that at a certain stage it rather conflicts with its further development.*

> Finally, Marx concretely analyzes the "internal contradictions" of the law of the falling rate of profit. The essential contradiction of capitalism is that it drives towards unlimited increase of production—"towards production as an end in itself"—while the express purpose of capital is to be self-expanding, i.e., profit-making. Unlimited productivity—at the expense of the great mass of impoverished and often unemployed workers—contradicts the purpose of profit. Marx argues that it is impossible for capital accumulation to limit itself, since the organic composition of capital rises inexorably. Thus the expansion of productivity and the profitable reinvestment of capital, Marx claims, are mutually exclusive aims. "The *real barrier* of capitalist production is *capital itself.*"

The decrease of variable in relation to constant capital, which goes hand in hand with the development of the productive forces, stimulates the growth of

---

*From Karl Marx, *Capital,* Vol. III (Moscow: Foreign Languages Publishing House, 1962), pp. 236–37.

the labouring population, while continually creating an artificial over-population. The accumulation of capital in terms of value is slowed down by the falling rate of profit, to hasten still more the accumulation of use-values, while this, in its turn, adds new momentum to accumulation in terms of value.

Capitalist production seeks continually to overcome these immanent barriers, but overcomes them only by means which again place these barriers in its way and on a more formidable scale.

The *real barrier* of capitalist production is *capital itself*. It is that capital and its self-expansion appear as the starting and the closing point, the motive and the purpose of production; that production is only production for *capital* and not vice versa, the means of production are not mere means for a constant expansion of the living process of the *society* of producers. The limits within which the preservation and self-expansion of the value of capital resting on the expropriation and pauperization of the great mass of producers can alone move—these limits come continually into conflict with the methods of production employed by capital for its purposes, which drive towards unlimited extension of production, towards production as an end in itself, towards unconditional development of the social productivity of labour. The means—unconditional development of the productive forces of society—comes continually into conflict with the limited purpose, the self-expansion of the existing capital. The capitalist mode of production is, for this reason, a historical means of developing the material forces of production and creating an appropriate world-market and is, at the same time, a continual conflict between this its historical task and its own corresponding relations of social production.*

Marx, it must be emphasized, is concerned with tendencies for capitalism to generate internal crises. Although he terms these tendencies "laws," he implies that these laws do not possess the same mechanical motion as the laws of physics. Human beings must grasp these "laws" and carry them through to their logical conclusion—in the case of capitalism, the emancipation of labor through revolutionary activity. Marx's crisis-theory does not predict the collapse of capitalism but only points the way towards possible scenarios of crisis and transformation. He did not preclude the development of new forms of crisis and transition in later stages of the development of capitalism.

Capital maps out both the internal contradictions of capitalism and possible modes of its breakdown. For our purposes as North American Marxists in the late 1970s, the most useful dimension of *Capital* is its superbly detailed articulation of capitalist contradictions; less useful is Marx's optimism that these contradictions would emerge in a final cataclysm that would bring the dawn of a new socialist age. While capitalism has outlived the crises Marx predicted would befall it in the late nineteenth century, the contradictions remain, renewing our optimism about socialist possibility and forcing us to reexamine the crisis-tendencies these contradictions breed, in quest of new and more appropriate forms of socialist class-radicalism.

---

*From Karl Marx, *Capital,* Vol. III (Moscow: Foreign Languages Publishing House, 1962), pp. 244–45.

GUIDE TO FURTHER READING*

BERTELL OLLMAN *Alienation,* is a useful and comprehensive introduction to Marx's theory of alienation.

HERBERT MARCUSE "The Foundations of Historical Materialism," in his *Studies in Critical Philosophy,* published as an essay in 1932 immediately following the unearthing of the "Economic and Philosophical Manuscripts," is a definitive appreciation of Marx's early works and of their relationship to the later scientific analysis of capitalism.

M. M. BOBER *Karl Marx's Interpretation of History,* contains succinct summaries of Marx's economic theories, concentrating on Marx's theories of crises and his views on the breakdown of capitalism and transition to communism. See especially Chapters IX—XIV of the Second Edition.

NICHOLAS LOBKOWICZ *Theory and Practice,* offers a history of the concept of praxis from Aristotle to Marx. He provides a careful analysis of Marx's meaning of praxis in the third section of his book.

JEAN HYPPOLITE *Studies on Marx and Hegel,* offers original and important reflections on differences and similarities between Marx and Hegel by a French existentialist Marxist.

JEAN-PAUL SARTRE *Critique of Dialectical Reason,* is a brilliant, if obscure, reinterpretation of Marx's dialectical method. Sartre unites existentialist and Marxist philosophy through his reading of Marx's dialectical method.

GEORGE LICHTHEIM *Marxism* originally published in 1961, is the most comprehensive history of the development of Marxian theory yet to appear. Lichtheim is especially clear in his exposition of the "scientific socialism" of the Second International.

KARL MARX *Economic and Philosophical Manuscripts,* is the first significant writing of Marx, containing primarily the manuscripts composed in Paris between 1843 and 1844. This work develops Marx's critique and theory of alienation.

KARL MARX *Capital,* Volumes 1, 2, and 3, is the most coherent systematic expression of Marx's critique of capitalism, especially Marx's notion of the unavoidable "internal contradictions" of capitalism such as the incongruity between the socialization of production and the private ownership of the means of production.

KARL MARX AND FRIEDRICH ENGELS *The German Ideology* (including "Theses on Feuerbach"), is considered as part of Marx's "early writings." Here Marx and Engels develop their seminal theory of ideology, based on the proposition that the ruling ideas of every historical period are always the ideas of the ruling-class.

MARX AND ENGELS *The Communist Manifesto,* published in 1848, contains a systematic statement of the dialectical method and offers a glimpse of Marx's vision of revolutionary transformation. Later, Marx shed many of the Blanquist-Jacobin formulations about revolutionary violence and dictatorship found in the *Manifesto.*

KARL MARX *Grundrisse,* drafted between 1857 and 1858, represents a bridge of sorts between Marx's early works and *Capital.* These lengthy manuscripts do not form a coherent single work but nonetheless abound with Marx's insights about technological development and domination.

KARL KORSCH *Karl Marx,* offers an interesting introduction to Marx's thought, colored by Korsch's gradual disenchantment with original Marxism.

OSCAR LANGE *On the Economic Theory of Socialism.*

ROBERT C. TUCKER *The Marxian Revolutionary Idea.*

LOUIS BOUDIN *The Theoretical System of Karl Marx in the Light of Recent Criticism.*

EMILE BURNS *An Introduction to Marxism.*

MAURICE DOBB *On Economic Theory and Socialism.*

---

*See Bibliography for full publication references.

QUESTIONS FOR FURTHER DISCUSSION

1. Why are latter-day Marxists often sharply divided over the internal division within Marx's own work between philosophical and scientific components?
2. How does this division effect contemporary Marxism?
3. What was Marx's greatest contribution to the development of social science?
4. What does Marx's oft-cited admission, "I am not a Marxist" mean?
5. Did Marx believe in the inevitability of the breakdown of capitalism? Cite textual evidence from his writings to substantiate your position.
6. Did Marx believe that the overthrow of capitalism would be violent? Did he base his view of the revolutionary transition on a prior historical example, such as the Jacobin episode in the aftermath of the French revolution?
7. Explain how Marx's theory of alienation must be modified today.

2

Twentieth Century Reformers and Radicals:Scientific Marxism in the Second International

HISTORICAL OVERVIEW

Early market capitalism reached its zenith during the Second International (1889–1914). Marxists during this period created theories that heralded the imminent collapse of the capitalist system. They also developed versions of "scientific socialism" that likened Marxism to the natural and physical sciences in its predictive reliability. The prospect of an imminent collapse of capitalism led thinkers like Karl Kautsky to develop systems of economic determinism that argued that there was little room for political spontaneity in hastening the collapse of the system. Kautsky implied that Marxists like himself should instead passively await the "inevitable" breakdown of the system. Eduard Bernstein argued against the scientific socialists that capitalism was not nearing its final collapse but was instead changing gradually into socialism. Bernstein advocated the democratic class struggle, carried on through parliamentary and electoral means, to create a practicable form of social democracy. Rosa Luxemburg stood on the left wing of the German Social Democratic Party, opposing both Bernstein's parliamentary socialism and Kautsky's scientific Marxism. Luxemburg argued that there must be an organic relationship between the revolutionary working class and certain revolutionary leaders. She attacked Lenin's concept of revolutionary leadership as overly authoritarian and elitist, arguing that the period of revolutionary transition—the so-called "dictatorship of the proletariat"—must be very short and must be quickly democratized in order to prevent the erection of an authoritarian socialist state (such as arose in Russia). The concept of a "scientific socialism" that charted the allegedly imminent breakdown of capitalism was born in 1891 when the Erfurt Programme was published. Engels and Kautsky attempted to provide Marxism with the same scientific legitimacy as the natural and physical sciences, ignoring Marx's own Hegelian inheritance and his idea of the dialectical method that was opposed to the deterministic character of the natural sciences. The scientific Marxism of the Second International gradually withered away as the outbreak of the First World

War split the International asunder, giving way to the Marxism-Leninism of the Bolsheviks who came to exercise dominance in the Third or Communist International, created in 1919. The so-called "revisionist controversy," begun in 1899 by Bernstein's rejection of Marxian crisis-theory and economic determinism, arose out of the peculiarities of Germany at the turn of the century. Germany lagged behind France, Britain, and the United States in terms of industrial and political development, and leaders of the Second International recognized that the achievement of parliamentary democracy was a necessary prerequisite of broader social transformation. Thus the socialist movement in Germany was not hinged on the aim of achieving immediate socialism but rather merely on modernizing the backward, authoritarian German political structure. The primary difference between Bernstein on the one hand and Kautsky, the Austro-Marxists, and Luxemburg on the other was the emphasis each placed on revising orthodox Marxian theory to fit the backward reality of Germany in the 1890s. Where Bernstein was honest about the necessity of creating liberal democracy before socialism, Kautsky tried to adhere theoretically to Marxian orthodoxy and economic determinism while strategically believing, with Bernstein, that the German workers' movement must fight not for their own Paris Commune but for democratic political participation.

GENERAL INTRODUCTION

By 1900 Marxism was certifiably a major social force in western Europe, and soon to become a major force in eastern Europe. Between about 1900 and 1920 Marxism both as theory and practice underwent significant changes. The western European working class had grown in number and appeared ready to assume the revolutionary responsibility that Marx had outlined. The two decades between the beginning of the twentieth century and the outbreak and consolidation of the Russian Revolution provided a revolutionary environment not soon to be matched. Marxian theory emerged from this environment deeply and irrevocably changed.

These two decades were pivotal in the way that they afforded a proving-ground for many of Marx's hypotheses about revolutionary transformation. Between the time that Marx and Engels completed the *Communist Manifesto* (1848) and the time that Marx published Volume 1 of his last great work, *Capital* (1867), the European political situation had become hostile to socialist change. The failure of the Paris Commune in 1871 may have forced Marx to reevaluate his initial response to the Commune, which was to announce with exuberance that communism had finally dawned on Europe. That the communist movement was not significantly spurred on by the example of the Communards led Marx to step back and adopt a longer-term perspective on the imminence of radical socialist change.

We argued in Chapter 1 that the development of Marxian theory cannot be understood apart from the changing context of economic and political reality. Marx's own development as a theorist provides eloquent proof of this assertion. *The Communist Manifesto* was written in a spirit of revolutionary exuberance, capturing shifting realities in European social and political life that indicated to Marx and Engels that a workers' revolution was at hand. By contrast, works like the *Grundrisse* (1857-1858) and the first volume of *Capital* were written in periods of class compromise, attempting not to foment and guide short-term political rebellion but to comprehend longer-term developments in the dialectical movement of capitalism.

Marx was acutely aware of the relationship between theoretical optimism and the immediacy of political rebellion; when sharp class-struggle is absent, theory will take on a more circumspect attitude towards revolutionary possibility. This is not to say that Marx became totally fatalistic after the collapse of the Paris Commune but only that he modified the emphasis of his theory better to suit the changing reality of industrial capitalism during a period of international consolidation and class compromise.

For deep and fundamental structural reasons, relating to the historical development of capitalism, the "contradictions" of capitalism did not fully mature. The working-class became an integral part of bourgeois society and not its fundamental antithesis, as Marx hoped and expected it might. Thus capitalism temporarily averted the deadly fate Marx argued it could not avoid, given the internal contradictions of a profit-system. This integration of the proletariat into the capitalist system provided the point of departure for Eduard Bernstein's social democratic revision of Marxism, to which Kautsky and Engels' subsequent scientific Marxism was a response.

Eduard Bernstein is considered to be the founder of parliamentary or "evolutionary" socialism, eventually becoming what we know today as modern social democracy (e.g., embodied in the program of the British Labour Party). Bernstein's influence in the Second International was paramount because Bernstein articulated certain fundamental differences with the assumptions of original Marxism.

It is unjustified to assert that Bernstein's concept of a parliamentary — an evolutionary, not revolutionary — socialism is inherently "un-Marxist." Such claims assume that there can be only one route to socialism and thus only one "correct" type of theory. This book argues against a monolithic model of Marxism, suggesting instead that Marxism is inherently historical. Thus Bernstein's parliamentary socialism, continually shifting its political and theoretical terms of reference, is not necessarily a clear-cut departure from Marx's goal of socialsim but perhaps only a different strategy for achieving it.

Bernstein's idea that socialism could be achieved through parliamentary means and without a violent revolution led by a tightly organized vanguard is not the source of significant Marxian criticism of his position. Instead many Marxists reject Bernstein's position because they see it as a significant departure from Marx's final aim of a classless society and, instead, endorsing accommodation to capitalism and other forms of class compromise. Most disputes over political strategies and tactics concern the meaning and substance of a classless society and the meaning of terms like socialism, communism, liberation, and emancipation. When certain Marxists attack Bernsteinian socialism they attack not primarily the means for achieving socialism but his very conception of *what* is to be achieved. Bernstein's critics have often asserted that parliamentary socialism and social democracy preserve capitalism and only effect cosmetic political changes (e.g., replacing the Conservative Party in Great Britain with the Labour Party).

Western Marxists are as much divided over conceptions of ultimate goals as over revolutionary tactics; strategic disputes often conceal larger theoretical differences. Marx refrained from making detailed projections about the blueprint of future communism and thus caused his followers to spend the next hundred years arguing about the "true meaning" of Marxism. Today, for many, this true meaning seems as elusive as ever.

Bernstein's conception was opposed largely because it was seen to be merely cosmetic in its effect on capitalism. The modern "welfare state" (found in Sweden, Great Britain, the United States, and Canada, for example) represents an uneasy coalition between business interests, labor interests, and the interests of the government (or "state," in Marxist parlance). Essentially, the welfare state tries to compensate the poor for injustices suffered by providing all citizens with social services and unemployment assistance. It is thought that Bernstein gave license to this conception of welfare-state socialism through his notion that class struggle would be displaced into the electoral arena, thus ensuring that class conflict could be blunted by compromises between the political representatives of capital and labor.

This concept of socialism, in a narrow strategic sense, has worked quite well, as evidenced by the growing number of nations with "parliamentary socialist" political systems. The lot of workers, both employed and unemployed, has improved considerably since Marx's time, at least inasmuch as there is little absolute deprivation, such as starvation and high infant mortality, in most industrial welfare states. Social services of all kinds have improved as a result of heavy government taxation that serves to redistribute (if not equalize) social wealth, especially where the very rich are taxed at much higher rates than the poor and middleclass (as in Great Britain).

Many thoughtful western radicals believe that parliamentary socialism is a practicable alternative to more drastic and authoritarian kinds of radical change. They argue that it is impossible to level all economic differences; and that it would be undesirable to create an overly centralized "workers state" such as exists in the Soviet Union. This belief about the practicability and even, in an ultimate sense, the desirability of welfare-state socialism is fundamentally rooted in the quite reasonable fear that to move beyond the democratic socialist welfare state towards more radical socialist forms would endanger individual civil liberties. The Soviet Union is always invoked in this context as an example of a society that has by-passed Bernstein's type of democratic socialism for more centralized forms (requiring economic planning, severe forms of work discipline, and the bureaucratic regulation of consumption and personal expression). The Soviet Union never passed through democratic, parliamentary socialism because there was no liberal-democratic tradition in pre-revolutionary Russia such as existed in the United States and Great Britain. In addition, Russia in 1917 was industrially underdeveloped and therefore the Bolsheviks felt that they could not afford the luxury of granting certain civil liberties such as the freedoms of speech and dissent.

It is difficult for a western Marxist to ignore the anxiety of Bernsteinian socialists about civil liberties; few radicals in the west would prefer to be radicals in the Soviet Union today (for their radicalism would be harshly punished by the Soviet authorities). In liberal, albeit capitalist, democracies such as our own leftist thinkers are even encouraged to write books about Marxism and to sell their books for a profit!

However there are real differences in perspective between Bernsteinians and more orthodox "scientific" Marxists that transcend the issue of strategy (and yet that are often reflected in differences on the issue of strategy). For example, many contend that the social democratic welfare-state allows capitalism to coexist with a limited degree of socialist planning and government intervention in the economy. The capitalist profit-motive is not eradicated by the welfare state; in fact, the policies of the welfare state contribute to the survival of capitalism, generating large capital expenditures and creating jobs for the structurally un- employed and underemployed (i.e., for those who Marx said would be forced out of the labor-force as the rate of profit began to fall).

Additionally, the welfare state strengthens capitalism by integrating global economies through the multi-national corporation. The nation-state legitimizes international capitalism and thus a new type of class conflict: that which takes place between developed, capital-owning nation-states and underdeveloped, capital-poor nation-states. It is possible to argue that the United States facilitates and protects the international commercial activities of the Exxon Corporation by allowing the Exxon Corporation's economic interests to become a constituent feature of American foreign policy. Although this smacks of conspiracy-theory, which Marx persistently opposed (wanting to analyze capitalism as a dynamic, if self-contradictory, social-economic structure and not as a creation of a few malevolent human beings), there is something of value in this type of analysis. *It might be said that modern capitalism is an interlocking system of nation-states, corporations, the military, unions, and individual consumers.* Without the com- pliance of any of these interest groups, the consensus upon which modern capitalism rests would begin to break down (see Chapter 7, especially the seg- ment on Jürgen Habermas, for further discussion of this point).

Those Marxists who oppose Bernsteinian Marxism do so not because electoral strategies *cannot* be successful but because socialist political parties do not usually effect radical socialist change once elected. In the late 1970s, a crucial test of this hypothesis may occur in Italy. The Communist Party in Italy is near the threshold of power, having already formed a coalition government with the bourgeois Christian Democrats and with the Socialist party (which is tiny and politically powerless). The burning issue for modern Marxists is how far a democratically-elected Communist Party can move towards significant socialist change. Can they abolish the system of private property and reduce class- differences while preserving participatory democracy? Many western Marxists fear that the exigencies of electoral politics in Italy will prevent the CPI from effecting these changes; after all, as a democratically-elected government, the Communists must be responsive to the wishes of the voters, only a small minor- ity of whom presently embrace the stated ideology of the CPI. Furthermore, the American-dominated NATO forces will not look with favor upon a Communist Italy, democratically elected or not (the American Central Intelligence Agency demonstrably subverted the democratically-elected regime of Salvador Allende in Chile, preferring the near-fascism of his military opponents).

There are other, deeper barriers to a genuinely socialist Italy. Many worry that the CPI is basically committed to Soviet-style Marxism ("Marxism- Leninism") and, once in power, will abolish most civil liberties, such as the right of dissent. This represents the inversion of the Bernsteinian problem: While social democratic parties often do not go far enough towards Marxist change, it is feared that the CPI will go too far towards the Soviet extreme of authoritarian socialism.

It may be that what we called the Bernsteinian problem—how to effect radical change electorally and peacefully, from within a capitalist system—will only be solved empirically, by experimenting with different types of socialist institutions. It is difficult to think of any intrinsic limits to socialism beyond which social democratic parties cannot go. It may be that there is nothing wrong with Bernstein's gradualist parliamentary approach but simply that there have been few socialist parties worth supporting by one who holds genuinely Marxist ideals.

At the same time as Bernstein outlined his parliamentary socialism, Karl Kautsky, with the help of Engels, attempted to rewrite Marx's theory of dialectical materialism. Kautsky tried strictly to separate the scientific from the ethical and political dimensions of Marx's theory, suggesting that the "political" goal of socialism must necessarily be separated from the methods (including theoretical and scientific activity) used to achieve it.

This separation was thought by Engels and Kautsky to provide Marxism with an improved scientific status. As we noted in Chapter 1, this debate about the scientific status of Marxism echoes throughout the history of left-wing thought. Indeed, the effects of this splitting of Kautsky's scientific concept of Marxism from original Marxism methodology, based upon what we earlier called a dialectical concept of theory, are still being felt (as we will observe in Chapter 7).

The splitting of social science from left-wing political movements closely resembles the stance taken by Max Weber in his writings on the philosophy of the social sciences. Weber argued that the ethics and political values of the social scientist must not be allowed to muddy his research and teaching. Weber's 1919 essay on "Science as a Vocation" is the classical expression of the modern-day dictum of scientific "value-freedom." Weber opposed Marxism on political and scientific grounds. The scientific Marxists of the Second International led by Kautsky, located themselves *between* Weber and Marx, combining Weber's concern with scientific impartiality and Marx's ethical-political vision of socialism. The possibility of combining Marxian political ideals (a classless society) with Weber's value-neutrality is not as problematic as it appears for Marx often suggested that dialectical materialism was a "natural science of history," attempting to claim for it the same lawful, objective reliability achieved by the natural and physical sciences.

This question of whether Marxism is a science or an ethical, moral philosophy is crucial today. Those Marxists who claim a certain scientific status for Marxism, suggesting that Marxian theory charts "laws" of social movement, often endorse Marxian determinism. Those Marxists willing to revise Marx's particular crisis-theory and his concept of a workers' revolution, instead searching for other revolutionary agents and forces, have also been generally willing to abandon the idea that Marxian theory is a type of deterministic "natural science."

At issue here is the question of Marxian determinism. Many opponents of Marxism have argued that Marxism robs the human being of revolutionary free will; certain scientific Marxists counter this perspective by claiming for Marxism precisely the predictive reliability enjoyed by the natural sciences. Those who take the orthodox view of Marxism, contending that Marxism is a natural science of history, *also* tend to adopt a relatively passive political stance. If the revolution is bound to happen and if its happening is beyond the control and choice of individuals, a passive politics is required. These Marxists suggest that the most important revolutionary task in the short run is not to devise new forms and agencies of class-radicalism but to develop a structural theory of what will happen during and after the revolution, in the transition period between capitalism and socialism.

Revisionist Marxists who reject this concept of deterministic orthodoxy and its implicit assumption that the revolution is inevitable (and predictable in the same way that the weather can be predicted using meteorological science), seek new and different forms of change, often arguing that crisis-forms have fundamentally changed since Marx. No longer, they argue, is the industrial working class, as it is presently constituted, the respository of all revolutionary possibilities; in fact, in nation-states like the United States, the working class is often politically and socially conservative, rejecting revolutionary theory as a threat to their new-found affluence.

This split between orthodox and revisionist Marxists that surfaced during the early twentieth century reduces to the dispute over whether Marxism can be a science in the sense of containing predictive statements about social reality. If Marxism is that type of social science, then theorists need not take an active part in change itself but rather they might stand back and attempt merely to comprehend pre-determined social processes. In this view Marxism must read reality as reality transforms itself automatically (through the allegedly natural, automatic collapse of capitalism). Determinist Marxists do not oppose socialist change but believe rather that the change will occur as a function of certain natural economic processes — "internal contradictions," as Marx termed them — that will veritably force the working class to revolt and abolish capitalism. Revisionist Marxists, like Bernstein, believe that there is nothing natural or inevitable about the process of socialist transformation and, further, that the working class today is not the most likely agent of socialist radicalism.

Between Bernsteinian revisionism and revolutionary theorists like Rosa Luxemburg and Antonio Gramsci stood Kautsky, who represented a type of social democracy that was peculiarly indebted both to revisionism and to a deterministic concept of Marxian science. Ultimately Kautsky broke ranks with thinkers such as Luxemburg who were more sympathetic to the early revolutionary experiments of the Bolsheviks than were most others in the German Social Democratic Party.

Kautsky seriously disagreed with Bernstein's evolutionary socialism, arguing that Marxism is a form of natural science that documents the inevitable and necessary breakdown of capitalism; paradoxically, Kautksy also believed that democratic means of struggle were not to be rejected out of hand. He separated Marxian ethics from Marxian science, creating the puzzling appearance of a coexistent economic determinism and ethical idealism and humanism. Kautsky has been described as occupying the center of German Social Democracy, flanked on the right by Bernstein and on the left by Luxemburg.

Kautsky believed that contradictions in capitalism were sharpening and that the proper stance of Marxists was to chart the natural maturation and revolutionary resolution of these contradictions. He opposed Bernstein both because Bernstein appeared to reject the ultimate aims of socialism (a debatable issue, at best) and because Bernstein did not believe that capitalism was approaching its inexorable, final breakdown. The Kautskyian scientific Marxists of the Second International were convinced that the breakdown, as Marx had projected it, was close at hand: Theoretical Marxism would document this final collapse as it happened; it would not intervene and foster revolutionary fervor because it saw the breakdown as unavoidable.

We have suggested before that those thinkers who conceive of Marxism as a form of "scientific socialism" (like Kautsky and Engels) often tend to be politically apathetic or reformist (Kautsky felt that Marxism must be an objective science and at the same time that parliamentary socialism was an unavoidable strategic necessity). However, in our first chapter on Marx's dialectical materialist concept of history, we appeared to take precisely the opposite position—that philosophical Marxists are apolitical and resigned to a "praxis-less" type of Marxian theory. We do not want to contradict outselves! We are arguing that scientific Marxism arises in turbulent, crisis-ridden historical periods as an expression of the imminence of large-scale socialist transformation. However *scientific Marxism often fails to rise above a pure determinism, thus cancelling its potential to guide and assist incipient revolutionary class struggle.*

It will be recalled that Marx's theory of capitalism contained both a theory of human alienation and a theory of the self-contradictory "laws" of capitalism. These two dimensions were connected by the theory of crisis, suggesting the empirical conditions in which revolutionary struggle could transform capitalist "laws." The Kautskyian Marxists of the Second International failed to develop the theory of crisis that would have related subjective and objective dimensions of Marxism; Bernstein explicitly argued that there would be *no* crisis of the sort Marx expected; Luxemburg argued that Marxists must seize upon the occurrence of crisis with revolutionary vigor and commitment, for she argued that the revolution would not occur automatically, as Kautsky suggested, but required theoretically-informed class-radicalism.

While a more scientific, deterministic strain of Marxism tends to emerge during crisis-ridden, historical periods, scientific Marxism is rarely engaged in fomenting class struggle. Kautsky's scientific Marxism was a "pure" form of Marxian determinism, likening itself to the natural sciences in its scientific predictability and reliability. It is the peculiar characteristic of scientific Marxism, as outlined by Engels and Kautsky, and even by Marx in those places where he claimed that Marxism is a "natural science of history," charting the "immanent laws" of capitalism, to refrain from entering the political fray: *Scientific Marxists believe that the revolution will occur naturally, with the same inevitability as the law of gravity.* Kautsky's dilemma was that his scientific Marxism bound him to do *nothing* to assist and expedite the revolutionary forces he perceived to be brewing around him.

Early capitalism was a period of revolutionary possibility, producing at once Bernstein's parliamentary socialism, Kautsky's dualism of scientific determinism and ethical humanism, and Luxemburg's and Gramsci's revolutionary vigor. Early twentieth century European capitalism perhaps more than any other period in recent history gave rise to a variety of hotly contested versions of Marxism. This is because early capitalism, between about 1880 and 1920, subsisted in a period of intense political turmoil and, most important, a period during which the structural arrangement of important social forces was being worked out. The proletariat in Bernstein's eyes should accommodate itself to the process of electoral politics and the gradual metamorphosis of capitalism into social democracy; the proletariat in Luxemburg's eyes should develop an action-oriented theory of class-radicalism to guide it in the radical reconstruction of all capitalist institutions; the proletariat in Kautsky's eyes will *naturally* emerge as a revolutionary force. This variety of theoretical programs does not represent merely the differing temperaments of thinkers but rather the real multiplicity of *possible* Marxisms during a turbulent period of economic and political crisis. For Marxists like Rosa Luxemburg a socialist revolution of a lasting, democratic kind was a realistic possibility. For Bernstein, similarly, the prospect that a revolution might be achieved by internal adjustments and modifications within a capitalist structure appeared feasible.

Kautsky occupies the territory between Bernstein and Luxemburg, unable to abandon revolutionary hopes (as evidenced in his scathing attack on Bernstein's gradualism) and also unable to move towards Luxemburg's more dialectical analysis, which joined revolutionary theory and revolutionary practice, and which implicitly denied that Marxism could be deterministic.

For Kautsky and the Austro-Marxists (who further divided Marxian science and Marxian ethics), a Weberian type of Marxism, split between empirical causality and ethical optimism and values, could avoid Luxemburg's activism while remaining faithful to Marx, combining socialist "values" and Marxian "science." Yet Kautsky did not find much of specific utility in Marx's works to guide him in his decision about whether or not to support the national chauvinism triggered by the outbreak of the First World War. Kautsky agonized over what Marx might have done had he been in Kautsky's own shoes. The point here is that those Marxists of the Second International like Kautsky, Renner, Hilferding and Adler who tried to reconcile the ethical goal of socialism with the practical expediencies of the time found themselves in a tortuous dilemma.

This raises the question about whether communism in Marx's terms is or should be conceived as an "ethical ideal." Marx implied in numerous places that capitalism was headed on a road to disaster and that the advent of socialism was virtually unavoidable. This formulation allowed many Marxists of the Second International like Kautsky to reinterpret Marxism as a social science variant of the natural and physical sciences. Earlier, however, we noted that many of the thinkers of the Second International like Kautsky separated the ethical ideal of communism from the movement to achieve it. Kautsky was a Weberian Marxist in this sense. While Kautsky thought that the breakdown of capitalism was inevitable in the sense that it could not be determined, effected, or delayed by human intervention, he possessed no criteria with which to determine whether the breakdown was actually happening, and thus what he as a theorist could do to foster class-radicalism.

A caricature of Kautsky, but one that captures his essential predicament, would reveal him asking the ghost of Marx why the revolution was not occurring in western Europe as Marx had "promised." Bernstein in a sense was less deterministic than Kautsky inasmuch as he took the non-existence of class struggle as a symptom of the basic illness of determinist Marxism as a whole. Bernstein broke with scientific Marxism when he saw that significant socialist goals could be achieved through parliamentary means. In retrospect, Bernstein may have possessed a certain profundity and depth of insight in this regard. Bernstein, unlike Kautsky and other Marxists divided between faith in inevitable revolution and a realistic empirical scepticism generated by the observation of reality, was able to free himself from the ghost of Marx sufficiently to offer original suggestions about ways of revising Marxism and generating new forms of class-radicalism.

The scientific Marxism of Kautsky could not harness revolutionary dynamics, in spite of his belief that Marxism must remain empirical and analytical. Kautsky was unable to apply his scientific Marxism to European society in such a way as to assist and guide class struggle. Scientific Marxism, when divorced from the subjective dimension of revolutionary motivation, can do little more than observe and chart the predetermined movement of capitalist structures. Kautsky could not connect his democratic political program with his scientific Marxism because he failed to grasp the dialectical foundation of Marxism. Although Kautsky ridiculed Bernstein's reformist program, he could go little further in developing a cogent model of class-based political action.

Luxemburg explicitly opposed the theory of the inevitable breakdown of capitalism because such a theory, she felt, degraded the contribution to be made by theoretically articulate, struggling workers. Again, the issue of the Marxian method arises: *Is Marxism a version of the natural sciences that charts the predetermined motion of a society that defies guidance by particular human beings? Or is Marxism a subjective orientation of the human being towards his own alienation?*

Luxemburg tried to resolve this dilemma by indicating that Marxism could be *both* a structural theory of contradictions and a theory of class struggle. She said that there could be no appropriate Marxism without both structural and subjective aspects: The system would not collapse of its own accord; nor would the system change merely because human beings recognized their own alienation. Instead workers must theorize about and comprehend the logical contradictions of capitalism while at the same time trying to imagine how the world today could be changed tomorrow. Marx's method, Luxemburg argued, combines both scientific objectivity and a type of utopian imagination that goes beyond the distorted appearance of objective reality towards the possibility of a new reality.

The Russian Revolution was initially invigorating for western Marxists like Luxemburg who took inspiration from Lenin's courage and tenacity. Although the Bolshevik insurrection did not actually fit Marx's model of revolution (which held that revolution will tend to happen in industrialized and not in agrarian societies, wherein "internal contradictions" between capital and labour were sharp), it was nonetheless the first blow against capitalism. The Bolsheviks sent shock waves through the western European working classes, truly "shaking the world" as one author described it. There had been no significant Marxian political success since the short-lived Paris Commune in 1871.

Lenin's political acumen and organizational skills are indisputable. He was a revolutionary genius who overcame heavy odds against his eventual success. Equally as important for the western European Marxists like Luxemburg and Gramsci who witnessed the Russian developments were the theoretical and ideological dimensions of Bolshevik political activity.

Partly because the Russian Revolution occurred in a backward society, Lenin felt it necessary to accelerate the contradictions that Marx suggested were latent in every capitalist system. He created a type of "state capitalism," as he called it, wherein the revolutionary workers' state was directed by a few strong leaders and where the first-order social priority was the creation of an industrial economy based on sufficient capital accumulation. Lenin temporarily instituted a New Economic Plan that borrowed significant features from the market capitalist free enterprise system.

Lenin organized his workers' state through the institution of what he termed "democratic centralism." Only by strict organizational discipline imposed on politically recalcitrant, backward workers by the vanguard of the Communist Party could the industrial infrastructure be created. Lenin's democratic centralism emerged out of political expediency of sorts, not simply out of a malevolent desire to oppress the new Russian working and peasant classes. Yet democratic centralism fundamentally altered Marx's ideal of the revolutionary workers' control of the production process. Lenin felt that he could legitimately interpose "democratic centralism" as a way of achieving the tight socialist organization of labor and industrial productivity while retaining the "democratic" ideal of a workers' state, if only in name.

The Russian Revolution guaranteed that workers in general could legally own the means of production; however, Lenin's democratic centralism also ensured that particular workers would *not* have any say in organizing society and the economy from below. According to Lenin, the Communist Party could provide workers with the theoretical mentality and work discipline allegedly required to build a new industrial society.

However the theory of democratic centralism, used to legitimize Lenin's model of socialism, proved to be much more than a practical expedient. There is every reason to believe that Lenin eventually wanted to transcend harsh central authority and move towards democratic socialism. But Lenin never completed his dream. Power struggles ensued between the early Bolshevik leaders, pitting Lenin variously against Bukharin, Trotsky, and finally Stalin, requiring on this basis the tightening of iron-fisted rule. These struggles revolved around the question of who would set policy for the creation of an industrialized Soviet Union. Bukharin, who urged the rapid democratization of the USSR, eventually was forced to admit to political "crimes"; and Lenin himself warned just before his death against Stalin's unbridled thirst for personal power.

But in spite of these warnings against the consequences of too much centralism and not enough democracy, the centralization of power proceeded unabated. This centralization required certain crucial adjustments in Marxian theory, such as the aforementioned additions of "state capitalism" and "democratic centralism." The Bolsheviks also required a theory of Soviet truth according to which political and social reality could be assessed and legitimated. Lenin himself wrote a number of philosophical and theoretical works (among them the1908 book *Materialism and Empirio-Criticism* and after he had become acquainted with Hegel, the *Philosophical Notebooks*) that served as the foundation of a Marxist-Leninist ideology.

Marxism-Leninism has thus a political and a philosophical component. Its political component involves Lenin's theories about democratic centralism, state capitalism, and the vanguard party allegedly required to lead the backward proletariat and peasantry. It was not this political theory in and of itself that proved to be explosive in western European Marxism; it was rather the perplexing Marxist-Leninist ideology developed by Lenin and Stalin that served to legitimize "socialist" reality in the Soviet Union, fundamentally altering the terms of reference of western European Marxism, that put democratically minded Marxists like Luxemburg on the defensive.

This official Soviet ideology protected the Soviet experiment by suggesting that every act of the regime could be philosophically and theoretically justified. Thus Marxism-Leninism became more than a theory about how to seize power. It quickly became a theory to justify peculiarities of the Bolshevik ascension to power and the centralized, authoritarian version of socialism that resulted. Anyone who quarrelled with Marxism-Leninism was said to be anti-Soviet, even an enemy of socialism and Marxism. After 1919, when the Bolshevik ideologist Zinoviev took over the leadership of the Third International, criticism of the Soviet Union became tantamount to treason.

This created grave ambivalence and ambiguity within the ranks of western

Marxism. Not only were Leninist political strategies often inappropriate to indus- trially developed and democratic western Europe, the Soviet concept of "socialist" truth, defined in terms of allegiance to the Soviet regime, forced western Marxists to fall into line with Moscow or to break ranks and risk excom- munication. For some western Marxists, Marx's original theories already seemed outmoded and thus they had little trouble in opposing Marxism-Leninism. For others, like Luxemburg and Gramsci, there was a real reluctance to criticize socialism for fear of strengthening western capitalism and counterrevolutionary forces within the Soviet Union. This reluctance on the part of western Marxists to criticize the Soviet Union lasted until after Stalin's death in the early 1950s and, in some quarters, persists to the present day.

The Soviet ideology was unsavoury to many in the west because it justified an authoritarian, even totalitarian reality. For thinkers like Luxemburg and Gramsci the essence of Marxism is radical democracy and "self-management" (i.e., the direct control of social institutions by those involved in them, especially in the realm of industrial production). Soviet centralism tended to delay and even postpone indefinitely the prospect of direct workers' democracy in the name of certain developmental imperatives. For discerning critics, however, the real rea- son for Stalin's decision to tighten central authority was not to create the condi- tions for democratic Marxism but instead to strengthen his own political hand. Again, in many quarters, it was incredibly difficult to believe that Stalin did *not* have the best interests of the Soviet working class at heart and was acting out of self-serving motives.

By 1919, when the Soviet influence began to be felt outside the territorial Soviet Union, the western working class movement had basically crumbled and turned towards trade-union activity and parliamentary strategies. The First World War shattered the internationalist aspirations of Luxemburg, further dividing each national working-class from one another, failing to unite them around the common purpose of destroying international capitalism. The prospects for a Marxian revolution diminished both because the structures of western capitalism were changing and because the Soviets distracted those Marxists by imposing upon them a peculiar, authoritarian model of socialism.

Marxism has not been the same since the Russian Revolution. Despite disagreements about matters of style and emphasis between Bernstein, Kautsky, and Luxemburg, the three important thinkers in German Social Democracy, they all related their theory directly to the on-going political reality in European society. After the breakdown of the Second International, Marxism in western Europe went "underground," shedding many of the appearances of original Marxian theory. Theorists rethought and rewrote Marx's analysis of capitalism by examining reasons for the revolutionary delay in western Europe. This is not to say that the Marxism that arose out of the ashes of original Marxism was inferior theoretically to the Marxisms of the Second International. In significant respects the "Hegelian Marxism" that followed the demise of the Second Interna- tional was a cogent response to Marxism-Leninism and its authoritarian logic. Indeed the aspirations of Luxemburg's revolutionary Marxism were largely pre- served in the form of Georg Lukács and Karl Korsch's Hegelian Marxist recon- struction of Marx's theory, examined in Chapter 3.

The period of the Second International instructs us that Marxian theory must take an active role in analyzing and assisting class-radicalism, refusing to endorse strict determinism; this balance between political engagement with the class struggle and analytical rigor in analyzing internal contradictions has been difficult to attain. Kautsky erred by upholding a deterministic concept of socialist change, failing to grasp the particular historical circumstances of the proletariat in Europe. Luxemburg, had she not been murdered mid-stream in her political career, might have proven to be more adept than Kautsky at uniting the analytical and revolutionary dimensions of Marxian theory, at the same time working against Lenin's highly centralized model of vanguard socialism.

BERNSTEIN: EVOLUTIONARY SOCIALISM

Eduard Bernstein took issue with the revolutionary core of original Marxism, suggesting that capitalism might gently slide towards socialism, without class warfare and revolutionary violence. Bernstein is considered to be the father of social democracy, embraced in varying degrees by the labor parties of Britain, Canada, Sweden, and even the United States (where the Democratic Party is a pale copy of the British Labor Party, endorsing a watered-down version of social democracy inspired by Franklin Roosevelt's progressivism).

Bernstein was attacked from all sides for (a) suggesting that Marxian theory required revisions, especially as class contradictions were being blunted by the gradual embourgeoisement of the working class, and (b) for apparently returning to Kant's conception of value-free empirical science, rejecting the dialectical and value-committed core of original Marxism. Bernstein's *Evolutionary Socialism*, first published in 1899, is admittedly weak on philosophy and stronger on his arguments about the outmoded character of orthodox Marxism; it is difficult to sustain the argument that Bernstein was a profound and systematic thinker. However his historical importance lies in his courageous and fundamental attack on orthodox deterministic models of revolutionary change. Much of Bernstein's vaunted "revisionism" appears to have become a component of neo-Marxist conventional wisdom, even that of the Frankfurt School, to which he otherwise bears scant resemblance. Bernstein, unlike most other thinkers of the Second and Third Internationals, was not afraid to confront the reality of failed revolutionary expectations, admitting to himself that the revolution, as Marx may have expected it, did not occur and that perhaps the Marxist theory itself required serious revisions.

Bernstein argues that Marxism cannot be economic determinism because "purely economic causes create . . .only a disposition for the reception of certain ideas, but how these then arise and spread and what form they take depend on the co-operation of a whole series of influences."

Historical materialism by no means denies every autonomy to political and ideologic forces—it combats only the idea that these independent actions are unconditional, and shows that the development of the economic foundations of social life—the conditions of production and the evolution of classes—finally exercises the stronger influence on these actions.

But in any case the multiplicity of the factors remains, and it is by no means always easy to lay bare the relations which exist among them so exactly that it can be determined with certainty where in given cases the strongest motive power is to be sought. The purely economic causes create, first of all, only a disposition for the reception of certain ideas, but how these then arise and spread and what form they take depend on the co-operation of a whole series of influences. More harm than good is done to historical materialism if at the outset one rejects as eclecticism an accentuation of the influences other than those of a purely economic kind, and a consideration of other economic factors than the technics of production and their foreseen development. Eclecticism—the selecting from different explanations and ways of dealing with phenomena—is often only the natural reaction from the doctrinaire desire to deduce everything from one thing and to treat everything according to one and the same method. As soon as such desire is excessive the eclectic spirit works its way again with the power of a natural force. It is the rebellion of sober reason against the tendency inherent in every doctrine to fetter thought. *

> Bernstein suggests that phenomena such as growing wealth in the hands of numerous capitalists, refuting the orthodox propositions about falling rate of profit and increasing concentration of capital, must not be ignored simply because they weaken the original dialectical scheme.

Nothing confirms me more in this conception than the anxiety with which some persons seek to maintain certain statements in *Capital,* which are falsified by facts. It is just some of the more deeply devoted followers of Marx who have not been able to separate themselves from the dialectical form of the work— that is the scaffolding alluded to—who do this. At least, that is only how I can explain the words of a man, otherwise so amenable to facts as Kautsky, who, when I observed in Stuttgart that the number of wealthy people for many years had increased, not decreased, answered: "If that were true then the date of our victory would not only be very long postponed, but we should never attain our goal. If it be capitalists who increase and not those with no possessions, then we are going ever further from our goal the more evolution progresses, then capitalism grows stronger, not socialism."

That the number of the wealthy increases and does not diminish is not an invention of bourgeois "harmony economists," but a fact established by the boards of assessment for taxes, often to the chagrin of those concerned, a fact which can no longer be disputed. But what is the significance of this fact as regards the victory of socialism? Why should the realisation of socialism depend on its refutation? Well, simply for this reason: Because the dialectical scheme seems so to prescribe it; because a post threatens to fall out of the scaffolding if one admits that the social surplus product is appropriated by an increasing instead of a decreasing number of possessors. But it is only the speculative theory that is affected by this matter; it does not at all affect the actual movement. Neither the struggle of the workers for democracy in politics nor their struggle for democracy in industry is touched by it. The prospects of this struggle do not depend on the theory of concentration of capital in the hands of a diminishing number of magnates, nor on the whole dialectical scaffolding of which this is a plank, but on the growth of social wealth and of the social productive forces, in conjunction with general social progress, and, particularly, in conjunction with the intellectual and moral advance of the working classes themselves. †

---

* From Eduard Bernstein, *Evolutionary Socialism* (New York: Schocken, 1961), pp. 13–14.

† From Eduard Bernstein, *Evolutionary Socialism* (New York: Schocken, 1961), pp. 211–13.

"We cannot demand from a class . . .the high intellectual and moral standard which the organization and existence of a socialist community presupposes." Bernstein suggests that the real condition of the working-class, no matter how unrevolutionary it may appear, should not be obscured merely for reasons of wishing to uphold the orthodox faith about revolutionary inevitability. Marxism requires a figure like Kant, Bernstein submits, who could see the world with a sober, non-dogmatic eye. Bernstein believes that this Kantian empiricism would oppose "the magnifying of material factors until they become omnipotent forces of evolution . . .," failing to consider the consciousness (or lack of it) of the working-class.

One has not overcome Utopianism if one assumes that there is in the present, or ascribes to the present, what is to be in the future. We have to take working men as they are. And they are neither so universally pauperised as was set out in the *Communist Manifesto,* nor so free from prejudices and weaknesses as their courtiers wish to make us believe. They have the virtues and failings of the economic and social conditions under which they live. And neither these conditions nor their effects can be put on one side from one day to another.

Have we attained the required degree of development of the productive forces for the abolition of classes? In face of the fantastic figures which were formerly set up in proof of this and which rested on generalisations based on the development of particularly favoured industries, socialist writers in modern times have endeavoured to reach by carefully detailed calculations, appropriate estimates of the possibilities of production in a socialist society, and their results are very different from those figures. Of a general reduction of hours of labour to five, four, or even three or two hours, such as was formerly accepted, there can be no hope at any time within sight, unless the general standard of life is much reduced. Even under a collective organisation of work, labour must begin very young and only cease at a rather advanced age, if it is to be reduced considerably below an eight-hours' day. Those persons ought to understand this first of all who indulge in the most extreme exaggerations regarding the ratio of the number of the non-propertied classes to that of the propertied. But he who thinks irrationally on one point does so usually on another. And, therefore, I am not surprised if the same Plechanow, who is angered to see the position of working men represented as not hopeless, has only the annihilating verdict, "Philistine," for my conclusions on the impossibility at any period within sight of abandoning the principle of the economic self-responsibility of those capable of working. It is not for nothing that one is the philosopher of irresponsibility.

But he who surveys the actual workers' movement will also find that the freedom from those qualities which appeared Philistine to a person born in the bourgeoisie, is very little valued by the workers, that they in no way support the morale of proletarianism, but, on the contrary, tend to make a "Philistine" out of a proletarian. With the roving proletarian without a family and home, no lasting, firm trade union movement would be possible. It is no bourgeois prejudice, but a conviction gained through decades of labour organisation, which has made so many of the English labour leaders—socialists and non-socialists—into zealous adherents of the temperance movement. The working class socialists know the faults of their class, and the most conscientious among them, far from glorifying these faults, seek to overcome them with all their power.

We cannot demand from a class, the great majority of whose members live under crowded conditions, are badly educated, and have an uncertain and insufficient income, the high intellectual and moral standard which the organisation and existence of a socialist community presupposes. We will, therefore, not ascribe it to them by way of fiction. Let us rejoice at the great stock of intelligence, renunciation, and energy which the modern working class movement has partly revealed, partly produced; but we must not assign, without discrimination to the masses, the millions, what holds good, say, of hundreds of thousands. I will not repeat the declarations which have been made to me on this point by working men verbally and in writing; I do not need to defend myself before reasonable persons against the suspicion of Pharisaism and the conceit of pedantry. But I confess willingly that I measure here with two kinds of measures. Just because I expect much of the working classes I censure much more everything that tends to corrupt their moral judgment than I do similar habits of the higher classes, and I see with the greatest regret that a tone of literary decadence is spreading here and there in the working class press which can only have a confusing and corrupting effect. A class which is aspiring needs a sound morale and must suffer no deterioration. Whether it sets out for itself an ideal ultimate aim is of secondary importance if it pursues with energy its proximate aims. The important point is that these aims are inspired by a definite principle which expresses a higher degree of economy and of social life, that they are an embodiment of a social conception which means in the evolution of civilisation a higher view of morals and of legal rights.

From this point of view I cannot subscribe to the proposition: "The working class has no ideas to realise." I see in it rather a self-deception, if it is not a mere play upon words on the part of its author.

And in this mind, I, at the time, resorted to the spirit of the great Königsberg philosopher, the critic of pure reason, against the cant which sought to get a hold on the working-class movement and to which the Hegelian dialectic offers a comfortable refuge. I did this in the conviction that social democracy required a Kant who should judge the received opinion and examine it critically with deep acuteness, who should show where its apparent materialism is the highest—and is therefore the most easily misleading—ideology, and warn it that the contempt of the ideal, the magnifying of material factors until they become omnipotent forces of evolution, is a self-deception, which has been and will be exposed as such at every opportunity by the action of those who proclaim it. *

> Bernstein, finally, believed that "goals are nothing, movement is every-thing." By this he meant that it is useless to speculate only about the distant future of socialism and to ignore the immediate requirements of political strategy. "The conquest of political power by the working classes, the expropriation of capitalists, are no ends in themselves but only means for the accomplishment of certain aims and endeavours."

I have at no time had an excessive interest in the future, beyond general principles; I have not been able to read to the end any picture of the future. My

---

* From Eduard Bernstein, *Evolutionary Socialism* (New York: Schocken, 1961), pp. 219-23.

thoughts and efforts are concerned with the duties of the present and the nearest future, and I only busy myself with the perspectives beyond so far as they give me a line of conduct for suitable action now.

The conquest of political power by the working classes, the expropriation of capitalists, are no ends in themselves but only means for the accomplishment of certain aims and endeavours. As such they are demands in the programme of social democracy and are not attacked by me. Nothing can be said beforehand as to the circumstances of their accomplishment; we can only fight for their realisation. But the conquest of political power necessitates the possession of political *rights;* and the most important problem of tactics which German social democracy has at the present time to solve, appears to me to be to devise the best ways for the extension of the political and economic rights of the German working classes.*

> The fact that the revolution has been postponed means that the development of models of change must "take upon itself *forms* and lead to forms that were not foreseen and could not be foreseen then." This is a crucial aspect of Bernstein's revisionism. Today it is difficult to refute Bernstein's argument about the need to amend Marxian models of change as social structural conditions themselves evolve and advance and as new forms of crisis emerge.

I set myself against the notion that we have to expect shortly a collapse of the bourgeois economy, and that social democracy should be induced by the prospect of such an imminent, great, social catastrophe to adapt its tactics to that assumption. That I maintain most emphatically.

The adherents of this theory of a catastrophe base it especially on the conclusions of the *Communist Manifesto*. This is a mistake in every respect.

The theory which the *Communist Manifesto* sets forth of the evolution of modern society was correct as far as it characterised the general tendencies of that evolution. But it was mistaken in several special deductions, above all in the estimate of the *time* the evolution would take. The last has been unreservedly acknowledged by Friedrich Engels, the joint author with Marx of the *Manifesto*, in his preface to the *Class War in France*. But it is evident that if social evolution takes a much greater period of time than was assumed, it must also take upon itself *forms* and lead to forms that were not foreseen and could not be foreseen then.†

KAUTSKY: MARXISM AS ETHICS AND SCIENCE

Karl Kautsky, in his 1906 work *Ethics and the Materialist Conception of History*, outlined the dichotomy between "scientific socialism" and ethics that characterized the thinking of most members of the Second International. Kautsky was in the peculiar position of (a) on the one hand upholding a rigorous scientific conception of Marxism, virtually reducing consciousness to material conditions possessing a logic and vitality of their own and (b) on the other hand advocating a peaceful, democratic model of the transition to socialism. Kautsky fiercely op-

---

*From Eduard Bernstein, *Evolutionary Socialism* (New York: Schocken, 1961), pp. *xvii-xviii*.
†From Eduard Bernstein, *Evolutionary Socialism* (New York: Schocken, 1961), p. *xii*.

posed the Marxist-Leninist justification of the dictatorship of the proletariat and its vanguard model of the role of the Communist Party.

Kautsky's work on ethics stressed the need for a moral ideal with which to orient the struggles of the proletariat. This moral ideal is to appear at the end of the historical process, after the proletariat has been emancipated. " . . .this ideal has nothing to find in scientific socialism, which is the scientific examination of the laws of the development and movement of the social organism. . . ." Here Kautsky presents the classical distinction between a Marxian ethics and Marxian social science. "Science has only to do with the recognition of the necessary," echoing Hegel and Engels' concept of scientific inquiry. Finally, "science stands above Ethics."

The ethical ideal of Marxism is the abolition of class, according to Kautsky. " . . .that ideal we can now recognize for the first time in the history of the world as a necessary result of the economic development, viz.: the abolition of class." Kautsky intimates that the abolition of class will be a necessary result of historical progress; Marxian social science gains insight into this necessity.

Kautsky depicts this historical necessity in terms of the growing productivity of industrial technology. "The productivity of labor is grown so huge that today already a considerable diminution of the labor time is possible for all workers." He argues that the ethical goal of Marxism is not the elimination of the division of labor per se but abolition of the distinction between rich and poor. Kautsky suggests that historical necessity will reveal itself as the productivity of labor grows, diminishing human labor time and thus freeing workers for socialist creativity.

The moral ideal of socialism is "won from sober economic considerations" — considerations about economic necessity and the inevitable growth of industrial productivity as the source of socialist liberation. Kautsky concludes with the sentiment that "socialism is inevitable because the class struggle and the victory of the proletariat is inevitable." He claims that this is not a "fatalist" necessity, although it is not exactly clear what other kind of necessity it could be. Perhaps Kautsky means that socialism is not a necessity in the sense that it will definitely become a reality in five years or ten years or a hundred years; rather, *because* the growth of industry and productivity is allegedly inevitable, so too is the eventual outcome of socialism.

Even the Social Democracy as an organization of the Proletariat in its class struggle cannot do without the moral ideal, the moral indignation against exploitation and class rule. But this ideal has nothing to find in scientific socialism, which is the scientific examination of the laws of the development and movement of the social organism, for the purpose of knowing the necessary tendencies and aims of the proletariat class struggle.

Certainly in Socialism the student is always a fighter as well, and no man can artificially cut himself in two parts, of which the one has nothing to do with the other. Thus even with Marx occasionally in his scientific research there breaks through the influence of a moral ideal. But he always endeavors and rightly to banish it where he can. Because the moral ideal becomes a source of error in science, when it takes it on itself to point out to it its aims. Science has only to do with the recognition of the necessary. It can certainly arrive at prescribing a shall, but this dare only come up as a consequence of the insight into the necessary. It must decline to discover a "shall" which is not to be recognized as a necessity founded in the world of phenomena. The Ethic must always be only an object of science; this has to study the moral instincts as well as the moral ideals and explain them; it cannot take advice from them as to the results at which it is to arrive. Science stands above Ethics, its results are just as little moral or immoral as necessity is moral or immoral.

All the same even in the winning and making known scientific knowledge morality is not got rid of. New scientific knowledge implies often the upsetting of traditional and deeply rooted conceptions which had grown to a fixed habit. In societies which include class antagonisms, new scientific knowledge, especially that of social conditions, implies in addition, however, damage to the interests of particular classes. To discover and propagate scientific knowledge which is compatible with the interests of the ruling classes, is to declare war on them. It assumes not simply a high degree of intelligence, but also ability and willingness to fight as well as independence from the ruling classes, and before all a strong moral feeling: strong social instincts, a ruthless striving for knowledge and to spread the truth with a warm desire to help the oppressed uprising classes.

But even this last wish has a misleading tendency if it does not play a simple negative part, as repudiation of the claims of the ruling conceptions to validity, and as a spur to overcoming the obstacles which the opposing class interests bring against the social development, but aspires to rise above that and to take the direction laying down certain aims which have to be attained through Social Study.

Even though the conscious aim of the class struggle in Scientific Socialism has been transformed from a moral into an economic aim it loses none of its greatness. Since what appeared to all social innovators hitherto as a moral ideal, and what could not be attained by them, for this the economic conditions are at length given, that ideal we can now recognize for the first time in the history of the world as a necessary result of the economic development, viz.: the abolition of class. Not the abolition of all professional distinctions. Not the abolition of division of labor, but certainly the abolition of all social distinctions and antagonisms which arise from the private property in the means of production and from the exclusive chaining down of the mass of the people in the function of material production. The means of production have become so enormous, that they burst today the frame of private property. The productivity of labor is grown so huge that today already a considerable diminution of the labor time is possible for all workers. These grow the foundations for the abolition not of the division of labour, not of the professions, but for the antagonism of rich and poor, exploiters and exploited, ignorant and wise.

At the same time, however, the division of labor is so far developed as to embrace that territory which remained so many thousands of years closed to it, the family hearth. The woman is freed from it and drawn into the realm of division of labor, so long a monopoly of the men. With that naturally the natural distinctions do not disappear which exist between the sexes: it can also allow many social distinctions, as well as many a distinction in the moral demands which are made to them to continue to exist or even revive such, but it will certainly make all those distinctions disappear from state and society which arise out of the fact that the woman is tied down to the private household duties and excluded from the callings of the divided labor. In this sense we shall see not simply the abolition of the exploitation of one class by another, but the abolition of the subjection of woman by man.

And at the same time world commerce attains such dimensions, the international economic relations become so close that therewith the foundation is laid for superseding private property in the means of production, the overcoming of national antagonisms, the end of war, and armaments, and for the probability of permanent peace between the nations.

Where is such a moral ideal which opens such splendid vistas? And yet they are won from sober economic considerations and not from intoxication through the moral ideals of freedom, equality and fraternity, justice, humanity!

And these outlooks are no mere expectations of conditions which only ought to come, which we simply wish and will, but outlooks at conditions which must come, which are necessary. Certainly not necessary in the fatalist sense, that a higher power will present them to us of itself, but necessary, unavoidable in the sense, that the inventors improve technic and the capitalists in their desire for profit revolutionize the whole economic life, as it is also inevitable that the workers aim for shorter hours of labor and higher wages, that they organize themselves, that they fight the capitalist class and its state, as it is inevitable that they aim for the conquest of political power and the overthrow of capitalist rule. Socialism is inevitable because the class struggle and the victory of the proletariat is inevitable.*

KAUTSKY: DEMOCRACY VERSUS DICTATORSHIP

While Kautsky favored "scientific socialism" with its rigid determinism, he also advocated social democracy and not the vanguardism of the Bolsheviks. Kautsky in his 1918 *The Dictatorship of the Proletariat* outlined his differences with the Russian Bolsheviks and with the concept of revolutionary dictatorship construed in its elitist authoritarian sense.

"We understand by Modern Socialism not merely social organization of production, but democratic organization of society as well." Kautsky cites Marx's speech to the Congress of the International at The Hague in 1872 where Marx suggested that revolutionary means must "fit" the nation in question. " . . .we do not assert that the way to reach this goal is the same everywhere," Marx is quoted as saying. Especially in Britain and the United States, where long democratic traditions already exist, it would be foolish to hold dogmatically to the concept of vanguard dictatorship. Kautsky argues for an open-minded approach to developing appropriate political forms of the transition period.

The distinction is sometimes drawn between democracy and Socialism, that is, the socialisation of the means of production and of production, by saying that the latter is our goal, the object of our movement, while democracy is merely the means to this end, which occasionally might become unsuitable, or even a hindrance.

To be exact, however, Socialism as such is not our goal, which is the abolition of every kind of exploitation and oppression, be it directed against a class, a party, a sex, or a race.

---

*From Karl Kautsky, *Ethics and the Materialist Conception of History* (Chicago: Kerr, 1918). pp. 202–206.

We seek to achieve this object by supporting the proletarian class struggle, because the proletariat, being the undermost class, cannot free itself without abolishing all causes of exploitation and oppression, and because the industrial proletariat, of all the oppressed and exploited classes, is the one which constantly grows in strength, fighting capacity and inclination to carry on the struggle, its ultimate victory being inevitable. Therefore, today every genuine opponent of exploitation and oppression must take part in the class struggle, from whatever class he may come.

If in this struggle we place the Socialist way of production as the goal, it is because in the technical and economic conditions which prevail today Socialistic production appears to be the sole means of attaining our object. Should it be proved to us that we are wrong in so doing, and that somehow the emancipation of the proletariat and of mankind could be achieved solely on the basis of private property, or could be most easily realised in the manner indicated by Proudhon, then we would throw Socialism overboard, without in the least giving up our object, and even in the interests of this object. Socialism and democracy are therefore not distinguished by the one being the means and the other the end. Both are means to the same end. The distinction between them must be sought elsewhere. Socialism as a means to the emancipation of the proletariat, without democracy, is unthinkable.

Social production, it is true, is also possible in a system other than a democratic one. In primitive conditions communistic methods became the basis of despotism, as Engels noted in 1875, when dealing with the village communism which has existed in India and Russia down to our own day.

Dutch colonial policy in Java for a long time based the organisation of agricultural production under the so-called "culture" system upon land communism for the profit of the government who exploited the people.

The most striking example of a non-democratic organisation of social work was furnished in the eighteenth century by the Jesuit State of Paraguay. There the Jesuits, as the ruling class, organised with dictatorial power the labour of the native Indian population, in a truly admirable fashion, without employing force, and even gaining the attachment of their subjects.

For modern men, however, such a patriarchal regime would be intolerable. It is only possible under circumstances where the rulers are vastly superior to the ruled in knowledge, and where the latter are absolutely unable to raise themselves to an equal standard. A section or class which is engaged in a struggle for freedom cannot regard such a system of tutelage as its goal, but must decisively reject it.

For us, therefore, Socialism without democracy is unthinkable. We understand by Modern Socialism not merely social organisation of production, but democratic organisation of society as well. Accordingly, Socialism is for us inseparably connected with democracy. No Socialism without democracy. But this proposition is not equally true if reversed. Democracy is quite possible without Socialism. A pure democracy is even conceivable apart from Socialism, for example, in small peasant communities, where complete equality of economic conditions for everybody exists on the basis of participating in privately owned means of production.

In any case, it may be said that democracy is possible without Socialism, and precedes it. It is this pre-Socialist democracy which is apparently in the minds of those who consider that democracy and Socialism are related to each other as the means to an end, although they mostly hasten to add that, strictly speaking, it is really no means to an end. This interpretation must be most emphatically repudiated. because, should it win general acceptance, it would lead our movement into most dangerous tracks.

Why would democracy be an unsuitable means for the achievement of Socialism?

It is a question of the conquest of political power.

It is said that if in a hitherto middle-class democratic State the possibility exists of the Social Democrats becoming the majority at an election, the ruling classes would make use of all the forces at their command in order to prevent democracy asserting itself. Therefore, it is not by democracy, but only by a political revolution that the proletariat can conquer the political power.

Doubtless, in cases where the proletariat of a democratic State attains to power, one must reckon with attempts of the ruling classes to nullify by violence the realisation of democracy by the rising class. This, however, does not prove the worthlessness of democracy for the proletariat. Should a ruling class, under the suppositions here discussed, resort to force, it would do so precisely because it feared the consequences of democracy. And its violence would be nothing but the subversion of democracy. Therefore, not the uselessness of democracy for the proletariat is demonstrated by anticipated attempts of the ruling classes to destroy democracy, but rather the necessity for the proletariat to defend democracy with tooth and nail. Of course, if the proletariat is told that democracy is a useless ornament, the needful strength for its defence will not be created. The mass of the people are everywhere too attached to their political rights willingly to abandon them. On the contrary, it is rather to be expected that they would defend their rights with such vigour that if the other side endeavoured to destroy the people's privileges, a political overthrow would be the result. The higher the proletariat values democracy, and the closer is its attachment to its rights, the more may one anticipate this course of events.

On the other hand, it must not be thought that the forebodings above mentioned will everywhere be realised. We need not be so fainthearted. The more democratic the State is, the more dependent are the forces exerted by the Executive, even the military ones, on public opinion. These forces may become, even in a democracy, a means of holding down the proletarian movement, if the proletariat is still weak in numbers, as in an agrarian State, or if it is politically weak, because unorganised, and lacking self-consciousness. But if the proletariat in a democratic State grows until it is numerous and strong enough to conquer political power by making use of the liberties which exist, then it would be a task of great difficulty for the capitalist dictatorship to manipulate the force necessary for the suppression of democracy.

As a matter of fact, Marx thought it possible, and even probable, that in England and America the proletariat might peacefully conquer political power. On the conclusion of the Congress of the International at the Hague in 1872, Marx spoke at a meeting, and among other things said:

"The worker must one day capture political power in order to found the new organisation of labour. He must reverse the old policy, which the old institutions maintain, if he will not, like the Christians of old who despised and neglected such things, renounce the things of this world.

"But we do not assert that the way to reach this goal is the same everywhere.

"We know that the institutions, the manners and the customs of the various countries must be considered, and we do not deny that there are countries like

England and America, and, if I understood your arrangements better, I might even add Holland, where the worker may attain his object by peaceful means. But not in all countries is this the case."

It remains to be seen whether Marx's expectations will be realised.*

As for Marx's comment in 1875 that the period of revolutionary transformation between capitalism and communism "requires a political transition, which
can be nothing else than the revolutionary dictatorship of the proletariat,"
Kautsky argues that Marx did not literally mean that a single dictator or dictatorial
party must arise to take over the reins of power. Instead, Marx referred to
proletarian dictatorship "as a condition" and not as a definite "form of government." By "dictatorship" Marx meant the hegemony or dominance of the
working-class, to be democratically constituted and imposed, a dictatorship of
the *majority.* During the Paris Commune, which collapsed in 1871, Marx
suggested that the working class held power in such a way as to constitute a
majoritarian dictatorship: in this sense, the dictatorship of the proletariat is "the
political form under which the freedom of labor could be attained." Kautsky
concludes by saying that democracy as a specific form of government is not
incompatible with the dominance of the proletariat as a general condition of
socialism, especially in nations where democratic political traditions already
exist.

In spite of other substantive theoretical differences, Kautsky and Luxemburg both shared this notion of proletarian democracy. Luxemburg specifically
reinterpreted Marx's concept of the dictatorship of the proletariat as implying a
majoritarian model of socialism. Kautsky joined Luxemburg in his stress on the
necessity of creating a radical democratic foundation on which socialism would
eventually be built. The so-called dictatorship of the proletariat in this sense
would be a dictatorship of the *majority* and not, as in class-society, a dictatorship
imposed by a concerted elite upon the masses. This is highly important for it
blunts one of the standard critiques of Marxism, namely, that Marxism is authoritarian and elitist. Indeed theorists like Kautsky and Luxemburg made it clear
that majoritarian proletarian dictatorship was necessary as a *transitional* stage
on route to full socialism or communism, in which the state would wither away
and power would dissolve. The eastern European Marxian humanists (see Chapter 5) make this notion of a majoritarian democratic socialism the central feature
of their critique of the Soviet model. Especially in modern Yugoslavia is this
concept of a workers' controlled, majoritarian democratic socialism accepted, as
a way of legitimizing the Yugoslav path towards socialism, which departs significantly from that of the Soviet Union and other eastern bloc countries.

Democracy is the essential basis for building up a Socialist system of production. Only under the influence of democracy does the proletariat attain that
maturity which it needs to be able to bring about Socialism, and democracy
supplies the surest means for testing its maturity. Between these two stages, the
preparation for Socialism and its realisation, which both require democracy,
there is the transition state when the proletariat has conquered political power,
but has not yet brought about Socialism in an economic sense. In this interven-

---

*From Karl Kautsky, *The Dictatorship of the Proletariat* (London: The National Labour Press, n.d.). pp. 4–10.

ing period it is said that democracy is not only unnecessary, but harmful.

This idea is not new. We have already seen it to be Weitling's. But it is supposed to be supported by Karl Marx. In his letter criticising the Gotha party programme, written in May, 1875, it is stated: "Between capitalist and communist society lies the period of the revolutionary transformation of the one into the other. This requires a political transition stage, which can be nothing else than the revolutionary dictatorship of the proletariat."

Marx had unfortunately omitted to specify more exactly what he conceived this dictatorship to be. Taken literally, the word signifies the suspension of democracy. But taken literally it also means the sovereignty of a single person, who is bound by no laws. A sovereignty which is distinguished from a despotism by being regarded as a passing phase, required by the circumstances of the moment, and not a permanent institution of the State.

The expression "Dictatorship of the Proletariat," that is the dictatorship not of a single person, but of a class, excludes the inference that Marx thought of dictatorship in the literal sense.

He speaks in the passage above quoted not of a form of government, but of a condition which must everywhere arise when the proletariat has conquered political power. That he was not thinking of a form of government is shown by his opinion that in England and America the transition might be carried out peacefully. Of course, Democracy does not guarantee a peaceful transition. But this is certainly not possible without Democracy.

However, to find out what Marx thought about the dictatorship of the proletariat, we need not have recourse to speculation. If in 1875 Marx did not explain in detail what he understood by the dictatorship of the ptoletariat, it might well have been because he had expressed himself on this matter a few years before, in his study of the Civil War in France. In that work, he wrote: "The Commune was essentially a government of the working class, the result of the struggle of the producing class against the appropriating class, the political form under which the freedom of labour could be attained being at length revealed."

Thus the Paris Commune was, as Engels expressly declared in his introduction to the third edition of Marx's book, "The Dictatorship of the Proletariat."

It was, however, at the same time not the suspension of democracy, but was founded on its most thoroughgoing use, on the basis of universal suffrage. The power of the Government was subjected to universal suffrage.

"The Commune was composed of town councillors, chosen by general suffrage in the various departments of Paris.

"Universal suffrage was to serve the people, constituted in Communes, as individual suffrage serves every other employer in the search for the workmen and managers in his business."

Marx constantly speaks here of the general suffrage of the whole people, and not of the votes of a specially privileged class. The dictatorship of the proletariat was for him a condition which necessarily arose in a real democracy, because of the overwhelming numbers of the proletariat.

Marx must not, therefore, be cited by those who support dictatorship in preference to democracy. Of course, this does not prove it to be wrong. Only, it must be demonstrated on other grounds.*

---

*From Karl Kautsky, *The Dictatorship of the Proletariat* (London: The National Labour Press, n.d.). pp. 42–45.

GRAMSCI: THE PHILOSOPHY OF PRAXIS

Antonio Gramsci, imprisoned by Mussolini in 1926 for alleged political crimes as head of the Italian Communist Party (1924-26), is one of the strangest and yet also one of the most important figures from early twentieth century Marxism. Gramsci's *Prison Notebooks,* running well over 2,000 pages in handwritten form, contain important, if unsystematic, reflections on the nature of revolutionary movements. It is convenient for chronological reasons to consider Gramsci's theoretical contribution in the context of the Second International, although many of his ideas deviate significantly from the "scientific socialism" that predominated in that International.

Gramsci, with Rosa Luxemburg, believed that socialism must be achieved through the active participation of the working class in its own emancipation. He avoided economic determinism and the Bolshevik concept of vanguardism or "democratic centralism," substituting instead a model of revolutionary change termed by him "the philosophy of praxis." This philosophy stressed the cooperation of the masses with certain critical intellectuals who together could comprehend alienation and act to overcome it.

Gramsci joined Kautsky and Luxemburg in urging a majoritarian democratic concept of socialism. Specifically Gramsci grappled with the problem of the relationship between intellectual revolutionary "experts" and the uneducated, atheoretical proletarian masses; his model of the socialist transition assumed that there would have to be *both* an intellectual leadership cadre, which developed a theory of socialism and a blueprint for achieving it, and an insurgent working class, which would cooperate with intellectual leaders in working towards socialism. For many other Marxists this has created the serious problem of vanguardism. Gramsci argued that it was possible for there to be a mutually supportive, non-authoritarian relationship between revolutionary elites and masses, the masses learning theoretically about the contours of domination and the possibilities of socialism and the masses teaching radical intellectuals about the actual circumstances and life-situations of the dominated. Gramsci's approach demonstrates that theory and praxis need to be dialectically unified in such a way that organization and planning are not imposed on the proletariat but rationally accepted by workers as a necessary expedient in the creation of socialism.

Gramsci believed that "all men are intellectuals." Unfortunately, not all "have in society the function of intellectuals." Gramsci felt that by mobilizing the inherent intellectual lurking within each human being the aims of the class struggle could be significantly furthered. Gramsci reformulated Marx's injunction about uniting manual and mental labor under socialism.

All men are intellectuals, one could therefore say, but not all men have in society the function of intellectuals.

When one distinguishes between intellectuals and non-intellectuals, one is referring in reality only to the immediate social function of the professional category of the intellectuals, that is, one has in mind the direction in which their specific professional activity is weighted, whether towards intellectual elaboration or towards muscular-nervous effort. This means that, although one can speak of intellectuals, one cannot speak of non-intellectuals, because non-intellectuals do not exist. But even the relationship between efforts of intellectual-cerebral elaboration and muscular-nervous effort is not always the same, so that there are varying degrees of specific intellectual activity. There is no human activity from which every form of intellectual participation can be excluded: *homo faber* cannot be separated from *homo sapiens.* Each man, finally, outside his professional activity, carries on some form of intellectual activity, that is, he is a "philosopher," an artist, a man of taste, he participates in a particular conception of the world, has a conscious line of moral conduct, and therefore contributes to sustain a conception of the world or to modify it, that is, to bring into being new modes of thought.

The problem of creating a new stratum of intellectuals consists therefore in the critical elaboration of the intellectual activity that exists in everyone at a certain degree of development, modifying its relationship with the muscular-nervous effort towards a new equilibrium, and ensuring that the muscular-nervous effort itself, in so far as it is an element of a general practical activity, which is perpetually innovating the physical and social world, becomes the foundation of a new and integral conception of the world. The traditional and vulgarised type of the intellectual is given by the man of letters, the philosopher, the artist. Therefore journalists, who claim to be men of letters, philosophers, artists, also regard themselves as the "true" intellectuals. In the modern world, technical education, closely bound to industrial labour even at the most primitive and unqualified level, must form the basis of the new type of intellectual.*

> Furthermore, Gramsci felt that this inherent intellectuality of the masses must be harnessed politically. He discusses the relationship between the masses and intellectuals, attempting to resolve the meaning of "spontaneity" in revolutionary struggle. Gramsci believes, against those orthodox Marxists for whom the revolution will be an automatic process, that the spontaneous behavior of the masses must not be ignored in favor of the imposed plans of theorists and tacticians. "There exists a scholastic and academic historico-political outlook which sees as real and worthwhile only such movements of revolt as are one hundred percent conscious, i.e., movements that are governed by plans worked out in advance to the last detail or in line with abstract theory. . ."

At this point, a fundamental theoretical question is raised: Can modern theory be in opposition to the "spontaneous" feelings of the masses? ("Spontaneous" in the sense that they are not the result of any systematic educational activity on the part of an already conscious leading group, but have been formed through everyday experience illuminated by "common sense," i.e., by the traditional popular conception of the world—what is unimaginatively called "instinct," although it too is in fact a primitive and elementary historical acquisition.) It cannot be in opposition to them. Between the two there is a "quantitative" difference of degree, not one of quality. A reciprocal "reduction" so to speak, a passage from one to the other and vice versa, must be possible. (Recall that Immanuel Kant believed it important for his philosophical theories to agree with common sense; the same position can be found in Croce. Recall too Marx's assertion in *The Holy Family* that the political formulae of the French Revolution can be reduced to the principles of classical German philosophy.) Neglecting,

---

*From Antonio Gramsci, *Selections from the Prison Notebooks* (London: Lawrence and Wishart, 1971), p. 9.

or worse still despising, so-called "spontaneous" movements, i.e., failing to give them a conscious leadership or to raise them to a higher plane by inserting them into politics, may often have extremely serious consequences. It is almost always the case that a "spontaneous" movement of the subaltern classes is accompanied by a reactionary movement of the right-wing of the dominant class, for concomitant reasons. An economic crisis, for instance, engenders on the one hand discontent among the subaltern classes and spontaneous mass movements, and on the other conspiracies among the reactionary groups, who take advantage of the objective weakening of the government in order to attempt *coups d'état*. Among the effective causes of the *coups* must be included the failure of the responsible groups to give any conscious leadership to the spontaneous revolts or to make them into a positive political factor. N.B., the example of the Sicilian Vespers, and the arguments among historians about whether this was a spontaneous movement or one planned in advance. In my view the two elements were combined in the case of the Vespers. On the one hand, a spontaneous rising of the Sicilian people against their Provençal rulers which spread so rapidly that it gave the impression of simultaneity and hence of preconcertation; this rising was the result of an oppression which had become intolerable throughout the national territory. On the other hand, there was the conscious element, of varying importance and effectiveness, and the success of Giovanni da Procida's plot with the Aragonese. Other examples can be drawn from all past revolutions in which several subaltern classes were present, with a hierarchy determined by economic position and internal homogeneity. The "spontaneous" movements of the broader popular strata make possible the coming to power of the most progressive subaltern class as a result of the objective weakening of the State. This is still a "progressive" example; but, in the modern world, the regressive examples are more frequent.

There exists a scholastic and academic historico-political outlook which sees as real and worthwhile only such movements of revolt as are one hundred percent conscious, i.e., movements that are governed by plans worked out in advance to the last detail or in line with abstract theory (which comes to the same thing). But reality produces a wealth of the most bizarre combinations. It is up to the theoretician to unravel these in order to discover fresh proof of his theory, to "translate" into theoretical language the elements of historical life. It is not reality which should be expected to conform to the abstract schema. This will never happen, and hence this conception is nothing but an expression of passivity.*

Gramsci envisages an "intellectual-moral bloc" composed of theorists and activists. He believes that it is possible to achieve "the intellectual progress of the mass," tapping everyman's intrinsic intellectuality by liberating him from the ideologically fostered narrowness and stupidity of the prevailing common sense. " . . .there is no organization without intellectuals, that is without organizers and leaders," according to Gramsci. Intellectuals must not dominate non-intellectuals for the political goal of democratic Marxism is to provide every human being with the possibility of controlling his own intellectual life. Gramsci calls for a "dialectic between the intellectuals and the masses."

---

*From Antonio Gramsci, *Selections from the Prison Notebooks* (London: Lawrence and Wishart, 1971), pp. 198–200.

The position of the philosophy of praxis is the antithesis of the Catholic. The philosophy of praxis does not tend to leave the "simple" in their primitive philosophy of common sense, but rather to lead them to a higher conception of life. If it affirms the need for contact between intellectuals and simple, it is not in order to restrict scientific activity and preserve unity at the low level of the masses, but precisely in order to construct an intellectual-moral bloc which can make politically possible the intellectual progress of the mass and not only of small intellectual groups.

The active man-in-the-mass has a practical activity, but has no clear theoretical consciousness of his practical activity, which nonetheless involves understanding the world in so far as it transforms it. His theoretical consciousness can indeed be historically in opposition to his activity. One might almost say that he has two theoretical consciousnesses (or one contradictory consciousness): one which is implicit in his activity and which in reality unites him with all his fellow-workers in the practical transformation of the real world; and one, superficially explicit or verbal, which he has inherited from the past and uncritically absorbed. But this verbal conception is not without consequences. It holds together a specific social group, it influences moral conduct and the direction of will, with varying efficacity but often powerfully enough to produce a situation in which the contradictory state of consciousness does not permit of any action, any decision or any choice, and produces a condition of moral and political passivity. Critical understanding of self takes place therefore through a struggle of political "hegemonies" and of opposing directions, first in the ethical field and then in that of politics proper, in order to arrive at the working out at a higher level of one's own conception of reality. Consciousness of being part of a particular hegemonic force (that is to say, political consciousness) is the first stage towards a further progressive self-consciousness in which theory and practice will finally be one. Thus the unity of theory and practice is not just a matter of mechanical fact, but a part of the historical process, whose elementary and primitive phase is to be found in the sense of being "different" and "apart", in an instinctive feeling of independence, and which progresses to the level of real possession of a single and coherent conception of the world. This is why it must be stressed that the political development of the concept of hegemony represents a great philosophical advance as well as a politico-practical one. For it necessarily supposes an intellectual unity and an ethic in conformity with a conception of reality that has gone beyond common sense and has become, if only within narrow limits, a critical conception.

However, in the most recent developments of the philosophy of praxis the exploration and refinement of the concept of the unity of theory and practice is still only at an early stage. There still remain residues of mechanicism, since people speak about theory as a "complement" or an "accessory" of practice, or as the handmaid of practice. It would seem right for this question too to be considered historically, as an aspect of the political question of the intellectuals. Critical self-consciousness means, historically and politically, the creation of an *élite* of intellectuals. A human mass does not "distinguish" itself, does not become independent in its own right without, in the widest sense, organising itself; and there is no organisation without intellectuals, that is without organisers and leaders, in other words, without the theoretical aspect of the theory-practice nexus being distinguished concretely by the existence of a group of people "specialised" in conceptual and philosophical elaboration of ideas. But the process of creating intellectuals is long, difficult, full of contradictions, advances and retreats, dispersals and regroupings, in which the loyalty of the masses is often sorely tried. (And one must not forget that at this early stage loyalty and discipline are the ways in which the masses participate and collaborate in the development of the cultural movement as a whole.)

The process of development is tied to a dialectic between the intellectuals and the masses. The intellectual stratum develops both quantitatively and qualitatively, but every leap forward towards a new breadth and complexity of the intellectual stratum is tied to an analogous movement on the part of the mass of the "simple," who raise themselves to higher levels of culture and at the same time extend their circle of influence towards the stratum of specialised intellectuals, producing outstanding individuals and groups of greater or less importance.*

> The masses possess "feeling" while intellectuals possess "knowledge." Without the masses, intellectuals descend to "pedantry"; without the intellectuals, the masses descend to "blind passion and sectarianism." The task of intellectuals is to translate the alienation and frustration of workers into a coherent theoretical system that articulates these experiences in historical and structural terms, pointing the way towards the possibility of socialism.

The popular element "feels" but does not always know or understand; the intellectual element "knows" but does not always understand and in particular does not always feel. The two extremes are therefore pedantry and philistinism on the one hand and blind passion and sectarianism on the other. Not that the pedant cannot be impassioned; far from it. Impassioned pedantry is every bit as ridiculous and dangerous as the wildest sectarianism and demagogy. The intellectual's error consists in believing that one can know without understanding and even more without feeling and being impassioned (not only for knowledge in itself but also for the object of knowledge): in other words that the intellectual can be an intellectual (and not a pure pedant) if distinct and separate from the people-nation, that is, without feeling the elementary passions of the people, understanding them and therefore explaining and justifying them in the particular historical situation and connecting them dialectically to the laws of history and to a superior conception of the world, scientifically and coherently elaborated—i.e., knowledge. One cannot make politics-history without this passion, without this sentimental connection between intellectuals and people-nation. In the absence of such a nexus the relations between the intellectual and the people-nation are, or are reduced to, relationships of a purely bureaucratic and formal order; the intellectuals become a caste, or a priesthood (so-called organic centralism).

If the relationship between intellectuals and people-nation, between the leaders and the led, the rulers and the ruled, is provided by an organic cohesion in which feeling-passion becomes understanding and thence knowledge (not mechanically but in a way that is alive), then and only then is the relationship one of representation. Only then can there take place an exchange of individ-

---

*From Antonio Gramsci, *Selections from the Prison Notebooks* (London: Lawrence and Wishart, 1971), pp. 332–35.

ual elements between the rulers and ruled, leaders [*dirigenti*] and led, and can the shared life be realised which alone is a social force—with the creation of the "historical bloc."*

LUXEMBURG: THE MAJORITARIAN DICTATORSHIP OF THE PROLETARIAT

One of the profoundest critics of the economic determinism of the Second International was Rosa Luxemburg, a leader of the so-called Spartacusbund that became the Communist Party of Germany in 1919. Luxemburg contributed much to an adequate theory of the structural crisis-tendencies of capitalism and to a theory of mass movements. Her famous *Junius Pamphlet,* written in 1915, remains a seminal attack on the downfall of European social democracy and its involvement in the divisive war effort. Luxemburg believed that socialist revolution would only occur through the cooperation and comradeship between the revolutionary mass and leaders like herself who did not impose on workers their own "correct" vision of political struggle.

Luxemburg, like Gramsci, believed that there must be dialectical reciprocity between the spontaneity of the masses and intellectual and political leadership. Her *Accumulation of Capital* is an excellent example of Marxian scholarship, while the *Junius Pamphlet* is more directly engaged with the political questions of her day. Luxemburg opposed the quietism and determinism of thinkers like Kautsky and the Austro-Marxists because they failed to take an active role in furthering the revolutionary effort. Luxemburg did not believe that capitalism would collapse without the combined efforts of the masses *and* their non-authoritarian leaders.

In the *Junius Pamphlet* Luxemburg articulated this relationship between the masses and their leaders. "Revolutions are not 'made' and great movements of the people are not produced according to technical recipes that repose in the pockets of the party leaders." Luxemburg emphasized the necessity of spontaneity in the revolutionary movement, without which the leaders would have no one to lead towards the creation of socialism.

Furthermore, she adds that "the great historical hour itself creates the forms that will carry the revolutionary movements to a successful outcome." These forms cannot be legislated by armchair speculation: Revolutionary forms of action and organization spring from historical circumstances; they must be seized upon and bent to the purposes of class struggle, not ignored merely because they do not fit orthodox or traditional models of revolutionary change.

But what action should the party have taken to give to our opposition to the war and to our war demands weight and emphasis? Should it have proclaimed a general strike? Should it have called upon the soldiers to refuse military service? Thus the question is generally asked. To answer with a simple yes or no, were just as ridiculous as to decide: "When war breaks out we will start a revolution." Revolutions are not "made" and great movements of the people are not produced according to technical recipes that repose in the pockets of

---

*From Antonio Gramsci, *Selections from the Prison Notebooks* (London: Lawrence and Wishart, 1971), p. 418.

the party leaders. Small circles of conspirators may organize a riot for a certain day and a certain hour, can give their small group of supporters the signal to begin. Mass movements in great historical crises cannot be initiated by such primitive measures. The best prepared mass strike may break down miserably at the very moment when the party leaders give the signal, may collapse completely before the first attack. The success of the great popular movements depends, aye, the very time and circumstance of their inception is decided, by a number of economic, political, and psychological factors. The existing degree of tension between the classes, the degree of intelligence of the masses and the degree or ripeness of their spirit of resistance—all these factors, which are incalculable, are premises that cannot be artificially created by any party. That is the difference between the great historical upheavals, and the small show-demonstrations that a well-disciplined party can carry out in times of peace, orderly, well-trained performances, responding obediently to the baton in the hands of the party leaders. The great historical hour itself creates the forms that will carry the revolutionary movements to a successful outcome, creates and improvises new weapons, enriches the arsenal of the people with weapons unknown and unheard of by the parties and their leaders.

What the Social Democracy as the advance guard of the class conscious proletariat should have been able to give was not ridiculous precepts and technical recipes, but a political slogan, clearness concerning the political problems and interests of the proletariat in times of war.*

Luxemburg's vigorous denunciation of Leninism took the following form:

If we assume the viewpoint claimed as his own by Lenin and we fear the influence of intellectuals in the proletarian movement, we can conceive of no greater danger to the Russian party than Lenin's plan of organization. *Nothing will more surely enslave a young labor movement to an intellectual elite hungry for power than this bureaucratic straitjacket, which will immobilize the movement and turn it into an automaton manipulated by a Central Committee.* On the other hand, there is no more effective guarantee against opportunist intrigue and personal ambition than the independent revolutionary action of the proletariat, as a result of which the workers acquire the sense of political responsibility and self-reliance.

What is today only a phantom haunting Lenin's imagination may become reality tomorrow.

Let us not forget that the revolution soon to break out in Russia will be a bourgeois and not a proletarian revolution. This modifies radically all the conditions of socialist struggle. The Russian intellectuals, too, will rapidly become imbued with bourgeois ideology. The social democracy is at present the only guide of the Russian proletariat. But on the day after the revolution, we shall see the bourgeoisie, and above all the bourgeois intellectuals, seek to use the masses as a steppingstone to their domination.

The game of the bourgeois demagogues will be made easier if at the present stage, the spontaneous action, initiative, and political sense of the advanced sections of the working class are hindered in their development and restricted by the protectorate of an authoritarian Central Committee.

More important is the fundamental falseness of the idea underlying the plan

*From Rosa Luxemburg, *The Junius Pamphlet* (London: The Merlin Press, n.d.), pp. 114–15.

of unqualified centralism—the idea that the road to opportunism can be barred by means of clauses in a party constitution.

Impressed by recent happenings in the socialist parties of France, Italy, and Germany, the Russian social democrats tend to regard opportunism as an alien ingredient, brought into the labor movement by representatives of bourgeois democracy. If that were so, no penalties provided by a party constitution could stop this intrusion. The afflux of nonproletarian recruits to the party of the proletariat is the effect of profound social causes, such as the economic collapse of the petty bourgeoisie, the bankruptcy of bourgeois liberalism, and the degeneration of bourgeois democracy. It is naive to hope to stop this current by means of a formula written down in a constitution.

A manual of regulations may master the life of a small sect or a private circle. A historic current, however, will pass through the mesh of the most subtly worded statutory paragraph. It is furthermore untrue that to repel the elements pushed toward the socialist movement by the decomposition of bourgeois society means to defend the interests of the working class. The social democracy has always contended that it represents not only the class interests of the proletariat but also the progressive aspirations of the whole of contemporary society. It represents the interests of all who are oppressed by bourgeois domination. This must not be understood merely in the sense that all these interests are ideally contained in the socialist program. Historic evolution translates the given proposition into reality. In its capacity as a political party, the social democracy becomes the haven of all discontented elements in our society and thus of the entire people, as contrasted to the tiny minority of the capitalist masters.

But socialists must always know how to subordinate the anguish, rancor, and hope of this motley aggregation to the supreme goal of the working class. The social democracy must enclose the tumult of the nonproletarian protestants against existing society within the bounds of the revolutionary action of the proletariat. It must assimilate the elements that come to it.

This is only possible if the social democracy already contains a strong, politically educated proletarian nucleus class conscious enough to be able, as up to now in Germany, to pull along in its tow the declassed and petty bourgeois elements that join the party. In that case, greater strictness in the application of the principle of centralization and more severe discipline, specifically formulated in party bylaws, may be an effective safeguard against the opportunist danger. That is how the revolutionary socialist movement in France defended itself against the Jauresist confusion. A modification of the constitution of the German social democracy in that direction would be a very timely measure.

But even here we should not think of the party constitution as a weapon that is, somehow, self-sufficient. It can be at most a coercive instrument enforcing the will of the proletarian majority in the party. If this majority is lacking, then the most dire sanctions on paper will be of no avail.

However, the influx of bourgeois elements into the party is far from being the only cause of the opportunist trends that are now raising their heads in the social democracy. Another cause is the very nature of socialist activity and the contradictions inherent in it.

The international movement of the proletariat toward its complete emancipation is a process peculiar in the following respect. For the first time in the history of civilization, the people are expressing their will consciously and in opposition to all ruling classes. But this will can only be satisfied beyond the limits of the existing system.

Now the mass can only acquire and strengthen this will in the course of the day-to-day struggle against the existing social order—that is, within the limits of capitalist society.

On the one hand, we have the mass; on the other, its historic goal, located outside of existing society. On one hand, we have the day-to-day struggle; on the other, the social revolution. Such are the terms of the dialectical contradiction through which the socialist movement makes its way.

It follows that this movement can best advance by tacking betwixt and between the two dangers by which it is constantly being threatened. One is the loss of its mass character; the other, the abandonment of its goal. One is the danger of sinking back to the condition of a sect; the other, the danger of becoming a movement of bourgeois social reform.

That is why it is illusory, and contrary to historic experience, to hope to fix, once for always, the direction of the revolutionary socialist struggle with the aid of formal means, which are expected to secure the labor movement against all possibilities of opportunist digression.

Marxist theory offers us a reliable instrument enabling us to recognize and combat typical manifestations of opportunism. But the socialist movement is a mass movement. Its perils are not the product of the insidious machinations of individuals and groups. They arise out of unavoidable social conditions. We cannot secure ourselves in advance against all possibilities of opportunist deviation. Such dangers can be overcome only by the movement itself—certainly with the aid of Marxist theory, but only after the dangers in question have taken tangible form in practice.

Looked at from this angle, opportunism appears to be a product and an inevitable phase of the historic development of the labor movement.

The Russian social democracy arose a short while ago. The political conditions under which the proletarian movement is developing in Russia are quite abnormal. In that country, opportunism is to a large extent a by-product of the groping and experimentation of socialist activity seeking to advance over a terrain that resembles no other in Europe.

In view of this, we find most astonishing the claim that it is possible to avoid any possibility of opportunism in the Russian movement by writing down certain words, instead of others, in the party constitution. *Such an attempt to exorcise opportunism by means of a scrap of paper may turn out to be extremely harmful— not to opportunism but to the socialist movement.*

Stop the natural pulsation of a living organism, and you weaken it, and you diminish its resistance and combative spirit—in this instance, not only against opportunism but also (and that is certainly of great importance) against the existing social order. The proposed means turn against the end they are supposed to serve.

In Lenin's overanxious desire to establish the guardianship of an omniscient and omnipotent Central Committee in order to protect so promising and vigorous a labor movement against any misstep, we recognize the symptoms of the same subjectivism that has already played more than one trick on socialist thinking in Russia.

It is amusing to note the strange somersaults that the respectable human "ego" has had to perform in recent Russian history. Knocked to the ground, almost reduced to dust, by Russian absolutism, the "ego" takes revenge by turning to revolutionary activity. In the shape of a committee of conspirators, in the name of a nonexistent Will of the People, it seats itself on a kind of throne and proclaims it is all-powerful. But the "object" proves to be the stronger. The knout is triumphant, for czarist might seems to be the "legitimate" expression of history.

In time we see appear on the scene an even more "legitimate" child of history—the Russian labor movement. For the first time, bases for the formation of a real "people's will" are laid in Russian soil.

But here is the "ego" of the Russian revolutionary again! Pirouetting on its head, it once more proclaims itself to be the all-powerful director of history— this time with the title of His Excellency the Central Committee of the Social Democratic Party of Russia.

The nimble acrobat fails to perceive that the only "subject" which merits today the role of director is the collective "ego" of the working class. The working class demands the right to make its mistakes and learn in the dialectic of history.

Let us speak plainly. Historically, the errors committed by a truly revolutionary movement are infinitely more fruitful than the infallibility of the cleverest Central Committee.*

The passage above contains the profound idea that Marxian theorists might *learn* from revolutionary struggle; this theory must follow a course between vanguardism—which threatens the "mass character" of the revolution— and the abandonment of the final goal of socialism in favor of reformism and opportunism—which turns the revolutionary workers' movement into merely another species of bourgeois democracy. "Historically, the errors committed by a truly revolutionary movement are infinitely more fruitful than the infallibility of the cleverest Central Committee." Therein lies the core of Rosa Luxemburg's theory of non-authoritarian, majoritarian socialism.

Luxemburg also develops the notion that socialist transformation cannot follow ready-made plans and blueprints. We possess "but a few main signposts" on the road towards socialism. We know only what we must eliminate in order to create the conditions for socialist emancipation. Socialism will be "a historical product," adjusted to local cultural, political, and economic circumstances. It cannot successfully be imposed from on high, "by a dozen intellectuals."

Luxemburg further developed this important reflection on the relationship between leaders and the masses in her critique of Lenin and Russian Bolshevism. Nowhere has the concept of a vanguard party and of democratic centralism (as Lenin ironically termed it) been so systematically attacked. Luxemburg criticized Lenin not from the standpoint of the threatened bourgeoisie, as a deep-seated enemy of socialism and Marxism. Rather she argued that Lenin's dictatorial route to socialism was not compatible with the final aim of a socialist society, but merely introduced another form of oppression to replace that of the czar. "The fact is that the social democracy is not *joined* to the organizations of the proletariat. It is itself the proletariat . . . Social democratic centralism . . . can only be the concentrated will of the individuals and groups representative of the most

---

*From Mary-Alice Waters, Editor, *Rosa Luxemburg Speaks* (New York: Pathfinder Press, 1970), pp. 126–30.

class-conscious, militant, advanced sections of the working class." Luxemburg in this vein did not separate the dictatorial party from the masses as sharply as did Lenin.

The tacit assumption underlying the Lenin-Trotsky theory of the dictatorship is this: that the socialist transformation is something for which a ready-made formula lies completed in the pocket of the revolutionary party, which needs only to be carried out energetically in practice. This is, unfortunately—or perhaps fortunately—not the case. Far from being a sum of ready-made prescriptions which have only to be applied, the practical realization of socialism as an economic, social, and juridical system is something which lies completely hidden in the mists of the future. What we possess in our program is nothing but a few main signposts which indicate the general direction in which to look for the necessary measures, and the indications are mainly negative in character at that. Thus we know more or less what we must eliminate at the outset in order to free the road for a socialist economy. But when it comes to the nature of the thousand concrete, practical measures, large and small, necessary to introduce socialist principles into economy, law, and all social relationship, there is no key in any socialist party program or textbook. That is not a shortcoming but rather the very thing that makes scientific socialism superior to the utopian varieties.

The socialist system of society should only be, and can only be, a historical product, born out of the school of its own experiences, born in the course of its realization, as a result of the developments of living history, which—just like organic nature of which, in the last analysis, it forms a part—has the fine habit of always producing along with any real social need the means to its satisfaction, along with the task simultaneously the solution. However, if such is the case, then it is clear that socialism by its very nature cannot be decreed or introduced by *ukase* [proclamation]. It has as its prerequisite a number of measures of force—against property, etc. The negative, the tearing down, can be decreed; the building up, the positive, cannot. New territory. A thousand problems. Only experience is capable of correcting and opening new ways. Only unobstructed, effervescing life falls into a thousand new forms and improvisations, brings to light creative force, itself corrects all mistaken attempts. The public life of countries with limited freedom is so poverty-stricken, so miserable, so rigid, so unfruitful, precisely because, through the exclusion of democracy, it cuts off the living sources of all spiritual riches and progress. (Proof: the year 1905 and the months from February to October 1917.) There it was political in character; the same thing applies to economic and social life also. The whole mass of the people must take part in it. Otherwise, socialism will be decreed from behind a few official desks by a dozen intellectuals.

Public control is indispensably necessary. Otherwise the exchange of experiences remains only with the closed circle of the officials of the new regime. Corruption becomes inevitable (Lenin's words, Bulletin No. 29). Socialism in life demands a complete spiritual transformation in the masses degraded by centuries of bourgeois class rule. Social instincts in place of egotistical ones, mass initiative in place of inertia, idealism which conquers all suffering, etc. No one knows this better, describes it more penetratingly; repeats it more stubbornly than Lenin. But he is completely mistaken in the means he employs. Decree, dictatorial force of the factory overseer, Draconic penalties, rule by terror—all these things are but palliatives. The only way to a rebirth is the school of public life itself, the most unlimited, the broadest democracy and public opinion. It is rule by terror which demoralizes.*

> Luxemburg finally grapples with the thorny (and seemingly eternal) contradiction between democracy and dictatorship in revolutionary struggle. Here she evokes Marx's comment about the necessity of an interim "dictatorship of the proletariat" required to intervene between the passing of capitalism and the dawn of socialism. Luxemburg asserts that socialism is not "something which begins only in the promised land after the foundations of socialist economy are created"; it is not a "Christmas present"! Marxian dictatorship requires the application of democracy in majoritarian fashion upon the crumbling institutions of capitalist society.

The basic error of the Lenin-Trotsky theory is that they too, just like Kautsky, oppose dictatorship to democracy. "Dictatorship or democracy" is the way the question is put by Bolsheviks and Kautsky alike. The latter naturally decides in favor of "democracy," that is, of bourgeois democracy, precisely because he opposes it to the alternative of the socialist revolution. Lenin and Trotsky, on the other hand, decide in favor of dictatorship in contradistinction to democracy, and thereby, in favor of the dictatorship of a handful of persons, that is, in favor of dictatorship on the bourgeois model. They are two opposite poles, both alike being far removed from a genuine socialist policy. The proletariat, when it seizes power, can never follow the good advice of Kautsky, given on the pretext of the "unripeness of the country," the advice being to renounce the socialist revolution and devote itself to democracy. It cannot follow this advice without betraying thereby itself, the International, and the revolution. It should and must at once undertake socialist measures in the most energetic, unyielding and unhesitant fashion, in other words, exercise a dictatorship, but a dictatorship of the *class*, not of a party or of a clique— dictatorship of the class, that means in the broadest public form on the basis of the most active, unlimited participation of the mass of the people, of unlimited democracy.

"As Marxists," writes Trotsky, "we have never been idol worshippers of formal democracy." Surely, we have never been idol worshippers of formal democracy. Nor have we ever been idol worshippers of socialism or Marxism either. Does it follow from this that we may also throw socialism on the scrap-heap, à la Cunow, Lensch, and Parvus, if it becomes uncomfortable for us? Trotsky and Lenin are the living refutation of this answer.

"We have never been idol worshippers of formal democracy." All that that really means is: We have always distinguished the social kernel from the political form of *bourgeois* democracy; we have always revealed the hard kernel of social inequality and lack of freedom hidden under the sweet shell of formal equality and freedom—not in order to reject the latter but to spur the working class into not being satisfied with the shell, but rather, by conquering political

---

*From Mary-Alice Waters, editor, *Rosa Luxemburg Speaks* (New York: Pathfinder Press, 1970), pp. 390–91.

power, to create a socialist democracy to replace bourgeois democracy—not to eliminate democracy altogether.

But socialist democracy is not something which begins only in the promised land after the foundations of socialist economy are created; it does not come as some sort of Christmas present for the worthy people who, in the interim, have loyally supported a handful of socialist dictators. Socialist democracy begins simultaneously with the beginnings of the destruction of class rule and of the construction of socialism. It begins at the very moment of the seizure of power by the socialist party. It is the same thing as the dictatorship of the proletariat.

Yes, dictatorship! But this dictatorship consists in the *manner of applying democracy*, not in its *elimination*, in energetic, resolute attacks upon the well-entrenched rights and economic relationships of bourgeois society, without which a socialist transformation cannot be accomplished. But this dictatorship must be the work of the *class* and not of a little leading minority in the name of the class—that is, it must proceed step by step out of the active participation of the masses; it must be under their direct influence, subjected to the control of complete public activity; it must arise out of the growing political training of the mass of the people.*

LENINISM: DIALECTICAL MATERIALISM AS A VANGUARD SCIENCE

Although Lenin's theory of imperialism is itself an important contribution to Marxian theory, providing an understanding of how international capitalism could almost indefinitely postpone the collapse of the system (and falling rates of profit as a catalyst of collapse), there are other dimensions of Lenin's reinterpretation of Marxism even more significant to western Marxists. Foremost among these is Lenin's model of Marxism as a science, an inheritance that has survived to the present day as the Soviet theory of dialectical materialism.

Lenin argued that Marxism is a form of natural science that "reads" social reality in much the same manner as science reads nature. In his 1908 work, *Materialism and Empirio-Criticism,* Lenin outlined a theory of Marxian science based on this so-called reflection-theory of knowledge. This concept of science was important in the development of the Second International, closely resembling that created by Lenin for the Third International.

Most members of the Second and Third Internationals agreed that Marxism is a form of what Engels termed "scientific socialism", charting laws of societal motion and predicting the collapse of the capitalist system based on an understanding of these laws. Kautsky and Lenin endorsed virtually the same model of Marxian science, although their political programs differed, with Kautsky endorsing democratic means of change and Lenin advocating the dictatorial vanguardist role of the Communist Party.

During the Second International, this scientific concept of Marxism heralded the apparently imminent breakdown of the capitalist economic system. To thinkers like Kautsky and the neo-Kantian Austro-Marxists, no less than to Rosa Luxemburg, capitalism appeared to be reaching the end of its "natural" life, beset by deep crises. As we argued in our first chapter, and, above, in our general introduction to this chapter, scientific Marxism appeared when the revo-

---

*From Mary-Alice Waters, editor, *Rosa Luxemburg Speaks* (New York: Pathfinder Press, 1970). pp. 393–94.

lutionary climax seemed close at hand; a more philosophically oriented Marxism arose when capitalism seemed "solid" and relatively crisis-free. We have argued that these two modes of Marxism are not incompatible and, indeed, we will argue in our concluding chapter that they must come into phase with each other, and even learn to complement each other, if Marxism is to be effective in comprehending and guiding radical movements in the future. Thus Kautsky's scientific Marxism was a symptom of the general turmoil of European society directly before World War I, the outbreak of which virtually ended these revolutionary expectations and itself produced a period of Marxist quiescence and philosophical introspection giving rise first to Lukács and Korsch's Hegelian Marxism and eventually to the critical theory of the Frankfurt School.

Lenin's scientific Marxism, however, served an entirely different political purpose in the hands of the Bolsheviks. The theory of Marxian science sketched in his aforementioned 1908 book was later resuscitated, after the Bolshevik seizure of power, as a new theory of dialectical materialism. This theory was to be used first by Lenin himself and later by Stalin as a form of justification of Bolshevik political practices. In essence, Lenin argued that science was a form of knowledge of the natural necessity of social dynamics. " . . .consciousness is only the reflection of being, at best, an approximately true . . .reflection of it."

Materialism in general recognises objectively real being (matter) as independent of consciousness, sensation, experience, etc., of humanity. Historical materialism recognises social being as independent of the social consciousness of humanity. In both cases consciousness is only the reflection of being, at best an approximately true (adequate, perfectly exact) reflection of it.*

Stalin employed sentiments such as these in arguing that Marxism can make "use of the laws of development of society for practical purposes."

Hence the science of the history of society, despite all the complexity of the phenomena of social life, can become as precise a science as, let us say, biology, and capable of making use of the laws of development of society for practical purposes.†

Only members of the Communist Party vanguard know these "laws," which they invoke to justify their political actions. Specifically, Stalin employed "dialectical materialism" whenever he needed to ground his often perverse political purges and reign of terror in Marxian theory. He could justify these practices on the basis of a kind of natural-scientific necessity, arguing that they *must* take place in order for socialism to exist—according to a theory only Stalin fully understood. If this seems like a caricature of Stalin's position in this regard, the reader need only turn to transcripts of the proceedings of the famous "show trials" during the mid and late 1930s where Stalin's political opponents were made to confess their alleged "crimes" and to ground their confessions in the "necessity" of dialectical materialism. (Especially poignant in this respect is the

---

*From V. Lenin, *Materialism and Empirio-Criticism* (Moscow: Foreign Languages Publishing House, 1952), p. 159–60.

†From J. V. Stalin, *Dialectical and Historical Materialism* (New York: International Publishers, 1940), p. 20.

confession of Stalin's competitor Nikolai Bukharin in 1938.)

Leninism was a form of political strategy which suggested that the Russian masses were incapable of theorizing about their own exploitation; they needed tight discipline and leadership "from without," from Marxian thinkers and intellectuals. These leaders were to form a "vanguard" that would lead the revolutionary movement and that would then represent the "dictatorship of the proletariat" immediately after the coup d'état. Lenin himself may have secretly recognized the need to make this period of vanguard-dictatorship as brief as possible, and to move quickly towards direct democracy and industrial self-management. Yet he postponed radical democracy for the seven years after the 1917 revolution, until his death in 1924. At that point, Stalin rapidly consolidated his own power, utilizing Lenin's earlier natural science-model Marxian theory to justify his every purge and execution.

Leninism thus has two integrated components: (a) the theory of the vanguard party, required to show the working class and peasantry what to do in the way of revolutionary and post-revolutionary activity; (b) the system of philosophical and theoretical justifications rooted in Lenin's concept of Marxism as a reflection-theory that provides insight into the necessities of societal "motion". The second component—Marxian science as a form of justifying ideology—legitimizes the elitist character of the first component, the vanguard model of socialism. The vanguard, in particular, the Communist Party of the Soviet Union, can do anything it wants politically *because* it holds a monopoly on social scientific truth.

We have seen that the conduct of the broadest political agitation and, consequently, of all-sided political exposures is an absolutely necessary and a *paramount* task of our activity, if this activity is to be truly Social-Democratic. However, we arrived at this conclusion *solely* on the grounds of the pressing needs of the working class for political knowledge and political training. But such a presentation of the question is too narrow, for it ignores the general democratic tasks of Social-Democracy, in particular of present-day Russian Social-Democracy. In order to explain the point more concretely we shall approach the subject from an aspect that is "nearest" to the Economist, namely, from the practical aspect. "Everyone agrees" that it is necessary to develop the political consciousness of the working class. The question is *how* that is to be done and what is required to do it. The economic struggle merely "impels" the workers to realise the government's attitude towards the working class. Consequently, *however much we may try* to "lend the economic struggle itself a political character," we *shall never be able* to develop the political consciousness of the workers (to the level of Social-Democratic political consciousness) by keeping within the framework of the economic struggle, for *that framework is too narrow*. The Martynov formula has some value for us, not because it illustrates Martynov's aptitude for confusing things, but because it pointedly expresses the basic error that all the Economists commit, namely, their conviction that it is possible to develop the class political consciousness of the workers *from within*, so to speak, from their economic struggle, i.e., by making this struggle the exclusive (or, at least, the main) basis. Such a view is radically wrong. Piqued by our polemics against them, the Economists refuse to ponder deeply over the origins of these disagreements, with the result that we simply cannot understand one another. It is as if we spoke in different tongues.

Class political consciousness can be brought to the workers *only from without,* that is, only from outside the economic struggle, from outside the sphere of relations between workers and employers. The sphere from which alone it is possible to obtain this knowledge is the sphere of relationships of *all* classes and strata to the state and the government, the sphere of the interrelations between *all* classes. For that reason, the reply to the question as to what must be done to bring political knowledge to the workers cannot be merely the answer with which, in the majority of cases, the practical workers, especially those inclined towards Economism, mostly content themselves, namely: "To go among the workers." To bring political knowledge to the *workers* the Social-Democrats must *go among all classes of the population;* they must dispatch units of their army *in all directions.* *

Lenin's theory of reflection need not be politically conservative. Only when it was used by certain Bolsheviks and especially by Stalin as a weapon with which to justify their own totalitarian actions did Marxian science — "Marxism-Leninism" — become a form of ideology. Luxemburg and Gramsci broke with Leninism precisely because they felt that each proletarian must become an active contributor not only to the creation of socialism but also to the creation of socialist *truth.* Luxemburg opposed Lenin because she did not believe that it was desirable for the Communist Party to impose its will upon the masses. Antonio Gramsci, as we noted above, believed that every human being could become an intellectual, opposing Lenin's vanguard model of politics and truth and the Stalinist uses to which it has been put in the USSR.

GUIDE TO FURTHER READING

V. I. LENIN   *What is to be Done?,* offers Lenin's definitive statement about the relationship between a revolutionary Communist party and the insurgent working class and peasantry.

V. I. LENIN   *The State and Revolution.*

KARL KAUTSKY   *Ethics and the Materialist Conception of History,* is a foremost expression of Kautsky and Engels' concept of a scientific Marxism, resembling the natural and physical sciences in its rigid determinism.

EDUARD BERNSTEIN   *Evolutionary Socialism,* is the major statement of the so-called revisionist position, arguing that sharp contradictions in capitalism have been blunted and stressing that the transformation to socialist institutions can occur gradually, through purely parliamentary means.

MARY-ALICE WATERS, ed.   *Rose Luxemburg Speaks,* is a collection of Luxemburg's essays containing some of her most important expressions of her opposition to Lenin's vanguardism and her belief that there must be an organic, reciprocal relationship between leaders and the masses.

ROSA LUXEMBURG   *The Junius Pamphlet.*

ANTONIO GRAMSCI   *Selections from the Prison Notebooks,* represents Gramsci's most significant original writings on Marxism, Italian history, and political theory.

---

*From V. I. Lenin, *What is to Be Done?* (Moscow: Progress Publishers, 1973), pp. 78–79.

GEORGE LICHTHEIM   *Marxism,* noted in Chapter 1, contains valuable chapters on Kautsky, Engels, and revisionism. Lichtheim's discussion of the immense gap between early Marxism, represented by the *Manifesto,* and the Marxism of the Second International, social democratic in nature, is among the best anywhere.

FRIEDRICH ENGELS   *Anti-Dühring,* outlines the basic principles of dialectical materialism as it was transformed into a form of scientific Marxism during the Second International.

PETER GAY   *The Dilemma of Democratic Socialism,* is a readable history of social democracy, concentrating on Bernstein's revisionism.

C. WRIGHT MILLS   *The Marxists,* contains an insightful section on the Marxism of the Second International.

KARL KAUTSKY   *The Labor Revolution.*

EMIL LEDERER   *State of the Masses.*

ROSA LUXEMBURG   *The Mass Strike.*

ROSA LUXEMBURG   *The Accumulation of Capital,* contains Luxemburg's theory of imperialism and her model of capitalist crisis and breakdown.

CARL BOGGS   *Gramsci's Marxism.*

FRANZ BORKENAU   *The Communist International.*

KARL KAUTSKY   *Class Struggle,* contains the Erfurt Programme, the most programmatic statement of the principles of Engels' and Kautsky's version of scientific socialism (published in 1891).

QUESTIONS FOR FURTHER DISCUSSION

1. Does the "scientific Marxism" of Kautsky and Engels faithfully represent Marx's own views on the character of his dialectical method? Cite textual evidence from Bernstein, Kautsky, and Luxemburg to support your view.

2. Why did Bernstein, Kautsky, and Luxemburg all oppose Lenin's vanguard-concept of the revolutionary transition?

3. What was the "revisionist controversy"?

4. How could theorists like Kautsky advocate "scientific socialism" and at the same time remain politically passive or advocate political democracy and parliamentary reform in Germany around 1910?

5. Explain how the German social democrats could advocate liberal democracy as a *revolutionary* strategy at the turn of the century

6. Why did the social democratic mass movement that existed during the Second International fail to achieve significant revolutionary aims?

7. Did Lenin preserve the essence of Marx's dialectical method in his own theorizing about the Bolshevik revolution?

Hegelian Marxism I: The Role of Class Consciousness

HISTORICAL OVERVIEW

The outbreak of the First World War in 1914 sent the Second International to a sudden death. Early market capitalism was able to survive the Marxist threat primarily because the First World War splintered the cause of international socialism into antagonistic national fragments. Rosa Luxemburg was unsuccessful in opposing the war effort on the grounds that Marxists should fight capitalism and not each other. After the war ended, and as the revolution was occurring in Russia in 1917, capitalism began to consolidate itself by developing more sophisticated industrial processes, by expanding internationally through colonialism and by mitigating the tension between capitalist and working classes. The aftermath of the First World War saw the emergence of the powerful political nation-state that soon appeared as a new and important force in the economic affairs of capitalism. Early capitalism also began to lose many of its features of open free market competition as capital became concentrated and centralized in the hands of a few large capitalists. This centralization of capital and the subsequent deterioration of economic competition in the open marketplace was predicted by Marx in the first volume of his Capital, published in 1867. Yet the capitalist system became temporarily stronger and more consolidated with the rise of what we term "early monopoly capitalism," predicated on the further concentration and centralization of capital, on the rise of the powerful nation-state and on increasing state intervention in the economy. Capitalism's "internal contradictions," resulting in what Marx called the law of the tendency of the rate of profit to fall, did not materialize in the final, devastating breakdown of the system. Indeed capitalism emerged from this period of internal and international consolidation on a stronger footing than it had enjoyed previously.

> *Early monopoly capitalism was a product of the consolidation of international capitalism that occurred after the Great Depression in the early 1930s and that reached its peak directly after the Second World War. Franklin Roosevelt's economic reconstruction of the American economy after the Depression served as a model for this new form of capitalism, which rested on a coalition between big business, labor, government, and the military. The rise of early monopoly capitalism caused many European Marxists, such as Georg Lukács, Karl Korsch and theorists of the Frankfurt School, to reassess scientific socialism and to inject a more psychological and philosophical tenor into Marxism. These "Hegelian Marxists" believed that the breakdown of capitalism did not occur in the period of intense turmoil of the 1920s because the working class did not develop sufficient class consciousness of its possible mission as a revolutionary political agent.*

GENERAL INTRODUCTION

In the preceding chapter we assessed Marxism as a strategic theory of class struggle. We could not escape the impression that this kind of scientific Marxism was directly oriented to the imminent possibility of socialist change, either of a reformist or revolutionary type. Although Eduard Bernstein, Karl Kautsky, and Rosa Luxemburg may have adopted differing strategic stances, they nonetheless shared a common activist purpose growing out of crisis periods in European capitalism. Their Marxism was oriented to the concrete situation of the western European proletariat and to its potential for class-radicalism. Debates during the Second International between reformist and revolutionary Marxists were mainly cast in terms of the differing stances to be taken by the revolutionary theorist. In this sense early twentieth century scientific Marxism was characterized by its close relationship to the class struggle.

Early twentieth century Marxism arose out of entrepreneurial, market capitalism. However, after World War I, capitalism quickly began to consolidate itself and to expand internationally. The very terms of the relationship between "capital" and "labor," as Marx called them, had begun to change, requiring, some thought, modifications of the analytical basis of Marxian theory. While certain Marxists (the author included) have retained Marx's basic dichotomy between capital and labor as the linchpin of their analysis of capitalist contradictions, other theorists have attempted to surpass the original assumptions of Marxism such as the theory of internal contradictions in attempting to capture what they believe is the changing reality of western capitalism.

The first requirement of these new types of Marxism, which were generally not to take form until the late 1920s and 1930s, was to explain the failure of western European working classes to shun the war effort in 1914 and instead to contribute to an international socialist revolution. Marx's theory tottered on the brink of oblivion because his theory of the crisis, only sketchily developed in *Capital,* did not explain the growing conservatism and "integrationist" tendencies of the working class in western Europe and in the United States. To rescue Marx's dialectical method and his vision of socialist change theorists were forced to reassess the pitfalls of the Second International and of Kautsky's scientific Marxism.

Furthermore, Marxist thinkers in central and western Europe were increasingly hostile to the Third or Communist International that had taken the place of the Second International in 1919. As we noted in Chapter 2, Marxism-Leninism became an ideology to justify a particular vanguard model of socialism as developed in the Bolsheviks' political struggle in Russia. This ideology had little immediate political relevance to western European societies. Moreover, it contained dogmatic assumptions about the authoritarian relationship between the Communist Party and the proletarian masses that repelled certain Marxists who lived in nation-states with liberal-democratic political traditions. Although many Marxists felt that Bernsteinian revisionism was *too* conservative and gradualist, few (including Kautsky and Luxemburg) wished to replace Bernstein's evident concern with the democratic process and parliamentary politics with the Bolsheviks' obvious authoritarianism.

Many leftists in western and central Europe disliked Marxism-Leninism because it was authoritarian and fundamentally elitist. Others found it repugnant because it apparently violated certain basic Marxian assumptions about socialist transformation. The Marxist-Leninists in the Soviet Union, fueled by Lenin's reinterpretation of aspects of Marx's theory of historical development, believed that the transition to full socialism or communism would need to be protracted, requiring an intermediate "dictatorship of the proletariat" organized by a Communist Party vanguard during the period of what Lenin called "state capitalism." This latter term referred to the way in which the Soviet leaders rushed to industrialize the Soviet economy, even operationalizing certain capitalist programs (such as Lenin's New Economic Policy) in order to generate capital accumulation and to facilitate the creation of an industrial infrastructure.

Russia in 1917 was a backward, industrially rudimentary, capital-poor nation. Lenin's argument for quick industrialization made good sense in the context of Russian backwardness. Yet Lenin *justified* brutal authoritarian rule by a Communist Party vanguard on the basis of this backwardness, arguing that an interim period of harsh dictatorship was necessary in order to enforce policies of rapid industrialization and capital accumulation. While Lenin may personally have hoped for the eventual abolition of this type of dictatorship, justified initially on the basis of Russia's industrial backwardness, events overtook him and by the time of his death in 1924 the ideology of Marxism-Leninism was firmly in place, ready for Stalin's consolidation of the centralized terror of the Communist Party of the Soviet Union.

Marxism-Leninism thus had a questionable strategic value even within the USSR. Outside the USSR, in liberal-democratic capitalist countries, its value, some held, was downright detrimental to the cause of socialism. The Third International was disastrous in western Europe and in the United States because the vanguard-model of the Russian Communists was either irrelevant to the situation of the increasingly affluent working class or else subversive of the valuable liberal-democratic traditions of western nation-states. These traditions guarded the democratic process against incipient authoritarianism resulting from the vanguard-model of revolutionary dictatorship.

Western Marxists in the period after 1920 located themselves between the scientific Marxism of the Second International and the ideological Marxism of the Soviet-dominated Third International. They attempted to defend a democratic socialist movement and to salvage Marx's dialectical method that, they argued, preserved both objective-scientific and subjective-philosophical dimensions of theoretical analysis. Implicitly the subjective dimension was seen to preserve the notion of the ultimate political and moral freedom of the individual, drawing upon Hegel's assumption that the human being must himself confront and overcome his own alienation. It will be recalled from our discussion in Chapter 1 that Hegel located alienation in the realm of the mind, explaining it in terms of the "externalization" of labor outside the domain of the mind and body. Hegel thought that all human activity entails a degree of alienation in this sense.

Marx differed from Hegel in suggesting that alienation was a historical and not a philosophical phenomenon, existing under class societies, where systems of wage-labor transform labor into an inhuman thing-in-itself standing outside the worker and defying his control of it. Marx suggested that alienation could be overcome not merely through philosophical and theoretical comprehension (although that was required as a prelude to revolutionary action) but through socialist transformation.

Although Hegel and Marx differed in their characterization of alienation, they shared the belief that human beings can resolve and overcome alienation. Hegel in the *Science of Logic,* his ultimate philosophical statement, suggested that the essence of being could be revealed through the philosophical attempt to comprehend the self-externalization of human beings and of whole societies and historical ages. Freedom, he asserted, would arise on the basis of comprehension and reason. Marx argued that human beings could liberate themselves by grasping the reason of history, and thus the possibility of their own emancipation, acting upon that vision of possible socialist change. Marx was Hegelian precisely to the degree to which he located self-emancipation within the activity of human beings and not in a deterministic historical process. Following Hegel, Marx felt that human beings could realize their freedom through productive, externalizing activity.

Western Marxists after World War I revived this aspect of Marx's dialectical method, bringing into light the Hegelian foundations of Marx's socialist vision. Theorists like Georg Lukács and Karl Korsch stressed the philosophical dimensions of the dialectical method because they wanted to avoid (a) the deterministic fatalism of the Second International's prevalent interpretation of Marxism as a form of natural science (drawing upon Kautsky and Engels' version of Marxism as "scientific socialism"), and, at the same time, (b) the authoritarianism of Marxism-Leninism that attempted to "speed up" historical dynamics through forced industrialization and capital accumulation at the expense of the working class and peasantry. Lukács and Korsch felt that the deterministic fatalism of the Second International and the authoritarian centralism of the Third International had a *common* source in the mechanistic, deterministic interpretation of Marxism. By reinvigorating the Hegelian foundations of Marxism, centered around the theory of alienation and the concept of creative praxis found in the early writings of Marx, Lukács, and Korsch could restore the dialectical foundations of Marx's vision of emancipation without at the same time re-idealizing his theory of socialist transformation. Lukács and Korsch remained dialectical materialists; *they merely hoped to restore the subjective dimension of class consciousness to a Marxism that had been denuded of this creative dimension by thinkers who felt that socialist change would result purely from the maturation of predetermined structural tendencies.*

The Second International's brand of scientific Marxism failed to energize the socialist revolution it felt was inevitable. The Third International's brand of Marxism—"Marxism-Leninism"—failed to involve the Russian worker and peasant in the democratic construction of Russian socialism, instead imposing the dictatorship of the proletariat from above. Hegelian Marxism was not primarily a theoretical or intellectual project designed merely to introduce a "correct" interpretation of Marx's thought. It was rather a theoretical-political attempt to explain reasons for the failure of the two European Internationals as these were related to mistakes made by past Marxists. Lukács was not a professor who was content to have his ideas evaluated purely by dispassionate criteria of professional scholarship (although, later in his career, his work gradually lost its revolutionary quality as he became accommodated to the ideologically rigid reality of Hungarian state-socialism). Lukács wanted to have a hand in restoring "class consciousness" in a historical situation when the overthrow of capitalism appeared possible and perhaps, to some, even likely. Both he and Korsch were personally involved both in the politics of European social democracy and in the politics of their home countries, Hungary and Germany respectively. It is difficult to separate the political and intellectual dimensions of Hegelian Marxism, and in any case it is undesirable because Lukács and Korsch were among the last western Marxists to be so close to the pulse of revolutionary class struggle. After capitalism had consolidated its expansion into the international sphere, the close relationship between intellectual Marxism and political Marxism was to be lost, regained only recently during the crisis-periods of monopoly capitalism in the late 1970s (as we will discuss in Chapter 7). It is hardly an exaggeration to say, as one recent commentator has said, that Lukács represents the "Grand Central Station of western Marxism," having redeveloped the dialectical method of Marx and the necessarily historical roots of Marxian theory.

In this chapter, we will explain and analyze the gradual transformation of Marxism from a revolutionary theory of class struggle to a theory and critique of ideology largely divested of its intimate connection to the working class. "Hegelian Marxism" is a term used to describe the theory developed during the early 1920s by Georg Lukács and Karl Korsch in opposition to the type of Marxism developed by Bernstein and other parliamentary socialists and in opposition to the "scientific socialism" of Engels, Kautsky, and the Austro-Marxists.

In the first place, both Lukács and Korsch were deeply sympathetic to the revolutionary class struggle endorsed by Luxemburg and Gramsci. Indeed, Lukács' most significant work, *History and Class Consciousness,* provided a philosophical foundation for the type of activist Marxism endorsed by Luxemburg. Yet both Lukács and Korsch rejected the kind of Marxism tied deterministically to the economic circumstances of the working class. Lukács explicitly rejected economism and determinism, believing that they placed insufficient emphasis on the voluntaristic aspect of the revolutionary process. Lukács took inspiration from Hegel in articulating a theory of revolutionary class consciousness.

Determinism to Lukács and Korsch was not only inadequate on theoretical grounds; it failed politically because it did not inspire the class consciousness and class-radicalism required to energize the revolution. By 1920, it was clear to Lukács that the western European revolution had failed, and that Russian Bolshevism was becoming the sole voice of European Marxism. The Communist International, or Comintern, had been founded in 1919 under the leadership of the Soviet official Zinoviev, a proponent of Marxism-Leninism. The growing influence of this official Soviet orthodoxy on the western communist movement disturbed Lukács and Korsch and convinced them that the dialectical foundations of Marxism needed to be revived.

Lukács attempted to counter deterministic tendencies in western Marxism because he felt that determinism underestimated the revolutionary role of class consciousness. The vehicle for Lukács' opposition to what he called automatic Marxism — scientific Marxism without a conception of active class consciousness — was his revival of the philosophical foundation of Marxism, involving the reappropriation of Hegel's creative concept of human self-consciousness. Lukács' interest in Hegel was both philosophical and political; Lukács attempted to comprehend the political failure of the working class in western Europe as a product of determinist Marxism that eliminated the revolutionary role of class-consciousness.

Lukács delved into abstruse philosophical sources, such as Hegel, in order to counter the political and organizational failure of the class struggle in western and central Europe. Lukács and Korsch believed that there was something intrinsic to

Marxian determinism that generated the failure of the working class to revolt in western Europe, or to repeat the apparent (but short-lived) success of the Bolsheviks in Russia. "Automatic" Marxists assumed that the socialist revolution would necessarily emerge from the resolution of "contradictory" economic forces, such as the falling rate of profit and immiserization of the urban proletariat. Lukács held that the revolution did not occur in western Europe because class consciousness was immature and because a deterministic concept of Marxism held sway, thus providing no mediations between Marx's crisis-theory and the creation of a new order.

Korsch explicitly argued that Bernstein's reformism and the economic orthodoxy of Kautsky, Engels, and Lenin were similar in that both ignored class consciousness. Automatic Marxists held that the transition to socialism would occur naturally: reformists believed that this would be an evolutionary process involving social democratic parliamentary means; scientific Marxists believed that this would be a process taking place purely on a structural-economic level.

Korsch approached the problem of class consciousness from a somewhat different direction. He argued that Marxism in its original formulation by Marx and Engels was inherently dialectical. Class consciousness was a material social force and not to be ignored in the belief that consciousness merely springs from economic conditions, as determinist Marxists assume. Korsch felt that he was faithful to Marx in arguing that there was a dialectical relationship between socio-economic conditions and class consciousness: The one could not be reduced to the other.

The Hegelian Marxists did not abandon Marxism by developing their theory of class consciousness; Lukács and Korsch both remained quite orthodox in their analyses of internal contradictions. It was only later, during the consolidation of what we term early monopoly capitalism in the 1930s and 1940s, that certain European theorists attempted to revise Marx's theory of class consciousness and ideology in a more fundamental way. The Institute for Social Research located in Frankfurt, Germany in the late 1920s and 1930s was the site of the development of "critical theory," which extended and deepened Lukács and Korsch's theory of ideology and class consciousness. The Frankfurt critical theorists, led by Max Horkheimer, the Director of the Institute from 1930 to 1958, and including Theodor W. Adorno (who replaced Horkheimer as Director in 1958), Herbert Marcuse, Erich Fromm, Walter Benjamin, Henryk Grossman, and Friedrich Pollock, took the dialectical Marxism developed by Lukács and Korsch as their point of departure.

The Hegelian Marxists believed that they were defending Marx against those whom they perceived as distorting Marx's basic doctrine in the direction of a passive determinism. Lukács and Korsch submitted that Marx and Engels paid ample attention to ideological factors and thus they read Marx not as an economic determinist but as a dialectical methodologist. A Marxist analysis of Marxism might show that the idea of the deterministic inevitability of the revolution is an illusion, never endorsed by Marx. As we noted in Chapter 1, Marx attempted to demonstrate that capitalism contained self-contradictory elements that threatened to subvert the profit-system. Yet according to Lukács and Korsch Marx also suggested that certain adjustments could be made that would postpone the collapse.

Lukács believed that he was merely salvaging Marx's dialectical method by developing the theory of class consciousness. Lukács opposed the mechanistic approaches of theorists of the Second International such as Kautsky because he believed that they misread Marx's concept of the dialectic between subjective and objective dimensions of the class struggle. Luxemburg, of all the thinkers of the Second International, was closest to Lukács in this respect, stressing the necessary reciprocity between the economic theory of the crisis and the spontaneity of class action required to lay the foundation for a socialist order.

We recall from Chapter 1 how Marx transformed Hegel's philosophical idealism into historical materialism. Lukács also returned to Hegel's terminology in developing the concept of a revolutionary "collective subject," the working class, that alone could transform capitalist society. Lukács was clearly not an idealist in that he did not impute a trans-individual consciousness or spirit to the working class, as Hegel might have done. Rather he treated the working class as the living embodiment of a kind of historical reason that he felt was embedded in the dynamics of capitalist society; this historical reason emerged from the pervasive reality of alienation and exploitation, providing hope that a new socialist order was indeed possible.

Not only was a new order possible, but the revolutionary "collective subject" could achieve consciousness about historical reason and its own role in actualizing or bringing into being the "truth" of that reason. Lukács did not suggest that history was a process of straightforward necessity, containing a hidden purpose having only to be revealed by idealist philosophers (a view that Hegel shared). Rather, history moved in comprehensible ways both according to its own intrinsic dynamic and according to the wills and desires of human beings. Lukács felt that Marx was the first to recognize that a revolutionary collective subject, through insight into the "reason" of the historical process unfolding in the early twentieth century, could harness historical dynamics and indeed move them forward, uncovering and actualizing their revealed purpose.

In this sense Lukács flirted with a deterministic vision of historical change, in much the same way as did Marx, as has often been noted by those who reject economic determinism. What saved Lukács from determinism was his recognition that there is no mechanistic relationship between conditions and class consciousness. Indeed, much of Lukács' earliest theoretical effort was oriented to explaining why the working class *failed* to grasp its possible historical mission and instead fell victim to class apathy and the divisive nationalism of the First World War.

The Frankfurt thinkers did not question Marx's assumption about the relentless drive for capital accumulation. However they questioned his assumption, expressed most cogently in Volume III of *Capital,* about the existence of "internal contradictions" in a capitalist economy. The Frankfurt theorists did not agree with the tenor of Marx's and Lukács' crisis-theories, for they believed that monopoly capitalism, especially after the Second World War, was capable of forestalling the manifestations of these "internal contradictions" such as would emanate from the growing organic composition of capital as well as from its centralization and concentration. While in a strict sense they did not suggest that the contradictions had disappeared, they argued that the contradictions were now contained (mainly via an interventionist state that, as Marx noted, was an "executive committee of the bourgeoisie") in such a way as to prevent the emergence of destructive crisis-tendencies. Two significant developments separated monopoly capitalism from the crisis-bound "early" capitalism Lukács confronted.

First, as Lenin recognized, capitalism became imperialist in order to extract cheap raw materials from underdeveloped countries and to find new foreign markets for manufactured goods. Second, and most important, human tastes could be manipulated in such a way that people would consume endlessly, protecting the economy against stagnation and thus a falling rate of profit. Marx failed to pay serious attention to the sphere of consumption, for he did not foresee that the manipulation of taste would become an important factor in sustaining and enhancing profitability and in achieving social control. (See Chapter 7 for a further discussion of this issue.)

The Frankfurt theorists attempted to provide the analysis of the consumption sphere and of ideology that orthodox Marxists had neglected. The Frankfurt theorists took note of the new roles of ideology and false consciousness in dampening working-class radicalism. Although Max Horkheimer was a contemporary of Lukács and Korsch, he quickly became more distant than they from the class struggle. Horkheimer recognized that the "ideological crisis of the proletariat," as Lukács called it, had grave consequences for Marx and Engels' model of the crisis and socialist class-radicalism. It appeared that the western working classes in the 1930s and 1940s were far from being the revolutionary agent that Marx had expected in *The Communist Manifesto* and, later, in *Capital*. Reification and false consciousness took a heavy toll in manipulating the potentially revolutionary spirit of the working class.

In this context, Horkheimer developed a position-piece on Marxism entitled "Traditional and Critical Theory" (first published in 1937) in which he attempted to change the terms of reference of Marxism. He felt that the revolutionary consciousness of the working class could not be assumed and that the class struggle would initially take the form of political education and the critique and demystification of ideologies. The manipulation of consciousness had to be countered by a critical theory that abandoned the deterministic strains of Marx's *Capital*. Instead, consciousness would have to be rehabilitated in such a way that the false consciousness of bourgeois existence could be revealed and reversed.

No longer was there an automatic or even plausible relationship between economic contradictions and the political situation of the working class. Horkheimer and his colleagues recognized that the rates of profit were not falling, and moreover, that the working class was not being immiserated. On the contrary, owing to imperialism, the expansion of war economies, and unionization, workers were entering into a class compromise with capitalists. The service sector in society was growing rapidly, weakening the strict distinctions between manual and mental work. These developments, coupled with the rise of Keynes' new analyses of the necessity of state intervention in the economy and the consequent weakening of economic liberalism and the ideology of laissez faire, threatened to subvert crucial aspects of Marx's analysis of economic crisis.

This area of investigation has created grave analytical difficulties for western Marxists. There has been much dispute over the Frankfurt allegation that economic crisis could be contained by the capitalist state through various programs of stimulation and fiscal adjustment. Perhaps the most telling difference between original Marxism, whether the scientific socialism of Engels and Kautsky or the Hegelian Marxism of Lukács and Korsch, and post-orthodox Frankfurt Marxism is this issue of the capitalist state's ability to contain and thus defuse "contradictions." The Frankfurt theory became a generalized critique of bourgeois existence, losing its specifically class-based focus because it assumed that crises could be contained indefinitely, and thus requiring that Marx's entire model of socialist transformation be seriously modified.

It is not obvious to all Marxists that either early or late monopoly capitalism is devoid of contradictions, eventually to result in sharp clashes between capital and labor. Even a member of the second generation of the Frankfurt School, Jürgen Habermas, argues that crisis has merely been *displaced* from the economic to the socio-political and cultural realms, emerging in modern capitalism as "legitimation crisis" (see Chapter 7). His argument is that the capitalist state, in order to avoid the type of crises that Marx in *Capital* suggested were unavoidable, such as falling rate of profit and immiseration of the working class, must continuously intervene in capitalist economic life to keep wages high and inflation reasonably low. This is a precarious activity for it contravenes the stated ideology of the free enterprise system, which warrants very limited government intervention in a free market economy. Workers increasingly find that the spreading controls of the welfare-governmental sectors over everyday social and economic life are undesirable, especially as they are victimized by inflation and periodic recession. The "legitima-tion" of liberal-capitalist governments is thus rendered problematic. This legitima-tion is required by democratically elected governments, which need to preserve the semblance (if not always the reality) of liberal democracy. In other words, serious confusion is created in an advanced capitalist system that requires ever increasing government stimulation in order to ward off economic crisis-tendencies but that at the same time requires a publically legitimated ideology of individual initiative and free enterprise—an ideology that is a product of a much earlier, late nineteenth century stage of capitalism.

Legitimation is difficult to obtain in light of the evident contradiction between Chamber of Commerce ideologies (belief in "free enterprise") and the interven-tionist economic policies of the bourgeois-democratic state. Serious crises are generated by the almost "socialist" appearance of the modern welfare state; this appearance clashes with the "old" capitalist ideology still in place in most western societies, repelling those who blame their own economic insecurity on "creeping socialism" and the like—not recognizing that this "creeping socialism" (the capitalist welfare state) is the *salvation* of modern-day capitalism, which would otherwise be torn apart by severe class conflict and falling rates of profit.

Habermas' analysis revises and salvages the economic crisis-theory of ear-lier Marxists, brings it forward into the 1970s and the era of late monopoly capitalism. He raises an issue largely glossed over by other members of the Frankfurt School: the inability of capitalism to contain crises that, he argues, are structurally produced by a capitalist economy.

Lukács himself, much earlier than Habermas, believed that the original Marx-ian theory of internal contradictions was valid; he *expected* the eventual break-down of the system. By contrast the Frankfurt theorists felt that crisis was no longer structurally threatening to the capitalist system and that advanced capitalism could be technocratically administered through the creation of the so-called infinite consumer, deep-seated commodity fetishism and false needs. Today the Frankfurt theory is widely rejected because it is said to "harmonize" the contradictions of the capitalist system, having become purely a critique of bourgeois ideology, losing touch with the Marxian theories of crises and class-radicalism.

Lukács brilliantly added the theory of class consciousness to Marxism, when it was in danger of being ignored completely in favor of a totally deterministic "scientific socialism." The Frankfurt theorists did not deny the reality of economic exploitation—indeed, they felt that economic exploitation and "reification," as Lukács called it, had become nearly total in monopoly capitalism. Rather they argued that economic and (in Habermas' terms) legitimation crisis could be indefi-nitely forestalled by the "administered" consciousness of bourgeois everyday life.

Although initially in the 1920s and 1930s Horkheimer, Adorno, and Marcuse were genuinely committed to the Marxist theory of internal contradictions, they quickly rejected Marx's particular version of crisis and class struggle, arguing that domination had invaded the very character structures of workers, rendering the prospects of class consciousness very dim indeed. The key to understanding differences between Lukács and the Frankfurt School is in their differing analysis of ideology. Lukács saw ideology in the traditional Marxian sense, viewing it as a system of fictions designed to mystify the reality of class exploitation. The Frankfurt thinkers instead saw ideology as a deeper, "self-inflicted" phenomenon that was not simply thrown up to mystify economic exploitation. They argued that differences between reality and appearance had been blurred, allowing human beings, who are still objectively dominated according to Marxist criteria, to believe that they are basically free. While Lukács' concept of reification pointed the way towards this understanding of "self-inflicted" ideological domination, Lukács was concerned with a more clear-cut type of ideology that blunted the radicalism of the working class.

The Frankfurt thinkers felt that pervasive bourgeois ideology (systematically analyzed in Chapter 4) vitiated the possibility of system-wrenching crisis and class-radicalism. Lukács' post-mortem of the Second International was carried out within the context of a form of early market capitalism when internal contradictions were coming to the surface as crisis-tendencies, as Marx expected they would. The Frankfurt School theorists developed their critique of ideology primarily in the 1930s and early 1940s, when capitalism was already well on its way, they felt, towards consolidating its contradictions by expanding internationally, by shifting from labor-intensive to capital-intensive modes of production and by manipulating the preferences of the consumer, creating within him a set of "false needs" that guide him in a pattern of endless consumption.

In a basic sense, Horkheimer and Adorno felt that domination under capitalism was "worse" than Lukács had believed. Differences here reflect the fact that Lukács was squarely rooted in early market capitalism and in 1923 had not yet been confronted with the metamorphosis of market capitalism consolidated monopoly forms (which arose after about 1920, coming into full maturity only after World War II), while Horkheimer and Adorno had already "moved" analytically into the later phase of monopoly capitalism (termed here, only for the sake of analytical convenience, early monopoly capitalism, which lasted until the 1950s and early 1960s, when "late" monopoly capitailsm arose). Lukács did not minimize capitalist domination, he simply believed that the revolutionary "collective subject" could emerge from its false consciousness through a proper appreciation of its historical mission based on an understanding of the process of dialectical development.

These are not mutually exclusive positions. We prefer to locate Lukács and the original Frankfurt School on a continuum, where Lukács' concept of reification and false consciousness was deepened and extended by the Frankfurt thinkers, forcing them to abandon the prospect of a revolutionary collective subject and class-radicalism. Had Lukács not become embroiled in a variety of embarrassing self-critiques, designed to accommodate himself to the ideological authority of state socialism, he might have reached the same conclusions as the Frankfurt thinkers about the difficulty of generating class consciousness through the critique of objective ideology and through the analysis of historical reason. He remained a creature of an earlier period of capitalism than Horkheimer and Adorno, perhaps reflecting the different stages of development reached by Lukács' Hungary and the Frankfurt School's Germany.

In spite of the differences between the first Hegelian Marxists, they all believed that Marx was a dialectician who never ignored the subjective and ideological dimensions of socialist change. The Hegelian Marxists endorsed a type of Marxism that necessarily adjusts itself to particular historical contexts and refuses to remain static in its analytical and political orientation. Differences between Lukács' stress on the revolutionary and "collective subject" and Horkheimer and Adorno's stress on the dominated personal subject reflect the differing historical contexts out of which their respective theories grew. They were joined by the common assumption that a truly dialectical theory must never overlook the potential for revolt existing at particular historical junctures; Horkheimer and Adorno went as far as to suggest that Marxism in early monopoly capitalism must appear pessimistic with respect to the then-existing potential for class-conscious revolutionary activity. They believed that Marxism was distinguished not by its headlong rush into political activity but rather by careful analysis of the structural possibilities of successful class-radicalism in particular historical contexts. It was left for later Marxists, in the 1960s and 1970s, to redevelop crisis-theory and new strategies of class-radicalism in response to further internal transformations of advanced capitalism.

LUKACS: ON CLASS CONSCIOUSNESS

The following passage is excerpted from Lukács' essay "Towards a Methodology of the Problem of Organization" in his book, *History and Class Consciousness*. Lukács analyzes what he calls "the ideological crisis of the proletariat," issuing in the failure of the working class to revolt. He attacks "fatalistic" Marxism that assumes the inevitability of the proletariat revolution.

Lukács suggests that the proletariat does not inevitably take control of its objective economic situation through inexorable "natural laws." The crisis of economic contradiction is produced by the breakdown of capitalism; and yet the crisis can only be resolved through "free action of the proletariat," taken on the basis of critical class consciousness.

In the context of this argument, Lukács attacks Engels' notion that with the revolution humanity will "leap from the realm of necessity into the realm of freedom." Lukács suggests that this is an inappropriate metaphor because it fails to recognize that the revolution will be a process and not a single event, a "leap." He dismisses as "utopian" any theory that separates the final goal of communism from the movement to achieve it. Lukács attacks economism, a deterministic theory of revolution that discounts the elements of collective choice and purpose required to resolve the crisis of capitalism.

Lukács describes the "unity of theory and practice," that is, the coupling of the recognition of economic crisis with the will and action to transform a crisis-ridden social order. Marxism for Lukács, thus, emerges *both* as a scientific and practical orientation: Crisis-theory prepares the proletariat for effective revolutionary action.

Lukács here introduces the foundations of his dialectical Marxism, rooted in subject-object dialectics. This dialectics relates the objective situation of the working class, determined by the crisis-tendencies of capitalism, to its subjective potential for formulating a "class conscious" account of domination and liberation. Subject-object dialectics opposed the automatic, deterministic Marxism of the Second International that, in spite of evident revolutionary intentions, ignored the requirements of class consciousness and reduced the collapse of capitalism (and the subsequent transition to socialism) to a given logical necessity, to be grasped by Marxian science.

Our aim here is to point out that the class consciousness of the proletariat does not develop uniformly throughout the whole proletariat, parallel with the objective economic crisis. Large sections of the proletariat remain intellectually under the tutelage of the bourgeoisie; even the severest economic crisis fails to shake them in their attitude. With the result that the standpoint of the proletariat and its reaction to the crisis is much less violent and intense than is the crisis itself.

This state of affairs, which makes possible the existence of Menshevism, is doubtless not lacking in objective economic bases. Marx and Engels noted very early on that those sections of the workers who obtained a privileged place vis-à-vis their class comrades thanks to the monopoly profits of the England of that time tended to acquire bourgeois characteristics. With the entry of capitalism into its imperialist phase this stratum came into being everywhere and is without a doubt an important factor in the general trend in the working class towards opportunism and anti-revolutionary attitudes.

In my opinion, however, this fact alone does not provide an adequate explanation of Menshevism. In the first place, this privileged position has already been undermined in many respects while the position of Menshevism has not been correspondingly weakened. Here too, the subjective development of the proletariat has in many ways lagged behind the tempo of the objective crisis. Hence we cannot regard this factor as the sole cause of Menshevism unless we are to concede it also the comfortable theoretical position arrived at by inferring the absence of an objective revolutionary situation from the absence of a thorough-going and clear-cut revolutionary fervour in the proletariat. In the second place, the experiences of the revolutionary struggles have failed to yield any conclusive evidence that the proletariat's revolutionary fervour and will to fight corresponds in any straightforward manner to the economic level of its various parts. There are great deviations from any such simple, uniform parallels and there are great divergencies in the maturity of class consciousness attained by workers within economically similar strata.

These truths only acquire real significance in the context of a non-fatalistic, non-"economistic" theory. If the movement of history is interpreted as showing that the economic process of capitalism will advance automatically and inexorably through a series of crises to socialism then the ideological factors indicated here are merely the product of a mistaken diagnosis. They would then appear simply as proof that the objectively decisive crisis of capitalism has not yet appeared. For in such a view there is simply no room for the idea of an ideological crisis of the proletariat in which proletarian ideology lags behind the economic crisis.

The position is not so very different where, while retaining the basic economic fatalism, the prevailing view of the crisis becomes revolutionary and optimistic: i.e., where it is held that the crisis is inevitable and that for capitalism there can be no way out. In this case, too, the problem examined here is not admitted to be a problem at all. What before was "impossible" is now "not yet" the case. Now, Lenin has very rightly pointed out that there is no situation from which there is no way out. Whatever position capitalism may find itself in there will always be some "purely economic" solutions available. The question is only whether these solutions will be viable when they emerge from the pure theoretical world of economics into the reality of the class struggle. For capitalism, then, expedients can certainly be thought of in and for themselves. Whether they can be put into practice depends, however, on the proletariat. The proletariat, the actions of the proletariat, block capitalism's way out of the crisis. Admittedly, the fact that the proletariat obtains power at that moment is due to the "natural laws" governing the economic process. But these "natural laws" only determine the crisis itself, giving it dimensions which frustrate the "peaceful" advance of capitalism. However, if left to develop (along capitalist lines) they would not lead to the simple downfall of capitalism or to a smooth transition to socialism. They would lead over a long period of crises, civil wars, and imperialist world wars on an ever-increasing scale to "the mutual destruction of the opposing classes" and to a new barbarism.

Moreover, these forces, swept along by their own "natural" impetus have brought into being a proletariat whose physical and economic strength leaves capitalism very little scope to enforce a purely economic solution along the lines of those which put an end to previous crises in which the proletariat figures only as the object of an economic process. The newfound strength of the proletariat is the product of objective economic "laws." The problem, however, of converting this potential power into a real one and of enabling the proletariat (which today really is the mere object of the economic process and only potentially and latently its co-determining subject) to emerge as its subject in reality, is no longer determined by these "laws" in any fatalistic and automatic way. More precisely: The automatic and fatalistic power of these laws no longer controls the essential core of the strength of the proletariat. In so far as the proletariat's reactions to the crisis proceed according to the "laws" of the capitalist economy, in so far as they limit themselves at most to spontaneous mass actions, they exhibit a structure that is in many ways like that of movement of pre-revolutionary ages. They break out spontaneously almost without exception as a defence against an economic and more rarely, a political thrust by the bourgeoisie, against the attempts of the latter to find a "purely economic" solution to the crisis. (The spontaneity of a movement, we note, is only the subjective, mass-psychological expression of its determination by pure economic laws.) However, such outbreaks come to a halt no less spontaneously, they peter out when their immediate goals are achieved or seem unattainable. It appears, therefore, as if they have run their "natural" course.

That such appearances may prove to be deceptive becomes clear if these movements are regarded not abstractly but in their true context, in the historical totality of the world-crisis. This context is the extension of the crisis to every class and not just the bourgeoisie and the proletariat. Where the economic process provokes a spontaneous mass-movement in the proletariat there is a fundamental qualitative distinction to be made between a situation in which the society as a whole is basically stable and one in which a profound regrouping of all social forces and an erosion of the bases of the power of the ruling class is taking place.

It is for this reason that an understanding of the significant role played by non-proletarian strata during a revolution and an understanding of its non-proletarian character is of such decisive importance. The exercise of power by a minority can only perpetuate itself if it can contrive to carry the classes that are not directly and immediately affected by the revolution along with it ideologically. It must attempt to obtain their support or at least their neutrality. (It goes without saying that there is also an attempt to neutralise sections of the revolutionary class itself.)

This was especially true of the bourgeoisie. The bourgeoisie had far less of an immediate control of the actual springs of power than had ruling classes in the past (such as the citizens of the Greek city-states or the nobility at the apogee of feudalism). On the one hand, the bourgeoisie had to rely much more strongly on its ability to make peace or achieve a compromise with the opposing classes that held power before it so as to use the power-apparatus they controlled for its own ends. On the other hand, it found itself compelled to place the actual exercise of force (the army, petty bureaucracy, etc.) in the hands of petty bourgeois, peasants, the members of subject nations, etc. If, following a crisis, the economic position of these strata were to alter and if their naive, unthought-out loyalty to the social system led by the bourgeoisie were shaken, then the whole apparatus of bourgeois domination might collapse, as it were, at a single blow. In that event the proletariat might emerge as the only organised power, as the victor without its having fought a serious battle let alone having really gained a victory.

The movements of these intermediate strata are truly spontaneous and they are nothing but spontaneous. They really are nothing more than the fruits of the natural forces of society obedient to "natural laws." As such they are themselves—socially—blind. These strata have no class consciousness that might have any bearing on the remoulding of society. As a result of this they always represent particular class interests which do not even pretend to be the objective interests of the whole of society. The bonds that join them to the whole objectively are only causal, i.e., they are caused by movements within the whole but they cannot be directed towards changing it. Hence both their concern with the whole and the ideological form it assumes have something adventitious about them even though their origins can be conceived in terms of causal necessities. Because of the nature of these movements their actions are determined by factors external to themselves. Whatever direction they finally choose, whether they attempt to hasten the dissolution of bourgeois society, whether they again acquiesce in their own exploitation by the bourgeoisie, whether they sink back into passivity as the result of the frustration of their efforts, nothing that they do is implicit in their inner nature. Instead everything hinges on the behaviour of the classes capable of consciousness: the bourgeoisie and the proletariat. Whatever form their later fate may take the very explosion of such movements can easily lead to the paralysis of all the machinery that holds bourgeois society together and enables it to function. It is enough to reduce the bourgeoisie to immobility at least for a time.

From the Great French Revolution on, all revolutions exhibit the same pattern with increasing intensity. When revolution breaks out the absolute monarchy, and later the semi-absolute, semi-feudal military monarchies upon which the economic hegemony of the bourgeoisie was based in Central and Eastern Europe, tend "all at once" to lose their hold over society. Social power lies abandoned in the street without an owner so to speak. A Restoration only becomes possible in the absence of any revolutionary class to take advantage of this ownerless power.

The struggles of a nascent absolutism against feudalism were on very different lines. For there the opposing classes could create organs of force much more directly from their own ranks and hence the class struggle was much more a struggle of one power against another. One recalls, for instance, the battles of the Fronde at the birth of absolutism in France. Even the downfall of English absolutism ran a similar course, whereas the collapse of the Protectorate and even more the—much more bourgeois—absolutism of Louis XVI were closer to the pattern of modern revolutions. There direct force was introduced from "outside," from absolute states that were still intact or from territories that had remained feudal (as in La Vendée).

By contrast, purely "democratic" power complexes may easily find themselves in a similar position in the course of a revolution: whereas at the moment of collapse they came into being of their own accord, as it were, and seized the reigns of power, they now find themselves no less suddenly stripped of all power—in consequence of the receding movement on the part of the incubate strata that bore them up and onward. (Thus Kerensky and Karolyi.) It is not yet possible to discern with complete clarity the pattern of future developments in the bourgeois and democratically progressive states of the West. Despite this Italy has found itself in a very similar situation since the end of the war and up to about 1920. The power organisation that it devised for itself since that time (Fascism) constitutes a power apparatus which is relatively independent of the bourgeoisie. We have as yet no experience of the effects of the symptoms of disintegration in highly developed capitalist countries with extensive colonial possessions. And in particular, we do not know what will be the effects of colonial revolts, which to a certain extent play the part of internal peasant uprisings, upon the attitude of the petty bourgeoisie, the workers' aristocracy (and hence, too, the armed forces, etc.)

In consequence the proletariat finds itself in an environment which would assign a quite different function to spontaneous mass movements than they had possessed in the stable capitalist system. This holds good even where these mass movements, when viewed in isolation, have preserved their former characteristics. Here, however, we observe the emergence of very important quantitative changes in the opposing classes. In the first place, the concentration of capital has made further advances and this in turn results in a further concentration of the proletariat—even if the latter is unable wholly to keep pace with this trend in terms of its consciousness and its organisation. In the second place, the crisis-ridden condition of capitalism makes it increasingly difficult to relieve the pressure coming from the proletariat by making minute concessions. Escape from the crisis, the "economic" solution to the crisis can only come through the intensified exploitation of the proletariat. For this reason the tactical theses of the Third Congress very rightly emphasise that "every mass strike tends to translate itself into a civil war and a direct struggle for power."

But it only tends to do so. And the fact that this tendency has not yet become reality even though the economic and social preconditions were often fulfilled, that precisely is the ideological crisis of the proletariat. This ideological crisis manifests itself on the one hand in the fact that the objectively extremely precarious position of bourgeois society is endowed, in the minds of the workers, with all its erstwhile stability; in many respects the proletariat is still caught up in the old capitalist forms of thought and feeling. On the other hand, the bourgeoisification of the proletariat becomes institutionalised in the Menshevik workers' parties and in the trade unions they control. These organisations now consciously labour to ensure that the merely spontaneous movements of the proletariat (with their dependence upon an immediate provocation, their fragmentation along professional and local lines, etc.) should remain on the level of pure spontaneity. They strive to prevent them from turning their attention to the totality, whether this be territorial, professional, etc., or whether it involves synthesising the economic movement with the political one. In this the unions tend to take on the task of atomising and depoliticising the movement and concealing its relation to the totality, whereas the Menshevik parties perform the task of establishing the reification in the consciousness of the proletariat both ideologically and on the level of organisation. They thus ensure that the consciousness of the proletariat will remain at a certain stage of relative bourgeoisification. They are able to achieve this only because the proletariat is in a state of ideological crisis, because even in theory the natural—ideological—development into a dictatorship and into socialism is out of the question for the proletariat, and because the crisis involves not only the economic undermining of capitalism but, equally, the ideological transformation of a proletariat that has been reared in capitalist society under the influence of the life-forms of the bourgeoisie. This ideological transformation does indeed owe its existence to the economic crisis which created the objective opportunity to seize power. The course it actually takes does not, however, run parallel in any automatic and "necessary" way with that taken by the objective crisis itself. This crisis can be resolved only by the free action of the proletariat.

"It is ridiculous," Lenin says in a statement that only caricatures the situation formally, not essentially, "to imagine an army taking up battle positions somewhere and saying: 'We are for Socialism' while somewhere else another army will stand and declare: 'We are for Imperialism' and that such a situation should constitute a social revolution." The emergence of revolutionary and counter-revolutionary fronts is full of vicissitudes and is frequently chaotic in the extreme. Forces that work towards revolution today may very well operate in the reverse direction tomorrow. And it is vital to note that these changes of direction do not simply follow mechanically from the class situation or even from the ideology of the stratum concerned. They are determined decisively by the constantly changing relations with the totality of the historical situation and the social forces at work. So that it is no very great paradox to assert that, for instance, Kemal Pasha may represent a revolutionary constellation of forces in certain circumstances whilst a great "workers' party" may be counter-revolutionary.

Among the factors that determine the direction to be taken, the proletariat's correct understanding of its own historical position is of the very first importance. The course of the Russian Revolution in 1917 is a classic illustration of this. For we see there how at a crucial moment, the slogans of peace, self-determination and the radical solution to the agrarian problem welded together an army that could be deployed for revolution whilst completely disorganising the whole power apparatus of counter-revolution and rendering it impotent. It is not enough to object that the agrarian revolution and the peace movement of the masses would have carried the day without or even against the Communist Party. In the first place this is absolutely unprovable: as counter-evidence we may point e.g., to Hungary where a no less spontaneous agrarian uprising was defeated in October 1918. And even in Russia it might have been possible to crush the agrarian movement or allow it to dissipate itself, by achieving a "coalition" (namely a counter-revolutionary coalition) of all the "influential" "workers' parties." In the second place, if the "same" agrarian movement had prevailed against the urban proletariat it would have become counter-revolutionary in character in the context of the social revolution.

This example alone shows the folly of applying mechanical and fatalistic criteria to the constellation of social forces in acute crisis-situations during a social revolution. It highlights the fact that the proletariat's correct insight and correct decision is all-important; it shows the extent to which the resolution of the crisis depends upon the proletariat itself. We should add that in comparison to the western nations the situation in Russia was relatively simple. Mass movements there were more purely spontaneous and the opposing forces possessed no organisation deeply rooted in tradition. It can be maintained without exaggeration, therefore, that our analysis would have an even greater validity for western nations. All the more as the undeveloped character of Russia, the absence of a long tradition of a legal workers' movement—if we ignore for the moment the existence of a fully constituted Communist Party—gave the Russian proletariat the chance to resolve the ideological crisis with greater dispatch.

Thus the economic development of capitalism places the fate of society in the hands of the proletariat. Engels describes the transition accomplished by mankind after the revolution has been carried out as "the leap from the realm of necessity into the realm of freedom." For the dialectical materialist it is self-evident that despite the fact that this leap is a leap, or just because of it, it must represent in essence a process. Does not Engels himself say in the passage referred to that the changes that lead in this direction take place "at a constantly increasing rate"? The only problem is to determine the starting-point of the process. It would, of course, be easiest to take Engels literally and to regard the realm of freedom simply as a state which will come into being after the completion of the social revolution. This would be simply to deny that the question had any immediate relevance. The only problem then would be to ask whether the question would really be exhausted by this formulation, which admittedly does correspond to Engels' literal statement. The question is whether a situation is even conceivable, let alone capable of being made social reality, if it has not been prepared by a lengthy process which has contained and developed the elements of that situation, albeit in a form that is inadequate in many ways and in great need of being subjected to a series of dialectical reversals. If we separate the "realm of freedom" sharply from the process which is destined to call it into being, if we thus preclude all dialectical transitions, do we not thereby lapse into a utopian outlook similar to that which has already been analysed in the case of the separation of final goal and the movement towards it?

If, however, the "realm of freedom" is considered in the context of the process that leads up to it, then it cannot be doubted that even the earliest appearance of the proletariat on the stage of history indicated an aspiration towards that end—admittedly in a wholly unconscious way. However little the final goal of the proletariat is able, even in theory, to influence the initial stages of the early part of the process directly, it is a principle, a synthesising factor and so can never be completely absent from any aspect of that process. It must not be forgotten, however, that the difference between the period in which the decisive battles are fought and the foregoing period does not lie in the extent and the intensity of the battles themselves. These quantitative changes are merely symptomatic of the fundamental differences in quality which distinguish these struggles from earlier ones. At an earlier stage, in the words of the Communist Manifesto, even "the massive solidarity of the workers was not yet the consequence of their own unification but merely a consequence of the unification of the bourgeoisie." Now, however, the process by which the proletariat becomes independent and "organises itself into a class" is repeated and intensified until the time when the final crisis of capitalism has been reached, the time when the decision comes more and more within the grasp of the proletariat.

This state of affairs should not be taken to imply that the objective economic "laws" cease to operate. On the contrary, they will remain in effect until long *after the victory* of the proletariat and they will only wither away—like the state—when the classless society wholly in the control of mankind comes into being. What is novel in the present situation is merely—merely!!—that the *blind forces of capitalist economics are driving society towards the abyss.* The bourgeoisie no longer has the power to help society, after a few false starts, to break the "deadlock" brought about by its economic laws. And the proletariat has the *opportunity* to turn events in another direction by the conscious exploitation of existing trends. This other direction is the conscious regulation of the productive forces of society. To desire this consciously, is to desire the "realm of freedom" and to take the first conscious step towards its realisation.

This step follows "necessarily" from the class situation of the proletariat. However, this necessity has itself the character of a leap. The practical relationship to the whole, the real unity of theory and practice which hitherto appeared only unconsciously, so to speak, in the actions of the proletariat, now emerges clearly and consciously. At earlier stages, too, the actions of the proletariat were driven to a climax in a series of leaps whose continuity with the previous development could only subsequently become conscious and be understood as the necessary consequence of that development. (An instance of this is the political form of the Commune of 1871.) In this case, however, the proletariat must take this step consciously. It is no wonder, therefore, that all those who remain imprisoned within the confines of capitalist thought recoil from taking this step and with all the mental energy at their disposal they hold fast to necessity which they see as a law of nature, as a "law of the repetition" of phenomena. Hence, too, they reject as impossible the emergence of anything that is radically new of which we can have no "experience." It was Trotsky in his polemics against Kautsky who brought out this distinction most clearly, although it had been touched upon in the debates of the war: "For the fundamental Bolshevist prejudice consists precisely in the idea that one can only learn to ride when one is sitting firmly on a horse." But Kautsky and his like are only significant as symptoms of the state of affairs: they symbolise the ideological crisis of the working class, they embody that moment of its development when it "once again recoils before the inchoate enormity of its own aims," and when it jibs at a task which it must take upon itself. Unless the proletariat wishes to share the fate of the bourgeoisie and perish wretchedly and ignominiously in the death-throes of capitalism, it must accomplish this task *in full consciousness.* *

KORSCH: PHILOSOPHY AND MARXISM

The following is excerpted from Korsch's *Marxism and Philosophy,* where Korsch argues against the "minimization of philosophical problems" by Marxists of the Second and Third Internationals. He attempts to reverse the tendency to see Marxism as a "pure" science merely reflecting social facts. He contraposes the dialectical materialism of Marx to the "vulgar-marxism" of the "epigones" of Marx such as Kautsky and the Austro-Marxists.

      The focus for Korsch's critique of economic determinism is the problematic of non-economic (or, in Marx's terms, "superstructural") forms like philosophy and religion. He suggests that Marx and Engels developed a "theory of social revolution that comprises all areas of society as a totality." The key term here is "totality". Like Lukács, Korsch borrows this Hegelian term to describe the complex, non-reductionist dialectical materialism that Marx inspired. Certain phenomena like philosophy and religion must not be minimized or reduced to linear reflections of economic circumstances; that reduction, according to Korsch, would fail to restore Marxism as an activist, revolutionary social science and would instead license a passive, disengaged type of theorizing.

      Korsch characterizes Marxism as a "revolutionary philosophy," drawing on *Theses on Feuerbach* (discussed in Chapter 1). He argues that for Marx the "abolition of philosophy did not mean . . . its simple negation," Instead, philosophy was to be comprehended as ideology that would only disappear with the abolition of capitalism. Korsch believed that Marx and Engels were never as reductionist as some of their followers; Marx stated that "philosophy could not be abolished without being realized."

      Korsch's analysis allowed later theorists like Horkheimer and Marcuse to amplify this insight into the dialectical complexity of advanced capitalism. Ideology came to have new, stronger powers of mystification, preventing the development of revolutionary class consciousness.

This transformation and development of Marxist theory has been effected under the peculiar ideological guise of a return to the pure teaching of original or true Marxism. Yet it is easy to understand both the reasons for this guise and the real character of the process which is concealed by it. What theoreticians like Rosa Luxemburg in Germany and Lenin in Russia have done, and are doing, in the field of Marxist theory is to liberate it from the inhibiting traditions of the Social Democracy of the second period. They thereby answer the practical needs of the new revolutionary stage of proletarian class struggle, for these traditions weighed "like a nightmare" on the brain of the working masses whose objectively revolutionary socio-economic position no longer corresponded to these evolutionary doctrines. The apparent revival of original Marxist theory in the Third International is simply a result of the fact that in a new revolutionary period not only the workers' movement itself, but the theoretical conceptions of communists which express it, must assume an

---

* From Georg Lukács, *History and Class Consciousness* (London: Merlin, 1971), pp. 304-314.

explicitly revolutionary form. This is why large sections of the Marxist system, which seemed virtually forgotten, are come to life again. It also explains why the leader of the Russian Revolution could write a book a few months before October in which he stated that his aim was "in the first place to restore the correct Marxist theory of the State." Events themselves placed the question of the dictatorship of the proletariat on the agenda as a practical problem. When Lenin placed the same question theoretically on the agenda at a decisive moment, this was an early indication that the internal connection of theory and practice within revolutionary Marxism had been consciously re-established.

A fresh examination of the problem of Marxism and philosophy would also seem to be an important part of this restoration. A negative judgement is clear from the start. The minimization of philosophical problems by most Marxist theoreticians of the Second International was only a partial expression of the loss of the practical, revolutionary character of the Marxist movement which found its general expression in the simultaneous decay of the living principles of dialectical materialism in the vulgar-marxism of the epigones. We have already mentioned that Marx and Engels themselves always denied that scientific socialism was any longer a philosophy. But it is easy to show irrefutably, by reference to the sources, that what the revolutionary dialecticians Marx and Engels meant by the opposite of philosophy was something very different from what it meant to later vulgar-marxism. Nothing was further from them than the claim to impartial, pure, theoretical study, above class differences, made by Hilferding and most of the other Marxists of the Second International. The scientific socialism of Marx and Engels, correctly understood, stands in far greater contrast to these pure sciences of bourgeois society (economics, history, or sociology) than it does to the philosophy in which the revolutionary movement of the Third Estate once found its highest theoretical expression. Consequently, one can only wonder at the insight of more recent Marxists who have been misled by a few of Marx's well-known expressions and by a few of the later Engels, into interpreting the Marxist abolition of philosophy as the replacement of this philosophy by a system of abstract and undialectical positive sciences. The real contradiction between Marx's scientific socialism and all bourgeois philosophy and sciences consists entirely in the fact that scientific socialism is the theoretical expression of a revolutionary process, which will end with the total abolition of these bourgeois philosophies and sciences, together with the abolition of the material relations that find their ideological expression in them.

A re-examination of the problem of Marxism and philosophy is therefore very necessary, even on the theoretical level, in order to restore the correct and full sense of Marx's theory, denatured and banalized by the epigones. However, just as in the case of Marxism and the State, this theoretical task really arises from the needs and pressures of revolutionary practice. In the period of revolutionary transition, after its seizure of power, the proletariat must accomplish definite revolutionary tasks in the ideological field, no less than in the political and economic fields—tasks which constantly interact with each other. The scientific theory of Marxism must become again what it was for the authors of the Communist Manifesto—not as a simple return but as a dialectical development: a theory of social revolution that comprises all areas of society as a totality. Therefore we must solve in a dialectically materialist fashion not only "the question of the relationship of the State to social revolution and of social revolution to the State" (Lenin), but also the "question of the relationship of ideology to social revolution and of social revolution to ideology." To avoid these questions in the period before the proletarian revolution leads to opportunism and creates a crisis within Marxism, just as avoidance of the problem of State and revolution in the Second International led to opportunism and indeed provoked a crisis in the camp of Marxism. To evade a definite stand on these ideological problems of the transition can have disastrous political results in the period after the proletarian seizure of State power, because theoretical vagueness and disarray can seriously impede a prompt and energetic approach to problems that then arise in the ideological field. The major issue of the relation of the proletarian revolution to ideology was no less neglected by Social Democrat theoreticians than the political problem of the revolutionary dictatorship of the proletariat. Consequently in this new revolutionary period of struggle it must be posed anew and the correct—dialectical and revolutionary—conception of original Marxism must be restored. This task can only be resolved by first investigating the problem which led Marx and Engels to the question of ideology: How is philosophy related to the social revolution of the proletariat and how is the social revolution of the proletariat related to philosophy? An answer to this question is indicated by Marx and Engels themselves and may be deduced from Marx's materialist dialectics. It will lead us on to a larger question: how is Marxist materialism related to ideology in general? . . .

It is essential for modern dialectical materialism to grasp philosophies and other ideological systems in theory as realities, and to treat them in practice as such. In their early period Marx and Engels began their whole revolutionary activity by struggling against the reality of philosophy; and it will be shown that, although later they did radically alter their view of how philosophical ideology was related to other forms within ideology as a whole, they always treated ideologies—including philosophy—as concrete realities and not as empty fantasies. . . .

The dialectical materialism of Marx and Engels is by its very nature a philosophy through and through, as formulated in the eleventh thesis on Feuerbach and in other published and unpublished writings of the period. It is a revolutionary philosophy whose task is to participate in the revolutionary struggles waged in all spheres of society against the whole of the existing order, by fighting in one specific area—philosophy. Eventually, it aims at the concrete abolition of philosophy as part of the abolition of bourgeois social reality as a whole, of which it is an ideal component. In Marx's words: "Philosophy cannot be abolished without being realized." Thus just when Marx and Engels were progressing from Hegel's dialectical idealism to dialectical materialism, it is clear that the abolition of philosophy did not mean for them its simple rejection. Even when their later positions are under consideration, it is essential to take it as a constant starting point that Marx and Engels were dialecticians before they were materialists. The sense of their materialism is distorted in a disastrous and irreparable manner if one forgets that Marxist materialism was dialectical from the very beginning. It always remained a historical and dialectical materialism, in contrast to Feuerbach's abstract-scientific materialism and all other abstract materialisms, whether earlier or later, bourgeois or vulgar-marxist. In other words, it was a materialism whose theory comprehended the totality of society and history, and whose practice overthrew it. It was therefore possible for philosophy to become a less central component of the socio-historical process for Marx and Engels, in the course of their development of materialism, than it had seemed at the start; this did in fact occur. But no really dialectical materialist conception of history (certainly not that of Marx and Engels) could cease to regard philosophical ideology, or ideology in general, as a material component of general socio-historical reality—that is, a real part which had to be grasped in materialist theory and overthrown by materialist practice. . . .

Economic ideas themselves only appear to be related to the material relations of production of bourgeois society in the way an image is related to the object it reflects. In fact they are related to them in the way that a specific, particularly defined part of a whole is related to the other parts of this whole. Bourgeois economics belongs with the material relations of production to bourgeois society as a totality. This totality also contains political and legal representations and their apparent objects, which bourgeois politicians and jurists—the "ideologues of private property" (Marx)—treat in an ideologically inverted manner as autonomous essences. Finally, it also includes the higher ideologies of the art, religion and philosophy of bourgeois society. If it seems that there are no objects which these representations can reflect, correctly or incorrectly, this is because economic, political, or legal representations do not have particular objects which exist independently either, isolated from the other phenomena of bourgeois society. To counterpose such objects to those representations is an abstract and ideological bourgeois procedure. They merely express bourgeois society as a totality in a particular way, just as do art, religion, and philosophy. Their ensemble forms the spiritual structure of bourgeois society, which corresponds to its economic structure, just as its legal and political superstructure corresponds to this same basis. All these forms must be subjected to the revolutionary social criticism of scientific socialism, which embraces the whole of social reality. They must be criticized in theory and overthrown in practice, together with the economic, legal and political structures of society and at the same time as them. Just as political action is not rendered unnecessary by the economic action of a revolutionary class, so intellectual action is not rendered unnecessary by either political or economic action. On the contrary it must be carried through to the end in theory and practice, as revolutionary scientific criticism and agitational work before the seizure of state power by the working class, and as scientific organization and ideological dictatorship after the seizure of state power. If this is valid for intellectual action against the forms of consciousness which define bourgeois society in general, it is especially true of philosophical action. Bourgeois consciousness necessarily sees itself as apart from the world and independent of it as pure critical philosophy and impartial science, just as the bourgeois State and Bourgeois Law appear to be above society. This consciousness must be philosophically fought by the revolutionary materialistic dialectic, which is the philosophy of the working class. This struggle will only end when the whole of existing society and its economic basis have been totally overthrown in practice, and this consciousness has been totally surpassed and abolished in theory. "Philosophy cannot be abolished without being realized."*

---

* From Karl Korsch, *Marxism and Philosophy* (New York: Monthly Review Press, 1970), pp. 67-71, 72-73, 75-77, 96-97.

HORKHEIMER: TRADITIONAL AND CRITICAL THEORY

In essays from the 1930s, many of which were published in the journal of the Frankfurt Institute for Social Research, *Zeitschrift für Sozialforschung,* Max Horkheimer attempted to develop a systematic critical theory, preserving Lukács and Korsch's emphasis on the importance of ideology and class consciousness. Horkheimer returned to Marx's concept of the dialectical relationship between theoretical knowledge and political action, reiterating that action in any historical context must be inspired and informed by the theoretical comprehension of domination.

Although Horkheimer writes about social science in general, Marxist and non-Marxist, he implicitly launches an attack on that species of "automatic," scientific Marxism; critical theory intervenes in the historical process, refusing merely to reflect it. In this sense, Horkheimer returns to Marx's *Theses on Feuerbach* in suggesting that truth can only be assessed in terms of the accomplishment of certain political goals. Thus the ultimate goal of Marxian science is not merely the correct perception of reality but rather "the abolition of social injustice." Like Lukács and Korsch, Horkheimer counters the assumption that arose during the Second and Third Internationals that Marxism is "value-free," allegedly resembling the natural sciences.

The traditional idea of theory is based on scientific activity as carried on within the division of labor at a particular stage in the latter's development. It corresponds to the activity of the scholar which takes place alongside all the other activities of a society but in no immediately clear connection with them. In this view of theory, therefore, the real social function of science is not made manifest; it speaks not of what theory means in human life, but only of what it means in the isolated sphere in which for historical reasons it comes into existence. . . .

We must go on now to add that there is a human activity which has society itself for its object. The aim of this activity is not simply to eliminate one or other abuse, for it regards such abuses as necessarily connected with the way in which the social structure is organized. Although it itself emerges from the social structure, its purpose is not, either in its conscious intention or in its objective significance, the better functioning of any element in the structure. On the contrary, it is suspicious of the very categories of better, useful, appropriate, productive, and valuable, as these are understood in the present order, and refuses to take them as nonscientific presuppositions about which one can do nothing. . . .

Critical thinking is the function neither of the isolated individual nor of a sum-total of individuals. Its subject is rather a definite individual in his relation to other individuals and groups, in his conflict with a particular class, and finally, in the resultant web of relationships with the social totality and with nature. The subject is no mathematical point like the ego of bourgeois philosophy; his activity is the construction of the social present. Furthermore, the thinking subject is not the place where knowledge and object coincide, nor consequently the starting-point for attaining absolute knowledge. Such an illusion about the thinking subject, under which idealism has lived since Descartes, is ideology in the strict sense, for in it the limited freedom of the bourgeois individual puts on the illusory form of perfect freedom and autonomy. . . .

But it must be added that even the situation of the proletariat is, in this society, no guarantee of correct knowledge. The proletariat may indeed have experience of meaninglessness in the form of continuing and increasing wretchedness and injustice in its own life. Yet this awareness is prevented from becoming a social force by the differentiation of social structure which is still imposed on the proletariat from above and by the opposition between personal class interests which is transcended only at very special moments. . . .

When the optimism is shattered in periods of crushing defeat, many intellectuals risk falling into a pessimism about society and a nihilism which are just as ungrounded as their exaggerated optimism had been. They cannot bear the thought that the kind of thinking which is most topical, which has the deepest grasp of the historical situation, and is most pregnant with the future, must at certain times isolate its subject and throw him back upon himself. . . .

Above all, however, critical theory has no material accomplishments to show for itself. The change which it seems to bring about is not effected gradually, so that success even if slow might be steady. The growth in numbers of more or less clear-minded disciples, the influence of some among them on governments, the power position of parties which have a positive attitude towards this theory or at least do not outlaw it—all these are among the vicissitudes encountered in the struggle for a higher stage of man's life in community and are not found at the beginnings of the struggle. Such successes as these may even prove, later on, to have been only apparent victories and really blunders. . . .

The hostility to theory as such which prevails in contemporary public life is really directed against the transformative activity associated with critical thinking. Opposition starts as soon as theorists fail to limit themselves to verification and classification by means of categories which are as neutral as possible, that is, categories which are indispensable to inherited ways of life. Among the vast majority of the ruled there is the unconscious fear that theoretical thinking might show their painfully won adaptation to reality to be perverse and unnecessary. . . .

There are no general criteria for judging the critical theory as a whole, for it is always based on the recurrence of events and thus on a self-reproducing totality. Nor is there a social class by whose acceptance of the theory one could be guided. It is possible for the consciousness of every social stratum today to be limited and corrupted by ideology, however much, for its circumstances, it may be bent on truth. For all its insight into the individual steps in social change and for all the agreements of its elements with the most advanced traditional theories, the critical theory has no specific influence on its side, except concern for the abolition of social injustice. This negative formulation, if we wish to express it abstractly, it is the materialist content of the idealist concept of reason.*

THE FRANKFURT INSTITUTE FOR SOCIAL RESEARCH:
IDEOLOGY AND THE ECLIPSE OF SUBJECTIVITY

In the general introduction to this chapter, it was noted that the Frankfurt School

---

*From Max Horkheimer, *Critical Theory* (New York: Herder and Herder, 1972), pp. 197, 206, 207, 210, 211, 213, 214, 218, 219, 232, 242.

extended and transformed Lukács and Korsch's analysis of ideology and false class consciousness. Horkheimer, Marcuse, and Adorno believed that false consciousness in late capitalism was more widespread and located deeper in the individual's structure of needs than in the past, necessitating the abandonment of the model of working-class radicalism as the unchanging essence of Marxism.

Horkheimer and Adorno went as far as to assert that human individuality was "in decline," even that it was non-existent. They suggested that late capitalist society had been levelled into a flat, harmonious, "one-dimensional" order (as Marcuse was later to call it; see Chapter 4 on his ideas in this regard). "Reification" (in Lukács's sense) was perceived to be all-powerful, eliminating every feature of negative thought and political opposition.

Consciousness is gradually eliminated as ideology and reality become indistinguishable. Horkheimer and Adorno extended Lukács and Korsch's analysis of the new powers of ideology by arguing that there are no longer any credible criteria with which to distinguish false consciousness from true consciousness; subjectivity has been eliminated, holding open no promise of radical opposition.

This pessimism initially was not discontinuous with Lukács and Korsch's orientations in the 1920s; at the time of their publication in 1923, *History and Class Consciousness* and *Marxism and Philosophy* had nearly lost touch with the working class. Horkheimer and Adorno register theoretically the disappearance of the working class when they deepen the analysis of ideology. Ideology has engulfed all sources of class-radicalism, destroying the organic relation between theory and practice. Negative thinking, which for Lukács and Korsch could be harnessed by a potentially activist working class as a stimulant to self-conscious revolt, now—post-1923—appears out of touch with political agents. In this context, Hegelian Marxism fell into a disillusioned, but perhaps in that sense historically honest, account of the demise of critical consciousness.

The disillusionment of the Frankfurt School can be explained by examining their terminological revisions of Marx's concept of alienation: for Marx, alienation was the process of the estrangement of the working class from the means and products of capitalist labor; for Lukács, reification was the false consciousness of the working class about the causes and possible transformations of alienation (in Marx's sense); for the Frankfurt School, domination was the penetration of reification into the innermost layers of human personality, preventing not only class struggle but all self-emancipatory activity, both class-based and individual.

Under the influence of liberalism, of its doctrine of free competition, we have become fully accustomed to thinking of the Monad as an absolute, existing for and by itself. Therefore the achievement of sociology and, prior to that, of speculative social philosophy, in shaking this faith and in showing that the individual is itself socially constituted, cannot be evaluated too highly. Because sociology, as theory of society, developed during the individualistic era, it is hardly surprising that the mutual relations between the individual and society came to represent practically its central theme, and that the depth and fruitfulness of all sociological theory were measured by the extent to which it was capable of penetrating this relationship. But the dynamics of the inner composition of the individual were taken up only at the end of the theory.

Human life is essentially, and not merely accidentally, social life. But once this is recognized, the concept of the individual as the ultimate social entity becomes questionable. . . .

The faith in the radical independence of the individual from the whole is indeed mere illusion. The form of the individual itself is one proper to a society which maintains its life by means of the free market, where free and independent economic subjects come together. The more the individual is strengthened, the more the power of the society increases, due to the relationship of exchange which forms the individual. . . . [F]or the totally internalized individual, reality becomes appearance and appearance reality. In asserting his existence, which in fact is isolated and dependent on society, and indeed only conditionally tolerated, as absolute, the individual makes himself into an absolute cliché: the "individual" of Stirner. The spiritual medium of individuation, art, religion, science atrophies to become the private property of a few individuals, whose subsistence today is only at times assured by society. And society, which produced the development of the individual, now is developing by alienating and fragmenting this individual. At the same time, the individual, for his part, misconstrues the world, on which he is dependent down to his innermost being, mistaking it for his own. . . .

With the crisis of bourgeois society, the traditional concept of ideology itself appears to lose its subject matter. Spirit is split into critical truth, divesting itself of illusion, but esoteric and alienated from the direct social connections of effective action, on the one hand, and the planned administrative control of that which once was ideology, on the other. If one defines the heritage of ideology in terms of the totality of those intellectual products, which to a large extent occupy the consciousness of human beings today, then by this should be understood, not so much the autonomous spirit, blind to its own social implications, as the totality of what is cooked up in order to ensnare the masses as consumers and, if possible, to mold and constrain their state of consciousness. The socially conditioned false consciousness of today is no longer objective spirit, not in that sense either, as crystallized blindly and anonymously out of the social process, but rather is tailored scientifically to fit the society. That is the case with the products of the culture industry, film, magazines, illustrated newspapers, radio, television, and the best-seller literature of various types, among which biographical novels play a special role. That the elements in this ideology, uniform in itself, are not new, in contrast to the multiple techniques of its dissemination, but that many are actually calcified, is self-understood. This is linked to the traditional distinction already marked in Antiquity, between the higher and lower spheres of culture, in which the lower are rationalized and integrated with debased residues of the higher spirit. Historically the schemata of the contemporary culture industry can be traced back especially to the early period of English vulgar literature around 1700. This already has at its disposal most of the stereotypes which grin at us today from the screen and the television tube. But the social examination of this qualitatively novel phenomenon must not allow itself to be duped by references to the venerable age of its components and the arguments, based on this, of the satisfaction of alleged primal and fundamental needs. For it is not these components which matter, nor that the primitive traits of contemporary mass culture have remained the same throughout all the ages of a mankind deprived of adult rights, but rather that today they all have been placed under a central direction and that a closed system has been fabricated out of the whole. Escape from it is hardly tolerated anymore, the human beings are encircled from all sides, and by means of the achievements of a perverted social psychology—or, as it has been so aptly called, an inverted psychoanalysis—the regressive tendencies, which the growing social pressures release in any case, are reinforced. Sociology has taken over this sphere under the title of communication research, the study of the mass media, and has placed special emphasis on the reactions of the consumers and the structure of the interaction between them and the producers. That such investigations, which hardly seek to deny their parentage in market research, have a certain value as insights is not to be denied; however, it would appear to be of greater importance to treat the so-called mass media in the sense of the critique of ideology, rather than to remain content with their mere existing nature. The tacit affirmation of the latter approach, in its purely descriptive analysis, itself constitutes an element of the ideology.

In the face of the indescribable power which these media exercise over human beings today—and here sport, which for a long time already has gone over into ideology in the broader sense, must also be included—the concrete determination of their ideological content is of immediate urgency. This content produces a synthetic identification of the masses with the norms and the conditions which either stand anonymously in the background of the culture industry, or else are consciously propagated by it. All that is not in agreement is censured, conformism down into the most subtle impulses of the psyche is inculcated. In this the culture industry can pretend to the role of objective spirit insofar as it is linked at the time to those anthropological tendencies which are active in the awareness of those whom it services. It seizes on these tendencies, reinforces and confirms them while all that is rebellious is either deleted or explicitly condemned. The rigidity, devoid of any experience, of the thinking that predominates in mass society, is hardened still further, if possible, while at the same time a sharpened pseudorealism which in all its externals furnishes the precise reproduction of empirical reality, prevents any insight into the character of the preformation, in accord with the social control, of that which is offered. The more alienated from human beings the fabricated cultural products are, the more these human beings are persuaded that they are being confronted by themselves and their own world. What one sees on the television tube is similar to what is only too familiar, while the contraband of slogans, such as that all foreigners are suspect or that success and career offer the highest satisfaction in life are smuggled in as though they were evident and eternal truths. If one were to compress within one sentence what the ideology of mass culture adds up to, one would have to represent this as a parody of the injunction: "Become that which thou art": as the exaggerated duplication and justification of already existing conditions, and the deprivation of all transcendence and all critique. In this limiting of the socially effective spirit to once again presenting to the human beings only what in any case already constitutes the conditions of their existence, but at the same time proclaiming this present existence as its own norm, the people are confirmed in their faithless faith in pure existence.

Nothing remains then of ideology but that which exists itself, the models of a behavior which submits to the overwhelming power of the existing conditions. It is hardly an accident that the most influential philosophers today are those who attach themselves to the word "existence," as if the reduplication of mere present existence, by means of the highest abstract determinations which can be derived from this, were equivalent with its meaning. This corresponds to a great degree to the state within men's minds. They accept the ridiculous situation, which every day, in the face of the open possibility of happiness, threatens them with avoidable catastrophe; to be sure, they no longer accept it as the expression of an idea, in the way that they may still feel about the bourgeois system of national states, but make their peace in the name of realism, with that which is given. From the outset the individuals experience themselves as chess pieces, and yet become acquiescent to this. However, since new ideology hardly says more than that things are the way they are, its own falsity also shrinks away to the thin axiom that it could not be otherwise than it is. While human beings bow to this untruth, at the same time they still see through it secretly. The glorification of power and of the irresistible nature of present existence is at the same time the condition for divesting it of its magic. The ideology is no longer a veil, but the threatening face of the world. It is not only due to its involvement with propaganda, but due to its own character, that it goes over into terror. However, because ideology and reality are converging in this manner, because reality, due to the lack of any other convincing ideology, becomes its own ideology, it requires only a small effort of mind to throw off this all-powerful and at the same time empty illusion; but to make this effort seems to be the most difficult thing of all.*

GUIDE TO FURTHER READING

MARTIN JAY, *The Dialectical Imagination,* provides an excellent and lucid introduction to the development of the Frankfurt School between 1923 and 1950. He situates the School in the context of twentieth-century Marxism and thus he emphasizes the continuity between the Hegelian Marxism of Lukács and Korsch and Frankfurt "critical theory."

ISTVÁN MÉSZÁROS, *Lukács' Concept of the Dialectic,* deals with the theoretical orientation of Lukács by one of his former students.

GEORG LUKACS, *History and Class Consciousness,* also contains Lukács' 1967 Preface in which he engages in a thoroughgoing self-criticism.

KARL KORSCH, *Marxism and Philosophy,* contains an interesting 1930 Postscript in which Korsch attacks Lenin from the perspective of Korsch's 1923 text.

MAX HORKHEIMER, *Critical Theory,* comprises essays from the 1930s, including the programmatic "Traditional and Critical Theory."

Aspects of Sociology, written and edited by the Frankfurt Institute for Social Research, is a volume of essays from the 1940s and 1950s, applying the theoretical insights of Hegelian Marxism to the analysis of contemporary sociological concepts.

TRENT SCHROYER, *The Critique of Domination,* provides a useful, if somewhat technical and abstract, account of the rise of critical theory and its relationship to classical Marxism. Schroyer also attempts an application of recent critical theory to the American circumstance.

ALBRECHT WELLMER, *Critical Theory of Society,* introduces the themes of critical theory from the perspective of Jürgen Habermas, whose work is examined in Chapter 7.

---

*From Frankfurt Institute for Social Research, editor, *Aspects of Sociology* (London: Heinemann Educational Books, 1973), pp. 39, 45, 48, 199-203.

GEORGE LICHTHEIM, *Lukács,* is a brief account of Lukács' life and work, worthwhile as a basic introduction.

GEORGE LICHTHEIM, *From Marx to Hegel,* is a collection of essays on the Hegelian roots of philosophical Marxism.

On Critical Theory, edited by John O'Neill, presents reflections on the contemporary implications of critical theory.

Telos, a Quarterly Journal of Radical Social Theory, is an indispensable source of original works of Hegelian Marxism and commentaries on them. See especially *Telos* Nos. 10 and 11, which are special numbers on the work of Lukács. Also see *Telos* No. 26, a special number on the work of Korsch. *Telos* will prove useful to the advanced student of contemporary Marxism in that most important recent works on Marxism are reviewed and assessed in it.

DICK HOWARD and KARL KLARE, editors, *The Unknown Dimension,* is an advanced-level introduction to western Marxism after Lenin. While the pieces included in it are generally of a quite sophisticated tone, this work will serve the upper-division undergraduate well in pursuing recent developments in Marxism further than we have.

JÜRGEN HABERMAS, *Theory and Practice,* is another advanced-level collection of Habermas' writings that may be of significance to the more sophisticated student of recent Marxism.

QUESTIONS FOR FURTHER DISCUSSION

1. Why did Lukács and Korsch distance themselves *both* from German social democracy (especially in Kautsky's formulation of it) and from Marxism-Leninism?

2. Explain Lukács' concept of "reification."

3. Was Lukács correct to think that a "class conscious" proletariat could be realistically created? Did Lukács retain the right to instruct the working class about the truth of history and thus implicitly introduce an elitist concept of the revolutionary struggle?

4. What separated the original Frankfurt School from Lukács and Korsch?

5. What is Hegelian Marxism? Which elements of Hegel's philosophy did Marx preserve?

6. Is *History and Class Consciousness* a relevant work today, in advanced capitalist societies? Why?

7. Does the Frankfurt School's concept of "domination" differ from or add to Marx's concept of "alienation"? What is the historical lineage of the term "domination"?

Hegelian Marxism II: The Theory of Domination

HISTORICAL OVERVIEW

By the end of World War II, early monopoly capitalism had fully matured. The period from about 1945 to the 1960s was a period of relative harmony and productivity for international capitalism. During this period, the United States emerged as the most powerful industrial and military power on earth, rivalled only by the Soviet Union. The victory over Nazi Germany, Japan, and the other Axis nations generated industrial productivity that was vastly advanced over that of early capitalism. The war effort required a tremendous build-up of productive capacity that was turned to peaceful purposes after the war. Consumption for personal use came into its own following the war effort, benefitting consumers who during the war engaged in abstinence from most aspects of pleasurable consumption (submitting to tight rationing in most industrial nations) and also benefitting capitalists who saw their levels of profit rise following the changeover to a peace-time economy. The "internal contradictions" of capitalism that Marx had outlined about eighty years before were apparently a thing of the past, as capitalism rolled on harmoniously with only minor periods of recession and stagnation. Roosevelt's alliance between business, labor, government, and the military had now become a stock-in-trade of western capitalism. Class conflict had all but disappeared from the western scene, as members of the working class who returned from the war in the mid- and late 1940s found themselves much better off than before the war. The industrial boom of the late 1940s was enjoyed both by ruling class and working class. This period of relative stability for capitalism produced Marxisms that only remotely resembled that sketched by Marx and Engels. Members of the Frankfurt School of critical theory, such as Max Horkheimer, Theodor Adorno, and Herbert Marcuse, argued that the system had lost many of its "contradictions" and that false consciousness had become nearly universal. They doubted that revolutionary consciousness could be stimulated, *certainly not among the industrial working classes. Instead they retreated into a philosophical mode of Marxian critique that attempted not to lay political plans for action but rather to destroy the illusion that paradise had been found in American society of the 1950s.*

GENERAL INTRODUCTION

Lukács and Korsch developed a theory of class consciousness in response to the deterministic Marxism of the Second and Third Internationals. They wanted to reground Marxism in the dialectical assumptions of Marx in order to explain why the working class failed to revolt in the early 1920s.

Lukács and Korsch in their path-breaking 1923 works related class struggle to theoretical analyses that they felt could organize and direct working-class radicalism. This did not resemble Lenin's vanguard-concept of the Communist Party in that Lukács did not believe that Marxist intellectuals or Communist politicians were privileged possessors of historical truth. Lukács, like Luxemburg earlier, urged the working classes of western Europe to achieve consciousness of their own alienation and then, via sustained theoretical comprehension, to work towards a socialist alternative. Lukács refused to reduce the possibility of socialist change either to purely objective or subjective factors—either alienation *or* the theoretical comprehension of alienation.

The Frankfurt School theorists appropriated Lukács and Korsch's stress on the strategic implications of a "reified" human consciousness. We recall that reification in Lukács' use refers to the way in which the alienation of labor extends to consciousness itself, turning human relationships into relations between things, rendering workers unable to rebel against alienation.

Lukács was primarily concerned with explaining why the industrial proletariat failed to recognize and act upon the historical mission laid out for it by Marx. In this sense, Lukács took his theoretical and political reference from Marx's original crisis-theory, and accepted Marx's idea that the working class would ultimately respond to creeping immiserization by overthrowing the capitalist system. Korsch likewise took his bearings from Marxism and its hypothesis about the revolutionary centrality of the working class, although later in his career he became deeply dissatisfied with dialectical materialism and before his death composed his provocative "Ten Theses on Marxism," which systematically outlined his differences with original Marxism.

Interestingly, Lukács grew closer to orthodox Marxism as he aged. He repudiated his 1923 book *History and Class Consciousness* soon after its publication, arguing that the work was flawed by its idealist theory of knowledge. Lukács became increasingly orthodox politically as he lived through the creation of a socialist state in his native Hungary, rejecting his explosive 1923 work because it did not appear to "fit" the distinctly unrevolutionary atmosphere in post-war Hungary. Lukács' journey from revolutionary Marxism to a more conservative, or "apologetic," type of Marxism had disappointed many initially attracted to his earlier vigorous theorizing. In many ways, the personal career of Lukács closely parallels the career of western Marxism as a whole after 1919: some western Marxists became social democrats and parliamentarians, while others like Lukács shifted toward a state socialist vanguard Marxism.

The Frankfurt theorists managed to avoid both of these alternatives, instead producing their own peculiar synthesis of Marxian theoretical undercurrents. Although Horkheimer and Marcuse may have appeared to deviate radically from revolutionary Marxism, it is also true that they thought that they were rescuing Marxism from both social democratic reformism and "apologetic" state socialism. We concluded our last chapter by noting that there seemed to be significant discontinuity between Lukács and Korsch's brand of Marxism and that of the Frankfurt School. While the "critical theorists" took their orientation directly from the Hegelian reconstruction of Marxism, they arrived at a new, pessimistic synthesis that only barely resembled old-style Marxism, whether of Marx or Lukács and Korsch.

Political history here is required to explain the Frankfurt School synthesis that differed so much from what had gone before. As we noted in Chapter 2, the year 1919 represented the final splitting of western and Soviet-style Marxism. The possibilities of revolutionary theory and politics that abounded during the Second International, in spite of conflicts and confusions within it, were drastically diminished by the collapse of that International caused in large part by the outbreak of World War I. By the end of the war, and certainly by 1919 when Moscow's influence in the newly-minted Third or Communist International had become strikingly evident, it was clear that western social democracy no longer had the same revolutionary potential that it enjoyed during the Second International. There were three reasons for this: (a) Above all, early capitalism was beginning successfully to integrate the European working classes into the political and economic system, thus blunting class conflict; (b) the nationalist ardor aroused by the war demonstrated the weakness of internationalist Marxism; (c) the Soviet "experiment" threatened to discredit western Marxism by emphasizing armed insurrection and not the long-term structural change projected by Marx.

Theorists of the Second International like Kautsky believed that parliamentary democracy was a necessary step along the way towards the final overthrow of capitalism. Kautsky and the Austro-Marxists combined, as we noted earlier, economic determinism with a democratic political ideology. This emerged from Kautsky's perception that the revolution in western Europe would not be violent or cataclysmic but would build, in almost evolutionary fashion, upon liberal democracy. This is why Kautsky and others who shared his theoretical orientation struggled to bring into being a full-fledged democratic workers' movement. Only by doing so could capitalism slide gradually towards socialism.

Kautsky's hope was destroyed by the nationalist sentiments of European working classes and by the failure of capitalism to reach the end of its "natural life." *There proved to be no automatic tendency of capitalism to slide gently towards socialism,* as Kautsky had believed (and according to his scientific Marxism). For the three reasons mentioned above, the working class ignored the historical mission laid out by Marx, Engels, and later by Kautsky.

Theorists like Luxemburg thought they knew all along that this "automatic Marxism" could never work. Lukács and Korsch followed Luxemburg in this respect, rejecting both Bernsteinian revisionism and Kautskyian scientific Marxism.

While Lukács developed the theory of class consciousness, the Frankfurt thinkers rebuilt the entire Marxian edifice. Lukács did not tamper with this edifice, defending Marx's non-deterministic theory against members of the Second International who felt that Marxism was a "pure" social science, devoid of political commitments in the sense that Marxism describes inevitable capitalist breakdown and does not need to further that breakdown.

The Frankfurt theorists did not feel that Marxist theory was viable in the context of an ever-changing capitalism that after about 1920 appeared to be more harmonious than ever, better able to fend off the threat of economic depression and better able to appease the working class by raising the material standard of living for most. Marxists in western Europe and North America had the choice of (a) following the Soviet, Marxist-Leninist model, (b) joining the parliamentary struggle to elect social democratic and labor parties in the West or (c) fundamentally modifying the Marxian theory of socialist transformation.

It may be apparent that strategies (b) and (c) are not mutually exclusive. However few Hegelian Marxists believe that parliamentary strategies hold much promise of achieving radical goals, for reasons explained in Chapter 2. Social democracy, the theory and ideology of most parliamentary socialists today, tends to accommodate itself to the reality of capitalism. Increasingly western industrial states are becoming "mixed economies," combining private ownership in some spheres with public ownership in others. Although some economies are more "mixed" than others, it is still nearly impossible for social democratic parties to campaign seriously for the fundamental socialist transformation of capitalism. Most workers appear to be satisfied with the balance between public and private control, with the 1970s seeing conservatism spreading throughout western Europe and North America triggered by deepening mistrust of big government. (However, it is our argument in Chapter 7 that this cynicism about government and bureaucracy could conceivably, if linked to a Marxist understanding, blossom forth as a hybrid North American Marxist-populism.)

Many workers feel that mixed economies should not relinquish their fundamental grounding in capitalist ideology. Social democratic parties must increasingly bend to these shifts in public opinion. For example, the Democratic Party in the United States (which traditionally has embodied a watered-down social democratic theory, taking its inspiration from Franklin Roosevelt's crusading progressivism in the 1930s and 1940s) has become far more conservative politically in order to create a new coalition of working-class and middle-class voters.

While social democracy in the period of the Second International was truly revolutionary (if often strategically confused, because of its confused allegiance to original Marxism), social democracy today, in the United States, Canada, Sweden, and Great Britain, has become an "establishment" ideology, although not for that reason devoid of progressive, even radical, ideological components (as we argue in Chapter 7). A Marxist would prefer Britain's mixed economy, built upon an infrastructure of civil liberties and a democratic tradition, to the centralized "command economy" of the present-day Soviet Union. But is it necessary, many critical Marxists would ask, to settle for a mixed economy with all of its vestiges of industrial capitalism when there may be other, more truly revolutionary alternatives? It is precisely this question to which we will address ourselves in Chapter 5, when we go outside the ambit of western Marxism in seeking viable concepts of Marxist change taken from dissident Marxian humanist voices in eastern Europe.

The Frankfurt School thinkers did not believe that social democracy was a revolutionary doctrine, especially in the period after the Second World War. The inspiring victory over fascism served to strengthen an emerging type of international capitalism. The second generation of Hegelian Marxists felt that World War II allowed western capitalist nations to avoid the deep economic crisis Marx felt would be unavoidable in a simpler form of purely domestic capitalism that had not yet reached the global monopoly stage. The war between the Allied and Axis nations created the conditions for the vast expansion of the western capitalist state, both in terms of international "economic imperialism" and in terms of its domestic scope and reach. Early capitalism was finally transformed into "late" or "monopoly" capitalism following World War II in the sense that the political state came to play a much more direct and important role in economic life, and in the sense that monopolization in many sectors of the economy proceeded unabated.

The bourgeois state came into its own with the victory over fascism, realizing its capacity to mobilize productive forces and at the same time to create an expanded realm of future consumption. The industrial infrastructure quickly created to beat back the Nazi advances was transformed into a more consumer-oriented production system following the war. In fact, consumers who had to undergo a degree of abstinence from personal consumption during the war were no longer content to remain "deprived" once the war had been won. Late capitalism was distinguished in large measure by its hugely expanded markets for goods and services, both in international and domestic spheres.

The rise of the capitalist state, which intervened in stimulating and managing certain features of economic activity, coupled with the rise of a hungry western consumer, created new political conditions in the west. The industrial working class no longer seemed the likely agent of revolutionary struggle, especially in the United States where the post-war boom contributed greatly to working class affluence and conservatism. Western Marxists were confronted with the strange reality of a type of capitalism that appeared to have "solved" the problem of class conflict, having achieved class compromise. World War II created economic and political conditions in which working class and middle class alike could benefit from newfound productive capacity. In the United States, the Eisenhower years were among the least revolutionary periods in the history of the nation.

Many western Marxists had emigrated from Nazi Germany and other European trouble spots before the war broke out. The so-called Frankfurt School moved its base of operations from Frankfurt to New York City, bringing with it not only the best radical thinkers from Europe but also vestiges of the Marxian tradition that had survived the demise of the Second International. Theorists like Max Horkheimer and Herbert Marcuse were personally confronted with the new political and economic situation in the United States as they bore first-hand witness to the emergence of late capitalism.

Hegelian Marxism, conceived in Budapest and in the context of the Central European political situation around 1915 and 1920, changed significantly as it became Americanized in the 1940s and 1950s. The theory of domination was transformed to fit the new reality of government intervention in post-war capitalist economies, to fit the new reality of apparent affluence for all classes, and to fit the new reality of expanded consumerism. Horkheimer, Marcuse, and Adorno believed that if revolutionary hopes were to be reinvigorated the entire theory of internal contradictions developed by Marx would have to be revised drastically. Just how drastic this revision was going to be was not immediately apparent. Essays by Horkheimer and his associates in the 1920s and 1930s, before the American exodus, were reminiscent of the more orthodox Marxism of Lukács and Korsch; the Frankfurt "critical theory" initially appeared to be the German equivalent of Lukács' Hungarian Marxism, firmly grounded in Marx's theory of class struggle. However, as Hegelian Marxists crossed the Atlantic and surveyed the new post-war reality of the United States, the remnants of original Marxism began to recede and new concepts were developed to describe these profoundly strange realities.

Lukács explicitly argued in his *History and Class Consciousness* that economic exploitation was deepened by what he termed "reification," or self-inflicted alienation. Lukács, as we noted, analyzed reasons for revolutionary delay in Western and Central Europe. His theory of reification provided answers to the question of why the working class did not revolt in the way Marx expected.

The Frankfurt thinkers, however, took Lukács' insight much further than Lukács' intended. They applied the theory of reification to the subjective human being as well as to the working class as a whole (as Lukács did). On this basis, Horkheimer and Adorno created a theory of domination that joined Marx's theory of alienation with Lukács' concept of reification. Domination expresses the way in which the human being fails to perceive his own alienation and relishes capitalist productivity and its material abundance. Domination is alienation that the person "does" to himself in a condition of false consciousness.

Marx himself offered the concept of false consciousness to explain the powerful hold of religion and a philosophy on the exploited class. He suggested that every form of class society produces a system of ideological justification. In the early capitalist system, bourgeois political economy and social science served as a type of ideology that could explain social reality to exploited human beings, showing them that capitalism is a just and even an inevitable social order. Lukács' theory of reification was heavily indebted to Marx's theory of ideology, as we noted in Chapter 3.

Hegelian Marxism in its first, European, phase analyzed ideology as a set of deliberate distortions of social reality, subject to rational scrutiny and unmasking. Hegelian Marxism in its second, American, phase saw ideology not as a system of deliberate distortions of an exploitative reality but as a form of consciousness unable to grasp the "reality" of modern capitalism. This is a crucial difference in emphasis. Lukács' implied that reification, or false consciousness of the working class, could be dispelled by rationally explaining the historical mission of the proletariat. The Frankfurt thinkers, by contrast, did not believe that a deeply institutionalized false consciousness could be eradicated merely by rational analysis and critique. Lukács understood that early capitalist ideology was intrinsically weak because early capitalism was rooted in sharp class conflict and deepening crises. Later capitalism, however, was not as evidently a system of social and economic injustice inasmuch as all classes were further integrated into the class compromise that emerged with the Second World War. It was more difficult to dispel ideology because it was no longer clear that "reality" was as personally damaging and alienating as in earlier stages of capitalism.

Reification in Lukács' sense could be eliminated by careful, rational analysis. Domination resisted this careful analysis because it appeared not to be domination at all. The Frankfurt theorists were saying that it is nearly impossible to convince workers that they are alienated when their economic lot is clearly improving. This transformation of the concept of alienation into domination provided the dynamic of theoretical reinterpretation that occurred between the two distinct phases of Hegelian Marxism.

The earliest work of members of the Frankfurt school involved the psychological study of the "authoritarian personality," which ultimately emerged in the famous work *The Authoritarian Personality* published during the early 1950s after Theodor Adorno had relocated in southern California. The "studies in prejudice," as they were called, connected the earlier European phase of the Frankfurt School with the later American phase. At issue was the type of human being who agrees to go along with fascist political ideology, who even realizes aspects of his innermost personality through identification with Hitler figures. Erich Fromm, who was closely allied with other more psychologically oriented members of the early Frankfurt School, carried out important theoretical and empirical investigations that gave substance to Adorno and Horkheimer's speculations about the bourgeois origins of fascism.

This interest in an authoritarian personality became the linchpin of a new type of Hegelian Marxism. Horkheimer and Adorno argued that the appearance of late capitalism, based upon the post-war constellation of big government, business, and organized labor, created conditions in which human psychology became an increasingly important political form. In Chapter 6 we will examine in greater detail Herbert Marcuse's synthesis of psychoanalysis and Marxism.

The study of bourgeois authoritarianism provided the theoretical underpinning of a new theory of capitalist domination. We recall that the Frankfurt theorists took Lukács' concept of reification to its ultimate conclusions, thus changing Marxian theory substantially. This took the concrete form of the concept of the "decline of the individual," as Horkheimer characterized it in lectures given in New York in the 1940s. Where Lukács felt that the working class had temporarily declined as a theoretically and politically conscious radical agent, the latter-day Hegelian Marxists like Horkheimer and Marcuse argued that the individual human being had itself "declined," or fallen under the sway of what they called "domination." Lukács' declining proletariat was temporarily unable to break through ideological mystifications fostered by capitalist ideologists and even by certain reformist social democrats like Bernstein and "pure Marxists" like Kautsky. The declining human being, in Frankfurt School terms, was unable to separate the appearances of late capitalist social reality from the alienating character of that reality.

Declining, dominated consciousness was a product of a new combination of social forces peculiar to a more advanced stage of capitalism. Marx theorized that as capitalism developed greater productive capacity it would become more crisis-prone, provoking renewed class-radicalism. Latter-day Hegelian Marxism takes exactly the opposite position: As long as capitalism does not collapse, the longer it survives, the *less* chance there is of crisis and subsequent revolutionary transformation.

The emergence of what some sociologists have called "mass society" signalled the end of traditional communities and institutions. The individual human being was left on his own, no longer insulated by protective institutions like the church or family. The decline of the individual, in the face of these huge, impersonal realities produced by late capitalist society, was hastened by the decline of the family. Curiously the Frankfurt thinkers did not believe that the nuclear family, which developed in early industrial Europe, was merely an agent of capitalism, producing industrious little workers and keeping women and children repressed. Instead the family was seen as one of the few sheltered harbors for human beings threatened by the facelessness and soullessness of bureaucratic-capitalist organizations.

The family declined, according to Horkheimer and his associates, because the father lost the economic independence he enjoyed under entrepreneurial capitalism (e.g., the industrious, self-determining small businessman). This economic independence allowed the father to mediate between the family group and society as a whole: the father was perceived by family members as a strong, self-sufficient, basically authoritarian figure who could protect the family against manipulation by external social forces. The family in early capitalism was a haven of escape from workaday social reality, if only in the evenings and on weekends. Gradually, however, the entrepreneur was phased out in favor of the "organization man" who worked not for himself but within the confines of a complex bureaucracy. The father was no longer independent in the sense that he succeeded or failed financially through his own effort; he was now, in advanced capitalism, merely a wage earner, dependent on the good graces of his immediate bosses and on the financial stability of the company as a whole.

The concept of the decline of individual autonomy is peculiar to the period of consolidation of early monopoly capitalism, roughly stretching from 1930 until the 1950s and early 1960s. During this period capitalism turned the individual into a virtually mindless and for that reason unquestioning and willing consumer, a citizen who took orders and helped capitalist society function efficiently. The concept of domination is useful in describing the development of early monopoly capitalism during a period when there was a good deal of ideological conformity and economic expansion. We will argue in our final chapter that this period of consolidation has passed and that there are new opportunities for radical transformation.

The working class in the United States has been primarily oriented to the Democratic Party, embracing the most tepid of social democratic ideologies. However, in western Europe, especially in France and Italy, the working class today is confronted with a fundamental choice between the Communist tradition and social democratic parties. Although there have been a number of important American Marxists (like Daniel De Leon), the Marxian tradition in North America has never been significant, thus deflating the potential class consciousness of the working class and forcing workers into the fold of the Democratic Party. During Franklin Roosevelt's presidency, the American working class was brought further into the capitalist system through traditional social democratic means. Roosevelt's progressivism was all that the American working class could hope for in light of the absence of a radical left-wing tradition in the ranks of American labor. Roosevelt was an extremely shrewd proponent of a "mixed economy," although in the basically conservative American context his opponents charged that he was a Marxist and Communist! Roosevelt struck a long-lasting alliance between American business and American labor, all the while expanding the scope and power of the federal government. The class compromise that emerged, between business, labor and government, is the modern-day essence of social democracy, nearer capitalism than socialism.

The lack of radical political consciousness in the American working class forced the Frankfurt thinkers to reappraise the crucial assumptions and categories of Marxism. This in no way implies that Horkheimer, Marcuse, and Adorno abandoned Marxist ideals, for the Frankfurt thinkers remained more orthodox in their Marxist aspirations than other, less philosophically inclined radicals willing to compromise their socialist ideals and join the parliamentary process. The Frankfurt thinkers were unable to "see" the possibility of socialist change in the American context because they were oriented to European modes of Marxism. Critical theory *sounded* so pessimistic because the Frankfurt thinkers could recognize little in the American context that corresponded to their experience of European working-class radicalism. In this sense, their concept of a "declining," increasingly dominated, and coopted human being indicated merely that a European human being did not exist in American mass society in the 1950s, which tended to level and not enhance cultural and intellectual pursuits. The Frankfurt thinkers often implied that Americans, unlike bourgeois Europeans, knew nothing else besides consumption.

An American Marxism might preserve the radical populist spirit of American political culture, as we argue in Chapter 7. This issue demands careful consideration because we wish to argue explicitly, in our concluding chapter, that Marxists must abandon dated models of crisis and instead seize upon examples of existing socialist revolt in creating new visions and models of radicalism. Soviet Marxism-Leninism has been unable to move towards socialist democracy and away from centralized authoritarianism because Russian political culture has never enjoyed a liberal democratic tradition.

The possibility of non-authoritarian Marxism requires the pre-existence of a democratic political culture. The United States might be precisely the proving ground for such a socialist model, given the deep-seated tradition of grass-roots democracy and public mistrust of centralized, bureaucratized government. In this regard, movements to decentralize Marxism might arise in the American context before they arise in more traditional and hierarchical European societies. When we examine "individualized Marxism" in Chapter 6, we will come to grips with Herbert Marcuse's fascinating attempt to Americanize Hegelian Marxism in precisely the sense that we would recommend, applying Marxian categories to the New Left in 1960s America.

This may be to say nothing more than that the theory developed by the Frankfurt thinkers in the 1940s and 1950s, stressing the decline of the dominated individual, has become dated. When we look back at the political culture that existed during the Eisenhower presidency we might recognize precisely the symptoms of deep-seated domination that Adorno and Horkheimer attacked. The quiescent period of the 1950s in the United States and western Europe was a period of consolidation for capitalism following the turbulent war years, which, we have argued, were a significant watershed for capitalism, prolonging its life and requiring new theories of crisis and models of class-radicalism.

Other aspects of the analysis of domination developed by the Frankfurt School theorists in the 1940s and 1950s include their critique of instrumental rationality. This type of rationality is thought to be the *modus operandi* of large, modern-day corporations, the terms of which were first outlined systematically by the German sociologist Max Weber, who suggested that the rise of an industrialized society requires the abandonment of traditional forms of political authority such as religious and charismatic rule. Weber suggested that bureaucratic organizations require a type of instrumental rationality characterized by a preoccupation with efficiency and productivity. Weber described this type of rationality as one that distinguished between means and ends. He argued that there has to be a certain separation of means and ends in industrial organizations, a distinction between the accomplishment of tasks and the intrinsic or political value of those tasks (e.g., to build a bridge there need to be engineers who carefully plan the details of construction; these engineers as engineers do not worry about whether the bridge is paid for by local tax-monies, by the federal government, or by a user tax collected at a toll station: They simply focus on building the bridge with competence). Weber was *not* oblivious to non-instrumental values, such as the question about how the bridge should be financed. He believed, rather, that the questions of financing and competent construction should be separated in the interests of technical efficiency.

Weber noted that this type of instrumental rationality, involving the separation of means and ends, tends to become an overwhelming concern in industrial civilizations. Weber has been described as a "nostalgic liberal," a creature and theorist of industrial capitalism, yet also nostalgic for certain qualitative dimensions of culture threatened by the relentless march of industrial progress.

The Frankfurt interpretation of Marxism rests heavily upon the twin concepts of domination and instrumental rationality. We have said that domination is alienation that the person "does" to himself in a condition of false consciousness; instrumental rationality is the framework within which domination is carried out. The ordinary citizen, thus, is seen to be motivated not by a clear conception of ultimate purposes or a systematic definition of personal happiness but merely by the spirit of efficiency and technical competence. This type of person consumes merely in order to possess, not in the interests of improving his life in a clearly demonstrable way. Consumption in late capitalist society becomes an addiction, far exceeding the requirements of a relatively comfortable lifestyle and instead being carried out for its own sake and for the sake merely of possessing things. Similarly, the motivation to work has become means-oriented. Most citizens of capitalistic societies work not for themselves in their own businesses but for large institutions that demand a certain output in the framework of a clearly defined and hierarchically arranged set of responsibilities. Human beings work not to fulfill a deep need to express themselves creatively but to achieve a certain consumerist lifestyle made possible by the expectation of a wage.

Horkheimer and his associates believed that "instrumentality" had virtually overtaken the profit motive as the moving force of late capitalism. This suggested that capitalist society could no longer be seen as class-stratified in Marx's sense for there was no simple opposition (or contradiction) between capitalist and working classes. Instead, there was a growing middle stratum of white-collar workers who were well paid but who did not own or control their production, being the proverbial "organization men." If conflicts between classes did not exist, or at least if they were muted by a rapidly expanding Gross National Product, then Marx's theory of socialist revolution cried out for amendment. It was not enough to wait in anticipation for falling levels of profit and the working-class insurrection that Marx felt would be catalyzed as a result.

The critique of instrumental rationality was developed to fill the vacuum left by the evident disintegration of Marx's theory of class struggle. There are those who argue that the critique of instrumental rationality ultimately failed because it was a "negative" theory, that is, it failed to provide directives to socialist class-radicalism. During the late 1940s and 1950s, there were evidently few revolutionary agents to replace the proletariat. The Frankfurt critique of capitalist mass society, hinged upon efficiency and self-preserving domination, was a negative critique because they could provide few practical directives to workers apparently satisfied with 1950s capitalism.

The critical theory developed by the Frankfurt thinkers has also been accused of a certain philosophical abstractness. Their theory of domination and critique of instrumentality were cast in a deeply philosophical language unfamiliar to many Americans untrained in recondite Continental philosophy and social theory. Further, many of the concepts employed by the Frankfurt thinkers defied precise operationalization and empirical testing. The very idea of domination—self-inflicted alienation—implies that the human being does not know what is good for him, or alternatively, bad for him. This has been a fundamental theme in the theory of the Frankfurt School surfacing in many different formulations. Their critique of domination and instrumental rationality is firmly rooted in the assumption that late capitalism has produced "false needs," as Herbert Marcuse characterized them in his 1964 work *One-Dimensional Man*.

We noted earlier how human satisfaction in advanced capitalism is often equated with consumption. The Frankfurt theorists argued that this conception of human needs was imposed on human beings by dominant economic interests, creating a type of infinite consumer of commodities. They believed that the human being was manipulated to want commodities he did not truly need. The theory of false needs rests on the argument that consumption in advanced capitalist society diverts the human being from his own alienation in the sphere of work. The progressive rationalization of capitalism, in Weber's sense of the proliferation of rules to govern human activity and in the French sociologist Émile Durkheim's sense of the increasing division of labor, strips the human being of deep creative purpose. Marx in his early writings indicated that alienation could only be reversed if the person controlled his entire existence, his work as well as his leisure. Marx refused to distinguish work from leisure because he felt that it was possible to emancipate human beings for lives of creative work, i.e., for lives in which work and leisure are virtually identical.

Domination is the outcome of "administered leisure"; false needs are the specific form of domination in late capitalist society. The needs are false because the human being is unable to relate means and ends in his own existence, failing to translate personal consumption into human satisfaction. False needs, thus, are intrinsically unsatisfying, failing adequately to compensate the worker for having to endure alienated labor.

We are left with the Frankfurt School's critique of domination, based upon the concepts of false needs, instrumental rationality, and declining individuality. While their critique may accurately capture aspects of contemporary domination, it says little about how workers might begin to transform advanced capitalism. Implicitly human beings with false needs can do nothing to overcome their domination; but Marxism relates alienation and domination, and the crisis-tendencies they produce, to the possibility of class-radicalism. The Frankfurt School's critique of domination fails if it cannot go beyond abstract concepts that indicate only that domination *exists*. Below we will examine various ways in which human beings are already beginning to overcome "false needs" and use that type of evidence, and those examples, to redevelop Marxian theory. The critical theory of the Frankfurt School should not be discarded out of hand but stands as a remembrance of early monopoly capitalism when the capitalist totality conspired to dominate the singular, defenseless human being.

ADORNO: NEGATIVE DIALECTICS

Adorno's 1966 work *Negative Dialectics* stands at the crossroads between early and late monopoly capitalism, between its crisis-free and crisis-ridden modes. According to our earlier terminological discussion, the dividing line between these two periods is less a precise chronological one than a substantive, structural one. The Frankfurt School's critique of instrumental rationality was developed during capitalism's international expansion and consolidation between about 1930 and 1945. During this period, capitalism expanded territorially, colonizing underdeveloped nations to exploit their natural resources and to create new markets for manufactured commodities; in addition to territorial expansion, however, capitalism invaded the consciousness of western man, creating an infinite consumer and passive citizen, willing to live in accord with its ideological principles.

In this context, Theodor Adorno, Max Horkheimer, and Herbert Marcuse argued that traditional Marxism had become largely irrelevant owing to the new reality of domination. They suggested that alienation, in the original Marxian sense, had undergone a metamorphosis of sorts as it had become a psychological as well as strictly class-based phenomenon. In the general introduction above, we discussed the contributions made by theorists from the Frankfurt School in their attempt to comprehend the political nature of early monopoly capitalism. In Chapter 3, we developed a number of important differences between Lukács, Korsch, and the Frankfurt School. Now we will examine in greater detail the Frankfurt School's analysis of domination.

Adorno's *Negative Dialectics* summarizes many of the theoretical assumptions of the Frankfurt School. "Theory does not contain answers to everything; it reacts to the world, which is faulty to the core." Adorno suggested that Marx's dialectical method must become negative, revealing and criticizing the domination of the human being without exploring possible strategies of class-based emancipation. Theory was meant to be an exercise in "negative dialectics," relentlessly speaking the truth about the pervasive character of instrumental rationality without pretending that there are easy, recipe-like solutions to the problem of domination.

Ideology lies in wait for the mind which delights in itself like Nietzsche's Zarathustra, for the mind which all but irresistibly becomes an absolute to itself. Theory prevents this. It corrects the naïve self-confidence of the mind without obliging it to sacrifice its spontaneity, at which theory aims in its turn. For the difference between the so-called subjective part of mental experience and its object will not vanish by any means, as witness the necessary and painful exertions of the knowing subject. In the unreconciled condition, nonidentity is experienced as negativity. From the negative, the subject withdraws to itself, and to the abundance of its ways to react. Critical self-reflection alone will keep it from a constriction of this abundance, from building walls between itself and the object, from the supposition that its being-for-itself is an in-and-for-itself. The less identity can be assumed between subject and object, the more contradictory are the demands made upon the cognitive subject, upon its unfettered strength and candid self-reflection.

Theory and mental experience need to interact. Theory does not contain answers to everything; it reacts to the world, which is faulty to the core.*

"Philosophy, which once seemed obsolete, lives on because the moment to realize it was missed." This sentiment opens the book and speaks directly to Marx's dream of realizing philosophy in the world as communism. Further, Adorno suggests that critical philosophy must not measure its value only in terms of its relevance to revolutionary praxis (which has all but disappeared) but rather it must become self-reflective and self-critical.

Philosophy, which once seemed obsolete, lives on because the moment to realize it was missed. The summary judgment that it had merely interpreted the world, that resignation in the face of reality had crippled it in itself, becomes a defeatism of reason after the attempt to change the world miscarried. Philosophy offers no place from which theory as such might be concretely convicted of the anachronisms it is suspected of, now as before. Perhaps it was an inadequate interpretation which promised that it would be put into practice. Theory cannot prolong the moment its critique depended on. A practice indefinitely delayed is no longer the forum for appeals against self-satisfied speculation; it is mostly the pretext used by executive authorities to choke, as vain, whatever critical thoughts the practical change would require.

Having broken its pledge to be as one with reality or at the point of realization, philosophy is obliged ruthlessly to criticize itself.†

In Adorno's formulation the dialectical method lost its praxis component. We recall that Marx, Lukács, and Korsch argued that there must be interaction and feedback between theory and praxis, the one stimulating class consciousness and the other carrying out the revolutionary deed. In the work of the Frankfurt School, theory was gradually divorced from praxis in the original Marxian sense as thinkers like Adorno became increasingly convinced that alienation had spread dangerously beyond the economic domain. In Adorno's eyes, the most plausible revolutionary resistance against domination lay in a critical, negative philosophy that relentlessly exposed the untruth of early monopoly capitalism (and, similarly, of eastern European state socialism). "Thought, as such, . . . is an act of negation." This negation tends "beyond that which merely exists." Like Hegel, Adorno felt that thought could rescue the ideal of freedom from bland reduction into positive homilies about the formal justice of liberal-capitalist society. "Accompanying irreconcilable thoughts is the hope for reconcilement"; this is Adorno's peculiar way of stating his case for the revolutionary resistance to be attained by critical philosophy: by being scrupulously objective about the reality of pervasive domination, thought could escape a dominating and corrupting system of power.

Thought as such, before all particular contents, is an act of negation, of resistance to that which is forced upon it; this is what thought has inherited from its archetype, the relation between labor and material. Today, when ideologues tend more than ever to encourage thought to be positive, they cleverly note that positivity runs precisely counter to thought and that it takes friendly persuasion by social authority to accustom thought to positivity. The effort implied in the concept of thought itself, as the counterpart of passive

---

*From Theodor Adorno, *Negative Dialectics* (New York: Seabury, 1973), pp. 30-31.

†From Theodor Adorno, *Negative Dialectics* (New York: Seabury, 1973, p. 3.

contemplation, is negative already—a revolt against being importuned to bow
to every immediate thing. Critical germs are contained in judgment and inference, the thought forms without which not even the critique of thought can do:
they are never definite without simultaneously excluding what they have failed
to achieve, and whatever does not bear their stamp will be denied—although
with questionable authority—by the truth they seek to organize. The judgment
that a thing is such and such is a potential rebuttal to claims of any relation of its
subject and predicate other than the one expressed in the judgment. Thought
forms tend beyond that which merely exists, is merely "given." The point which
thinking aims at its material is not solely a spiritualized control of nature. While
doing violence to the object of its syntheses, our thinking heeds a potential that
waits in the object, and it unconsciously obeys the idea of making amends to the
pieces for what it has done. In philosophy, this unconscious tendency becomes
conscious. Accompanying irreconcilable thoughts is the hope for reconcilement, because the resistance of thought to mere things in being, the command-
ing freedom of the subject, intends in the object even that of which the object
was deprived by objectification.*

    Where Marx saw capitalists motivated by quest for profit, Adorno believes
that the profit motivation has been largely displaced (if not replaced) by the need
for social control in a system where there exists the prospect of generalized
affluence and thus the possibility of emancipation from alienated labor. Early
monopoly capitalism differs from nineteenth century market capitalism in that it
demands greater ideological compliance from human beings; according to
Adorno, the triumph of "positive thinking" is the most dangerous aspect of
modern ideology—the inability to comprehend reality and to speak intelligently
about freedom.

    This inability to pierce the ideological veil of the "positive" can only be
remedied by negative thinking. "Today the thwarted possibility of something
other has shrunk to that of averting catastrophe in spite of everything." For
Adorno, Marxism has failed to realize "something other" than a system of alienation; so too have the Soviets failed. Marx and Engels, he claims, "could not
foresee what became apparent later, in the revolution's failure even where it
succeeded: that domination may outlast the planned economy . . ." Adorno here
suggests that Marx and Engels succumbed to a naive optimism about Marxian
revolution; socialism did not automatically become a better world than the
capitalism it replaced. Adorno suggests that Marx and Engels did not adequately
understand the psychologically damaging effects of capitalist ideology: where
Marx believed that ideology was merely the weight of ruling-class ideas (recall
our discussion of *The German Ideology* in Chapter 1), Adorno presented a
different theory and critique of ideology, stressing the subliminal effects of
"identity-theory" on human beings. Identity-theory is the philosophical assumption about a perfect congruence between subject and object—or less abstractly
stated, between the individual and society.

    Negative Dialectics charts the philosophical justifications of this victory of
society over the individual, rescuing critical thought from the clutches of total
identity with the surrounding social order. Philosophy for Adorno became an
active vehicle for salvaging damaged personality, fighting absorption into the

---

*From Theodor Adorno, *Negative Dialectics* (New York: Seabury, 1973), p. 19.

totality of capitalism through dialectical negation. Where Marx fought ideology by way of the rational analysis of historical possibilities, passing on this message to the potentially insurgent proletariat, Adorno resisted ideology by attacking the philosophical identity-theory that threatened to destroy the individual in the name of "absolute integration."

Identity-theory functions as ideology by convincing each person of his or her own political and social autonomy. Adorno, like the other Frankfurt theorists, felt that individual autonomy had been virtually eliminated under early monopoly capitalism. The "nominalistic consciousness" treats each individual as unique and self-determining; but "it is ideology" to think that individual autonomy exists.

Adorno criticized identity between subject and object because he contended that the object (capitalism) dominated the subject (human beings). He felt that ideology in advanced capitalism took the form not of class unconsciousness (as it did for Marx and Lukács) but of the illusions that (a) the individual is autonomous and that (b) the social system is harmoniously ordered (having achieved perfect identity, to use Adorno's own formulation). This illusion of subjective autonomy and of subject-object identity is created in the interests of domination, misleading the human being about the heavy preponderance of the capitalist order.

A candid look at the predominance of the universal does all but unbearable psychological harm to the narcissism of all individuals and to that of a democratically organized society. To see through selfhood as nonexistent, as an illusion, would easily turn all men's objective despair into a subjective one. It would rob them of the faith implanted in them by individualistic society: that they, the individuals, are the substance. For the functionally determined individual interest to find any kind of satisfaction under existing forms, it must become primary in its own eyes; the individual must confuse that which to him is immediate with the πρώτη οὐσία. Such subjective illusions are objectively caused: it is only through the principle of individual self-preservation, for all its narrowmindedness, that the whole will function. It makes every individual look solely upon himself and impairs his insight into objectivity; objectively, therefore, it works only so much more evil. The nominalistic consciousness reflects a whole that continues by virtue of obdurate particularity. Literally it is ideology; socially, it is a necessary semblance.*

In one of Adorno's most telling passages, he describes the new ideology of capitalism as a "spell." "The reified consciousness has become total. The fact of its being a false consciousness holds out a promise that it will be possible to avoid it . . ." Adorno does not cancel out hope; the fact that critical consciousness exists, even in obscure philosophical forms such as *Negative Dialectics,* suggests that human beings still might wrest a degree of autonomy from the surrounding social totality. " . . . total socialization objectively hatches its opposite, and there is no telling yet whether it will be a disaster or a liberation." Revolution could yet occur, although it will not be a conscious product of socialist class-radicalism.

Human beings, individual subjects, are under a spell now as ever. The spell is

---

*From Theodor Adorno, *Negative Dialectics* (New York: Seabury, 1973), p. 312.

the subjective form of the world spirit, the internal reinforcement of its primacy over the external process of life. Men become that which negates them, that with which they cannot cope. They do not even have to cultivate a taste for it any more, as for the higher thing which indeed it is, compared with them in the hierarchy of grades of universality. On their own, a priori, so to speak, they act in line with the inevitable. While the nominalist principle simulates individualization for them, they act as a collective. This much of Hegel's insistence on the universality of the particular is true: in its perversion, as impotent individualization at the universal's mercy, the particular is dictated by the principle of perverted universality. The Hegelian doctrine of the universal's substantiality in the individual adopts the subjective spell; what is presented there as metaphysically worthier owes this aura chiefly to its opaqueness and irrationality, to the opposite of the mind which metaphysics would have it be.

The basic stratum of unfreedom—one that in the subjects lies even beyond their psychology, which it extends—serves the antagonistic condition now threatening to destroy the subjects' potential to change it. Expressionism, a spontaneous form of collective reaction, jerkily registered some of that spell, which has since become as omnipresent as the deity whose place it is usurping. We do not feel it any more because hardly anything and hardly anyone escapes it far enough to make the difference show it. Yet mankind still keeps dragging itself along as in Barlach's sculptures and in Kafka's prose, an endless procession of bent figures chained to each other, no longer able to raise their heads under the burden of what is. Mere entity, the opposite of the world spirit according to the highminded doctrines of idealism, is the incarnation of that spirit—coupled with chance, which is the form of freedom under the spell.

The spell seems to be cast upon all living things, and yet it is probably not—as in Schopenhauer's sense—simply one with the *principium individuationis* and its mulish self-preservation. Something compulsive distinguishes animal conduct from human conduct. The animal species *homo* may have inherited it, but in the species it turned into something qualitatively different. And it did so precisely due to the reflective faculty that might break the spell and did enter into its service. By such self-perversion it reinforces the spell and makes it radical evil, devoid of the innocence of mere being the way one is. In human experience the spell is the equivalent of the fetish character of merchandise. The self-made thing becomes a thing-in-itself, from which the self cannot escape any more; in the dominating faith in facts as such, in their positive acceptance, the subject venerates its mirror image.

In the spell, the reified consciousness has become total. The fact of its being a false consciousness holds out a promise that it will be possible to avoid it—that it will not last; that a false consciousness must inevitably move beyond itself; that it cannot have the last word. The straighter a society's course for the totality that is reproduced in the spellbound subjects, the deeper its tendency to dissociation. This threatens the life of the species as much as it disavows the spell cast over the whole, the false identity of subject and object. The universal that compresses the particular until it splinters, like a torture instrument, is working against itself, for its substance is the life of the particular; without the particular, the universal declines to an abstract, separate, eradicable form. In *Behemot,* Franz Neumann diagnosed this in the institutional sphere: Disintegration into disjoint and embattled power machineries is the secret of the total fascist state. In line with this is anthropology, the chemism of humankind. Resistless prey of the collective mischief, men lose their identity.

It is not altogether unlikely that the spell is thus breaking itself. For the time being a so-called pluralism would falsely deny the total structure of society, but its truth comes from such impending disintegration, from horror and at the same time from a reality in which the spell explodes. Freud's *Civilization and Its Discontents* has a substance that was scarcely in the author's mind: It is not only in the psyche of the socialized that aggressiveness accumulates into an openly destructive drive. Instead, total socialization objectively hatches its opposite, and there is no telling yet whether it will be a disaster or a liberation. An involuntary schema of this was designed by the philosophical systems; they too have been increasingly united in disqualifying their heterogeneities—whether called "sensation," "not-I," or whatever—down to that "chaos" whose name Kant used for heterogeneity at large. What some like to call *angst* and to ennoble as an existential is claustrophobia in the world: in the closed system. It perpetuates the spell as coldness between men, without which the calamity could not recur. Anyone who is not cold, who does not chill himself as in the vulgar figure of speech the murderer "chills" his victims, must feel condemned. Along with *angst* and the cause of it, this coldness too might pass. *Angst* is the necessary form of the curse laid in the universal coldness upon those who suffer of it.*

> Reification, he maintains, penetrates into every last recess of human consciousness. The ultimate reification is death. We increasingly fear death the less we enjoy life.

As the subjects live less, death grows more precipitous, more terrifying. The fact that it literally turns them into things makes them aware of reification, their permanent death and the form of their relations that is partly their fault. The integration of death in civilization, a process without power over death and a ridiculous cosmetic procedure in the face of death, is the shaping of a reaction to this social phenomenon, a clumsy attempt of the barter society to stop up the last holes left open by the world of merchandise.†

> Adorno's final, obscure thought is that dialectics might struggle to liberate consciousness, and eventually, possibly, all humanity, by its ruthless negativity that uncovers the parallel today between reified life and living death. Dialectics is the "self-consciousness of the objective context of delusion." It is a form of thought that recognizes how damaged thought and life have become, pretending no ready solutions and little uninformed optimism.

To this end, dialectics is obliged to make a final move: Being at once the impression and the critique of the universal delusive context, it must now turn even against itself. The critique of every self-absolutizing particular is a critique of the shadow which absoluteness casts upon the critique; it is a critique of the fact that critique itself, contrary to its own tendency, must remain within the medium of the concept. It destroys the claim of identity by testing and honoring it; therefore, it can reach no farther than that claim. The claim is a magic circle that stamps critique with the appearance of absolute knowledge. It is up

---

*From Theodor Adorno, *Negative Dialectics* (New York: Seabury, 1973), pp. 344–47.

†From Theodor Adorno, *Negative Dialectics* (New York: Seabury, 1973), p. 370.

to the self-reflection of critique to extinguish that claim, to extinguish it in the very negation of negation that will not become a positing.

Dialectics is the self-consciousness of the objective context of delusion; it does not mean to have escaped from that context. Its objective goal is to break out of the context from within. The strength required from the break grows in dialectics from the context of immanence; what would apply to it once more is Hegel's dictum that in dialectics an opponent's strength is absorbed and turned against him, not just in the dialectical particular, but eventually in the whole. By means of logic, dialectics grasps the coercive character of logic, hoping that it may yield—for that coercion itself is the mythical delusion, the compulsory identity. But the absolute, as it hovers before metaphysics, would be the nonidentical that refuses to emerge until the compulsion of identity has dissolved. Without a thesis of identity, dialectics is not the whole; but neither will it be a cardinal sin to depart from it in a dialectical step.

It lies in the definition of negative dialectics that it will not come to rest in itself, as if it were total. This is its form of hope.*

> In this sense, Adorno and the other Frankfurt theorists were more concerned with preserving their individual sensibilities as critical intellectuals than with stimulating class-based revolutionary struggle. Adorno's work after World War II fell under the shadow of Auschwitz, as he noted time and again. Instead of invoking the possibility of positive freedom, as Marx invoked in his 1844 images of communism, Adorno's negative philosophy attempted to *avoid* the totality of evil represented by the deeds and atrocities of the fascists. "A new categorical imperative has been imposed by Hitler upon unfree mankind: to arrange their thoughts and actions so that Auschwitz will not repeat itself, so that nothing similar will happen."
>
> Adorno felt deeply anguished about surviving the concentration-camps, as did many European Jews who either escaped or were spared while their families and neighbours died. Throughout Adorno's thought runs the comparison between bourgeois subjectivity, created under early monopoly capitalism, and the fascist subjectivity that put millions of Jews to death. "Genocide is the absolute integration." By this Adorno means that the identity of subject and object, the goal of all western philosophy according to him, was achieved by the Nazis. Adorno's philosophy resisted "identity between subject and object" for he felt that this identity would always be achieved at the expense of human beings. The perfectly harmonious society was an illusion, an aspect of bourgeois ideology predicated on the metaphor of the "invisible hand" of market capitalism designed to benefit everyone. Adorno's theory evoked the screams of the tortured instead of portraying a communist utopia lying in the distant future; he felt that it would be untruthful to ignore the continuity between fascist irrationality and the pseudo-rationality of capitalists, both motivated by the vision of "absolute integration," as he termed it.

...it is not wrong to raise the less cultural question whether after Auschwitz you can go on living—especially whether one who escaped by accident, one who by rights should have been killed, may go on living. His mere survival calls for the coldness, the basic principle of bourgeois subjectivity, without which

---

*From Theodor Adorno, *Negative Dialectics* (New York: Seabury, 1973), p. 406.

there could have been no Auschwitz; this is the drastic guilt of him who was spared. By way of atonement he will be plagued by dreams such as that he is no longer living at all, that he was sent to the ovens in 1944 and his whole existence since has been imaginary, an emanation of the insane wish of a man killed twenty years earlier.*

HORKHEIMER: ECLIPSE OF REASON

Max Horkheimer's *Eclipse of Reason,* published in 1947 and drawn from public lectures delivered at Columbia University in 1944, is both the most accessible and the most programmatic of the book-length Frankfurt works. Horkheimer tersely summarizes the major themes of the Frankfurt School's theory of domination: the critique of instrumental rationality that blurs the distinction between means and ends; the domination of human and nonhuman nature; the decline of the autonomous individual. Although Horkheimer does not take up an explicit dialogue with original Marxism, he nonetheless constantly evokes the nuances of difference between the Frankfurt critical theory and Marx's original theory of capitalism. Remaining in common is the vision of emancipation presupposed by Marx's critique of capitalist alienation.

Horkheimer briefly states the main focus of the Frankfurt School's theory and analysis:

It seems that even as technical knowledge expands the horizon of man's thought and activity, his autonomy as an individual, his ability to resist the growing apparatus of mass manipulation, his power of imagination, his independent judgment appear to be reduced. Advance in technical facilities for enlightenment is accompanied by a process of dehumanization. Thus progress threatens to nullify the very goal it is supposed to realize—the idea of man. Whether this situation is a necessary phase in the general ascent of society as a whole, or whether it will lead to a victorious re-emergence of the neo-barbarism recently defeated on the battlefields, depends at least in part on our ability to interpret accurately the profound changes now taking place in the public mind and in human nature.†

Horkheimer is puzzled by the apparent paradox of industrial capitalism's vast capacity for satisfying basic material needs and the co-existent reality of increasing human misery and social irrationality. Members of the Frankfurt School felt that Marxism underwent a serious crisis as early market capitalism expanded after the victory over the European fascists and gradually took monopoly forms. Instead of improving the democratic heritages of western industrial nations, primed by the immense sacrifices of the war effort and consequent creation of vast industrial capacity, the victory over fascism only introduced new forms of domination. We have already noted the further development by the Frankfurt School theorists of Marx's concept of alienation; this concept was expanded into the concept of domination because it now appeared that

---

*From Theodor Adorno, *Negative Dialectics* (New York: Seabury, 1973), pp. 362-63.
†From Max Horkheimer, *Eclipse of Reason* (New York: Seabury, 1974), pp. v-vi.

human beings were consciously *refusing* the prospect of their own emancipation.

Domination was primarily an individual phenomenon, where Marx's concept of alienation was rooted in the exploitation and domination of the working class. There is no necessary contradiction between these two levels of analysis: Horkheimer argued that individual domination reinforced the political apathy and conservative-integrationist character of the working class.

Under a system of domination, Horkheimer suggests, "reason has become an instrument." He adds that truth no longer motivates human intellectual activity: "In so far as words are not used obviously to calculate technically relevant probabilities or for other practical purposes, among which even relaxation is included, they are in danger of being suspect as sales talk of some kind, for truth is no end in itself."

Having given up autonomy, reason has become an instrument. In the formalistic aspect of subjective reason, stressed by positivism, its unrelatedness to objective content is emphasized; in its instrumental aspect, stressed by pragmatism, its surrender to heteronomous contents is emphasized. Reason has become completely harnessed to the social process. Its operational value, its role in the domination of men and nature, has been made the sole criterion. Concepts have been reduced to summaries of the characteristics that several specimens have in common. By denoting a similarity, concepts eliminate the bother of enumerating qualities and thus serve better to organize the material of knowledge. They are thought of as mere abbreviations of the items to which they refer. Any use transcending auxiliary, technical summarization of factual data has been eliminated as a last trace of superstition. Concepts have become "streamlined," rationalized, labor-saving devices. It is as if thinking itself had been reduced to the level of industrial processes, subjected to a close schedule—in short, made part and parcel of production. Toynbee has described some of the consequences of this process for the writing of history. He speaks of the "tendency for the potter to become the slave of his clay . . . In the world of action, we know that it is disastrous to treat animals or human beings as though they were sticks and stones. Why should we suppose this treatment to be any less mistaken in the world of ideas?"

The more ideas have become automatic, instrumentalized, the less does anybody see in them thoughts with a meaning of their own. They are considered things, machines. Language has been reduced to just another tool in the gigantic apparatus of production in modern society. Every sentence that is not equivalent to an operation in that apparatus appears to the layman just as meaningless as it is held to be by contemporary semanticists who imply that the purely symbolic and operational, that is, the purely senseless sentence, makes sense. Meaning is supplanted by function or effect in the world of things and events. In so far as words are not used obviously to calculate technically relevant probabilities or for other practical purposes, among which even relaxation is included, they are in danger of being suspect as sales talk of some kind, for truth is no end in itself.

In the era of relativism, when even children look upon ideas as advertisements or rationalizations, the very fear that language might still harbor mythological residues has endowed words with a new mythological character. True, ideas have been radically functionalized and language is considered a mere tool, be it for the storage and communication of the intellectual elements of production or for the guidance of the masses. At the same time, language takes its revenge, as it were, by reverting to its magic stage. As in the days of magic, each word is regarded as a dangerous force that might destroy society and for which the speaker must be held responsible. Correspondingly, the pursuit of truth, under social control, is curtailed. The difference between thinking and acting is held void. Thus every thought is regarded as an act; every reflection is a thesis, and every thesis is a watchword. Everyone is called on the carpet for what he says or does not say. Everything and everybody is classified and labeled. The quality of the human that precludes identifying the individual with a class is "metaphysical" and has no place in empiricist epistemology. The pigeon-hole into which a man is shoved circumscribes his fate. As soon as a thought or a word becomes a tool, one can dispense with actually "thinking" it, that is, with going through the logical acts involved in verbal formulation of it. As has been pointed out, often and correctly, the advantage of mathematics—the model of all neo-positivistic thinking—lies in just this "intellectual economy." Complicated logical operations are carried out without actual performance of all the intellectual acts upon which the mathematical and logical symbols are based. Such mechanization is indeed essential to the expansion of industry; but if it becomes the characteristic feature of minds, if reason itself is instrumentalized, it takes on a kind of materiality and blindness, becomes a fetish, a magic entity that is accepted rather than intellectually experienced.

What are the consequences of the formalization of reason? Justice, equality, happiness, tolerance, all the concepts that, as mentioned, were in preceding centuries supposed to be inherent in or sanctioned by reason, have lost their intellectual roots. They are still aims and ends, but there is no rational agency authorized to appraise and link them to an objective reality. Endorsed by venerable historical documents, they may still enjoy a certain prestige, and some are contained in the supreme law of the greatest countries. Nevertheless, they lack any confirmation by reason in its modern sense. Who can say that any one of these ideals is more closely related to truth than its opposite? According to the philosophy of the average modern intellectual, there is only one authority, namely, science, conceived as the classification of facts and the calculation of probabilities. The statement that justice and freedom are better in themselves than injustice and oppression is scientifically unverifiable and useless. It has come to sound as meaningless in itself as would the statement that red is more beautiful than blue, or that an egg is better than milk.*

The power of science replaces the classical pursuit of truth. Reason is degraded into verifiable technical operations performed on a world which exists only to be manipulated, processed and consumed. Horkheimer believes than an objective concept of reason has been lost as reason is increasingly "formalized," i.e., reduced to a series of operations performed on the world.

This might imply that the Frankfurt thinkers opposed technology and science in general. Horkheimer, however, makes it clear that he does not oppose technological advancement but only the fixation on this advancement as the sole rationale of science and intellectual activity. He believes that concepts such as

---

*From Max Horkheimer, *Eclipse of Reason* (New York: Seabury, 1974), pp. 21-24.

freedom and justice, while not subject to scientific operationalization, are valuable in themselves. It will be recalled that Marx believed that communism would contain a balance between industrial productivity, able to satisfy all basic needs, and social freedom. Horkheimer echoes this sentiment as he investigates the paradox, noted above, of the co-existent realities of industrial progress and growing irrationality.

Rationality has become merely the individual's capacity for adapting to the requirements of the surrounding social order. To be rational is to be realistic. " ...the life of each individual, including his most hidden impulses, which formerly constituted his private domain, must now take the demands of rationalization and planning into account: the individual's self-preservation presupposes his adjustment to the requirements for the preservation of the system." Here Horkheimer further elucidates differences between early market capitalism and monopoly capitalism; under early capitalism, social order and civic harmony were to be achieved through the free play of producing and consuming individuals. Freedom would automatically produce order, according to the prevailing ideology of the free market. In monopoly capitalism, where the free market has been transformed through state intervention in economic life and by the blunting of conflict between classes, individual "adjustment becomes the standard for every conceivable type of subjective behavior." Adaptability to reality is the hallmark of modern reason, where before, in early market capitalism, rationality involved the careful weighing of economic costs and benefits.

Just as all life today tends increasingly to be subjected to rationalization and planning, so the life of each individual, including his most hidden impulses, which formerly constituted his private domain, must now take the demands of rationalization and planning into account: the individual's self-preservation presupposes his adjustment to the requirements for the preservation of the system. He no longer has room to evade the system. And just as the process of rationalization is no longer the result of the anonymous forces of the market, but is decided in the consciousness of a planning minority, so the mass of subjects must deliberately adjust themselves: the subject must, so to speak, devote all his energies to being 'in and of the movement of things' in the terms of the pragmatistic definition. Formerly reality was opposed to and confronted with the ideal, which was evolved by the supposedly autonomous individual; reality was supposed to be shaped in accordance with this ideal. Today such ideologies are compromised and skipped over by progressive thought, which thus unwittingly facilitates the elevation of reality to the status of ideal. Therefore adjustment becomes the standard for every conceivable type of subjective behavior. The triumph of subjective, formalized reason is also the triumph of a reality that confronts the subject as absolute, overpowering.*

Horkheimer grapples seriously with the apparent trade-off between consumer freedom, occasioned by industrial and technological progress, and the types of emotional and moral sacrifices required by the complex reality of industrial-capitalist society. On the one hand, human beings have been liberated from medieval codes of conduct and obedience to the church; moral and ethical absolutism has given way to relativism. "Paradoxically, however, this increase of

---

*From Max Horkheimer, *Eclipse of Reason* (New York: Seabury, 1974), pp. 95-96.

independence has led to a parallel increase of passivity." Because society today is all-powerful with respect to the individual, the concept of individual freedom loses much of its substance. "Economic and social forces take on the character of blind natural powers that man, in order to preserve himself, must dominate by adjusting himself to them." Thus freedom today is largely a function of being a clever manipulator of existing forces and institutions. The capacity to reason is less important than a clever ability to adapt to changing circumstances and to compromise with dominant institutions.

"For the average man self-preservation has become dependent upon the speed of his reflexes. Reason itself becomes identical with this adjustive faculty." We will argue below, especially in our Chapters 6 and 7, that Horkheimer was describing a particular stage in the development of monopoly capitalism, its more harshly repressive period during which it sought the "absolute integration" of every aspect of human individuality into an harmonious social system (as Adorno termed its purpose in *Negative Dialectics*).

While we have wider consumer choice than before, we must also adapt to the technical processes involved in the consumption of modern commodities. The freedom to own a private automobile, for example, entails the cost of adjusting to speed limits and adopting a careful demeanour when on the road. While human beings are free to escape noisy cities, this freedom is exchanged at the price of having to rivet our attention on the highway and on surrounding cars in order not to destroy ourselves and our passengers. Horkheimer's contention is that industrial progress and advances in commodity production are mixed blessings, with consequences for the autonomy of the human personality.

Man has gradually become less dependent upon absolute standards of conduct, universally binding ideals. He is held to be so completely free that he needs no standards except his own. Paradoxically, however, this increase of independence has led to a parallel increase of passivity. Shrewd as man's calculations have become as regards his means, his choice of ends, which was formerly correlated with belief in an objective truth, has become witless: the individual, purified of all remnants of mythologies, including the mythology of objective reason, reacts automatically, according to general patterns of adaptation. Economic and social forces take on the character of blind natural powers that man, in order to preserve himself, must dominate by adjusting himself to them. As the end result of the process, we have on the one hand the self, the abstract ego emptied of all substance except its attempt to transform everything in heaven and on earth into means for its preservation, and on the other hand an empty nature degraded to mere material, mere stuff to be dominated, without any other purpose than that of this very domination.

For the average man self-preservation has become dependent upon the speed of his reflexes. Reason itself becomes identical with this adjustive faculty. It may seem that present-day man has a much freer choice than his ancestors had, and in a certain sense he has. His freedom has increased tremendously with the increase in productive potentialities. In terms of quantity, a modern worker has a much wider selection of consumer goods than a nobleman of the *ancien régime*. The importance of this historical development must not be underestimated; but before interpreting the multiplication of choices as an increase in freedom, as is done by the enthusiasts of assembly-line production, we must take into account the pressure inseparable from this increase and the change in quality that is concomitant with this new kind of choice. The pressure consists in the continual coercion that modern social conditions put upon everyone; the change may be illustrated by the difference between a craftsman of the old type, who selected the proper tool for a delicate piece of work, and the worker of today, who must decide quickly which of many levers or switches he should pull. Quite different degrees of freedom are involved in driving a horse and in driving a modern automobile. Aside from the fact that the automobile is available to a much larger percentage of the population than the carriage was, the automobile is faster and more efficient, requires less care, and is perhaps more manageable. However, the accretion of freedom has brought about a change in the character of freedom. It is as if the innumerable laws, regulations, and directions with which we must comply were driving the car, not we. There are speed limits, warnings to drive slowly, to stop, to stay within certain lanes, and even diagrams showing the shape of the curve ahead. We must keep our eyes on the road and be ready at each instant to react with the right motion. Our spontaneity has been replaced by a frame of mind which compels us to discard every emotion or idea that might impair our alertness to the impersonal demands assailing us.*

> The decline of autonomous individuality is achieved through fundamental shifts of economic power. Horkheimer argues that "individuality loses its economic basis," meaning that the age of the individual entrepreneur, buying and selling on the open market, is largely behind us and that large corporations have taken over, reducing the human being to the proverbial "organization man." In a brilliant and novel analysis, Horkheimer suggests that the modern human being can survive only through "mimicry," imitating and thus accommodating himself to dominant power structures. "By echoing, repeating, imitating his surroundings, by adapting himself to all the powerful groups to which he eventually belongs . . .he manages to survive."

In this age of big business, the independent entrepreneur is no longer typical. The ordinary man finds it harder and harder to plan for his heirs or even for his own remote future. The contemporary individual may have more opportunities than his ancestors had, but his concrete prospects have an increasingly shorter term. The future does not enter as precisely into his transactions. He simply feels that he will not be entirely lost if he preserves his skill and clings to his corporation, association, or union. Thus the individual subject of reason tends to become a shrunken ego, captive of an evanescent present, forgetting the use of the intellectual functions by which he was once able to transcend his actual position in reality. These functions are now taken over by the great economic and social forces of the era. The future of the individual depends less and less upon his own prudence and more and more upon the national and international struggles among the colossi of power. Individuality loses its economic basis.

There are still some forces of resistance left within man. It is evidence against social pessimism that despite the continuous assault of collective patterns, the spirit of humanity is still alive, if not in the individual as a member of social groups, at least in the individual as far as he is let alone. But the impact of the existing conditions upon the average man's life is such that the submissive type

---

*From Max Horkheimer, *Eclipse of Reason* (New York: Seabury, 1974), pp. 97-98.

mentioned earlier has become overwhelmingly predominant. From the day of his birth, the individual is made to feel that there is only one way of getting along in this world—that of giving up his hope of ultimate self-realization. This he can achieve solely by imitation. He continuously responds to what he perceives about him, not only consciously but with his whole being, emulating the traits and attitudes represented by all the collectivities that enmesh him—his play group, his classmates, his athletic team, and all the other groups that, as has been pointed out, enforce a more strict conformity, a more radical surrender through complete assimilation, than any father or teacher in the nineteenth century could impose. By echoing, repeating, imitating his surroundings, by adapting himself to all the powerful groups to which he eventually belongs, by transforming himself from a human being into a member of organizations, by sacrificing his potentialities for the sake of readiness and ability to conform to and gain influence in such organizations, he manages to survive. It is survival achieved by the oldest biological means of survival, namely, mimicry.*

> Horkheimer argues that "labor and capital are equally concerned with holding and extending their control." He adds that "efficiency, productivity, and intelligent planning are proclaimed the gods of modern man."

At the present time, labor and capital are equally concerned with holding and extending their control. The leaders in both groups contend to an increasing extent that theoretical critique of society has become superfluous as a result of the tremendous technological progress that promises to revolutionize the conditions of human existence. The technocrats maintain that superabundance of goods produced on super-assembly lines will automatically eliminate all economic misery. Efficiency, productivity, and intelligent planning are proclaimed the gods of modern man; so-called "unproductive" groups and "predatory" capital are branded as the enemies of society.

It is true that the engineer, perhaps the symbol of this age, is not so exclusively bent on profitmaking as the industrialist or the merchant. Because his function is more directly connected with the requirements of the production job itself, his commands bear the mark of greater objectivity. His subordinates recognize that at least some of his orders are in the nature of things and therefore rational in a universal sense. But at bottom this rationality, too, pertains to domination, not reason. The engineer is not interested in understanding things for their own sake or for the sake of insight, but in accordance with their being fitted into a scheme, no matter how alien to their own inner structure; this holds for living beings as well as for inanimate things. The engineer's mind is that of industrialism in its streamlined form. His purposeful rule would make men an agglomeration of instruments without a purpose of their own.†

> Horkheimer appears at times to agree with those Marxists who view instrumental rationalization and profit-maximization as fundamentally interdependent. He states that "there are still some forces of resistance left within man." Yet this appears to have no basis in class-based political activism for Horkheimer

---

*From Max Horkheimer, *Eclipse of Reason* (New York: Seabury, 1974), pp. 140-42.

†From Max Horkheimer, *Eclipse of Reason* (New York: Seabury, 1974), p. 151.

or Adorno; the only remaining form of resistance is a kind of relentless cerebral radicalism. The preponderance of Horkheimer's argument is captured in the passage: "The age of vast industrial power, by eliminating the perspectives of a stable past and future that grew out of ostensibly permanent property relations, is in process of liquidating the individual." He adds: "Every instrumentality of mass culture serves to reinforce the social pressures upon individuality, precluding all possibility that the individual will somehow preserve himself in the face of all the atomizing machinery of modern society."

We recall that Adorno hoped that a type of negative philosophy could prolong political optimism by revealing and articulating prevailing domination. Adorno continuously grappled with the stark images of Auschwitz in attempting to reckon the meager prospects of radical change. Horkheimer, too, argues that the task of philosophy is to evoke the suffering of the "anonymous martyrs of the concentration camps."

The real individuals of our time are the martyrs who have gone through infernos of suffering and degradation in their resistance to conquest and oppression, not the inflated personalities of popular culture, the conventional dignitaries. These unsung heroes consciously exposed their existence as individuals to the terroristic annihilation that others undergo unconsciously through the social process. The anonymous martyrs of the concentration camps are the symbols of the humanity that is striving to be born. The task of philosophy is to translate what they have done into language that will be heard, even though their finite voices have been silenced by tyranny.*

HORKHEIMER AND ADORNO:
MARXISM AS POSITIVIST MYTHOLOGY

Inherent in the Frankfurt School's theory of domination is a critique of prevailing standards of reason. Instrumental rationality (the logic of "getting things done") was perceived to be implicitly irrational by Horkheimer and Adorno. Lukács' penetrating concept of reification—literally meaning "thing-ification"—applied to tendencies within late capitalism to transform consciousness into an instrument. (While the Frankfurt thinkers drew upon Lukács' concept of "reification" in developing their own theory of domination, they did not uphold his revolutionary optimism.)

The reification of consciousness, to the Frankfurt theorists, was not simply a form of what Marx and Lukács had termed false consciousness, for false consciousness to Marx could be abolished through the uncovering of mystifying ideology: This was precisely the source of Lukács' optimism about awakening the working classes to their historical mission explicated in Marxian theory. Horkheimer and Adorno did not consider false consciousness to be primarily a phenomenon of class unconsciousness but instead a generalized individual phenomenon. They suggested that human beings could no longer reason because reason had been integrated into capitalist society and reduced to an instrument for taming nature and enforcing social control.

They indicated that science and especially mathematics had become new forms of mythology—mythical because they operate as forms of false con-

---

*From Max Horkheimer, *Eclipse of Reason* (New York: Seabury, 1974), p. 161.

sciousness. "In the most general sense of progressive thought, the Enlightenment has always aimed at liberating men from fear and establishing their sovereignty. Yet the fully enlightened earth radiates disaster triumphant." Scientific enlightenment has not emancipated men from dogmatic ideology and mythic belief but merely substitutes one form of myth for another, less systematic and pervasive, form.

Francis Bacon, in his *Novum Organum,* first gave voice to this concept of enlightenment. Bacon suggested that mind would become "patriarchal" with respect to nature, controlling and exploiting it—*taming* nature. The scientist could control nature by comprehending its laws of operation; "power and knowledge are synonymous."

Despite his lack of mathematics, Bacon's view was appropriate to the scientific attitude that prevailed after him. The concordance between the mind of man and the nature of things that he had in mind is patriarchal: The human mind, which overcomes superstition, is to hold sway over a disenchanted nature. Knowledge, which is power, knows no obstacles: neither in the enslavement of men nor in compliance with the world's rulers. As with all the ends of bourgeois economy in the factory and on the battlefield, origin is no bar to the dictates of the entrepreneurs: Kings, no less directly than businessmen, control technology; it is as democratic as the economic system with which it is bound up. Technology is the essence of this knowledge. It does not work by concepts and images, by the fortunate insight, but refers to method, the exploitation of others' work, and capital. The "many things" which, according to Bacon, "are reserved," are themselves no more than instrumental: The radio as a sublimated printing press, the dive bomber as a more effective form of artillery, radio control as a more reliable compass. What men want to learn from nature is how to use it in order wholly to dominate it and other men. That is the only aim. Ruthlessly, in despite of itself, the Enlightenment has extinguished any trace of its own self-consciousness. The only kind of thinking that is sufficiently hard to shatter myths is ultimately self-destructive. In face of the present triumph of the factual mentality, even Bacon's nominalist credo would be suspected of a metaphysical bias and come under the same verdict of vanity that he pronounced on scholastic philosophy. Power and knowledge are synonymous.*

Enlightenment banished fear of the unknown by evaluating the world with respect to the operational norms of "computation and utility"; positivism is the theory of knowledge most characteristic of this attitude of enlightenment. Positivism suggests that ideas which do not admit of operationalization and testing in the world are worthless—literally non-sense. When Horkheimer and Adorno say that "enlightenment is totalitarian" they do not mean that knowledge in scientific and mathematical forms necessarily acts as a pernicious form of ideology but that science, in positivist form, *rejects* that which cannot be quantified and measured. In this way, science is less open-minded than its partisans contend; indeed, science is a new form of ancient mythology.

For the Enlightenment, whatever does not conform to the rule of computation

---

*From Max Horkheimer and Theodor W. Adorno, *Dialectic of Enlightenment* (New York: Herder and Herder, 1972), p. 4.

and utility is suspect. So long as it can develop undisturbed by any outward repression, there is no holding it. In the process, it treats its own ideas of human rights exactly as it does the older universals. Every spiritual resistance it encounters serves merely to increase its strength. Which means that enlightenment still recognizes itself even in myths. Whatever myths the resistance may appeal to, by virtue of the very fact that they become arguments in the process of opposition, they acknowledge the principle of dissolvent rationality for which they reproach the Enlightenment. Enlightenment is totalitarian.*

> "Enlightenment behaves toward things as a dictator toward men. He knows them in so far as he can manipulate them." Thus, enlightenment exists only as an instrument, not as a value in itself. Bacon himself suggested that the truth-value of knowledge is its practical efficacy.

Myth turns into enlightenment, and nature into mere objectivity. Men pay for the increase of their power with alienation from that over which they exercise their power. Enlightenment behaves toward things as a dictator toward men. He knows them in so far as he can manipulate them. The man of science knows things in so far as he can make them. In this way their potentiality is turned to his own ends.†

> Writing at the opening of the computer age Horkheimer and Adorno argue that mathematics is the ultimate form of enlightened reason. Mathematics "turns thought into a thing." Their argument here represents the core of their attack on modern reason: Where objective reason should grasp the totality of reality, the "given as such," mathematical formalism subjects "reason to what is directly given." Real knowledge arises, the authors suggest, not from determination of the "abstract spatio-temporal relations of the facts" but "on the contrary [from grasping them] as mediated conceptual moments which come to fulfillment only in the development of their social, historical, and human significance." In the end, "factuality wins the day" as "cognition is restricted to its repetition."
>
> The authors attack positivist science as a mode of ideology. Marx and Lukács saw ideology as a mystifying veil thrown up by the ruling class to explain away injustice as a fact of nature, as fate; Marx felt that ideology could be banished by explaining "reality" to the exploited class, employing a theoretical and empirical language of analysis and critique. Horkheimer and Adorno see ideology not as a conscious mystification of reality, easily banished through rational critique and analysis, but a "spell," a trap into which all have fallen unwittingly. Cognition merely mirrors reality, failing to grasp its historical and structural character. Positivism, the modern philosophical underpinning of science, banishes historical and theoretical explanation as non-empirical and hence invalid. Science, instead of piercing the ideological haze, cannot distinguish ideology from reality because it does not see facts as "mediated conceptual moments" — pieces of *history* — bit as mere data, things without a past and future.
>
> Enlightenment in this sense is basically ahistorical. Modern domination is

---

*From Max Horkheimer and Theodor W. Adorno, *Dialectic of Enlightenment* (New York: Herder and Herder, 1972), p. 6.

†From Max Horkheimer and Theodor W. Adorno, *Dialectic of Enlightenment* (New York: Herder and Herder, 1972), p. 9.

perpetuated by this ahistorical cast of mind: The present reality cannot be analyzed dialectically, in terms of its past and future motion, but only mirrored and reproduced.

Mathematical procedure became, so to speak, the ritual of thinking. In spite of the axiomatic self-restriction, it establishes itself as necessary and objective: it turns thought into a thing, an instrument—which is its own term for it. But this kind of mimesis, in which universal thought is equalized, so turns the actual into the unique, that even atheism itself is subjected to the ban on metaphysics. For positivism, which represents the court of judgment of enlightened reason, to digress into intelligible worlds is no longer merely forbidden, but meaningless prattle. It does not need—fortunately—to be atheistic, because objectified thinking cannot even raise the problem. The positivist censor lets the established cult escape as willingly as art—as a cognition-free special area of social activity; but he will never permit that denial of it which itself claims to be knowledge. For the scientific mind, the separation of thought from business for the purpose of adjusting actuality, departure from the privileged area of real existence, is as insane and self-destructive as the primitive magician would consider stepping out of the magic circle he has prepared for his invocation; in both cases the offense against the taboo will actually result in the malefactor's ruin. The mastery of nature draws the circle into which the criticism of pure reason banished thought. Kant joined the theory of its unceasingly laborious advance into infinity with an insistence on its deficiency and everlasting limitation. His judgment is an oracle. There is no form of being in the world that science could not penetrate, but what can be penetrated by science is not being. According to Kant, philosophic judgment aims at the new; and yet it recognizes nothing new, since it always merely recalls what reason has always deposited in the object. But there is a reckoning for this form of thinking that considers itself secure in the various departments of science—secure from the dreams of a ghost-seer: World domination over nature turns against the thinking subject himself; nothing is left of him but that eternally same *I think* that must accompany all my ideas. Subject and object are both rendered ineffectual. The abstract self, which justifies record-making and systematization, has nothing set over against it but the abstract material which possesses no other quality than to be a substrate of such possession. The equation of spirit and world arises eventually, but only with a mutual restriction of both sides. The reduction of thought to a mathematical apparatus conceals the sanction of the world as its own yardstick. What appears to be the triumph of subjective rationality, the subjection of all reality to logical formalism, is paid for by the obedient subjection of reason to what is directly given. What is abandoned is the whole claim and approach of knowledge: to comprehend the given as such; not merely to determine the abstract spatio-temporal relations of the facts which allow them just to be grasped, but on the contrary to conceive them as the superficies, as mediated conceptual moments which come to fulfillment only in the development of their social, historical, and human significance. The task of cognition does not consist in mere apprehension, classification, and calculation, but in the determinate negation of each immediacy. Mathematical formalism, however, whose medium is number, the most abstract form of the immediate, instead holds thinking firmly to mere immediacy; Factuality wins the day; cognition is restricted to its repetition; and thought becomes mere tautology. The more the machinery of thought subjects existence to itself, the more blind its resignation in reproducing existence. Hence enlightenment returns to mythology, which it never really knew how to elude.*

The *Dialectic of Enlightenment* wants to reverse the "self-destructiveness of enlightenment," its regression into mythology and ideology as positivism. The linear reason of mathematics is inferior to the dialectical reason of Marxian theory. Where ideology in an earlier historical period could be broken and banished through critical rationality, possessed by the working class and its leaders, today critical rationality threatens to vanish. Horkheimer and Adorno defy the conventions of the new ideology, an ideology of positive thinking, by attempting to rescue thought and language from immediate identification of the given reality. This is why their works are often tortured and obscure, barely accessible to the reader. The authors claim that this obscurity has a purpose:

When public opinion has reached a state in which thought inevitably becomes a commodity, and language the means of promoting that commodity, then the attempt to trace the course of such depravation has to deny any allegiance to current linguistic and conceptual conventions, lest their world-historical consequences thwart it entirely.†

They worry that the "dutiful child of modern civilization is possessed by a fear of departing from the facts [and that] this anxiety is none other than the fear of social deviation." Horkheimer and Adorno attempt to overcome this fear through an analysis and critique of modern reason, which, they argue, has become fundamentally irrational.

It is characteristic of the sickness that even the best-intentioned reformer who uses an impoverished and debased language to recommend renewal, by his adoption of the insidious mode of categorization and the bad philosophy it conceals, strengthens the very power of the established order he is trying to break. False clarity is only another name for myth; and myth has always been obscure and enlightening at one and the same time: always using the devices of familiarity and straightforward dismissal to avoid the labor of conceptualization.‡

Modern ideology holds men in bondage to the *given,* to immediate reality: Change appears to be an impossibility. The authors claim that this ideology is the dominating rationality of positivist science and mathematics, substituting the mere reflection of reality for its dialectical, historical comprehension. Much of the work of the Frankfurt School can be read as a refusal to participate in this culture of "absolute integration"; by writing obscure philosophical works Adorno and Horkheimer hope to rescue thought and reason from the clutches of positivist mythology. Instrumental rationality avoids the "labor of conceptualization" required to speculate intelligently about the contours and possibilities of radical social change.

---

*From Max Horkheimer and Theodor W. Adorno, *Dialectic of Enlightenment* (New York: Herder and Herder, 1972), pp. 25-27.

†From Max Horkheimer and Theodor W. Adorno, *Dialectic of Enlightenment* (New York: Herder and Herder, 1972), pp. *xi-xii.*

‡From Max Horkheimer and Theodor W. Adorno, *Dialectic of Enlightenment* (New York: Herder and Herder, 1972), p. *xiv.*

Adorno and Horkheimer attack alienation not in terms of a direct critique of the capitalist production process (as Marx did) nor in terms of a critique of class unconsciousness (as Lukács and Korsch did) but in terms of the forces that prevent human beings from thinking about their own liberation—from seeing the world as a non-eternal reality, subject to radical transformation. The authors of *Dialectic of Enlightenment* did not reject science and technology as such but only the ideological auras that surrounded their uses in advanced capitalism, such as the positivist philosophy of science that implicitly banishes metaphysical ideas in favor or precise, quantifiable operations. Adorno and Horkheimer argued, in a peculiar twist, that science no longer serves to enlighten men about reality (as Marx had intended that his science would do) but rather deceives them about the lawfulness of what they see. With Marx, Adorno and Horkheimer contend that capitalism is not a necessary or eternal social order, a product of perfectly harmonious laws, but a fractured, distorted order that can be changed. Although they abandon the scientific character of Marxian theory, they do not abandon Marx's intention to demystify ideology that, now as before, keeps men in bondage to the given.

MARCUSE: ONE-DIMENSIONAL SOCIETY*

The most coherent expression of the Frankfurt School's theory of domination is found in Herbert Marcuse's 1964 work *One-Dimensional Man.* Marcuse systematically outlines "the ideology of advanced industrial society," developing and extending earlier themes of the Frankfurt School such as the critique of instrumental rationality and the blurring of the distinction between means and ends. Marcuse has gained considerable notoriety for this thesis that critical consciousness has nearly evaporated in advanced industrial society, occasioned by the totalization of domination and the subsequent demise of the person's ability to evaluate social reality critically and rationally.

Marcuse's key assumption, shared by Horkheimer and Adorno, is that the advancement of technology has not liberated human beings but only served to create "new, more effective, and more pleasant forms of social control and social cohesion." Marcuse argues that capitalist domination extends into the individual's innermost psyche, programming him to be an obedient subject of the capitalist reality principle and engendering "false needs." This proceeds on the basis of the obliteration of the distinction between private and public existence, with private existence being assimilated into the irrationality of the repressive whole. This is Marcuse's reformulation of Adorno and Horkheimer's thesis of the decline of individuality under late capitalism.[1]

He argues that there exists a deep-seated paradox between the ability of the technological production system to satisfy basic human needs and the inability of human beings to think critically about their own domination in the midst of plenty. Marcuse suggests that "freedom from want," increasingly achieved through the "total mobilization" of advanced industrial society, both capitalist and state-socialist, contradicts individual liberty. Advancing productivity, according to Marcuse, brings advancing conformity and civic obedience. Paradoxically, people are losing the powers of individual initiative on which early market capitalism had been built; the rationality of the pliant organization man replaces

* In this section, footnotes are guides to further reading in the original sources.

1. Herbert Marcuse, *One- Dimensional Man* (Boston: Beacon, 1974), p. xv.

the entrepreneurial spirit. While Marcuse does not glorify rugged individualism (being a Marxist who sees personal freedom as social freedom), he feels that it was an improvement over the civic obedience of individuals in late capitalism who lack the psychic resilience to refuse the imperatives of imposed corporate rationality.[2]

Marcuse, like other Frankfurt School theorists, broadens the concept of alienation into the larger category of domination. He characterizes advanced industrial society as "totalitarian," not for its political or economic repression but for the very structures of domination inherent in the processes of production and consumption. Technological domination now manipulates the human being into a kind of emotional and political passivity that renders him helpless in face of the vast institutional complexes of industrial capitalist society. " . . .this productivity mobilizes society as a whole, above and beyond any particular individual or group interests." Marcuse suggests that this mobilization was effected primarily to serve the interests of capital; he suggests that the interests of the ruling class now require the mobilization of the totality of human behavior, emotion, and thought in order to achieve deep social control.

This social control, "absolute integration" to employ Adorno's term, can be broken only through the depiction of an order not rooted in domination. "Such new modes can be indicated only in negative terms because they would amount to the negation of the prevailing modes." In this sense, Marcuse defines liberation "negatively," with reference not to positive attributes of freedom but to the absence of domination.

Marcuse argues that the "totalitarianism" of late capitalism is not equivalent to the political terrorism of Nazi Germany but is rather an insidious terrorism enforced by "economic-technical coordination" of human needs. This coordination denies the possibility of the human experience of liberation; it reduces the given reality to ultimate rationality by convincing people that this is the best of all possible worlds, the apex of all previous social development. This reduction of reality to rationality and its coordination of human needs undercuts organized opposition to the present order. Modern totalitarianism, to Marcuse, is achieved not by conscious propaganda campaigns masterminded by some latter-day Goebbels but by the subtle manipulation of human needs.

By one-dimensionality Marcuse refers to this insidious coordination of all human experience by the technological-economic apparatus of modern capitalism. A two-dimensional social order would preserve the difference between private and public experience, thus allowing men and women to think rationally and critically about their needs. A one-dimensional order cultivates particular needs that are then internalized in such a way as to preclude their critical scrutiny.[3]

Marcuse, in what many contend is his most important contribution to the development of critical theory, distinguishes between true and false human needs. "False are those which are superimposed upon the individual by particular social interests in his repression: the needs which perpetuate toil, aggressiveness, misery, and injustice." In an evocative phrase, Marcuse defines the satisfaction of these false needs as "euphoria in unhappiness," willing bondage. False needs are not false merely because Marcuse does not "like" them — large automobiles, gadgets, chic clothes, and television — but because they are imposed

2. Ibid., p. 1.
3. Ibid., pp. 3–4.

on a pliable consumer as a substitute for more substantive freedom (such as non-alienated labor). "The development and satisfaction of these needs is heteronomous." False needs are false not because their content displeases Marcuse but because they are cultivated by dominant interests and not freely self-determined. False needs are characterized by their contribution to civic and ideological order: They enable the individual to escape temporarily from the work-a-day world, on vacation or via the consumption of certain commodities in leisure time. But they do not enable him to transform his lived-experience of work and leisure; they merely substitute for freedom already lost. True needs are those that drive towards liberation from the present order and are arrived at through critical analysis and personal struggle.[4]

Marcuse has been criticized for the implicitly elitist tendency of his argument against false needs. After all, how does he know that present-day "euphoria," as he terms it, is necessarily tainted with deep-seated unhappiness, that needs are false? He answers these critics by cautioning that "no tribunal can justly arrogate to itself the right to decide which needs should be developed and satisfied."

"All liberation depends on the consciousness of servitude": and yet "the emergence of this consciousness is always hampered by the predominance of needs and satisfactions which, to a great extent, have become the individual's own." In other words, human beings must undo their own false needs, recognizing the requirement of their liberation. But they are unable to grasp this requirement when their lives are administered by interests predisposed not to liberation but to profit and social control. Even the appearances of liberal democracy can be bent to these purposes of social control. The illusion of personal autonomy today deceives individuals about the real substance of their dominated lives. "Free election of masters does not abolish the masters or the slaves." The illusion of personal autonomy is a powerful agency of social control, especially in liberal-democratic nation-states like the United States where individualism is ideologically sanctioned. But this is illusory freedom, according to Marcuse, for it may only elect new "masters" and not transform the system as a whole. Put simply, we cannot vote capitalism out of existence, at least in those social orders where Marxist and socialist political parties are weak or non-existent. We can merely elect the political representatives of capital, choosing between essentially homogenous candidates from "competing" political parties.[5]

Marcuse adds that social control is achieved by the "transplantation of social into individual needs." He does not blame advertising and the media as conspirators who mechanically create false needs, imposing them upon blind and ignorant individuals. Rather he argues that human beings are subtly "pre-conditioned" to want the commodities and life-styles offered by the media and corporate producers. When the corporate executive and the manual worker "enjoy the same television program and visit the same resort places" crucial cultural distinctions between socio-economic classes are blurred and the illusion of a classless, post-industrial society is reinforced.

"The people recognize themselves in their commodities." This recognition of essential self-hood in commodities anchors modern social control "in the new needs which it has produced." The "preconditioning," a life-long process comprised of numerous experiences of childhood and adult socialization, creates

4. Ibid., pp. 4–5.

5. Ibid., pp. 6–8.

these new needs. Marcuse indicates that there is no longer an inviolable core of personal autonomy capable of resisting this sort of preconditioning. This gives rise to the striking paradox of growing material abundance in the midst of social irrationality: to the fact "that people find their soul in their automobile, hi-fi set, split-level home, kitchen equipment."[6]

Marcuse argues that men identify themselves with their consumption because they lack the inner strength required to think rationally about the satisfaction of their needs. Marcuse suggests that a "private space" in which individual sensibility remains inviolable no longer exists: It has been "invaded and whittled down by technological reality." The resulting personality structure is characterized by "mimesis," immediate identification of the individual and the surrounding society achieved through imitation of its central values. It will be recalled that this concept of mimesis as a means of psychic survival in a totally integrated society appeared twenty years earlier, in Max Horkheimer's *Eclipse of Reason.* Marcuse repeats one of the central themes of the Frankfurt School, the reduction of reason into a mechanism for adjusting to the prevailing social order. "The impact of progress turns Reason into submission to the facts of life. . . ."

Marcuse summarizes his arguments by challenging the sociological assumption, developed in the 1950s and early 1960s, that ideology in advanced capitalism had disappeared. Theorists like Daniel Bell argued that the so-called "end of ideology" had been occasioned by the fundamental reconciliation of class conflict in advanced industrial-capitalist societies. Marcuse opposes the thesis of the end of ideology, arguing that the peculiar characteristic of one-dimensional society is the "absorption of ideology into reality," the blurring of distinctions between the ideological and the real. One-dimensional consciousness is deceived not merely by the ideological falsification and mystification of reality (according to Marx's understanding of ideology); this consciousness is seduced into a way of life predicated on the endless consumption of unneeded—or rather *falsely* needed—commodities. Ideology, according to Marcuse, is no longer only a system of mystifying ideas. It has become instead a feature of reality itself, located in the very production process of advanced industrial society. "The products indoctrinate and manipulate; they promote a false consciousness which is immune against the falsehood." He goes on to define one-dimensionality as the reduction of "ideas, aspirations, and objectives that, by their content, transcend the established universe of discourse and action" into "terms of this universe."

In other words, reality can no longer be evaluated by traditional criteria of rationality and justice. The appearance of modern life, and, specifically, the appearance of commodities, cannot be pierced by discerning thought. In this sense, social control is enforced by dispossessing men not of their labor-power (which still happens, ours being a capitalist system) but first and foremost of their *rationality,* manifested in their inability to break the hold of a life given over to endless consumption, "euphoria in unhappiness."

JACOBY: SOCIAL AMNESIA

Finally, Russell Jacoby in a 1975 work entitled *Social Amnesia* has synthesized major themes of the original Frankfurt School. Jacoby draws upon Horkheimer

6. Ibid., pp. 8–9.

and Adorno's arguments about mythology and enlightenment, on Adorno's concept of a negative philosophy and on Marcuse's theses about the one-dimensionality of modern consciousness. While the book is primarily concerned with a critique of post-Freudian and humanist psychology, arguing that Freud perspicaciously foresaw tendencies in late capitalist society to obliterate the individual—and that to ignore or dismiss Freud is tantamount to ignoring contemporary social reality—Jacoby manages to weave together the diverse elements of the Frankfurt theory of domination.

Social amnesia refers to our collective forgetting of the past in the spirit of what Jacoby believes is a naive progressivism. He relies on the sentence in Horkheimer and Adorno's *Dialectic of Enlightenment* that suggests that "all reification is a forgetting." Marx himself was seriously concerned with the bond between past and future in terms of the legacy left by dead labor in the form of commodities and machines. He termed the past a "nightmare on the brain of the living"; at the same time, Marx argued that the past was a burden that tied people to an alienated human condition. Jacoby, following the lead of other Frankfurt School theorists, argues that there can be no liberation without coming to grips with the dead and silent past: " . . .a past which the present still suffers."

Historical consciousness is necessary for a critical theory that does not reduce liberation merely to the "positive thinking" of individuals. Current trends in post-Freudian and neo-Freudian psychology rely on the "power of positive thinking" to liberate men. Jacoby believes that a truly dialectical theory does not ignore structures of domination inherited from the past and thus cannot reduce emancipation purely to good revolutionary intentions. He further argues that Freudian psychoanalysis contains a "revolutionary core" in its attempt to grapple with the seemingly eternal demands of "civilization" upon the psycho-social needs of the individual.

"Today criticism that shelves the old in the name of the new forms part of the *Zeitgeist;* it works to justify and defend by forgetting." Jacoby considers ahistorical thought to be "apologetic," blending in with dominant social institutions by neglecting to uncover their roots in the history of class society. Marx's dialectical method projected future social possibilities from the evidence of past and present reality. "The syndrome is a general one. In brief, society has lost its memory, and with it, its mind. The inability or refusal to think back takes its toll in the inability to think." Jacoby perceives modern social amnesia, as he characterizes it, as a form of contemporary alienation—in this case, alienation from the *past.*

More concretely, social amnesia preserves "the status quo by presenting the human and social relationships of society as natural—and unchangeable—relations between things." As such, amnesia is an instance of reification, the process of life becoming a thing, distant from human control. Thought that ignores the past tends to perceive the present social order as finished and final, obliterating the possibility of continuous dialectical motion and the uncovering of new social relationships.

Jacoby links his analysis of social amnesia as a latter-day form of reification with the Marxist theory of political economy. "This form of reification is rooted in the necessities of the economic system. The intensification of the drive for surplus value and profit accelerates the rate at which past goods are liquidated to make way for new goods; planned obsolescence is everywhere." As we remarked above, Marxism is grounded in the "notion that dead labor dominates living labor . . .and the past commands the present." Jacoby terms social amnesia "a psychic commodity of the commodity society," produced to protect the society from being seen as a historical, noneternal order, subject to a variety of possible future transformations.

Today criticism that shelves the old in the name of the new forms part of the *Zeitgeist;* it works to justify and defend by forgetting. In making only a fleeting gesture toward the past, or none at all, social and psychological thought turn apologetic. The heroic period of militant, materialistic, and enlightened bourgeois thought, if there ever was one, is no more. The "law" once enunciated on "the dwindling force of cognition in bourgeois society" can be confirmed daily. In the name of a new era past theory is declared honorable but feeble; one can lay aside Freud and Marx—or appreciate their limitations—and pick up the latest at the drive-in window of thought.

The syndrome is a general one. In brief, society has lost its memory, and with it, its mind. The inability or refusal to think back takes its toll in the inability to think. The loss of memory assumes a multitude of forms, from a "radical" empiricism and positivism that unloads past thought like so much "intellectual baggage" to hip theories that salute the giants and geniuses of the past as unfortunates born too soon. The latter, more important in the context of this book, in the impatience to contrive new and novel theories, hustle through the past as if it were the junk yard of wrecked ideas. "In every era," wrote Walter Benjamin, "the attempt must be made to wrest tradition away from a conformism that is about to overcome it."

The general loss of memory is not to be explained solely psychologically; it is not simply childhood amnesia. Rather it is *social* amnesia—memory driven out of mind by the social and economic dynamic of this society. The nature of the production of social amnesia can barely be suggested here; such an explanation would have to draw upon the Marxist concept of reification. Reification in Marxism refers to an illusion that is objectively manufactured by society. This social illusion works to preserve the status quo by presenting the human and social relationships of society as natural—and unchangeable—relations between things. What is often ignored in expositions of the concept of reification is the psychological dimension: amnesia—a forgetting and repression of the human and social activity that makes and can remake society. The social loss of memory is a type of reification—better: It is *the* primal form of reification. "All reification is a forgetting."

To pursue this for a moment: This form of reification is rooted in the necessities of the economic system. The intensification of the drive for surplus value and profit accelerates the rate at which past goods are liquidated to make way for new goods; planned obsolescence is everywhere, from consumer goods to thinking to sexuality. Built-in obsolescence exempts neither thought nor humans. What is heralded as new or young in things, thoughts, or people masks the constant: this society. Inherent in Marxism is the notion that dead labor dominates living, things dominate activity, the past commands the present. "The domination of capitalist over workers is the domination of things over men, dead labor over the living, products over producers. . . ." Exactly because the past is forgotten, it rules unchallenged; to be transcended it must first be remembered. Social amnesia is society's repression of remembrance—society's own past. It is a psychic commodity of the commodity society.*

---

*From Russell Jacoby, *Social Amnesia* (Boston: Beacon Press, 1975), pp. 3-5.

Marcuse's one-dimensional man is a victim of this collective loss of memory. Jacoby does not glorify the past — nor did Marx — but believes that emancipation is impossible without appreciating the historical nature of the present. He suggests, in a pivotal chapter, that the New Left unwittingly succumbed to social amnesia and eschewed traditional Marxian theory in favor of "instant" solutions to domination. The North American New Left, Jacoby argues, was unable to escape the pervasive amnesia — or the "spell," as Adorno called it — with respect to prior social and intellectual traditions such as Marxism.

"Attending to the emergency of the individual has absorbed sustained political energy and theory." Jacoby analyzes the demise of the New Left and its often naive glorification of personal revolt as the equivalent of significant radical change. "The rejection of theory and theorizing is grounded in the affirmation of subjectivity. Theory seems politically impotent and personally unreal and distant. Only human subjectivity — the personal life — is meaningful and concrete." Here Jacoby argues that forms of cultural opposition such as rock music and the more politicized sectors of the drug culture have fallen victim to amnesia and its reduction of political activism to immediate personal rebellion and liberation. Theory appears to members of the New Left as an "old," "bourgeois" encumbrance that fails to bridge the gap between theory and action.

Jacoby, like Marx, wants to restore the dialectic between theory and action. Without comprehending the historical structures of late capitalist society, action cannot find its bearing; it degenerates into repetitive slogans and the cult of the rebellious individual. Jacoby argues, persuasively, that the individual always loses at the hands of bourgeois society. Thus successful insurrection must take forms that protect the meager individual against the whirlpool of social amnesia and reification that is virtually all-powerful.

As alienation spreads, "the cult of subjectivity is a direct response to its eclipse." The more that human beings are turned into agents of their own social control, the more they clamor to escape. Jacoby wants to restore "a subject-object dialectic," relating personal alienation to larger structures that produce that alienation.

The political left has not escaped the ravages of social amnesia and subjective reductionism. The very effort to think through and back, which in different forms belongs to the best of psychoanalytic and Marxist thought, is undermined by the individual in crisis unable to think beyond itself. Evidence of this is everywhere, in revisionist and conformist psychology as well as in the left. The crisis is no fraud; the chill of social relations numbs the living. The effort to keep psychically warm, to stave off the cold that seeps in, shunts aside any time for or possibility of sustained thought and theory. The permanent emergency of the individual blocks the permanent and social solution.

Within the left this assumes a definite form. Because the political left is a left it retains a social analysis of society. The very problem, however, is that this social analysis decays more and more into slogans, thoughtless finds of the moment. The individual stripped of memory and mind magnetically attracts reified slogans that serve more to sort out one's friends and enemies than to figure out the structure of reality. This is a dynamic that keeps society rattling along; the very breathing space that could give life to critical theory is lost in the desperate search for life itself. The search without reflection grooves along in the ruts of society.

Social amnesia takes two forms within the left: the construction of instant and novel theories of reform and revolution, and, recently and increasingly, the hasty refurbishing of older slogans and tactics. Both proceed simultaneously because both live off the suppression of the past. The pop theories are fabricated out of scraps and pieces of personal experience and the morning news. Jaded ones are picked out of left archives and, once cleansed of their historical context, content, and critique, are restored to service. These forms of social forgetting render a discussion of trends in the left doubly irrelevant; not only is such a discussion distant from the immediate needs of the individual, but it is obsolete, examining political thought and slogans that have already been discarded and forgotten. So rapidly does the left change that discussion and analysis seem doomed to lag behind.

Evidently this is part of the problem: Attending to the emergency of the individual has absorbed sustained political energy and theory. The slogans that replace and dislodge theory shift with the moment. These shifts are not made through choice, discussion, and thought, but "automatically"—thoughtlessly and unconsciously. If the latest political opinions are improvements over former ones, it is not because the latter have been surpassed, but because they have been forgotten. They pass as they arose, uncritically, and promise to return. The hex that haunts left thought is the hex of bourgeois society: memoryless repetition. Thinking falls under the sway of fashion: change without change. If ideas such as "smash monogamy" are not promoted with the same vigor as previously this does not mean that they have been critically transcended, but simply that they have been dropped, to be elsewhere and later recycled and reused. Inasmuch as this discarding and forgetting is a continuing process, an examination of slogans, even if they are obsolete—which is by no means certain—may indicate forces that are hardly obsolete, that are as vital as society itself.

This analysis does not intend to simply equate developments within the left proper with those outside it, as if the two canceled each other out, confirming the wisdom that it is best to do nothing. That a political left and non-left participate in the same drive toward subjectivity, that both suffer from social amnesia, is proof only of the virulence of society, not of the meaninglessness of political distinctions.

Further, it need hardly be said, the left itself is more and more fragmented; these thoughts are concerned with *trends* which tend to exert themselves, but are not evident everywhere. Such an analysis does not claim universal validity. It should be noted also that while it is impossible to discuss the left without drawing material from the women's movement, Weathermen, and so on, it would violate the very spirit and intent to read this as an indictment of specific groups. At best, one can say certain groups express with greater clarity trends that are present everywhere. But nothing more; neither that such developments are restricted to particular groups or, more erroneously, that these groups brought them about. Here, as elsewhere, the issue is society as a whole.

The rejection of theory and theorizing is grounded in the affirmation of subjectivity. Theory seems politically impotent and personally unreal and distant. Only human subjectvity—the personal life—is meaningful and concrete. The personal is said (or was said?) to be political, the political, personal. The identity of the two eliminates the need to pursue either separately. Theory and critical thought give way to human relations, feelings, and intuitions. The immediacy of these cuts to the quick of theory and thought: mediacy. The presence of the here and now in the form of subjective feelings banishes thoughts to afterthoughts and second thoughts. It instills an immediacy that stills reflection.

The promise held out by a focus on human subjectivity is lost if no attention is given to its place within society in general. Here the relation of phenomena within and outside a left is at once critical and fluid. For the cult of human subjectivity is not the negation of bourgeois society but its substance. Against a Marxist dogma that proscribed all subjectivity in the name of science, its articulation within the left was progress; but when this articulation becomes an exclusive pursuit it courts a regression that constitutes bourgeois society's own progress. The fetish of subjectivity and human relationships is progress in fetishism. The rejection of theory which seeks insight into objectivity in favor of subjective feelings reconstitutes a suspect Cartesian tradition in the reverse. I feel, therefore I am. The inner drive of bourgeois society was to throw the human subject back on itself. Descartes's thought illustrates this tendency. "My third maxim was to endeavor always to conquer myself rather than fortune, and to change my desires rather than the order of the world." Human subjectivity was left to shift for itself: to examine and transform the self, not the universe of the self. To prescribe more subjectivity as aid to the damaged subject is to prescribe the illness for the cure.

The wholesale rejection of theory incurs the constitutional failing of the individual retailer; apparently free to buy and sell he is a victim of objective laws without knowing them. The private individual, free to pick and choose, was a fraud from the beginning; not only were the allotments already picked and chosen, but the contents of the choice followed the dictates of the social not the individual world. The "private interest is already a socially determined interest, which can be achieved only within the conditions laid down by society and with the means provided by society. . . . It is the interest of private persons; but its content, as well as the form and means of its realization, is given by social conditions independent of all." Even as society announced it, the idea of the individual as an autonomous being was ideological. The unemployed, like the employed, were to think that their lack of luck, or their luck, was due to private abilities and was not determined by the social whole. No less are the private hopes, desires, and nightmares cued by public and social forces. The social does not "influence" the private; it dwells within it. "Above all we must avoid postulating 'Society' again as an abstraction vis-à-vis the individual. The individual *is the social being*."

The fetish of human relations, responses, emotions, perpetuates the myth; abstracted from the social whole they appear as the individualized responses of free men and women to particular situations and not, as they are, the subhuman responses to a nonhuman world. As noted previously, a rat psychology befits humans only when a suffocating world has transformed men and women into rats. The endless talk on human relations and responses is utopian; it assumes what is obsolete or yet to be realized: *human* relations. Today these relations are inhuman; they partake more of rats than of humans, more of things than of people. And not because of bad will but because of an evil society. To forget this is to indulge in the ideology of sensitivity groups that work to desensitize by cutting off human relations from the social roots that have made them more brutal. More sensitivity today means revolution or madness. The rest is chatter.

The cult of subjectivity is a direct response to its eclipse. As authentic human experience and relationships disappear, they are invoked the more. Autobiographical accounts replace analysis because autobiographies as the history of a unique individual cease to exist. "To get in touch with one's feelings"—a slogan picked up by parts of the women's movement—hopes to affirm an individual existence already suspect. Self and mutual affirmation and confirmation work to revitalize experience denatured long ago. Bewitched by the commodity, the individual turns into one. The atomized particle called the individual gains an afterlife as an advertisement for itself.

The exclusive pursuit of subjectivity insures its decline. Not against the drive of society but in tune with it, it judges a social product to be a private woe or utopia. What was exacted from the individual at the beginning of its history— that the individual's freedom, labor, and so on, were only subjective and personal—is promoted later as its salvation. That parts of the women's movement have made subjectivity programmatic, repudiating all objective theoretical thought, indicates only the extent to which the revolt recapitulates the oppression: Women, allegedly incapable of thought and systematic thinking but superior in sentiments and feelings, have repeated this in their very rebellion. Yet the point is not to resuscitate an official orthodoxy that eliminated any role for the subject. Critical theory and viable Marxist thought have worked precisely against this orthodoxy; it is a question of restoring a subject-object dialectic. The alternatives of pure subjectivity and pure objectivity are the alternatives of positivist thought itself. Marxist and critical thought must use another logic, dialectical logic.

The promise of radical subjectivity to escape political and personal irrelevancy is unfulfilled. While there was positive progress against an older, scientific Stalinist orthodoxy, it repeated in reverse the same sin: an indifference toward the content of bourgeois society that perpetuates this content. "The passage to theory-less praxis was motivated by the objective impotence of theory," wrote T.W. Adorno, "and multiplied that impotence by the isolation and fetishization of the subjective moment of the historical movement." Subjectivity that forsakes sustained theory gravitates toward slogans that are not the crystallizations of discussion and thought but secretions of the existing society. As such they serve not to popularize thought, but to replace it. From "armed struggle" to "smash monogamy" they are not necessarily wrong in themselves, but wrong insofar as they are blank labels, indifferent, or rather antagonistic, toward content. They are to be applied anywhere and everywhere, as if indifference to concrete and definite conditions were the hallmark of revolutionary theory and not its negation.

Blindness to content is the social logic of a society that deals in exchange values: how much? No matter their tone, blank categories of affirmation (or condemnation) of armed struggle, the third world, leadership, men, and the rest, do not resist, but succumb to the inner mechanism of this society. The preservation of concrete dialectical analysis, even in idealistic form—to follow Lenin—makes intelligent idealism closer to dialectical materialism than vulgar materialism that is primitive and indifferent. The former, in its loyalty to the particular, preserves what a crude materialism, blind to distinctions, loses.

What Lenin said of idealism can be said perhaps, for the same reason, of pacifism. Intelligent pacifism is closer to revolution than simplistic and armed struggle.*

> Social amnesia reached its zenith in hippiedom and the drug culture of the 1960s. "A cult of subjectivity—complete with drugs—dopes the discontented into taking their own death, figuratively and in fact, for life itself." The final form of damaged subjectivity is "rampant narcissism," according to Jacoby. The destruction of individuality, exhaustively charted earlier by Horkheimer, Adorno, and Marcuse, produces aberrant forms of subjectivity in the late 1960s and 1970s. What Tom Wolfe calls the "Me decade" is a product of the progressive deterioration of autonomous personality, the ability to perceive one's own liberation in historical, social and structural terms.
>
> Jacoby suggests that hope lies in a restoration of the dialectic between theory and praxis that Marx developed a century ago. "...efforts must remain continually alive to the tension between the 'personal' and the 'political' without abdicating either or reducing one to the other." The New Left can fight reification most effectively by combatting social amnesia through the rejuvenation of the dialectical method and Marxian critique.

If the intensification of subjectivity is a direct response to its actual decline, it ultimately works to accelerate the decline. To the damaged subject it proposes more of the same. The objective loss of human relationships and experience is eased by their endless pursuit. A cult of subjectivity—complete with drugs—dopes the discontented into taking their own death figuratively and in fact, for life itself. The immediacy of it all drives out mediacy of any of it. Sustained political and theoretical thought is not simply rejected but forgotten and repressed. The slogans and rhetoric that replace it are as vacant and thoughtless as the society that tosses them up. The specter not only of society, but of its opposition, that has lost its memory and mind, haunts history.

The tone of the slogans notwithstanding, their collaboration with society is barely hidden. Empty concepts, too often fired by resentment and envy, perpetuate the essential content of this society. A critique of monogamy, theory, leadership, relationships between two people as forms of exclusion and privilege is a critique that falls behind bourgeois society, not advances over it; it is akin to the "thoughtless" communism outlined by Marx. What is perpetually lost under the sway of immediacy is a dialectical analysis: monogamy as both human and inhuman—as the bad refuge from a worse world and a bad solution for a better world; theory as insight into objectivity as well as elitism. To see only one moment is to trade the worse for the bad: no theory instead of elitist theory, inhuman fragmented relations for damaged human ones. The dialectical path is elsewhere.

The depletion of political concepts in favor of psychological and subjective ones is a by-product of the scramble for the remnants of human experience. Yet the subjectivization of objective concepts is not the repudiation of the loss of human experience but forms its prehistory. The reduction of the Marxist theory of alienation to a subjective condition by liberal sociologists has its counterpart in the left in the reduction of oppression to a whim of the individ-

---

*From Russell Jacoby, *Social Amnesia* (Boston: Beacon Press, 1975), pp. 101-107.

ual. Alienation becomes a headache and oppression mere annoyance. "I'm oppressed," announces someone, and that's that.

Inside and outside the left radical subjectivity announces its own end; it resists reification by colluding with it. Hence the totalitarian urge of radical subjectivity to control everything. Endless talk about human relationships within the closed group promotes domination. Bad subjectivity seeks the bad collective that secures subjectivity by annihilating it. "Collectivism and individualism complete each other in the false." The bourgeois individual whittled down to identical monads pursues its last fragments in and for a public only too anxious to share the remains. The individual goes public in a desperate attempt to maintain solvency. Blank and vacant affirmations or condemnations of the women's movement, men, armed struggle, recent political and personal events serve as tools of interpersonal relations. Thought is reduced to slogans and slogans to symbols of mutual- and self-confirmation.

Rampant narcissism surfaces as the final form of individualism; it at once negates the ego and perpetuates its mangled form. Vague conceptions of guilt, the universal oppression of women by men, one's "own" oppression, function as instruments of an ego that is regressing in the face of a disintegrating society. That men, too, have suffered and died in the massacre of history is affirmed or denied, but is in any case irrelevant. What counts is the immediate, and here an economism-turned-feminism is promoted as if the blind endorsement of what every worker did or thought is improved when it is as blindly applied to women. Social analysis decays into group loyalty. The jealousy with which the oppression of women, children, homosexuals, and so on, is defended as a private preserve, off-limits to others, expresses an urge to corner the market of oppression.

Again, the point here is not to argue for a return to a "scientific" objective theory that proscribed any role for the subject; and again, the alternatives of pure subjectivity and pure objectivity are the either/or of bourgeois culture itself. The choice between instant subjectivity and instant slogans; between unorthodox individual needs and political orthodoxy is no choice at all. Nor are the practical and communal attempts to overcome the deadly privacy and coldness of existence to be rejected. Rather they are to be advanced; but advanced not by a mode of thought and action that damns them to be more of the same. The political and personal praxis that is sustained by bad subjectivity and abstract slogans issues into the very prison that is the bourgeois world. What is to be sought is a concrete subject/object dialectic that reconstructs the new out of the decay; only the praxis that shuns the fetish can hope for liberation. There are no guarantees nor tried-and-tested methods. Mistakes have been and will be made; but the efforts must remain continually alive to the tension between the "personal" and the "political" without abdicating either or reducing one to the other.

The line that inspired the Weatherman name suggested one metaphor for the path of theory and praxis: you don't need a weatherman to know which way the wind is blowing. In classical Marxist theory this metaphor indicates opportunism, that is, subjectivism or the lack of principles; the willingness to swim with the current, be what it may. Obviously, Weatherman was a direct repudiation of social-democratic opportunism; not only by their actions and program, but also by their courage and dedication. And yet, as argued here, they as others unwittingly collapse into a subjectivity and abstract sloganeering that is part and parcel of bourgeois society itself. The Lukács of *History and Class Consciousness* suggested another metaphor for revolutionary theory and praxis; he wrote there of the sailor. The sailor, like the weatherman, takes exact readings from the wind—but with a decisive difference: "without letting the wind determine his direction, on the contrary, he defies and exploits it so as to hold fast to his original course." *

GUIDE TO FURTHER READING

PHIL SLATER *Origins and Development of the Frankfurt School,* self-consciously bears the subtitle "a Marxist perspective." Slater's work offers a contrast to the dominant outlook of the Frankfurt School. This work is not a definitive exegesis of Frankfurt School themes but rather a polemical attempt to demonstrate the "un-Marxian" roots of the School.

THEODOR ADORNO *Prismen,* is a collection of Adorno's essays on aesthetics and social history.

RUSSELL JACOBY *Social Amnesia,* is a "critique of conformist psychology from Adler to Laing." Jacoby's book applies the central insights of the Frankfurt critique of instrumental rationality to an analysis of trends in post-Freudian psychology. Jacoby takes to its logical conclusion Adorno and Horkheimer's argument that the human subject had been virtually eliminated by late capitalism.

THEODOR ADORNO *Negative Dialectics,* written in the mid-1960s, is the ultimate theoretical statement of the Frankfurt School's revision of original Marxism. Adorno goes to great lengths to explode positivistic Marxism from the perspective of a dialectical method that is relentlessly "negative," i.e., oriented to the critique of ideology. Adorno's Marxism gave up its political relationship to the working class, or to any other revolutionary agents for that matter, in favor of a critique of domination.

MAX HORKHEIMER *Eclipse of Reason,* is undoubtedly the clearest statement of the Frankfurt position. Originally presented as lectures at Columbia University in 1944, and published in English in 1947, this work was reissued in 1974. Horkheimer concludes with a statement about the "rise and decline of the individual" under advanced capitalism.

MAX HORKHEIMER *Critique of Instrumental Reason,* collects certain of Horkheimer's earliest essays outlining the gap between original Marxism and Frankfurt critical theory.

MAX HORKHEIMER AND THEODOR ADORNO *Dialectic of Enlightenment,* is the seminal 1944 work by the two leading members of the Frankfurt School that criticizes the positivism and false enlightenment of advanced capitalist culture. The authors argue that myth and enlightenment are dialectically interrelated and that modern scientific method contains elements of myth and ideology. The publication of this work signalled the final rupture between original Marxism and the Frankfurt critical theory, abandoning many aspects of Marx's own revolutionary optimism.

---

*From Russell Jacoby, *Social Amnesia* (Boston: Beacon Press, 1975), pp. 115-18.

HERBERT MARCUSE   *One-Dimensional Man,* published in 1964, was Marcuse's last major work before he developed his concept of the "new sensibility." It can be located squarely within the mainstream of Frankfurt theory, advancing Marcuse's hypothesis that the human individual has become a "one-dimensional" subject, captive of pervasive ideological forces. Yet even here Marcuse argues that this is an "ambiguous' situation and that one-dimensionality may in fact be subject to transcendence through critical philosophy and art.

THEODOR ADORNO   *Philosophy of Modern Music,* articulates Adorno's thesis that opposition to domination can best be captured in non-discursive forms like music (and especially in the atonal music of composers like Arnold Schoenberg). This amplifies his insight in *Negative Dialectics* that Marxism—or rather critical theory—can no longer work with fixed positive concepts of social change but must instead attempt to negate ideological illusion and distortion. In the opinion of this author, Adorno's position is fundamentally undialectical in the Marxian sense, breaking off the relationship between theory and praxis that is the core of Marx's dialectical method.

QUESTIONS FOR FURTHER DISCUSSION

1. Is it meaningful to characterize the Frankfurt School theorists as Marxists? In what sense did Horkheimer, Adorno, and Marcuse preserve the aims or method of Marx?
2. What is the significance of the term "instrumental rationality"? Relate this concept to Max Weber's discussion of bureaucratic, rule-bound types of authority.
3. Explain Horkheimer and Adorno's concept of the decline of the individual.
4. Explain the preoccupation of the Frankfurt theorists with the phenomenon of fascism as a constituent element of their analysis of advanced capitalism.
5. What political role for the critical intellectual have the Frankfurt theorists mapped out to replace the model of the revolutionary class struggle?
6. Explain the concept of the dialectic of myth and enlightenment, expressed in Horkheimer and Adorno's *Dialectic of Enlightenment.*
7. Expand on your answer to question six by developing the substance of the Frankfurt School's critique of the positivist philosophy of science.

Eastern European
Revisionism: Marxian
Humanism

HISTORICAL OVERVIEW

*During the 1960s and into the 1970s, certain eastern European Marxist intellectu-
als challenged the authority of the official state ideology of Marxism-Leninism, an
ideology created in the early 1920s by Lenin and the Bolsheviks to protect his
political leadership and the centralized dominance of the Communist Party of the
Soviet Union. Soviet-style state-socialism was a peculiar form of socialist political organization that rested on the paradoxical concept of "democratic centralism," essentially utilized to defend the Bolsheviks' centralization of all political
power in the name of the so-called "dictatorship of the proletariat." Although
Marx suggested that eventually the socialist state would wither away, replaced
by the self-management of all social institutions, the Soviets felt that a strong
centralized state, led by a vanguard party, was necessary to mobilize an industrial
work force and to coordinate the accumulation of capital. Lenin argued that the
rudimentary state of industrialization in 1917 forced him to direct the working
class, exacting terrible human sacrifices and years of penury in return for a fully
industrialized society. In the 1960s, certain renegade Marxist humanists in eastern Europe took stock of the Stalinist period, ending with Stalin's death in 1953,
and decided that Soviet state-socialism bore virtually no resemblance to Marx's
projected model of a free workers' state in which fundamental civil liberties
would be guaranteed. In the mid and late 1960s in countries such as Czechoslovakia, Poland, and especially Yugoslavia (which in the early 1950s broke from
the Soviet Union's political authority, creating a system of workers' self-management as a direct counter to the Leninist concept of a vanguardist "democratic
centralism") theorists attacked Marxism-Leninism in the name of the Marxist
heritage. They argued that Marx's early writings authorize a democratic,
humanist interpretation of Marxism that places the individual at the center of the
socialist vision. These dissidents felt that Marxism-Leninism indefinitely post-*

pones the humanization of socialism in the name of certain developmental imperatives. They attack the state-socialist system for being fundamentally as alienated and exploitative as capitalism. Marxian humanism of this kind favors greater democracy and workers' control of industry as a practical way of decentralizing political power. This species of Marxism suggests that the most important aspect of communism is the overcoming of alienation and the creation of a society of "praxis" – self-expressive and self-creating labor.

GENERAL INTRODUCTION

While this book is basically concerned with western European and North American Marxism, there have been recent developments in eastern Europe that warrant our attention. The hiatus between Marx's original works and the Second and Third Internationals and, later, the rise of western Marxism in its Hegelian variants should not obscure the reality of the Russian experience with Marxist theory and with various models of socialism. Indeed, much of Hegelian Marxism, as we noted earlier, was formulated in response to the dogmatic "Marxism-Leninism" created by Lenin and his Bolshevik followers.

Marxism-Leninism has been both an original political theory of the Bolshevik revolution and, in its more sordid apologetic versions, an ideology used to justify the purges of Stalin. In Chapter 2, we described the way Lenin's theories of revolution and his concept of Marxian science became influential in the Third International, further splintering social democratic factions that had been fatally weakened by the outbreak of the First World War. Lenin's theoretical justification of a "vanguard party" became a dominant form of revolutionary Marxism during the years following 1919.

In the eastern countries, and especially in the Soviet Union, Marxism-Leninism was much more than a theory concerned with sketching the conditions for revolution. It was a justifying ideology used to explain the peculiarities of Soviet political behavior. While to outsiders this might seem to be largely a meaningless issue, at least in a theoretical sense, in the Soviet Union, where the revolution and its political aftermath had to be explained in terms of revolutionary ideology, this issue has had great impact. Even today, political actions taken by the Soviet state are always carefully measured in terms of Marxist-Leninist ideology. Pictures of Lenin adorn most public buildings and Marxist-Leninist slogans appear on roadside billboards, indicating the extent to which the people still perceive him as the father of Soviet socialism to whom they must address all ideological appeals for sanctification.

The structure of the present-day Soviet Union was legitimated by Lenin's twin concepts of the vanguard party (providing the theoretically and politically "naive" working class with tight discipline and ideological direction) and of democratic centralism (a euphemism for authoritarian bureaucratic and political centralization, carried out by the Communist Party in the name of the workers of the Soviet Union who theoretically and legally own the means of production). Today the Soviet Union is a highly centralized, industrialized, energy-wasteful society. While the rise of a consumerist ethic has not been as rapid as in western societies, much of the extant productive capacity having been given over to the production of armaments, it is clear that the Soviet Union is becoming basically a consumption-oriented economy. Recent books about the Soviet Union and its way of life (see the Guide to Further Reading at the end of this chapter for references in this regard) clearly demonstrate that there is a growing "convergence" between the Soviet and American consumer and their lifestyles. The past ten years in the USSR have witnessed an incredible boom in the production and distribution of commodities for personal use, most notable among these being the private car (the Russian version of the Italian Fiat), western-style clothes (especially bluejeans among the younger generation), western records, cosmetics, and a variety of other goods heretofore reserved strictly for members of the Party elite (who have never lived in penury).

The black market for consumer goods in the Soviet Union provides those commodities not produced or openly distributed by the regular economy. The Soviet consumer is demanding more goods for personal consumption, arguing that years of abstinence and hard work should now be compensated. The Soviet regime, although constantly preoccupied with arms production, is coming around to this way of thinking for they recognize that they can gain more social and political control by providing enhanced levels of consumption for the individual. Alienation and disaffection can be mitigated to some extent by providing a high-intensity market setting in which the Soviet consumer can spend the rubles accumulated after years of paid labor. The central economic dilemma in the Soviet Union today is not grinding poverty, as it was under Stalin, but rather the unavailability of high-quality commodities. Many Soviet workers have large bank accounts but little possibility of spending their savings. The distribution of goods in the Soviet Union is still highly inefficient, mainly because the centrally planned economy is cumbersome and unresponsive to consumer preferences.

The picture we are trying to draw is of a society both politically and economically centralized, and in which the individual is only considered as an ideologically obedient consumer. These two dimensions feed into each other, for it is thought that the happy consumer is the solid citizen. This formula applies both to the Soviet Union and to the United States and other western capitalist societies. The difference between the two industrial systems at present is that in the west the citizen-as-consumer has experienced decades of material abundance, while the Soviet citizen-consumer is only beginning to come into his own and for that reason may be seen as "hungrier" for consumer goods.

As we noted in Chapter 3, the analysis of "legitimacy crisis" in western societies is a variant of modern Marxism, to be surveyed more systematically in our concluding chapter. Theorists such as Jürgen Habermas argue that economic crises are now largely secondary to political crises, most notably the crisis in obtaining enough public legitimacy for western capitalist governments to function successfully. Precariously caught between the interests of capital and labor, western political states rely upon doses of "legitimation" to support them. Legitimation in this context is a synonym for "popular support," derived mainly from the provisioning of enough goods and services to satisfy the hungry consumer and alienated worker.

Legitimation is given in exchange for the promise of high-intensity consumption. This consumption in western capitalist societies compensates the worker for sacrifices of alienation made in the workplace. The bureaucratic organization of labor further robs the human being of creativity in work. Thus consumption, carried out in so-called leisure time, is a compensation for the long hours put in at the office or factory. Capitalist societies require, in addition, that workers allow the government to intervene in economic life in order to redress the grievances of the most exploited classes in society (through welfare-state measures) and to keep employment as high as possible while at the same time keeping the rate of inflation as low as possible. In other words, legitimation is required in order for the capitalist state to function as an agency of arbitration and mediation between capitalist and working classes.

In the Soviet Union, perhaps even more than in capitalist societies, legitimation is a function of the guarantee of rising levels of personal consumption. Where in a capitalist society consumption must be accompanied by the maintenance of democratic pretenses—inasmuch as liberal democracy must not appear to be compromised by the capitalist state's essentially "pro-capitalist" political role—this is not the case in the Soviet Union. Leaders in the Kremlin were reportedly puzzled by the Watergate crisis for they could not comprehend why Nixon did not merely imprison or ignore those who criticized his behavior. They did not understand that legitimation in the United States depends upon a certain adherence to the constitutional principles of liberal democracy and thus that Nixon could not merely send his enemies to the American equivalent of Siberia! This is not to say that the tradition of liberal democracy is merely superficial, for at least Nixon's enemies could effectively depose him without resorting to a violent insurrection or a coup d'état as would have been required in an authoritarian political culture without a democratic underpinning.

In eastern Europe, thus, legitimation crisis is met by providing human beings with rising levels of consumption. However certain internal critics of state-socialist societies argue that this is not enough to legitimate the state-socialist model; these critics take the position that Marxism is a theory of humanism and socialist democracy that is being fundamentally undermined by the Marxist-Leninist ideology of vanguardism and democratic centralism. They oppose the Leninist justification of a hierarchical, bureaucratized political structure that placates alienated workers with periodic doses of consumption and further argue that Leninism is no longer a valid "revision" of original Marxism.

Today these internal critics of eastern European state-socialism parallel the internal critics of late capitalism. Both the Frankfurt School theorists and eastern European "Marxian humanists" argue that the individual is fundamentally dominated by highly centralized political structures in basic violation of Marx's democratic vision of socialism. There are significant parallels between the western Marxist critique of bureaucratic domination and the eastern Marxist critique of state-socialism, as we will see below.

"Marxian humanism" is the name usually given in the west to these internal critics of state-socialism. This is a useful term for the variety of such critics, although in a literal sense it is often inadequate to characterize the particular versions of Marxism developed in the east. In fact many eastern European critics of Marxism-Leninism such as the Polish philosopher Adam Schaff take the position that "humanism" is contained *within* Marxism in its original form and that it need not be introduced from outside. They take the position that Marxism-Leninism overrides the individual and ignores the requirements of revolutionary democracy. The resurrection of Marxian humanism, or "socialism with a human face" as Alexander Dubček, one of the architects of the short-lived democratization in Czechoslovakia in 1968, called it, pits one version of Marxism against another version: It pits Marx's early philosophical concerns with the general principles of socialism against the structuralist-determinist perspective that sees

Marxism only as an economic critique of capitalist exploitation.

Marxist-Leninist state-socialism has produced its own "theory of opposition," paralleling the way in which later capitalism has produced internal radical opposition (which, in theoretical form, is what we in Chapter 6 call individualist Marxism). *In eastern Europe, individualist Marxism becomes "Marxian humanism," an ethical theory of socialism that emphasizes the civil liberties of the person against the claims made by the state.* In this sense Marxian humanism, as it has been termed, is not primarily a theory of socialist change but rather a theory of *protest* that attempts to resurrect the rights of the person in the name of authentic Marxism.

There appears little desire on the part of Marxian humanists to eradicate the "Marxian" nature of their societies, no matter how imperfect it may be; few Marxian humanists wish to introduce capitalism in place of state-socialism. Admittedly, however, there are dissidents, especially in the Soviet Union, who are blatantly anti-socialist and who would prefer either liberal democracy or even authoritarian religious regimes to state-socialism. (In the USSR, Alexandr Solzhenitsyn represents the latter position, Andrei Sakharov the intermediate position, being a liberal democrat of sorts, and Roy Medvedev takes the position, common to "Marxian humanism," that socialism must be preserved.) The Soviet dissidents, because of the restrictive nature of their system, have not been able to theorize systematically about the possibility of a different social system and thus their opposition has taken the form mainly of protest against the abuses of the regime in the violation of human rights.

In other, less restrictive eastern European societies, however, more systematic types of opposition and protest have been mounted, usually from within the university and academy. The two breeding grounds for Marxian humanism—Czechoslovakia in 1968 and Yugoslavia today—are social systems in which there is greater freedom of speech and dissent than exists either in the Soviet Union or East Germany. Although the Czech experience proved to be unsuccessful, as Soviet tanks crushed the liberalization of Dubček and Svoboda, Czech intellectuals had more freedom of speech during the "thaw" than their counterparts in the Soviet Union or other Soviet-bloc countries. In Yugoslavia, a one-party system that combines a deep-rooted tradition of democratic socialism and anti-Soviet international politics, freedom to criticize socialism has been almost "western" in its scope. Admittedly, there are still limits to this dissidence, as evidenced in the political incarcerations that persist in Yugoslavia. Yet Yugoslavia is fundamentally a self-critical socialist society, not content with the officially imposed Marxist-Leninist ideology of the Soviet Union that white-washes all social contradictions with the prevailing Party line. It is not surprising that Yugoslavian socialism is patterned on industrial self-management and workers' control: The freedom of criticism appears to go hand in hand with the very concept of workers' control.

Many Marxists find in modern Yugoslavia *too* much western liberalism. The system of workers' control, operative in the industrial workplace but not in the overall political system, which is still directed by the League of Communists, tends to be anarchic and often begs for centralization and planning. A current dispute in Yugoslav society is being carried on between technocrats and communist politicians who forged the identity of Yugoslav, fighting beside Tito in World War II. These technocrats emphasize industrial efficiency where political interests emphasize the ideological value of workers' control as an end in itself.

The Yugoslavs today are experiencing acute dilemmas with respect to the very nature of their socialism. Marx was ambiguous in his projections of a future socialist regime of workers' ownership of the means of production. In Yugoslavia there seem to be severe tensions between the requirements of industrial production, and the high levels of consumption it tends to presuppose, and the requirements of democratic, self-managed socialism, achieved through the workers' control of production. Many workers have expressed the opinion that they would trade rising incomes for personal participation on workers' councils, providing demonstrable evidence of this tension between technocratic and Marxian humanist interests.

In the Soviet Union and most other state-socialist societies, with planned economies and no workers' control in production, Marxian humanism is directed *not* against this economic centralization but rather against the political domination of the Communist Party. In Yugoslavia, by contrast, Marxian humanism more often attacks technocratic and bureaucratic domination and not the political hegemony of the League of Communists. Few doubt that the League of Communists in the Yugoslav context is intrinsically necessary in a hostile international situation where the very survival of the Yugoslav nation-state depends on the centralized political state's monopoly of armaments and its guarantee of territorial integrity. Others add, however, that as long as there is economic democracy (in the form of workers' councils) and political authoritarianism (in the form of the preeminence of the League of Communists), real socialism will be impossible to achieve. Yet in spite of these reservations it is true that Marxian critique in the Yugoslav context primarily takes the form of a critique of bureaucratization and not a critique of the absence of civil rights. Any western traveller to Yugoslavia will note immediately that there are an abundance of western newspapers, symbolizing the open borders between Yugoslavia and other nations. While the League of Communists still holds central political power, refusing to allow a multi-party electoral system, it is apparent that there are other, more direct, threats to socialist democracy in Yugoslavia in the form of those technicians and professionals who would eliminate workers' control in favor of a high-consumption, efficiency-oriented economy.

Marxian humanism is not primarily concerned with socialist transformation but with a type of personal liberation from "bureaucratic collectivism," as many have termed the Soviet-style centralized political and economic structure. In our next chapter, we will examine the nature of western theories of "individualist Marxism," developed in the late 1950s and 1960s during the maturity of a highly organized and monolithic form of capitalism when individual rebellion was "coopted" by dominant interests and ideologies; individualist Marxism stressed personal liberation as the source of socialist transformation. Thinkers like Herbert Marcuse proposed modes of escape from patterns of what he termed "one-dimensionality," a characterization that in certain respects resembled that of "mass society," devised in the 1950s by non-Marxist sociologists to capture the monolithic complexity and cultural homogeneity of North American society. One-dimensional society, according to Marcuse, dominates the human being, in spite of the existence of liberal freedoms of speech and choice, offering no fundamental alternatives to the predominant styles of conformist thought and action; indeed, it consumes these deviant styles and even merchandises them, thus cancelling out their political content (e.g., the cultural phenomena of the hippie generation in the 1960s, such as rock music and "liberated" sexual behavior).

The individual Marxists like Marcuse argue that "mass society" is not an improvement on early capitalism, where capital and labor were more sharply divided. Sociologists like Daniel Bell suggest that the "end of ideology" has accompanied the rise of mass society in that early capitalist modes of political and economic contradictions have been blunted by the rise of a social and economic system that is fundamentally egalitarian. Marcuse disputes this claim because he believes that mass society—or one-dimensional society, as he prefers to call it—is still class-stratified. He argues that there is a certain ideological value in persuading human beings that working class and ruling class alike benefit from the system, and that the period of ideological conflict has passed, as Bell avers.

Marxian humanism in state-socialist societies takes basically the same stance with respect to socialist "mass society." Thinkers like Gajo Petrović and Rudi Supek in Yugoslavia, Karel Kosík and Radovan Richta in Czechoslovakia, and Leszek Kolakowski in Poland criticize state-socialist models from the vantage point of the human individual. They have centered their critique of socialist "mass society" around the assumption that Marxism is a theory of the emancipation of the human being and the community; Marxian humanism in this sense is a theory of "praxis," endorsing a concept of man's creative essence to be unveiled by the advent of socialism.

Marxists have traditionally been wary about specifying a theory of human nature, believing that the creation of a viable model of socialist revolution was to have critical and political priority. The eastern European Marxian humanists argue that in a state-socialist context Marxism must be a theory of praxis, an outline of ideal and ethical human nature. In this way people could develop a mode of everyday life that would actualize Marx's vision of socialist freedom and community. The theory of praxis takes the form of (a) a theory of "socialist" human nature and (b) a critique of the authoritarian violations of that potential human nature.

Thinkers like Petrović, who is one of the leading figures of the Yugoslav *Praxis* group, attack state-socialism and its undemocratic political structure by assessing the potential (and lack of it) for creative human "praxis" under that structure. Soviet-style socialism, according to Petrović, frustrates human praxis by denying fundamental human rights and creative freedom. Petrović argues that Marx's concept of praxis involves "self-creativity," a notion of the way in which free human beings express their essential "humanness" through non-alienated labor.

This theory of praxis takes its point of departure from Marx's writings in the Paris manuscripts about the essential character of human labor. There, it will be recalled from Chapter 1, Marx developed a vision of socialist freedom and non-authoritarian community that was seen to depend on emancipating the human being from alienated labor. The root characteristic of human beings, according to Marx, is "externalizing" activity that projects human personality, design and purpose onto nature. Marx characterized the essence of man as productive activity; yet he defined production not in terms of prevailing concepts of economic profit-making activity (i.e., production for exchange-value as against use-value) but more broadly in terms of man's generic capacity for externalization. Marx believed that the distinguishing feature of homo sapiens is the capacity of man for self-expressive activity, changing the natural and social world by externalizing outward the human personality.

Praxis has been stunted, however, by the reality of class society. Marx borrowed from Hegel's theory of consciousness in developing a more historical theory of labor and externalization. Hegel described "alienation," Marx's core analytical concept, as any activity that externalizes aspects of human personality in the outside world. Hegel argued that an emancipated, mature human consciousness could only develop in the interplay between externalization, alienation (which for Hegel was the inevitable by-product of all externalization), and the recovery or "transcendence" of alienation through philosophical self-consciousness.

Marx took Hegel's embryonic theory of alienation and transformed it into a dialectical theory of socialist revolution. Marx, following the inspiration of Ludwig Feuerbach in this regard, felt that Hegel wrongly equated all externalizing activity with the "loss of the object" — as Hegel was to characterize alienation. The human spirit, Hegel felt, must undergo a necessary process of estrangement from its origins in order for the process of *Aufhebung* (the negation-preservation-transcendence of alienation) to be authentic. Hegel thought that large-scale social history could be interpreted in terms of this process of the necessary alienation of externalized products; he saw rationalist philosophy as a vehicle for negating-preserving-transcending the externalizations of personal and social history, a way of achieving that unity of being that lies at the core of all western philosophy.

While Hegel was a philosopher concerned with the development of individual and collective consciousness of the oneness of the realm of spirit, Marx was a socialist revolutionary. Marx took issue with Hegel's assumptions (a) that all externalization of man into nature was alienating and (b) that philosophy alone could overcome alienation. Marx argued that there are possible social orders that do not require the oppression of human beings (alienation) and that these orders could be achieved through active political struggle designed to effect the structural transformation of society. Marx took his inspiration from Hegel's profound theory of externalizing activity, found mainly in his *Phenomenology of Mind*; he felt that Hegel deeply understood the way human beings must externalize themselves to fulfill their essential natures as creatures of self-creative praxis.

But Marx refused on this basis to offer a theory of human nature defined in traditional terms. Many latter-day opponents of Marxism criticize Marx for having offered no theory of human nature and, at the same time, for presupposing a certain "goodness" in humanity that will make a socialist order possible. Those critics reject Marx's hypothesis that it is possible to eliminate class stratification and economic competition, believing that man is "naturally" acquisitive and competitive.

Marx's concept of human nature was based upon human potentials he felt could be released under a socialist order. As a developmental, dialectical theorist, Marx's view of "possible" man was fundamentally open-ended in the sense that Marx's image of socialist freedom was never spelled out in detail. Marx felt that he could not "predict" dimensions of the personality of a communist human being. He suggested rather that the essence of human emancipation was the multiplicity of choices that free human beings would make once liberated from alienation and domination. Marx suggested that human nature, in a state of freedom, would *create itself.*

Praxis, or free human activity, was the vehicle and the source of human emancipation. Men would define themselves through their externalization, produced without compulsion, strict supervision, or authoritarian "imperative coordination." Work, in the capitalist sense of the production of commodities to be exchanged for money, would become a form of art in that it would express the purposes, images, and values of the worker. Ultimately the distinction between work and art would fade as human beings learned to express themselves both in areas of production for use and for exchange. Furthermore, people would cooperate in production, often deriving as much satisfaction from the act of social cooperation as from the work itself.

Marx may have gone too far in arguing that all work could be fully humanized and rendered a form of creative "praxis," suggesting that necessary labor (i.e., required for human survival) and free labor would completely merge. Modern technological production may require more imperative coordination and a more severe division of labor than can feasibly exist under a non-alienated order; there may be certain intrinsic limits to the degree to which work can be transformed into a form of artistic, self-expressive, and self-externalizing praxis. There may also be ecological limits to the extent to which human beings can turn the natural world into a gigantic canvas on which to express their sensibilities. Yet for all of his optimism about transforming alienated labor into free labor, Marx offered a powerful and innovative theory of praxis that preserved the best elements of Hegel's theory of externalization while moving beyond Hegel's narrow philosophical concerns towards a broader and more historical theory of social change.

Certain eastern European Marxism humanists found Marx's theory of praxis and self-externalization to be a significant weapon with which to fend off Marxist state-socialists and those who stress the purely economic dimensions of Marxism. The eastern European praxis philosophers have found that Soviet ideologists often ignore praxis completely in their rush to legitimize the peculiar state-socialism that grew out of the Bolshevik experience. Not only have the basic human rights of eastern European citizens been violated by the peculiarly authoritarian Soviet version of the so-called "dictatorship of the proletariat" and the hegemony of the various national Communist Parties, but the fundamental possibility of self-creative praxis envisioned by Marx has been denied by socialist technocrats and politicians concerned with industrial efficiency and social control and not human emancipation.

There are two grounds on which the Marxian humanists indict state-socialism: (a) in the first place, state-socialism denies fundamental human rights; (b) in the second place, state-socialism does not sufficiently emancipate the person from alienated labor. Marxian humanism is concerned primarily with the latter violation of Marx's concept of emancipation. While recent developments in East-West relations have centered on the issue of human rights (stemming from the Helsinki conference in 1976), this issue for most Marxian humanists is not as critical as the broader issue of the violation of Marxian emancipatory principles by state-socialist regimes.

Human rights, a concept taken from liberal democratic political theory, is not in itself a critical or dialectical concept; it is not a concept that attacks fundamental dimensions of alienation. Civil liberties can be provided in capitalist democracies without altering the basic nature of capitalist class domination. Others who blend the Marxian and human rights perspectives argue that alienation itself, however it is defined, is a violation of human rights, taken in the most rudimentary and fundamental sense of the term. Marxian humanists have not attacked state-socialist domination through a human rights critique largely because the avowed ideological traditions of state-socialist regimes are Marxist and not liberal democratic. In North America and Western Europe, where traditions of democracy have grown up side by side with industrial capitalism, feeding back and forth into each other, the human rights concept has been more powerful. This is to say that domination in the West is often attacked as a violation of basic human rights—the right to substantive political and social freedom as well as to certain limited electoral rights. Few critics of American society would still accept the prevalent ideological definition of political freedom merely as the right to elect representative officers of the state and local community. Most of these critics, especially in the post-Vietnam and post-civil rights eras, recognize that the concept of human rights must have a more substantive (even socialist) meaning, going beyond the ideal of citizen-as-voter.

In eastern Europe, the violation of human rights and of socialist possibilities is best exposed within the frame of reference of original Marxism. Nothing is as powerful as showing that Marx or Engels or Lenin would not have endorsed particular state actions; political legitimation in Soviet-bloc countries stems from appeal to the tradition of Marxism-Leninism. In the USSR, Lenin is the final court of appeals for adjudicating ideological claims. (Marx is less important in the USSR today for the perpetuation and further development of state-socialist ideology than is Lenin, who personally helped give birth to the Russian model of vanguard socialism. Marx wrote much less about the political measures to be taken in the event of a revolutionary coup d'état than did Lenin. Many argue that Marx did not endorse the concept of a revolutionary and post-revolutionary vanguard party, believing that it would have been a fundamental violation of his socialist principles.)

Nonetheless Marx and Marxism are still powerful ideological reference points in all Soviet-bloc nations. Political education in high schools and universities proceeds on the basis of studying Marx's theories of historical and dialectical materialism. The reading of Marx and Lenin's collected works constitutes the core of basic ideological education. Young members of the Soviet Communist Party know as much about the ideological principles and program of Marx as young Americans know about the Constitutional founding fathers. While Marx is a more distant source of inspiration for present-day Soviet ideologists than Lenin, he still exerts a powerful influence over Soviet thought and action.

This enables the Marxian humanists to criticize Soviet socialism by appealing to Marx's theoretical and ideological authority. By showing that Marx was concerned with socialist freedom and with praxis, these critics can attack bureaucratic and Party domination. By resurrecting Marx's theory of alienation, Marxian humanists can justify their claim that alienation still exists in Soviet society. Officially, of course, alienation *cannot* exist in a state-socialist society because the workers legally own the means of production. But by referring to Marx's early theory of alienation, a broader concept of alienation, involving the dehumanizing character of the socialist labor process, can be developed that will allow the analysis of Soviet "contradictions" to proceed unhindered. Marx, Marxist humanists contend, felt that alienation was basically a result of loss of control of one's work-life, one's community, and the product and means of one's labor. Alienation does not refer only to private ownership of the means of production by capitalists but to all social arrangements that strip the human being of control of his productive existence.

The expansion of the concept of alienation beyond its strictly economic significance, in terms of the degree to which workers own capital, has been a theoretical priority for all western Marxists, especially for those within the Hegelian tradition. Hegel himself talked about *Herrschaft* as a form of political domination, rendered in English by the words "power" and "authority." Hegel and Weber both broadened the concept of domination and, implicitly, moved it beyond narrowly economic terms. By expanding the concept of alienation, which was drastically narrowed from what Marx had originally intended by determinists of the Second International, Marxian humanists implicitly create the foundation of their own critique of state-socialism. They can now discover alienation in Moscow as well as in New York.

Marxian humanism within the Soviet bloc testifies to the fact that even state-socialist societies are subject to internal opposition and revolt. It is facetious to suggest parallels between the present-day USSR and Orwell's *1984*, with thought control and total police surveillance; there are crucial differences between present-day state-socialism and Stalinism. To this extent Marxian humanists hope to introduce a more democratic, decentralized, and debureaucratized model of socialism to societies that are "Marxist" in name only. Marxian humanism is both a useful political force of internal opposition within eastern-bloc countries and a theoretical contribution to Marxism in the West, emphasizing Marx's theory of praxis as the revolutionary core of dialectical materialism. It restores Marx and Hegel's concept of the self-externalizing individual and to that extent revives Marx's vision of the possible identity of work and art.

This type of theoretical contribution may become fundamentally crucial for western Marxists in the next decade. In Chapter 7, we will examine ways in which creative human "praxis" might arise in response to political, economic, and ecological realities. Marxian humanism might be a type of socialist ethics that places greater value on the choices and decisions made by individual producers and consumers. The shift from an energy-wasteful, highly centralized capitalist system to decentralized craft-oriented socialism might be urged by a Marxian humanist ethics that informs human beings of their own responsibilities for democratic socialist change.

In this sense, a Marxian ethics, built around the concepts of praxis and of democratic community, found in the early Marx and remaining the essence of Marx's dialectical vision, might bridge the gap between personal liberation and structural transformation. When we examine individualist Marxists in our next chapter we will note that many of these 1960s theories of personal liberation fell short of socialist change because they were unable to relate the personal to the political, structural dimensions of change. Marxian humanism, based on a philosophy of praxis and a concept of democratic community, might be precisely the link between personal liberation and structural transformation western Marxists are seeking; at the very least, it is important to recognize that there are important currents within Marx's thought that stress the ethical responsibility of the human being for refusing to dominate others in the name of distant future liberation. The poetic and artistic images Marx employed to characterize a society beyond alienation might have been developed precisely in conjunction with an ethical theory of socialism. Marxian humanism opposes those who endorse a vanguard model of socialism by stressing that people can only achieve socialism in a total sense by choosing to *act* like socialists—refusing to oppress others, even "class enemies," in the immediate present. This ethics obviously pertains both to eastern European state-socialism and to monopoly capitalism (where, in some quarters, Stalinism and authoritarian socialism are making a comeback of sorts). Marxian humanism as a living concept of ethical responsibility might oppose authoritarian socialism in the West as well as in the East.

Another dimension of Marxian humanism, pertaining to a new ethics of socialist behavior, is the concept of nature found in the early Marx. The theory of praxis and democratic community contains important ideas about the relationship between human beings and surrounding nature. Again, these ideas are relevant to eastern and western societies, both of which will soon have to confront the "limits to industrial growth."

Marx in the Paris manuscripts wrote about the fundamental bond between human beings and nature, suggesting that the emancipation of human nature would require the emancipation of non-human nature. In this regard Marx anticipated later developments in individualist Marxism and, most notably, in existentialism and phenomenology, that stress the embodied, nature-bound character of human existence. Marx recognized that people are "sensuously" imbedded in nature and that human praxis always mediates between human creative purposes and nonhuman nature. Marx went beyond Hegel's philosophical idealism by stressing that externalization always takes place in the context of material nature. The concept of the emancipation of nature is thus another fundamental aspect of Marxian humanism. While ecological crises have not caused the same political and theoretical reaction in eastern European industrial societies as in the West (at least not *yet*), Marxian humanists have also sought within early Marx an appreciation of the bond between humanity and nature that is the core of a left-wing ecological perspective. The creation of a Marxist ethics requires the revival of Marx's assumption that the emancipation of human and nonhuman nature are inseparable.

Finally, Marxian humanism is the most natural forum for discussing the relationship between politics and art in socialist theory. Although Marx did not explore the proper political role of the socialist artist, a subject that consumes many contemporary Marxist discussions of art, he indicated that creative praxis is a type of artistic activity (a) in that it is freely undertaken and not imposed on human beings by the powerful or dominating and (b) in that it represents and externalizes the inner being of the person in nature. Art is a representational, symbolizing activity. Marx suggested that work, when freed from alienation, could resemble art in its representational, self-creative character. Art represents the human being by projecting outward his or her inner realities. Non-alienated work, Marx felt, or "praxis," as he sometimes termed it, could become art under a socialist order.

Nature is the medium in which human beings through praxis realize their inner characters. Without nature, people would lack the (artistic) canvas upon which they project themselves in acts of self-creative externalization. While this dimension of Marxism is not usually deemed important in Marx's own political development or in the development of later Marxism, eastern European Marxian humanists like Kolakowski and Petrović (refusing to see nature as something merely to be mastered or conquered) have been concerned with art as a form of free human praxis and with nature as the "canvas" on which this praxis might take form.

The ecological implications of viewing human praxis as a form of art, respecting the aesthetic and ethical rights of the natural world, are obvious by now. There are also deeper political implications. Marx indicated that the possible unity of work and art as forms of creative praxis would fundamentally change the way in which human beings defined themselves and their social roles. In later work, Marx said that the socialist person would be capable of a certain multi-dimensionality of role-playing, being variously a fisherman, hunter, and critic, without being identified totally with any single activity. By this he meant that the rigid industrial division of labor could be largely ameliorated by more rational and self-managed labor organization and, with it, the self-definitions of human beings who in capitalist society identify totally with their narrow productive roles. In this way Marx assailed one of the deepest structures of bureaucratically organized industrial society, both capitalist and state-socialist; he attacked the dehumanizing effects of a rigid division of labor that requires human beings to define themselves purely in terms of their particular task in bureaucratically organized offices and factories.

Marx felt that human beings could express themselves freely through their praxis; free work could become a representational, symbolizing activity. The very character of work would change in the process. While Marx was vague about how the capitalist division of labor could be overcome, there are nonetheless ample hints and notes in his thought that serve as a point of departure for further speculation along these lines. Implicitly, creative socialist praxis cannot be bound to rigid institutional definitions of political, economic, and social roles for it is "total" in the sense that it blends a variety of creative purposes in a single, self-externalizing activity.

This is to suggest that alienation involves the fragmentation of labor. Marx opposed the division of labor because it splits work into incomplete parts and thus robs the human being of the freedom to create a totality of meaning and symbolism in his work-activity. Art necessarily externalizes this type of totality; in this sense art is not functional to some higher purpose. Workers on the assembly line or in the office do not "represent" themselves in the particular tasks laid out for them (and which are then imperatively coordinated by higher authorities). They merely perform given tasks in the expectation that their labor will be rewarded by a wage. Workers thus live not for the creativity of their work but for the wages they dispose of in their so-called leisure time.

Marx implied that the separation of (alienated) labor and leisure is fundamentally dehumanizing. The worker who enjoys his work, because it expresses the totality of his personality in externalized form, does not divide his time into work and leisure components, the one involving self-sacrifice and boredom and the other involving freedom and self-expression. The worker-artist who has control over his production and his product is not subject to the rigid division of labor and, within it, the division between labor and leisure.

This is not to say, as many Marxian humanists unwittingly imply, that there will be *no* socialist division of labor, no specialization of productive activities. There will have to be a degree of the coordination of separate producers, until that time when all aspects of production are automated. The division of labor will not be abolished but rather transformed in the sense that it will lose its imperatively coordinated character and be opened to workers' control and self-management. The human personality will no longer be defined in terms of a specific, narrowly conceived work-function; instead, production will take on an increasingly "artistic" quality as human beings engage in praxis that expresses the totality of their personalities.

A Marxian humanist perspective on labor will assess the extent to which labor is dehumanizing, fragmentary, and authoritatively controlled and coordinated. Where labor is dehumanizing, Marxian humanists will speculate about ways in which the production process can be made less fragmented and, to that extent, more artistic. Marxian humanism need not be seen as a purely philosophical and artistic perspective, without consequences for analyzing and abolishing the alienation of labor. The theory of praxis, as we have called it, adds an entirely new dimension to Marxian theorizing, which considers the human being in his totality in his relation to work and to nature. In this sense, Marxian humanists' concern with praxis may provide the missing link between personal liberation and structural transformation, relevant to the West as well as to the East.

Marxian humanism often appears to be a vision of personal protest and liberation and not a more systematic theory of institutional change, designed to offer guidelines for the transformation of socialist bureaucratic domination. The prominent exception to this has been in Yugoslavia, among Marxian theorists concerned with further democratizing the model of workers' self-management. Thinkers like Korać, Marković, and Stojanović, excerpted below, believe that the Yugoslav model, in spite of its many evident imperfections, some of which have been discussed above, offers a significant alternative both to the capitalist and Soviet models. They contend that the concept of self-management offers a new perspective on the problem of bureaucratic organization that, carried to its full extent, may provide a concrete model of a new socialist order.

Marxism attempts to relate personal liberation to social transformation of a broader and more structural kind. Marxian humanism stops short of offering a perspective that will relate individual protest and personal liberation to broader transformation. The Yugoslavs, however, have experimented for three decades with a type of socialism that departs radically from the Soviet model, predicated on the notion that industrial production should be broken down into small, self-managed enterprises of cooperative producers. This perspective on socialist organization might prove to be the key to broadening personal liberation into the larger dimension of structural social transformation.

The idea of "praxis" is abstract unless it can be made to suggest possible forms of work and life that break out of the syndrome of alienation. Marx argued that work that takes on a life of its own, outside the ambit of the producer and his community, is alienated work. He did not agree with Hegel that all work must of necessity pass through a phase of self-alienation. Yet Marx did not introduce a fixed definition of praxis.

A positive formulation of the conditions for praxis and free human labor is required today in order for socialist theory to be developed more systematically. It is not enough to suggest that the elimination of capitalism (in narrow economic terms) will automatically produce a society of socialist praxis. There need to be intermediate links between the abolition of class society and the creation of a praxis-oriented socialist society.

Marxian humanism, like individualist Marxism in the West, has failed to rise above protest against alienation in drawing out these links between protest and structural change. The model of workers' self-management might be one such link, overcoming the subservience of workers to managers, administrators, and technocrats in the realm of the workplace and office. Workers' self-management stresses the importance of breaking down the division of labor and the structures of bureaucracy and professionalism which today reinforce capitalist alienation. Only when human beings comprehend the total conditions of their lives, refusing to allow experts to administer and coordinate every last detail of existence, will personal rebellion against alienation begin to broaden out into a larger socialist movement capable of transforming the deepest structures of class society. We will confront this theme again, as we assess the political and theoretical significance of individualist Marxism in the following chapter.

KORAĆ: ON SOCIALIST HUMANISM

Erich Fromm's edited *Socialist Humanism,* published in 1965, contains many of the original expressions of "Marxian humanism." Fromm brings together essays by leading social philosophers from Yugoslavia, Czechoslovakia, and Poland to develop the meaning of socialist or Marxian humanism. In our general introduction to this chapter, we argued that eastern European Marxian humanism has served essentially the same purpose in the East as individualized Marxism in the West. Marxian humanism appeals to Marx's own humanist anthropology in developing a standard of alienation and freedom that can be applied to state-socialist societies. The Yugoslav and Czech social philosophers have criticized the evident imperfections in their own societies from the standpoint of a fresh reading of Marx's philosophical humanism.

Veljko Korać opens Fromm's volume with an essay stressing Marx's intention not merely to abolish private property but also to emancipate human labor from exploitation and alienation. "Marx raised the question of abolishing all these forms of dehumanization, and the possibility of restoring *human* society. This is his basic problem." Korać argues that Marx's fundamental definition of liberation is the emancipation of human labor. "The abolition of private property and exploitation are only the first steps in that direction; the humanization of labor is the first immediate task of socialist practice."

This provides Korać and other Marxian humanists, with a standard by which to assess state-socialist practice. While state-socialists have abolished private property, at least in name, they have not abolished the alienation of labor. "Socialism is therefore not Marx's ultimate aim but an approximation. His ultimate aim is *human* society." This is a central formulation of Marxian humanism, declaring that alienation still exists under state-socialism.

Korać argues that Marxian humanism rescues the rights of the individual from the clutches of the bureaucratic, often despotic state apparatus. In state-socialist societies "individual man is increasingly deprived of his personality while mankind as a greater goal of history is increasingly emphasized." Stalinism served to "submerge the personality in the society, or in the people . . . in the name of higher interests which are also termed collective interests." This is remarkably similar to the Frankfurt School's critique of the tendencies of advanced capitalism towards the "absolute integration" of man and society, fundamentally overriding the rights and humanity of the individual in the process. As Marx stressed, the freedom of the individual is a condition of freedom for all.

Finally, "...Marx's philosophy cannot be reconciled with bureaucratic decrees which announce that socialism or communism in a certain country is already an accomplished fact. On the contrary, what is necessary, according to Marx, is unconditional and uncompromising criticism of everything existing."

Establishing through critical analysis man's alienation from man, from the product of his labor, even from his own human activity, Marx raised the question of abolishing all these forms of dehumanization, and the possibility of restoring *human* society. This is his basic problem. As critics of the existing society, other socialists also knew that the society of private property was nothing more than a society of merciless exploitation, dehumanization, and the deformation of man, but they never analyzed deeply the reasons for such a state of affairs. They believed that society could be transformed by an ideal plan of a more perfect form of social relationships which would be realized by the triumph of reason as soon as people comprehended what such a plan held out to them. The real liberating forces within society remained unknown to them, as did the real methods for overcoming existing dehumanization and inhumanity. For this reason all attempts to realize such projects very soon came to nothing.

Nevertheless, the idea of socialism was not compromised. Marx was completely aware of this when he confronted various communistic and socialistic doctrines. He criticized them from first to last, even rejecting some for their egalitarian dogmatism, illusionism, and other biases. Every notion of egalitarianism projected in advance he regarded as dogmatism. In place of this he chose consistent criticism of the inhumanity in existing society. Searching for the root of the basic contradictions in that society, he came to the phenomenon of the irreconcilable opposition of capital and labor. "In speaking of labor one deals directly with man himself," he observed, adding that "this new formulation of the problem already contains its solution." He wanted to discover why work wrought marvels for the wealthy but brought poverty and wretchedness to the laborer. What was the contradiction in work itself? If by his own labor man creates himself, why then is his own work something foreign, a hardship instead of a satisfaction? Why is man alienated from man and from his own humanity?

That all these questions necessarily followed from Marx's concept of man is more than obvious, and the answers he gave had a decisive meaning for his entire theory and the practice of it—for it was from these answers that he derived his socialist theory. Their essential content is that man creating himself through the social-historical process becomes only potentially more human because his way of life under the prevailing conditions of division of labor and class antagonism permits his humanity to manifest and confirm itself only partially. Increasing his power over nature, man develops the dimension of his species-being, but remains powerless to direct his social existence because his own being remains alien and unknown. In the society of private property and exploitation, universal alienation manifests itself as the alienation of those potentialities that raise man above all other living creatures. Even the advances of science and technology become instruments of inhumanity. That is why the problem of abolishing alienation and insuring free development presents itself as the problem of social freedom.

Ascertaining that all forms of alienation are a consequence of the alienation of man's working activity and that private property as "the sensuous material expression of estranged man's life gave rise to the stupid habit of regarding an object one's own only upon physical possession of it," Marx concluded that without complete and true emancipation of labor, people could not become human and society could not become human society. The abolition of private property and exploitation are only the first steps in that direction; the humanization of labor is the first immediate task of socialist practice. But to accomplish this it is necessary to know just which social forces can accomplish it. Starting with the fact of alienation, Marx showed that total estrangement and dehumanization (in his words "the complete loss of man") has become universal in modern society, causing universal suffering. Marx's aim was true *man*—living under emancipated conditions of labor and not disintegrated by the division of labor. His vision of humanity's future was founded on the assumption that such a man was not only possible, but the necessary result of social development and essential to the existence of a truly human society. It was in this spirit that he wrote that "the standpoint of the old materialism is 'bourgeois society'; the standpoint of the new materialism is *human* or socialized humanity."

Socialism is therefore not Marx's ultimate aim but an approximation. His ultimate aim is *human* society; society in which dehumanization ceases, human labor is truly emancipated, and man has all the conditions necessary to his development and self-affirmation. Marx does not propose an ideal society in which the freedom of the individual is automatically achieved. This he knows to be a delusion, for free society remains an abstraction if every member of that society is not free as an individual. Therefore he makes explicit that a new, *human* society can be only an association of men where *the freedom of each individual becomes the condition for the freedom of all.*

Freedom of human personality, for Marx, is not an empty abstraction, nor is it merely a youthful dream as his conservative detractors would like to maintain. In *Capital* he says clearly that freedom in social relations lies with freely associated men, associated producers, rationally regulating their exchange of matter with nature, bringing it under social control so as to effect the exchange with as little expenditure of energy as possible and under conditions most worthy of their human nature. Only thus can alienated labor, which impoverishes, deforms, and robs the worker of his humanity, come to an end. Hence when Marx speaks of the absolute impoverishment of the worker in capitalism and declares that the accumulation of capital is equaled by the accumulation of misery, he is thinking of the worker's inhuman life in all its aspects, not just of his economic poverty. This is what he has in mind when he writes that the accumulation of "drudgery, slavery, savagery, and moral decline are the lot of the very class which creates its own product in the form of capital."

Truly emancipated labor will provide the conditions for free social life because only then will work become *production,* i.e., a creative activity which transforms the individual into a personality. Marx saw the development of society as the development of each individual, hence the ultimate aim of society's development became the complete and true freedom of the personality, which is the essential condition of freedom for all.

The socialist and humanist theories with which Marx had occasion to deal gave very little attention to this problem; moreover, the majority of them postulated ideal socialism or communism in such a way as to eliminate freedom of the personality.

Marx was an energetic opponent and critic of all such forms of socialism and communism, as his attitude toward Cabet and Weitling well illustrates. Describing their system of ideal society as "primitive" or "crude" communism, Marx noted:

> This communism, which negates the *personality* of man in every sphere, is only the logical expression of private property, which is this negation. Universal *envy* setting itself up as a power is only a camouflaged form of cupidity which re-establishes itself and satisfies itself in a different way. The thoughts of every individual with private property are *at least* directed against any *wealthier* private property, in the form of envy and the desire to reduce everything to a common level; so that this envy and leveling in fact constitute the essence of competition. Crude communism is only the culmination of such envy and leveling-down on the basis of a *preconceived* minimum. How little this abolition of private property represents a genuine appropriation is shown by the abstract negation of the whole world of culture and civilization, and the regression of the *unnatural* simplicity of the poor and wantless individual who has not only not surpassed private property but has not yet even attained it.

Marx's socialism was thoroughly opposed to every form of unnatural simplicity, and to the leveling and complete loss of the individual in the impersonal and nameless collective. Instead he proposed the free and universal development of the individual as the underlying *condition* of freedom for all. Such an association of people calls first of all for the abolition of classes, but not in the sense of primitive egalitarianism as in Campanella's *Civitas Solis;* rather, as Friedrich Engels stresses, "the abolition of social classes presupposes a level of production at which the appropriation of the products and means of production, and with them political power, monopoly of education and spiritual guidance, by a special social class will be not only superfluous but a hindrance to economic, political, and intellectual progress." This is why Marx expected that the socialist revolution would begin in the most developed countries of the capitalist world.

However, contemporary history shows that socialist revolutions have not taken place in industrially developed countries but in those barely on the verge of industrial revolution; also that contemporary socialist practice often contains obvious digressions from some of Marx's basic principles of socialist theory. Furthermore, certain socialist developments that have occurred would be extremely difficult to reconcile with any, let alone Marx's, socialism. This, of course, is seized upon as an argument against socialism in general, and especially against Marx's socialism.

The dialectical philosophy on which Marx based his socialist theory cannot ignore these divergences, just as objections to his socialism cannot remain ignored. Critical and revolutionary, Marx's philosophy states that a theory comes to life in a people only to the extent to which it is a realization of that people's needs.

The question thus arises as to what and how great is the need for socialism in an underdeveloped country which finds itself on the threshold of industrial revolution. What are the primary needs of such countries? Whether they call themselves socialist or capitalist, there is no doubt that their primary needs are bound up with the development of material production. For this reason the problems of industrialization outweigh all others, even human relationships. Belief in a better life, which has arisen in all parts of the world after victorious socialist revolutions, is a powerful stimulus to action and becomes a potent element in social practice, accelerating social development. But with limited possibilities of realization that belief must of necessity remain restricted to ideologies of human happiness. So it has been in the past and so it is today. For a poor society, as for a poor man, the primary consideration is the satisfaction of elementary needs and the experience of elementary material enjoyment. Since the contemporary socialist and communist ideal of social order (as formulated by Marx and Engels on the basis of their critical analysis of existing society) presupposes a high level of development of productive forces, the potential danger of considering socialism in a purely economic sense as the only and ultimate aim of social progress is constantly present.

The often observed tendency in socialist countries to take technical advance and growth in productive forces (in themselves not an earmark of socialism, because they are just as important a feature of capitalism) as the index for the degree of socialism and social progress attained bears ample witness to this danger, especially as, at the same time, the progress of humanity and personal rights remain secondary. The less developed a country is, the greater its tendency toward primitive egalitarianism and the suppression of personal freedom. It has even come to the point where, in some countries, the ideal of socialism has taken shape in precisely the aspect that Marx most energetically criticized as the "regression to *unnatural* simplicity of the poor and wantless individual" and as "universal envy" (China). The wish to accelerate material technical achievement results in deliberate human sacrifice, and the attempt to justify such sacrifice by historical necessity. To make the justification convincing, fictitious history is substituted for the real. The present is sacrificed in the name of a bright future; living people are the victims to posterity's happiness—just as Christian ideologists promised the kingdom of heaven in reward for worldly suffering. Remote fictitious goals, which are favored over immediate objectives, are presented as absolute ideals for which it is necessary to sacrifice everything. Thus historical optimism, which motivated and still motivates people to strive for a better future, is reduced to a common instrument of current politics and loses all connection with socialist ideals.

There are more than enough examples to show how man becomes, in the name of socialism, a mere instrument for certain fixed aims without regard for objective reality. Man's and humanity's advancement become an adjunct of the advancement of an entity which stands above man, and which can be "society," "the state," "technology." etc. In any case, individual man is increasingly deprived of his personality while mankind as a "greater" goal of history is increasingly emphasized.

All this finds its expression in various sorts of ideological instrumentalism and conformism, in philosophy, science, art, literature—every variety of spiritual activity. Spiritual creativity is converted into an instrument of ideology and politics to become submerged by those elements of contemporary behavior that have come to be one of the essential marks of present-day bureaucratism, institutionalism, and totalitarianism. The high ethical standards of socialism are misapplied for entirely profane purposes, most often for those purposes that correspond to the interests of the bureaucracy, which thinks only of itself and identifies that self with society and socialism, speaking of an ideal future while enjoying *today's* pleasures and considering itself the single interpreter of historical laws.

The proportions reached by this tendency were demonstrated by Stalinist practice, which, of course, did not cease at the moment when Stalin's embalmed body was removed from Lenin's mausoleum on Red Square. The situation in contemporary China is the best evidence of the tendency toward the revival of Stalinist statism and its transformation into a specific model of primitive and poor egalitarianism. It is this model that wants to impose itself ruthlessly on contemporary mankind as the ideal of socialism—which means that Stalinistic practice wants to impose itself from an even lower level than it used to occupy, a level that really has nothing in common with Marx's ideas of *human* society. In Stalinist practice, faith in socialism was transformed into one of the main levers of despotic arbitrariness which, in the name of certain "greater" future goals, and the "future happiness of humanity," became antihuman and anticritical in the highest degree, until it finally turned into ruthless state idolatry.

Ideologists of bureaucratic-state tendencies have illustrated their departure from Marx's socialist theory on numerous occasions. An outstanding example of this is the following explanation of freedom of the personality in socialism:

> The personality in socialism is free by virtue of the fact that all of the people are free. Under the conditions of socialistic collectivism and socialistic democracy the freedom of one member of the society does not and cannot threaten the freedom of another.

Thus, the relationship between the personality and society is posed in such a way as absolutely to submerge the personality in the society, or in "the people," and this is brought about in the name of "higher" interests which are also termed collective interests. The fact that this "collective" interest ceases to be collective as soon as the individual or personal interest is excluded from it is forgotten. But this is the method whereby bureaucracy represents its own interests. It is more than apparent that, with a personality so described, nothing is left of Marx's association of men in which the freedom of each individual is the *condition* of the freedom for all. It is obvious then that practice has indeed become far separated from Marx's socialist theory, because his case is clear enough: Where there is no freedom of the personality, there is not and cannot be any freedom for "the people."

Critics and opponents of Marx's socialism would like to use just such practice as an argument against Marx's socialism, precisely as they would use the materialism of Karl Vogt as argument against Marx's materialism. They forget that this practice has abandoned Marx and set up its own ideology, which has nothing in common with Marx's ideas, regardless of what is attributed to him. If, in the countries that experienced socialist revolutions before they had had industrial revolutions, all kinds of distortions of socialist ideas appeared, this still does not speak against either the principles of Marx's socialism, or the possibility of realizing these principles under more developed or different conditions, and with different methods. The contradictions in contemporary trends to socialism appear mostly because some socialist practice wants to impose itself as the only possible model of socialism.

Tendencies to ignore or to conceal these contradictions are contrary to Marx's dialectic principles, which attempt to expose and resolve them—their creative strength lies in *precisely* this attempt. Therefore Marx's philosophy cannot be reconciled with bureaucratic decrees which announce that socialism or communism in a certain country is already an accomplished fact. On the contrary, what is necessary, according to Marx, is unconditional and uncompromising criticism of "everything existing." Only to the extent that such criticism exists can the principles of Marx's socialism be verified and affirmed. That is why such criticism increasingly assumes the characteristics of a humanist revolt against bureaucratic-technocratic pragmatism and against all forms of dehumanization and alienation—whatever the society to which it is applied.

Returning to Marx in the original and to the search for the anthropological and humanist principles of his socialism is not, therefore, an escape into the outlived past. Rather, it is the affirmation of the concept that, in socialism bearing Marx's name, man as man can never be sacrificed to the alleged "higher" interests of the future, but always remains the ultimate aim of *today's* tendencies toward *human* society, both theoretically and in practice. That is why interest in Marx's ideas is more alive today than it has been at any previous time.*

SCHAFF: MARXIAN HUMANISM AND THE PROBLEM OF HAPPINESS

Adam Schaff, the eminent Polish Marxist philosopher, has written the most systematic work on Marxist humanism, *Marxism and the Human Individual,* published in Polish in 1965 and translated into English in 1970. In the fourth chapter of that work, "Marxist Humanism," Schaff assesses the nature of human happiness under socialism through an analysis of the dimensions and modalities of Marxist humanism.

First, he asserts that "Marxism . . . is a *radical* humanism," grasping things by their roots—which, for Marx, was man himself. By transforming objective reality, man creates himself and his world. "Man . . . is . . . the autonomous forger of his destiny, the maker of his world and of himself."

Second, Marxism is "militant humanism," for which existential struggle is the key to the fulfillment of human personality. Man "must set about freeing himself." Superhuman or transhuman forces will not emancipate human nature: Human emancipation must be *self*-emancipation.

Third, Marxism is an integral humanism. ". . . Marxist socialism shuns all wishy-washy and abstract injunctions of the 'love thy neighbor' brand; it is a doctrine of struggle and so enjoins hatred of the enemy in the *name* of love of neighbor." Here Schaff develops one of the most critical themes of Marxian humanism. This humanism does *not* preach individual liberation as a sufficient political goal; it starts from the individual's alienation, dissects the causes of that alienation, structural and historical in nature, and finally returns to the individual: The goal of socialism is the emancipation of each person and *thus* the emancipation of society as a whole.

Schaff emphasizes that Marxian humanism, unlike traditional humanism which locates emancipation in the mind and will of the singular individual, aims

*From Erich Fromm, editor, *Socialist Humanism* (Garden City: Anchor Books, 1966), pp. 6-15.

to liberate the individual by the analysis and transformation of alienating social structures. While capitalist class society is the cause of general human alienation, the goal of Marxian humanism is the emancipation of each particular individual.

The final feature of Schaff's humanism is its optimistic character. Because "the world is a *product* of man and man himself is a product of *self-creation* ... man has in practice boundless possibilities of transforming himself." Schaff indicates that technological advances can be harnessed in the further development of human possibilities, giving substance to the implicit optimism of Marxian humanism.

Ours could easily be called an age of clashing humanisms: Not only are there many currents of thought that claim this name but they compete with one another or even fight each other. For we are living at a time when the growing importance of the problem of individual life often causes political struggle to take the form of mutual accusations of a lack of humanism, or even of anti-humanism. Such charges are not a proof that the accuser is himself a humanist, nor an insurance against countercharge. This popularity of humanism and the growing number of conflicting varieties show only one fact: Man, whose very existence is now threatened as never before, wants at least the consolation of hearing about human happiness.

Nor is there a shortage of phrases concerning man and his happiness, particularly in propaganda. This is probably why these words have now lost so much of their meaning, and it is surely because of this that men sceptically test words with actions. The conflict of humanisms is primarily resolved in practice. But this does not mean that theory has been completely devalued. For one thing, practice is seldom self-evident, nor does it provide direct solutions to our problems; and when we refer to the future we must resort to interpretation, and thereby to theory. Another reason is that, despite the growing incredulity of the public, ideologies still play a great role in shaping the minds and emotions of men—and every humanism is an ideology.

The ideological struggle has, therefore, been fought out with humanisms. Not surprisingly, all the sides are sharpening, or at least rattling, their weapons. The wonder is that Marxism held back for so long from this struggle, particularly since it is so well equipped for it.

What do we mean by humanism? Without an answer to this question the dispute—none too precise as it is—threatens to become completely confused.

The learned scholar could easily demonstrate that the word "humanism" has more than one meaning. This is certainly the case, and I do not intend to enter upon a semantic analysis of the word. Instead, I will try to distinguish its meaning more accurately as it is used in such phrases as "Marxist humanism," "Catholic humanism," etc.

Thus, by humanism we mean a system of reflections about man that regard him as the supreme good, and aim to guarantee in practice the best conditions for human happiness. Within this broad humanist framework, there is naturally room for various currents of thought, and, depending on their interpretation of the individual, society, and human happiness, and on their assessment of the effectiveness of the various paths to happiness, they may not only differ considerably but even be directly contradictory. Hence the controversy about which of the rival varieties of humanism is "true" or right. Naturally, this depends on what definitions are accepted, and these in turn depend upon an accepted philosophical system and its related system of values. It is, therefore, a debate that cannot be decided on its own merits, in isolation from a wider theoretical context and from practice. On the other hand, what can be done is to argue about effectiveness from the point of view of the ultimate goal, which is to create the best conditions for human happiness, and thus to win people's minds to a system of values related to one particular version of humanism.

Marxism is humanism, a *radical* humanism, which through its theoretical consistency and its organic unity with practice and action, is greatly superior to all its rivals. Therein lies its attraction to all the oppressed who seek not only verbal consolation, but actual liberation from everything that bars the road to happiness.

"To be radical," Marx wrote, "is to grasp things by the root. But for man the root is man himself. . . . The criticism of religion ends with the doctrine that *man is the supreme being for man.* It ends therefore with the *categorical imperative to overthrow all those conditions* in which man is an abased, enslaved, abandoned, contemptible being. . . .""

This is precisely—as we have repeatedly pointed out—the point of departure of Marxism: man as the supreme good, and the struggle for the changing of the social relations that debase him. This starting point, which bestows on the whole Marxist system of thought its special character, also gives it its humanism. Marxism is humanism—but, naturally, humanism of a specific kind. The most important thing is to pin down this difference which earmarks Marxist humanism and distinguishes it from the many other varieties of humanism.

Above all, then it is a *real* humanism, as Marx himself once described it, although it should more properly be called *materialist,* in contradistinction to the idealist, or even spiritualist, types. As it happens, Marx himself emphasized the contrast. *"Real humanism,"* he wrote, "has no more dangerous enemy in Germany than *spiritualism* or *speculative idealism* which replaces the *actual, individual man* with 'self-consciousness' or 'spirit.'. . ."

Here clearly the character of humanism is associated with the conception of the human individual, which Marx takes as his point of departure: If the starting point is provided by the real, concrete individual (concrete from the point of view of his social ties as well) then this humanism is *real;* but when we start from the idealist speculation about "self-consciousness," "spirit," and the like, the humanism constructed on such foundations is *spiritualist.*

With which of them Marx sides is obvious—it is only real humanism that can be coherently related to his views about the world and society.

Closely connected with the reality of Marx's humanism is another of its most characteristic features: It is consistently *autonomous.*

This question has been discussed in detail in an earlier chapter, and need only be briefly recapitulated. Marxist humanism starts from the real individual and real society, and its doctrine is based on the assumption that man, in the course of *transforming* objective reality, *creates* his world and indirectly influences his own development. Hence this humanism is consistently *autonomous* in the sense of interpreting the human world as a result of the play of its own forces, without resorting to any ultra-humanism and thus heteronomous forces. This divorces Marxist humanism not only from all speculation of a religious nature, but also from objective idealism, which, for instance, takes a *heteronomous* view of the world of objective values. Man, real man, is not only the point of departure, but also the autonomous forger of his destiny, the maker of his world and of himself. Only such a humanism that denies interference in human affairs by forces *over* man can be described as consistent. This is the only possible humanism *sensu proprio*.

To this fundamental feature, this world view of Marxist humanism a further characteristic is wedded: It is a *militant* humanism.

Objections are often raised, particularly by Catholic philosophers, to the appropriation of the adjective "militant" for Marxist humanism alone. *Cannot*, for example, a humanism that is based on Catholic thought be described as militant? Certainly, and one could even quote examples. But what matters in this case is whether the attitude of a *militant* humanist is a logical consequence of his theoretical premises or is independent of them, an accidental appendage.

Viewed from this angle, a humanism based on real individuals and their social relations, and recognizing man as the supreme good, *must* challenge everything that debases man. The attitude of *militant* humanism is in this case resolutely logical: To abstain from the struggle would mean a lack of conviction, an inconsistency. On the other hand, if humanism proceeds from "spirit," "person," "self-consciousness," and the like, it *may* but *need not* oppose evil in *practical* life, since it is not practical life but philosophical speculation that is its province.

In this respect, Marxism is a full-blooded humanism and is deeply rooted in practice: It not only preaches certain principles but draws practical conclusions from them. This is precisely why Marx as a young man had already made *revolutionary struggle* a conclusion of his humanism.

> Just as philosophy finds its *material* weapons in the proletariat so the proletariat finds its intellectual weapons in philosophy. And once the lightning of thought has penetrated deeply into this virgin soil of the people, the Germans will emancipate themselves and become *men*...
>
> The emancipation of Germany is only possible in *practice* if one adopts the point of view of that theory according to which man is the highest being for man.... The *emancipation of Germany* will be an *emancipation of man*. Philosophy is the head of this emancipation, the proletariat is its heart. Philosophy can only be realized by the abolition of the proletariat, and the proletariat can only be abolished by the realization of philosophy.

There is no doubt that the militant attitude of Marx's humanism was an integral part of his temperament. A man who answered his daughter's "questionnaire" about "happiness" by saying that happiness meant "struggle" and unhappiness "surrender" could hardly be satisfied with merely contemplating the causes of human suffering. But this aspect of Marx's humanism is also a logical consequence of his theoretical presuppositions.

In elaborating his view of the world, Marx dissociated himself no less firmly from a purely contemplative position than from idealism. This, in fact, is closely connected with what we have already pointed out in earlier chapters: *that the key to Marx's view of the world should be sought in his theory of man.* Marx begins with the living, real individual, not from contemplation but from action, from transformation of the world. Like Goethe's Faust he says that "in the beginning was the deed," and the "deed" to him is human practice. Consequently, the passive speculation of traditional philosophy, materialism included, was alien to him. He acknowledged the superiority of idealism in this respect: It developed the active side of philosophy although it did not, and could not, arrive at a theory of practice. This trend in Marx's thought culminated in his critique of Feuerbach's philosophy, and the famous eleventh "Thesis on Feuerbach" contains his credo: "The philosophers have only *interpreted* the world in various ways; the point however is to *change* it." With *such* an approach to philosophy, Marx could not, naturally, be satisfied with a humanist contemplation of human fate. A man who saw philosophy as the spiritual weapon of the proletariat and the proletariat as the material weapon of philosophy *must* choose a *militant* humanism.

It must not be thought, however, that this trait of Marx's humanism was arrived at by deduction from his general philosophical premises. The reverse was rather the case, although it seems likely that this is a classic example of mutual interaction.

As already pointed out, *militancy* is the logical outcome, primarily of the starting point of Marx's humanism, a consequence of the fact that this was a *real* humanism, which interpreted the human world as an *autonomous* world, created by social man and only by him.

If the world of man and man himself are products of *self-creation,* then man cannot and should not expect to be liberated from his sufferings by some superhuman force—good or evil—but must set about freeing himself. In other words, belief in self-creation means that one must also accept the idea of self-emancipation. And it is precisely the basic idea of the self-emancipation of the proletariat that must liberate the whole of mankind in order to liberate itself as a class, that is at the foundation of Marx's socialism; consequently, his humanism must accept the principle of struggle for its fulfilment and thus become a *militant* humanism.

It is only on the basis of self-emancipation and militant humanism that one can understand the Marxian theory of class struggle and of the historic mission of the proletariat in the formation of a classless society—so masterfully condensed in the *Communist Manifesto.* It is only through these ideas that we can grasp the dialectic of that which is class conditioned and that which transcends classes, the dialectic of general social interests, in Marxian socialism, as well as the dialectic of love and hatred that comes to be in the course of its realization.

Man is the point of departure of Marx's socialism; and man is also its point of arrival, its goal.

We know already that the man of whom Marx speaks is no abstraction—indeed, he criticized such an approach—but a concrete, real individual, involved in social relations and the resulting conflicts and struggles. Thus, in proceeding from real individuals, Marx at the outset predicated his argument on actually existing social classes and social strata. In this way he made his discovery of the proletariat and its universal social function.

But Marx's point of arrival, the object of his endeavors, is man in general, the happiness of *every* human individual. This is where the profound meaning of the dialectic of his humanism lies: not in the purely sentimental theory "love thy neighbor" or with mumbo jumbo about "integral" humanism. It strives precisely toward the fulfillment of *integral* humanism, since it embraces the whole of mankind and is concerned with the full development of *every* personality. More than that: Thanks to its realism and its guarantee of fulfillment through a struggle, *only* this humanism can *truly* be called *integral* by virtue of its aims—although it is resolutely opposed to the catchword of integral humanism in the sense of a repudiation of a genuine struggle for realization of humanist aims.

With this dialectic of struggle, the interaction between what is class-conditioned and what is all-human, is connected the dialectic of love and hate in the pursuit of universal human ideals.

Since socialism—in *every* form—takes man and a revolt against the dehumanization of life as its point of departure, it thus starts with *love of man* and a sense of distress at man's dehumanization, debasement, unhappiness. Socialism *is* in a sense *identical* with love of man, while a socialism that hated man would be a contradiction in terms. Yet Marxist socialism shuns all wishy-washy and abstract injunctions of the "love thy neighbor" brand; it is a doctrine of struggle and so enjoins hatred of the enemy in the *name* of love of neighbor. A contradiction? Only on the surface. In fact, this is a far more consistent, and so authentic, conviction than the lukewarm slogans of "integral" humanism, which, while sometimes subjectively honest, are in most cases hypocritical and mendacious.

Socialism is a doctrine of neighborly love both in its point of departure and in its goals. But since it approaches the problem of love not abstractly but in a concrete way—that is, on the hard ground of struggle for its related basis and goals—Marxist humanism must struggle against what contradicts this love, and so against all that makes man debased, oppressed, exploited—in a word, unhappy. But "struggle" is not simply a phrase, it means *action* to frustrate and render harmless all those who, in the name of their private interests, bar men's way to happiness—and so deny love of mankind. For in a class society, there have been and still are *enemies* of this love—whether their behavior is conscious or unconscious. Anyone who understands that also understands that the enemies of brotherly love—enemies of the cause of humanity—must be fought actively—and this is inseparably connected with feelings of hate. Love of man is far from excluding—in fact, presupposes—hatred of those who act objectively in the name of hatred (and how much more abominable if subjective awareness goes along with it). The Nazis are the classic example of such men. Despite appearances, anyone who in such a situation denies the necessity of struggle—and so of hatred of the enemy—acts not as a humanist but as a typical *antihumanist*. For by preaching a love of man that forbids harming another human being under any circumstances, one *does harm* to thousands and millions of innocent people who are victims of class, national, racial, or other kinds of oppression and violence. That *no* sensible person would behave like this in practice is a different matter; but the very profession of such principles—and they are often put forward in self-interest to bring intellectual chaos and confusion among one's enemies—is tantamount to asserting antihumanist ideas. On this point there should be theoretical clarity.

And so we have a love of neighbor, a love of man, which does not exclude hatred, since it does not exclude struggle, but on the contrary postulates it. But having adopted such a position *and following it through in practice,* we must exercise particular caution, which is also indispensable in the development of the relevant theory. In both cases, the *most important* thing is to remember that the crux is man, while hatred is always subordinated to another cause—*the love of man.* Unfortunately, in matters like this, it is always difficult to keep within the proper limits. This is one more reason to remember and recall—if only for didactic purposes—that what is really decisive is the problem of man. . . .

Finally, there is one other characteristic that distinguishes Marxist humanism, particularly in our day: It is an *optimistic* humanism.

Reading the classic Marxist texts on man under communism, one sometimes gets the feeling that they are utopian. No doubt they do contain a residue of Utopia. But it may also be that, limited as we are by the narrow perspective of our own time, we lose sight of the more distant vistas adumbrated by the founders of the system. If it is advisable to beware of too bold flights of fantasy, it is equally necessary to avoid the mistake of keeping our feet too leadenly planted on the ground. In the light of the modern technical revolution, with automation of production and liberation of atomic energy, should we not take a different view of such goals as the elimination of the disparities between manual and mental labor, between work on the land and in the city, or the possibility of a practically limitless satisfaction of human needs—all of which only several decades ago belonged to the realm of fantasy?

Modern industrial technology certainly gives rise to a number of new problems, some of which were not foreseen. But if the right social context were created for it, technology also offers possibilities of solving ancient unsolved problems; if nothing else, it can bring a shorter working day.

It is interesting to see, particularly from the viewpoint of social psychology, how *the same* social phenomenon—industrialization and technical progress— can be interpreted in different ways according to the social perspective of the observer.

On the one hand, it forms the background of a philosophy of despair that treats society as a sum of isolated, atomized monads, moving meaninglessly on the stage of life in a setting of a depersonalized mass culture totally devoid of any human values. This is a grotesque exaggeration of certain features of the modern social and cultural situation in bourgeois society. That *only these* traits are perceived is undoubtedly due to a preoccupation with the perspective of a "dehumanized world"—to use a phrase of the young Marx. But this point of view makes for a pessimistic vision of the world. If existentialism is humanism—as Sartre with justice claims—it is the humanism of a dying world and therefore tragic and *pessimistic*.

But *the same* phenomenon can be seen in another light, as a harbinger of the new that the future will bring. This is the attitude of socialist humanism, whose perspective is determined by a completely new social situation, or at least by the prospects of such a situation. The technical revolution, which is disintegrating the old world, also holds out the possibility of creating a new world. For the first time in history there is a real chance of making mankind's most ancient dream—a happy life *for all men*—come true. Can this dream be *fully* realized? The future will show; personally, I am sceptical. But there is certainly the possibility of a *better, happier* life; this is already a great deal, and more can surely be expected. When things are viewed in this light—and this is feasible only from the appropriate social perspective—the vision of the further development of the individual and society at once changes.

This does not mean that the vision of Kafka's *Castle* or Sartre's *Nausea* must be replaced by a social-realist brand of optimism in which virtue always triumphs like the honest sheriff in American cowboy Westerns. Matters here are certainly—and fortunately—more complicated. But it is undoubtedly an *optimistic* humanism, not because it irrationally believes that man is good and that good must triumph (just as Sartre's existentialism holds, or held, the opposite belief), but because of its conviction that the world is a *product* of man and man himself is a product of *self-creation;* consequently, since his possibilities of transforming the world are practically boundless—as proved, among other things, before our eyes by the present technical revolution—man has in practice boundless possibilities of transforming himself.

Such optimism is not an act of faith but a *conviction* based on facts. Thus, it is not an axiom but a working hypothesis of high probability and tremendous practical importance from the point of view of mobilizing the social energies of man. Such a hypothesis is a component of ideology, but its heuristic value is no less great than many other propositions in the social sciences. And that is enough. *

> Schaff also proposes a "negative" theory of happiness to suit his vision of a Marxian humanism. ". . . A society that, to achieve a fusion of individual and public interests, strives to enforce a *generally binding* model of human happiness must inevitably end with a horrifying tyranny that stifles the individual with a totally dehumanized life." Schaff argues that a complete and total union of individual and society inevitably destroys human individuality. This argument is reminiscent of the Frankfurt School's critique of the decline of the individual, and its "absolute integration" into society, although Schaff implicitly believes that the individual can be "saved" (via revolution) where Adorno was more pessimistic in this respect.
>
> ". . . *there is not*—and fortunately *cannot be*—a single type of happiness for everybody," Schaff writes, ". . . let each person be happy in his own way, even if what he needs is a hobby, or if he insists on being slightly eccentric or different." Schaff thinks that Marxism can be more effective by eliminating existing alienation and impediments to happiness than by imposing its own fixed definitions of freedom and satisfaction. He feels that it is false to work towards a specific definition of the requirements of human happiness; instead Marxists should concentrate on removing impediments to the free and individual expression of human personality in all of its diversity.

Every fully developed system of humanism contains its own theory of happiness. In a sense, each humanism is a theory of happiness, for any reflection on man and his affairs must culminate in a discussion of the conditions for a happy life. Marxist humanism is no exception. It also contains a theory of happiness, or at any rate *implies* one; to make it *explicit* is indispensable for a better understanding of the character of this Marxist humanism.

The problem of happiness can be approached from either of two directions: its positive side—which we call "happiness"—or its negative side—which we describe as "unhappiness." The difference between these approaches is crucial, particularly from a practical point of view, and cannot be reduced to the simple matter of inserting a "not" in certain affirmative propositions.

The first method is the traditional one, tested in various theories of happiness that have made their appearance during the history of human thought. But experience has shown that the positive approach does not—and cannot—yield any results, or only very modest ones. What a wealth of pronouncements we have had on this subject and how different, even contradictory, have been the attitudes behind them! No wonder: A condition that basically consists of

---

subjective feelings, responses, and sensations can hardly be defined (apart from definitions that are so general as to be practically meaningless), and still less codified by means of norms and injunctions. I may go on for years telling somebody that he should be happy in a given situation, seeing his circumstances through *my* eyes, or thinking of one of the standard definitions of happiness— that of the Stoics, for example—and yet this will change nothing: The person in question will continue to be unhappy and may even commit suicide because in *his* mind the situation has become intolerable. It is in this discrepancy between *my* and *your* perception of a situation, one that cannot either be ignored or skirted, that the crux of the matter lies. For what is involved—and philosophers have often forgotten this—is not an abstraction, but living, real men who often enough differ from each other fundamentally as well as in details, men who constitute specific structures, specific microcosms. The problem of happiness may not be *fully* reducible to the subjective factor, but it is so closely, so organically linked with it that to take no account of this when trying to construct generally valid—and thus abstract—definitions is bound to be self-defeating. We all know, and need not be surprised, that what makes one person feel happy can make another unhappy, even within the same social framework, the same historical period, and the same system of social determinants. Some rejoice in exercising power, while it would make others suffer deeply; some delight in a permanent siesta, while others are driven to despair from lack of active work; one man will exult in promiscuous love affairs, another would regard it as intolerable drudgery. And so on, and so forth. It is also psychologically true, paradoxical as it may seem, that to feel contented some people must be un- happy, or at least have something to grumble about—and they go out of their way to find a cause for dissatisfaction. In a word, people are not alike and cannot find gratification in the same things. Since the feeling of happiness is always an individual sensation, which is organically bound to the psychophysi- cal structure of the perceiving subject, any attempt to settle the problem in a "general" way, by means of sweeping definitions, or even worse, by laying down when and in what circumstances people *should* be happy is doomed to failure; and in the case of a state embarking on *practical* activity to this effect, it may bring real human misery.

A socialist society should pay particular attention to this problem—not only because the possibilities of centralized action are greater under socialism than in other systems of government, but also because the temptation of trying to decree the conditions for human happiness is a real danger.

It is not irrelevant to point out that it is precisely this formula that has provided the basis for various anticommunist utopias: A society that, to achieve a fusion of individual and public interests, strives to enforce a *generally binding* model of human happiness must inevitably end with a horrifying tyranny that stifles the individual with a totally dehumanized life. Let me illustrate this with the example of a little-known book, Zamiatin's *We*, probably the most original work of its kind. I have chosen this novel not because I approve its tenor, but because, like Orwell's *1984*, it takes to their logical extreme some of the tendencies in socialist ideology and certain developments in socialist countries, and thus helps us better to visualize the dangers.

The message of Zamiatin's book is as follows: when the idea of a complete fusion of individual and society is carried to its extreme (note that the Marxist postulate of a fusion between the *interests of the individual* and society has been twisted into a non-Marxist notion implying the *disappearance of individuality;* without this intellectual trick, the novel would not work), this must necessarily result in a denial of the right to individuality and individual happiness. By abolishing individual identity, the state imposes the same stereotype of happiness on everybody (in the book this is carried as far as the compulsory removal from the brains of all citizens of their "imagination center," which is responsible for their individualistic tendencies). Hell begins here. Do not deprive individuals of their individuality, is the author's single message; do not enforce your own ideas of happiness, for in doing this you can only dehumanize human existence, only make man unhappy.

Zamiatin is right, although it could easily be objected that he is fighting shadows since nobody ever sought to bring about the situation he describes, or that he has deliberately distorted the Marxist ideals by talking of a fusion between individual and society in terms of the liquidation of individuality. These criticisms are to the point, but even so a hard core remains in the book and deserves meditation.

Working with a specific literary convention, Zamiatin reduces certain observed tendencies to absurdity and shows what would happen if they were given full rein. Later, the same procedure was adopted by Orwell. It is true that this results in a grotesque or tragicomic distortion of things as they are. But the fact remains that this mirror reflects a certain reality which deserves closer inspection.

Although Zamiatin's anticommunist utopia is false, there are some kernels of truth in this falsehood and these should not be ignored. When definitions of happiness begin to be elaborated and a corresponding code of behavior is made binding on all men for their own good, of course;—what has not been done in history in the name of salvation and happiness!—then people are threatened under socialism too, with the danger of being "made happy" by decree, forcibly, according to the accepted model of happiness; and this may lead to massive general unhappiness. After all, a certain restriction of human freedom is then required—and every such constraint tends to reduce rather than increase the chances of happiness. Fortunately, experience has shown that such tendencies are typically a symptom of the childhood diseases of left-wing communism and usually fade away with the stabilization of life under the new system of government. Consequently, it is enough to conclude these remarks with just one warning: Since *there is not*—and fortunately *cannot be*—a single type of happiness for everybody, any attempt to construct identical stereotypes should be avoided. Socialism does not oppose human individuality—on the contrary. Let us then give this individuality free play in the pursuit of happiness and let each person be happy in his own way—even if what he needs is a hobby, or if he insists on being slightly eccentric or different. That's his own business. Recognition of this freedom—which can do no harm to socialism—is one of the pre-conditions for genuine, authentic happiness of all men.

Thus, if the positive approach to the problem of human happiness does not yield any results—and even holds a danger of doing mischief—our interest should be all the greater in the opposite inquiry: What causes unhappiness, and what are the characteristics of this condition.

No generally binding definition of human happiness can be given, since, in view of its individual nature, such a definition is simply impossible. On the other hand, it is fairly easy to name the causes of general human unhappiness:

hunger, death, disease, imprisonment, all kinds of exploitation and oppression, etc. People have changing needs and they cannot be codified positively from the point of view of general happiness. But they can be codified *negatively*: no normal man can be happy unless he can satisfy a minimum of his own and his family's needs, if he suffers hunger and cold, if he is sick, if he is threatened with death in war, when his country is enslaved, when he cannot enjoy his freedom in various ways, etc.

Here is a reasonable basis for action on behalf of human happiness—not in the sense of making man happy, but of *eliminating the causes of general unhappiness.*

The militant character of Marxist humanism is closely connected with this concept of happiness: It calls for an uncompromising struggle against the causes of human misery as a mass phenomenon—and thus against its *social* roots. This is a realistic objective, the aim being to create the *chances* of a happy life. Nothing more can be achieved by any social order, since no one can *guarantee* happiness. This after all is an individual matter. Even in ideal social and economic conditions people can individually be unhappy —no economic or social system can protect them against disease, the death of their near ones, unrequited love, personal failures, etc. Nor is this the point—it would be as impossible and unpracticable an objective as trying to make people happy by force, or to eradicate all sources of individual misery. But it is fully possible and practicable to root out the causes of widespread mass misery, whose sources lie not in the individual, but outside him, in social conditions and relations. Thus Marxist humanism does not promise any utopian paradise and does not claim to provide a key to individual happiness for everybody. It does not even guarantee that new barriers to human happiness will not emerge in the future; even this cannot be guaranteed, although it is highly probable that a rationally organized society will consciously combat such situations. But Marxist humanism calls for something else: *the liquidation of the existing social causes of human unhappiness.* This is a great deal—and it gives this humanism its appeal to all those who suffer under the prevailing social relations. It is this that determines its rebellious and militant character, as it strives to fulfill Marx's words cited above: "The criticism of religion ends with the doctrine that *man is the supreme being for man;* it ends therefore with the *categorical imperative* to overthrow *all* those conditions in which man is an abused, enslaved, abandoned contemptible being. . . ."*

MARKOVIĆ: PARTICIPATORY DEMOCRACY AND BUREAUCRACY

With Gajo Petrović and Svetozar Stojanović, Mihailo Marković belongs to the "Praxis" school of social philosophers, comprised primarily of philosophy professors from the Universities of Zagreb and Beograd. This school first formed around the publication of an international theoretical journal, *Praxis,* published both in Serbo-Croat and in an international edition (with English, French, and German translations). In addition, this school grew around summer philosophy conferences held on the Adriatic island of Korčula, where western Marxists joined with Yugoslavs in discussing salient problems of Marxian humanism.

The Praxis group has two basic thrusts: (a) first, it relies on Marx's early humanism and his theory of alienation in developing a concept of free human activity, or "praxis"; (b) second, it relates this interpretation of Marxism as a philosophy of praxis to contemporary Yugoslav society. Praxis philosophy operates as a critique of alienation within socialist systems, measuring Yugoslav political and economic structures against the requirements of human freedom first developed by Marx in the early writings.

The Praxis philosophers support the Yugoslav experiments with workers' self-management; they believe that Yugoslav socialism in this regard represents a fundamental alternative to the Soviet model. However the Praxis philosophers have also been relentlessly critical of the insufficient development of self-management as an organizing principle for the entire Yugoslavian society. It is evident that elements of "statism" and centralized imperative coordination exist side by side with industrial self-management. The national political structure in modern Yugoslavia remains fundamentally hierarchical, as do the local and regional political structures. While many argue that Yugoslavia must remain vigilant in face of threatened Soviet invasion, thus requiring a strong centralized and authoritarian political structure, the Praxis philosophers contend that socialism will be incomplete until self-management becomes the organizing principle of the entire society.

Unfortunately, members of the philosophy faculty at the University of Beograd have lost their professorial posts in recent years because they have been labelled politically irresponsible by the League of Communists. While Yugoslavia is much freer domestically than the Soviet Union, with relatively open borders and free dissemination of information, especially foreign publications, there still exist numerous points of friction between the state apparatus, controlled by the Yugoslav League of Communists, and the requirements of self-management and critical discussion. The Praxis group has been threatened with extinction virtually since its inception, thus confirming its central contention that self-management and other non-authoritarian forms have been insufficiently developed in contemporary Yugoslavia.

Mihailo Marković in 1974 published *From Affluence to Praxis,* articulating the basic assumptions of praxis philosophy and raising questions about the future of self-management socialism generally. ". . . A permanent concentration of power in the hands of any particular social group would be an essential limiting factor of the whole further development." Marković in his final chapter, "The New Human Society and its Organization", asks whether "there [is] not always the need for some kind of elite in a complex modern society?" He worries that self-management contradicts the modern requirement of bureaucratic and technocratic organization, subverting the efficiency of modern industrial production processes and the hierarchical organization which they allegedly require.

Marković works towards a theory of the transcendence of socialist bureaucracy, a theory he argues Marxists have basically ignored. He states that "for the first time in history it becomes clear that in the social division of work there is no need for a special profession of people who decide and rule in the name of others. Bureaucracy as an independent, alienated, political subject becomes redundant." The Praxis philosophers criticize both the hierarchical political structure in Yugoslavia and the subtle but inexorable tendencies towards the technocratic management of labor in socialist societies. Workers' self-management threatens to become merely a cosmetic measure taken to appease workers and a few intellectuals; meanwhile, the real decisions about investment and production are made by trained economists and politicians. This tendency towards bureaucratic specialization and professionalism is the most worrisome aspect of modern Yugoslavia, contradicting and even reversing important gains of the self-management system.

Marković is careful to explain differences between himself and the "new left," which opposes all state apparatuses and seems to endorse an anarchist political program. (In this respect, it is possible that Marković is indirectly referring to Marcuse's later work.) Marković, like the other Praxis theorists, does not call for abolition of the state as an immediate, short-term policy; he "merely" advocates social and economic forms of organization that are optimally democratic and nonbureaucratic.

PARTICIPATORY DEMOCRACY AND THE PROBLEM OF BUREAUCRACY

The key problem which mankind will have to face for a long time is how to prevent the recurrence, even in new social models, of considering people as things.

This problem is of fundamental importance for any radical vision of the future. For the existence of alienated concentrated economic and political power in the hands of any ruling elite—of military leaders, private owners of the means of production, managers, professional politicians, or even scientists and philosophers—would impede any radical changes in the sphere of human relationships. The division of people into historical subjects and objects would entail a hypertrophy of the apparatus of power, a conservation of the ideological way of thinking, a control over the mass media of communication, a limitation of political and spiritual freedom. Consequently, a permanent concentration of power in the hands of any particular social group would be an essential limiting factor of the whole further development.

Fortunately, scientific and technological progress with all the far-reaching consequences in the economic, social, and cultural plane opens the historical possibilities for a radical supersession of those institutions which in past history have allowed certain privileged elites to rule over people, such as the state, political parties, army, political police, and security service.

These institutions are necessary to hold together, to protect, regulate, and direct society only while it is dismembered and disintegrated, which is the case with all backward and even semi-industrial societies. While there are a multitude of clashing particular interests—of various enterprises and economic branches, various regions and nationalities—a particular force is needed which will mediate, arbitrate, and direct in the name of the general interest, although the general interest has not yet been constituted. But one of the most important consequences of the present scientific and technological revolution is the dissolution of all artificial barriers and the integration of small, relatively autonomous economic systems into big ones.

Until recently big systems required big bureaucratic apparatuses. However, a profound change is taking place while we are entering a new phase of the technological revolution—the era of cybernetics. All routine administrative operations, including the analysis of information and the search for optimal solutions within some given programs, will be performed much faster and in a more accurate way by electronic computers. A considerable part of bureaucracy would thus lose any *raison d'être*.

Of all the various strata of contemporary bureaucracy the only one which will surely survive are the experts who make and test the alternative programs within the framework of the goals, criteria, and established priorities of the accepted general politics. It is essential that the only remaining professional politicians, highly skilled administrators and executives, be strictly subordinated to the elected political bodies. They will still maintain considerable power and influence. Unlike other citizens they have free access to all information. They have more time than others to study the data and to try to establish certain general trends. By mere selection and interpretation of data, by the choice of certain possibilities and elimination of others in the process of the preparation of alternative solutions, and finally, by a biased presentation of the results of accepted programs. Professional politicians will retain a considerable capacity to induce a desired course of action. In order to check this capacity and keep it within certain limits, several possibilities are open.

First, the subordination of professional politicians to the corresponding assemblies and councils of self-government must be as complete as to allow full responsibility and immediate replacement of any official.

Second, professional political experts will have different roles and to a certain extent different interests. They should not be allowed to form a political block or to control any kind of political organization. Their function of expertise will be best performed if they eliminate any personal or group loyalties and any ideological considerations, and if they would be obliged to follow the principle of technological rationality, that is, to try to find the most adequate means for the goals laid down by the elected representatives of the people.

Third, their whole work should be critically examined by the independent political scientists. Future society must pay very serious attention to the critical scientific study both of politics in general and of actual political practice embracing also its economic sociological and psychological aspects. In contrast to the present-day "politicology" which is either apologetic or focuses on remote events, future society will need a political theory which will try to discover limitations in the actual practice and which will not only study phenomena *a posteriori*, but will also make projections and prepare solutions parallel to the work of the experts in the state apparatus.

Fourth, the most important and indeed revolutionary change in the political organization of the future society should be concerned with the determination of general policies, with the definition of general goals, and with the criteria of evaluation of possible alternative political programs. These key political functions must be radically democratized: The very idea of politics implicit in them will be fundamentally altered. According to Weber, politics is (a) the set of efforts undertaken in order to participate in ruling or in order to influence the distribution of power either among the states or among different groups within one state; (b) this activity is basically the activity of the state; (c) the state is "a relationship of domination of man over other men, based on the means of legitimate violence." Politics in this sense, as compared with true *praxis*, was characterized by Marx as the sphere of alienation. Political activity could, then, become praxis under following conditions:

1. The political praxis is the domination of man over things. The things, however, in the human world are the products of objectified human work. Therefore, political praxis is essentially a control and a rational direction of the social forces which, in fact, are *les forces propres* of social man.

2. The criterion of evaluation among various alternatives of this process is the satisfaction of authentic human needs in all the richness of their specific manifestations in the given historical conditions.

3. The goal of political praxis is not the domination of one social group over the rest of society, but an activity which has *universal* character and concerns each human individual.

4. Political praxis is not isolated from other modes of praxis. Contrary to alienated political activity it is based on a philosophical vision of human nature and history, it need not violate moral norms, its choices presuppose a scientific knowledge of all real possibilities in the given historical situation. At last it also contains elements of a noble struggle, of a game, of an art. To act politically in a human way implies, among other things, "to create according to the laws of beauty."

5. The people would regard such an activity without subjugation, tutelage, and fear as extremely attractive. By participating in such an activity the individual develops an important dimension of his social being and acquires an ample opportunity to express many of his potential capacities and possibly to affirm himself as a gifted, strong, and creative personality.

This conception of political praxis is far from being an invention of pure imagination or a stanza of philosophical poetry.

All those who have participated in a really revolutionary movement have experienced what politics could be, for at least a limited period of time, when it is not a monopoly of a privileged elite. The questions arise, however: Is not every such attempt at the democratization and humanization of politics limited in time and eventually doomed to failure? Does not a moment come when the principle of freedom has to be replaced by the principle of order, when a new social organization begins to function, or when the revolutionary *avant-garde* becomes the new bureaucracy almost overnight? Is there not always the need for some kind of elite in a complex modern society?

The decisive new historical fact relevant to these questions is that the considerable reduction of compulsory work and production, which will take place on a mass scale in an advanced future society, will liberate enormous human energies and talents for political life. The general education and culture, including political knowledge of these potential political "amateurs," need not be inferior to that of "professionals." By participating in local communal life and in various voluntary organizations, many of them have acquired a satisfactory experience in public relations and the art of management. It should also not be overlooked that due to the penetration of modern mass media of communication into most of its corners and secrets, politics has been demystified to a large extent, and many of its institutions and personalities are losing the magical charm they had in the past. Thus the distance in competence between the leaders of political organizations and their rank and file, and, in general, between a political elite and the large masses of people, is eroding. For the first time in history it becomes clear that in the social division of work there is no need for a special profession of people who decide and rule in the name of others. Bureaucracy as an independent, alienated, political subject becomes redundant.

That the socialist movement up to the present has not succeeded in developing a consistent and concrete theory about the transcendence of bureaucracy and the political structure of the new society is the consequence of a really paradoxical development during the last two decades.

First, a series of revolutions took place in backward East European and Asian countries guided by a theory of democratic socialism, which was created in the conditions of relatively advanced Western capitalism. Marx would never call "socialism" an essentially bureaucratic society. He knew that in the initial phase of industrialization really communal social control over productive forces is not yet possible. That is why in *Grundrisse der Kritik des Politischen Oekonomie* he stated explicitly that such a possibility will be created in an advanced society in which "the relations of production will become universal, no matter how reified," in which man will no longer be directly governed by people but by "abstract reified social forces." Only then will the freely associated producers be able to put the whole process of social life under their conscious, planned control. But this requires a material basis "which is the product of a long and painful history of development."

It is pointless to argue now to what extent Lenin and the Bolshevik Party were aware of the essential difference between the conditions in their country in the period of 1917-22 and those conditions under which Marx's theory of self-government were applicable. The fact is that Lenin and his collaborators did not believe that socialist revolution in Russia would be successful without a revolution in all Europe. The institution of Soviets, introduced during the first Russian Revolution in 1905, was a specific form of self-government. Unfortunately, by the end of the civil war there were no longer Soviets, no longer a strong, organized working class. In order to survive, in order to defeat the external enemy, the counterrevolutionary forces, white terrorism, and hunger, and to overcome the total economic collapse, the Bolshevik Party had no other alternatives but to surrender or to proceed by military and bureaucratic methods. While this dilemma was a historical necessity, nothing of the sort can be said about Stalin's later crimes or about the purely ideological identification of this new type of postcapitalist bureaucratic society with socialism.

It follows then that the revolutionary movement in Russia, China, and other underdeveloped countries did not give rise to a theory about the supersession of bureaucracy by the system of self-government because historical conditions for such a radical change of the political structure did not yet exist.

Paradoxically enough, such a theory has not yet been developed by the *new left* in much more favorable conditions. Due to the high level of material development, economic integration, education, and also to the considerable democratic achievements in the past, at least in some Western countries, bureaucratization in the post-capitalist development is by no means the only and necessary way. Instead of looking for alternative forms of political organization based on the principle of self-government, a widespread attitude in the student movement and among the *new left* is a distrust of any kind of political institution. This kind of attitude is easy to understand as a violent reaction to the process of obvious degeneration of the revolutionary state in the victorious revolutions in the East. It involves, however, a mistaken generalization from experiences which have a specific regional character. A dialectical denial of the state is much less and at the same time much more than a *contestation totale*. It is much less because some of the functions and institutions of the state will have to survive and be incorporated into the new political structure. It is much more because a *total* negation of the establishment is practically no negation at all. A real negation of the state is the abolition of its essential internal limit—the monopoly of power in the hands of a particular social group, and the use of apparently legitimate violence in order to project and promote interests of this privileged elite. This abolition does not lead to anarchy and the lack of any organized authority, but to an alternative, really democratic system of management, without any external alienated power.*

STOJANOVIĆ: SELF-CRITIQUE OF SOCIALIST SOCIETY

Svetozar Stojanović's 1969 work, *Between Ideals and Reality* (translated into English in 1973), offers a useful discussion of the Praxis group's attitude towards the self-criticism of socialist society. Stojanović, like Marković, articulates the need for a Marxist critique of Marxism, directing this critique at the imperfections of both statist and self-management models of socialism. It is the latter target of critique that is more interesting in this context. Since Stalin, orthodox Marxists have been reluctant to hold up socialist society to the same critical standard as capitalist society—namely, the existence or absence of human alienation.

" . . . True Marxism will remain the merciless critique of all existing conditions." And "Marxism must relentlessly confront the reality of socialism with the ideals of humanism, unmasking newly constructed myths, fetishes, taboos, and sacred tenets in order to contribute thereby to the willingness of the people to continue their revolutionary activity." Stojanović here is referring not only to the apologetic character of Stalinism, with which Yugoslavia broke decisively in the early 1950s, but also to contemporary Yugoslavia. Stojanović views Marxism as a "moral-political-orientation" that must link theory and practice in the lives of individual human beings. In this sense, Stojanović, like the other Praxis philosophers, expresses impatience at delays in achieving full, and democratic, communism in Yugoslavia.

The critical faculty is an inherent, essential characteristic of the Marxist *Weltanschauung*. Thus, no one can call a person a Marxist while complaining that he is not critically oriented. This distinction derives from the dialectical nature of Marxism, of which Marx wrote:

> In its rational form it [dialectic] is a scandal and an abomination to the bourgeoisie and its doctrinaire professors, because it includes in its comprehension and affirmative recognition of the existing state of things, at the same time also, the recognition of the negation of that state, of its inevitable breaking up; because it regards every historically developed social form as in fluid movement, and therefore takes into account its

*From Mihailo Marković, *From Affluence to Praxis* (Ann Arbor: University of Michigan Press, 1974), pp. 226–33.

transient nature not less than its momentary existence; because it lets nothing impose upon it, and is in its essence critical and revolutionary.

Marx conceived of his mission as follows:

> If the construction of the future and its completion for all time is not our task, what we have to accomplish at this time is all the more clear: *the merciless critique of all existing conditions,* merciless in the sense that this critique is not afraid of its own findings and just as little afraid of conflict with the powers that be.

The Stalinists do not reject this formulation, but "merely" limit it to capitalism. After the revolution, Marxism must allegedly concentrate upon the study and evaluation of the stability, organization, and functioning of the new system.

In Yugoslavia such an understanding of the relationship of Marxism to socialism was rejected long ago. Disagreement has persisted, however, precisely on the demand for a "*merciless* critique of *all* existing conditions" in socialism, as well. It seems that the Czech Marxist Karel Kosík had this dilemma in mind when he wrote:

> The dialectic can justify morality only if it is itself moral. The morality of the dialectic is contained in its distinctive *continuum,* which stops before nothing and no one in its process of destruction and totalization. The nature and size of the spheres which the dialectic leaves outside this process correspond to the degree of its inconsistency and amorality.

As long as it exists, true Marxism will remain the merciless critique of all existing conditions. One might even add that Marxists must be even more critical in socialism than in capitalism, precisely because they are so concerned about socialism. Dialectical thought is inseparable from critical adventure, and it is as harmful to curb it in socialism as it is in capitalism. Those who stand opposed to the merciless critique of all existing conditions in socialism evidently seek to exclude certain persons or certain phenomena from criticism.

Marxism must relentlessly confront the reality of socialism with the ideals of humanism, unmasking newly constructed myths, fetishes, taboos, and sacred tenets in order to contribute thereby to the willingness of the people to continue their revolutionary activity. Socialist society, too, easily falls prey to ideological self-deception. Nor do we exclude the possibility that in the course of destroying the myths of the socialist state, of the communist party, of social planning and social interest, social self-government, the working class, commodity production, and group and personal interests will themselves become the subjects of new myths.

The obligation of the Marxist is solely to the truth of humanism and the humanism of truth. Complete and unadulterated truth threatens only the usurpers of the revolution, never the revolution itself. However, Marxists are interested not only in the relationship of the idea to reality, of reason to existence, but also in the converse relationship. Sometimes even the noblest ideas can be historically irrelevant. When this is not understood, theory easily falls prey to narcissism. Nevertheless, when we talk about the consideration which Marxists should give to historical possibility, we must take great care, because in the history of the communist movement opportunism has often been disguised as realism.

If one understands theory in the Marxist sense, one must live it. Being a Marxist is not a purely theoretical matter. Marxism is a moral-political orientation as well. The principle of the unity of theory and practice—upon which Marxists have insisted so strongly—must be embodied in their lives. Only those theorists whose conceptions are at the same time their convictions will fight for a revolutionary-humanist program, since convictions represent one's intrinsic dispositions for commitment and action.

Both when it is politically safe as well as when it is not, the Marxist must maintain his integrity. Since he knows that in socialism, too, "all great truths begin as blasphemies" (George Bernard Shaw), the Marxist must expect to be attacked for being ahead of his time.*

GUIDE TO FURTHER READING

ADAM SCHAFF   *Marxism and the Human Individual,* is an interesting appreciation by a leading eastern European philosopher of the significance of Marx's early writings on alienation. Schaff argues—in the tradition of all humanism—that the well-being of the human individual must be the ultimate value of any political system.

ERICH FROMM, editor   *Socialist Humanism,* is a work of considerable historical value as the first major work collecting various views on Marxian humanism, many of them from eastern European theorists. Fromm's 1965 book remains one of the most useful references for students of eastern European Marxian humanism.

SVETOZAR STOJANOVIĆ   *Between Ideals and Reality,* is one of the foremost expressions of the Yugoslavian "Praxis" group comprised of professors from Beograd and Zagreb. Members of the Praxis group have participated in editing the important international philosophical journal *Praxis* as well as in annual summer schools on the Yugoslav island of Korcula, bringing together leading theorists of Marxism.

GAJO PETROVIĆ   *Marx in the mid-twentieth Century,* is one of the first works of Yugoslavian Marxism to be translated into English. A member of the Praxis group, Petrović carries forth the argument that Marxism is a theory of freedom and praxis that must never rest in its critical evaluation of every form of human society.

MIHAILO MARKOVIĆ   *From Affluence to Praxis,* goes significantly beyond certain other works of the Praxis group in its ability to relate Yugoslavian Marxian humanism to the larger tradition of western Marxism (such as the Frankfurt School) and to the works of Marx themselves.

SHARON ZUKIN   *Beyond Marx and Tito,* is a sympathetic but critical appraisal of Yugoslavian political reality as well as of the intellectual efforts of Yugoslav philosophers and social theorists.

The *Praxis* journal is an indispensable source of writings on Marxian humanism and Marxian theory generally. It is published both in a Serbo-Croat and an international edition (with articles in French, English, and German). Unfortunately, the journal has temporarily ceased publication owing to political tensions in Yugoslavia and owing in particular to the increasing hostility of the political regime towards members of the Praxis group. The fate of *Praxis* itself demonstrates that the birth of Yugoslavian socialism has been turbulent and not entirely progressive in nature.

FRIEDRICH VON HAYEK   *Collectivist Economic Planning,* is an analysis and critique of centralized economic planning.

*From Svetozar Stojanović, *Between Ideals and Reality* (New York: Oxford University Press, 1973), pp. 13-16.

BRANKO HORVAT   *An Essay on Yugoslav Society,* is a very thoughtful collection of essays on the development of Yugoslavian self-management and democratic socialism by a leading Yugoslav economist.

RADOVAN RICHTA *et al.*   *Civilization at the Crossroads,* first published in Czech in 1967, is an explosive reexamination of Marxian dialectical materialism by a group of Czech social scientists and philosophers. It served as a manifesto of sorts for the architects of the "Prague Spring" in 1968. Richta argues that scientific-technical progress has fundamentally invalidated original Marxism and created new problems of technological society common both to capitalist and socialist systems.

MILOVAN DJILAS   *The New Class,* is the work by a former Yugoslav partisan and comrade of Tito that rocked the socialist world. Djilas postulated the existence of a new elite of Communist Party and military leaders that replaces the capitalist class. His book met with harsh criticism by Tito, and Djilas was subsequently jailed and his work banned from publication in Yugoslavia.

QUESTIONS FOR FURTHER DISCUSSION

1. Explain why eastern European Marxian humanism is more a form of protest against state-socialist regimes than a form of revolutionary Marxism.

2. Was Marx a "Marxian humanist," in Schaff's and Fromm's senses?

3. How does the Yugoslavian self-management system differ from Soviet state-socialism?

4. To what extent, if at all, is Marxian humanism relevant to western industrial societies?

5. Why has the development of Marxian humanism been retarded in the Soviet Union by comparison to its level of development in other eastern European countries like Yugoslavia, Poland, and Czechoslovakia?

6. Are Marxism and humanism inherently incompatible? Why?

Individualized Marxism: Class Radicalism in the 1960s

HISTORICAL OVERVIEW

The 1960s were a time of fundamental reordering of the western capitalist system. The harmony of early monopoly capitalism, culminating in the Eisenhower years in the United States, was exploded by a variety of unprecedented developments in the 1960s: In North America and Western Europe, students began to question many of the basic values of puritanism and the bourgeois work ethic, rejecting these values in favor of more meaningful ones relating to creativity and community; this questioning of the young arose largely in response to the political catastrophe of the United States' involvement in the protracted Indochina war and in the context of the American civil rights and black movements. The political consensus upon which early monopoly capitalism had been built began to erode as people became increasingly cynical about democratic politics, as a result of the assassinations of John Kennedy, Robert Kennedy, and Martin Luther King Jr., and as a result of the disastrous period of Watergate and the resignation of Richard Nixon from the American Presidency. Furthermore, developments in the international economic situation shook the liberal consensus in the West. Economic power began to shift in the early 1970s towards the Arab oil-producing states. In addition, ecological concerns have become highly visible, threatening the seemingly endless production and consumption of commodities upon which capitalism intrinsically rests. All of these developments have reintroduced the concept of crisis into recent Marxist analysis. The harmony of the 1950s is gone, replaced by impending economic and ecological crisis. Citizens of western industrial nations are beginning to question the values of early market capitalism such as personal frugality, hard work, and individual initiative. The intrinsic value of endless consumption is coming under scrutiny, both because endless consumption is threatening to the global ecosystem (using up valuable resources and, as a by-product of production, emitting heat into the atmosphere, threatening as a consequence to overheat the atmosphere and eventually to melt the polar ice caps) and because consumption is no longer viewed as the only possible source of human satisfaction and meaning. This weakening of the ideology of free enterprise and endless commodity production threatens the capitalist system both with a loss of public legitimacy and of profit. This leaves open the way for personal escape from the system. In the 1960s, social movements arose out of this personal rebellion against bourgeois values and life styles; these movements—such as the "hippie" phenomenon—were unable, divorced from systematic class-radicalism, to effect radical political and economic change, although they did serve as a reminder that all was not well with the liberal-capitalist consensus in the West.

GENERAL INTRODUCTION

In light of recent developments in Marxian theory it is necessary to survey conceptual and empirical innovations proposed by thinkers who have self-consciously departed from orthodox scientific Marxism and similarly from the Frankfurt School's Marxism. We have already noted that the critique of domination offered by Horkheimer and Adorno took Georg Lukács' insights further than Lukács intended, relinquishing both the crisis-theory of Marx and the theory of internal contradictions and class-radicalism. In Chapter 4, we argued that Horkheimer and his associates in the Institute for Social Research failed to repoliticize their Marxism once they decided that domination had fundamentally erased the critical autonomy of human beings in late capitalism.

The failure to move twentieth century Marxism beyond a stagnant, negative philosophy was not universal. In the late 1950s and 1960s there emerged a "deviant" strain of post-Hegelian Marxism that tried to steer a course between the Scylla of economic determinism and the Charybdis of the Frankfurt School's abject negative critique. This variant of Marxism was grounded in Marx's early philosophical writings and in the Freudian and existentialist reconstruction of Marxian theory. We term these efforts "individualized Marxism" in order to capture their common spirit. While the works of Herbert Marcuse figure most centrally in this type of Marxism, we will also assess the impact of phenomenological and existentialist currents within modern Marxism. These strains of thought are joined together by their common intention to overcome both the critique of domination (Frankfurt School) and stilted economic orthodoxy (determinism) through a renewed theory of non-authoritarian class-radicalism.

At first glance an individualized Marxism appears to be a contradiction in terms. Marx's analysis and critique of capitalism was carried out on the level of class analysis, making it unlikely that Marx seriously considered the possibility of political activity *beneath* the level of class struggle. This is not to say that Marx ignored the individual, for as we noted in the preceding chapter, it is possible to reconcile an ethical concept of socialist humanism with revolutionary class struggle. In Eastern Europe, Marxian humanism arose as a counterforce to state-socialism that overran the singular individual.

Thinkers like Marcuse do not *substitute* an individualized Marxism for class struggle in the traditional sense. Rather they attempt to join the human being's own responsibility for self-emancipation with socialist change in a larger structural sense. The individualized Marxists did not replace the class struggle with purely personal resistance (such as radical art, escapist philosophy, or drug-transcendence) but rather endeavored to map out a viable relationship between the struggling individual and class-radicalism in a larger sense. Marcuse, Sartre, and Merleau-Ponty believed that it was still possible to uphold the promise of the socialist class struggle; yet they wanted to inject democratic organizational forms into this new class-radicalism in order to avoid the vanguardism of Leninists. Marcuse believed that the struggling individual was the point of departure for significant class-radicalism, drawing theoretical inspiration from the protests of students and minorities against the North American power-systems in the 1960s. Marcuse believed that the so-called New Left was correct to reject "old" Marxian ideologies in favor of a non-authoritarian participatory socialism based on democratic processes and the elimination of bureaucratic organization. In short, Marcuse argued that class-radicalism was only possible if it was built on participatory foundations, drawing on personal frustration and resistance in generating new organizational forms of the class struggle.

Correct as Adorno may have been about the improbability of socialist change during the Eisenhower and Adenauer years, the 1950s and early 1960s, certain of his followers felt that Marxism was soon to reenter the realm of class-radicalism. Adorno's utterly negative conception of Marxian theory—Marxism seen as the critique and destruction of ideologies, not as a synthesis that could organize new struggle—was surpassed during the 1960s by a number of theorists working within the Freudian and existential-phenomenological traditions of western Marxism. These thinkers did not believe that the individual had "declined" in the way that Adorno suggested. Furthermore, they did not believe that Marxism should only rip apart bourgeois ideologies, given the impotence of more ordinary types of class-based political action. Marxists like Herbert Marcuse took the position that socialist change was not impossible (as the Frankfurt critique of domination largely assumed) but that change, if indeed possible, would have to take radically new forms.

Our historical schema based on our discussions up to this point indicates that Marxian theory in the West has passed through four distinct periods:

1. The theorists of the Second International developed Marxisms that were intimately related to the prospect of revolutionary struggle; in spite of temperamental and strategic differences between them, Bernstein, Kautsky, and Luxemburg all believed that early capitalism was nearing the end of its tether. Differences emerged around the issue of how best to *expedite* the incipient final crisis they felt was unavoidable; Bernstein submitted that parliamentary socialism could bring an end to capitalism; Kautsky said that the system would collapse of its own accord and that socialist democracy was an immediate requirement of the period of transition; Luxemburg took a somewhat less fatalistic view than Kautsky in arguing that there must be active proletarian intervention in structural dynamics, believing that capitalism would not simply self-destruct.

2. Lukács and Korsch suggested that the working class failed to fulfill the hopes of Marxists like Kautsky and Luxemburg because the working class lacked "class consciousness" about its imputed historical mission. Lukács stressed that there must be a dialectic between structural crisis-tendencies

and revolutionary voluntarism for the system would neither collapse by itself nor could it be transformed merely by the good intentions of a small vanguard of dedicated activists or "professional revolutionaries."

3. The early Frankfurt School theorists believed that because the working class had become an *un*revolutionary agent in early monopoly capitalism, the entire theory of internal contradictions would have to be transformed to suit the new reality of "domination" (a combination of outright economic exploitation and self-inflicted alienation such as unnecessary consumption and the belief in scientific and instrumental rationality as a panacea for all societal problems). They argued that the individual was more alienated than before and thus they saw few prospects for organized class struggle.

4. Individualized Marxism grew out of the 1960s when early monopoly capitalism underwent further structural changes. Herbert Marcuse attempted to locate new agents of a class-radicalism that in their very choice of post-bourgeois life styles created the infrastructure of socialism. This theory was paralleled in Eastern Europe by the rise of Marxian humanism, which tried to rescue the human being from the stranglehold of bureaucratically organized state-socialism. Where eastern European Marxism humanism was primarily an ethical theory, because it remained politically impotent in the face of the proponderant power of the Soviet state, individualized Marxism in the west took inspiration from the North American student movement, from the anti-war effort, and from the struggle of racial and sexual minorities.

Individualized Marxism arose not because thinkers like Marcuse in the quiet privacy of their offices decided that Adorno's critique of domination was sociologically invalid but because capitalist dynamics, in which Marcuse was inextricably involved, were producing new types of radical opposition. The function of Marxian theory in this context is of paramount importance; we can now better comprehend differences between scientific and dialectical Marxism. Engels and Kautsky felt that Marxist social science must only observe and document capitalist reality, charting and predicting self-generating structural contradictions. We have taken the position that this type of science was not endorsed by Marx because Marx felt that "scientific socialism" had a double character, only one aspect of which was observational and predictive in the former sense. Instead Marx felt that socialist theorists must also attempt to organize and to order that reality in urging along structural tendencies towards crisis and transformation.

Individualized Marxism is interesting because it draws together apparently dissimilar and even contradictory themes. Marcuse's synthesis of Freud and Marx appears to have little in common with Sartre's existentialist Marxism or Piccone's phenomenological Marxism. What unifies them is the assumption that the human being has not totally "declined," as members of the Frankfurt School asserted; instead, *the struggling individual is the starting point for any meaningful theory of class struggle.*

Individualized Marxism arose in response to deterministic Marxism, to Lukács' Hegelian Marxism, and to the historical pessimism of the Frankfurt School. Curiously, it opposed both the scientific determinism of Engels and Kautsky, who felt that revolutionary transformation need not involve individual human beings, and those Hegelian Marxists who conceive of historical change only in terms of massive socialist movements. While Lukács stressed the need to combine structural crisis with a willful and activist working class, opposing in this the mechanistic Marxism of Engels and Kautsky, he did not reduce the working class to particular individuals. He spoke of a revolutionary "collective subject," employing Hegelian terminology (and borrowing from Hegel's implicit assumption that history is made through the movement of large-scale social structures and rarely through the individual actions of ordinary men). While the Frankfurt School theorists rejected Lukács' version of revolutionary Marxism, they overreacted by suggesting not only that there is no revolutionary "collective subject" but that there is no personal subject capable of significant political radicalism.

Individualized Marxism opposes all theories that ignore the relationship between the struggling individual and class struggle. It does so because it contends that the fate of the individual is in some sense the fate of the revolution. The Soviet experience demonstrates the pitfalls of a vanguard model of socialism and its propensity for becoming merely another form of authoritarianism. Korsch indicted the Bolsheviks for having created "a dictatorship *over* the proletariat," stressing the need for revolutionary democracy throughout the process of socialist transition. Korsch reiterated Luxemburg's emphasis on proletarian democracy as an essential corrective to authoritarian state-socialism that denies the rights of the individual in the name of a purely collectivist regime. Lenin's apology for failing to democratize Russia quickly enough involved the claim that to industrialize rapidly, and to create the conditions for "state capitalism" from which Russia could then move beyond into real socialism, there had to be central dictatorship in the hands of a vanguard party. Earlier we suggested that although Lenin may have been correct in applying this assumption to Russia in 1917, the consequences for the future of Soviet socialism have been especially grave.

Lukács and Korsch resisted the authoritarian implications of Marxism-Leninism, arguing that there had to be immediate revolutionary democracy in order to prevent the "dictatorship over the proletariat" sanctioned by Lenin's vanguardist theory and his "democratic centralism." Essentially, Hegelian Marxists argued against theorists of the Second International that human consciousness was vital to *catalyze* and *carry forth* a socialist revolution; while, against the ideologists of the Third International, they argued that consciousness would *guarantee* revolutionary democracy and thus prevent the development of vanguard socialism.

The first generation of Hegelian Marxists, emerging from crisis-bound Central and Eastern Europe, struggled against the state-socialist submersion of the individual; paradoxically, the second generation of Hegelian Marxists, associated with the Frankfurt School, struggled against the domination of the individual by corporate capital. Individualized Marxism arose out of second generation Hegelian Marxism, while diverging from its negative critique of domination. Where Lukács opposed automatic Marxism and Marxist-Leninist vanguardism with the concept of a revolutionary "collective subject," the individualist Marxists like Herbert Marcuse transcended the Frankfurt theory of domination with a concept of a revolutionary *personal* subject, capable of contributing to new forms of the class struggle.

Some have argued that there have always been intrinsic elements in Hegelian Marxism inimical to the preservation of a concept of human consciousness and thus individual rebellion. Hegel's philosophy is interpreted by some as reducing everything to the "totality" that, he argued, was to be a perfect synthesis of ideal and real elements. Lukács employed Hegelian terminology in developing his theory of class consciousness, indicating that socialism would be a new totality, and creating the impression that his concept of a revolutionary "collective subject" largely ignored the individual; that in spite of Lukács' intention to reinvigorate Marxism he unwittingly ignored the personal subject, which proved to be both the ultimate insurance against state-socialist authoritarianism and the source of transcendence of the abject theory of domination.

In the wake of Lukács came the Frankfurt School's critique of domination during the period of early monopoly capitalism. Though this theoretical effort subjectivized Marxism for the first time, recognizing alienation or domination both as an individual and class phenomenon, it did not provide a basis for articulating the concept of a revolutionary individual. Hegelian Marxism in its Lukácsian and Frankfurt formulations failed to find a level of socialist opposition between the revolutionary class and the dominated individual.

To this extent, "individualized Marxism" may be a misnomer. Theorists like Marcuse do not believe that socialist change will result only from personal resistance; they argue rather that change will emerge from personal resistance and rebellion that is expanded into structural transformation through the reorganization of class struggle. Marcuse was explicitly concerned in the 1960s with the problem of achieving revolutionary solidarity without introducing vanguardism, which would have the effect of closing off the democratic character of socialist change. Marcuse, in his 1969 work *An Essay on Liberation,* tries to steer a course between anarchist spontaneity, for which all revolutionary planning and organization is anathema, and the rigid vanguard model. Marcuse writes eloquently about how socialist change must be prefigured in the "sensibilities" of human beings who internalize the ethics and aesthetics of a nonrepressive socialist order *during* the very process of transformation, lest the socialist "cure" be as dismal as the capitalist "disease."

In this sense, Marcuse refuses to separate individual from structural change and, similarly, to return to our opening chapter on Marx, to separate philosophical from scientific dimensions of Marxism. Although Marcuse's own work has its roots in the Hegelian Marxism of the early Frankfurt School, and although Marcuse's earliest work took its reference from the existential-phenomenologies of Husserl and Heidegger, he eventually moved away from Hegelian Marxism and towards a Freudian Marxist theory of the "new sensibility" as an intermediate level of class-radicalism capable of relating individual frustration and alienation to large-scale structural transformation.

The difference between Hegelian Marxism and individualized Marxism revolves around the question, raised in Chapter 4 in the context of our discussion of the Frankfurt School's theory of domination, of whether the individual is capable of revolt and of organizing that revolt collectively and politically. Adorno and Horkheimer in abandoning Marx and Lukács' theory of class struggle denied the possibility of a new type of, perhaps initially individualized, class-radicalism, believing that the individual had become merely a puppet of capitalist domination.

Marcuse and other post-Hegelian theorists are reluctant to accept the judgement that the prospect of effective class-radicalism has disappeared. They argue that Hegelian Marxism both in its revolutionary and pessimistic phases— Lukács and the Frankfurt School, respectively—had always been hindered by the Hegelian dichotomy of "universal" and "particular," or of "class" and "individual" in Marxist language. In this sense Adorno's pessimism about the fully dominated individual was not a significant departure from the Hegelian Marxism of Lukács and Korsch: Adorno did not speculate about new forms of the class struggle once he saw that late capitalism had "integrated" the working class; rather he concluded that class-radicalism was entirely absent, except perhaps in the most remote artistic terms (such as in Schoenberg's disharmonic music).

If individual human beings are capable of revolt, contra the Frankfurt School, *then* they could organize socialist class-radicalism in a non-authoritarian spirit. Events in the Soviet Union convinced thinkers like Marcuse that socialist change would be worthless if it did not proceed from participatory foundations, creating organizational forms that did not require a political and theoretical vanguard. Marcuse's concept of a "new sensibility," requiring a new ethics and aesthetics of personal existence, was the foundation stone of his argument that new forms of socialist class-radicalism could be created that did not impose heavy bureaucratic obligations and imperatives on human beings. Marcuse returned to Marx's early concept of socialism as a democratically organized community of men and women working together in peaceful coexistence. Marxism in this sense, as it grew out of the American political experience of the 1960s and the various protest movements directed against the American political and cultural establishment, became a democratic class-radicalism.

Marcuse, Sartre, Merleau-Ponty, and Piccone attempt to revise the theory of class struggle by developing an intermediate level of class-radicalism capable of relating large-scale socialist transformation to individual protest and rebellion against alienation. Moving Marxism onto this middle level guarantees that the class struggle will be optimally democratic, avoiding vanguardism and its rigid organizational requirements. The individualist Marxists, in different ways, all opposed the bureaucratization of socialism, both of Soviet and social democratic varieties, believing that socialist transformation must emerge from the everyday lives of struggling, frustrated human beings who attempt to liberate themselves from a rigid division of labor and from bureaucratic organizations. This individual rebellion, while not initially an aspect of significant class-radicalism, can be raised to the level of class-radicalism by theoretical and political organization that collects a variety of radical strategies and creates a new, multi-dimensional class struggle.

What Marcuse ultimately lacked was a systematic theory that could give further political form to his vision of the democratic class struggle, built from individualist foundations. Such a theory would offer a model of crisis-tendencies that can guide democratic class-radicalism (a theory further developed in Chapter 7). Marcuse's vision of small-scale, democratically structured emancipation—created by, and creating, what he called the socialist "new sensibility" that refuses to oppress others in the name of distant future liberation—was a significant improvement over past authoritarian and deterministic Marxisms. What he lacked was a crisis-theory that could raise up small-scale emancipation (e.g., the struggle of minority groups in 1960s America) to the level of full-blown class struggle, generating a coherent strategy of socialist transformation rooted in an understanding of advanced capitalist structural dynamics and crisis-forms. Individualist Marxism remains a suggestive image of future democratic class-radicalism, providing the theoretical inspiration for the subsequent development of a large-scale socialist movement.

All of the so-called individualist Marxists began from the foundation of the suffering, sensitive individual. They argued, from different psychological and philosophical foundations, that individuals create the categories of generalized class struggle and emancipation, based upon their own lived-experience of capitalist alienation. Without understanding alienation phenomenologically, in terms of this lived-experience, Marxists ignore a vital aspect of the socialist movement, just inviting the authoritarian determinisms that cede the responsibilities and rights of struggling workers to certain central political agencies, responsible for general (but often not particular) liberation. The bureaucratization of socialism, noted above, occurs when class struggle is unrelated to the struggle of individuals to comprehend and master their own damaged, dominated lives, and when socialism is seen as a distant end-point to be achieved only on the basis of immense short-term sacrifices — sacrifices of liberty, free will and perhaps life itself. The individualist Marxists invest the human individual with a good deal of practical competence to provide diagnoses and transformations of his own alienation, ultimately allowing us to build a generalized socialist movement on the basis of these numerous acts of self-emancipation. This does not abolish the class struggle but grounds it in the democratic free will of struggling individuals, guaranteeing that the class struggle will be an exercise in participatory democracy.

The prospect of a non-authoritarian, majoritarian North American Marxism, built on radical populist foundations, and implicitly opposed to the bureaucratization of socialism, will be explored in the final reading in Chapter 7. Our argument in that reading draws from the individualist Marxists, surveyed in this chapter; we will contend that the radical democratic underpinning of American populism can be linked to the Marxist class struggle in such a way as to build a significant socialist ideology on North American soil. This Marxist-populist synthesis will demonstrate that socialism need not be perceived as an intrinsically authoritarian, bureaucratic structure, thus potentially recapturing the support of American workers who have been convinced by the preponderant weight of American liberal political culture that socialism is equivalent to bureaucratic domination (as it is in the Soviet Union). The possibility of a non-authoritarian small-scale socialism that does not sacrifice the individual to the requirements of class struggle was first outlined by Marcuse and others who treat the individual as the point of departure for any socialist movement.

Individualized Marxism differs from Lukács' Marxism in that it locates the source of revolutionary dynamics in the individual and his immediate community. Individualized Marxism differs from the critical theory of the Frankfurt School for it assumes that the human being is still capable of throwing off the burden of alienation. Yet theorists like Marcuse, Sartre, and Merleau-Ponty have not developed a systematic model of class-radicalism based on a new theory of crisis. Marcuse has not systematically developed the concept of a "new sensibility" that could provide inspiration for the creation of new socialist forms that do not embody imperative coordination and hierarchy. His "new sensibility" largely remains a metaphorical ideal, lacking the concrete socio-political determinates necessary for developing a broadly based class struggle.

The individualist Marxists, in spite of their many valuable insights into the character of modern domination, both capitalist and socialist, have failed to develop the linkages between personal rebellion and structural transformation — linkages between the "new sensibility" of human beings unwilling to allow their lives to be administered by bosses, experts, and technocrats and a class-based political strategy with which to build new forms of socialist organization that are not hierarchical and dominating. Individualized Marxism can be read as restoring the human individual to the center of modern Marxism, unwilling to endorse Lukács' concept of the "collective subject" or Adorno's concept of the dominated subject. Individualized Marxism finds an intermediate level of radicalism above the pessimism of the Frankfurt School and below the class-based revolutionary strategies of Marx and Lukács. This restoration of the human being as the vehicle of opposition has been begun by Marcuse in the exuberant climate of the late 1960s. Yet the process of radical reinvigoration is incomplete, lacking the blueprints and strategies designed to provide a concrete model of democratic class-radicalism. In Chapter 7 we will attempt to develop these models further, going beyond Marcuse's pregnant vision of the new sensibility towards a crisis-theory that can allow for the creation of a new socialist movement.

The individualized Marxists were profoundly important for they brought the Marxian class struggle into the 1960s and 1970s, refusing to endorse worn-out revolutionary strategies drawn mainly from the context of early twentieth century Europe. By treating the individual as the point of departure for non-authoritarian forms of the class struggle, Marcuse, Merleau-Ponty, Sartre, and Piccone overcame both economic determinism and the Frankfurt School's deep-seated pessimism. But while the individualist Marxists injected new blood into Marxian theory, bending it to the North American context in the 1960s, they did not go all the way towards mapping out new models and strategies of socialist transformation. What they lacked was a crisis-theory that could allow them to organize class-radicalism around substantive themes of the 1970s, focusing this class-radicalism on specific crisis-points in advanced capitalism. In our concluding chapter we will map out new developments in Marxian crisis-theory, hoping to provide the foundation for new strategies of class struggle, inspired by Marcuse and others in the 1960s who first argued that the class struggle towards socialist transformation could be a genuine exercise in participatory democracy.

MARCUSE: FREUDIAN MARXISM *

The distance between the Frankfurt School's critique of instrumental rationality (emerging during the genesis of what we have termed early monopoly capitalism between about 1930 and 1950) and individualized Marxism (emerging during the genesis of late monopoly capitalism, post-1950) is the distance between the periods in Marcuse's own work. Marcuse is the only Frankfurt School theorist to have transcended his earlier preoccupation with the theory of domination and its pessimistic focus on the insufficiency of organized radical politics. Indeed in the 1960s and early 1970s Marcuse broke upon the North American scene labelled in some circles as the "guru" of the American New Left and the theorist of the counterculture. His 1969 work, *An Essay on Liberation,* remains the central programmatic work of individualized Marxism, articulating as it does a concept of personal radicalism that can initiate large-scale Marxist social transformation.

Before he embarked on his speculations about contemporary liberatory theory, culminating in works such as *An Essay on Liberation,* Marcuse composed a seminal study of the relationship between psychological and historical domination entitled *Eros and Civilization,* first published in 1955. While Marcuse's 1964 book, *One-Dimensional Man,* occupies a prominent place in Chapter 4, we wish

---

*In this section, page references are guides to further reading in the original source.

to treat his earlier book on Freud as the point of departure of individualized Marxism. In that book, Marcuse first examined psychological forms of capitalist domination and suggested possible routes of escape from what he termed "surplus repression."

Briefly, Marcuse argued that capitalism survives because workers have failed to seize upon emancipatory possibilities contained in the rapid development of industrial technology, capable of servicing most basic human needs. "Surplus repression" operates to orient the human being towards maintenance of the "performance principle," remaining obedient to the Protestant work ethic and the edicts of social control imposed by the so-called "superego" (a term used by Freud to describe a person's moral conscience and its internalization of societal expectations). Freud theorized that every human being must undergo a process of repression and sublimation of certain fundamental sexual (or "libidinal") impulses; this repression inhibits the aim of these sexual impulses that originally, Freud argued, were directed towards the world as a whole and towards the child's parents. Aim-inhibited sexuality is not a "bad" thing for it allows the human being to develop a sense of what is permissible and forbidden in the social world, acting as a vital "reality principle" as Freud characterized it.

Marcuse does not reject Freud's concept of necessary repression, enabling the human being to live sanely in the real world. He believes however that Freud was insufficiently historical in his analysis of the genesis and scope of repression, ignoring societally-induced variations over time in the degree of repression. Marcuse suggests that repression is *heightened* in advanced capitalism in order to prevent human beings from enjoying the possibilities inherent in a potentially super-productive technological order; furthermore, heightened repression keeps human beings in productive gear, preventing any significant decrease in the rate of production and consumption that would occur as a result of more rational, socialist uses of the technological apparatus. It is hoped by Marcuse that sexuality under socialism could be freed from purely genital modes of expression; he talks about "re-erotization" as the goal of socialist transformation, stressing that narrowly genital sexuality merely reproduces the performance principle of capitalism, limiting sexual expression and satisfaction both to narrow bodily zones and to a narrow time-frame (genital sexuality carried out in bed, usually at night). Marcuse argues that socialist people will be able to express their successfully repressed (but not surplus repressed) libidos in a variety of ways, only some of them involving narrow heterosexual genitality. Marcuse has been attacked from all sides for proposing that this socialist sexuality would be "polymorphous perversity," using Freud's term for the undifferentiated, total sexuality of the human infant. By polymorphous perversity Marcuse simply means that liberated human beings would be able to touch their loved ones, and to be touched, without shame. He does not, on this basis, endorse "free love" or counsel against monogamy but only attacks narrowly genital sexuality under capitalism for being libidinally and emotionally unfulfilling. By "re-erotization" Marcuse refers to the various ways in which people would infuse their various activities and relationships with tenderness and caring.

Marcuse's distinction between repression and surplus repression has created serious difficulties for many of his readers who mistakenly read him endorsing "total" liberation from civilizing repression (and not merely from surplus repression, or alienation, as Marcuse really argues). Those who read him as endorsing free love and the like do not realize that he is aiming to *retain* sublimation and repression while removing *only* surplus repression: Thus he calls not for a regression to uncivilized barbarism and animality but for progress towards responsible, mature adulthood predicated neither on insufficient repression nor on too much repression. Marcuse agrees with Freud that properly repressed libido will emerge both in free and erotized human relationships and in culture-building activities of all kinds. Freud felt that successfully repressed culture-building activity would require progressively larger doses of repression (as argued in his later work, *Civilization and Its Discontents*). Marcuse agrees with Freud that the purpose of successful repression is erotized human relationships and culture-creation (work, art, science, etc.) but disagrees that the progress of culture as a whole requires increasing repression. Marcuse argues that capitalist class society, which requires surplus repression, is not eternal (as Freud evidently assumed, pessimistically) but can be abolished in the direction of a non-authoritarian socialism rooted in successful (non-alienating) repression. The difference between Freud and Marcuse is simply that Freud was not a Marxist who could envision a social order in which human beings did not have to submit to tight regimentation of their instincts in order to contribute to the common weal through useful work.

Marcuse and other recent western Marxists have considered the possibility that human beings could be freed *today* from tightly organized industrial and bureaucratic routines. Contemporary domination increasingly takes the form of "imperative coordination" resulting from a rigid division of labor and a sharp dichotomy between work and leisure. Marcuse suggests that the potential exists for ending the most unpleasant features of human labor (utilizing the full productive capacities of technology and utilizing automation and cybernation in order to replace men with machines, wherever possible). This potential is not realized because the advanced capitalist social structure has further tied the human being to a "surplus repressive" regime of imposed discipline and self-discipline.

Here the novel character of domination according to Marcuse becomes clear: The exploitation and alienation of labor in Marx's original sense was obviously not "wanted" by the worker; it was immediately experienced as painful and undesirable. Today domination is often experienced as pleasant and desirable. This is termed by Marcuse "repressive desublimation," utilizing Freud's concept of sublimation to illuminate ways in which human beings are led to believe that they can be free *within* a system of exploited, coordinated labor. An example of repressive desublimation is the headlong rush to consume endlessly as a compensation for alienated labor. Recall Marcuse's analysis of "false needs" in *One-Dimensional Man,* discussed in Chapter 4; false needs are expressions of this type of desublimation.

Surplus repression—repression beyond the requirements of the maintenance of organized human personality—props up advanced capitalism by diverting and narrowing sexuality into system-supporting channels. Marcuse in 1955 tried to answer the question posed by Lukács and Korsch in the 1920s: Why has socialist liberation not occurred? Lukács' answer was that class consciousness had not developed in the ranks of the working class. Marcuse's answer is different in kind and in scope. He argues that liberation has been postponed because human beings are instinctively tied to work performance that is basically *unnecessary;* human beings are led to believe that they can be happy and free within a social order in which (alienated) work time is sharply divided from free time.

"The modes of domination have changed: They have become increasingly technological, productive, and even beneficial; consequently, in the most advanced areas of industrial society, the people have been co-ordinated and reconciled with the system of domination to an unprecedented degree." Marcuse argues that the realm of freedom is shrinking: The system is becoming more repressive as productivity grows, sharpening the contradiction between utopian possibility and the capitalist performance-principle.

For the first time in human history, freedom is objectively possible, owing to the capacity of automated technological production to liberate human beings from the realm of alienated work. Marcuse suggests that alienated work can be veritably eliminated under a social order in which there are no sharp distinctions between "necessary" work and "free" leisure or play. The prospect of automation threatens advanced industrial capitalism because it suggests the possibility of eliminating the strict boundaries between labor and leisure.[1]

The thrust of Marcuse's analysis is captured in the following statement: "Civilization has to defend itself against the specter of a world which could be free." Consciousness is controlled through "the promotion of thoughtless leisure activities." The liberation of sex has become merely an instrument of "repressive desublimation" as sexuality and social utility, the two opposing poles of Freud's psychoanalysis, have become thoroughly compatible. Sexuality becomes merely another form of alienation, a purely genital mode of conquest and submission.

Marcuse suggests that "totalitarianism spreads over late industrial civilization." This is facilitated by the "manipulation of consciousness" of individuals who otherwise might enjoy the forbidden fruits of advanced technology that can liberate them from the regime of scarcity and toil. The enormous paradox is increasing domination and alienation *within* the context of an unprecedented technological apparatus potentially capable of satisfying material needs the world over. Advanced capitalism, according to Marcuse, survives precisely because human beings introject the requirements of a repressive reality principle, abstaining from creative praxis and enjoyable, erotized leisure and instead continuing to perform thoughtlessly the productive functions set out for them by the administrators of domination.

While "sexual freedom has unquestionably increased . . .the sexual relations themselves have become much more closely assimilated with social relations; sexual liberty is harmonized with profitable conformity." The root of Marcuse's Freudian Marxism is the sentiment that Eros, when authentically liberated from surplus repression, will tend towards creative praxis and towards socialist emancipation. Vulgar sexual promiscuity, restricted to narrowly genital zones of the body, is not a hallmark of freedom but rather a way of falsely sublimating the quest for freedom. Rampant genital promiscuity is a symptom of surplus repression; liberated sexuality, according to Marcuse, would issue instead in new and durable work relations and in a generalized interpersonal sensitivity inimical to the interests of capitalist alienation and exploitation.[2]

"Consciousness . . .tends to be reduced to the task of regulating the coordination of the individual with the whole." The individual toils beyond the limits of natural necessity, endlessly reproducing commodities that are purchased and discarded according to the ceaselessly shifting whim of the consumer. A "general anaesthesia" prevails that allows knowledge to become merely a force for administering the laboring human being, making him or her face up to "duty" within

1. Herbert Marcuse, *Eros and Civilization* (New York: Vintage, 1955), pp. vii–viii.

2. Herbert Marcuse, *Eros and Civilization* (New York: Vintage, 1955) pp. 85–86.

a productive civilization: life exists for (alienated) production and consumption.

Relations between people become relations between things. Work is seen as drudgery, as unfulfilling. Marcuse adds that "this state of ossification also affects the instincts, their inhibitions and modifications." Human consciousness itself is eclipsed, and "reduced to the task of regulating the coordination of the individual with the whole." Here Marcuse echos the earlier Frankfurt thesis of the decline of human subjectivity under the sway of the preponderance of domination in late capitalism. "The individual does not really know what is going on," having been anaesthetized by the coercive ideological and material forces around him. The purpose of existence becomes adjustment to the given order and not its transformation through self-actualizing praxis (as in early Marx's sense.)[3]

Freud assumed that the reality principle would always enjoy superiority over the pleasure principle. Marcuse argues that this relationship can be reversed under a free social order, with the pleasure principle informing every aspect of human existence, work and non-work. Freud assumed that "free libidinal relations are essentially antagonistic to work relations, that energy has to be withdrawn from the former in order to institute the latter . . ." Marcuse suggests that instinctual domination results not from the necessity of labor *per se* but from a particular organization of labor imposed by the interests of domination.

He also grapples with the question of whether "civilization would explode and revert to prehistoric savagery" if material scarcity was overcome via automation and the rational disposition of the technological apparatus. Freud felt that people would have to undergo relatively severe forms of repression (in the psychoanalytic sense) if they were to engage in productive labor. Marcuse argues, dialectically, that it is not the fact of scarcity *per se* that requires men to suffer alienation but rather, again, the "specific social organization of labor imposed by the interest in domination." Thus Marcuse calls for the elimination of surplus repression (in the interest of domination) but not of repression, required for all civilizations. Marcuse is saying that Freud failed to distinguish carefully between alienated and creative work. He tended to see all work as the necessary result of sharp psychosocial repression and domination. Marcuse envisions "the emergence of a non-repressive reality principle," the result of which would not be apathetic laziness or renewed interpersonal barbarism but instead "new and durable work relations."

Here Marcuse is saying that work and sexuality are not intrinsically opposed, that the channeling of successfully repressed and sublimated sexuality (Eros) into constructive, nonaggressive activity will liberate labor and not eliminate it, as Freud had feared. Freud discounted the possibility of socialism and thus he failed to recognize the possibility of what Marcuse terms "erotized labor," i.e., labor performed without external compulsion and without harsh instinctual and psycho-social repression.[4]

Marcuse identifies a new principle of civilization, to come into being in a social order without surplus repression. He terms it the "play impulse," following the usage of the German philosopher Friedrich Schiller. "Nature . . . would . . . be experienced primarily, neither as dominating man (as in the primitive society), nor as an object of 'contemplation.'" Free human activity, termed by Marx

3. Herbert Marcuse, *Eros and Civilization* (New York: Vintage, 1955), pp. 93–94.
4. Herbert Marcuse, *Eros and Civilization* (New York: Vintage, 1955), pp. 139–40.

"praxis," is characterized by Marcuse as "display, the free manifestation of potentialities." The "play impulse" would not abolish work but would rather humanize work in such a way that the distinction between necessary work and free leisure disappears. Marcuse is not saying that work and play are identical but only that work can be creative praxis, "the free manifestation of potentialities." He suggests that the distinction between work and play can be blurred, if not utterly eliminated; he recognizes the difference (dialectical and not absolute) between the artist who paints the canvas and the child who finger-paints.[5]

Marcuse ends his book with a discussion of the forms emancipation might take. It is here that he goes beyond the Frankfurt School's theory of domination, appropriate primarily to the more repressive, one-dimensional period of early monopoly capitalism. In his Chapter 10, "The Transformation of Sexuality into Eros," Marcuse comes full circle in demonstrating the subversive, utopian possibilities inherent in the Freudian concept of Eros. He develops the notion of a "non-repressive reality principle," a "rationality of gratification," that would not be opposed to the pleasure principle, traditionally seen as opposed by Freudians and Marxists alike. He discusses what he terms "regression," indicating that instinctual liberation "would *regress* behind the attained level of civilized rationality."

The core of Marcuse's later work on sexuality and art, to be discussed in the next section of this chapter, is prefigured here, in his views on regression. This regression would restore the needs of the libido during early stages of its development, choked off under a surplus repressive order. ". . . The possibility of a non-repressive civilization is predicated not upon the arrest, but upon the liberation, of progress . . ." Gad Horowitz (author of *Repression,* a study of Marcuse's Freudianism) has termed Marcuse's concept of regression "dialectical regression," indicating that emancipation would be both "regress" and progress at once, realizing a new reality principle rooted in instinctual liberation and rationally harnessing existing technology in order to emancipate men from alienating labor.

By "regression" Marcuse evidently means that human beings could regain aspects of playful work activity known earlier in childhood. This would not be pure and simple regression, for, as we remarked above, the adult painter is not equivalent to the child who finger-paints. Marcuse advocates "dialectical regression," in Horowitz's terms, that is, regression that reintroduces the play impulse into mature adulthood and into the work that people will do in a non-surplus repressive social order. Marcuse believes that we can create a new form of rationality, a "rationality of gratification," that merges instinctual and intellectual reason towards the purpose of instinctually gratifying creative work. Marcuse in this sense rejects the long western tradition of separating mind and body, reason and instincts. He believes that it is possible to liberate Eros in such a way that its liberation produces not barbarism and childish narcissism but rather a new type of rationality and new work relations.[6]

In his closing sections of the book, Marcuse goes further in defining a new reality principle. He envisages a "rationality of gratification in which reason and happiness converge." Western philosophers have traditionally separated reason and sensual and aesthetic pleasure; Marcuse overcomes this dualism by arguing

5. Herbert Marcuse, *Eros and Civilization* (New York; Vintage, 1955), p. 173.
6. Herbert Marcuse, *Eros and Civilization* (New York: Vintage, 1955), p. 181.

that human freedom and the requirements of mature civilization might prove to be compatible. ". . . Mature civilization depends for its functioning on a multitude of coordinated arrangements. These arrangements in turn must carry recognized and recognizable authority. Hierarchical relationships are not unfree *per se.*" Marcuse does not believe that "rational authority" as such is a form of domination; he would not challenge the authority of the airplane pilot or the brain surgeon. He distinguishes between basic and surplus repression, the one required for mature rationality and responsible authority and the other a product of a particular social organization of labor—class society.

In a very important formulation, Marcuse argues that "the liberty of the individual and that of the whole may perhaps be reconciled by a 'general will' taking shape in institutions which are directed toward the individual needs." The authority generated by this general will must be democratically imposed. Many critics of Marcuse's emancipatory theory have charged that he endorses an irresponsible attitude of unbridled individualism, advocating the return to a prehistorical primitivism and narcissism, and presumably implying the renaissance of charismatic authoritarianism. Marcuse does not abandon work, authority, and organization but simply their distorted, dominated forms. He implies the possibility of what I call a non-authoritarian authority, such as the authority of the airplane pilot or of the traffic officer (that is, authority we willingly accept without worrying that we will be dominated by the pilot or the officer). Marcuse argues that the choice for western civilizations is not between sheer authoritarianism or utter individualism. Following Rousseau and Marx in this sense, he believes that we can create a socialist general will that will allow us to have authority and organization without class domination. These new forms of authority will be informed by what he terms the "rationality of gratification," rooted in a merger of reason and instincts.

Marcuse's vision of a socialist general will follows from Marx's own sentiments, expressed in the 1844 manuscripts, about the possibility of a nonantagonistic dialectic between the individual and the community. Marx suggested that human beings could only seek their humanity through social labor (labor that is creative and situated in a human community). Marcuse likewise believes that freedom is not individualistic in the strict sense: It is not a form of narcissism. Rather he argues that freedom can only be successfully found in human community, that ultimately it is impossible to distinguish between personal freedom and a general social or collective freedom. Thus, following Marx, he sees that individual liberty and social solidarity (general will) are not antithetical; indeed, he claims that they are interdependent.[7] Marcuse wants to break the hold of a surplus repressive reality principle not to send humanity back to animality but to go *beyond* class society that demands too much repression. With Freud, Marcuse sees that non-repressive sublimation transforms instinctual impulses into creative and productive activity. As a Marxist, Marcuse believes that people can coexist democratically, through the general will, without abandoning personal freedoms. He believes, beyond Freud, that work can be reconstructed, "erotized," in such a way that it becomes instinctually gratifying praxis in the Marxian sense. Marcuse builds on Freud and Marx in order to transcend their dualistic assumptions about the allegedly eternal split between reason and instincts (in the case of Freud) and between work and freedom (in the case of Marx).

7. Herbert Marcuse, *Eros and Civilization* (New York: Vintage, 1955), pp. 205–206.

MARCUSE: THE NEW SENSIBILITY*

Marcuse's *Eros and Civilization* was the first systematic attempt to analyze domination from a psychological perspective, combining Marx's theory of alienation and Freud's theory of repression. Marcuse's appreciation of the psychological foundation of domination—the reality of surplus repression beyond the basic requirements of mature civilization—provides the link between the Frankfurt School's theory of domination and later attempts to develop an individualized Marxism. Marcuse's vision of instinctual liberation as the catalyst of large-scale socialist transformation informs his recent work, most notably his 1969 book, *An Essay on Liberation,* which remains the most significant theoretical expression of individualized Marxism.

As Marcuse demonstrates in *Eros and Civilization,* there can be no clear-cut demarcation between structural and personal dimensions of Marxian theory. *An Essay on Liberation* is explicitly devoted to creating a model of change that surpasses Marx and Engels' class-based revolutionary strategies. Yet he retains Marx's model of the class struggle. As we discussed in the general introduction to this chapter, Marcuse wants to build new forms of democratic class-radicalism on the foundation of the struggling individual, the "new sensibility." By grounding it in the personal sensibility Marcuse guarantees that the class struggle will remain optimally democratic and attuned to particular human needs (and not ride roughshod over those needs in the name of higher, trans-individual developmental imperatives).

This surpasses the Frankfurt School's theory of the dominated individual for it provides modes of escape from what Adorno termed "absolute integration." Writing in the 1960s, Marcuse recognized aspects of cultural and personal rebellion that did not "fit" more orthodox models of Marxian change, such as the student movement (catalyzed by protest against the Vietnam war), racial movements, the women's movement, and the "counterculture". This is not to suggest that Marcuse felt that rock music and drugs were adequate forms of the "new sensibility," for he remained fundamentally within the European intellectual tradition of rationalism. Yet Marcuse at least considered these manifestations of changed personal sensibilities and life styles as important signals of possible socialist liberation in the 1960s and 1970s. Marcuse "arrived" on the North American scene before other members of the Frankfurt School because his theory of instinctual liberation evoked sympathetic responses from many American youth and intellectuals at a time when the liberal-democratic consensus of the 1950s was rapidly weakening.

The weakening of this consensus, which undoubtedly reached its peak during the Eisenhower presidency and which was shattered finally during the denouement of the Vietnam war, gave rise to new types of protest and rebellion against monopoly capitalism. Although American students and intellectuals for the most part remained ignorant of traditional Marxian theory, they nonetheless provided evidence that "absolute integration" had not been achieved and that there were still significant possibilities of radical change, albeit in forms unfamiliar to most European Marxists.

Marcuse confronted these cultural and political movements of resistance and tried to capture their Marxist potential. His *An Essay on Liberation* was

---

*In this section, page references are guides to further reading in the original source.

written at the height of the student movement and counterculture. While it has been read superficially as endorsing "free love," its importance lies in its attempt to bridge between traditional Marxian concerns, such as the theory of alienation, and a concept of personal liberation springing from the cultural formation of American populism.

He begins by arguing that "utopian possibilities are inherent in the technical and technological forces of advanced capitalism and socialism." Yet the rational disposition of these technological forces would not by itself guarantee liberation. Marx's pregnant phrase "to each according to his needs" is inadequate according to Marcuse. "What is now at stake are the needs themselves." This refers back to the discussion in *One-Dimensional Man* of "false needs" perpetuating domination within the realm of apparently "free" consumer choice. Marcuse asks how human beings can satisfy their needs without damaging themselves and prolonging domination.

Marx and Engels refrained from sketching a socialist blueprint of the future because they wanted to avoid utopianism and idle speculation. Marcuse argues that the further metamorphosis of capitalism since the time of Marx necessitates a new utopianism that considers the immense and unprecedented productive capacity of the existing technology. No longer is it unrealistic to dream of a world in which basic material needs could be satisfied without endless back-breaking toil. However socialists must ensure that a socialist technological order does not again enslave workers: "a bureaucratic welfare state would still be a state of repression." To guarantee a humane and democratic socialism human needs must themselves be transformed in such a way that the individual does not depend "on an exploitative apparatus which, in satisfying his needs, perpetuates his servitude." The *Essay on Liberation* is a document of Marxist utopianism that argues for the abolition of alienated labor (as a consequence of the rational harnessing of socialist technology) and for the transformation of human needs and the human sensibility in the direction of socialist humanism.[1]

The working class failed to develop appropriate consciousness about their political mission because "a vested interest in the existing system is fostered in [their] instinctual structure." Marcuse wants to add a "biological" dimension to Marxism, exploring the impact of false needs on concepts and strategies of liberation.

This preoccupation with false needs is a hallmark of Marcuse's recent work, prefigured first in *Eros and Civilization*. His notion is that human beings tend to reproduce their own alienation in the ways that they work and engage in consumer behavior. The repressive reality principle is thus reproduced on the level of the individual's own sensibility and in his everyday life. Thus workers do not desire Marxist revolution but color televisions and large cars, emulating the life styles of their bosses. Liberation tends to be defined not in terms of certain substantive properties of human action, such as in the Marxian sense of creative social praxis, but in terms of the acquisition of commodities. This fixation on commodities is eschewed by Marcuse because it represents an inauthentic type of liberation: Marx stressed that both capitalist and worker are alienated; thus to imitate the luxurious life style of the capitalist does not free the worker from his alienated work but merely relegates freedom to the ephemeral domain of after-hours leisuretime in which he can dress like his boss, drive the boss' car, and

---

1. Herbert Marcuse, *An Essay on Liberation* (Harmondsworth: Penguin, 1972), pp. 13-14.

watch the boss' favorite television shows.

False needs are those determined by the surrounding cultural and ideological definitions of commodity consumption. Marcuse as a Marxist believes that consumption is merely one aspect of human activity; more central to him is the way that people realize their creative humanity in their work. Needs are false if they restrict freedom to the realm of leisure; true needs are needs that flow from the individual's own determination of his or her creative productivity. For example, one person's artistry might be another person's carpentry or writing or sports.[2]

A new model of emancipation via creative praxis must be grounded in the objective possibilities latent in late capitalist society. Marcuse suggests that freedom today "depends largely on technical progress," echoing Marx's view in this regard that technological progress could, if guided rationally, bring an end to want and scarcity. Yet Marcuse adds the crucial condition for the rational use of technology: There must be a reconstruction of science and technology in accord with the life instincts and the "new sensibility." Marcuse describes what he calls a "vicious circle." On the one hand, new needs for creative work must prefigure the revolution; on the other hand, these needs can only come about in the crucible of class struggle. This paradox troubles Marcuse and yet he suggests that the vicious circle can be escaped if radical transformation has an "objective foundation in the production process" of late capitalism. This is why he argues that the "true" needs of the new sensibility must necessarily be harnessed to a new science and new technology that do not dominate nature and that admit of workers' control and non-authoritarian labor organization. This is crucial because it moves Marcuse's initially individualist Marxism into the dimension of structural political economy, offering possible mediations between the struggling individual and new types of class-radicalism. Marcuse, against the caricatures of many of his critics, both right-wing and left-wing, does not ignore labor but argues, following upon his insights in *Eros and Civilization,* that work can be "erotized" and merged with the play impulse.[3]

Marcuse outlines his fundamental departure from original Marxism. He suggests that Marx separated the realms of necessity and freedom, thinking that human liberation could only occur outside the realm of necessity (necessary production for the maintenance of human life). Marx could not adequately foresee new socialist forms of creative praxis because he did not recognize the possibility of overcoming the dualism between necessity and freedom. Marx implied, following most sociological theorists, that a "free" human being would still separate his existence into work and leisure components. "Marx rejects the idea that work can ever become play."

Marcuse harnesses Freudian insights into the fundamentally erotic nature of human beings to project a vision of emancipation in terms of the "play impulse," as he characterized it in *Eros and Civilization.* He submits that the very character of work could change, in accord with the non-distorted needs of the life instincts. It will be recalled how in his earlier work on Freud Marcuse suggested that the elimination of surplus repression would not abolish work, authority, and organization as such but "merely" class society and the alienation of labor. Here he gives fuller flesh to this ideal. He argues that the innermost character of

---

2. Herbert Marcuse, *An Essay on Liberation* (Harmondsworth: Penguin, 1972), p. 25.

3. Herbert Marcuse, *An Essay on Liberation* (Harmondsworth: Penguin, 1972), pp. 27–28.

production could be transformed; "instinctual transformation is conceivable as a factor of social change only if it enters the social division of labor, the production relations themselves."

Marx argued that social freedom would be manifested mainly as the shortening of the working day. Marcuse argues that the very character of the working day could be changed, blurring the clear-cut distinction between "necessary" work and "free" leisure. When Marcuse asserts that work can become play he does not trivialize the notion of non-alienated work; free work would have a deeply creative purpose under a new social order. Human production and human self-creation would lose their antithetical character as the very activity of work is liberated from tight emotional organization and instinctual regimentation allegedly required by bureaucratically organized production processes.

The reconstruction of work for Marcuse would invalidate one of Marx's central assumptions, namely, about the separability of labor and leisure. Marcuse suggests that unprecedented technological advancement will allow labor to be transformed into a veritable form of freedom—Marx's praxis. Marcuse suggests that there can be freedom *within* the realm of necessity and not beyond it as Marx had implied in his sketch of the shortening of the working day as a means of ameliorating the plight of labor. Marcuse suggests that the character of work can itself be transformed under a "rationality of gratification," informing new science and new technology. This new kind of work would require a new kind of worker, a "new sensibility" that would refuse to distinguish between the productive-utilitarian and creative aspects of the working process. But this new sensibility can be an effective political agent in the struggle for humane socialism "only if it enters the social division of labor, the production relations themselves." It must not remain a purely aesthetic ideal, a form of individual escape. Here again Marcuse hints that individualist Marxism lacks effective mediations between the struggling individual and the workers' class struggle as a whole.[4]

The "new sensibility" would join reason and happiness, *merging* work with play, traditionally defined. Marcuse calls for new modes of perception, feeling, and experience to "accompany the material and intellectual reconstruction of society." Yet he wants to avoid the "narcotic character" of the drug experience in order to avoid an irrationalism that shuns political change in favor of merely personal "transcendence." He argues for a "union of the new sensibility with a new rationality." Marcuse returns to his argument of fourteen years earlier in *Eros and Civilization* about the possible merger of intellectual reason and libidinal sensibility. The new sensibility is as much a new rationality as a new type of libido. The drug culture of the 1960s is indicted by Marcuse for possessing a "narcotic character" that brings release not only from repressive capitalist reason but from reason *per se.* Thus hippies failed to negate the dominant order but remained ensconsed within it, as merely marginal people lacking the radical power of collective negation. Hippie rationality was a rationality purely of the body and not of mind, as it needed to be in order to blossom into democratic forms of class struggle.[5]

A summary of Marcuse's concept of new sensibility is found in the following formulation: " . . .the economic, political, and cultural features of a classless society must have become the basic needs of those who fight for it." Otherwise

4. Herbert Marcuse, *An Essay on Liberation* (Harmondsworth: Penguin, 1972), pp. 28–30.
5. Herbert Marcuse, *An Essay on Liberation* (Harmondsworth: Penguin, 1972), pp. 43–44.

socialist revolution will fail to realize its ultimate purpose of human liberation; the society that emerges will be a carbon copy of the social order it replaced, replete with surplus repression and false needs. Marcuse suggests that exploitative relationships among radicals must be abandoned during the very process of transformation, and not retained as a short-term expedient lest they be internalized by those radicals. He ensures a democratic class struggle on the basis of the creation of new needs among the radicals who fight for humane socialism. What Karl Korsch called the "dictatorship over the proletariat" will be avoided by the internalization of non-exploitative, non-authoritarian needs on the part of radicals.[6]

The thrust of *An Essay on Liberation* is to argue for new bridges between individual and class radicalism, rooted initially in the struggling sensibility of the human being who, in his own everyday life and in his personal relationships, attempts to throw off the yoke of alienation and surplus repression. Marcuse does not discount these individuated moments of pre-political radicalism but harnesses them as the point of departure of a fuller-fleshed class struggle. This class struggle, by building on the individual's own self-transformation, will be optimally democratic and conducive to the fostering of "true" needs.

SARTRE AND MERLEAU-PONTY: EXISTENTIALIST MARXISM

In the 1940s and 1950s two French philosophers created their own synthesis of Hegel and Marx. Jean-Paul Sartre and Maurice Merleau-Ponty, lifelong friends and co-founders of the Parisian journal *Les Temps Modernes,* belong in any study of recent Marxism. Although much of Sartre's published work has been literary in nature, and although Merleau-Ponty has written extensively on the nuances of phenomenological philosophy, both have contributed valuable essays to the discussion of contemporary Marxism.

The fundamental contribution of Sartre and Merleau-Ponty lies in their critique of Marxist determinism. Both thinkers have tried to restore the philosophical foundation of Marx's critique of alienation through an appreciation of man's essential nature as a creature of self-creative praxis. Sartre and Merleau-Ponty composed their most telling critiques of Marxist-Leninist orthodoxy and the idea of "scientific socialism" during the period in the 1940s and early 1950s when the brutality of Stalinism was first being exposed in the West. Existentialism, a philosophical doctrine stressing the ultimate freedom and responsibility of the human being, was utilized by Sartre and Merleau-Ponty as a basis for criticizing the overly structural, bureaucratic, and deterministic character of Marxist orthodoxy. Although both Sartre and Merleau-Ponty believed that existentialism in pure form was an essentially idealistic bourgeois philosophical system, unable to comprehend human alienation in historical and structural terms, they also felt that an overly mechanical species of Marxism unnecessarily ignored the human foundation of Marx's dialectical materialism.

Existentialist Marxism belongs to the historical period covered in this chapter. Although Sartre and Marcuse seem to have little in common theoretically, and few personal connections apart from a rather distant respect for each other, there is a striking similarity between Marcuse's vision of a new sensibility and

6. Herbert Marcuse, *An Essay on Liberation* (Harmondsworth: Penguin, 1972), pp. 90–91.

Sartre and Merleau-Ponty's conception of Marxian praxis. This parallel can be explained partly with reference to historical circumstances: Both Marcuse and Sartre turned away from the rigid scientific determinism of orthodox Marxism, which seemed to ignore the individual, and from the proto-idealism and philosophical isolation of the Hegelian Marxism of the Frankfurt School. Although Sartre remained more traditionally Marxist in his conception of class-based political strategy than Marcuse, both thinkers attempted to restore individual praxis as the fundamental point of departure of the dialectical method.

This focus on individual praxis characterizes all of the theorists covered in this chapter. Sartre and Marcuse did not dispose of class analysis but argued rather that there must be new ways of relating the levels of the individual and the (class) collectivity. They contended that traditional class analysis ignores the requirements of participatory democracy by elevating the class, and its revolutionary exigencies, above the individual. This insight took its departure from Adorno and Horkheimer's critique of "absolute integration," surveyed in Chapter 4; it attempted to overcome the individual's victimization at the hands of monopoly capitalism by developing theories of self-emancipatory behavior that related the requirements of class struggle to the responsibilities and rights of the human being.

Sartre and Marcuse attempted to restore class analysis by resuscitating the dominated individual. Existentialism, psychoanalysis, and phenomenology all provided bases upon which this restoration could take place, each, in different ways, showing that there yet remains a core of personal autonomy and free will that can be the springboard for future class struggle of a kind desired by Marxists. In this way, individualist Marxism did not abandon the working class but rather tried to develop new ways of joining the struggling individual to meaningful class groupings.

As early monopoly capitalism (emergent from the victory over European fascism and strengthened by the industrial development and colonial expansion generated by the war effort) developed into a less "total" form in the late 1950s and 1960s, the prospects of human liberation appeared to grow. Sartre, like Marcuse in North America, has been very close to the student movement, even serving as its political and theoretical spokesman. Where Horkheimer and Adorno in the 1960s gradually withdrew from radical politics, Marcuse and Sartre found that radical political movements were highly significant for the future development of Marxian theory. In short, Sartre, like Marcuse, was a highly engaged theorist, always measuring the truth-value of his theory against its practical possibilities and strategic meanings.

Sartre begins his 1960 work, *Search for a Method* (the prefatory essay in his major *Critique of Dialectical Reason,* recently translated into English), with the sentiment that "Marxism, after drawing us to it as the moon draws the tides, after transforming all our ideas, after liquidating the categories of our bourgeois thought, abruptly left us stranded. . . . In the particular situation in which we were placed, it no longer had anything new to teach us, because it had come to a stop."

Marxism, after drawing us to it as the moon draws the tides, after transforming all our ideas, after liquidating the categories of our bourgeois thought, abruptly left us stranded. It did not satisfy our need to understand. In the particular situation in which we were placed, it no longer had anything new to teach us, because it had come to a stop.

Marxism stopped. Precisely because this philosophy wants to change the world, because its aim is "philosophy-becoming-the-world," because it is and wants to be *practical,* there arose within it a veritable schism which rejected theory on one side and *praxis* on the other. From the moment the USSR, encircled and alone, undertook its gigantic effort at industrialization, Marxism found itself unable to bear the shock of these new struggles, the practical necessities and the mistakes which are always inseparable from them. At this period of withdrawal (for the USSR) and of ebb tide (for the revolutionary proletariats), the ideology itself was subordinated to a double need: security (that is, unity) and the construction of socialism *inside* the USSR. Concrete thought must be born from *praxis* and must turn back upon it in order to clarify it, not by chance and without rules, but—as in all sciences and all techniques— in conformity with principles. Now the Party leaders, bent on pushing the integration of the group to the limit, feared that the free process of truth, with all the discussions and all the conflicts which it involves, would break the unity of combat; they reserved for themselves the right to define the line and to interpret the event. In addition, out of fear that the experience might not provide its own clarities, that it might put into question certain of their guiding ideas and might contribute to "weakening the ideological struggle," they put the doctrine out of reach. The separation of theory and practice resulted in transforming the latter into an empiricism without principles; the former into a pure, fixed knowledge.*

"Marxism stopped," he adds. Sartre throughout refers to "Marxism" as the system of apologies created by the Soviet leaders in order to legitimize and explain away the brutal reality of Leninism and Stalinism. For Sartre, there can be no Marxism apart from history, time, and place; Marxian theory is not a rarified theory of society, to be isolated from the context in which it gains life. Thus modern Marxism for Sartre has become unfortunately identified with the distorted ideology of the Soviets. ". . . The Party leaders, bent on pushing the integration of the group to the limit, feared that the free process of truth, with all the discussions and all the conflicts which it involves, would break the unity of combat; they reserved for themselves the right to define the line and to interpret the event."

Sartre, as a proponent of dialectical method, argues that theory and praxis are inseparable. The Soviets separated theory and praxis, reducing praxis to "an empiricism without principles" and reducing theory into "a pure, fixed knowledge," unable to learn from experience. "For years the Marxist intellectual believed that he served his party by violating experience, by overlooking embarrassing details, by grossly simplifying the data . . ." Sartre attacks the reduction of Marxian thought merely to the passive reflection of given circumstances, events, and policies. We can always learn from historical experience and thus we must not restrict our knowledge to narrow pigeonholes taken from a doctrinaire system of principles and assumptions.

Sartre eloquently defines the dialectical method: "The Marxist approaches the historical process with universalizing and totalizing schemata." The Marxist social scientist does not merely reflect reality, without preconceptions about the structure and meaning of events. "But in no case, in Marx's own work, does this

---

*From Jean-Paul Sartre, *Search for a Method* (New York: Vintage, 1963), pp. 21-22.

putting in perspective claim to prevent or to render useless the appreciation of the process as a *unique* totality." In other words, Sartre argues that Marx never reduced historical movement merely to laws of motion, as a physicist might. Events always have a uniquely human significance, a tragedy and beauty, that must be grasped concretely from the grounding of human experience. "...He gives to each event, in addition to its particular signification, the role of being revealing." A Marxist method requires both factual evidence—fragments of history—and, in order to comprehend the factual evidence, models, structures, and concepts with which to make sense of this evidence.

Today Marxian "analysis consists solely in getting rid of detail"; "the open concepts of Marxism have closed in." Marxist historians reduce everything to the relation between capital and labor, failing to read history as a process of human meaning as well as structural regularity. Sartre's final indictment is that "Marxism has reabsorbed man into the idea, and existentialism seeks him everywhere *where he is,* at his work, in his home, in the street ...We say only that [man] is not known." An arid Marxism loses its grasp on "particularity"—human experience and human meaning—in its quest "to search for the whole in its parts."

The heuristic principle—"to search for the whole in its parts"—has become the terrorist practice of "liquidating the particularity." It is not by chance that Lukács—Lukács who so often violates history—has found in 1956 the best definition of this frozen Marxism. Twenty years of practice give him all the authority necessary to call this pseudo-philosophy *a voluntarist idealism.*

Today social and historical experience falls outside of Knowledge. Bourgeois concepts just manage to revive and quickly break down; those which survive lack any foundation. The real attainments of American Sociology cannot hide its theoretic uncertainty. Psychoanalysis, after a spectacular beginning, has stood still. It knows a great many details, but it lacks any firm foundation. Marxism possesses theoretical bases, it embraces all human activity; but it no longer *knows* anything. Its concepts are *dictates;* its goal is no longer to increase what it knows but to be itself constituted a priori as an absolute Knowledge. In view of this twofold ignorance, existentialism has been able to return and to maintain itself because it reaffirmed the reality of men as Kierkegaard asserted his own reality against Hegel. However, the Dane rejected the Hegelian conception of man and of the real. Existentialism and Marxism, on the contrary, aim at the same object; but Marxism has reabsorbed man into the idea, and existentialism seeks him everywhere *where he is,* at his work, in his home, in the street. We certainly do not claim—as Kierkegaard did—that this real man is unknowable. We say only that he is not known. If for the time being he escapes Knowledge, it is because the only concepts at our disposal for understanding him are borrowed either from the idealism of the Right or from the idealism of the Left. We are careful not to confuse these two idealisms: The former merits its name by the *content* of its concepts, and the latter by the *use* which today it makes of its concepts. It is true also that among the masses Marxist *practice* does not reflect, or only slightly reflects, the sclerosis of its theory. But it is precisely the conflict between revolutionary action and the Scholastic justification of this action which prevents Communist man—in socialist countries as in bourgeois countries—from achieving any clear self-consciousness. One of the most striking characteristics of our time is the fact that history is made without self-awareness. No doubt someone will say this has always been the case; and this was true up until the second half of the last century—that is, until Marx. But what has made the force and richness of Marxism is the fact that it has been the most radical attempt to clarify the historical process in its totality. For the last twenty years, on the contrary, its shadow has obscured history; this is because it has ceased to live *with history* and because it attempts, through a bureaucratic conservatism, to reduce change to identity.*

Maurice Merleau-Ponty, like Sartre, was an existential philosopher who wedded certain existentialist assumptions about the human foundation of social reality with Marxian concepts of historical change. More explicitly than Sartre, Merleau-Ponty grasped the weaknesses of a scientific Marxism that ignored the philosophical and psychological dimensions of socialist transformation. In two essays written in 1945 and 1946, Merleau-Ponty clarified his relationship to existentialism. The first essay, "The Battle over Existentialism," was published in *Les Temps Modernes* as a defense of Sartre's first major philosophical work, *Being and Nothingness,* against orthodox Marxists like Henri Lefebvre who attacked it. Merleau-Ponty suggests that Marxism cannot avoid philosophy; he broadens Marx's observation that the only way to destroy philosophy is to realize it in the world.

Merleau-Ponty argues that the final outcome of communism is not inevitable. "...We still have to know *what to do*" in the way of grasping our revolutionary responsibility. Merleau-Ponty notes that because the achievement of class consciousness is not a straightforward necessity of history one must develop a concept of "individual man who retains his power to serve or to betray his class and who in this sense joins it of his own accord." The root of revolution is the experience of alienation and the human being's motivation to overcome that alienation.

Marxism "gives man a dizzying responsibility." Marxism is neither absolute idealism nor absolute materialism. Merleau-Ponty indicates that a middle ground between these two extremes is occupied by existentialism. "Such a philosophy continues to see the revolutionary event as contingent and finds the date of the revolution written on no wall nor in any metaphysical heaven."

Merleau-Ponty defines an existentialist Marxism as a theory of historical change that embraces a conception of human consciousness rooted both in the human being's autonomy and his dependence. Men are determined *and* they are free: They are determined by what they have been in the past, and they are free to remake that past in creating new historical syntheses. "Marxism is unique in that it invites us to make the logic of history triumph over its contingency without offering any metaphysical guarantees." Here Merleau-Ponty suggests that determinism can be avoided only through an appreciation of the voluntarist bases of revolutionary struggle. Men must act with historical self-awareness to overcome the alienated condition that has turned them into puppets of social and economic forces. A "living Marxism" integrates existentialism, and learns from it, because existentialism remains a philosophical catalyst of revolutionary voluntarism.

If, in the name of Marxism, one wants to exclude the problems of subjectivity and, indeed, the very notion of it, it is not on these remnants of metaphysical

_____

*From Jean-Paul Sartre, *Search for a Method* (New York: Vintage, 1963), pp. 28-29.

materialism that one must base his case. Marxism contains a much deeper reason for abandoning the subject to concentrate on the object and history: the idea that we have no choice, that we are through and through the product of history, thrown without reservation into the world. For Marxism, whatever subjective justifications may be brought forth, exclusive reference to the interior is objectively an abstention and a way of avoiding the concrete tasks imposed on us from the outside. In a word, we are involved. It would be consistent with the purest Marxism to say that all philosophy is idealistic because philosophy always presupposes reflection, i.e., breaking with the immediate, and that therein lies the condemnation of philosophy. It is a special type of estrangement, a way of fleeing to the great beyond, a refusal to be, an anxiety in the face of revolution, a bourgeois guilty conscience. The philosopher who becomes aware of himself as nothingness and as freedom gives the ideological formula of his time, translating into concepts that phase of history where man's essence and existence are still separated, where man is not himself because he is bogged down in the contradictions of capitalism. The very idea of a *speculative* philosophy which would try to grasp an eternal essence of man and the world, testifies to the philosopher's existential refusal, underlying his ideas, to work at transforming the world, to his anxiety before the real humanity which *creates* itself through work and through praxis rather than seeking to define itself once and for all. The only way to obtain what philosophy seeks—a complete grasp of the world—is to connect ourselves with history instead of contemplating it. As Marx said in a famous text, the only way to fulfill philosophy is to destroy it.

Marxism's strongest argument against a philosophy of the subject is therefore an "existential" argument. It comes down to saying that any reflexive philosophy is inadequate to what it wants to grasp—that is, man's existence—because it itself is a certain way of existing apart from the world and history. "Philosophers," said Marx, "have only *interpreted* the world in various ways; the point, however, is to *change* it." Gabriel Marcel likewise criticizes Sartre for imprisoning himself within the vicious cycle of being and nothingness. "There would hardly be any point," he adds, "in claiming that he is forced into it by the given facts of the structural conditions of our existence. Isn't the one authentic transcendence (no doubt it would be better to say 'the one authentic transcending') that act by which we free ourselves from these data and these conditions, replacing them with fresh facts and conditions?" Both sides thus make the same appeal to action as the way of getting beyond dialectical oppositions (except that Marx does not claim that by earthly praxis we can rejoin a synthesis which has already been completed in heaven, and he situates synthesis in our future instead of outside time). At this point Kierkegaard and Marx, the two halves of Hegelian posterity, come together, but their very *rapprochement* is good evidence that Marxist praxis should become clearer about its own ends and means if it wishes to remain distinct from mystical action or pragmatism. It is all very well to invite us to be what we are, to become a conscious part of the movement of history in which we are involved in any case. But we still have to know what this movement of history is, who we can count on to help us complete it; we still have to know *what to do*. And from the minute these questions are raised, one invites the individual to understand and decide; in the last analysis one puts him back in control of his life and agrees that the meaning history will have for him depends on the meaning he sees in it. Every man, even a Marxist, is obliged to agree with Descartes that our knowledge of some outside reality depends on our having apprehended within ourselves that process by which we come to know. No *in itself* would be accessible to us if it were not at the very same time *for us*, and the meaning we find in it depends on our consent. No man can reject the *cogito* and deny consciousness, on pain of no longer knowing what he is saying and of renouncing all statements, even materialist ones. Marxist writers have said often and with good reason that Marxism does not deny the subjective conditions of history and is not a fatalism, that men create their history, and that ideologies, even if they express a clearly defined economic and social situation, have a bearing on history. But that is saying that they do not eliminate the subject as a factor in history. Let us remind those who shudder at the very word "subjectivity" of Marx's famous phrase: "The main thing wrong with all past materialism . . . is that it considers the thing, reality, the tangible world only as *object* or intuition, not as concrete human activity; as *practice,* not subjectively."

M. Lefebvre lives subjectivity just like everyone else, though he would like to ignore this fact. Even he must sometimes stop thinking about politics for a few hours and return to it afterwards as to a duty. If his life has for him a political meaning, it is because he gives it this meaning through decisions of his own. In the same way, not all proletarians are Communists, which is to say that we can slip away from our class and from what we are. The dialectic between being and nothingness takes place not only in Sartre's mind but also in the mind of the down-hearted worker who is withdrawing from the struggle. Who would dare insist that no condemned man feel anguish at his death, even if he dies for his class and, through it, for the future of mankind? As soon as man is introduced as the subject of history—and Marxism so portrays him—one is no longer bringing in merely collective man or class but is also including individual man who retains his power to serve or to betray his class and who in this sense joins it of his own accord. Marx gives us an objective definition of class in terms of the effective position of individuals in the production cycle, but he tells us elsewhere that class cannot become a decisive historical and revolutionary factor unless individuals become aware of it, adding that this awareness itself has social motives, and so on. As a historical factor, class is therefore neither a simple objective fact, nor is it, on the other hand, a simple value arbitrarily chosen by solitary consciousnesses. It is more in the nature of a fact-value or an incarnate value, for which the theory remains to be worked out. Today, when other oppositions (the national opposition of France and Germany, both of them worn out and stripped of social consciousness by Hitlerism and the Vichy regime; the opposition between the new world of America and the old Western world, between rich countries and those which have been bled to death) mask class relationships to a greater extent than ever, the French worker must make an individual effort to reestablish contact with the Italian worker despite the Fascist aggression of 1940; the individual Italian worker must make an effort to reforge the link with the French worker in spite of French projects to annex the Aosta Valley; restoring the ties between the American worker and his poor French relative, between the French worker and his rich American cousin, depends on the individual efforts of both, and the subject's role in establishing class as a historical factor is clearer than ever. We must analyze involvement, the moment when the subjective and objective conditions of history become bound together, how class exists before becoming aware of itself—in short, the status of the social and the phenomenon of co-existence. *L'Être et le néant* does not yet offer this social theory, but it does pose the problem of the reciprocal relations between consciousness and the social world as vigorously as possible by refusing to admit of freedom outside of a situation and by making the subject in no sense a reflection, as epiphenomenalism would have it, but a "reflecting reflection" in accordance with Marxism.

But there is more to be said. Marxism not only tolerates freedom and the individual but, as "materialism," even gives man a dizzying responsibility, as it were. Insofar as he reduced history to the history of the spirit, Hegel found the final synthesis heralded and guaranteed in his own consciousness, in his certainty at having understood history completely, and in the very realization of his philosophy. How could he help being optimistic, when history was consciousness's return to itself and the internal logic of the idea as he lived it in himself testified to the necessity of this return and to man's possibility of attaining totality and freedom from anxiety? That is the textbook Hegel, but there are other ways to interpret him: He could be, and we think he must be, made much more Marxist; one could base his logic on his phenomenology and not his phenomenology on his logic. But whether it bears the name of Hegel or Marx, a philosophy which renounces absolute Spirit as history's motive force, which makes history walk on its own feet and which admits no other reason in things than that revealed by their meeting and interaction, could not affirm *a priori* man's possibility for wholeness, postulate a final synthesis resolving all contradictions or affirm its inevitable realization. Such a philosophy continues to see the revolutionary event as contingent and finds the date of the revolution written on no wall nor in any metaphysical heaven. The breakdown of capitalism may lead the world to chaos instead of to the revolution if men do not understand the situation and do not want to intervene, just as childbirth may result in the death of both mother and baby if no one is there to assist nature. Although synthesis exists *de jure* in Hegel, it can never be more than *de facto* in Marxism. If there is a Hegelian quietism, there is necessarily a Marxist unrest. Although Hegel's solid and enduring foundation in theology makes it possible for him blindly to leave everything to the natural course of events, Marxist praxis—which can rely on nothing but coexistence among men—does not have the same resource. It cannot assign history a particular end in advance; it cannot even affirm the dogma of "total man" before he actually comes into being. If all our contradictions are someday to be resolved, then that day will be the first we know of it. Engels' learned talk about the way necessity reabsorbs historical accidents is much admired, but how does he know that history is and will continue to be rational if he is no longer a theist or an idealist? Marxism is unique in that it invites us to make the logic of history triumph over its contingency without offering any metaphysical guarantees.

One might ask why existentialism is so eager to conciliate Marxism. M. Lefebvre's gracious supposition is that it is the better to devour it. The truth—which, as we shall see, is much more straightforward—is that many readers of Marx are in absolute agreement with analyses like *XVIII Brumaire*, for example, but feel unsatisfied with certain of Marx's own theoretical formulas and above all with those of his commentators. According to these readers, the Marxist discovery of social existence as the most "interior" dimension of our life, of class dynamics as an integral process where economic and cultural determinations endlessly intersect and inter-signify, not only admits but demands a new conception of consciousness on the theoretical plane, which would establish a basis for both its autonomy and its dependence by describing it as a nothingness which comes into the world and which could not keep its liberty without engaging itself at every moment. According to them, this is the conception of consciousness which Marxism has at least *practiced* in its most powerful concrete analyses, if not formulated in theory. A living Marxism should "save" and integrate existentialist research instead of stifling it.*

> An existentialist Marxism occupies a middle ground between determinism and voluntarism. Marx felt that the dialectical method must integrate the structural analysis of historical dynamics with a concept of revolutionary praxis capable of overturning the past. Marxism is a doctrine that stresses the need to liberate men from their pasts, marred by domination. Marxism cannot be determinism, according to Merleau-Ponty, because it wants to break the spell of determinism through the chosen freedom of revolutionary activity. Marxism formulates "laws" of history only to show that these laws are impermanent and false. "Marx's entire effort in *Das Kapital* is directed precisely to showing that these famous laws, often presented as the permanent features of a 'social nature,' are really the attributes (and the masks) of a certain 'social structure,' capitalism, that is evolving towards its own destruction ... *A priori* scientism seems a conservative idea since it causes us to mistake the merely momentary for the eternal."
>
> Bourgeois political economy represented the workings of market capitalism as a lawful process of harmonious supply and demand relationships. This was portrayed as a harmony of *nature.* Marxism reveals that there is nothing "natural" about capitalism, that there can be other, qualitatively different, social and economic arrangements.

A Marxist conception of human society and of economic society in particular cannot subordinate it to permanent laws like those of classical physics, because it sees society heading toward a new arrangement in which the laws of classical economics will no longer apply. Marx's entire effort in *Das Kapital* is directed precisely to showing that these famous laws, often presented as the permanent features of a "social nature," are really the attributes (and the masks) of a certain "social structure," capitalism, which is evolving towards its own destruction. The notion of structure or totality, for which P. Naville has nothing but mistrust, is one of the basic categories of Marxism. A Marxist political economy can speak of laws only within qualitatively distinct structures, which must be described in terms of history. *A priori,* scientism seems a conservative idea since it causes us to mistake the merely momentary for the eternal. Throughout the history of Marxism, in fact, the fetishism of science has always made its appearance where the revolutionary conscience was faltering: The celebrated Bernstein exhorted Marxists to return to scientific objectivity. As Lukács notes, scientism is a particular case of alienation or objectification *(Verdinglichung)* which deprives man of his human reality and makes him confuse himself with things.†

---

*From Maurice Merleau-Ponty, *Sense and Non-Sense* (Evanston, Ill.: Northwestern University Press, 1964), pp. 78-82.

†From Maurice Merleau-Ponty, *Sense and Non-Sense* (Evanston, Ill.: Northwestern University Press, 1964), pp. 125-26.

These alleged "laws" of capitalism can only be abolished by free and conscious activity. Merleau-Ponty feels that Marxism needs to employ a theory of consciousness—existentialism—that stresses this relationship between history and praxis. Otherwise Marxism degenerates into an utterly mechanistic system of assumptions which treats the revolution as a fact of nature, as inevitable as the rising sun in the east.

PHENOMENOLOGICAL MARXISM

Existentialist Marxism is flanked on one side by the Freudian Marxism of Marcuse and on the other by the phenomenological Marxism developed by the Italian Marxist Enzo Paci and introduced into the United States in the late 1960s by Paul Piccone, founding editor of the neo-Marxist journal *Telos.* Phenomenological Marxism argues that Marxian theoretical concepts emerge from human "lifeworlds"—pre-theoretical grounds of everyday common sense and experience—and that revolutionary activity arises from this foundation in raw, untheorized human experience. Like existentialist Marxism, phenomenological Marxism attempts to reground Marxian theory in subjective experience and motivation, opposing deterministic versions of materialism that reduce revolutionary struggle purely to structural movements.

Phenomenological philosophy is rooted in the notion that all theoretical knowledge springs initially from pre-theoretical human experience (located in the "lifeworld"). In this sense, Marxism must be traced back to the lifeworld from which it springs, specifically the experience of alienation and the will towards emancipation. Like existentialism, phenomenology stresses that liberation is ultimately a *choice* (and not deterministically guaranteed by something above men).

Thus the phenomenological reconstruction of Marxism aims at restoring the dialectic between individual and class, arguing that the human being creates the categories for the analysis and critique of domination on the basis of his own experience of the capitalist lifeworld. Without an active, self-conscious human being, class struggle remains an abstraction devoid of subjectivity, consciousness, and will. Phenomenology joins psychoanalysis and existentialism, in their Marxist versions, in postulating that there must be a dialectic between the individual and the class; there must be individual rebellion in order for there to be universal emancipation.

Paci and Piccone argue that the human experience of alienation is the precondition of radical political activity. The so-called "lifeworld" from which all human expressions arise is the living basis of all theoretical and political projects. Marxism can only reorient its assumptions about radical change by reassessing the relationship between historical structures and the various human lifeworlds from which the revolutionary impulse must necessarily spring.

In a 1971 article, outlining the major theoretical assumptions of phenomenological Marxism, Paul Piccone begins by assessing the theoretical pitfalls of Lukács' Hegelian Marxism as a point of departure for phenomenological Marxism. Piccone argues that in spite of Lukács' great advances over the orthodox Marxism and social democarcy of the Second International there were serious problems with Lukács' analysis. Piccone claims that Lukács ignored "the concrete realities of the time" and thus unwittingly retained certain Marxian categories that had lost their relevance to Europe by the 1920s. Piccone argues that Lukács lacked a sufficient "grounding in socio-historical reality," to be remedied by a phenomenological Marxism that relentlessly revises Marxian theory with respect to the historical context, or "lifeworld," from which it arises.

Lukács sought to dialectically articulate a dynamic Marxism free of the metaphysical shackles of scientism and positivism. He did this by vindicating the Hegelian heritage of Marxism and uncompromisingly approaching every problem in terms of the Totality. His whole effort, however, was fundamentally vitiated by objective idealism, since it did not deal with the concrete realities of the time but instead substituted for them a set of highly articulate categories lifted out *tout court* from Marx's works. Although dynamic, these categories remained foreign to Lukács' historical situation and rendered his whole analysis hopelessly obsolete. This prevented Lukács from dealing with *real* historical forces and led him into political dead ends entailed by his uncritically accepted Marxist categories. Thus, it is not surprising that *History and Class Consciousness,* a work spouting revolutionary fire from every page, turned out to be the most untimely book of the period, appearing as it did precisely when it had already become evident that Marxist revolutions in Western Europe had been defeated and that there was absolutely no opportunity to carry them out for the next few years. The problem with Lukács' book was that despite all its rhetorical lip service to materialism, it operated entirely with an idealistic dialectic which brilliantly articulated Marxist categories transposed lock, stock, and barrel from Marx without, however, retaining their grounding in socio-historical reality, i.e., their materiality. Notwithstanding its penetrating philosophical analyses of reification, social democracy, and bourgeois thought, *History and Class Consciousness* was, in practice, a beautiful dream altogether lacking any mediation whereby it could meaningfully relate to the desperate realities of 1920 middle Europe. Lukács himself must have been painfully aware of this for, in the very last essay of the book, "Towards a Methodology of the Problem of Organization," and in another little booklet written immediately thereafter on *Lenin,* he practically repudiates his entire theoretical apparatus in favor of the Leninist notion of the party and its mechanistic consequences. Ironically, he gained the much needed mediation at the price of precisely the theoretical framework which had to be mediated.*

For Piccone phenomenological Marxism provides "mediations" between theoretical categories and human experience. In Chapter 7 we will further explore the possibilities of developing new mediations between contemporary Marxian theory and practice, appropriate to advanced capitalism in the late 1970s and 1980s. Here Piccone implies that Marxism is not a timeless set of assumptions valid once and for all but rather a set of provisional hypotheses that must be continuously referred back to the pre-theoretical reality that they describe and hope to change. Thus Lukács could not provide an adequate analysis of the downfall of class consciousness in his 1923 book *History and Class Consciousness.* Piccone thinks that the book was peculiar in that it came just *after* revolutionary possibilities had all but evaporated in western Europe; he argues that Lukács could not account for this development, and thus he failed to revise

---

*From Paul Piccone, "Phenomenological Marxism," *Telos,* No. 9, Fall 1971, pp. 8-9.

Marxian categories such as the concepts of class and class consciousness, because he did not adequately grasp relevant "mediations" between theory and praxis in that historical period.

Phenomenological Marxism grasps the creative human foundation of these mediations. "Phenomenology, critically understood, is the tracing back of all mediations to the human operations that constituted them." Lukács invested his faith in a class-conscious proletariat at precisely that moment when the proletariat was far from being a mature revolutionary subject (undergoing, as it was, a process of integration into the capitalist systems of each nation-state in Western Europe). Piccone argues that human beings construct the mediations that join theory and praxis and thus contribute to large-scale social change of a radical sort. Phenomenology enables Marxism to develop these mediations and thus to alter and modify its theory as circumstances dictate. In this sense, Piccone's phenomenological Marxism is highly relativistic, refusing to be an abstract system of fixed theoretical assumptions, relevant equally (although in different ways) in 1867 and 1977.

The crisis of Marxism today must be met both politically and theoretically, Piccone argues. "Phenomenological Marxism . . . [is] that approach which . . . reduces all theoretical constructs — including Marxism — to their living context in order to guarantee the adequacy of the concept not only to the object it claims to apprehend, but also to the goals it seeks to attain." A living Marxism, as both Sartre and Merleau-Ponty termed it, must adjust itself to the shifting contexts and forms of human alienation.

The most pressing problem facing any serious Marxist today is the crisis of Marxism, seen not only on a *practical* level dealing with the degeneration of the Soviet Union, but also on the theoretical level, since it would be abstract and idealistic to suppose that a fundamentally sound Marxism could have resulted in the unsound consequences that it has had: Something must have been wanting in Marxism from the very beginning. And it is precisely the locating of this original flaw which must allow an analysis of Stalinism and its consequences. Phenomenological Marxism can be preliminarily described as that approach which constantly reduces all theoretical constructs—including Marxism—to their living context in order to guarantee the adequacy of the concept not only to the object it claims to apprehend, but also to the goals it seeks to attain. In fact, its point of departure is precisely the rejection of that theory of reflection so dear to "orthodox" Marxists which, unfortunately, turns out to be an untenable positivistic leftover. Disclaimers to the contrary notwithstanding, Merleau-Ponty was right: "Marxism needs a theory of consciousness." And this is where phenomenology comes in.*

The central philosophical assumption of phenomenological philosophy is that human beings create the categories they use to conceptualize and transform their lived experience. Piccone suggests that people put in touch with this essential human faculty can begin to loosen the bonds of alienation. Phenomenology is a revolutionary philosophy for it argues that people must emancipate themselves from imposed knowledge and authority, regaining their own adequacy as living theorists and potential creators of their own futures. Like existentialism,

---

*From Paul Piccone, "Phenomenological Marxism," *Telos*, No. 9, Fall 1971, p. 15.

phenomenology grasps the possibility of human creativity and imagination as the ultimate resource for a "living Marxism."

THE DIALECTICAL SENSIBILITY

In a recent article in the *Canadian Journal of Political and Social Theory* we develop the concept of a radical social scientific empiricism that could further develop these "mediations" between the levels of individual experience and creativity and of social structure. We summarize many of the themes of individualized Marxism, as developed in this chapter, including the idea that theoretical developments dialectically interact with historical and political circumstances.

We outline a "radical empiricism" that links up the human experience of alienation and efforts to overcome that alienation with the theoretical orientations of radical thinkers. This radical empiricism comes close to Piccone's phenomenological Marxism, arguing that theory must always adjust itself to changes in the empirical and phenomenological basis of society. We add that theory can also guide and instruct grass-roots efforts to overcome alienation: "... out of struggle will spring the resources for improving and enhancing struggle."

We begin by developing a critique of the Frankfurt School's theory of domination. We argue that Horkheimer and Adorno failed to develop the concept of a creative human nature and thus they found no basis for supposing that the person could recognize and overturn his own alienation. Furthermore, the Frankfurt thinkers failed to adopt the "advisory" role of Marx's theory, providing mediations between individual rebellion and large-scale structural transformation. Our "radical empiricism" is the basis for moving beyond the Frankfurt theory of domination towards a more adequate conception of change in the 1980s.

Critical theory in Marcuse's hands has begun to transcend its pessimism about effecting social change in late capitalist society. The transcendence of pessimism, and the subsequent repoliticization of critical theory, turns on the concept of human nature adopted by theorists. If empirical subjectivity still exists, political radicalism again becomes a meaningful possibility.

I submit that critical theory can overcome its proclivity for abstract philosophical negation and cerebral radicalism (a) by developing a concept of subjectivity which allows it to recognize and locate empirical instances of struggle to create new institutions; (b) by developing an orientation to the relation between theory and practice which more nearly approximates Marx's own concept of the advisory role of theory.

The first task can be characterized as involving epistemological strategies, the second as involving political strategies. These tasks are intimately related, inasmuch as a Marxian theory of knowledge relates directly to its attitude towards stimulating social change. Objectivistic epistemology tends to reinforce a fatalistic attitude to social change, as I have argued elsewhere. Marxian positivism degrades the role of consciousness both epistemologically *and* politically, accepting an image of fully heteronomous subjectivity.

Again, I submit that the thorough-going critique of scientism by members of the original Frankfurt School led them to scrap the advisory role of theory and to abandon the prospect of effective radicalism. It is not the case that Adorno believed that change was impossible, for he remained a dialectical thinker, fundamentally uncertain about the future. He only abandoned the advisory role of theory (developed by Marx) in the belief that human subjectivity could not be perceived as revolutionary and thus theory could not improve and deepen its political possibilities. In overcoming the deep-seated historicism and purely cerebral orientation of the original Frankfurt School, critical theory will be able to develop a *possible concept of radicalism,* rooted in an image of constitutive subjectivity. Empiricism will take the form of uncovering the objective potential of radical activity. Radical social science will locate existing rebellion and thus counter its original tendency to view modern capitalism as a self-sufficient, automatic totality, capable of integrating all opposition.

Radical empiricism will construct the model of a constitutive human being. It will utilize particular examples of struggle to illuminate a broader theory of change. Epistemological strategies become relevant to political strategies in the sense that critical theory will *locate* empirical instances of rebellion in order to *illuminate* their radical potential. Theory will allow rebellion to think its own radicalism, to locate its sense of injustice and proposed alternative institutions in a theoretical totality. *Out of struggle will spring the resources for creating a theory to improve and to enhance struggle.*

Radical empiricism becomes a form of political activity as soon as it enters the dialectic of theory and practice (task number *b*). Radical empiricism sheds the disengagement of traditional, purely contemplative theories by *taking control* of the process of cognition. The division between manual and mental labour is overcome by what Gramsci called "organic intellectuals," intellectuals who refuse to remain aloof from human struggle. The organic intellectual does not rely on experts and dead authorities, believing that cognition is a constructive activity which must be renewed continuously, never able to rest with final and ultimate knowledge.

Radical empiricism is itself a political strategy; it challenges the scientistic concept of disinterested knowledge, taking inspiration from Marx's concept of "practical-critical activity" in *Theses on Feuerbach.* Radical empiricism eschews the abstract tendencies of traditional theory by overturning the dualism between contemplation and action, a dualism which Lukács characterized as an "antinomy of bourgeois thought."

Critical theory in this sense can converge with phenomenology and ethnomethodology by endorsing their concepts of cognition as a *practical,* as opposed to a transcendental, activity. Although phenomenology and ethnomethodology fail to develop a systematic critique of domination, they both implicitly subvert the contemplative disengagement of the traditional bourgeois intellectual. Radical empiricism is an "everyday" activity, a mode of self-objectification. It relates its theoretical constructs to the "lifeworld" from which human struggle springs, attempting to develop a structural understanding of the subjective roots of emancipatory activity. Radical empiricism studies subjective radicalism, attempting to articulate a theory of change, while it is *itself* a mode of radical subjectivity: This is the ineradicable dialectic between knowledge and action which lies at the heart of a repoliticized critical theory.

The radical empiricist is thus a *dialectical sensibility,* refusing to separate his activity into reflective and activist roles. The radical empiricist is a human being who studies and attempts to assist human beings in the process of their self-emancipation. As a dialectical sensibility, the radical empiricist does not separate his own liberation from the liberation of others: He attempts to provide others with subjective, constitutive autonomy so that they might help him create a dialogical community. The dialectical sensibility must be an empiricist because he does not believe that the particular, peculiar circumstances of human beings can be ignored by a theory of change. Institutional change is contingent on organizing and developing subjective sources of rebellion.

The dialectical sensibility goes *beneath* the appearances of domination, believing that contemporary society contains inchoate, even invisible tendencies towards its own transformation. The dialectical sensibility explains how social change—in the abstract—would have concrete consequences for particular human existences. The dialectical sensibility, through the filter of radical empiricism, *begins to live the revolution.*

Critical theory will shed pregiven, abstract models of change. The models will be suggested by what people do to improve their own lives. Marx, in a similar fashion, did not develop a speculative concept of proletarian radicalism, thinking that the proletariat was an ontologically necessary radical agent. Instead, Marx analyzed empirical developments in market society which *stimulated* proletarian radicalism; Marx created a theory of change by examining the genesis and potential of existing struggle, a theory which he then articulated in order to heighten and to rationalize the workers' movement. Marx learned from struggling workers in order to teach them about their possible historical mission.

Radical social science will create a theory of change from empirical evidence of existing struggle (task number *b*). In order to perceive existing struggle theorists must utilize a concept of constitutive subjectivity which *provides for* the possibility of radicalism (task number *a*). If society is fully one-dimensional (a thesis falsely ascribed to Marcuse, one which he has never endorsed), it would make no sense to harness examples of rebellion in creating a new theory of change. The issue here is that of the existence or absence of revolutionary agents. Critical theory stands or falls on its estimate of the *possibility* of social change. A theorist indulges his insight and imagination in taking a position on the possibility of change and, implicitly, on a concept of subjectivity. Once this step has been taken, certain empirical strategies suggest themselves. These strategies are oriented to developing a theory of change rooted in existing examples of rebellion.

My own position, with Marcuse and others, is that change is presently possible. My concept of subjectivity suggests the possibility that people can *and do* create alternative institutions. I am reluctant to accept the thesis of declining individuality; instead, I am concerned to locate existing rebellion in developing the foundations of a new, more relevant theory of change.

Once tasks numbers *a* and *b* have been accomplished, and a dialectical sensibility created, a radical social science can take wing. Assuming a concept of constitutive subjectivity *and* assuming an advisory role for a theory constructed with evidence from empirical cognition, a revised theory of change can be outlined.

However, there is a kind of Marxian empiricism which neither assumes the relevance of constitutive subjectivity nor conceives of theoretical cognition as advisory and practice-oriented. I submit that within bourgeois social science,

Marxism is usually viewed as this type of empiricism, being merely a variant of value-free social science. I characterize this version as *Weberian Marxism* because it rests upon Weber's concept of value-free scientific objectivity, rejecting Marx's concept of practice-oriented empiricism developed, if briefly, in *Theses on Feuerbach*. Weberian Marxism is a product of the neo-Kantian Marxism of the Second International, further developing its dichotomy of knowledge and action.

While Horkheimer and Adorno overstated their critique of scientism, or appeared to do so, Weberian Marxists have neglected the theoretical significance of the critique of scientism. Marxist empiricism can take a variety of forms, some of which depart from the dialectical epistemology embraced by Lukács and Korsch. Scientistic Marxism fails to endorse the practice-oriented implications of Marx's revolutionary science, believing that Marxian empiricism must take the form of value-neutral social science developed most systematically by Max Weber.

I contrapose Weberian Marxism to dialectical Marxism: Weberian Marxism separates Marxian social theory from radical political activity. Sociologists like Tom Bottomore follow Weber in arguing that Marxian empiricism must formulate causal relationships which can provide greater comprehension of social dynamics. While the radical empiricism which I propose does not abandon the cognitive purpose of science, it is a *dialectical* empiricism in that it *intervenes* in the social process which it cognizes. Marxist positivism, buttressed by Weber's canon of value-free objectivity, stands in a passive relationship to the objective world, failing to adopt the mediating, advisory role with respect to existing struggle that I believe Marx recommended.

Theory and practice are not identical, as certain critical theorists have unwittingly implied, believing that the critique of ideology and of captive subjectivity must *replace* political activism. But neither are theory and practice unconnected, as Weberian Marxists assume. Dialectical empiricism is unlike non-Marxist social sciences in that it seeks a particular type of information, namely, about how human struggle might be able to change society. Dialectical empiricism seeks to inform rebellion of its political possibilities. In this sense, Weberian Marxism does not think of itself as a special science—a science which struggles to make itself unnecessary by changing society—but only as an instance of value-neutral empiricism.

The Weberian Marxist *as a scientist* does not allow political commitments to affect his scientific cognition. However, the radical empiricist does not *separate* his life as a scientist from his life as a political partisan and activist. He does not make this separation because, as Marx bluntly reminded us, the point is to change the world, not only to interpret it.

Marxist social science either *acts* as a change-agent in society, advising and stimulating on-going rebellion; or it *reflects* social processes, refusing to unify cognitive and political roles.

I submit that the model of a revolutionary working class will be replaced by a model of revolutionary self-management and deprofessionalization. In this sense, the class-specific attack on the capitalist division of labour launched by Marx will be *generalized* into an attack on all aspects of the division of labour, involving every class.

Following Habermas and Mueller, I submit that economic crises, endemic to an earlier stage in the development of capitalism, have been displaced by new forms of crisis such as the crisis of *legitimacy*. This type of crisis has resulted from the near-collapse of liberalism and its ideology of individual initiative, a collapse which has eroded the bases of political and cultural legitimacy in advanced industrial societies. Legitimation crisis is peculiar to a form of capitalism which rests not on sharp class conflict but on expanding professional and service sectors. The ideology of liberalism, suitable to an earlier form of market capitalism, no longer elicits mass belief in the rationality of the social system. Affluence has not in its own right guaranteed a stable political system, especially when human dissatisfaction in the spheres of work and leisure has not been mitigated by mere consumption.

Class conflict is now largely replaced by cynicism about the rationality and humanity of the system. A cynical public fails to trust economic and cultural elites, and begins to reject the imposition of authority. In this sense, the locus of crisis and rebellion has changed since the time of Marx. Job dissatisfaction and moral anomie have largely replaced poverty in advanced industrial society as manifestations of alienation.

In this context, resentment of exploitative economic elites is replaced by resentment of *imposed authority*. People feel that they can have no input to complex decision-making processes, nor control over their work-places, communities, and social services. The world appears to be beyond the ken of subjective control, an illusion sustained knowingly by the ideology of scientism and technocracy which has largely superseded liberalism.

Marxism thus can be most effective by enhancing the struggle to *take control* over private and public existences. The on-going rebellion against authority imposed from above can be *mediated* and *organized* by modern critical theory, and raised to a higher level of theoretically self-conscious radicalism. For example, the movement to develop neighbourhood control in large urban centres can be seized upon by critical theory and informed about its own latent radicalism, its denial of imposed authority.

Instead of searching for a revolutionary working class, which becomes more and more bourgeois as the scope and powers of unions expand, Marxists will instead search for movements to *take control* of social and political processes. They will attempt to provide a theoretical framework within which efforts to decentralize and deprofessionalize modern life can be perceived as radical. They will refuse to minimize the "revolutionary" importance of these kinds of rebellion, no longer retaining the vocabulary of economistic radicalism appropriate to an earlier stage of capitalism.

Paradoxically, the original Frankfurt theorists remained *more* traditional in their concept of radical scholarship than perhaps appearances indicated. The pessimism which I have attributed to critical theory was a product of disappointment about a quiescent working class. Although the thesis of declining subjectivity seems to apply to all social groups, middle class and proletarian, I argue that it was secretly meant to apply only to the fallen working class. The critical theorists did not believe that critical consciousness *as such* had been eradicated, but only the critical consciousness of the working class. Horkheimer and Adorno believed that certain radical intellectuals were privileged in that they were not captives of instrumental rationality.

The original Frankfurt theorists were bourgeois intellectuals in the sense that they did not believe that intellectual theoretical practice was a political activity and, consequently, that their own activity needed to be transformed. In this regard, the critical theorists failed to develop new concepts of radical scholarship, falling back on the archetype of "critical criticism," as Marx called it, or disengaged intellectuality. Had the Frankfurt theorists actually *revised* Marx's revolutionary science, they could have developed a concept of intellectual deprofessionalization and even self-management, becoming "organic intellectuals" in Gramsci's terms. Shifting the analytic terms of Marxian theory, from the class-specific model of proletarian activism to the generalized model of revolutionary self-management, might have allowed the Frankfurt critics to shed their own self-identity as traditional scholars, disengaged from politics.

That Adorno and Horkheimer in the late 1960s felt threatened by the West German New Left, by their blatant eroticism and attack on authority-structures and professional roles *including* traditional Marxist scholarship, is comprehensible in light of this interpretation. Critical theory could not adequately shift gears in developing a radical empiricism which would allow the theory of social change to be appropriately transformed. This issued in the traditionalist concept of professional scholarship which Horkheimer and Adorno retained.

A radical empiricism based upon a concept of constitutive subjectivity requires that the role of the intellectual be rethought. An orthodox Marxist shies away from the demystification of authority-structures because he fears that his own authoritative role will be weakened in the process. A Marxist who is not reluctant to abandon faith in a proletarian revolution can become a practice-oriented intellectual, no longer reluctant to adjust his own intellectual and political self-image to the exigencies of on-going radicalism. I would argue that Marcuse could so readily come to terms with the New Left in the 1960s because he—alone among the Frankfurt theorists—was receptive to rebellion which did not fit traditional models, being a dialectical sensibility and radical empiricist.

Unless critical theory sheds its thesis of declining individuality and recaptures its advisory relationship to struggle (tasks numbers *a* and *b*, above) it will remain politically irrelevant. Marxists can either await a delayed revolution to be carried out by the working class, or they can return to the inspiration of Marx's revolutionary materialism and his idea that radicalism provides theory with empirical and political resources and not the other way around. Critical theory seeks the promise of emancipation in unorthodox forms of struggle, constantly putting intellectual radicalism to the test of social and political practice, becoming a *living theory* which refuses to separate cognitive and political roles.

The Marxist intellectual can become a dialectical sensibility, engaging in his own particular type of subjective revolt against imposed authority. The dialectical sensibility does not separate theory and practice, envisaging instead a radical intellectuality which itself contributes to social change. It remains for this type of theoretical practice to be articulated.*

"Dialectical sensibility" begins to "live the revolution" by attempting to rejoin thought and action, refusing to succumb to total domination. The dialectical sensibility struggles to take control of political, economic, technological, and scientific processes, wresting control from technocrats and bureaucrats. We thus

*From Ben Agger, "Dialectical Sensibility I: Critical Theory, Scientism, and Empiricism," *Canadian Journal of Political and Social Theory*, Vol. 1, No. 1, Winter 1977, pp. 24-31.

provide a basis for reevaluating the traditional role of the Marxist intellectual, suggesting that the theorist is always implicitly engaged in a kind of political praxis in the way in which he or she approaches social reality and relates to social change movements. The Marxist intellectual need not remain aloof from human struggle; indeed, the dialectical sensibility attempts to overcome alienation in its own life by challenging the imposed authority of experts and professionals.

The Marxist intellectual today would reexamine the mediations between theory and praxis. The traditional model of revolutionary class struggle appears to have lost much of its analytical and political utility. We end by suggesting that a concept of "revolutionary self-management" might be developed to replace earlier models of class struggle. In this sense, the Marxist intellectual will encourage radical self-management, and will practice it with respect to his or her own intellectual activity, as a route to significant radical change. The most important requirement in this sense is to put people in touch with their essential capacity for changing the present order and for making a new one. This theme will be rejoined in Chapter 7.

GUIDE TO FURTHER READING

HERBERT MARCUSE   *An Essay on Liberation*, published in 1969, is the most important statement of individualized Marxism, emerging out of the student and protest movements in the late 1960s. Marcuse here introduces his central concept of a "new sensibility" that begins to live in non-exploitative and non-dominating ways in the immediate present, refusing to postpone the achievement of socialism to a distant future time.

HERBERT MARCUSE   *Counterrevolution and Revolt*, published in 1973, amplifies the insights of his 1969 book, noted above, while expressing scepticism about the political self-consciousness of the American New Left. This work contains important chapters on art and nature in the revolutionary struggle.

HERBERT MARCUSE   *Eros and Civilization*, is Marcuse's signal attempt to synthesize Marxian and Freudian themes, published in 1955.

ENZO PACI   *The Function of Modern Science and the Meaning of Man*, is considered to be the classic synthesis of phenomenology and Marxism. Paci relies on a creative reinterpretation of Marx's early writings to blend phenomenological and dialectical materialist themes.

MAURICE MERLEAU-PONTY   *Signs* and *Sense and Non-Sense*, are collections of political, theoretical, and philosophical writings by one of the leading French existentialist Marxists. *Signs* contains important essays from the period 1945–1947 when Merleau-Ponty attempted to come to grips with the relationship between Hegelian and existential-phenomenological foundations of living Marxism.

JEAN-PAUL SARTRE   *Search for a Method,* a section of his larger 1960 work *Critique of Dialectical Reason,* outlines Sartre's reconciliation of existentialism and Marxism. Sartre argues that existentialism belongs to the Marxist philosophy of history, providing it with a crucial grasp on the source of individual meaning and thus offering a counterweight to Marxian economic and structural determinism. Unfortunately for the student of Marxism, Sartre's prose and conceptual vocabulary is much more difficult than Merleau-Ponty's.

PAUL PICCONE   The founding editor of *Telos,* the most important journal of radical social theory in North America, has extended many of Enzo Paci's insights in new directions. Although *Telos* now represents a variety of theoretical positions, ranging from Habermasian Marxism to Hegelian Marxism (of the Frankfurt species) to Piccone's own phenomenological Marxism, Piccone's seminal essay on "Phenomenological Marxism" (*Telos*, No.9) nicely summarizes current issues in Marxist disputation and especially the relationship between history and theory that lies at the center of the so-called "revisionist controversy." Also see Piccone's essay attacking the Hegelian Marxism of the Frankfurt School from the perspective of phenomenological Marxism, entitled "Beyond Identity Theory," in John O'Neill's edited collection *On Critical Theory.*

MARK POSTER   *Existential Marxism in Post-War France,* offers an authoritative intellectual and theoretical history of the group surrounding Sartre and Merleau-Ponty.

BEN AGGER   "Dialectical Sensibility I: Critical Theory, Scientism, and Empiricism," in *Canadian Journal of Political and Social Theory.* Vol. 1, No. 1, Winter 1977, contains a critique of the Frankfurt School's historical pessimism. The author proposes an "advisory" concept of the relationship between critical theory and human struggle as a way of circumventing the abject pessimism of Adorno and Horkheimer.

BEN AGGER   "Dialectical Sensibility II: Towards a New Intellectuality," in *Canadian Journal of Political and Social Theory,* Vol. 1, No. 2, Spring 1977, further develops the themes of the above article. The author calls for an "experimental Marxism," moving beyond the traditional model of the class struggle in the direction of revolutionary self-management as the organizing principle of a new and more relevant Marxism.

PAUL BREINES, editor   *Critical Interruptions,* is a useful collection of articles on Marcuse and critical theory, offering both sympathetic and critical perspectives.

PAUL PICCONE and BART GRAHL, editors   *Towards a New Marxism,* is a collection of papers drawn from the first *Telos* conference at the University of Waterloo, Canada in 1970.

MAURICE MERLEAU-PONTY   *Humanism and Terror,* contains the author's reflections on revolutionary terror and the creation of socialism.

GAD HOROWITZ   *Repression: Basic and Surplus Repression in Psychoanalytic Theory: Freud, Reich, Marcuse,* is a systematic analysis of Marcuse's synthesis of Marxism and psychoanalysis, offering a detailed examination of Freud's theory of basic repression and sublimation.

QUESTIONS FOR FURTHER DISCUSSION

1. Is Marcuse's concept of the "new sensibility" a fundamental departure from original Marxism or does Marx prefigure Marcuse's insights in certain of his works such as the early writings?

2. What is the significance of the concept of "mediation" for a discussion of individualist Marxism?

3. To what specific historical and cultural developments is individualist Marxism a response? Is it an adequate response from a Marxian point of view?

4. Explain why Marcuse's recent works have been the subject of such harsh criticism, from both right-wing and left-wing thinkers.

5. What are the essentials of Freudian Marxism and how does it contribute to the development of Marxism as a whole? Refer where necessary to Wilhelm Reich's posthumous collection of writings entitled *Sex-Pol* or to Marcuse's *Eros and Civilization.*

6. How have Sartre and Merleau-Ponty attempted to revive and reconstruct Marxism by employing insights from existential phenomenology? If necessary, refer also to Paul Piccone's essay on "Phenomenological Marxism" in *Telos* No. 9.

7

Returning to Crisis-Theory: The Many Faces of Modern Marxism

HISTORICAL OVERVIEW

The dawning of the 1960s did not bring the affluent, post-industrial society that sociologists in the 1950s had prophesied. Instead international capitalism was shaken by runaway inflation, high levels of unemployment and mounting threats from underdeveloped nations as well as from the Arab oil-producing states. Within western industrial societies, human beings have become increasingly dissatisfied with capitalist free enterprise both because many suffer deprivation at the hands of capitalism and because many of those who do not suffer as directly in an economic sense are bored with workaday routines and a shallow leisure-time existence. Legitimacy crisis, sparked in the 1960s by the Vietnam travesty, gathered momentum in the 1970s. Thus many Marxists are returning to Marx's original concept of crisis as an inevitable by-product of the capitalist production process. Crisis-theories today emphasize both the built-in structural contradictions in capitalism (resulting in what Marx termed the falling rate of profit) and the tendency for advanced capitalism to deepen alienation and to fragment human existence as well as to pollute the environment and to denude nature of its resources. The return to a theory of crisis indicates that late monopoly capitalism is ripe for fundamental transformations, on the level of its economic performance as well as on the level of human motivation and meaning. The endless production of commodities for profit is ending, as human beings express frustration with the monolithic reality of man-as-consumer. Large-scale social change in the 1980s may take the form of an "ecological Marxism" that stresses the need to decentralize technology and its bureaucratic infrastructure and thus to return control of production and consumption directly to small groups of people. Marxism today increasingly emphasizes the overcentralization of modern life and the sheer size of modern organizations as factors of alienation.

Many Marxists believe that radical change will spring from attempts to recapture control of the environment, workplace, and local communities; Marxian crisis-theory will organize these incipient social change movements into a concerted effort to transform the total social system. Marxists will tap existing sources of rebellion that largely take the form of efforts to overcome an overly centralized, bureaucratized, and fragmented human existence, inadequately compensated by leisure-time consumption.

GENERAL INTRODUCTION

In Chapter 6 we arrived at the crossroads of the 1960s and 1970s. The recent work of Marcuse, the French existentialists, and the phenomenological Marxists was surveyed in the context of what we termed individualist Marxism, which was itself a reaction to the pessimism of the Frankfurt School (Chapter 4). We must now go beyond the 1960s, a period that generated new types of Marxism directly responsive to the struggles of American students and minorities against the Indochina war effort and domestic power- and class-systems.

The deepening crises of the 1970s have modified the mood of romantic optimism in which theorists like Marcuse tried to devise new forms and strategies of class-radicalism, often intensely personal ones (e.g., his "new sensibility"). We do not proclaim the new sensibility dead; but merely recognize that Marcuse's *An Essay on Liberation* is an unfinished manifesto that must now be related to larger trends in the development of advanced capitalism. To put this matter differently, we contend that Marcuse's vision of the new sensibility can only be restored by locating its possibility in a macro-theory of capitalist crisis and socialist transition.

While the period of romantic exuberance, characteristic of youth culture in the late '60s and captured forever in the image of the Paris May movement in 1968, has passed, capitalism today is not a more stable system, intractable and crisis-free. Indeed the crises are more serious than the crises of the 1960s. The anti-war movement was sparked by opposition to the Indochina military involvement. Today, as we reach the end of the 1970s, the increasingly acute crises are in a sense "self-caused"; capitalism is on very rocky footing, with runaway inflation, aggravating (and humanly debilitating) unemployment, and a recessionary investment climate. While the exuberance of the '60s has temporarily passed, economic, ecological, and social crisis abounds, begging for a coherent perspective on the possibilities of radical transformation.

The individualist Marxism launched in the 1960s and the sober economic and ecological crisis-theory of the late 1970s (surveyed in the readings below) need not be seen as disjunctive alternatives. Indeed it is our argument here that modern crisis-theory will be politically ineffective *unless* it is linked with an exuberant, voluntaristic struggle for collective emancipation and self-emancipation; we hope to blend Marcuse's cry for a "new sensibility" with a more total socioeconomic theory within which the new sensibility becomes a meaningful possibility. It is to this task that we devote ourselves in this chapter introduction and in our brief commentaries on the particular readings to follow.

While this is a textbook, committed to the dispassionate presentation of theoretical and historical material, it is also a book about Marxist futures. Thus it is incumbent on us to develop our own argument, using past data and blending it in new syntheses, about the future of Marxism. Of particular importance for our argument is the relevance of a Marxist outlook to North Americans; implicit in our earlier discussions of Marxist theorists is a critique of the Eurocentric character of much of their work. The argument here rests on the assumption that capitalism in the West is in serious trouble and that an adequate crisis-theory (operating simultaneously on the level of politics, economics, and ecology) will attempt to comprehend the possibility of socialist change. But our argument does not end with the analysis of a collection of crisis-theories. It is also committed to the creation of a new ideology and vision, suitable to the North American context, that can stimulate radical activity. Marxism in its essentials is not deterministic and thus it requires that human beings engage in self-emancipatory attempts (for revolution will not fall from the sky or spring from the cosmic clash of self-contradictory economic structures, as thinkers like Kautsky sometimes intimated).

The product of this final chapter will be a new ideology of socialist change, blending modern crisis-theories with an analysis of the possibilities of self-emancipatory action in the North American context. The final reading, the author's own, will attempt to bring together these themes as a conclusion to this book.

Marx's methodology contained (a) a theory and critique of alienation, (b) a theory of the system's deep-seated internal contradictions, and (c) a theory of crisis and strategy of transition. Our discussions until now have concerned primarily the Marxian theories of alienation, domination, and reification as well as the theory of capitalism's internal contradictions. It is now the time to devote ourselves to a more concrete discussion of crisis-theory in the 1970s, in order both to assess recent developments within Marxian theory and to improve upon prior syntheses of Marxian theoretical undercurrents.

There are two distinctive, but complementary, strains in recent Marxism that warrant initial attention. The first is the attempt by theorists such as Jürgen Habermas, Claus Offe, Ernest Mandel, James O'Connor, Nicos Poulantzas, and Ralph Miliband to develop an adequate theory of the advanced capitalist state. They draw from Marxian political economy and particularly from Marx's theory of the capitalist state. Marx suggested that the political state is merely an "executive committee of the bourgeoisie" that necessarily acts to support the interests of capital. The neo-Marxian theory of the state attempts both empirically to document ways in which state intervention in the economy operates and also to articulate new crisis-problems that this state intervention engenders.

Below we will excerpt sections from Jürgen Habermas' recent *Legitimation Crisis,* which is the most advanced theoretical analysis of new crisis-tendencies generated by the malfunctioning of the capitalist state. Habermas argues (a) that state intervention in the capitalist economy is vitally important in order to stimulate capital expenditures (often through military-defense spending) and to maintain nearly full employment, as well as periodically to regulate wages and prices and (b) that this intervention creates serious crises primarily stemming from the ideologically incongruous appearance of a state-regulated "free market" economy. Writers like James O'Connor argue that this takes the form of "fiscal crisis," generated by the inability of the capitalist state to accumulate sufficient tax revenues to meet its interventionist commitments.

The neo-Marxist theory of the state, in short, assesses the potential for large-scale transformation created by the crisis-bound role of the capitalist state. Most neo-Marxist theorists of the state accept Marx's basic understanding of the state as the executive committee of the bourgeoisie but deny that crisis-forms described by Marx have much relevance today. The primary developments that invalidate Marx's own incomplete and insufficiently worked out crisis-theory have been (a) the creation of an interventionist state and (b) the existence of monopoly capitalism in most sectors of the economy. (While the entrepreneurial sector still exists, it is by no means the primary location of capitalist production, as documented by O'Connor in his *The Fiscal Crisis of the State.)*

Monopoly capitalism, as we know it today in the United States and elsewhere, is *not* the same as it was in Marx's time but it is *also* not different. By this we mean that the internal contradictions of the capitalist system still exist but that crisis-tendencies have changed significantly. It will be recalled from Chapter 1 that the primary internal contradiction of capitalism is the contradiction between the socialized character of the production process (its increasing interdependence and growing division of labor) and private ownership of the means of production and private appropriation of the surplus. While this contradiction still exists in all capitalist systems, regardless of their degree of monopolization, crisis-forms are only indirectly related to this contradiction, as Marx sketched it.

Marxism is not deterministic precisely because internal contradictions are not automatically related to corresponding forms of crisis: That capitalism is anarchic and irrational does not require that it "must" collapse in the immediate future. In spite of the fact that Marx argued that collapse was inevitable he did not believe that the collapse was preordained or unavoidable. Crises, according to Marx, *tend* to result from the working out of contradictions; but, as Merleau-Ponty once noted, "the date of the revolution is written on no wall." And so the neo-Marxian theory of the state searches for new ways to understand possible crises and modes of transition, triggered by shifting internal forces in capitalism—now monopoly capitalism.

Capitalist class society still exists but now its weaknesses are manifested in a variety of new ways, deviating significantly from Marx's own theories of crisis, which involved falling rates of profit and the creation of a vast industrial reserve army. The following is a list of models of crisis taken from the neo-Marxist theory of the state, of which two leading works are excerpted below:

1. The theory of fiscal crisis, authored by James O'Connor, suggests that the capitalist state is increasingly hard-pressed to collect sufficient revenues to meet its interventionist obligations.
2. The theory of legitimation crisis, authored by Jürgen Habermas, Ralph Miliband, and others, suggests that there is a basic incongruity between the capitalist state's interventionist role in monopoly capitalist systems and the ideology of free enterprise still in place in most western nation-states. Habermas argues that many wage-laborers are increasingly disenchanted with big business and government (as well as organized labor, but for different reasons) because they do not see that these large-scale forces are either manageable or rational; and, furthermore, the average laborer no longer sees the system as fair (for the prospect for the successful small-scale entrepreneur is now dim indeed).

Both of these theories of crisis stem from an appreciation that the vastly expanded role of the state has created new problems for capitalism, shifting the locus of crisis from the economy per se to political, ideological, and cultural spheres. The causes of fiscal and legitimation crises are the same as they were for Marx—the very structure of capitalism, precariously balanced between social production and private consumption. Now the *forms* differ, requiring new theories of crisis and eventually new strategies of social change.

The second contemporary theory of capitalist crisis is less sharply focused, if no less important, than the neo-Marxist crisis-theories rooted in an analysis of the state. This theory argues that there are deep-seated contradictions not only in the capitalist production process but also in the ways in which that production process interacts with the ecosystem as a whole. This ecological crisis-theory, or ecological Marxism as we prefer to term it, argues that the imperative need to limit industrial growth will create grave political pressures that may force a fundamental reevaluation of our goals and methods as an industrial-capitalist civilization.

Ecological Marxism is Marxist precisely because it locates the causes of wasteful industrial production in the expansionist dynamics of capitalism; it does not ignore class structure. Yet ecological Marxism recognizes the genesis of new crisis-dynamics triggered by what we term below the "dialectic of shattered expectations"—a process of sudden consumer disenchantment with capitalist production and consumption and the possible restructuring of our expectations about the meaning of happiness.

Ecological Marxists recognize that capitalism is predicated on the ceaseless expansion of commodity production as a source of profit, as Marx understood. However Marx and most recent Marxists have ignored, or simply not comprehended, the effect on our planetary ecosystem of this type of wasteful overproduction. Furthermore, the overproduction of commodities also involves a powerful dynamic of social control, located in the pacifying effects of endless consumption.

Below, in our final reading on crisis-theory, we will develop an analysis of what we term "alienated consumption," the logical counterpart of alienated labor, yet, we contend, a topic ignored by most Marxists. Ecological Marxism involves two analytical perspectives: (a) on the one hand, it assesses the environmental consequences of continued resource-depletion and atmospheric pollution generated by the expansionist dynamics of capitalist commodity production; (b) on the other hand, it attempts to assess modern forms of domination located in the way in which human beings become emotionally dependent on the alienated consumption of commodities, attempting to escape the authoritarian coordination and boredom of alienated labor. (The notion of alienated consumption is defined below, in our final reading.)

The aim of ecological Marxism is also twofold. It wants to plot a socialist future that breaks the hold of overproduction and overconsumption. Overproduction will be overcome by decentralizing and scaling down industrial production; overconsumption will be surpassed by providing human beings with meaningful, non-alienated work (in small-scale, democratically controlled associations of producers). Thus the argument is as follows: Ecological crisis will impel capitalists to scale down commodity production, and will urge human beings, through the dialectic of shattered expectations, as we have termed it, to restructure their needs and values and offer them the prospect of creative work and as a result liberation from unneeded (and ecologically harmful) consumption.

Ecological crisis-theory and the crisis-theories generated by examination of the role of the capitalist state are complementary. The theory of the state deals with capitalist power relationships while the theory of a small-scale non-authoritarian socialism, offered by ecological Marxism, provides state-analysts with a utopian dimension, allowing them to see beyond capitalism towards new social and economic structures. In this sense ecological crisis-theory works on a more utopian, future-oriented level than state-theory, which deals primarily with the description of class- and power-systems in monopoly capitalism.

The fundamental theme of state-theory is the contradiction, increasingly manifested in monopoly capitalist societies, between state intervention in the economy and the ideological crisis generated by that intervention. O'Connor has termed this the tension between the state's legitimizing and accumulation functions. In short, the capitalist state must appear to be nonpartisan while carrying out the mission of protecting corporate capital from underconsumption, underinvestment, and general stagnation. It cannot brook deep-seated public cynicism about its legitimacy, for it cannot risk sparking radical revolt that would challenge its very reason for being. Yet it *also* cannot stop protecting corporate capital lest it invite depressions and the threat of workers' insurrection.

Ecological Marxism understands contradiction on a different, deeper level of advanced capitalism. It locates contradiction on the level of the basic tension between capitalist production and the ecosystem as a whole, arguing that the expansionist dynamics of capitalist production must be eventually stopped owing to inevitable, intractable environmental limits to growth.

These two levels of contradiction, and the crisis-theories they support, are not mutually exclusive. As we remarked above, capitalism is *both* the same and different as when Marx first analyzed it as a system of inexorable internal contradictions. The development of monopoly capitalism has created two levels of crisis, one involving the tension between the state's legitimizing and accumulation functions and the other involving the tension between capitalist production and consumption and a threatened ecosystem. While Marx did not explicitly foresee either of these modes of crisis, it is clear, at least to most Marxists, that both kinds of crisis stem from the central contradiction, as Marx saw it, between socialized production and private appropriation.

What do these complementary crisis-theories say about the future? Where do they lead us in the way of intelligent and reasonable speculation about the future of socialism? On the one hand, the state-theories stress the need for new types of planning with which to overcome the anarchy of the market and with which to conquer state power in periods of crisis. On the other hand, ecological crisis-theory implicitly urges the decentralization, deconcentration, and direct workers' control of the production process both in order to avoid ecological disaster via irrational overproduction and to put workers in touch with their essential competence to self-manage their own work- and leisure-lives. Thus the image of future socialism that results from working out both levels of crisis-theory is one of workers' self-managed, non-authoritarian, decentralized, debureaucratized socialism that scales down commodity production and dealienates labor and leisure.

This introduces the issues raised by Harry Braverman in one of the excerpts. Braverman is not a crisis-theorist, although his work meshes with both state-theory and ecological Marxism. Braverman, in his influential *Labor and Monopoly Capital,* argues that the most debilitating aspect of the capitalist wage-labor system is the way in which the very labor process itself is highly fragmented and controlled from above. Braverman argues convincingly that alienation is still with us in spite of what many western sociologists tell us about the imminent dawning of a post-industrial age. Braverman says that the working class now includes many white-collar workers such as stenographers, waitresses, and keypunch operators, all of whom are as dominated as workers a century ago.

The thrust of Braverman's argument is to show that alienation resides in the very division of labor in the modern office and factory, which has been developed along lines of Taylorist "scientific management." Braverman opposes hierarchy in the organization of labor and fragmentation in the working process itself. Implicitly he argues that capitalist alienation can only be blunted by allowing workers to organize their labor in such a way as to abolish both hierarchy and fragmentation in the workplace.

The impact of Braverman's critique is to show us how the working process must be reconstructed in a post-capitalist society. Capitalist crisis is to be resolved in the direction of returning control of the working process to workers, allowing them to plan their production rationally and allowing them to realize their desires and fulfill their needs in non-alienated work.

Braverman's perspective is vital for neo-Marxists because he shows that socialism must be non-authoritarian in its very organization and coordination of labor. It is not enough (nor was it enough for Marx) for workers to own the means of production; they must also *control* the production process, breaking down the debilitating effects of a rigid, narrow division of labor within the office or factory and effectively challenging the hierarchical organization of work. Marx's theory of alienation developed in the 1844 manuscripts emphasized this requirement of direct workers' control from which Braverman implicitly draws.

This perspective is important because it assists us in speculating intelligently about the future of socialism; it is imperative that socialism should not develop new relations of domination. Braverman argues convincingly that workers must not only own the means of production but that they must also control the democratic, non-authoritarian organization of their labor.

The writers excerpted below attack the problem of modern domination from different, but not mutually exclusive, perspectives. Miliband and Habermas develop a theory of the state that provides insights into the self-contradictory and crisis-bound interventionist role of the state in monopoly capitalism; Braverman provides a critique of the fragmentation and hierarchical coordination of labor in advanced capitalism, urging an end, under socialism, to the rigid division of labor; Leiss probes the problem of ecological crisis from a Marxist perspective, developing crisis-theory on a different level from that of the state-theorists. There is no compelling reason to see any one of these works as more important or more pressing than any other. Marxists in the 1970s are potentially joined together in a theoretical-ideological "united front" by a shared Marxist critique of class society, for, as we noted above, the contradictions in the system remain. They are divided (but not isolated) by the particular levels upon which they analyze crisis.

Ecological crisis-theory requires state-theory and class-theory of the kind that Habermas and Braverman provide, respectively, because the "dialectic of shattered expectations" (developed in the final reading, below) would otherwise remain an ideological mystification. Ecological crisis can only be turned towards socialist change by (a) directing state power towards the reconstruction of the capitalist relations of production and (b) by reconstructing the labor process itself to make it less alienating and more responsive to human needs. The shattered expectations of western consumers can only be guided in a socialist direction by mounting a full-blown critique of capitalism (which causes overconsumption as an "escape" from alienated labor). This requires a new ideology of radical social change that can harness popular frustration with centralist bigness and with bureaucracy to a socialist critique of the capitalist power- and class-systems.

The crisis-theoretic investigations reported below, in the selections from various authors, ultimately provide the resources for a new *model* of socialist change. Marx's dialectical method comprised a theory and critique of alienation and internal contradictions as well as a vision of a new order, to be built upon the ashes of the old. Neo-Marxist crisis-theories are important because they augur a possible socialist future people can begin to work towards in the context of their own lives.

When we talk about a new ideology of socialist change, we implicitly broaden Marx's notion of ideology as false consciousness. Ideology, in the non-Marxian sense, is any belief-system capable of guiding and organizing social action. Marxism is itself an ideological system (in the non-Marxian sense) for it "knows" the world in order to show men how to change it (cf., the eleventh thesis on Feuerbach). The critique of the state and ecological Marxism both serve as aspects of this new ideology that can energize future radical action.

A neo-Marxian ideology builds upon the frustration of workers with their dominated, coordinated lives. It explains their domination in terms of historical and structural forces, and it shows workers the possibility of radical change. Because Marxism in its very methodology is non-deterministic, requiring a reciprocity of theory and action, it is possible to relate a neo-Marxian ideology to the research findings of Marxian analysts. This relationship between ideology and research inspires people to act on their own experienced domination and to organize their social order in new ways. In this sense, ideology need not be seen, strictly speaking, as false consciousness but potentially as a belief-system that instills in individuals a sense of vision and of collective possibility allowing them to transcend their present alienation.

This ideology can conceivably grow on North American soil, joining traditional American populism with European Marxist themes. By itself, Marxism is foreign to American political culture, as is the state-theory developed by Habermas and others. Yet combined with the traditional populist underpinning of American life, which favors grass-roots democracy and political decentralization, Marxism can take on new life as an ideology that constructively confronts social and ecological crises with renewed vigor.

The blending of state-theory, class-theory, and ecological radicalism is especially appropriate to the American circumstance for it can build upon the deep-seated mistrust of centralist bigness that characterizes American populism. It can *bend* populism in a Marxist direction by showing consumers that limits-to-growth need not be seen as a heavy social cost but can rather be viewed as a fortuitous opportunity to transform society in radical ways. In isolation from the Marxist tradition, shattered consumer expectations, occasioned by the inevitable cooling down of industrial production, will generate no radical innovations. However when populist frustration with the overcentralization of modern life and with overproduction is joined to a critique that *explains* overproduction and environmental degradation as a function of the expansionist dynamics of capitalism then a new ideological synthesis begs to be born—one especially suited to the North American cultural and political soil.

Traditional Marxism remains distant from most Americans because they see it as intrinsically authoritarian. The prospect of a populist-inspired non-authoritarian socialism, of a kind desired by Marxian humanists and Frankfurt-oriented critical theorists, is heightened by joining different levels of crisis-theory, generating a theoretical eclecticism and a mixed strategy of class-radicalism. Domination can be challenged both on the level of power- and class-stratification systems, on the level of ecologically wasteful overproduction and overconsumption, and on the level of the alienating, hierarchically coordinated working process itself. An ideological synthesis of American populism and Marxism allows us to generate themes of everyday alienation not usually articulated by traditional Marxian theory. A North American Marxism can build upon the deep-seated cultural formation of populism in such a way as to create a non-authoritarian, decentralized, debureaucratized socialism—which blends (American) democracy and (European) socialism.

This ideological synthesis will show North Americans that socialism can be legitimately decentralized, energy-conserving, non-bureaucratic, and respectful of civil liberties. At the same time, it can nudge Americans frustrated by overcentralization and overcoordination of work and leisure towards a socialist perspective, without which American populism would lack a vital Marxist dimension. Populism, by itself, lacks a sufficient critique of the class- and power-systems of North American society; it resents the powers-that-be (bureaucrats, politicians, professionals) but it does not explain how they can be effectively challenged or, indeed, abolished.

Future neo-Marxian research will further develop different levels of crisis-theory, as surveyed below in the readings. An adequate understanding of crisis-tendencies in North American monopoly capitalism may give rise to a new ideological synthesis that can enable North American workers to reinterpret the frustrations of their work and leisure lives as a function of capitalist class society, its rigid division of labor, and its tendencies to overproduce commodities. The contemporary preoccupation with energy "crises" and with ecology generally can be the foundation stone of an American Marxism that "captures" these issues and bends them in a Marxist direction—without estranging those to whom Marxism has traditionally meant Soviet state-socialism. The future of American socialism depends in large measure on how traditional American themes are reinterpreted in Marxist fashion without at the same time ignoring the American cultural and ideological grounding in small-scale democracy and populist majoritarianism.

A living Marxism may indeed find its most propitious proving ground not in Europe, the birthplace of socialism and Marxism, but in the new world, traditionally seen by Marxists as the least likely site of class confrontation. But orthodox Marxists disregard the possibility that class confrontation may take new forms as the nature of capitalist crisis is itself altered by the further (unplanned, irrational) development of monopoly capitalism. An ecological Marxism, informed by the theory of the state and its legitimation and fiscal crises, might Americanize Marxism in such a way that class struggle can be redefined so as to make good sense to North American workers.

In summarizing the sources of the appeal of North American Marxism, we would list the following:

1. A critique of the legitimation and accumulation problems of the American state, built upon a populist-inspired critique of big government and big business (Habermas, Miliband, O'Connor)
2. A critique of the ecologically harmful effects of industrial overproduction and overconsumption (Leiss, Agger)
3. A critique of the rigid division of labor in the factory and office, based upon the populist-inspired critique of bureaucratic centralization (Braverman)

The readings that follow develop the analytical perspectives of each of these levels. It will be reiterated that these perspectives can be seen as mutually complementary and not as mutually exclusive, each adding to a more comprehensive crisis-theory and radical ideology that can both make sense to North Americans and generate political strategies that are not authoritarian or dogmatic. It remains for the ideological synthesis of American populism and Marxism to be sufficiently developed in a way that can utilize each of these perspectives on crisis in a directly practical fashion, suggesting to workers what they might actually do to create the infrastructure of future North American socialism.

Finally, our return to crisis-theories in the late 1970s should definitely be seen as a sign that many neo-Marxists are dissatisfied with traditional Marxist disputation, revolving around the question of what Marxism "really" means. The perspectives on crisis presented below, and our outline of a nondogmatic North American Marxism that combines the analysis of different levels of crisis in a systematic macro-theory, all stem from frustration with traditional Marxist argumentation. American populism and pragmatism stress the praxis-oriented dimensions of theory. Similarly, an American Marxism must dissociate itself from the scholastic style of much European Marxism where the meaning of books becomes more important than the application of theoretical knowledge in the realm of praxis.

The perspectives developed below all represent dissatisfaction with Marxist disputation of the usual sort and especially with the esoteric nuances of Hegelian Marxism and critical theory. While Habermas and Leiss both studied with original members of the Frankfurt School, they have self-consciously jettisoned many of the philosophical and textual preoccupations of the Frankfurt thinkers in attempting to reengage the empirical world. Crisis-theory talks about the world and not about books or ideas although it does not abandon model-building and systemizing in favor of atheoretical empirical research (of the kind reported in most mainstream, non-Marxist social science journals in North America).

Our call to reengage the empirical dimensions of capitalist functioning and crisis *assumes* that the Marxist theoretical perspective is basically sound. The style of empirical research advocated here is oriented not to the dispassionate accumulation of data (according to Weber's model of value-free social science) but to changing the capitalist world. However this research goes beyond theoretical and textual disputation in quest of practical, feasible strategies of socialist change rarely provided by purely theoretical perspectives.

The empirical research into capitalist crisis-tendencies, and on this basis construction of a North American Marxist-populist ideology, opposes two streams in western Marxism, surveyed in preceding chapters:

1. It opposes the disengaged philosophy of the original Frankfurt School and especially Adorno's critique of domination and his notion of declining subjectivity.
2. It opposes deterministic Marxism that sees the world narrowly in terms of a clash between "capital" and "labor," with the eventual outcome being predetermined by the very self-contradictory structure of capitalism.

The first outlook precludes meaningful analysis of possible crisis-tendencies and the development of political strategy; the second outlook precludes the development of a differentiated theory of class struggle, adopting a fatalistic outlook on socialist change.

In earlier chapters we developed a model for assessing the historical relationship between Marxian theory and practice, noting that periods of intense, crisis-triggered class struggle produce empirically oriented Marxian theory and research, while periods of capitalist "class compromise" generate abstract philosophical versions of theory. The pendulum in the late 1970s is swinging back towards crisis-triggered class struggle as the vaunted class compromise begins to erode and as monopoly capitalism triggers unforeseen deep crises in state functioning and in the ecosystem. A renewed Marxian empiricism is reemerging as an articulation of these newfound tendencies; not an empiricism devoid of theoretical and ideological commitment but an empiricism that builds a theory and ideology of change on the foundation of a non-doctrinaire analysis of social structural developments.

This renewal of empiricism fits well with the heritage of American pragmatism. It adds further weight to the ideological synthesis of populism and Marxism, continuously translating Marxian theoretical assumptions into analytical and strategic terms. Deepening crises in monopoly capitalism, both domestically and internationally, move us away from theory and towards an empiricism that utilizes research into crisis-tendencies to build a more global model of socialist change. The renewal of Marxian empiricism does not require that we shut out the long and varied history of Marxian theory but rather than we attempt wherever possible to relate theoretical concepts to their political referents.

The renewal of empiricism is reminiscent of the scientific Marxism of the Second International, yet it overcomes the political passivity of theorists like Kautsky. Scientific Marxism in the 1970s researches problems of crisis in order to generate political strategies; this is rooted not in fatalism about the inevitability of capitalism's breakdown but in the dialectical method. Scientific Marxism is a misnomer; the type of theory-research-action linkage we are describing would better be termed dialectical Marxism for it is founded on the reciprocity of theory and practice.

Once the question of Marxist methodology is settled, and the configuration of alienation-contradiction-crisis fully understood, research into action-strategies may begin. This book has explored the vicissitudes of Marxist methodology since the time of Marx. We have argued *both* that Marxism is alive and that parts of Marxism are dead. This is not a paradox but merely the recognition that contradictions remain (because capitalism remains) and that crisis-forms and appropriate types of radical practice must change. If Marxism is still alive, it is not because Marxists repeat tired slogans about the spectre of communism or the inevitability of socialism but because theorists are willing to reapply Marxian categories in new and creative ways. Where there is alienation, so, we hope, there will be Marxist possibility captured by new analytical and ideological vision.

MILIBAND: STATE INTERVENTION

One of the crucial problem areas for contemporary Marxists is the political and economic function of the capitalist state. While Marx postulated a role for the bourgeois state, characterizing the state as the "executive committee of the bourgeoisie," he did not fully develop an analysis of state functions in a capitalist economy. Furthermore, Marx could not have foreseen the extent to which the modern capitalist state would play a critical role in stimulating the economy, regulating wages and prices, and mediating between large corporations and unions.

As we noted in our general introduction to this chapter, Marxism today takes two primary forms: The first strain deals primarily with the development of empirical theory about the functions of the capitalist state, while the second strain builds what we have termed "ecological Marxism," investigating decentralized forms of technology and worker's organizations appropriate to a non-authoritarian socialist steady-state economy.

It is our contention in this concluding chapter that the structuralist theory of the capitalist state and the ecological crisis-theory sketched by Leiss and ourself, below, need not be seen as mutually exclusive. Indeed it is possible and necessary to allow them to complement each other, working on different levels of crisis-theory and together forming a more comprehensive analysis and critique of advanced capitalism. Miliband, Habermas, Braverman, Leiss, and we take different points of departure and converge on the same end-point—a critique of capitalism, a theory of its predominant crisis-forms and finally a model of how to move strategically towards future socialism. All of these authors have in common the desire to create a non-authoritarian socialism premised on optimally democratic foundations. It is the underlying premise of this final chapter that Marxism in the 1980s and beyond will be eclectic and multidimensional, working on a host of complementary levels of analysis and critique.

The first strain, as we indicated in our general introduction, retains a structuralist orientation to social change, deemphasizing the personal dimensions of liberation and emphasizing the large-scale economic forces at work in society, such as the role of an interventionist political state. It is argued that Marx's theory of capitalism was fundamentally correct in that Marx predicted falling rates of profit, the progressive immiserization of the proletariat, and rising unemployment. Indeed it is now apparent to most economists, Marxist and non-Marxist, that Keynesian economics has not been the salvation that it appeared to be during the expansionist periods of the late 1940s and early 1960s. High inflation and high unemployment now exist side by side in most capitalist democracies, contradicting the economic conventional wisdom of most Keynesians. Capitalist economies seem to have entered a period of acute and frequent crises, resulting from the "maturation" of the structural tendencies towards breakdown that Marx prophesied years ago.

The major revision of Marxian economics before the Second World War occurred during the period of the Bolshevik revolution, when Lenin developed his theories of imperialism. He suggested that capitalism would relentlessly expand to cover the globe in seeking out sources of cheap labor, cheap raw materials, and markets for manufactured goods in the underdeveloped nations of the world. Imperialism helped to forestall the breakdown Marx felt was due to occur in western and central Europe before the turn of this century. Instead of suffering a falling rate of profit occasioned by increasing concentration of capital in the hands of a few monopolistic capitalists, capitalism could expand into foreign markets and thus increase the rate of profit at the expense of underdeveloped countries.

The modern theory of the state builds upon Lenin's theory of imperialism. The nation-state plays a crucial role both as an economic agent—a giant capitalist, as it is said by some—and as a military agent that protects the interests of domestic capital. It should be noted that state-socialist political regimes play virtually identical roles with respect to their foreign interests.

The theory of the state builds upon Marx's original crisis-theory in attempting to chart new forms of probable crisis. Marx argued that the breakdown of capitalism would occur as a result of the internal pressures built up in a capitalist system suffering from falling profit and the immiserization of the working class. Violent insurrection would take place when workers could no longer tolerate their meager existences and either took to the barricades or else engaged in plundering and looting in order to survive, setting off a chain-reaction of police and military repression followed in turn by further insurrection and, ultimately, revolution.

Marxists who concentrate on the state suggest that economic crisis has only been temporarily and imperfectly delayed first by imperialism and then by the rise of the state acting as a giant capitalist. The recent recessions in the United States bode well for revolutionary expectations, as do the crises generated in the early 1970s by the Arab boycott of American oil markets.

Ralph Miliband in his influential *The State in Capitalist Society*, first published in 1969, attempts to unmask the modern functioning of the liberal-capitalist state. Miliband argues that no single interest group is capable of monopolizing power in advanced industrial democracies, being forced to compete with other, countervailing interest groups. Miliband argues persuasively that the state is basically a protector of capitalist interests. His most significant point reiterates the essence of Marxian political economy: "Economic life cannot be separated from political life." At the same time, Miliband realistically acknowledges the importance of democratic civil liberties that exist in most western capitalist states. "It is a dangerous confusion to believe and claim that, because 'bourgeois freedoms' are inadequate and constantly threatened by erosion, they are therefore of no consequence."

Miliband makes a crucial and telling point when he argues that there is presently a delicate balance between liberal-democratic institutions and the basically exploitative structure of capitalism. Miliband questions the assumptions of Daniel Bell and others who argue that the age of ideology has passed owing to the fundamentally harmonious character of pluralist, capitalist democracies. Miliband sees instead a growing despair about the evident discrepancy between "promise and performance" in advanced capitalist nations. ". . . A deep malaise, a pervasive sense of unfulfilled individual and collective possibilities penetrates and corrodes the climate of every advanced capitalist society." It is not inevitable that democracy and capitalism coexist permanently. Fundamental

disruptions have already been caused by runaway inflation and high unemployment. A new authoritarianism may yet emerge in capitalist societies, produced
by the irresolvable tensions created by the (a) disparity between rich and poor,
still existing, (b) by the increasing need for state intervention in the economy and
the problems that this causes for the maintenance of a laissez faire political
ideology (which countenances little state intervention in the alleged "free market"), and (c) by the likelihood of a "steady-state" economy in which the Gross
National Product is stabilized or even falls, causing severe dislocations for those
who are less-than-affluent and who recognize the fundamental inequity of
capitalism.

     This last point may be the most important of all. Below, we will examine in
greater detail the impact of slowing industrial growth on capitalist societies. At
first glance, it appears that the poor are kept in political check today by the
system's implicit promise of future wealth. What will happen when this promise
is withdrawn, as industrial progress slows? Will the economic elites and upper
middle classes be *willing* to divide their wealth in the interest of preserving
domestic peace? Might a new authoritarianism arise on this foundation, designed to keep an increasingly rebellious proletariat at bay? These are questions
for Marxists in the 1980s and beyond, according to Miliband.

The most important political fact about advanced capitalist societies, it has been
argued in this book, is the continued existence in them of private and ever more
concentrated economic power. As a result of that power, the men—owners and
controllers—in whose hands it lies enjoy a massive preponderance in society, in
the political system, and in the determination of the state's policies and actions.

     Given this permanent preponderance, the familiar claim, indeed the famil-
iar assumption, that these are countries which have long achieved political
equality, whatever may be the case in regard to economic and social equality,
constitutes one of the great myths of the epoch. Political equality, save in formal
terms, is impossible in the conditions of advanced capitalism. Economic life
cannot be separated from political life. Unequal economic power, on the scale
and of the kind encountered in advanced capitalist societies, inherently *produces*
political inequality, on a more or less commensurate scale, whatever the constitution may say.

     Similarly, it is the capitalist context of generalised inequality in which the
state operates which basically determines its policies and actions. The prevalent
view is that the state, in these societies, can be and indeed mostly is the agent of a
"democratic" social order, with no inherent bias towards any class or group;
and that its occasional lapse from "impartiality" must be ascribed to some
accidental factor external to its "real" nature. But this too is a fundamental
misconception: The state in these class societies is primarily and inevitably the
guardian and protector of the economic interests which are dominant in them.
Its "real" purpose and mission is to ensure their continued predominance, not
to prevent it.

     However, the manner in which the state fulfils that role and the degree to
which it manifests its bias differs greatly according to place and circumstance.
The maintenance of a social order characterised by class domination may
require the dictatorship of the state, the suppression of all opposition, the
abrogation of all constitutional guarantees and political freedoms. But in the
countries of advanced capitalism, it generally has not. With occasional and

notable exceptions, class rule in these societies has remained compatible with a wide range of civil and political liberties; and their exercise has undoubtedly helped to mitigate the form and content of class domination in many areas of civil society. The main agent of that mitigation has been the state, which helps to explain why it has been able to present itself, and why it has been widely accepted, as the servant of society. In fact, this mitigating function does not abolish class rule and even serves, at a price, to guarantee it. But this does not detract from its importance to the subordinate classes.

It is perfectly true that civil and political liberties in advanced capitalist regimes have been severely circumscribed by the economic, social, and political framework in which they have existed; that they have often been infringed in practice and, particularly in times of crisis, even more drastically narrowed; that constitutional guarantees have not prevented the systematic discrimination and oppression of such minorities as the black people in the United States; that the liberties enjoyed by the citizens of metropolitan capitalist countries were more often than not conspicuous by their absence in the territories which succumbed to imperialist occupation; and that, for all their democratic and liberal rhetoric, these regimes have shown themselves capable of massive crimes in the protection of sordid interests.

Yet, when all this and more has been said about the limits and contingent character of civic and political liberties under "bourgeois democracy," and when the fact has been duly noted that some of these liberties are a mere cloak for class domination, it remains the case that many others have constituted an important and valuable element of life in advanced capitalist societies; and that they have materially affected the encounter between the state and the citizen, and between the dominant classes and the subordinate ones. It is a dangerous confusion to believe and claim that, because "bourgeois freedoms" are inadequate and constantly threatened by erosion, they are therefore of no consequence. For all its immense limitations and hypocrisies, there is a wide gulf between "bourgeois democracy" and the various forms of conservative authoritarianism, most notably Fascism, which have provided the alternative type of political regime for advanced capitalism. The point of the socialist critique of "bourgeois freedoms" is not (or should not be) that they are of no consequence, but that they are profoundly inadequate, and need to be extended by the radical transformation of the context, economic, social, and political, which condemns them to inadequacy and erosion.

Indeed the largest of all questions about Western-type regimes is how long their "bourgeois-democratic" framework is likely to remain compatible with the needs and purposes of advanced capitalism; whether its economic, social, and political contradictions are of such a kind as to render unworkable the political order with which it has, in general, hitherto been able to accommodate itself.

This was the question which was asked, with anxious insistence, about capitalist regimes in the late twenties and thirties, when Fascism and Nazism appeared to many people on the Left, and not only on the Left, to foreshadow the direction in which "liberal capitalism" in many countries other than Italy and Germany was likely to travel. That question was, in subsequent decades, buried deep beneath the celebration of Western democracy, the free world, the welfare state, the affluent society, the end of ideology, and pluralistic equilibrium. To have posed it again even a few years ago would have appeared ludicrous or perverse but at any rate distinctly obsolete. Whatever might be said about the economic, social, and political deficiencies of Western capitalism (and the tendency was in any case to sing its praises, or rather the praises of "post-capitalist" society), at least its "democratic" and "liberal" foundations were held to be secure and beyond challenge, save of course for the threat posed to them from the Left.

In the recent past, however, that old question has again come to the surface, and been posed with growing frequency, again by no means exclusively on the Left. Nor is this surprising, given the tendencies which advanced capitalism and the political system associated with it have increasingly exhibited. The point is not that "bourgeois democracy" is imminently likely to move towards old-style Fascism. It is rather that advanced capitalist societies are subject to strains more acute than for a long time past, and that their inability to resolve these strains makes their evolution towards more or less pronounced forms of conservative authoritarianism more rather than less likely.

There are many reasons for taking this view of the political prospects of these societies. But the most fundamental of them all lies, by a fatal paradox, in their productive success. For as the material capacity of the economic system unfolds at an ever-increasing pace its immense promise of human liberation, so does its inability to match performance with promise become more blatant and obvious. The contradiction is not new; but it reveals itself more plainly with every productive and technological advance.

In order to fulfil their human potentialities, advanced industrial societies require a high degree of planning, economic coordination, the premeditated and rational use of material resources, not only on a national but on an international scale. But advanced capitalist societies cannot achieve this within the confines of an economic system which remains primarily geared to the private purposes of those who own and control its material resources.

Similarly, and relatedly, these societies require a spirit of sociality and cooperation from their members, a sense of genuine involvement and participation, which are equally unattainable in a system whose dominant impulse is private appropriation. It is forever said that industry is a partnership, a cooperative enterprise, a social venture, and so forth. This is certainly what it needs to be, yet which the very nature of the capitalist system renders impossible. The "two sides of industry" remain two conflicting sides, in permanent and inevitable opposition. Indeed, the whole of society, steeped as it is in a miasma of competition and commercialism, is a battlefield, now more active, now less, but with no prospect of genuine peace.

No doubt, the transcendence of capitalism—in other words, the appropriation into the public domain of the largest part of society's resources—cannot by itself resolve all the problems associated with industrial society. What it can do, however, is to remove the greatest of all barriers to their solution, and at least create the *basis* for the creation of a rational and humane social order.

It is the need for this transcendence of capitalism which all the agencies of legitimation seek to obscure. Yet they cannot obscure the discrepancy between promise and performance. They cannot obscure the fact that, though these are rich societies, vast areas of bitter poverty endure in them; that the collective provisions they make for health, welfare, education, housing, the social environment, do not begin to match need; that the egalitarian ethos they are driven to proclaim is belied by the privileges and inequalities they enshrine; that the structure of their "industrial relations" remains one of domination and subjection; and that the political system of which they boast is a corrupt and crippled version of a truly democratic order.

The consciousness of these discrepancies does not by any means automatically lead to a rejection of the social system which produces them; and even where it does lead to it, the rejection may often be in favour of pseudo-alternatives which are perfectly "functional" and therefore self-defeating. In fact, experience has sufficiently shown that the translation of a consciousness of deep ills into a will for *socialist* change is a painful, complex, contradictory, "molecular" process, which can be greatly retarded, deflected, and distorted by an endless variety of factors of the kind which were discussed in earlier chapters.

Yet, a deep malaise, a pervasive sense of unfulfilled individual and collective possibilities penetrates and corrodes the climate of every advanced capitalist society. Notwithstanding all the talk of integration, *embourgeoisement,* and the like, never has that sense been greater than it is now; and never in the history of advanced capitalism has there been a time when more people have been more aware of the need for change and reform. Nor has there ever been a time when more men and women, though by no means moved by revolutionary intentions, have been more determined to act in the defence and the enhancement of their interests and expectations. The immediate target of their demands may be employers, or university authorities, or political parties. But as was noted at the very beginning of this study, it is the state which men constantly encounter in their relations with other men; it is towards the state that they are increasingly driven to direct their pressure; and it is from the state that they expect the fulfilment of their expectations.*

HABERMAS: LEGITIMATION PROBLEMS IN LATE CAPITALISM

Jürgen Habermas, a member of the second generation of the Frankfurt School, has, in his 1975 book *Legitimation Crisis,* outlined the salient features of "late capitalism," differentiating it from earlier forms of market capitalism and, most significant for our purposes, assessing possible modes of its transformation.

Late capitalism, or "organized capitalism," as it is also termed, refers to (a) "the process of economic concentration—the rise of national and, subsequently, of multinational corporations—and to the organization of markets for goods, capital, and labor." It also refers to (b) "the fact that the state intervenes in the market as functional gaps develop." Organized capitalism is distinguished from earlier competitive capitalism by "the supplementation and partial replacement of the market mechanism by state intervention" in economic processes.

The emergence of organized capitalism has resulted in the collapse of the earlier liberal-capitalist ideology of just exchange—the exchange of labor-power for a living wage conducted in the open marketplace. The system's public legitimation now is contingent on "civil privatism," abstinence from politics coupled with a preoccupation with career, leisure, and consumption. The citizen believes in formal democracy, and perhaps even votes periodically, but does not see this participation as a source of personal meaning.

This results in a "structurally depoliticized public realm," which must itself be legitimated either through democratic elite theory or technocratic systems

---

*From Ralph Miliband, *The State in Capitalist Society* (London: Quartet Books, 1974), pp. 237-41.

theory. Both species of legitimation stress the need for experts and professionals to make complex decisions; they also stress the fundamental incompetence of the human being in the face of these alleged systemic requirements of a professional hierarchy and what Weber called "rational authority." Habermas argues that class conflict is blunted in organized capitalism and a "class compromise" of sorts arises.

In essence Habermas argues that legitimation has become increasingly difficult for the system to exact. In earlier periods of capitalism the ideology of free enterprise sufficed to keep the less-than-affluent fundamentally committed to the system, in spite of their own miserable working existences. The promise of future fortunes or a better life for their children kept them going. Indeed aspects of this ideology still exist in capitalist societies, especially in North America. Yet during the late 1960s and 1970s this ideology, essentially produced during the earliest periods of market capitalism, has considerably weakened, primarily as a result of (a) increased state intervention in the "free" economy coupled with (b) the twin realities of rising unemployment and inflation. Workers are increasingly unwilling to trust in the beneficent growth of the political state inasmuch as the state fails to compensate them successfully for escalating inflation and high taxes. To this extent, Habermas argues, legitimation crisis, occurring primarily in the political sphere, has replaced economic crisis of the kind prophesied by Marx. In order to *avert* serious economic crisis, such as falling rates of capital investment and retarded job-creation, the democratic capitalist state must *violate* the ideology of free enterprise, mediating precariously between the interests of capital, the interests of labor (which must be placated, lest the "class compromise" crumble) and the interests of consumers in general.

State intervention in economic life, as Miliband noted, is not a recent development. What is unique about late capitalism is the way in which state intervention has failed to resolve the more serious economic crises of capitalism, giving the average worker nightmares about galloping inflation and producing skepticism about the legitimacy of the capitalist state.

This has emerged in unprecedented public cynicism about the capitalist political and economic system as a whole. Although vestiges of belief in private enterprise obviously still exist (in North American Chambers of Commerce, presumably!) the average worker has become extremely skeptical about all political parties, whether they be left or right of center. This is an extremely dangerous development, as Miliband and Habermas both acknowledge, for while the return to a grass-roots individualism could conceivably follow from this cynicism about political structures and leadership, it may also spawn a more authoritarian reaction on the part of those threatened by the potentially insurgent underclasses.

In a world of dwindling resources and shrinking GNPs, political legitimation may become increasingly difficult to obtain. The poor and dispossessed will become more mistrustful of democratic regimes—recognizing that the American state, for example, merely exists to protect American capital—while the wealthier classes will argue for *stronger* government to control these increasingly radicalized lower classes. The outcome might be a renewed class polarization. At the same time, this class polarization would not be a stand-off between two equal forces, for in today's industrial civilization the wealthy and powerful control much of the military technology and weaponry necessary to put down incipient rebellion.

The growing tenacity of racism and ethnic mistrust, and the increasingly harsh reaction in North America against what is euphemistically called "bleeding heart liberalism," is evidence of a new type of authoritarianism. Both poor and wealthy alike are seeking scapegoats for their economic misery and uncertainty. A new McCarthyism may be on the rise in North America, with resentment building against professors, students, and the liberal left generally. This is the seamy side of legitimation crisis.

There also exists, as we mentioned earlier, the potential to turn legitimation crisis into a healthy stock-taking and reassessment of liberal capitalist society. Marxism might return to the fore as a renewed critique of bureaucratic society and technocratic elitism. An alternative social order might appear to be a realistic and desirable alternative to the present corporate structures. *A grass-roots movement might take form around the issues of political and economic decentralization, local democracy, and workers' control.* The return to community, so often invoked during the late 1960s, might be resurrected as a response to legitimation crisis. We will develop this idea below, in our discussion of the ecological Marxism of William Leiss.

A DESCRIPTIVE MODEL OF ADVANCED CAPITALISM

The expression "organized or state-regulated capitalism" refers to two classes of phenomena, both of which can be attributed to the advanced stage of the accumulation process. It refers, on the one hand, to the process of economic concentration—the rise of national and, subsequently, of multinational corporations—and to the organization of markets for goods, capital, and labor. On the other hand, it refers to the fact that the state intervenes in the market as functional gaps develop. The spread of oligopolistic market structures certainly means the end of *competitive capitalism.* But however much companies broaden their temporal perspectives and expand control over their environments, the steering mechanism of the market remains in force as long as investment decisions are made according to criteria of company profits. Similarly, the supplementation and partial replacement of the market mechanism by state intervention marks the end of *liberal capitalism.* Nonetheless, no matter how much the scope of the private autonomous commerce of commodity owners is administratively restricted, political planning of the allocation of scarce resources does not occur as long as the priorities of the society as a whole develop in an unplanned, nature-like manner—that is, as secondary effects of the strategies of private enterprise. In advanced-capitalist societies the economic, the administrative, and the legitimation systems can be characterized, approximately and at a very general level, as follows.

The Economic System.
During the sixties, various authors, using the United States as an example, developed a three-sector model based on the distinction between the private and the public sectors. According to the model, private production is market-oriented, one sub-sector still being regulated by competition while the other is determined by the market strategies of oligopolies that tolerate a "competitive fringe." By contrast, in the public sector, especially in the armaments and space-travel industries, huge concerns have arisen whose investment decisions can be made almost without regard for the market. These concerns are either

enterprises directly controlled by the state or private firms living on government contracts. In the monopolistic and public sectors, capital-intensive industries predominate; in the competitive sector, labor-intensive industries predominate. In the monopolistic and public sectors, companies are faced with strong unions. In the competitive sector workers are less well organized, and wage levels are correspondingly different. In the monopolistic sector, we can observe relatively rapid advances in production. In the public sector, companies do not need to be rationalized to the same extent. In the competitive sector, they cannot be.

The Administrative System.

The state apparatus carries out numerous imperatives of the economic system. These can be ordered from two perspectives: By means of global planning, it regulates the economic cycle as a whole; and it creates and improves conditions for utilizing excess accumulated capital. Global planning is limited by the private autonomous disposition of the means of production (for the investment freedom of private enterprises cannot be restricted) and positively by the avoidance of instabilities. To this extent, the fiscal and financial regulation of the business cycle, as well as individual measures intended to regulate investment and overall demand—credits, price guarantees, subsidies, loans, secondary redistribution of income, government contracts guided by business-cycle policy, indirect labor-market policy, etc.—have the reactive character of avoidance strategies within the framework of a system of goals. This system is determined by a formulistically [*leerformelhaft*] demanded growth, stability of the currency, full employment, and balance of foreign trade.

While global planning manipulates the boundary conditions of decisions made by private enterprise in order to correct the market mechanism with respect to dysfunctional secondary effects the state actually *replaces* the market mechanism whenever it creates and improves conditions for the realization of capital:

—through "strengthening the competitive capability of the nation" by organizing supranational economic blocks, securing international stratification by imperialist means, etc.;

—through unproductive government consumption (for example, armaments and space exploration);

—through guiding, in accord with structural policy, the flow of capital into sectors neglected by an autonomous market;

—through improvements of the material infrastructure (transportation, education, health, recreation, urban and regional planning, housing construction, etc.);

—through improvement of the immaterial infrastructure (general promotion of science, investments in research and development, provision of patents, etc.);

—through heightening the productivity of human labor (general system of education, vocational schools, programs for training and re-education, etc.);

—through relieving the social and material costs resulting from private production (unemployment compensation, welfare, repair of ecological damage).

Improving the nation's position in the international market, government demand for unproductive commodities, and measures for guiding the flow of capital, open up or improve chances for capital investment. With all but the last of the remaining measures this is indeed a concomitant phenomenon; but the goal is to increase the productivity of labor and thereby the "use value" of capital (through provision of collective commodities and through qualification of labor power).

The Legitimation System.

With the appearance of functional weaknesses in the market and dysfunctional side effects of the steering mechanism, the basic bourgeois ideology of fair exchange collapses. Re-coupling the economic system to the political—which in a way repoliticizes the relations of production—creates an increased need for legitimation. The state apparatus no longer, as in liberal capitalism, merely secures the general conditions of production (in the sense of the prerequisites for the continued existence of the reproduction process), but is now actively engaged in it. It must, therefore—like the pre-capitalist state—be legitimated, although it can no longer rely on residues of tradition that have been undermined and worn out during the development of capitalism. Moreover, through the universalistic value-systems of bourgeois ideology, civil rights—including the right to participate in political elections—have become established; and legitimation can be dissassociated from the mechanism of elections only temporarily and under extraordinary conditions. This problem is resolved through a system of formal democracy. Genuine participation of citizens in the process of political will-formation [*politischen Willensbildungsprozessen*], that is substantive democracy, would bring to consciousness the contradiction between administratively socialized production and the continued private appropriation and use of surplus value. In order to keep this contradiction from being thematized, then the administrative system must be sufficiently independent of legitimating will-formation.

The arrangement of formal democratic institutions and procedures permits administrative decisions to be made largely independently of specific motives of the citizens. This takes place through a legitimation process that elicits generalized motives—that is, diffuse mass loyalty—but avoids participation. This structural alteration of the bourgeois public realm [*Öffentlichkeit*] provides for application of institutions and procedures that are democratic in form, while the citizenry, in the midst of an objectively [*an sich*] political society, enjoy the status of passive citizens with only the right to withhold acclamation. Private autonomous investment decisions thus have their necessary complement in the civic privatism of the civil public.

In the structurally depoliticized public realm, the need for legitimation is reduced to two residual requirements: The first, civic privatism—that is, political abstinence combined with an orientation to career, leisure, and consumption—promotes the expectation of suitable rewards within the system (money, leisure time, and security). This privatism is taken into account by a welfare-state substitute program, which also incorporates elements of an achievement ideology transferred to the educational system. Secondly, the structural depoliticization itself requires justification, which is supplied either by democratic elite theories (which go back to Schumpeter and Max Weber) or by technocratic systems theories (which go back to the institutionalism of the twenties). In the history of bourgeois social science, these theories today have a function similar to that of the classical doctrine of political economy. In earlier phases of capitalist development, the latter doctrine suggested the "naturalness" of the capitalist economic society.

Class Structure.
While the political form of the relations of production in traditional societies permitted easy identification of ruling groups, in liberal capitalism manifest domination was replaced by the politically anonymous power of civil subjects. (Of course, during economically induced social crises these anonymous powers again assumed the identifiable form of a political adversary, as can be seen in the fronts of the European labor movement.) But, while in organized capitalism the relations of production are indeed repoliticized to a certain extent, the political form of the class relationship is not thereby restored. Instead, the political anonymity of class domination is superseded by social anonymity. That is, the structures of advanced capitalism can be understood as reaction formations to endemic crisis. To ward off system crisis, advanced capitalist societies focus all forces of social integration at the point of the structurally most probable conflict—in order all the more effectively to keep it latent. At the same time, in doing so they satisfy the political demands of reformist labor parties.

In this connection, the quasi-political wage structure, which depends on negotiations between companies and unions, plays a historically epochmaking role. "Price setting" [*Machtpreisbildung*, W. Hofmann], which replaces price competition in the oligopolistic markets, has its counterpart in the labor market. Just as the great concerns quasi-administratively control price movements in their markets, so too, on the other side, they obtain quasi-political compromises with union adversaries on wage movements. In those branches of industry belonging to the monopolistic and the public sectors, which are central to economic development, the commodity called labor power receives a "political price." The "wage-scale partners" [*Tarifpartner*] find a broad zone of compromise, since increased labor costs can be passed on through prices and since there is a convergence of the middle-range demands of both sides on the state—demands that aim at increasing productivity, qualifying labor power, and improving the social situation of the workers. The monopolistic sector can, as it were, externalize class conflict.

The consequences of this immunization of the original conflict zone are: (a) disparate wage developments and/or a sharpening of wage disputes in the public service sector; (b) permanent inflation, with corresponding temporary redistribution of income to the disadvantage of unorganized workers and other marginal groups; (c) permanent crisis in government finances, together with public poverty (that is, impoverishment of public transportation, education, housing, and health care); and (d) an inadequate adjustment of disproportional economic developments, sectoral (agriculture) as well as regional (marginal areas).

In the decades since World War II the most advanced capitalist countries have succeeded (the May 1968 events in Paris notwithstanding) in keeping class

conflict latent in its decisive areas; in extending the business cycle and transforming periodic phases of capital devaluation into a permanent inflationary
crisis with milder business fluctuations; and in broadly filtering the dysfunctional secondary effects of the averted economic crisis and scattering them over
quasi-groups (such as consumers, schoolchildren and their parents, transportation users, the sick, the elderly, etc.) or over natural groups with little organization. In this way the social identity of classes breaks down and class consciousness is fragmented. The class compromise that has become part of the structure
of advanced capitalism makes (almost) everyone at the same time both a
participant and a victim. Of course, with the clearly (and increasingly) unequal
distribution of wealth and power, it is important to distinguish between those
belonging more to one than the other category.*

> Habermas outlines four forms of possible crisis specific to the system
> (excluding, for the moment, international and ecological dimensions of crisis).
> Economic crisis refers to inadequate "output" of consumable values such as
> goods and services. Political crisis results from the failure of the administrative
> system to fulfill imperatives received from the economic system. Rationality
> crisis, the form of political crisis-tendencies, results when there is tension be-
> tween systems of private property and private ownership of capital, on the one
> hand, and, on the other hand, the increasing need in advanced capitalism for
> "administrative planning" and state intervention. Capitalism cannot do away
> with either of these functions. Socio-cultural crisis-tendencies refer to the way in
> which the breakdown of the economic and political systems results in either the
> withdrawal of legitimation or the weakening of the motivation to perform (to
> work, to obey orders, etc.)

Economic Crisis Tendencies.

The economic system requires an input of work and capital. The output
consists in consumable values, which are distributed over time according to
quantity and type among social strata. A crisis that derives from inadequate
input is atypical of the capitalist mode of production. The disturbances of
liberal capitalism were output crises. The crisis cycle again and again placed in
question the distribution of values in conformity with the system. ("In conformity with the system" here means all patterns of distribution of burdens and
rewards permissible within the range of variation of the legitimating value
system.) If economic crisis tendencies persist in advanced capitalism, this indicates that government actions intervening in the realization process obey, no
less than exchange processes, spontaneously working economic laws. Consequently, they are subject to the logic of the economic crisis as expressed in the
law of the tendential fall of the rate of profit. According to this thesis, the state
pursues the continuation of the politics of capital by other means. The altered
forms of appearance (such as crises in government finances, permanent inflation, growing disparities between public poverty and private wealth, etc.) are
explained by the fact that self-regulation of the realization process now also
operates through legitimate power as a medium of control. But since the crisis
tendency is still determined by the law of value—that is, the structurally
necessary asymmetry in the exchange of wage labor for capital—the activity of
the state cannot compensate for the tendency of the falling rate of profit. It can

---

*From Jürgen Habermas, *Legitimation Crisis* (Boston: Beacon Press, 1975), pp. 33-39.

at best mediate it, that is, itself consummate it by political means. Thus, economic crisis tendency will also assert itself as a social crisis and lead to political struggles in which class opposition between owners of capital and masses dependent on wages again becomes manifest. According to another version, the state apparatus does not obey the logic of the law of value in an unplanned, nature-like manner, but consciously looks after the interests of united monopoly capitalists. This agency theory, tailored to advanced capitalism, conceives of the state, not as a blind organ of the realization process, but as a potent collective capitalist [*Gesamtkapitalist*] who makes the accumulation of capital the substance of political planning.

Political Crisis Tendencies.

The political system requires an input of mass loyalty that is as diffuse as possible. The output consists in sovereignly executed administrative decisions. Output crises have the form of a *rationality crisis* in which the administrative system does not succeed in reconciling and fulfilling the imperatives received from the economic system. Input crises have the form of a *legitimation crisis;* the legitimizing system does not succeed in maintaining the requisite level of mass loyalty while the steering imperatives taken over from the economic system are carried through. Although both crisis tendencies arise in the political system, they differ in their form of appearance. The rationality crisis is a displaced systemic crisis which, like economic crisis, expresses the contradiction between socialized production for non-generalizable interests and steering imperatives. This crisis tendency is converted into the withdrawal of legitimation by way of a disorganization of the state apparatus. The legitimation crisis, by contrast, is directly an identity crisis. It does not proceed by way of endangering system integration, but results from the fact that the fulfillment of governmental planning tasks places in question the structure of the depoliticized public realm and, thereby, the formally democratic securing of the private autonomous disposition of the means of production.

We can speak of a rationality crisis in the strict sense only if it takes the place of economic crisis. In this case, the logic of problems of capital realization is not merely reflected in another steering medium, that of legitimate power; rather, the crisis logic is itself altered by the displacement of the contradictory steering imperatives from market commerce into the administrative system. This assertion is advanced in two versions. One version starts with the familiar thesis of the anarchy of commodity production that is built into market commerce. On the one hand, in advanced capitalism the need for administrative planning to secure the realization of capital grows. On the other hand, the private autonomous disposition of the means of production demands a limitation to state intervention and prohibits planned coordination of the contradictory interests of individual capitalists. Another version has been developed by Offe. While the state compensates for the weaknesses of a self-blocking economic system and takes over tasks complementary to the market, it is forced by the logic of its means of control to admit more and more foreign elements into the system. The problems of an economic system controlled by imperatives of capital realization cannot be taken over into the administratively controlled domain, and processed there, without the spread of orientations alien to the structure.

A rationality deficit in public administration means that the state apparatus cannot, under given boundary conditions, adequately steer the economic system. A legitimation deficit means that it is not possible by administrative means to maintain or establish effective normative structures to the extent required. During the course of capitalist development, the political system shifts its boundaries not only into the economic system but also into the socio-cultural system. While organizational rationality spreads, cultural traditions are undermined and weakened. The residue of tradition must, however, escape the administrative grasp, for traditions important for legitimation cannot be regenerated administratively. Furthermore, administrative manipulation of cultural matters has the unintended side effect of causing meanings and norms previously fixed by tradition and belonging to the *boundary* conditions of the political system to be publicly thematized. In this way, the scope of discursive will-formation expands—a process that shakes the structures of the depoliticized public realm so important for the continued existence of the system.

Socio-Cultural Crisis Tendencies.

The socio-cultural system receives its input from the economic and political systems in the form of purchasable and collectively demandable goods and services, legal and administrative acts, public and social security, etc. Output crises in both of the other systems are also input disturbances in the socio-cultural system and translate into withdrawal of legitimation. The aforementioned crisis tendencies can break out only through the socio-cultural system. For the social integration of a society is dependent on the output of this system—directly on the motivations it supplies to the political system in the form of legitimation and indirectly on the motivations to perform it supplies to the educational and occupational systems. Since the socio-cultural system does not, in contrast to the economic system, organize its own input, there can be no socio-culturally produced input crises. Crises that arise at this point are always output crises. We have to reckon with cultural crisis tendencies when the normative structures change, according to their inherent logic, in such a way that the complementarity between the requirements of the state apparatus and the occupational system, on the one hand, and the interpreted needs and legitimate expectations of members of society, on the other, is disturbed. Legitimation crises result from a need for legitimation that arises from changes in the political system (even when normative structures remain unchanged) and that cannot be met by the existing supply of legitimation. Motivational crises, on the other hand, are a result of changes in the socio-cultural system itself.

In advanced capitalism such tendencies are becoming apparent at the level of cultural tradition (moral systems, world-views) as well as at the level of structural change in the system of childrearing (school and family, mass media). In this way, the residue of tradition off which the state and the system of social labor lived in liberal capitalism is eaten away (stripping away traditionalistic padding), and core components of the bourgeois ideology become questionable (endangering civil and familial-professional privatism). On the other hand, the remains of bourgeois ideologies (belief in science, post-auratic art, and universalistic value systems) form a normative framework that is dysfunctional. Advanced capitalism creates "new" needs it cannot satisfy.

Our abstract survey of *possible* crisis tendencies in advanced capitalism has served an analytic purpose. I maintain that advanced-capitalist societies, assuming that they have not altogether overcome the susceptibility to crisis intrinsic to capitalism, are in danger from at least one of these possible crisis tendencies. It is a consequence of the fundamental contradiction of the capitalist system that, other factors being equal, either

—the economic system does not produce the requisite quantity of consumable values, or;

—the administrative system does not produce the requisite quantity of rational decisions, or;

—the legitimation system does not provide the requisite quantity of generalized motivations, or;

—the socio-cultural system does not generate the requisite quantity of action-motivating meaning. *

The gist of Habermas' argument is captured in his discussion of "motivation crisis," the predominant form of legitimation crisis, which, he argues, has largely replaced economic crisis in late capitalism. "The most important motivation contributed by the socio-cultural system in advanced capitalist societies consists of syndromes of civil and familial-vocational privatism." Civil privatism means that human beings believe in the system but do not participate actively in its political processes. Familial-vocational privatism indicates a process of upbringing that emphasizes consumption, leisure, career, and status.

I speak of a motivation crisis when the socio-cultural system changes in such a way that its output becomes dysfunctional for the state and for the system of social labor. The most important motivation contribution by the socio-cultural system in advanced capitalist societies consists of syndromes of civil and familial-vocational privatism. Civil privatism here denotes an interest in the steering and maintenance [*Versorgung*] performances of the administrative system but little participation in the legitimizing process, albeit participation appropriate to institutionally provided opportunities (high-output orientation versus low-input orientation). Civil privatism thus corresponds to the structures of a depoliticized public realm. Familial-vocational privatism complements civil privatism. It consists in a family orientation with developed interests in consumption and leisure on the one hand, and in a career orientation suitable to status competition on the other. This privatism thus corresponds to the structures of educational and occupational systems that are regulated by competition through achievement.

Both patterns of motivation are important to the continued existence of the political and economic systems.†

Habermas concludes by suggesting that "a legitimation crisis can be avoided in the long run only if the latent class structures of advanced capitalist societies are transformed or if the pressure for legitimation to which the administrative system is subject can be removed." His work ends with a diagnosis of this problem but with few definitive suggestions about new forms of legitimation and motivation to replace the ideology of just exchange.

Habermas' work is important because he modifies the original Marxian

---

*From Jürgen Habermas, *Legitimation Crisis* (Boston: Beacon Press, 1975), pp. 45-49.

†From Jürgen Habermas, *Legitimation Crisis* (Boston: Beacon Press, 1975), p. 75.

theory of crisis. Habermas believes that crisis today takes primarily the form of legitimation and motivation crisis, forms into which economic crisis is increasingly translated. In short, he argues that the traditional legitimating belief in free enterprise has been significantly weakened under organized capitalism, where the state increasingly intervenes in the marketplace and where the "old" belief in individual initiative and advancement is collapsing. The crisis of late capitalism is now manifested in terms of the periodic withdrawal of legitimation by citizens uncertain about the fundamental "goodness" and rationality of the system, and about their roles in it.

Habermas in later work has speculated about new forms of human motivation that can replace "civil privatism." These forms of motivation might be grounded in the desire to seek democratic consensus about the purposes of social life. At root, Habermas believes that new forms of rational, democratic community might arise that will abolish the class-system of private enterprise and eliminate its potential for serious crisis. His recent work has focused on "communication theory," further developing a new theory of rationality to replace instrumental rationality. Habermas argues that the crisis in contemporary motivation, and the weakening of the privatistic achievement ethic of earlier forms of capitalism, might be overcome by creating a new source of motivation such as the interest in interpersonal discussion and in community. Communicative competence, as he has called it, might serve both as a vehicle for reordering social and political priorities, challenging the technocratic structure of modern capitalism, and as an end in itself, a pursuit which will be its own reward in terms of human satisfaction.

BRAVERMAN: AGAINST THE THEORY OF THE "NEW WORKING CLASS"

Harry Braverman's recent *Labor and Monopoly Capital* (1974) has quickly become one of the seminal works of recent Marxism. Braverman reappropriates Marx's theory of class and reapplies it to late capitalist society. His work represents a seriously argued critique of the concept of a "new working class" that enjoyed a wide currency in the 1950s and 1960s. Braverman debunks those sociological analyses that suggest that an entirely autonomous middle class had emerged to take its place between the working class, traditionally defined, and the capitalist class.

The thrust of Braverman's argument is twofold: First, he argues that the working class has expanded since Marx and not shrunk as so many theorists have attested. Many new occupations—primarily office and clerical jobs such as keypunch operator and filing clerk—have emerged with the development of the computer and its advanced technology. Braverman feels that these occupations do not constitute the basis for the concept of a "new working class" but remain as fundamentally exploited as other wage-laborers.

Second, Braverman contends that alienation has become more severe since early market capitalism. These office proletarians are increasingly subject to severe work discipline and rationalization, organized by administrators of time and motion studies. Braverman does not feel that he can meaningfully talk about the "post-industrial" society, beyond class contradictions, as long as wage-laborers toil in unfulfilling, imperatively coordinated occupations, whether they be factory workers or office workers. In this sense Braverman launches a systematic attack on the technical division of labor, as he terms it, which he feels has only increased human alienation.

He argues that the fragmentation of labor has been accelerated under advanced capitalism. He distinguishes here between the industrial or general division of labor—the existence of separate professions and occupations (e.g., lawyers, farmers, teachers, mechanics)—and the technical division of labor, which refers to the splitting of each occupation into a multitude of separate but interrelated functions. (For example, the production of automobiles on the assembly line is highly fragmented.)

Braverman sees the increasing technical division of labor in this sense as an advanced form of capitalist domination. He does not object to the general division of labor that, in principle, is socially necessary in an urbanized industrial society (although that, too, may be questionable). Rather he objects to the way in which labor is increasingly subject to fragmentation and imperative coordination by managers, supervisors, technocrats, and bosses. These phenomena of (a) the fragmentation of labor into increasingly "small" and routinized units and (b) the coordination and integration of this labor from above, carried out by the bureaucratic and technocratic representatives of capital, define the modern character of alienation, according to Braverman. This analysis rebuts those theories that argue that work has become more "meaningful" for members of the "new working class" and middle class. Indeed a very small proportion of workers in capitalist society truly enjoy their work in the sense that they find it self-directing and creative. As long as work is drudgery, requiring little skill or psychic attachment, domination survives.

Braverman argues that one cannot comprehend modern alienation without understanding alienation from the perspective of the labor process itself. This alienation comes at the hands of the "detail" or "technical" division of labor that fragments the working process in order to cheapen labor's component parts (he terms this Babbage's law, after Charles Babbage, who first analyzed this tendency). Braverman's thesis can be elaborated as follows: The level of skill of modern labor is *lower* than in earlier periods of capitalism when the worker had more craft-knowledge of the production process. Contrary to the "post-Marxian" sociologies of work, Braverman argues that further rationalization of the technical division of labor makes the worker more passive and less skillful, and thus more alienated, than ever before.

The earliest innovative principle of the capitalist mode of production was the manufacturing division of labor, and in one form or another the division of labor has remained the fundamental principle of industrial organization. The division of labor in capitalist industry is not at all identical with the phenomenon of the distribution of tasks, crafts, or specialties of production throughout society, for while all known societies have divided their work into productive specialties, no society before capitalism systematically subdivided the work of each productive specialty into limited operations. This form of the division of labor becomes generalized only with capitalism.

This distinction is made clear, for instance, in Herskovits' description of the division of labor in primitive societies:

Only rarely is any division of labor within an industry—or, as it might be termed, subdivision of labor—encountered among nonliterate folk. Such intra-industrial specialization would be encountered only in the production of such larger capital goods as houses, canoes, or fish-weirs. Even here, it is the rule in such cultures that an arrangement of this sort is temporary; moreover, each worker devoting himself to a part of a specific task is most often competent to perform other phases of the work besides that on which he may at the moment be engaged.... Thus in groups where the primary division of labor is along sex lines, every man or woman not only will know how to do all those things that men or women habitually do among them, but must be able to do them efficiently. As we move to societies of somewhat greater economic complexity, we find that certain men may spend a larger proportion of their time than others doing wood-carving or iron-working, or certain women making pots or weaving cloth; but all the members of the groups will have some competence in the techniques controlled by those of a given sex. In still other nonliterate societies, certain men and women specialize not only in one technique, but in a certain type of product, as, for instance, where one woman will devote her time to the production of pots for everyday use and another make pottery exclusively for religious rites. It must again be stressed that, except under the most unusual circumstances, we do not find the kind of organization where one woman characteristically specializes in gathering the clay, another in fashioning it, and a third in firing the pots; or, where one man devotes himself to getting wood, a second to roughly blocking out the proportions of a stool or figure, and a third to finishing it.

Herskovits gives us here a picture of a division of labor into crafts, a differentiation which in the beginning owes much to sex roles. By and large, however, there is no division of tasks within the crafts. While men or women may habitually be connected with the making of certain products, they do not as a rule divide up the separate operations involved in the making of each product.

This form of division of labor, characteristic of all societies, is, if we follow Marx's terminology, called the *social division of labor*. It is a derivative of the specific character of human work: "An animal forms things in accordance with the standard and the need of the species to which it belongs, whilst man knows how to produce in accordance with the standard of every species." The spider weaves, the bear fishes, the beaver builds dams and houses, but the human is simultaneously weaver, fisherman, builder, and a thousand other things combined in a manner which, because this takes place in, and is possible only through, society, soon compels a social division according to craft. Each individual of the human species cannot alone "produce in accordance with the standard of every species" and invent standards unknown to any animal, but the species as a whole finds it possible to do this, in part through the social division of labor. Thus the social division of labor is apparently inherent in the species character of human labor as soon as it becomes social labor, that is, labor carried on in and through society.

As against this general or social division of labor, there stands the division of labor in detail, the manufacturing division of labor. This is the breakdown of the processes involved in the making of the product into manifold operations performed by different workers.

The practice of regarding the social and the detailed divisions of labor as a single continuum, a single abstract technical principle, is by far the greatest source of confusion in discussions of this subject. The division of labor in society is characteristic of all known societies; the division of labor in the workshop is the special product of capitalist society. The social division of labor divides society among occupations, each adequate to a branch of production; the detailed division of labor destroys occupations considered in this sense, and renders the worker inadequate to carry through any complete production process. In capitalism, the social division of labor is enforced chaotically and anarchically by the market, while the workshop division of labor is imposed by planning and control. Again in capitalism, the products of the social division of labor are exchanged as commodities, while the results of the operation of the detail worker are not exchanged within the factory as within a marketplace, but are all owned by the same capital. While the social division of labor subdivides *society,* the detailed division of labor subdivides *humans,* and while the subdivision of society may enhance the individual and the species, the subdivision of the individual, when carried on without regard to human capabilities and needs, is a crime against the person and against humanity.

The view which ignores the distinction between the social and detailed divisions of labor is given typical expression in the following comments: "Social differentiation and division of labor are universal attributes of human society. Contrary to the view persisting into the recent past that primitive man lives in completely homogeneous and amorphous groups, modern knowledge of primitive and peasant communities reveals much complexity and specialization. . . . Modern specialization cannot therefore be contrasted with an assumed society or period having no division of labor. The difference is one of degree and not of kind." Wilbert Moore here forces us to assume that the division of society among trades, crafts, professions "cannot be contrasted" with the breakup of those occupations, that there is no difference "in kind" between the practice of farming, cabinetmaking, or blacksmithing, and the repeated tightening of a single set of bolts hundreds of times each day or the key punching of thousands of cards each week throughout a lifetime of labor, because *all* are expressions of the "division of labor." On this level of abstraction, obviously, nothing can be learned about the division of labor, except the banal and apologetic conclusion that being "universal," each of its manifestations is probably inevitable. Needless to say, this is precisely the conclusion that bourgeois society prefers.

It is for this reason that the popularity of Émile Durkheim's work, *The Division of Labor in Society,* has grown as its applicability to the modern world has dwindled. Durkheim adopts just such a level of abstraction in his approach: "The only way to succeed in objectively appreciating the division of labor is to study it first in itself, entirely speculatively, to look for its use, and upon what it depends, and finally, to form as adequate a notion as possible of it." He proceeds in this fashion, determinedly avoiding the specific social conditions under which the division of labor develops in our epoch, celebrating throughout his proposition that "the ideal of human fraternity can be realized only in proportion to the progress of the division of labor," until in the last tenth of his work he discovers the division of labor in the factories and offices of modern capitalism, and dubs them "abnormal forms." But, as has been noted by a recent critic, M. C. Kennedy, "when we inspect these abnormal forms throughout the world, it becomes difficult to find one clear-cut case of the normal division of labor." Kennedy is absolutely right when he calls Durkheim's "normal" form of the division of labor "the ideal of a moralistic sociologist and not a sociologist of morals."

Our concern at this point, therefore, is not with the division of labor in society at large, but within the enterprise; not with the distribution of labor among various industries and occupations, but with the breakdown of occupations and industrial processes; not with the division of labor in "production in general," but within the capitalist mode of production in particular. It is not "pure technique" that concerns us, but rather the marriage of technique with the special needs of capital.

The division of labor in production begins with the *analysis of the labor process*—that is to say, the separation of the work of production into its constituent elements. But this, in itself, is not what brings into being the detail worker. Such an analysis or separation, in fact, is characteristic in every labor process organized by workers to suit their own needs.

For example, a tinsmith makes a funnel: He draws the elevation view on sheetmetal, and from this develops the outline of an unrolled funnel and its bottom spout. He then cuts out each piece with snips and shears, rolls it to its proper shape, and crimps or rivets the seams. He then rolls the top edge, solders the seams, solders on a hanging ring, washes away the acid used in soldering, and rounds the funnel to its final shape. But when he applies the same process to a quantity of identical funnels, his mode of operation changes. Instead of laying out the work directly on the material, he makes a pattern and uses it to mark off the total quantity of funnels needed; then he cuts them all out, one after the other, rolls them, etc. In this case, instead of making a single funnel in the course of an hour or two, he spends hours or even days on each step of the process, creating in each case fixtures, clamps, devices, etc. which would not be worth making for a single funnel but which, where a sufficiently large quantity of funnels is to be made, speed each step sufficiently so that the saving justifies the extra outlay of time. Quantities, he has discovered, will be produced with less trouble and greater economy of time in this way than by finishing each funnel individually before starting the next.

In the same way a bookkeeper whose job it is to make out bills and maintain office records against their future collection will, if he or she works for a lawyer who has only a few clients at a time, prepare a bill and post it at once to the proper accounts and the customer statement. But if there are hundreds of bills each month, the bookkeeper will accumulate them and spend a full day or two, from time to time, posting them to the proper accounts. Some of these postings will now be made by daily, weekly, or monthly totals instead of bill by bill, a practice which saves a great deal of labor when large quantities are involved; at the same time, the bookkeeper will now make use of other shortcuts or aids, which become practicable when operations are analyzed or broken up in this way, such as specially prepared ledger cards, or carbon forms which combine into a single operation the posting to the customer's account and the preparation of a monthly statement.

Such methods of analysis of the labor process and its division into constituent elements have always been and are to this day common in all trades and crafts, and represent the first form of the subdivision of labor in detail. It is clear that they satisfy, essentially if not fully, the three advantages of the division of labor given by Adam Smith in his famous discussion in the first chapter of *The Wealth of Nations:*

> This great increase in the quantity of work, which, in consequence of the division of labour, the same number of people are capable of performing, is owing to three different circumstances; first, to the increase of dexterity in every particular workman; secondly, to the saving of the time which is commonly lost in passing from one species of work to another; and lastly, to the invention of a great number of machines which facilitate and abridge labour, and enable one man to do the work of many.

The example which Smith gives is the making of pins, and his description is as follows:

> One man draws out the wire, another straightens it, a third cuts it, a fourth points it, a fifth grinds it at the top for receiving the head; to make the head requires two or three distinct operations; to put it on, is a peculiar business, to whiten the pins is another; it is even a trade by itself to put them into the paper; and the important business of making a pin is, in this manner, divided into about eighteen distinct operations, which, in some manufactories, are all performed by distinct hands, though in others the same man will sometimes perform two or three of them.

In this example, the division of labor is carried one step further than in the examples of the tinsmith and the bookkeeper. Not only are the operations separated from each other, but *they are assigned to different workers.* Here we have not just the analysis of the labor process but the creation of the detail worker. Both steps depend upon the scale of production: Without sufficient quantities they are impracticable. Each step represents a saving in labor time. The greatest saving is embodied in the analysis of the process, and a further saving, the extent varying with the nature of the process, is to be found in the separation of operations among different workers.

The worker may break the process down, but he never voluntarily converts himself into a lifelong detail worker. This is the contribution of the capitalist, who sees no reason why, if so much is to be gained from the first step—analysis—and something more gained from the second—breakdown among workers—he should not take the second step as well as the first. That the first step breaks up only the process, while the second dismembers the worker as well, means nothing to the capitalist, and all the less since, in destroying the craft as a process under the control of the worker, he reconstitutes it as a process under his own control. He can now count his gains in a double sense, not only in productivity but in management control, since that which mortally injures the worker is in this case advantageous to him.

The effect of these advantages is heightened by still another which, while it is given surprisingly little mention in economic literature, is certainly the most compelling reason for all for the immense popularity of the division of tasks among workers in the capitalist mode of production, and for its rapid spread. It was not formulated clearly nor emphasized strongly until a half-century after Smith, by Charles Babbage.

In "On the Division of Labour," Chapter XIX of his *On the Economy of Machinery and Manufactures,* the first edition of which was published in 1832, Babbage noted that "the most important and influential cause [of savings from the division of labor] has been altogether unnoticed." He recapitulates the classic arguments of William Petty, Adam Smith, and the other political economists, quotes from Smith the passage reproduced above about the "three different circumstances" of the division of labor which add to the productivity of labor, and continues:

> Now, although all these are important causes, and each has its influence on the result; yet it appears to me, that any explanation of the cheapness of manufactured articles, as consequent upon the division of labour, would be incomplete if the following principle were omitted to be stated.
>
> *That the master manufacturer, by dividing the work to be executed into different processes, each requiring different degrees of skill or of force, can purchase exactly that precise quantity of both which is necessary for each process; whereas, if the whole work were executed by one workman, that person must possess sufficient skill to perform the most difficult, and sufficient strength to execute the most laborious, of the operations into which the art is divided.*

To put this all-important principle another way, in a society based upon the purchase and sale of labor power, dividing the craft cheapens its individual parts. To clarify this point, Babbage gives us an example drawn, like Smith's, from pin manufacture. He presents a table for the labor employed, by type (that is, by age and sex) and by pay, in the English manufacture of those pins known in his day as "Elevens."

Drawing wire	Man	3s.3d.per day
Straightening wire	Woman	1s.0d.
	Girl	0s.6d.
Pointing	Man	5s.3d.
Twisting and cutting	Boy	0s.4½d.
heads	Man	5s.4½d.
Heading	Woman	1s.3d.
Tinning or whitening	Man	6s.0d.
	Woman	3s.0d.
Papering	Woman	1s.6d.

It is clear from this tabulation, as Babbage points out, that the minimum pay for a craftsman capable of performing all operations is no more than the highest pay in the above listing, and if such craftsmen are employed exclusively, then the labor costs of manufacture would be more than doubled, *even if the very same division of labor were employed and even if the craftsmen produced pins at the very same speed as the detail workers.*

Let us add another and later example, taken from the first assembly line in American industry, the meatpacking conveyor (actually a *disassembly* line). J. R. Commons has realistically included in this description, along with the usual details, the rates of pay of the workers:

> It would be difficult to find another industry where division of labor has been so ingeniously and microscopically worked out. The animal has been

surveyed and laid off like a map; and the men have been classified in over thirty specialties and twenty rates of pay, from 16 cents to 50 cents an hour. The 50-cent man is restricted to using the knife on the most delicate parts of the hide (floorman) or to using the ax in splitting the backbone (splitter); and wherever a less-skilled man can be slipped in at 18 cents, 18½ cents, 20 cents, 21 cents, 22½ cents, 24 cents, 25 cents, and so on, a place is made for him, and an occupation mapped out. In working on the hide alone there are nine positions, at eight different rates of pay. A 20-cent man pulls off the tail, a 22½-cent man pounds off another part where good leather is not found, and the knife of the 40-cent man cuts a different texture and has a different "feel" from that of the 50-cent man.

Babbage's principle is fundamental to the evolution of the division of labor in capitalist society. It gives expression not to a technical aspect of the division of labor, but to its social aspect. Insofar as the labor process may be dissociated, it may be separated into elements some of which are simpler than others and each of which is simpler than the whole. Translated into market terms, this means that the labor power capable of performing the process may be purchased more cheaply as dissociated elements than as a capacity integrated in a single worker. Applied first to the handicrafts and then to the mechanical crafts, Babbage's principle eventually becomes the underlying force governing all forms of work in capitalist society, no matter in what setting or at what hierarchical level.

In the mythology of capitalism, the Babbage principle is presented as an effort to "preserve scarce skills" by putting qualified workers to tasks which "only they can perform," and not wasting "social resources." It is presented as a response to "shortages" of skilled workers or technically trained people, whose time is best used "efficiently" for the advantage of "society." But however much this principle may manifest itself at times in the form of a response to the scarcity of skilled labor—for example, during wars or other periods of rapid expansion of production—this apology is on the whole false. The capitalist mode of production systematically destroys all-around skills where they exist, and brings into being skills and occupations that correspond to its needs. Technical capacities are henceforth distributed on a strict "need to know" basis. The generalized distribution of knowledge of the productive process among all its participants becomes, from this point on, not merely "unnecessary," but a positive barrier to the functioning of the capitalist mode of production.

Labor power has become a commodity. Its uses are no longer organized according to the needs and desires of those who sell it, but rather according to the needs of its purchasers, who are, primarily, employers seeking to expand the value of their capital. And it is the special and permanent interest of these purchasers to cheapen this commodity. The most common mode of cheapening labor power is exemplified by the Babbage principle: Break it up into its simplest elements. And, as the capitalist mode of production creates a working population suitable to its needs, the Babbage principle is, by the very shape of this "labor market." enforced upon the capitalists themselves.

Every step in the labor process is divorced, so far as possible, from special knowledge and training and reduced to simple labor. Meanwhile, the relatively few persons for whom special knowledge and training are reserved are freed so far as possible from the obligations of simple labor. In this way, a structure is given to all labor processes that at its extremes polarizes those whose time is infinitely valuable and those whose time is worth almost nothing. This might even be called the general law of the capitalist division of labor. It is not the sole force acting upon the organization of work, but it is certainly the most powerful and general. Its results, more or less advanced in every industry and occupation, give massive testimony to its validity. It shapes not only work, but populations as well, because over the long run it creates that mass of simple labor which is the primary feature of populations in developed capitalist countries.*

Braverman also adds that "Taylorism," the first important theory of the scientific management of labor, is by no means a thing of the past, and that Taylorism has invaded the service industries and clerical professions. Taylorism consists of three interrelated principles: (a) the dissociation of the labor process from the skills of the workers; (b) the separation of conception from execution; (c) the use of management's monopoly of knowledge to control each step of the labor process and its mode of execution.

First Principle
"The managers assume . . .the burden of gathering together all of the traditional knowledge which in the past has been possessed by the workmen and then of classifying, tabulating, and reducing this knowledge to rules, laws, and formulae. . . ." We have seen the illustrations of this in the cases of the lathe machinist and the pig-iron handler. The great disparity between these activities, and the different orders of knowledge that may be collected about them, illustrate that for Taylor—as for managers today—no task is either so simple or so complex that it may not be studied with the object of collecting in the hands of management at least as much information as is known by the worker who performs it regularly, and very likely more. This brings to an end the situation in which "Employers derive their knowledge of how much of a given class of work can be done in a day from either their own experience, which has frequently grown hazy with age, from casual and unsystematic observation of their men, or at best from records which are kept, showing the quickest time in which each job has been done." It enables management to discover and enforce those speedier methods and shortcuts which workers themselves, in the practice of their trades or tasks, learn or improvise, and use at their own discretion only. Such an experimental approach also brings into being new methods such as can be devised only through the means of systematic study.

This first principle we may call the *dissociation of the labor process from the skills of the workers.* The labor process is to be rendered independent of craft, tradition, and the workers' knowledge. Henceforth it is to depend not at all upon the abilities of workers, but entirely upon the practices of management.

Second Principle
"All possible brain work should be removed from the shop and centered in the planning or laying-out department. . . ." Since this is the key to scientific management, as Taylor well understood, he was especially emphatic on this point and it is important to examine the principle thoroughly.

---

*From Harry Braverman, *Labor and Monopoly Capital* (New York: Monthly Review Press, 1974), pp. 71-82.

In the human, as we have seen, the essential feature that makes for a labor capacity superior to that of the animal is the combination of execution with a conception of the thing to be done. But as human labor becomes a social rather than an individual phenomenon, it is possible—unlike in the instance of animals where the motive force, instinct, is inseparable from action—to divorce conception from execution. This dehumanization of the labor process, in which workers are reduced almost to the level of labor in its animal form, while purposeless and unthinkable in the case of the self-organized and self-motivated social labor of a community of producers, becomes crucial for the management of purchased labor. For if the workers' execution is guided by their own conception, it is not possible, as we have seen, to enforce upon them either the methodological efficiency or the working pace desired by capital. The capitalist therefore learns from the start to take advantage of this aspect of human labor power, and to break the unity of the labor process.

This should be called the principle of the *separation of conception from execution,* rather than by its more common name of the separation of mental and manual labor (even though it is similar to the latter, and in practice often identical). This is because mental labor, labor done primarily in the brain, is also subjected to the same principle of separation of conception from execution: Mental labor is first separated from manual labor and, as we shall see, is then itself subdivided rigorously according to the same rule.

The first implication of this principle is that Taylor's "science of work" is never to be developed by the worker, always by management. This notion, apparently so "natural" and undebatable today, was in fact vigorously discussed in Taylor's day, a fact which shows how far we have traveled along the road of transforming all ideas about the labor process in less than a century, and how completely Taylor's hotly contested assumptions have entered into the conventional outlook within a short space of time. Taylor confronted this question— why must work be studied by the management and not by the worker himself; why not *scientific workmanship* rather than *scientific management?*—repeatedly, and employed all his ingenuity in devising answers to it, though not always with his customary frankness. In *The Principles of Scientific Management,* he pointed out that the "older system" of management

> makes it necessary for each workman to bear almost the entire responsibility for the general plan as well as for each detail of his work, and in many cases for his implements as well. In addition to this he must do all of the actual physical labor. The development of a science, on the other hand, involves the establishment of many rules, laws, and formulae which replace the judgment of the individual workman and which can be effectively used only after having been systematically recorded, indexed, etc. The practical use of scientific data also calls for a room in which to keep the books, records, etc., and a desk for the planner to work at. Thus all of the planning which under the old system was done by the workman, as a result of his personal experience, must of necessity under the new system be done by the management in accordance with the laws of the science; because even if the workman was well suited to the development and use of scientific data, it would be physically impossible for him to work at his machine and at a desk at the same time. It is also clear that in most cases one type of man is needed to plan ahead and an entirely different type to execute the work.

The objections having to do with physical arrangements in the workplace are clearly of little importance, and represent the deliberate exaggeration of obstacles which, while they may exist as inconveniences, are hardly insuperable. To refer to the "different type" of worker needed for each job is worse than disingenuous, since these "different types" hardly existed until the division of labor created them. As Taylor well understood, the possession of craft knowledge made the worker the best starting point for the development of the science of work; systematization often means, at least at the outset, the gathering of knowledge which *workers already possess*. But Taylor, secure in his obsession with the immense reasonableness of his proposed arrangement, did not stop at this point. In his testimony before the Special Committee of the House of Representatives, pressed and on the defensive, he brought forth still other arguments:

> I want to make it clear, Mr. Chairman, that work of this kind undertaken by the management leads to the development of a science, while it is next to impossible for the workman to develop a science. There are many workmen who are intellectually just as capable of developing a science, who have plenty of brains, and are just as capable of developing a science as those on the managing side. But the science of doing work of any kind cannot be developed by the workman. Why? Because he has neither the time nor the money to do it. The development of the science of doing any kind of work always required the work of two men, one man who actually does the work which is to be studied and another man who observes closely the first man while he works and studies the time problems and the motion problems connected with this work. No workman has either the time or the money to burn in making experiments of this sort. If he is working for himself no one will pay him while he studies the motions of some one else. The management must and ought to pay for all such work. So that for the workman, the development of a science becomes impossible, not because the workman is not intellectually capable of developing it, but he has neither the time nor the money to do it and he realizes that this is a question for the management to handle.

Taylor here argues that the systematic study of work and the fruits of this study belong to management for the very same reason that machines, factory buildings, etc., belong to them; that is, because it costs labor time to conduct such a study, and only the possessors of capital can afford labor time. The possessors of labor time cannot themselves afford to do anything with it but sell it for their means of subsistence. It is true that this is the rule in capitalist relations of production, and Taylor's use of the argument in this case shows with great clarity where the sway of capital leads: Not only is capital the property of the capitalist, but *labor itself has become part of capital*. Not only do the workers lose control over their instruments of production, but they must now lose control over their own labor and the manner of its performance. This control now falls to those who can "afford" to study it in order to know it better than the workers themselves know their own life activity.

But Taylor has not yet completed his argument: "Furthermore," he told the Committee, "if any workman were to find a new and quicker way of doing work, or if he were to develop a new method, you can see at once it becomes to his interest to keep that development to himself, not to teach the other workmen the quicker method. It is to his interest to do what workmen have done in all times, to keep their trade secrets for themselves and their friends. That is the old idea of trade secrets. The workman kept his knowledge to himself instead of developing a science and teaching it to others and making it public property." Behind this hearkening back to old ideas of "guild secrets" is Taylor's persistent and fundamental notion that the improvement of work methods by workers brings few benefits to management. Elsewhere in his testimony, in discussing the work of his associate, Frank Gilbreth who spent many years studying bricklaying methods, he candidly admits that not only *could* the "science of bricklaying" be developed by workers, but that it undoubtedly *had been*. "Now, I have not the slighest doubt that during the last 4,000 years all the methods that Mr. Gilbreth developed have many, many times suggested themselves to the minds of bricklayers." But because knowledge possessed by workers is not useful to capital, Taylor begins his list of the desiderata of scientific management: "First. The development—by the management, not the workmen—of the science of bricklaying." Workers, he explains, are not going to put into execution any system or any method which harms them and their workmates: "Would they be likely," he says, referring to the pig-iron job, "to get rid of seven men out of eight from their own gang and retain only the eighth man? No!"

Finally, Taylor understood the Babbage principle better than anyone of his time, and it was always uppermost in his calculations. The purpose of work study was never, in his mind, to enhance the ability of the worker, to concentrate in the worker a greater share of scientific knowledge, to ensure that as technique rose, the worker would rise with it. Rather, the purpose was to cheapen the worker by decreasing his training and enlarging his output. In his early book, *Shop Management*, he said frankly that the "full possibilities" of his system "will not have been realized until almost all of the machines in the shop are run by men who are of smaller calibre and attainments, and who are therefore cheaper than those required under the old system."

Therefore, both in order to ensure management control and to cheapen the worker, conception and execution must be rendered separate spheres of work, and for this purpose the study of work processes must be reserved to management and kept from the workers, to whom its results are communicated only in the form of simplified job tasks governed by simplified instructions which it is thenceforth their duty to follow unthinkingly and without comprehension of the underlying technical reasoning or data.

Third Principle

The essential idea of "the ordinary types of management," Taylor said, "is that each workman has become more skilled in his own trade than it is possible for any one in the management to be, and that, therefore, the details of how the work shall best be done must be left to him." But, by contrast: "Perhaps the most prominent single element in modern scientific management is the task idea. The work of every workman is fully planned out by the management at least one day in advance, and each man receives in most cases complete written instructions, describing in detail the task which he is to accomplish, as well as the means to be used in doing the work. ...This task specifies not only what is to be done, but how it is to be done and the exact time allowed for doing it. . . .Scientific management consists very largely in preparing for and carrying out these tasks."

In this principle it is not the written instruction card that is important. Taylor had no need for such a card with Schmidt, nor did he use one in many other instances. Rather, the essential element is the systematic pre-planning and pre-calculation of all elements of the labor process, which now no longer exists as a process in the imagination of the worker but only as a process in the imagination of a special management staff. Thus, if the first principle is the gathering and development of knowledge of labor processes, and the second is the concentration of this knowledge as the exclusive province of management—together with its essential converse; the absence of such knowledge among the workers—then the third is the *use of this monopoly over knowledge to control each step of the labor process and its mode of execution.*

As capitalist industrial, office, and market practices developed in accordance with this principle, it eventually became part of accepted routine and custom, all the more so as the increasingly scientific character of most processes, which grew in complexity while the worker was not allowed to partake of this growth, made it ever more difficult for the workers to understand the processes in which they functioned. But in the beginning, as Taylor well understood, an abrupt psychological wrench was required. We have seen in the simple Schmidt case the means employed, both in the selection of a single worker as a starting point and in the way in which he was reoriented to the new conditions of work. In the more complex conditions of the machine shop, Taylor gave this part of the responsibility to the foremen. It is essential, he said of the gang bosses, to "nerve and brace them up to the point of insisting that the workmen shall carry out the orders exactly as specified on the instruction cards. This is a difficult task at first, as the workmen have been accustomed for years to do the details of the work to suit themselves, and many of them are intimate friends of the bosses and believe they know quite as much about their business as the latter."

Modern management came into being on the basis of these principles. It arose as theoretical construct and as systematic practice, moreover, in the very period during which the transformation of labor from processes based on skill to processes based upon science was attaining its most rapid tempo. Its role was to render conscious and systematic, the formerly unconscious tendency of capitalist production. It was to ensure that as craft declined, the worker would sink to the level of general and undifferentiated labor power, adaptable to a large range of simple tasks, while as science grew, it would be concentrated in the hands of management.*

This argument about the continued viability of Taylorism as an ideology of labor in late capitalism is applied to an analysis of the technologization of the production process. Braverman explodes the sociological discovery of the so-called "new working class" that emerged in the context of Daniel Bell's twin theses of the "end of ideology" and "post-industrial society." Bell and others argued that class conflict had been ended in late capitalism, with generalized

---

*From Harry Braverman, *Labor and Monopoly Capital* (New York: Monthly Review Press, 1974), pp. 112-21.

affluence for almost everyone, leaving only minor problems of "fine tuning" to be confronted by omniscient technocrats.

The shortcoming of Bell's analysis, according to Braverman, is that he overestimates the qualitative shift from industrial growth to post-industrial "scientific-technological" growth. While capitalist economies have indeed been rehinged around planned technological growth and science-based productivity, along with rapid expansion of the service sector of the economy, this has *not*, according to Braverman, emancipated most human beings from alienated wage-labor. Instead the further technologization of industrial production has *decreased* the need for skilled human labor (raising the so-called organic composition of capital, as Marx predicted), throwing many out of work or forcing them into low-paid, non-unionized service industries. The engineer and technician remain minority figures in the work force; their growing predominance has not eliminated alienated labor, as many like Bell and Herman Kahn have optimistically projected ("post-industrial society"), but merely shifted labor out of capital-intensive industries into low-skill, labor-intensive industries where alienation is still found and experienced. Braverman argues that the scientific-technological revolution, in short, has not freed workers from labor but has merely taken them out of factories and put them into the clerical professions or set them to work as janitors and waitresses, lowering both their wages and their levels of training, skill, and craftsmanship.

This displacement of labor as the subjective element of the process, and its subordination as an objective element in a productive process now conducted by management, is an ideal realized by capital only within definite limits, and unevenly among industries. The principle is itself restrained in its application by the nature of the various specific and determinate processes of production. Moreover, its very application brings into being new crafts and skills and technical specialties which are at first the province of labor rather than management. Thus in industry all forms of labor coexist: the craft, the hand or machine detail worker, the automatic machine or flow process. But far more important than this relative restraint on the operation of the principle is the resulting continual shifting of employment. The very success of management in increasing productivity in some industries leads to the displacement of labor into other fields, where it accumulates in large quantities because the processes employed have not yet been subjected—and in some cases cannot be subjected to the same degree—to the mechanizing tendency of modern industry. The result therefore is not the *elimination* of labor, but its *displacement* to other occupations and industries . . .*

LEISS: TECHNOLOGY, ECOLOGY, AND HUMAN NEEDS

The analysis of the state in late capitalist society leads directly to the second strain of recent Marxism, termed above ecological Marxism. Miliband's discussion of the probability of a new authoritarianism and abolition of the liberal-democratic

---

*From Harry Braverman, *Labor and Monopoly Capital* (New York: Monthly Review Press, 1974), p. 172.

underpinning of capitalist nation-states rests primarily on the ability of the economy to satisfy a variety of human needs, both of rich and poor.

Ecological Marxists examine this question from a different perspective. They start from the assumption that a "steady-state" economy will become an unavoidable necessity, requiring a shrinkage of capitalist productivity and perhaps a broader regulatory role for the capitalist state. Furthermore, material human needs will have to be drastically reassessed and scaled down. A new asceticism may yet be required in face of energy shortages, the "shrinking" nature of the planet, and the growing interdependence of its ecological support systems.

The democratic legitimacy of an interventionist state was formerly achieved via the promise that workers could aspire to growing wealth. This source of legitimacy has begun to evaporate in light of the various economic crises experienced by the capitalist system. In the next few decades, it is argued by some, this type of legitimacy-crisis will only become more severe in light of the inevitability of an inexorable slowdown of economic growth. The promise of nearly unlimited consumption, a promise tendered as much to the poor as to the wealthy, will have to be withdrawn and a new frugality may take its place.

The scaling down of human needs—and perhaps their displacement into more spiritual and cultural realms (termed "qualitative growth" by some economists)—will require more than good intentions on the part of consumers. It may also require a fundamental transformation of the very class-system, requiring redistribution of wealth designed to placate the poor and to bind them back into the political and economic system. Legitimation in the next few decades may depend on satisfying the dispossessed that a "steady-state" economy will not spell the sudden end of their ideologically-fostered dreams of personal affluence.

Ecological Marxism enables us to develop the theory of the state in a new direction. Increasing state intervention in the economy may be required to regulate the consumption of precious resources. Furthermore, personal consumption may have to be scaled down and redistribution of wealth, achieved perhaps through a more progressive tax system and a guaranteed annual income, undertaken to prevent the insurrection of the lower classes in capitalist society. What Miliband termed a new authoritarianism may be avoided only through the internal transformation of the class-system and the wholesale transformation of human needs. Ecological Marxists suggest that this scenario may constitute the only hope for the survival of industrial civilization as we know it.

William Leiss, one of the most articulate and systematic of the ecological leftists, outlines two possible scenarios for the genesis of the steady-state economy: On the one hand, "the coming of the stationary state may occasion heightened conflict and attempts at authoritarian political solutions, as Heilbroner has intimated (in his very alarming *An Inquiry into the Human Prospect,* in which he argues that a steady-state global system can only come about through the imposition of authoritarian world government and vastly increased state intervention in domestic economies)." On the other hand, there exists a "subterranean" tradition that argues that "the stationary state would afford an opportunity for qualitative improvement." This is the tradition of what we have called ecological Marxism, numbering among its ranks Fourier, Marx, Ruskin, Morris, Kropotkin, Bookchin, Fromm, Illich, Goodman, Macpherson, and Marcuse. Leiss suggests that the general unifying assumption of this tradition is that "the possibilities of human satisfaction must be rooted in the creation of a well-functioning sphere of shared activity and decision making within which individuals would forge the means for satisfying their needs."

Ecological Marxists stress that human satisfaction ultimately lies in production activity and not in consumption activity (although, as Leiss notes, consumption will obviously not be eliminated under a socialist steady-state economy). The goal of this type of scaled-down social order "is gradually to dismember the massive institutional structures of the industrialized economy and to reduce, so far as possible, the dependence of individuals on them." We have spoken above about how certain contemporary Marxists such as the Frankfurt School theorists see alienation now primarily as a phenomenon of human powerlessness and helplessness before the vast institutions of corporate society. Leiss argues that this powerlessness could conceivably be remedied through the decentralization of the polity and economy and by shifting away from high-consumption life styles.

Industrial societies today, both capitalist and state-socialist, are characterized by (a) large-scale technologies, (b) high energy demands, (c) centralization of production and population, (d) increasing specialization of functions, and (e) a growing assortment of commodities for personal consumption. Leiss argues that human happiness tends to be defined solely in terms of frenetic consumption activity. He feels that this is a symptom of contemporary alienation. The measurement of satisfaction solely in terms of consumption is intrinsically confusing in the modern setting because commodities embody a complex "package" of meanings and symbols that are often difficult to disentangle and then to relate to human needs. In other terms, the human being, who probably does not enjoy his job, struggles to satisfy his needs in the consumption of name brands that continuously lose and acquire allure as taste makers determine fads and trends in the marketplace.

Leiss states that "the relentless expansion of industrial production and human numbers has rudely shifted the locus of concern [about the steady-state economy] from aesthetic education to biological survival." Ecological Marxists combine these two concerns by arguing that impending ecological catastrophe impels us to rethink our patterns of industrial life, allowing us to move towards more decentralized, scaled-down patterns of social and economic organization. The recognition of ecological limits provides the opportunity for fundamental social transformation of a kind called for by many radicals since Fourier and Marx.

John Stuart Mill included a brief chapter entitled "Of the Stationary State" in his *Principles of Political Economy,* which advocated a stabilization of economic progress and population growth. In it he proposed the audacious notion that the productive capacities and population level existing at that time need not expand any further. Of course he recognized the gross inequities in the distribution of life's amenities and the opportunities for self-fulfillment among the population, but he contended that these could only be remedied by more rational forms of social organization. He maintained—correctly, as it turned out—that quantitative increases would not necessarily improve the lot of mankind as a whole. Finally, he argued that a turn from quantitative to qualitative criteria was the primary desideratum for further social progress.

For over a century thereafter the predominant traditions of social thought have maintained a conspiracy of silence with regard to Mill's suggestion. Recently it has been resurrected and applied in the context of contemporary issues. This recent discussion, however, only tends to confirm Mill's fear that the idea of the stationary state would be taken seriously only in response to pressing necessity, rather than being freely adopted as a desirable framework for qualitative improvement. In a situation of bitter competition over the disposition of resources and wealth, the coming of the stationary state may occasion heightened conflict and attempts at authoritarian political solutions, as Heilbroner has intimated.

The other alternative—the expectation that the stationary state would afford an opportunity for qualitative improvement—remains hidden in the subterranean regions of contemporary discussion. Mill himself did not indicate what kinds of innovative social practices might be appropriate for the positive accomplishments of the stationary state—or, to use a more adequate current expression, for the objectives of a conserver society. Suggestions that are relevant to this point can be found in the writings of other nineteenth- and twentieth-century thinkers, even though these suggestions were not advanced as a direct response to Mill's idea. They may be found in the works of earlier thinkers such as Fourier, Marx, Ruskin, Morris, and Kropotkin (as well as in other writings by Mill), and in the works of contemporary authors such as Bookchin, Fromm, Illich, Goodman, Macpherson, and Marcuse. I wish to refer to them not to advocate the adoption of any specific practical proposals, but only to illustrate some general characteristics of one set of possible alternative directions for social change.

The positive ideals and values that have informed this alternative tradition of thought have always centred on the emerging dimension of human individuality. These thinkers were never exclusively preoccupied—as I have been in this essay—with the negative aspects of the high-intensity market setting as such. The common focus of their positive ideals has been the assertion that a social transformation could make possible a rich dimension of genuine satisfaction in both the labour activities and the free time of all individuals. If there is one basic proposition that forms the cornerstone of this tradition, it is the idea that the possibilities of human satisfaction must be rooted in the creation of a well-functioning sphere of shared activity and decision making within which individuals would forge the means for satisfying their needs.

For this tradition qualitative differences in the mode of organization of socially necessary labour, and the relation of this labour to play and leisure activities, are the decisive element in the problem of satisfaction that arises in various forms of production and consumption activities. The organization of labour through a network of non-hierarchical, community-based associations, for example, would constitute a concrete form of social practice very different from the prevailing one. Such a decision-making structure, it is argued, would allow individuals to determine their needs under conditions of freedom and autonomy. In other words, what is most important for this tradition is a change in the mode of expressing and satisfying needs, not a definition or predetermination of an alternative set of needs as such. As the outcome of qualitatively different conditions of life, the new structures of needing could not be specified in advance. The "negative theory of needs" mentioned earlier is thus an essential element in this tradition.

In this perspective the possibility of satisfaction would be primarily a function of the organization of productive activity, and not—as in our society today—primarily a function of consumption. There is some evidence to show that individuals are aware of the fact that increasing rates of consumption are supposed to compensate for frustrations experienced in other domains of social life. The argument of this essay, which has emphasized the ambiguities inherent in the consumption process, has tried to show why this is a fruitless endeavour. If this argument is correct, then we have reason to believe that the possibilities for progressive social change are dependent upon identifying other spheres of activity, apart from the consumption process, in which the sense of satisfaction and well-being also may be grounded. A full-length study would be required in order to provide a critical review of the proposals made in this regard within the tradition of thought under discussion; this cannot be attempted here. A few brief remarks must suffice just to indicate the tenor of these proposals.

On the level of individual activity, the possibilities of satisfaction in an alternative setting would be related to overcoming the extreme specialization of work in the provisioning of goods and services (especially the methodical separation of mental and manual labour) and a consequent limitation of the sphere of commodity exchange. This has been a consistent theme in the tradition, and recently Ivan Illich has given it a new designation, *conviviality*. Illich uses this term to describe a social fabric based upon "autonomous and creative intercourse among persons, and the intercourse of persons with their environment." The goal of a convivial society is gradually to dismember the massive institutional structures of the industrialized economy and to reduce, so far as possible, the dependence of individuals on them: "People have a native capacity for healing, consoling, moving, learning, building their houses, and burying their dead. Each of these capacities meets a need. The means for the satisfaction of these needs are abundant so long as they depend primarily on what people can do for themselves, with only marginal dependence on commodities. These activities have use-value without having been given exchange-value. Their exercise at the service of man is not considered labor. These basic satisfactions become scarce when the social environment is transformed in such a manner that basic needs can no longer be met by abundant competence." The current organization of producing and consuming activity inhibits the development of the individual's talents and capacities for participating directly in activities that provide the means for satisfying a wide range of needs (building a home, growing food, making clothing), and instead orients his activity exclusively around market purchases. The convivial society would encourage individuals to engage directly in productive activities to the greatest degree possible.

There is nothing inherently evil in commodities and market exchanges as such, and there is no reason to believe that it would be desirable to extirpate them completely. There is cause for concern only when commodity exchange tends to become the *exclusive* mode for the satisfaction of needs. Nor is there any profit in attempting to specify a universally valid pattern for the relative significance of the sphere of market exchange in the overall economic calculus of every society. We may assume that the degree of significance of commodity production will vary widely according to specific historical circumstances and variations in social organization and personal desires. There need not be any uniform pattern even within a particular society, if that society is sufficiently decentralized to allow wide variations in the choices available to its members. The simple rule governing such choices may be stated as follows: Reliance on access to complex manufactured objects through market exchanges is inversely related to the degree of local, direct control over the means of satisfying needs.

Obviously these choices of varying patterns could only become realistic alternatives after the present national concentrations of wealth and wide regional disparities had been overcome as a result of deliberate social policies. Promotion of a stultifying uniformity in types of material objects and life-situations, both within and among nations, is one of the primary tendencies of generalized market exchange in industrialized economies. This is not a necessary result of technological progress itself, but is rather a function of the social policies that favour massive, centralized technologies of production over intermediate and small-scale technologies. The pattern of public and private investment which results from such policies concentrates productive resources and undermines the viability of any social and economic activity outside the metropolis that is not directly connected to the organizing centres of production.

The objective of an alternative social policy would not be to return a larger portion of the population to the harshness of circumstances which in the past often characterized life in the hinterland, but to disperse the advantages of modern technology—deliberately sacrificing some of the dubious "efficiency" of centralized production—over a wider variety of situations. This exercise would indeed be self-defeating if another uniform pattern—for example, identical smaller-scale communities—were to be substituted for the prevailing one. At present life in a rural community is often simply a poorer version of the urban style. In order for a variety of equally viable life-situations to emerge, ranging from the city to the small community, a significant proportion of the investments currently favouring the concentration of production and generalized commodity exchange would have to be diverted to the support of alternative patterns of social organization.

The "ideal type" for existing social policy is a population which is concentrated in urban high-rise dwellings and is dependent upon massive, complex systems for its energy supply, food and other necessities, and waste disposal. Every aspect of this life situation is energy-intensive: heating and cooling of buildings, mechanized agriculture, transportation, manufacturing of commodities, and recycling of waste products. Huge investments for the continued provisioning of fossil fuels and now for nuclear generating plants will be required to sustain it. Those investments could be redirected to the support of efficient technologies for alternative ideals, for example the small dwelling or group of buildings which relied upon solar and wind energy sources, greenhouses, and the recycling of nutrients from wastes to provide a high proportion of the basic requirements of daily life. Further adaptations of new technologies in communications and local computer terminals linked to information storage banks could overcome some of the disadvantages formerly imposed upon scattered smaller communities.

The objective of an alternative social policy would not be to force all individuals to adopt a different uniform pattern of living, but rather to make other options more attractive than they are at present. Now investment decisions have the effect of making a single option—the high-intensity market setting of the concentrated urban population—the only viable one. But under alternative policies the positive features of industrialization and sophisticated technologies could offer to contemporary society a luxury not available to earlier societies, namely the ability to sustain a variety of life-situations that are more equally attractive for individuals. Different patterns of needing and satisfactions, responsive to differences in the needs of individuals, are a real possibility under present conditions. If the genius of modern productive technology were applied to the task of dispersing material and cultural accomplishments more equitably across a variety of life-situations instead of forcing them into a single mould, a wider range of realistic choices would be available to individuals. Under these circumstances individuals could choose, for example, to trade off at diverse levels the satisfactions gained by personal activity in the production of everyday requirements against the satisfactions of consumption in a generalized market setting.

The directions established by general social policies will fix the parameters within which the trade-offs made by individuals will occur. In other words, the relative attractiveness of different options for individuals will be determined in part by the options available to the society as a whole. The postwar rise in the standard of living in the industrialized nations was to some extent based on the availability of cheap energy and minerals; that situation is fast changing. The rising costs of energy, material resources, and environmental degradation soon will begin to constrict the promised delights of the high-consumption lifestyle. To sustain the mirage of ever more extensive forms of satisfaction there will be a progressive deterioration in the quality of goods and—following Martin Krieger's scenario—an expansion of simulated gratification. In this context alternatives to the forms of satisfaction that are characteristic of the high-intensity market setting may appear more attractive, so long as they are not repressed by a social system which remains intent on enforcing the hegemony of that one path to happiness, no matter what the cost may be.

Opponents of the alternative tradition under discussion here have often castigated its ideals and values as "primitive," "romantic," and "reactionary." Therefore it is essential to stipulate at the outset that this perspective does not seek to glorify any earlier state of social development as a golden age to which we should return. It does not necessarily assume that any other earlier social pattern achieved a better realization of that "autonomous and creative intercourse" among persons and between persons and their environment of which it speaks. What it has suggested is that the present form of producing and consuming activity (including our dependence on energy-intensive, large-scale industrial technology) discourages the growth of personal autonomy, creativity, and responsibility. To be sure, some scope for the expression of these traits has existed in most forms of social organization, including the one analyzed in this essay; moreover, some of the achievements of modern industrialism have opened up new possibilities for their expression and realization. Thus we need not adopt the stance that our existing society represents a scene of unrelieved repression of individual self-fulfilment nor that any set of alternative proposals promises an instant and complete cure for all the ills of humanity. My own assumptions here are simply that the time when we could afford to indulge ourselves in certain illusions about the prevailing pattern is fast running out, and that recalling the challenge of an alternative tradition can broaden the ... of the future options which we may wish to consider.

At present the direction of social change is governed by the ideal of an unlimited expansion of material production and its supporting infrastructure (more elaborate large-scale technologies, higher energy demands, centralization of production and population, increasing specialization of functions, and a wider assortment of commodities). I have argued that the negative aspects of this ideal introduce certain dangers whose potential dimensions are so vast that it may be impossible to deal with them effectively once their nature becomes evident. These negative features of the dominant ideal are inherent in its very structure and are magnified in direct proportion to the success and prosperity of the high-intensity market setting. Should that system begin to falter as a result of certain constraints, such as the rising costs mentioned earlier, other difficulties would arise.

In general there are two possible ways of responding to this situation. The social ideal of the high-consumption lifestyle may be upheld in the face of emerging constraints for as long as possible. Existing inequalities would persist and perhaps worsen as the overall standard of living—measured in terms of the accumulation of commodities—ceased to rise or began to decline. Since the operative principle of this social ideal is the tendency to channel all desires and aspirations toward the sphere of consumption, anxieties and frustrations would be exacerbated as the realm of promised satisfactions shrank. Social tensions would increase rapidly, because the general level of material expectations is so much higher now than it was in the past, for example in the period preceding the Great Depression. To maintain that ideal under such circumstances would inevitably require the imposition of more repressive and authoritarian forms of political rule, managed by the agents of the privileged minority.

Another way is open, although greater courage and foresight are necessary in order to follow it. The talents and instrumentalities required for undertaking the journey already exist. As indicated above, one aspect of this way involves the development of alternative situations in which more direct and personal participation in activities related to the satisfaction of needs is encouraged, in opposition to the prevailing tendency to route all aspects of needing through the increasingly ambiguous world of commodities. If this alternative is to have any chance of success, the first steps in this direction should be taken now, before the accumulating confusions and frustrations that arise in the existing system produce a mood of sullen despair among the citizenry.

The specific forms of such activities cannot be displayed for selection in the pages of a theoretical treatise, as if what we required were a different version of the department store catalogues that appear regularly in our mailboxes. The intention of the critical analysis undertaken in this essay is to detail the structural faults of the social practice that orients needs exclusively toward commodities, a redirection of social policies and capital investment so as to reduce our reliance on that mechanism is essential. The result would be an attempt to satisfy our needs in ways that require far less energy and fewer material resources. The new routes would vary considerably in relation to socio-economic, political, technological, cultural, and geographical peculiarities. They cannot be mapped in advance as an inducement to the undertaking. They would be quite different from any of the detailed prescriptions found in the alternative traditions of thought, such as the one that has been mentioned for illustrative purposes in the foregoing remarks. But I cannot believe that we lack the ingenuity to construct any such routes at all.

After experiencing another century of "development" we can give a more precise general guideline for a decisive shift in the direction of social change than could Mill. The conserver society is the ensemble of social policies in the industrially developed nations whose objective would be to lessen the importance of commodities as factors in the satisfaction of human needs and to minimize per capita energy and materials demands. Most future technological innovation would be designed to assist the realization of this objective and to combat the accumulated effects of residual industrial wastes in the environment. One further point is especially important: The transition to the conserver society would represent a form of social progress only if a series of related policies, such as the gradual overcoming of the endemic poverty that exists even in the richest industrialized nations, were an integral part of the objective stated above. If this were not the case, quite obviously the conserver society would simply be another form of impoverished existence for the disadvantaged elements in society.

The two basic points I wish to make about the idea of the conserver society may be summarized as follows. First, it is not an end in itself, but rather an organizing frame of reference for a reorientation of social policy away from quantitative criteria of well-being and toward qualitative criteria. Therefore it should be conceived positively as an intensely dynamic phase of social reorganization, rather than being viewed negatively as the sign of defeat for our cherished ambitions. Second, it is unimportant whether at any particular time the conserver society is characterized by an economic situation of growth, stabilization, or decline in the Gross National Product, for this situation must vary with particular circumstances and needs. The primary desideratum is a reallocation of resources and a reorientation of policies so that the problem of the satisfaction of needs is no longer viewed exclusively as a function of consumption activity. There is a growing tendency among individuals and social agencies, for example, to pay more attention to job satisfaction and shared decision making in production activity. This is the kind of tendency we should strive to encourage.

Mill stipulated that a decent measure of social justice must be a feature of his stationary state. Not absolute social equality, but a "well-paid and affluent body of labourers," a limitation on the accumulation of wealth, and a modest income for those engaged in intellectual pursuits constituted for him some of the social policies to be implemented. Population would also be stabilized: Mill thought that already in his day the desirable level had been reached almost everywhere on the planet. But there is another dimension as well: "Nor is there much satisfaction in contemplating the world with nothing left to the spontaneous activity of nature, with every rood of land brought into cultivation, which is capable of growing food for human beings, every flowery waste or natural pasture ploughed up, all quadrupeds or birds which are not domesticated for man's use exterminated as his rivals for food, every hedgerow or superfluous tree rooted out, and scarcely a place left where a wild shrub or flower could grow without being eradicated as a weed in the name of improved agriculture." The basis of Mill's plea was an aesthetic notion, shared by a number of thinkers in his day, which expressed their belief that the finer sensibilities of mankind were tutored by the experience of undomesticated nature. Today there are different reasons for recalling Mill's concern for the relation of man and nature in the context of a conserver society. The relentless expansion of industrial production and human numbers has rudely shifted the locus of concern from aesthetic education to biological survival. The problem of the impact of human demands on the natural environment has now reached such a magnitude that we must consider the question of human needs as an integral part of a larger network of ecological interactions.*

TOWARDS AN ECOLOGICAL MARXISM

Alienated Consumption and the Dialectic of Shattered Expectations

Our central thesis is that historical changes have invalidated the original Marxian theory of crises as belonging solely to the realm of industrial capitalist production. Today crisis-tendencies have been displaced into the sphere of consumption, replacing economic crisis with ecological crisis. This crisis springs from the inability of capitalism to maintain its present rate of industrial growth required to provision human beings with an endless stream of commodities, provided in the interest of mitigating their alienation. We are going to start from Marx's insight into the nature of capitalist production and attempt to unravel the connection between production, consumption, human needs, commodities, and the environment.

If we are successful in this, we will emerge with a clearer understanding of the imperatives of socialist change. It is our contention that the Marxian theory of alienated production by itself is no longer useful for analyzing modern capitalist crisis-tendencies. We wish to examine shortcomings in Marx's analysis, which, we argue, belongs to an earlier stage in the history of capitalism. It is our argument that the dynamics of social change are embedded in the process of interaction between human needs and commodities and that this process is located in a finite ecosystem.

A Marxian framework for thinking about human needs may enable us to surpass two seemingly conflicting, but implicitly, similar trends in recent Marxism. The first trend can be termed economistic or determinist Marxism (Chapter 2), rooted in the original economic crisis-theory sketched by Marx and Engels. The second trend is exemplified by members of the Frankfurt School such as Max Horkheimer and Theodor Adorno, who were oriented to the critique of domination (Chapter 4), which they articulated in terms of an abstract negation of the present system (offering only meager hopes for radical change). It is our dissatisfaction with the politically disengaged frameworks of both approaches that motivates our search for a concept of human needs that can provide the missing link between a contemporary crisis-theory, not Marx's own, and desiderata of modern class-radicalism.

While many critics have accused Adorno and his Frankfurt colleagues of endorsing a "praxis-less" Marxism, it is our view that what went wrong with the Frankfurt critical theory was its tendency to view all human activity as controlled by the dominating forces emanating from advanced capitalist production. This prevented Adorno from creating a new crisis-theory and a new framework for examining emancipatory thrusts directed against a dominant system. Adorno believed that human beings in advanced capitalism did not, and could not, desire

---

*From William Leiss, *The Limits to Satisfaction* (Toronto: University of Toronto Press, 1976), pp. 104-13.

their own liberation, owing to peremptory ideological forces that fundamentally distorted human needs.

The position advanced here is that Adorno failed to develop a new framework of needs, generating certain self-emancipatory thrusts and class-radicalism, the vital center of Marx's dialectical method, because he and Hork-heimer could not develop a new crisis-theory, to which the reassessment of human needs would be a probable response. Marx did not theorize about needs because he assumed that economic crisis would generate self-emancipatory thrusts required to make a new social order. Adorno believed that in the absence of evident crisis-tendencies in advanced capitalism, self-emancipatory thrusts such as new types of class-radicalism were not forthcoming, allowing him to postulate the existence of self-inflicted domination or what Marcuse later called "false needs."

Our position is that Adorno was not wrong about the praxis-less situation in the United States during the Eisenhower era, or in West Germany during the Adenauer era, but only that he did not foresee new crisis-tendencies looming on the horizon of late capitalism. The purpose of this argument is to relate these crisis-tendencies to the prospect of generating new self-emancipatory thrusts, premised on a framework of needs that are not "false," in Marcuse's sense, and that can therefore underpin the development of these thrusts towards a socialist order.

A theory of needs is essential for understanding the rationale behind social change movements, created in response to severe systemic crises. Needs are molded and transformed in the crucible of structural dynamics (Marx's "internal contradictions"). We wish to show that new crisis-tendencies may produce new constellations of needs that can then provide the dynamics of radical social and political change. Marx's implicit theory of needs, found somewhere beneath the surface of *Capital*, held that members of the working class would revolt because they were unemployed or otherwise impoverished. He did not need to make this assumption explicit for it was, he felt, patently obvious that serious economic crisis, caused by a falling rate of profit, would set the working class into concerted action. His theory of needs in this sense was not "wrong"; rather his estimation of the incipient crisis-tendencies of late nineteenth century capitalism overesti-mated the severity of crises, as it turned out.

A theory of needs illuminates the capacity for self-initiated emancipatory action of human beings in a crisis situation. It is our underlying assumption that human beings derive satisfaction from creative, non-alienated work but not from the endless consumption of symbolically mediated commodities. This sentiment fuels our sketch of explosive crisis-tendencies emerging presently from the wasteful overproduction of these commodities the provisioning of which com-pensates human beings for their time spent in alienated labor. *Because* human beings need creative work and leisure, as our framework of needs suggests, they might react to commodity shortages with a willingness to adopt a radically new style of existence characterized by small-scale, democratically organized produc-tion and "intrinsic" consumption, in which the symbolically mediated appear-ance of commodities is not as important as their substantive use-value.

Thus we would argue that a theory of needs is essential for a post-orthodox socialist theory. Without it, we would have little reason to expect human beings to react to the shattering of their consumer expectations with anything other than resentment and a renewed desire for authoritarian regimes that would supervise the distribution of increasingly scarce commodities.

It was Marx's assumption that capitalism would tend to break down because the accumulation of capital would depress wages and force workers into the ranks of the unemployed. Marx did not foresee the ability of the capitalist mode of production to survive its internal, built-in tendency to accumulate capital at a rate too fast for it to be profitably utilized. It is our argument, amplified in Chapter 3, that socialist revolution did not occur as Marx expected because capitalism consolidated itself between World Wars I and II. This consolidation took the form of the replacement of entrepreneurial, market capitalism with what we term early monopoly capitalism, in which contradictions between capital and labor, abounding during entrepreneurial capitalism, were gradually blunted, if not eliminated altogether. The tendency for the accumulation of capital to outstrip the ability of capitalists to utilize it profitably was reversed during this period, issuing in a realignment of classes and, as a consequence, a fundamental shift in the character of capitalist crisis.

Two developments intervened to postpone capitalism's final collapse: (a) first, the working class in Europe did not seize upon its revolutionary mission, as outlined by Marx and Engels, because it lacked sufficient class consciousness and theoretical and political direction (this is Lukács' argument in his 1923 work, *History and Class Consciousness;* this was due in part to the divisive effects of the outbreak of the First World War, which compromised the international solidarity of western European proletariats); (b) second, capitalist productivity expanded in such a way as to guarantee the provisioning of members of the working class with commodities heretofore reserved for capitalist elites. We must not exaggerate the suddenness of this process, for it occurred very gradually and even imperceptibly at first. Yet Marx's assumption that the fall in the rate of profitability would issue in a final crisis and allow for the transition to socialism went by the boards as market capitalism underwent transformation into a more sophisticated international version, with greater concentration and centralization of capital. Marx exaggerated the tendency of capital to be systematically underutilized. Indeed, capital expanded precisely because the working class, through slow and steady embourgeoisement, was able to afford commodities the exchange of which created greater profit for the capitalist.

A close reading of *Capital* leaves this reader with the impression that Marx simply did not know *how* the system, via crises, would "contradict" itself and collapse. This is not to diminish the analytic profundity of Marx's accomplishment for, more clearly than anyone else, he depicted the fundamentally irrational and anarchic process of social production for private consumption. We would argue that the radically Jacobinesque language of *The Communist Manifesto* (written in 1848) had long since disappeared by 1867, when Marx published the first volume of *Capital* revealing his growing uncertainty about the concrete empirical forms that crisis would take. As we noted in Chapter 1, *Capital* is more an exercise in unravelling the complicated (internally contradictory) logic of capitalist production than a revolutionary blueprint designed to show the working class exactly what to do in the way of freeing itself.

Marx did not adequately analyze the realm of consumption, believing, erroneously, as it turned out, that crisis-tendencies solely within the realm of production (e.g., tendency for the organic composition of capital to rise, tendency for the rate of profit to fall) would spell the collapse of capitalism. As capitalism proved to be more resilient than Marx evidently imagined, his sketchy crisis-theory became even more remote from the concrete circumstance of advanced capitalism. By the end of the Second World War, at the very latest, original Marxism had little to say about strategies of socialist emancipation through crisis-triggered class-radicalism.

It is our contention that the Marxian theory of crises can be reapplied to the present social system. Because we abandon Marx's economic crisis-theory does not mean that we abandon his theory of non-alienated human activity or his theory of contradictions: On the contrary, the only way to salvage Marx's vision and to avoid utopianism is to analyze new forms of crisis such as exist presently in the relationship between symbolically mediated consumption and the threatened environment. Our analysis in this regard assumes that it is possible and even desirable to separate Marx's dialectical method from specific historical applications of his crisis-theory (which animates his dialectical method by allowing us to relate the abstract prospect of class liberation to the concrete forms it might take).

In this sense we contend, albeit polemically, that the continued fixation on the model of class struggle, maintained in the face of large-scale social transformation simply unforeseen by Marx, is the *more* utopian strategy: utopian precisely in the sense of failing to unite crisis-dynamics with a political theory of emancipatory class-praxis. We believe that the ecological crisis-theory developed here is more sensitive to the "internal contradictions" of advanced capitalism, providing a specific empirical outlook on strategies of socialist change.

Replacing the original Marxian model of socialist change, rooted in an archaic crisis-theory, will be a model of change through what we will term *the dialectic of shattered expectations.* This refers to the way in which crisis in the provisioning of goods taken for granted during periods of industrial boom and relative abundance may indeed provoke, willingly or unwillingly, fundamental reassessment of the means to satisfaction. Shattered expectations about the capability of our advanced industrial society to provide us with an endless stream of commodities may eventually turn into its opposite, an appreciation, hard-won, admittedly, of the possibilities for human satisfaction in a world of less-than-total abundance. This is not to argue for a new penury as the means to instill a renewed puritanical spirit but rather for a restructuring of human expectations regarding the nature and quality of the good life. Indeed, the dialectic of shattered expectations may see us through this first period of enforced abstinence (a period we believe is well nigh unavoidable given the current rate of growth of industrial societies and the corresponding rate of waste). Eventually, we submit, people may come to enjoy this newfound simplicity and begin to derive pleasure no longer from symbolically mediated consumption but from small-scale production and from a craft-type of consumption. We do not believe that human beings are creatures with insatiable wants and needs, as the economic conventional wisdom would have it. People can *learn* how much is "enough."

Ecological crisis today requires industrial production to be systematically scaled down. We term this the "ecological imperative" because we agree, following authors like Robert Heilbroner, that industrial civilizations have little alternative to a fundamental reduction of commodity production and consumption. Heilbroner's argument is that unlimited, geometrically expanding industrial growth will result in (a) a shrinking of the world's supply of nonrenewable resources or (b) the overheating of the atmosphere caused by the industrial production process. "Thermal pollution," as Heilbroner has termed it, threatens eventually to melt the polar ice caps. Related to both of the above is the rapid growth of the world's human population, putting added demands on the ecosystem and the atmosphere.

Additionally, Heilbroner feels that growing tensions between developed and underdeveloped nations will result in wars of preemptive seizure. He argues that there is currently a shifting balance of world power created by the energy crisis and the newfound affluence of the Arab oil-producing states. He suggests that these nations could effectively hold up the more advanced and oil-poor nations for ransom. Furthermore, the spread of nuclear technology threatens to generate global terrorism virtually uncontrollable by the present-day nuclear super-powers.

The most compelling part of Heilbroner's argument, and the source of his striking pessimism about the future of the human prospect, is his claim that a new authoritarianism and global dictatorship will be required to reorder global priorities. Heilbroner feels that ecological and political crisis can be averted only by the further centralization of political and economic authority in a super-government that would wield nearly total power. As compelling as his view is, we wish to offer an alternative scenario, not relying on further global centralization to achieve a "no-growth" economy and to scale down industrial production. It is our view that the cooling down of industrial economies requires not the further centralization of political-economic structures but rather their radical decentralization, debureaucratization, and socialization. Our argument is that the best way to control the processes of production and distribution, avoiding wasteful over-production, is to shatter the bureaucratic centralization of capitalist political economies that have grown large and cumbersome. We start from the rudimentary assumption that people directly involved in the production and distribution of commodities can best determine the nature of production; that large, centrally administered political economies suffer both from imperfect knowledge about consumer preferences and from a highly coordinated and manipulative character. Where Heilbroner feels that a degree of political authoritarianism is a practical expedient required to save the planet and the human race, we will argue that there are other possible modes of political and social reorganization that are more decentralized and thus less authoritarian.

At first glance, it appears that Heilbroner's argument is reasonable, to wit, that the ecological imperative can best be mastered through the centralized manipulation of global economies. It is our contention that further centralization of an already centralized global economic system would only have the effect of making people more dependent on a type of alienated consumption designed to compensate them for a nonparticipatory and alienated work-life. Greater dependence on the good graces of central global authorities would *increase* the tendency to equate consumption with happiness and thus to place demands on social systems to produce a never-ending variety of commodities. Heilbroner's further centralization of global political economies would immediately set up countervailing pressure from consumers who would work off their dissatisfaction about political authoritarianism by throwing themselves even more maniacally into consumption behavior. It might be responded that Heilbroner's political authoritarianism allegedly required to bring into being a no-growth economy, and thus saving the ecology of the planet, would brook no such "demands" from below. Our answer is that either political authoritarianism must be total, all socio-economic decisions being taken by a small centralized elite, or else there will be a tendency for public demands on the system to escalate rapidly. An example of this latter process is in the Soviet Union where the loosening of totalitarian controls since the death of Stalin has allowed consumer demand to reach an all-time high level. The current Soviet regime finds that it is politically unwise to ignore forever the demands of the man or woman in the street for more and better shoes, clothes, washing machines, and cars.

We argue that on its own terms the further global centralization of production and consumption would prove inefficient in terms of the ecologically sane allocation of commodities. It would also prove to be inimical to the purpose of creating a democratic community and of reeducating the consumer away from endless, addictive consumption and towards other modes of the pursuit of satisfaction. Heilbroner ends his book with the wistful hope that human beings might eventually come to define happiness less in terms of qualitative consumption (how many things) and more in terms of quantitative consumption (better culture, art, spiritual enjoyment, and fulfillment). We argue that his authoritarian political solution to the ecological imperative will have the effect of accelerating the tendency to define happiness purely in terms of expanding consumption, creating severe political tensions when centralized global authorities decide that human beings have had "enough" of a certain commodity.

Our argument for decentralization does not mean that we necessarily oppose any concept of central socialist planning; we do not advocate a return to the fabled pure marketplace of entrepreneurial capitalism when supply allegedly would meet demand. Instead there may exist an intermediate organizational format, in between total planning and the anarchy of the marketplace, that can allow production and consumption to be rationally determined.

Our argument is hinged on the notion that the structural weaknesses of capitalism and state-socialism create a situation in which human beings are impelled to seek satisfaction through high-intensity personal consumption, thus accelerating the growth of industry and placing further pressures upon an already fragile ecosystem. In short, *lack of self-expressive freedom and meaning in work results in a debilitating dependence on consumption behavior.*

Economic crises of the sort Marx envisaged have not wrecked the system. In the intervening years the manipulation and coordination of consumption has prolonged the life of the capitalist system. This has taken place in two interrelated ways:

1. First, the manipulation of consumption has allowed the rate of profit to remain relatively high, checking the tendency for a capitalist system to overproduce unwanted commodities.
2. Second, and most important here, the manipulation of consumption has allowed human beings to satisfy themselves without being directly involved in the management of the production process.

In other words, the reason for the geometric expansion of industrial productivity, in Heilbroner's sense, is precisely located in the political function of alienated consumption. Both capitalist and socialist states protect their public legitimacy by providing a nearly constant flow of commodities for personal consumption. Marx neglected the analysis of this process because he felt that the central internal contradiction in capitalism was not the distorted relationship between production and consumption (and the ability of managed consumption to bleed off potentially revolutionary human alienation) but the contradiction within the realm of production itself between the private nature of ownership and the increasingly socialized nature of the production process.

Thus we reject Heilbroner's argument for further centralization of global economies because we believe that only by decentralizing these economies can a viable, non-distorted relationship be restored between production and consumption. We have two motives in mind:

1   We wish, along with Heilbroner, to halt the trend towards endless industrial growth; we contend that the best way to halt exponential growth is to realign production and consumption in such a way as to allow consumers to tell producers "how much is enough" for a decent level of material well-being.
2. We wish to transform social systems that frustrate human desires for freedom and creativity—Marx's vision of "praxis"—by managing consumption in such a way as to leave human beings few media for the satisfaction of needs other than personal consumption.

Alienated consumption, as we term it, refers to the way in which human beings compensate themselves for boring, uncreative, and often underpaid work-lives by engaging in the acquisition of commodities. This process of acquisition is not a straightforward fitting needs to the mundane appearance of commodities. The more complex process involves the fitting of needs to certain brand-name products and not the "pure" products themselves. While all consumption involves a certain matching of needs to the appearance of commodities (hunger to the appearance of bread, for example) the unique features of advanced industrial society and its high-intensity market setting are (a) the complexity of the relationship between needs and commodities, mediated through advertising, and (b) the preoccupation of people with consumption as the sole source of the satisfaction of needs.

Marx wrote in an era when capitalism had not advanced to the point where there was either a complex relationship between needs and the appearance of commodities, presented in advertising, or a near-total identification of human satisfaction and consumption. In advanced capitalist society alienation also takes the form of human dissatisfaction with the world of work and the corresponding tendency to derive meaning purely from the consumption of symbolically mediated commodities. Human beings live for leisure-time when they can escape a highly coordinated and centralized production process (be they blue-collar or white-collar workers) and when they can fulfill their nascent creativity through consumption.

This is not a totally unhappy picture for those who in earlier times might have been destitute at the hands of a burgeoning capitalism, when contradictions, in Marx's sense, were sharper. In no sense are we indicting the productive capacity of capitalism to satisfy basic material needs. We are questioning only the tendency to overproduce symbolically mediated commodities in order to appease human beings basically frustrated by routinizing, imperatively coordinated, and alienated occupations. This tendency towards overproduction is both ecologically disruptive and wasteful and "bad" in itself, inadequately compensating human beings for alienated, managed work-lives.

The casual reader might construe our argument as a plea for regression to a pre-industrial past, not "cursed" with abundance. Others might imagine that we intend to offer a set of particular "true" consumer needs that will not result in environmental or moral degradation. We wish to do neither. Ours is more a descriptive than a prescriptive exercise. We must now explain what we think will happen when the industrial production of symbolically mediated commodities begins to slow.

Initially (and there is already substantial evidence for this, culled from the recent energy crisis in North America in the early 1970s) human beings might react with despair to the shrinking supply of commodities. They have, reasonably in many cases, come to expect their "dose" of material abundance as a reward for ungratifying labor. Expectations about the promise of eternal abundance will be rudely shattered by incipient ecological crises, met, inexorably, by a cooling down of industrial production. However, it is our view that these shattered expectations may have their own unintended consequences: We suspect that the initially rude awakening to a world of limited supplies will eventually create an entirely new set of responses and hopes within human beings conditioned to equate happiness with symbolically mediated consumption.

Shattered expectations may soon pass as human beings adjust, almost naturally, it may be hoped, to a steady-state economy. The cooling down of industrial production need not return us to the proverbial dark ages, for we will be able to live off the accumulated wealth of our incomparably rich industrial civilization. What we are saying is that human beings might begin systematically to rethink their values with respect to the relationship between human needs and commodities once this reality of a no-growth economy is perceived as a *fait accompli,* as inevitably it must be. The reliance on symbolically mediated consumption as the sole means of human satisfaction may be broken as people formulate new expectations about what their lives should offer.

It is in this dynamic process, termed here the dialectic of shattered expectations, that we find the most compelling impetus to socialist change. There must be no misunderstanding about the effects of ecological crisis, for they will initially destroy many of our time-worn values and concepts, throwing many of us into a state of serious bewilderment about our collective future. It takes little imagination to recognize that the cooling down of industrial production will force us to get by with fewer modern "conveniences," requiring us to spend more time performing rudimentary chores such as baking our own bread, walking instead of driving, and eating less grain-fed meat in favor of more nutritious and ecologically less wasteful non-meat sources of protein. For many this will seem like the end of the world. Yet the limiting of symbolically mediated consumption may force us towards a fundamental reevaluation of the realm of work, from which endless consumption is only a temporary escape.

In spite of our reluctance to develop a definitive list of "true needs," we believe that human happiness consists in a combination of fulfilling labor and rewarding consumption—in this we draw our inspiration from Marx's 1844 manuscripts. Symbolically mediated consumption that provides the sole source of human meaning for many is alienated, in our terminology, precisely because it accepts an alienated work-life as an inevitable condition of material abundance. Marx in his early writings offers a perspective on human freedom that stresses the self-expressive, self-externalizing character of non-alienated production. In this sense, he implicitly rejects the dualism of necessity and freedom that is often used as a justification of the division of human existence into work and leisure components (work being "necessary labor" and leisure being "freedom").

The key to breaking through alienated consumption, which we contend is but a pale copy of real freedom and which, in any case, must soon come to a halt given certain ecological imperatives, is the reconstruction of production to make it less alienating. By so doing, we could allow people to scale down their consumption needs and to break through an over-reliance on symbolically mediated consumption. As we conceive of it, this process, in rough outline form, would have three interrelated steps:

1. The inability of the ecosystem to support endless growth will require the cooling down of industrial production oriented to providing an endless stream of symbolically mediated commodities for personal consumption.
2. This will require that human beings initially scale down their needs and ultimately rethink their patterns of need, shifting away from the identification of happiness purely with symbolically mediated consumption.
3. This rethinking of patterns of need might allow alienated consumption to become what we call "productive leisure" and "creative work." Human beings would reenter the realm of work no longer perceiving it as a source of wealth to be applied to future consumption. They could realize their own essential desires and values in the activity of socially useful production (and, indeed, this would change the very meaning of social utility, including certain nonmaterial values such as the arts).

The dialectic of shattered expectations might allow people to realign their values and desires. While we do not value penury in itself, it just might be that a diminished sense of material abundance could initiate this process of the reevaluation of the means to satisfaction. In this way, social change might result from human efforts to master the real threat of ecological crisis, allowing us to emerge from a crisis period with newfound resilience and additional flexibility in the ways we derive meaning and satisfaction from our behavior.

This would in part depend upon a *further* rationalization and automation of industrial production. Ours is not, as we noted above, a pre-industrial scenario; but nor is it post-industrial in that it presupposes thoroughgoing automation of every productive task (a sheer impossibility at this point). Instead, we envision a *mixed* technology that combines automation in certain sectors of production with small-scale technology in other sectors. The schema demands a reconceptualization of the traditional outlook on the relationship between production and consumption, shared by most Marxists and non-Marxists alike.

The traditional view holds that socially necessary labor (defined in terms of the production of what Marx called use-values, required for the reproduction of human life) requires the abandonment of personal creativity, spontaneous thought and action, and a non-authoritarian relationship with fellow workers. Marx in later works inclined to this view, although our intention here is to use early Marx's insights into the possible identity of work and leisure against the later Marx's more traditional views on the dualism of work and leisure.

The traditional view, as we have called it, assumes that freedom can only exist outside of work, in the domain of leisure time. Our argument is that leisure time in the contemporary world tends to be filled with symbolically mediated consumption as the sole source of its meaning. The imperatively coordinated, authoritarian character of work forces human beings to seek their satisfaction in leisure-time consumption. Marxists have ignored this because they felt that internal contradictions within production would produce revolutionary transformation. As we have argued, this has not occurred because capitalism managed to shunt off its crisis-tendencies into the realm of consumption, rewarding people for lives of imperatively coordinated labor with time away from work spent in symbolically mediated consumption.

Because most Marxists have apparently accepted the traditional view, that labor and freedom are fundamentally incompatible, they have neglected the realm of consumption. Specifically, they have not attended to an analysis of the possible reconstruction of the realm of consumption, assuming, wrongly, we argue, that once alienation in the sphere of production has been eliminated then human needs will be able to attain free expression and satisfaction. This has not happened because alienated consumption only *fuels* the system of alienated production, allowing capital accumulation and reinvestment to continue and, more crucially, compensating people for frustrating, unfulfilling labor. Those Marxists who persist in concentrating only on crises in the realm of production fail to see that these crisis-tendencies have shifted into the realm of consumption, replacing economic crisis with ecological crisis.

We contend that the resolution of ecological crisis will feed back into the realm of production, ultimately (a) destroying the imperatively coordinated character of certain types of work by debureaucratizing and democratizing the production process (via small-scale technology and workers' control), or (b) automating those sectors of production that resist debureaucratization and democratization.

The impetus for this feedback will come not from the suddenly changed consciousness of consumers (trained for years in the expectations and values of alienated consumption) but from the imperious character of ecological crisis (supply and resource shortages) that will force a change of consumer behavior and, if we are lucky, a transformation of the capitalist world of work.

The dialectic of shattered expectations may produce, first, a reformulation of human needs, and, second, a revised attitude towards the possibilities of attaining satisfaction from labor. A non-alienated society, in our mind's eye, is not merely one that has achieved a no-growth economy; it must also allow people self-expression through their productive activity.

Decentralizing and Debureaucratizing Industrial-Capitalist Society

Our prior analysis of alienated consumption and the ecological pressures it generates leads us to more concrete speculation about the reorganization of advanced industrial-capitalist society. Our two key concepts, "decentralization" and "debureaucratization," apply equally to technical (production) processes and to social and political processes. We contend that by decentralizing and debureaucratizing modern life we can preserve the integrity of the environment (limiting industrial growth), and, in the process, qualitatively transform the dominant socio-economic-political institutions of advanced capitalist society.

The influential book by the late E. F. Schumacher, *Small Is Beautiful: Economics As If People Mattered,* has defined the terms of what we shall call small-scale technology. Schumacher's argument is that there is no compelling rationale for the highly centralized character of large-scale industrial production. He calls for an "appropriate technology," which shifts away from the highly centralized character of modern industrial production, arguing from a variety of moral and political premises that bigness is not necessarily best. Schumacher suggests that the goal of human life should not be the endless acquisition of commodities but the discovery of harmonies between needs and consumption. In this sense Schumacher is fundamentally dissatisfied with the process of alienated consumption we described in the preceding section. However, Schumacher's critique of industrial bigness and of the consumerist life styles it generates is not a radical one. He is unable to link his concept of a small-scale technology to the qualitative transformation of dominant socio-political institutions.

We wish to "borrow" Schumacher's vision of a new kind of technological organization and put it to use within our radical theory of technology and ecology. Schumacher is not enough of a Marxist in the way he approaches the subject of technology; he does not come to grips with the nature of a capitalist society that *relies upon* the centralization of production as a stock-in-trade of its social control of human beings, who become dependent on these centralized mechanisms for their livelihood and for their consumer activities. Schumacher, in short, does not adequately grasp the interlocking character of technology and social structure and thus he is prevented from making his critique of industrial bigness a central weapon in the creation of a socialist theory of technological change.

It is unclear just how Schumacher would apply the concept of a small-scale technology in advanced industrial-capitalist society; indeed he often seems more concerned with the "development" of underdeveloped Third World nations than with First and Second World industrialized societies. Schumacher, with many others, suggests cogently that development of backward societies need not be premised on the type of industrialization that took place in the West. Indeed small-scale technology draws heavily from the particular cultural and socio-political circumstances of societies in adjusting itself to those circumstances, and not riding roughshod over cultural habits and norms by imposing a single model of industrial organization. But the Schumacherian perspective is ill-equipped to explain how the immense power of capitalism can be dented in order to re-organize industrial-capitalist society along the lines of small-scale technology.

By radicalizing Schumacher's vision, we can uncover the sociopolitical significance of small-scale technology. In other words, we can explore the interlocking character of technical and sociopolitical dimensions with respect to the notion of a decentralized technology. Small-scale technology, in the capitalist context, implies not only a reorganization of the technical process of capitalist industrial production but also a reorganization of the power relations of that social order.

The justifying theory of large-scale centralized technology has always been that it is more "efficient" than dispersed regional and local technologies. The sociological justification of this approach is found in the long tradition of Weberian sociology, rooted in Max Weber's seminal writings on bureaucracy and authority. Weber suggested that the requirements of modern industrial society were for hierarchical, impersonal organizations of producers called "bureaucracies." While Weber personally had reservations about how humane these forms would ultimately be, he gave rise to a tradition of sociology built upon the alleged necessity of bureaucracies in industrial social orders. Our concept of a small-scale technology fundamentally opposes the Weberian sociology of bureaucracy because we argue that it is *possible* to organize the production process democratically *given* its decentralization. Our approach depends upon developing an anti-bureaucratic theory of industrial production, in this way underpinning our notion that Schumacher's concept of small-scale technology can indeed be radicalized (and, on that basis, grounding the contention we make that the ecology movement in general can be radicalized).

Weber said that bureaucracy was characterized by political hierarchy and a top-to-bottom chain of command. The industrial process was to be managed by experts and professionals who would imperatively coordinate the mass of laborers "below" them. Each of these laborers, be they office workers or manual workers, would contribute his or her small share to the total production process, engaging in a highly fragmented task that would have to be coordinated from above for the final product to emerge at the end (the final product could be a memorandum or an automobile; the principle in each case is the same).

We have two objections to the Weberian scheme. First, it is unconvincing to say that hierarchical, top-to-bottom control is necessary for industrial production. Second, we do not accept the high degree of the fragmentation of labor the bureaucratic form most often presupposes.

We would contend that the hierarchical coordination of labor is unnecessary where the workers trust each other and do not fear exploitation from outside. Industrial production, we contend, does not depend on "smart" people telling "stupid" people what to do. The distinction between mental and manual labor is fundamental to the rise of industrial-capitalist society. It is a distinction that keeps the worker in bondage, requiring him to submit to imperative coordination by managers, bosses, and professionals.

Furthermore, hierarchical organizations establish their legitimacy on the basis of this distinction between the smart and the stupid. It is a powerful aspect of capitalist ideology, as Marx would have termed it, that some are unable to make decisions about the production process and therefore must be relegated to positions of manual work and political passivity. Bureaucracy in this sense is a self-fulfilling prophecy: If people believe that bureaucracy is necessary for industrial organization, they tend to accept the hierarchical chain of command and the separation of manual and mental labor bureaucracy presupposes.

Our second objection to the Weberian approach is its fragmentation of the labor process. It is not self-evident that industrial production must be minutely subdivided for sophisticated production. As with the hierarchical forms of bureaucracy, we contend that the highly developed division of labor into myriad separate tasks only serves to keep the worker essentially powerless in face of managerial expertise that organizes that divided labor. Recent experiments in the Volvo automobile plants in Sweden indicate that the assembly-line system may be no more efficient than a smaller-scale, more democratized system of production (where small teams of workers produce a finished automobile, participating in a whole variety of subdivided tasks). It is our central assumption that the more labor is divided and fragmented, the more that it is experienced as uncreative and unfulfilling by the worker. This should not be taken to mean that we oppose the division of labor in general (i.e., the division of society into different productive roles) but rather that we oppose the fragmentation of the labor process with respect to the production of a particular product, like the Volvo automobile. Numerous industrial sociologists in western countries have shown that the more the worker participates in the total production process, the less estranged he will subsequently be from his work as a whole.

Thus we oppose the two central assumptions of the Weberian theory of bureaucracy, which in turn underpins the centralization and bureaucratization of the industrial production process as we know it in advanced capitalist society (and, parenthetically, as it has developed also in the Soviet Union, where Weberian bureaucracy and the so-called "scientific management" ideology it generates are held in esteem by the ruling communists). We believe that there is nothing intrinsic to industrial production that requires workers to be powerless with respect to decisions taken in the factory or office or that requires workers to be subject to a highly fragmented production process. It is our contention that there can be a democratically organized and coordinated production process developed in the context of small-scale technology that liberates workers from bureaucratic organizations.

Where small-scale technology results from the decentralization of technology, the democratization of the working process results from the debureaucratization of industrial organizations. Without the one there cannot be the other. Decentralization by itself is not a revolutionary concept; it needs to be accompanied by direct *workers' control* of the production process (i.e., the debureaucratization and self-management of the production process).

The notion of workers' control arises from the political traditions of Marxism, anarcho-syndicalism and anarchism. Workers' control has been instituted in modern Yugoslavia as a way of creating a non-authoritarian alternative to the Soviet system, which venerates the Weberian concept of bureaucratic organization. We can learn much about the possibility of radicalizing the conserver society from the Yugoslavian experience with workers' control and industrial self-management. Schumacher's insights, on this view, need to be joined with the Yugoslavian system of workers' control.

Workers do not control the means of production in capitalist economies (and they obviously do not own those means of production). Marx in his earlier philosophical manuscripts argued that control of the means of production was every bit as important as ownership of those means in terms of the liberation of the working class. Conceivably, the working class could legally own the factories, as in the Soviet Union, and yet remain captive victims of a system of alienated production (where the real control of the factories resides with a Communist Party vanguard and their appointed bureaucrats).

Our earlier discussion of Weber's concept of bureaucracy must now be shifted into more political terms. We argued that effective decentralization of industrial production would only lead to socialist change if it were accompanied by the abolition of: (1) the hierarchical organization of labor and (b) the minute fragmentation of the working process. We must now add a third feature of radical social change: (c) the transformation of imposed capitalist control into self-imposed workers' control. This third feature "Marxizes" the notion of debureaucratization; without it we would be left with the possibility that the working process might be suitably democratized and rendered small-scale while the external relations of the workers with capitalists would remain intact. It is possible to have decentralization and debureaucratization in a prison. We must develop the notion that the democratization of the working process can be coupled with a political-economic program that returns ownership (as well as control) to the worker. In Yugoslavia, the debureaucratization of the working process has not been advanced far enough; workers still remain largely captive of a system of imperatively coordinated and minutely subdivided labor. What is distinctive about the

Yugoslav system is the way in which workers own the means of production cooperatively and thus to some extent make fundamental decisions about the disposition (and investment) of the so-called surplus product of their labor.

In Yugoslavia workers' control involves primarily the elimination of the political control of the production process by the Soviet-style state. Indeed in Yugoslavia the free market is utilized to depoliticize economic decision making as much as possible. It does not do this completely for workers do not, in each and every factory, spontaneously determine the amount and character of their production. An uneasy balance has been struck between sociopolitical requirements, determined centrally, and direct workers' control in each enterprise.

The working process in Yugoslavia has not been debureaucratized in the first two senses noted above. There is still a fragmented division of labor in every enterprise (many of which are rooted in the assembly-line system). There is also bureaucratization (or the chain-of-command pattern) of authority and decision making. The concept of the workers' council, on which each worker sits for a limited period of time, eliminates the external manipulation of the working process by the state, but it does *not* prevent the specialization and professionalization of technical decision making within the plant. In others words, barriers still remain between professional managers and manual laborers (although these lines are more blurred than in either capitalist or Soviet-style societies).

Workers' control defuses the utter centralization and politicization of the production process. In this way the concept of workers' control "Marxizes" our program of radical social change via ecological crisis theory. It is the missing link between decentralization and debureaucratization, on the one hand, and the traditional Marxist goal of non-alienated labor on the other.

We take Marx's vision of socialist freedom to mean that workers, under communism, must be directly involved in managing their own labor process. Workers' control, in the Yugoslavian sense, goes *part* way towards that goal. Marx gave equal weight to ownership and control of the means of production. The Yugoslavian model allows workers to link the abstract goal of the socialist ownership of the means of production with a politically decentralized type of structure (the workers' council). The Yugoslavs, however, have not been able to move toward full decentralization and debureaucratization of the working process because they are still concerned to preserve the central authority of the League of Communists (whose hegemony would be clearly threatened by full debureaucratization).

The Yugoslavian system of socialist ownership is rooted in workers' control (via the workers' council), while the Soviet system (the predominant model of state-socialist societies today) is rooted in state control. The orthodox Marxian conception, developed during the Second and Third Internationals, endorsed the model of state control ("dictatorship of the proletariat" interpreted as government by a vanguard party) as an intermediate stage on the route to full socialism. In the Soviet Union, the state owns the means of production and the workers "are" the state (as the official ideology has it). In Yugoslavia the workers own the means of production: This is termed "social ownership" to distinguish it from socialist ownership that the Soviets interpret as *state* control.

Our point here is that socialist ownership can itself be understood in terms of a continuum between centralized and decentralized polarities. Socialist ownership in the Soviet Union is highly centralized (concentrating political and economic authority in the Kremlin) while socialist ownership in Yugoslavia is highly decentralized (authority to make investment decisions and the like residing in the workers' councils of each industrial enterprise). We would contend that the degree of decentralization of socialist ownership relates positively to the degree of debureaucratization. In other terms, the potential for full-scale debureaucratization of social life is much greater in a system of decentralized socialist ownership (workers' control) than in a system of centralized socialist ownership (state control).

Decentralization *in vacuo* can exist in any type of ideological system. Decentralization coupled with socialist ownership *tends* to produce full debureaucratization. In terms of our ecological concerns, decentralization might be sufficient to ensure environmental protection (e.g., solar energy employed in the North American capitalist system). This decentralization, coupled with workers' control appropriately understood, might also produce radical social change in the direction of debureaucratized socialism.

Exactly how does decentralized socialist ownership become full debureaucratization? What does the Yugoslav system lack? First, it lacks full technological-industrial decentralization. Second, it has not abolished the technical division of labor, the regime of technocrats, the assembly-line system, etc. In terms of the first consideration—decentralization—it is feared that there must be some degree of political and economic centralization in a society threatened by foreign powers. Many Yugoslavian industrial sociologists worry that the workers' council system is rapidly becoming an ideological prop that conceals deep-seated bureaucratic domination.

The basic lesson to be learned from our discussion of socialist ownership is that there is no single model after which radical change might be patterned. Our interest here is to *link* Marxist change with an ecological crisis-theory and thus our interests are best served by a combination of decentralized socialist ownership (contra-state control) and debureaucratization of the division of labor. We oppose the political centralization of "socialist" societies (e.g., the USSR) and we oppose the technological centralization of large-scale, energy-wasteful production processes. As we cautioned above, it may be possible to have a decentralized (or at least an energy-conserving) technology in a capitalist society. As Heilbroner argues, it may be possible to have a steady-state capitalism, with no industrial growth. Thus the technological-ecological issue of centralization cannot be considered in isolation from the sociological-political issue of bureaucratization. What is compelling about the notion of workers' control is that it so easily lends itself *both* to the decentralization of industrial production and to the full debureaucratization and dealienation of modern social life.

Marx's basic model of human needs stressed the need for creative labor. Our non-authoritarian socialism would allow and indeed encourage human beings to seek alternatives to commodity consumption as the means to their satisfaction. Small-scale, debureaucratized, collectively organized production would become an end in itself. The work-leisure dichotomy would be abolished as the barrier between "necessary" work and "free" work was blurred. The solution to the problem of alienated consumption is not to eliminate fast-food restaurant chains or advertising but to provide people with fundamental alternatives to this type of consumption. It is our contention that these alternatives will probably not be provided within a capitalist system of wage-labor but only in a system of decentralized socialist ownership (with a requisite degree of debureaucratization). The capitalist system requires the separation of work and leisure and thus it has no "interest" in providing workers with fundamental alternatives to alienated consumption.

How, exactly, might the ecology movement be guided in a Marxist direction so that we can develop this "third way" between energy-wasteful capitalism and energy-wasteful authoritarian socialism? Answers at this point are difficult to formulate. We are *not* saying that the whole system can be moved towards ecological socialism simply because small pockets of human beings in capitalist society are able to overcome alienated consumption and to find non-alienated work. This strikes us as a naive and idealistic scenario that will shatter in the face of massive corporate power. To put this differently, how do we convince workers not only that their alienated consumption is energy-wasteful and personally stultifying but *also* that qualitative change lies in a system of decentralized socialist ownership? Even if we convince workers of this, how do we emancipate them from their alienated jobs (in the office or factory)?

How, in general terms, can the class-struggle be made to focus on issues of ecological radicalism? Our answer is tinged with pessimism for we see no appreciable evidence that socialist political parties or trade unions have moved very far towards a concept of non-authoritarian decentralized socialist ownership. What would be required is a fundamental restructuring of socialist theory in a direction that would make compatible Marx's theory of alienated labor and a critique of ecological crisis-tendencies. Until workers see the fundamental *relatedness* of their lives as producers and as consumers they will not appreciate ecological Marxism. A left-wing ecology movement need not abandon traditional Marxist goals such as socialist ownership; we contend precisely that by reformulating socialist ownership as the foundation stone of a decentralized and debureaucratized social order we strengthen its roots in the non-authoritarian tradition to which Marx definitely belongs. By developing the concept of a decentralized socialism we protect Marx's vision of socialist ownership against those centralists who interpret socialist ownership as state control.

This may all sound too good to be true — the perfect harmony of man and nature, snatching socialist ideals from the jaws of ecological crisis. Our conceptual model is indeed the epitome of harmony in this regard. However, we would readily admit that there is as yet no suitable program of class-radicalism through which to bring this into being. We are not sanguine that these radical measures can spring from within the heart of capitalism or that, if they can, they will have much systematic impact. What is needed is a coherent and pragmatic theory of how we move towards socialist ownership in advanced capitalist systems. Our optimism is about the conceptual dynamics of a non-authoritarian, ecologically-sane socialism: Our pessimism comes in face of the present-day realities of power and ideology that seem to prevent its realization.

The likely response of the large corporations to our radical challenge, and of their political representatives in Washington and Ottawa, would be towards political authoritarianism and not towards emancipation. We could envisage a contraction of civic freedoms in face of the popular demand for the end of a system of alienated wage-labor (and the abolition of alienated consumption). Heilbroner, too, worries that the authoritarian tendencies of capitalist society would come to the fore if a stationary-state were to be instituted. Limits to growth would mean the end of the working class dream of further embourgeoisement. The working class is kept at bay by the abstract promise of further enrichment by a capitalist system that depends on endless production and consumption. This promise would be dashed if a stationary capitalism were to emerge. This would spell an authoritarian political solution, for the dominant classes would not brook, and this is precisely our fear, the egalitarian redistribution of wealth and power. The class-interest of capitalists would prevent them from advocating non-authoritarian steady-state socialism. They would have no alternative but to repress the socialist demands of the working class.

We fear that this solution is the more probable one. While Heilbroner's pessimism flows from his assumption that a super-national global dictatorship will be required to prevent ecological catastrophe, we worry that capitalist nation-states will still continue to resist the move towards socialist ownership (required, we believe, to abolish alienated labor and also to save our ecosystem by abolishing wasteful overproduction). The cycle of repression and domination will be perpetuated. Breaking this cycle depends on the overthrow of capitalist power, a difficult task at best.

A non-authoritarian system, if it could be built on the grounds of vanished capitalism, could also be an energy-conserving, small-scale, debureaucratized social order. We do not accept Heilbroner's notion that socialist societies are monolithic and would all respond weakly to the so-called ecological imperative; we can *imagine* a type of socialism that is energy-conserving. A particular type of decentralized, debureaucratized socialism would be the perfect breeding ground for a new ecological consciousness, which would arise both as a response to the ecological imperative and in opposition to what we have termed alienated consumption.

The liberal-left ecology movement stagnates because it fails to link up its twin goals of decentralization and debureaucratization with the traditional Marxist goal of socialist ownership. The stark reality of capitalist power prevents the ecological left from moving beyond Schumacher's "small-scale technology" towards a full-blown concept of workers' controlled socialism. Capitalism flourishes even where it overproduces and overpollutes: This reality frames our discussion, below, about a new socialist ideology, arising from North American soil, that can take into account the reality of capitalist power.

Populism and Marxism

Let us now reconsider the class struggle from a different vantage point. Let us speculate not about how we can dislodge corporate power but rather about the ideological requirements of this new movement of ecological radicals. We have assumed that traditional Marxists will open their minds to an ecological radicalism; we must now discuss ways in which non-Marxists might adopt this perspective, beginning with liberal and even conservative assumptions about industrial society and socialist change.

Socialist ideology, traditionally conceived, is an ineffective means for promoting new speculation about the relationship of ecology and socialist change. A different basis must be found for fomenting organized resistance to the capitalist system of wage-labor and to the alienated consumption it generates. We will argue below that a combination of populism and Marxism might be a more opportune basis for creating a North American Marxism. This is not to ignore the aims of socialist ideology, which we have sketched in our preceding section, but rather to reformulate the theoretical and political vocabulary in which these aims are usually articulated. Marxism has lost touch with organized labor in the United States and Canada (except in its most watered-down forms of parliamentary social democracy). For this reason, we will go outside the Marxist political tradition in seeking a new basis for an ideology that might generate the type of organized class-radicalism we desire.

Instead of starting with the goal of socialist ownership, the zero point for most Marxists, we start at the other end of the continuum we described in the preceding section. We will instead begin with the notion of debureaucratization and attempt to work back towards socialist ownership. If it is possible to stimulate workers' consciousness with the prospect of a debureaucratized and decentralized society, then the process of socialist change might feasibly begin not with the traditional socialist program (nationalization of industry, workers' control, general strikes, and the like) but rather with different types of emancipatory ideologies.

This new ideology can emerge, we believe, from the cultural and political basis of American populism. This basis provides the foundation for a sustained critique of *centralist bigness* from which ecological Marxism might then proceed. The ingrained suspicion of big government and big business in the United States can be bent in a socialist direction. The deep-seated populism of American political life lends itself well to our ecological radicalism hinged on the three fundamental notions of decentralization, debureaucratization, and socialist ownership. What is missing from American populism, in both its right- and left-wing variants, is the socialist component (Marxism). Our consideration in this concluding section is the possibility of grafting Marxism onto American populism in such a way as to provide this missing link that, we contend, will generate a full-blown radical critique of ecology and socialist change.

Modern alienation involves a feeling of helplessness in face of the bureaucratization of all forms of existence, work and non-work. It may be possible to tap these sources of alienation by showing workers that a debureaucratized socialist order would liberate them from stultifying office and factory routines and from the technical division of labor. Advanced capitalism might be shown to be first and foremost a system that depends for its functioning on the fragmentation and imperative (bureaucratic) coordination of labor. If workers could mount a critique of this process of the fragmentation and bureaucratization of labor, then they could generate demands for new forms of sociopolitcal organization and, ultimately, for socialist ownership (conceived in terms of workers' control and not state control). At present, North American workers have only the vaguest ideas about what a non-capitalist order would look like, employing traditional formulations like the dictatorship of the proletariat to flesh out these vague images. It is our purpose to provide a theoretical vocabulary more suitable to North Americans in which these images might be expressed.

The critique of bureaucratization might initially proceed on the basis of a critique of the division of labor. The helplessness of the average citizen in face of technocracy and professionalism, bureaucratically organized and institutionalized, might be the point of ingress of this critique. The wage-labor relationship is the fundamental economic relationship of our social order (pertaining to production); the most fundamental relationship pertaining to consumption and culture is the relationship between the expert and nonexpert. We maintain that a social change movement might be erected on the basis of a critique of the second relationship, which could then spill over into a critique of the wage relationship (as the critique of bureaucratization moved beyond into a critique of capitalist ownership).

Our notion here is that emancipatory impulses may emerge not from the experiences of alienated labor per se but from the experience of alienated, coordinated *consumption*. Workers are increasingly dissatisfied with the way all aspects of social life require bureaucratization and the development of expert-nonexpert relationships. This is why we suggest that the "other" face of alienated labor is the feeling of existential helplessness and incompetence in face of institutions organized hierarchically in terms of the hegemony of experts. The experience of this incompetence might be the point of departure for a new socialist ideology that begins with a critique of bureaucracy and the division of labor and ends with a full-blown critique of capitalism.

In our section on alienated consumption, above, we indicated that the dialectic of shattered expectations might move people to think beyond capitalist socioeconomic arrangements. But this is not to happen without bringing into being a new emancipatory ideology on the basis of which frustrated consumers can mount a critique of the existing capitalist system in its entirety. In our earlier section we appeared to say that the frustrated expectations of infinite consumers would unproblematically issue in socialist change. It is now necessary to develop the meaning of a legitimation-crisis in the realm of consumption, for on its basis we can better understand the prospects of socialist change as they relate to the ecological imperative.

Ecological crisis-tendencies, we have averred, will force industrial economies to undergo a process of cooling down with respect to commodity production. This will initially frustrate workers for whom, in systems of alienated labor, endless consumption is perceived as the only source of meaning and purpose. But we are arguing that this frustration might eventually take the form of a critique of capitalism, ultimately abandoning alienated consumption as an insufficient "escape" from alienated labor.

Such a critique would be rooted in the frustration that most working people feel at the hands of authorities and experts who administer nearly every aspect of everyday life. Social change may arise out of demands that professionals and experts not be allowed to usurp all decision-making functions in consumption and production; that many of these functions can be returned to groups of self-determining human beings. Liberation thus *begins* not with socialist owner-ship but with the restructuring of the division of labor and its bureaucratic elements.

Socialist ideology often lacks sufficient focus on the internal aspects of the working process; Marx never reduced alienation to economic exploitation but rather argued convincingly that alienated labor was the result of systems of wage-labor and class domination that both bound the worker to the capitalist through the wage relationship and to a production process that he could not control. Our earlier discussion of workers' control clarified various dimensions of alienated labor. We argued that socialist ownership implies either state control of the means of production or direct workers' control of the means of production. In the former case, socialist ownership remains fundamentally alienating for work-ers do not control the production process. Thus alienated labor exists under the Soviet system despite the fact that workers legalistically own the means of production (via the state, which represents them, according to Soviet ideology and law).

We argued that socialist ownership must be conceived in terms of workers' control (and, further, in terms of industrial-technological decentralization and, finally, debureaucratization). Similarly, a critique of the division of labor can broaden out into the endorsement of a non-authoritarian type of socialist ownership. In cultures where Marxist traditions are weak, such as in the United States and Canada, the critique of bureaucracy might precede the endorsement of socialist ownership. Workers might rebel first against their frustration at the hands of a highly fragmented division of labor and against its bureaucratization. Their critique of alienation might initially take the form of a generalized critique of bureaucratic organization (only later being narrowed into a coherent perspective on the possibilities of debureaucratized socialist ownership).

For most North Americans socialism is a vague and somewhat threatening prospect because they think of socialism in terms of vanguard models or in terms of other distorted fragments of European socialist traditions. Our purpose here is to salvage the emancipatory elements of Marx's critique of capitalism by blending them with a theory of ecological crisis. This may appeal to those North Americans who have been conditioned to think of socialism as an obscure European system that would threaten civil liberties.

If people could see socialism not as more and bigger government but potentially as a system of direct workers' and consumers' control, then this populism might be bent in a radical direction. It is on this hope that we base our argument for a new ideology with which to organize modern frustration with alienation into a concerted political effort to transform large-scale industrial capitalism into small-scale non-authoritarian socialism.

Some of the most powerful critiques of industrial-capitalism have come not from traditional Marxists but from thinkers like Ivan Illich and Paulo Freire. They have argued that the domination and mystification of nonexpert by expert perpetuates alienation. Illich has analyzed the medical profession as a culprit in the process of mystification with respect to its clients (its patients). Freire has attempted to understand the process of becoming literate as a political process, allowing illiterate and dominated Latin peasants to regain a measure of intellectual, and thus potentially political, competence and, thus, liberation.

Illich and Freire in different ways stress that powerlessness stems from cognitive domination as much as from political and economic domination. Thus we reverse the order of traditional Marxian change: Instead of starting with the deepest structural causes of alienation we start with the manifestations of contemporary alienation such as the self-imposed cognitive "stupidity" of modern workers. By formulating a critique of professionalism and the hegemony of the expert, we appeal to the frustration experienced by the modern worker; *later,* we can show this worker how the hegemony of the expert stems from the very nature of the capitalist wage relationship.

Thus we do not conceive of class struggle and a critique of the division of labor as disjunctive alternatives. They are merely different emphases in the critique of capitalism. In the absence of a concerted working class, in the traditional Marxian sense, the process of socialist transformation can begin by attacking aspects of alienation traditional Marxists have ignored.

The class struggle continues, albeit with a variety of forms and manifestations not imagined by Marx. While we accept Marx's theories of the internal contradictions of the capitalist system, we need to go beyond his specific theories of crisis. The internal contradictions still exist, but the external manifestations differ. Ecological crisis now replaces economic crisis (falling rate of profit, immis-erization, formation of the industrial reserve army, etc.), forcing us to rethink the agencies and forms by which crisis can be turned into full-blown socialist trans-formation.

The notions of decentralization and debureaucratization contain a powerful emancipatory content in that they both presuppose precisely the cognitive self-management we urged above. Decentralized technology and the debureau-cratized organization of labor both presume the competence of people effectively to play the multi-faceted roles required by each of these processes. We are not calling merely for "renaissance men" but rather for a type of cognitive universal-ity that is able to resist the limiting, constricting, and coordinating forces of the rigid division of labor. For workers to formulate a critique of bureaucratic-capitalist society, they must be able to think beyond the narrow roles, in produc-tion and consumption, they presently occupy. They must *want* a new social order (including definite new roles within it).

A human being must *need* liberation from domination; this need must be embodied in a self-image of potential freedom. Our argument is that this libera-tory need is carried in the idea that people have of themselves as potential self-managers of their social existences. Without experiencing this need to live a debureaucratized, self-managed life, the person will be unable to move beyond his initial frustration engendered by bureaucratic domination. This frustration, if unconnected to a positive need for self-liberation, will remain simply a form of bitterness, finding no coherent expression as a movement towards socialist change.

Our basic assumption about the possibilities inherent in human nature is that people are self-determining and indeed *want* to be self-determining. Our model of the human is different from Heilbroner's and Weber's in that we believe that people will choose self-directive freedom over the total administration of their lives by experts and professional coordinators. This is not a dichotomous choice—a choice between complete personal autonomy and utter helplessness in face of bureaucracy. We are suggesting merely that human beings, if given the choice and the circumstance, will probably choose to exercise their freedom in a self-managing way.

Instead of returning the means of production to workers (although not obviating that as a feasible political goal), we would call for the return of creative rationality and self-directiveness to human beings who for too long have been in the thrall of experts. We attack bureaucratic domination *first* and then we move on to the critique of capitalism in its entirety. Our guess is that working men and women in North America will respond to the call for the democratization of expertise more quickly than they would respond to the traditional socialist pro-gram (which, to many, only symbolizes a new form of the dictatorship of experts).

Thus we contend that populism and Marxism may meet in the new world, joining together a grass-roots democratic ethos (particularly American in charac-ter) and a critique of capitalism taken from the European socialist tradition. Marxism in its traditional clothing has never had much patience with anarcho-syndicalism or populism, preferring the more centralist ethos of the tradition of German philosophical reason (loosely translated by Lenin into the notion of a vanguard party). While Marx tried to conceptualize a form of socialism that would be democratic in its essentials, the Marxists of the Second and Third Internation-als (with only a few exceptions such as Rosa Luxemburg and Antonio Gramsci) transformed socialism into a new form of hierarchy (albeit "socialist" hierarchy).

A dose of populism might also allow the Marxist tradition to be Americanized in such a way as to build upon the traditional American mistrust of big government and expansive bureaucracies. Were North Americans to reinterpret capitalist alienation as bureaucratic domination and centralization (instead of the more narrowly construed economic exploitation indicated by members of the Second International and other "vulgar" Marxists), they might not view the concept of socialist ownership as authoritarianism—or as just another form of centralist bigness. The constructive reinterpretation of Marxism, to allow for populist nuances and undercurrents, would allow us to build on existing North American frustration with centralist bigness in creating a constituency for ecological radicalism.

The democratic ethos of American populism can be the point of departure for this radicalism; the next step is to tap into existing frustration about what we have termed alienated consumption. There are straws in the wind indicating that the era of the endless consumer is nearly over, and that human beings are searching for alternative modes of satisfaction, beyond the realm of consumption proper. The counterculture movement of the late 1960s in North America was not merely a passing fancy. It left many with the sentiment that "more" is not necessarily better; and that highly centralized and bureaucratized lives stunt the development of human personality. The counterculture, we would contend, is as much an integral part of American populism as the original Jacksonian political ideology.

Class struggle can proceed under a variety of banners. In the absence of a viable left-wing tradition in American political thought, we must instead concentrate on radicalizing aspects of populism such as they exist, bending this populism to the purposes of a sustained critique of industrial-capitalist society.

Points of leverage here are provided by the twin concepts of decentralization and debureaucratization. American populism is characterized (at least historically) by a healthy mistrust of centralized and bureaucratized organizations. Out of this mistrust springs both the unreconstructed free enterprise Republicanism of Barry Goldwater and the 1960s counterculture. While traditional Marxists see this as evidence of the intrinsically liberal (and not radical) character of American populism, we take it to mean that populism can contain a radical perspective on bureaucracy and technology, no matter how inchoate that perspective is initially. We would be quick to admit that the romanticism of the counterculture is an inadequate form of "class struggle" today; yet in the counterculture's frustration with the traditional politics of bigness there are seeds awaiting further radicalization. It is this task that might conceivably cement populism to Marxism in a way that broadens the Marxist critique of capitalism and activates populism in a significantly new and even revolutionary direction.

The counterculture is merely a symbol of the frustration the cycle of overproduction and endless consumption breeds. Herbert Marcuse, in *An Essay on Liberation,* tries to capture the genuinely radical content of hippiedom by moving it in a more Marxist direction. Marcuse says that the traditional Marxian separation of the realms of freedom and necessity (consumption and production) ignores the real possibility of creating freedom within the realm of production. The new sensibility experiences work as creative and not compelled by the edicts of bosses and managers—as a form of the artistic self-expression described so powerfully by Marx in the early manuscripts.

Marcuse opposes vulgar Marxism (and its essentially Weberian concept of industrial organization) by arguing that the revolutionary transition must begin in the self-transformation of individual consciousness. He then attempts to harness this self-emancipation to the notion of class struggle, creating, if successful, a new revolutionary class. While many critics view Marcuse as hopelessly post-Marxist, his *An Essay on Liberation* is one version of how populism (via the American counterculture) and Marxism might meet and cross-fertilize.

Marcuse's "new sensibility" has been attacked for falsely universalizing aspects of the 1960s counterculture. But his new sensibility might equally well herald the transformation people undergo as they move from populist frustration towards socialist critique and action. Marcuse did not abandon the class struggle but only indicated that there may be new cultural and ideological forms for fostering class consciousness, building upon populist frustration and its democratic ethos (and not disregarding the populist currents in American life).

The synthetic combination of populism and Marxism could produce pressure for the decentralization, debureaucratization, and socialization of the means and relations of production. Consumer movements are not intrinsically reformist or conservative; the populist frustration that often binds them together (e.g., the enormous popularity of Ralph Nader in his crusades against American corporations) can conceivably give rise to new types of class consciousness that can be the point of departure for ecological radicalism. It may be premature to dismiss American populism, such as it exists, as an irrelevant, purely reformist ideology, for this populism, we contend, contains valuable critical and radical elements such as the tradition of grass-roots democracy and the mistrust of centralist bigness (both being aspects of our ecological radicalism).

Creative Marxists could tap these sources of frustration and in the process radicalize those who express populist frustration with centralist bigness. This radicalization might be accelerated by economic crises in advanced capitalist societies. Coexistent high inflation and high unemployment might make the populist frustration with centralist bigness intolerable, pushing people over the crest separating mere populism from socialism and Marxism. Theorists of the advanced capitalist state contend that economic and political crises of this sort are unavoidable in the long term, as the government is increasingly torn between its intrinsically noninterventionist political ideology and the growing necessity of state intervention in economic life. As pressures upon the capitalist state reach the critical point, workers may no longer accept the (capitalist) "mixed economies" that exist at present. The vaunted "class compromise" the American system has produced may erode as the political state finds itself precariously torn between the ideology of free enterprise and the *realpolitik* of state intervention; and as the system of wage-labor is increasingly perceived and experienced as alienating.

This latter phenomenon gives us the greatest hope about the possible overthrow of the capitalist system. As consumers become sated with consumption, and as eco-pressures descend upon us to force the curtailing of "endless" production, new human values and human needs may emerge to take the place of consumerism. On the surface, this may seem like a romantic dream. But we contend that the dialectic of shattered expectations may allow dashed consumer dreams to resurface in terms of a radical critique of a social order that forces people to seek meaning in commodity consumption. There is not much distance, we contend, between shattered consumer expectations as these take the form of the demand for commodities and shattered expectations as these take the form of a socialist critique of capitalism.

Marxists of a more traditional type would not worry about shattered expectations but would instead continue to foment workers' class consciousness. Our position is that these are complementary strategies: Frustrations with centralist bigness, especially in a situation of relative deprivation caused by the slowing of industrial growth, may become a radical critique of the capitalist order *if* it is shown that energy-wasteful centralist bigness is a product of the capitalist system. Thus populism (shattered consumer expectations) and Marxism (radical critique of capitalism) can be joined via an appreciation of the socialist possibilities opened up by attempts to resolve capitalist ecological crises.

GUIDE TO FURTHER READING

LOUIS ALTHUSSER *For Marx* and his *Reading Capital* (with Étienne Balibar), argues that Marxism must be an objective science, without a philosophical underpinning. Althusser, unlike the author of this book, believes that Marx jettisoned his "early philosophical" period and subsequently became a structuralist in his later economic writings. Althusser opposes the individualist Marxists on the ground that they are allegedly unfaithful to Marx's deep-seated materialism and structuralism.

JÜRGEN HABERMAS *Legitimation Crisis,* offers an analysis of the shifting terms of Marxian crisis-theory in late capitalism. Habermas argues that economic crisis has been largely displaced into the sociopolitical realm, with the weakening of early capitalist ideologies such as the belief in free enterprise and the equation of supply and demand.

WILLIAM LEISS *The Limits to Satisfaction,* argues that the relationship between needs and commodities has become confused in the "high-intensity market setting" of late capitalism (and, for that matter, state-socialism). He believes that present and future Marxists will need to pay more attention to the relationship between nature and society, devising significant alternatives to the high-intensity market setting. Leiss sets the terms for what we have termed an "ecological Marxism."

RALPH MILIBAND *The State in Capitalist Society,* analyzes the role of the state in advanced capitalism. He concludes with the thought that Marx's early understanding of the political state merely as an "executive committee" of the bourgeoisie (found in the *Communist Manifesto*) is still largely true today. The documentation he provides of his argument is interesting and useful.

HARRY BRAVERMAN *Labor and Monopoly Capital,* is one of the most influential and important Marxist works of the decade. Braverman re-analyzes the class structure of advanced capitalism, finding that capitalist society is still class-stratified and that the working class has not shrunk but rather that the working class occupational structure has changed to include certain "white-collar" workers such as secretaries, clerks, waitresses, salespeople, and keypunch operators. Braverman argues that the plight of labor in advanced capitalism has not improved much since Marx's time. He stresses that human alienation from both the product and process of production has not decreased.

MAURICE GODELIER *Radionality and Irrationality in Economics.*

LUCIO COLLETTI *Marxism and Hegel,* is an important book by a leading Italian Marxist that argues that many western Marxists, beginning with Engels and Lukács, have not abandoned Hegelian idealism and thus have allowed members of the Frankfurt School to replace Marx's materialist critique of alienation with a proto-idealist critique of science and technology. Colletti calls for a return to Gramsci's and Luxemburg's crisis-theories and to their direct engagement with the political context of capitalist contradictions.

JAMES O'CONNOR   *The Fiscal Crisis of the State,* first published in 1973, argues that the modern capitalist state is increasingly crisis-bound because it cannot easily raise enough revenues, via taxation, to meet its massive expenditures.

ERNEST MANDEL   *Marxist Economic Theory,* is an indispensable guide to recent developments in Marxian economic theory. Mandel, a Belgian Marxist economist, offers a wide-ranging study of the functioning of the modern capitalist economy, building upon Marx's own insights into the workings of the capitalist system.

ERNEST MANDEL   *Late Capitalism,* is a massive work that goes beyond *Marxian Economic Theory* in analyzing specific differences and similarities between early market capitalism and more sophisticated state-interventionist versions.

NICOS POULANTZAS   *Political Power and Social Classes,* is a rather technical attempt to develop a Marxian theory of the political state. In general, this book does not compare favorably to that of Ralph Miliband, noted above in this section.

The journals *Politics and Society, Kapitalistate, New Left Review, Telos, New German Critique,* and *Canadian Journal of Political and Social Theory* are all concerned, in different ways, with the development of modern critical theory. There remain theoretical differences between certain of these journals, making it difficult for the reader to know exactly the ideological orientation of the journal in question. Broadly speaking, *Telos* and *New German Critique* are closest in orientation to the general theme of this work, being rooted in the tradition of nonorthodox western Marxism and not in economic determinism.

QUESTIONS FOR FURTHER DISCUSSION

1. Why has recent Marxism returned to crisis-theory and to class-radicalism, abandoning the pessimism of the Frankfurt School and the deterministic fatalism of "scientific" Marxists?

2. What is "ecological Marxism"?

3. Does Ralph Miliband's analysis of the capitalist state add to Marx's own analysis of the state or is it merely a continuation of it, building upon categories and assumptions already present in Marx's writings?

4. In your opinion, is Marxism still relevant to advanced capitalist societies? If so, does the meaning of "socialism" today necessarily differ from what it meant for Marx?

5. Is modern capitalism by its continued existence disproving Marx's idea that capitalism is beset by "internal contradictions" that, he felt, would eventually cause the system to collapse? Can the notion of internal contradictions be disproven, or verified, and if so, how?

6. What do modern Marxists mean by "the state"? How, if at all, does this differ from what Marx meant by the term?

GLOSSARY

alienation This describes the way the worker's work, and its product, becomes estranged from him and takes on a life of its own. Capitalism produces alienation, according to Marx.

automatic Marxism This is the version of Marxism developed by Kautsky and others during the Second International. They argued that capitalism would inevitably collapse, without the assistance of a struggling, class-conscious proletariat.

capital Marx referred to accumulated labor, in the form of money and machinery, as "capital."

class Marx saw the world divided into antagonistic groups of people who either worked for a wage or owned the means of production. He termed these groups "classes."

class struggle Marx argued that working class and capitalist class were pitted in an inexorable "class struggle." He believed that this class struggle was the motive force of all human history.

collective subject Georg Lukács, following Hegel in this vein, used the term collective subject to describe an organized working class that in a sense has a mind and purpose of its own. He believed that this collective subject would, through revolutionary action, realize the truth of a certain built-in historical reason, which tended in the direction of socialism.

commodity A commodity is anything to be exchanged on the open market.

crisis A "crisis," in Marxian terminology, is any severe disturbance in capitalist functioning, threatening to give rise to a workers' revolution.

crisis-tendencies Crisis-tendencies are the empirical manifestations of internal contradictions. They are the real outgrowths of these internal contradictions, refracted through history, culture and everyday life. Although internal contradictions are buried deep below the surface of empirical reality, possessing a structural reality often inaccessible to the human eye, crisis-tendencies, such as depressions and high unemployment, are empirically visible.

critical theory   This is another term for the version of Marxian theory centered around the theory of domination, developed by the Frankfurt School theorists.

declining subjectivity   This term is used by the Frankfurt School theorists to describe the condition of the individual who is so dominated that he can no longer recognize his own captivity by corporate capital.

democratic centralism   This is Lenin's euphemism for the type of socialism that exists in the Soviet Union. It combines the notion of the democratic dictatorship of the proletariat and the centralization of political and economic power in the hands of the Communist Party.

dialectical materialism   This is Marx's own philosophical system, rooted in the presupposition that socio-economic conditions shape men but that men can consciously change the existing socio-economic conditions.

domination   The Frankfurt School theorists defined domination as alienation a person unwittingly inflicts on himself by participating in the capitalist consumption process. Domination is more an individual than a collective concept; its collective counterpart is Lukács' reification.

ecological crisis   This is a notion developed by Marxists who argue that capitalism will soon have to confront environmental limits to industrial growth that will create new and unforeseen societal and psychological pressures.

existentialism   This is a philosophical world view that stresses the person's responsibility for his own fate and for his own liberation. In this book, it relates to the work of Sartre and Merleau-Ponty, who attempted to unite Marxism and existentialism, arguing that the human being must actively struggle to liberate himself (and his class) from capitalist alienation.

externalization   All human activity involves "externalization," or the self-expression of people in their work and art, projected outwards onto nature.

Freudian Marxism   This perspective was developed by Herbert Marcuse and Wilhelm Reich, who argued, in different ways, that capitalist alienation was perpetuated by repressing the person's erotic nature, thus transforming workers into willing agents of capitalist social control.

general will   This is the French political philosopher Jean-Jacques Rousseau's term for the democratic spirit underlying our systems of representative democracy. The general will is more than mere electoral democracy achieved through means of voting, it refers to our collective solidarity and willingness to be led by leaders whom we trust to represent our best interests.

Hegelian Marxism   This refers to the species of Marxism developed by Lukács and Korsch in the 1920s, centered around the theory of class consciousness they developed to explain why the working class had failed to revolt against capitalism.

hegemony   This is a concept used by Gramsci to describe Marx's notion that the ruling ideas in a given historical period are always the ideas of the ruling class.

idealism   This is a philosophical doctrine that says that the world can be transformed through mere thought. Marx opposed idealism, instead creating what he termed dialectical materialism.

imperative coordination   This is the translation, by Talcott Parsons, of Max Weber's concept of *Herrschaft* (which is also translated as "power" and "authority"). Imperative coordination refers to the way in which labor is organized in industrial societies on the basis of bureaucracies and on the basis of the rigid division of labor.

individualist Marxism   This perspective argues that Marxian revolution can only stem from the individual's own personal struggles in his everyday life against alienation.

internal contradictions   These are features of capitalism that predispose the system to collapse. The central internal contradiction for Marx was the contradiction between capital and labor.

labor   Marx argued that capital could only be activated and expanded by the force of human work or "labor." He wrote that the only source of capitalist profit is human labor.

legitimation crisis   This is Jürgen Habermas' term for a prevalent mode of social crisis today, involving the weakening of public belief in the advanced capitalist system. Legitimation crisis is triggered, he contends, by further state intervention in political and economic life, explicitly contradicting the ideology of the free market and of laissez faire.

lived-experience   This is a term used by phenomenologists to describe the pre-theoretical flow of experience that makes up all of our perceptions of the world. Lived-experience is sometimes used synonymously with everyday life.

Marxian humanism   This is the eastern European version of individualist Marxism, rooted in Marx's 1844 manuscripts and in his notion that creative praxis is the essential feature of socialism. It opposes official state-socialism of the Soviet variety.

mediation   A "mediation" is any entity that joins the relationship between two other entities. In the Marxist sense, mediation is the process of relating economic to socio-cultural and ideological realities. For Marx, the world is always a mediated world, for there is no automatic or unilinear relationship between economic and ideological-cultural realities.

negative dialectics   Theodor Adorno describes his philosophical outlook with this term. It is characterized by a ruthless negativity and not by positive and definite assumptions about the nature of truth, meaning, and value. Adorno wanted his negative dialectics to pierce the veil of ideological falsehood he felt to be characteristic of late capitalism.

new sensibility   This is Herbert Marcuse's term for the kind of human sensibility that refuses to dominate others in the name of distant future liberation.

one-dimensional society   Marcuse uses this term to describe a social order that closes off the possibility of successful revolt by dispossessing the people who are able to criticize that order.

parliamentary socialism   Eduard Bernstein's argument that socialism could be achieved through the electoral process and not with a violent revolution is termed parliamentary socialism.

phenomenology   This is a philosophical system that stresses the way all knowledge is grounded in the immediate personal experience of daily life.

populism   This is an ideology and social movement that arose in the United States under the Presidency of Andrew Jackson but that survives, in terms of its cultural and political influences, to the present day. A populist believes that "the people" should be actively involved in determining their own social fate and should refuse to allow themselves to be manipulated by experts, professionals, and bosses. It can be used as a synonym for radical democracy.

praxis   Praxis is a Greek word for human activity. Marx argued that the essence of human freedom, to be realized under socialism, is praxis — the ability to realize ourselves in our work, our interactions with nature.

profit   The capitalist makes "profit" by paying the worker a wage that compensates for only part of the work he does during the workday. The remainder, "profit," is pocketed by the capitalist.

psychoanalysis   This is the science of the mind and the unconscious developed by Sigmund Freud.

reification   Georg Lukács developed the concept of "reification" to refer to the false consciousness of the working class. Strictly, he defined reification as the objectification of human relationships such that they appear to be relations between things. Reification is virtually synonymous with Marx's concept of alienation.

revisionism   This term refers originally to the kind of socialist theory offered by Eduard Bernstein at the turn of the century. Generally, it refers to any version of Marxian theory that deviates from Marx and Engels' original concepts.

scientism   This is a term used to describe the view that social reality can be known scientifically (as in the natural sciences) and that social reality is thoroughly objective.

social democracy   This refers to the political movement that arose during the Second International under the influence of Eduard Bernstein and his parliamentary socialism. Social democracy is a compromise of sorts between capitalism and socialism, combining features from both systems. It is often characterized by a "mixed economy," combining state ownership in some sectors of the economy with private ownership in other sectors. Today, nations such as Sweden and Great Britain can be called social democracies, with relatively large degrees of governmental regulation of social and economic life (as compared to the United States).

state-socialism   This is the official ideology of the Soviet Union, also known as Marxism-Leninism. Its essential assumption is that there must be a protracted period in between capitalism and full communism during which the workers' state, run by the Communist Party, must be tightly organized and administered in the interests of full development of its industrial potential.

subjectivity   This concept refers to the human being's experience and action in the world. It usually refers to personal as opposed to collective modes of experience and action.

surplus repression   This is the central analytic concept of Marcuse's Freudian Marxism. It refers to the phenomenon of a willing acceptance of the dominant ways of life of advanced capitalism, such as the work ethic, by human beings who are objectively free to engage in non-alienated labor owing to advanced technological capacity. Surplus repression is alienation the person "does" to himself.

surplus value   This concept refers to Marx's notion that the capitalist could extract an unpaid portion of surplus labor from the worker. For example, if the worker works for ten hours but his work for eight of those hours will feed him and clothe him (in terms of his wages), then the extra two hours work goes towards the production of surplus value. The only source of surplus value, according to Marx, is labor-power.

vanguardism   This is Lenin's theory of socialist transformation, to be achieved by the rigid organization of the proletariat and peasantry by a small group of dedicated revolutionary tacticians.

Bibliography

ADORNO, THEODOR *Negative Dialectics.* New York: Seabury, 1973.

———. *Philosophy of Modern Music.* London: Sheed and Ward, 1973.

———. *Prismen.* Frankfurt Am Main: Suhrkamp, 1955.

AGGER, BEN "Dialectical Sensibility I: Critical Theory, Scientism, and Empiricism." *Canadian Journal of Political and Social Theory,* Vol. 1, No. 1, Winter 1977.

———. "Dialectical Sensibility II: Towards a New Intellectuality." *Canadian Journal of Political and Social Theory,* Vol. 1, No. 2, Spring–Summer, 1977.

———. "On Happiness and the Damaged Life," *On Critical Theory.* John O'Neill, editor. New York: Seabury, 1976.

———. "Marcuse and Habermas on New Science," *Polity,* Vol. 9, No. 2, Winter 1976.

ALTHUSSER, LOUIS *For Marx.* London: Allen Lane, 1969.

ALTHUSSER, LOUIS, AND ÉTIENNE BALIBAR *Reading Capital.* London: NLB, 1970.

BERNSTEIN, EDUARD *Evolutionary Socialism.* New York: Schocken, 1961.

BOBER, M.M. *Karl Marx's Interpretation of History.* Cambridge: Harvard University Press, 1962.

BOGGS, CARL *Gramsci's Marxism.* New York: Urizen Books, 1976.

BORKENAU, FRANZ *The Communist International.* London: Faber and Faber, 1938.

———. *World Communism.* Ann Arbor: University of Michigan Press, 1962.

BOTTOMORE, T.B., editor *Karl Marx: Early Writings.* New York: McGraw-Hill, 1964.

BOUDIN, LOUIS *The Theoretical System of Karl Marx in the Light of Recent Criticism.* New York: Monthly Review Press, 1967.

BREINES, PAUL, editor *Critical Interruptions.* New York: Herder and Herder, 1970.

BRAVERMAN, HARRY *Labor and Monopoly Capital.* New York: Monthly Review Press, 1974.

BURNS, EMILE *An Introduction to Marxism.* New York: International Publishers, 1957.

COLLETTI, LUCIO *Marxism and Hegel.* London: NLB, 1973.

DJILAS, MILOVAN *The New Class.* New York: Praeger, 1964.

DOBB, MAURICE *On Economic Theory and Socialism.* London: Routledge and Kegan Paul, 1955.

ENGELS, FRIEDRICH *Anti-Duhring.* Moscow: Foreign Languages Publishing House, 1962.

FEUER, LEWIS, editor *Basic Writings on Politics and Philosophy.* Garden City: Anchor, 1959.

FRANKFURT INSTITUTE FOR SOCIAL RESEARCH, editor *Aspects of Sociology.* London: Heinemann, 1973.

FROMM, ERICH, editor *Socialist Humanism.* Garden City: Anchor, 1966.

GAY, PETER *The Dilemma of Democratic Socialism.* New York: Collier, 1961.

GODELIER, MAURICE *Rationality and Irrationality in Economics.* London: NLB, 1972.

GRAMSCI, ANTONIO *Selections from the Prison Notebooks.* London: Lawrence and Wishart, 1971.

HABERMAS, JÜRGEN *Legitimation Crisis.* Boston: Beacon, 1975.

_____. *Theory and Practice.* Boston: Beacon, 1973.

VON HAYEK, FRIEDRICH *Collectivist Economic Planning.* New York: A.M. Kelley, 1935.

HEILBRONER, ROBERT *An Inquiry into the Human Prospect.* New York: Norton, 1974.

HORKHEIMER, MAX *Critical Theory.* New York: Herder and Herder, 1972.

_____. *Critique of Instrumental Reason.* New York: Seabury, 1974.

_____. *Eclipse of Reason.* New York: Seabury, 1974.

HORKHEIMER, MAX, AND THEODOR ADORNO *Dialectic of Enlightenment.* New York: Herder and Herder, 1972.

HOROWITZ, GAD *Repression: Basic and Surplus Repression in Psychoanalytic Theory.* Toronto: University of Toronto Press, 1977.

HORVAT, BRANKO *An Essay on Yugoslav Society.* White Plains: International Arts and Sciences Press, 1969.

HOWARD, DICK, AND KARL E. KLARE, editors *The Unknown Dimension.* New York: Basic Books, 1972.

HYPPOLITE, JEAN *Studies on Marx and Hegel.* New York: Basic Books, 1969.

JACOBY, RUSSELL *Social Amnesia.* Boston: Beacon, 1975.

JAY, MARTIN *The Dialectical Imagination.* Boston: Little, Brown, 1973.

_____. *The Dictatorship of the Proletariat.* London: The National Labour Press, no date; and Ann Arbor: University of Michigan Press, 1964.

KAUTSKY, KARL *Class Struggle.* New York: Norton, 1971.

_____. *Ethics and the Materialist Conception of History.* Chicago: Kerr, 1918.

_____. *The Labor Revolution.* London: Allen and Unwin, 1925.

KORSCH, KARL *Karl Marx.* New York: Russell and Russell, 1963.

_____. *Marxism and Philosophy.* New York: Monthly Review Press, 1970.

LANGE, OSCAR *On the Economic Theory of Socialism.* Minneapolis: University of Minnesota Press, 1952.

LEDERER, EMIL *State of the Masses.* New York: Fertig, 1967.

LEISS, WILLIAM *The Limits to Satisfaction.* Toronto: University of Toronto Press, 1976.

LENIN, V. *Materialism and Empirio-Criticism.* Moscow: Foreign Languages Publishing House, 1952.

LENIN, V.I. *The State and Revolution.* Moscow: Foreign Languages Publishing House, n.d.

LENIN, V.I. *What Is to Be Done?* Moscow: Progress Publishers, 1973.

LICHTHEIM, GEORGE *From Marx to Hegel and Other Essays.* London: Orbach and Chambers, 1971.

_____. *Lukacs.* London: Fontana, 1970.

_____. *Marxism.* London: Routledge and Kegan Paul, 1964.

LOBKOWICZ, NICHOLAS *Theory and Practice.* Notre Dame: University of Notre Dame Press, 1967.

LUKACS, GEORG *History and Class Consciousness.* London: Merlin, 1971.

LUXEMBURG, ROSA *The Accumulation of Capital.* New York: Monthly Review Press, 1973.

_____. *The Junius Pamphlet.* London: Merlin, n.d.

_____. *The Mass Strike.* New York: Harper & Row, 1971.

MANDEL, ERNST *Late Capitalism.* London: NLB, 1975.

_____. *Marxist Economic Theory.* New York: Monthly Review Press, 1969.

MARCUSE, HERBERT *Counterrevolution and Revolt.* Boston: Beacon, 1969.

_____. *Eros and Civilization.* New York: Vintage, 1955.

_____. *An Essay on Liberation.* Harmondsworth: Penguin, 1972.

_____. *One-Dimensional Man.* Boston: Beacon, 1964.

_____. *Studies in Critical Philosophy.* London: NLB, 1972.

MARKOVIĆ, MIHAILO *From Affluence to Praxis.* Ann Arbor: University of Michigan Press, 1974.

MARX, KARL *Capital.* Vol. 1. Moscow: Progress Publishers, n.d.

_____. *Capital.* Vol. 2. Moscow: Foreign Languages Publishing House, 1961.

_____. *Capital.* Vol. 3. Moscow: Foreign Languages Publishing House, 1962.

_____. *Economic and Philosophical Manuscripts.* Moscow: Foreign Languages Publishing House, 1961.

_____. *Grundrisse.* London: Allen Lane, 1973.

MARX, KARL AND FRIEDRICH ENGELS *The Communist Manifesto.* New York: Washington Square Press, 1965.

_____. *The German Ideology.* New York: International Publishers, 1949.

MERLEAU-PONTY, MAURICE *Humanism and Terror.* Boston: Beacon, 1972.

_____. *Sense and Non-Sense.* Evanston, Ill.: Northwestern University Press, 1964.

_____. *Signs.* Evanston, Ill.: Northwestern University Press, 1964.

MÉSZÁROS, ISTVÁN *Lukács' Concept of Dialectic.* London: Merlin, 1972.

MILIBAND, RALPH *The State in Capitalist Society.* London: Quartet, 1974.

MILLS, C. WRIGHT *The Marxists.* New York: Dell, 1962.

O'CONNOR, JAMES *The Fiscal Crisis of the State.* New York: St. Martin's, 1973.

OLLMAN, BERTELL *Alienation.* Cambridge: Cambridge University Press, 1976.

O'NEILL, JOHN, editor *On Critical Theory.* New York: Seabury, 1976.

PACI, ENZO *The Function of Modern Science and the Meaning of Man.* Evanston, Ill.: Northwestern University Press, 1972.

PETROVIĆ, GAJO *Marx in the Mid-twentieth Century.* Garden City: Anchor, 1967.

PICCONE, PAUL "Beyond Identity Theory." John O'Nell Editor. *On Critical Theory.* New York: Seabury, 1976.

_____. "Phenomenological Marxism." *Telos.* No. 9, Fall 1971.

PICCONE, PAUL, AND BART GRAHL, editors *Towards a New Marxism.* St. Louis: Telos Press, 1973.

POSTER, MARK *Existential Marxism in Post-War France.* Princeton: Princeton University Press, 1975.

POULANTZAS, NICOS *Political Power and Social Classes.* London: NLB and Sheed and Ward, 1973.

REICH, WILHELM   *Sex-Pol: Essays 1929 – 1934,* Lee Baxandall, editor. New York: Random House, 1972.

RICHTA, RADOVAN *ET AL.*   *Civilization at the Crossroads.* White Plains: International Arts and Sciences Press, 1969.

SARTRE, JEAN-PAUL   *Critique of Dialectical Reason.* London: NLB, 1976.

————. *Search for a Method.* New York: Vintage, 1963.

SCHAFF, ADAM   *Marxism and the Human Individual.* New York: McGraw-Hill, 1970.

SCHROYER, TRENT   *The Critique of Domination.* New York: Braziller, 1973.

SCHUMACHER, E.F.   *Small Is Beautiful: Economics As If People Mattered.* New York: Harper & Row, 1973.

SCHWARTZ, JESSE   *The Subtle Anatomy of Capitalism.* Santa Monica, Calif.: Goodyear, 1977.

SHER, GERSON   *Praxis.* Bloomington: Indiana University Press, 1978.

SLATER, PHIL   *Origin and Significance of the Frankfurt School.* London: Routledge and Kegan Paul, 1977.

STALIN, J.V.   *Dialectical and Historical Materialism.* New York: International Publishers, 1940.

STOJANOVIĆ, SVETOZAR   *Between Ideals and Reality.* New York: Oxford University Press, 1973.

TUCKER, ROBERT C.   *The Marxian Revolutionary Idea.* New York: Norton, 1969.

WARD, DWAYNE   *Toward a Critical Political Economics.* Santa Monica, Calif.: Goodyear, 1977.

WATERS, MARY-ALICE, editor   *Rosa Luxemburg Speaks.* New York: Pathfinder, 1970.

WELLMER, ALBRECHT   *Critical Theory of Society.* New York: Herder and Herder, 1971.

ZUKIN, SHARON   *Beyond Marx and Tito.* London: Cambridge University Press, 1975.

Index

A

Adler, Max 83
Adorno, Theodor 121, 125, 126, 140, 145, 149, 150, 151, 152, 153, 156, 157, 158, 159, 161, 162, 167, 170, 171, 172, 174, 175, 179, 185, 216, 230, 231, 234, 235, 237, 240, 244, 249, 260, 278, 316, 317
Agger, Ben 277
alienated consumption 316, 320, 322, 324, 330, 331, 332, 334, 337
alienation 1, 3, 7, 8, 9, 10, 12, 14, 16, 17, 28, 33, 43, 55, 65, 66, 67, 118, 119, 122, 140, 146, 150, 154, 155, 156, 157, 163, 164, 176, 179, 181 196, 197, 198, 199, 200, 201, 203, 210, 220, 225, 236, 244, 248, 257, 259, 270, 274, 294, 295, 309, 316, 333, 334, 335
Austro-Marxists 12, 76, 83, 104, 111, 120, 134, 147

B

Babbage, Charles 295
Bacon, Francis 171, 172
Bakunin, Milkail 5

Bell, Daniel 178, 195, 280, 306, 307
Benjamin, Walter 121
Bernstein, Eduard 75, 77, 80, 81, 82, 83, 84, 86, 87, 88, 89, 90, 91, 117, 118, 121, 151, 231
Blanquist 5
Bolsheviks 75, 78, 81, 84, 85, 94, 108, 112, 114, 118, 121, 197, 233, 279
Bookchin, Murray 308
Braverman, Harry 17, 273, 274, 279, 294, 295, 306, 307
Bukharin, Nikolai 85, 113

C

collective subject 122, 125, 126, 233, 234, 237
communicative competence 294
Communist League 5
crises 1, 2, 15, 36, 72, 111, 124, 276, 280, 308, 316, 318, 321, 338, 339
crisis 10, 11, 13, 15, 43, 66, 91, 123, 125, 149, 153, 229, 231, 233, 237, 268, 269, 270, 271, 272, 275, 277, 290, 294, 319, 325, 335, 336
critical theory 121, 138, 145, 150, 153, 155, 163, 276, 277, 316
critique of ideology 28

De Leon, Daniel   152
democratic socialism   78
determinism   9, 10, 11, 12, 67, 75, 76,
   80, 82, 87, 94, 99, 120, 121, 134, 237,
   248, 256
dialectic of shattered expectations
   316, 319, 323, 324, 325, 334, 338
dialectical materialism   27, 67, 80,
   111, 134, 199
dialectical method   2, 9, 10, 11, 12,
   13, 14, 27, 28, 30, 31, 32, 33, 36, 43,
   65, 66, 118, 156, 157, 250, 275, 278,
   317, 319
dialectical regression   242
dialectical sensibility   260, 265
division of labor   6, 17, 63, 201, 239,
   274, 276, 277, 295, 327, 329, 330,
   333, 334, 335
domination   8, 16, 28, 55, 125, 140,
   149, 150, 152, 154, 155, 156, 157,
   158, 163, 164, 170, 172, 175, 176,
   179, 181, 231, 232, 233, 234, 238,
   239, 242, 244, 260, 274, 276, 295
Dubcek, Alexander   192
Durkheim, Emile   29, 155

early market capitalism   5, 116, 125,
   163, 166
early monopoly capitalism   116, 117,
   121, 125, 126, 145, 152, 157, 158,
   159, 162, 229, 232, 234, 249, 318
ecological imperative   319, 320, 321,
   324, 332
ecological Marxism   268, 272, 273,
   274, 276, 279, 286, 308, 309
emancipation of nature   200
Engels, Friedrich   5, 8, 9, 13, 28, 29,
   31, 32, 35, 36, 40, 66, 77, 80, 81, 119,
   120, 121, 123, 126, 134, 147, 158,
   198, 232, 233, 244, 245, 316, 318
Erfurt Programme   75
evolutionary socialism   77, 81
exchange value   45
existentialism   248, 249, 251, 252,
   257, 259

false consciousness   8, 32, 145, 150,
   159, 170, 275
false needs   124, 125, 155, 175, 176,
   177, 239, 245, 246, 317
Feuerbach, Ludwig   196, 275
Fourier, Charles   308, 309
Frankfurt School   11, 14, 15, 16, 41,
   87, 112, 117, 125, 126, 138, 140, 145,
   146, 147, 148, 149, 151, 155, 156,
   157, 163, 170, 174, 175, 176, 178,
   179, 192, 203, 216, 230, 232, 233,
   234, 235, 237, 242, 244, 249, 260,
   269, 277, 278, 284, 309, 316
Freire, Paulo   335
Freud, Sigmund   238, 239, 240, 241,
   243, 244, 246
Freudian Marxism   234, 237, 240
Fromm, Erich   121, 151, 308

general law of capitalist accumula-
   tion   6, 10, 58, 63, 65, 67
German idealism   27, 29
German Social Democratic Party   75
Goodman, Paul   308
Gramsci, Antonio   81, 86, 99, 100,
   101, 104, 114, 120, 336
Grossman, Henryk   121

Habermas, Jürgen   79, 123, 124, 191,
   270, 271, 274, 275, 277, 279, 284,
   285, 290, 293, 294
Hegel, G.W.F.   27, 28, 29, 118, 119,
   120, 122, 196, 197, 199, 233, 248
Hegelian Marxism   16, 86, 112, 117,
   119, 120, 121, 123, 126, 140, 148,
   149, 150, 151, 153, 190, 230, 232,
   233, 234, 249, 257, 277
Heidegger, Martin   234
Heilbroner, Robert   308, 319, 320,
   321, 331, 332, 336
Helsinki Conference   197
Hilferding, Rudolf   83
historical materialism   35

Horkheimer, Max   121, 123, 125, 126, 134, 138, 140, 145, 147, 149, 150, 151, 152, 153, 154, 155, 156, 163, 164, 165, 166, 167, 168, 169, 170, 171, 172, 174, 175, 178, 185, 230, 234, 249, 260, 316, 317
Horowitz, Gad   242
human rights   197, 198
Husserl, Edmund   234

idealism, 28, 31, 33, 122, 200
identity-theory   158, 159
Illich, Ivan   308, 335
immanent laws   7
individualist (or individualized) Marxism   2, 15, 33, 153, 193, 194, 195, 199, 203, 230, 231, 232, 233, 234, 235, 236, 237, 238, 249, 269
industrial reserve army   60, 61, 63, 65
The Institute for Social Research   121, 138, 230
instrumental rationality   16, 153, 154, 155, 156, 163, 170
internal contradictions   1, 5, 7, 8, 9, 10, 11, 12, 13, 14, 15, 43, 65, 66, 71, 72, 81, 87, 116, 117, 121, 122, 124, 125, 145, 270, 325, 335

J

Jacobin   5
Jacoby, Russell   178, 179, 181, 185

K

Kahn, Herman   307
Kant, Immanuel   87, 89
Kautsky, Karl   12, 14, 15, 75, 76, 77, 80, 81, 82, 83, 84, 86, 87, 91, 92, 94, 97, 104, 111, 112, 117, 118, 119, 120, 121, 123, 134, 147, 151, 231, 232, 233, 270, 278
Keynes, John Maynard   123
Kolakowski, Leszek   195, 200
Korać, Veljko   202, 203

Korsch, Karl   86, 112, 117, 119, 120, 121, 123, 134, 138, 140, 146, 147, 150, 156, 157, 175, 231, 233, 235, 239, 248
Kosík, Karl   195
Kropotkin, Peter   308

labor-power   44, 45, 49, 55, 57, 58, 60
late monopoly capitalism   124, 125, 156
Lefebvre, Henri   252
legitimation crisis   124, 191, 268, 271, 272, 285, 286, 293, 294, 308
Leiss, William   274, 277, 279, 286, 307, 308, 309
Lenin, V.I.   9, 27, 84, 85, 87, 108 109, 111, 112, 113, 114, 118, 121, 122, 146, 189, 190, 198, 279, 280, 336
Lukács, Georg   15, 86, 87, 112, 117, 119, 120, 121, 122, 123, 124, 125, 126, 134, 138, 140, 146, 147, 150, 156, 157, 159, 170, 172, 175, 230, 231, 232, 233, 234, 235, 236, 237, 239, 257, 258, 259, 318
Luxemburg, Rosa   75, 76, 81, 82, 83, 84, 85, 86, 97, 99, 104, 105, 108, 109, 110, 111, 114, 116, 117, 118, 120, 121, 146, 231, 233, 336

M

Macpherson, C.B.   308
Mandel, Ernest   270
Mannheim, Karl   29
Marcuse, Herbert   2, 15, 121, 125, 134, 140, 145, 147, 149, 151, 152, 153, 155, 156, 175, 176, 177, 178, 179, 181, 185, 195, 221, 230, 231, 232, 233, 234, 235, 236, 237, 238, 239, 240, 241, 242, 243, 244, 246, 247, 248, 249, 268, 308, 317, 337, 338
Marković, Mihailo   202, 219, 221, 225
Marxian humanism   189, 190, 192, 193, 194, 195, 197, 198, 199, 200, 201, 202, 203, 209, 210, 230, 232
Marxian political economy   270

Marxism-Leninism   75, 79, 85, 86, 92, 114, 117, 118, 119, 120, 153, 189, 190, 198
Mao Tse-Tung   27
materialism   31, 33, 67, 122
Medvedev, Roy   193
Merleau-Ponty, Maurice   15, 231, 235, 236, 237, 248, 249, 252, 256, 257, 259, 271
Miliband, Ralph   270, 271, 274, 277, 279, 280, 281, 285, 307
Morris, William   308
Mussolini, Benito   99

Nader, Ralph   338
necessary labor   55
negative dialectics   156
new sensibility   235, 236, 244, 246, 247, 269
new working class   294, 295, 306

O'Connor, James   270, 271, 273, 277
Offe, Claus   270
one-dimensional(ity)   140, 176, 178, 179, 186, 194, 242
organic composition of capital   68, 69, 70, 71, 122
Owen, Robert   18

P

Paci, Enzo   257
Paris Commune   5, 76, 77, 84, 97
parliamentary socialism   77, 78, 82
Petrović, Gajo   195, 200, 219
phenomenological Marxism   257, 258, 259, 260
phenomenology   259
Piccone, Paul   235, 237, 257, 258, 259, 260
Pollock, Friedrich   121
populism   2, 3, 148, 236, 245, 275, 276, 277, 278, 332, 333, 335, 337, 338, 339
Poulantzas, Nicos   270

praxis   9, 16, 28, 33, 43, 99, 119, 157, 185, 190, 195, 196, 197, 198, 199, 200, 201, 202, 219, 220, 225, 241, 242, 246, 247, 248, 249, 250, 259, 266, 316
productive consumption   57

reflection-theory of knowledge   111, 113
reification   123, 124, 125, 140, 150, 151, 161, 170, 179, 181, 185
Renner, Karl   83
repressive desublimation   239
revisionist controversy   76
Richta, Radovan   195
Rousseau, Jean-Jacques   243
Ruskin, William   308
Russian Revolution   16, 76

Sakharov, Andrei   193
Sartre, Jean-Paul   15, 231, 235, 236, 237, 248, 249, 250, 251, 252, 259
Schaff, Adam   192, 209, 210, 216
Schiller, Friedrich   241
Schoenberg, Arnold   235
Schumacher, E.F.   325, 326, 327, 328, 332
scientific management   328
scientific socialism (or Marxism)   12, 75, 77, 81, 82, 83, 84, 91, 92, 94, 99, 111, 112, 117, 119, 120, 123, 124, 138, 147, 232, 248, 252, 278
Second International   2, 10, 11, 15, 75, 77, 80, 81, 82, 83, 86, 87, 91, 99, 111, 116, 117, 118, 119, 121, 125, 127, 134, 138, 146, 147, 148, 190, 199, 233, 257, 278, 329, 336, 337
self-management   86, 113, 189, 193, 202, 220, 221, 225, 266, 328
social amnesia   185
social democracy   77, 82, 87, 104, 147, 148, 152
Solzhenitsyn, Alexandr   193
Spartacusbund   104
Stalin, Joseph   85, 86, 112, 113, 114, 118, 189, 190, 225, 321

Stojanović, Svetozar 202, 219, 225
subject-object dialectics 126, 127, 181
surplus labor 55
surplus repression 238, 239, 240, 243, 248
surplus value 6, 48, 49, 54, 55, 66, 67, 68, 69
Svoboda, Ludvik 193

T

Taylorism 274, 306
theory of the state 270, 271, 273, 279, 280, 308
Third (or Communist) International 76, 85, 87, 111, 117, 118, 120, 134, 138, 146, 147, 190, 233, 329, 336
Trotsky, Leon 85

U

unproductive consumption 57
use-value 44, 45, 48
utopian socialists 55

V

value-freedom 80
voluntarism 11, 12, 232

W

Weber, Max 80, 153, 154, 155, 199, 277, 326, 327, 328, 336
Welfare state 78, 79, 124
Wolfe, Tom 185

Z

Zinoviev, Grigorii 85, 120